Scot land the Best

PETER
IRVINE

for **DON**

Published by Collins
An imprint of HarperCollins Publishers
Westerhill Road
Bishopbriggs
Glasgow G64 2QT
www.harpercollins.co.uk

13th edition 2019

A catalogue record for this book is available from the British Library.

ISBN 978-0-00-830774-5   10 9 8 7 6 5 4 3 2 1

First published in 1993 by Mainstream Publishing
Company (Edinburgh) Ltd

First published by HarperCollins Publishers in 1997

Printed and bound in China

If you would like to comment on any aspect of this book,
please contact us at the above address or online.
e-mail: **the.best@harpercollins.co.uk**

Contents

Section 3 *Glasgow*

Section 4 *Regional Hotels & Restaurants*

Section 5 *Particular Places to Eat & Stay in Scotland*

Section 6 *Good Food & Drink*

Section 7 *Outdoor Places*

Section 12 *Skye & The Islands*

Introduction

After another odyssey across Scotland, it's a pleasure to welcome again old friends, new readers and fellow travellers. Here I commend to you hundreds of places in Scotland that I can say with conviction are worth your while, bringing to your attention especially those that are new, independent and personally run. *Scotland the Best* continues to celebrate creative entrepreneurs, chefs, activists, people with commitment and ideas that put their lives into their work and put their city, village or area on the map.

Tourism in Scotland is a booming industry, as evidenced by the roaring success of the North Coast 500, the caravanserai from Edinburgh to Skye and the influx of hotel and high-street chains in our cities. But it's often the lesser known and distinctive places that enhance the visitor experience, and give depth to the authenticity that many visitors come to find.

So *StB* celebrates and encourages the independent, artisan and sometimes quirky enterprises that are proliferating too. 'Seasonal', 'locally sourced', home-made and home-grown are mantras that have been enthusiastically adopted throughout Scotland. From hipster coffee shops and bakeries, from bread and cheese to the mighty whisky and small single-batch gin distilleries, Scotland is on the leading edge of food tourism. In this edition, there are new categories and some that have been dropped. Chain businesses have been included only if they in some way make a unique contribution to their location. Both budget and deluxe hotel chains serve a purpose but can seem the same everywhere. *Scotland the Best* proclaims the places that are only here.

For new readers, please note that this is not your usual guide book. It's highly selective, a personal choice across a wide range of interests and price, but they're all special, (well, according to me). It's a book of impressions and opinions and while of course I'm not infallible, everywhere in these pages has been experienced and compared. I do believe we can identify and ascertain what is better than the rest and over 25 years it seems that readers agree. I try to be rigorous in my explorations and deliberations, comparing like with like within the categories I've determined and evaluating how we match up in a burgeoning world of old and new destinations. *Scotland the Best* is a guide to the good life not just to an amazing wee country.

Hotels, restaurants and walks have their own unique code system including less quantifiable aspects like atmosphere and location that are so important to the quality and to the total experience of being there.

Since I started compiling *Scotland the Best* 25 years ago standards in hospitality everywhere have improved hugely. So has 'the competition'. With our scenery, history and vibrant, accessible culture, Scotland has all the right ingredients to attract global and local visitors, but demand brings an increasing understanding of good service, the importance of food integrity and that the look, the feel, empathy and the vibe do count. I have tried to reflect increasingly sophisticated perceptions of what 'the best' requires and means. So in this edition there is a further refinement, an upscaling of what constitutes 'the Best'. While everywhere selected is clearly considered worthy of inclusion, I have honed *StB*'s 'tick' system. As you'll see on the codes pages (pages 11–12), some places are awarded 1, 2 or 3 ticks to further distinguish their excellence. In each successive edition, places may lose or gain ticks but this time I've been more resolved to reflect rising standards, and therefore, 2 ticks may have become 1, etc. I hope I don't lose any friends over this but the watchwords of Scotland's unique visitor appeal – authenticity, integrity, honesty – need to be apparent in these pages too.

I hope you have luminous and numerous memorable experiences in Scotland. Your feedback will be much appreciated and inform the reprints or next edition. In the meantime, enjoy it all and do discover: the Borders, the South West, Moray and Speyside, and the great cities that are not Edinburgh. And go find your own beach.

Edinburgh, 2019

How To Use This Book

There are three ways to find things in this book:

1. The book can be used by category – you can look up the best restaurants in the Borders or the best scenic routes in the whole of Scotland. Most entries have an item number in the outside margin. These are in numerical order and allow easy cross-referencing.

2. If out and about in Scotland, start with the maps and see how individual items are located, how they are grouped together and how much there is that's worth seeing or doing in any particular area. Then look up the item numbers. **I would urge you to use the maps and this method of finding the best of what an area or town has to offer. Top tip: numbers up to 1552, that is, in the earlier sections of the book, refer to hospitality places – hotels, restaurants, food and drink, etc.**

3. There's an index at the back.

All items have a code which gives (1) the specific item number; (2) the map on which it can be found; and (3) the map co-ordinates. For space reasons, items in Glasgow and Edinburgh are not individually marked on Map 8, although they do have co-ordinates in the margin to give you a rough idea of location. A typical entry is shown below, identifying the various elements that make it up:

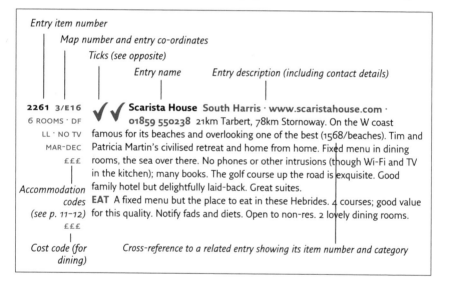

Entry item number

Map number and entry co-ordinates

Ticks (see opposite)

Entry name   Entry description (including contact details)

2261 3/E16
6 ROOMS · DF
LL · NO TV
MAR-DEC
£££

Accommodation codes
(see p. 11–12)
£££

Cost code (for dining)

Scarista House South Harris · www.scaristahouse.com · 01859 550238 21km Tarbert, 78km Stornoway. On the W coast famous for its beaches and overlooking one of the best (1568/beaches). Tim and Patricia Martin's civilised retreat and home from home. Fixed menu in dining rooms, the sea over there. No phones or other intrusions (though Wi-Fi and TV in the kitchen); many books. The golf course up the road is exquisite. Good family hotel but delightfully laid-back. Great suites.
EAT A fixed menu but the place to eat in these Hebrides. 4 courses; good value for this quality. Notify fads and diets. Open to non-res. 2 lovely dining rooms.

Cross-reference to a related entry showing its item number and category

A Note On Categories

Edinburgh and Glasgow, the destinations of most visitors and the nearest cities to more than half of the population, are covered in the substantial Sections 2 and 3. You will probably need a city map or smartphone/satnav to get around.

For the purposes of maps, and particularly in Section 4 (Regional Hotels & Restaurants), I have used a combination of the subdivision of Scotland based on current standard political regions and on historical ones, e.g. Argyll, Ayrshire. Section 4 is meant to give a comprehensive and concise guide to the best of the major Scottish towns in each area. Some recommended hotels and restaurants will be amongst the best in the region (or even amongst the best in Scotland) and have been selected because they are the best there is in the town or the immediate area.

From Sections 6 to 11, the categories are based on activities, interests and geography and are Scotland-wide. Section 12 covers the islands, with a page-by-page guide to the larger ones.

Ticks For The Best There Is

Although everything listed in the book is notable and remarkable in some way, there are places that are outstanding even in this superlative company. Instead of marking them with a rosette or a star, they have been 'awarded' a tick.

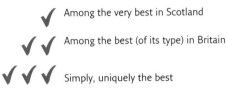

✓ Among the very best in Scotland

✓ ✓ Among the best (of its type) in Britain

✓ ✓ ✓ Simply, uniquely the best

Listings generally are not in an order of merit although if there is one outstanding item it will always be at the top of the page and this obviously includes anything which has been given ticks.

The Codes

1. The Item Code
At the left-hand margin of every item is a code which will enable you to find it on a map. Thus **1126** 5/M18 should be read as follows: **1126** is the item number, listed in simple consecutive order; 5 identifies the particular map at the back of the book; M18 is the map co-ordinate, to help pinpoint the item's location on the map grid.

2. The Accommodation & Property Code
Beside each recommended accommodation or property is a series of codes, as follows:

16 ROOMS	NO PETS
DF	NO KIDS
L, LL and LLL	NO TV
APR-OCT	**ATMOS**
NC500	HES/NTS
☕	

ROOMS indicates the current number of bedrooms in total (to give an idea of the size of the hotel). No differentiation is made as to the type of room.

NO PETS indicates that the hotel does not generally accept pets.

DF denotes a place that welcomes dogs, although often with conditions. Check in advance.

NO KIDS does not necessarily mean children are unwelcome, only that special provisions are not usually made; ask in advance. In other cases, children are welcome, often with special rates.

L, LL and LLL indicate places in outstanding locations. L is set in a great location; LL denotes a very special setting; and LLL indicates a world-class spot.

NO TV means there are no TVs in the bedrooms.

APR-OCT shows when the accommodation is open. No dates means it is open all year.

ATMOS indicates a place whose special atmosphere is an attraction in itself.

NC500 indicates a place that is on or close to the North Coast 500 route.

HES or NTS denotes a place in the care of Historic Environment Scotland or the National Trust for Scotland.

☕ indicates a property with an exceptional tearoom.

3. Accommodation and Dining Cost Codes

£, ££, £££ and £LOTS indicate the general cost of the **accommodation** based on a standard twin or double room rate, with breakfast included. Note, however, that many hotels change rates daily depending on occupancy. The broad prices associated with each band are: £ = under £100; ££ = £100-£175; £££ = £175-250; and £LOTS = over £250.

For **dining** £, ££, £££ and £LOTS refer to the cost of an average dinner per person with a starter, main course and dessert. Wine, coffee and extras are excluded. The prices associated with each band are: £ = under £25; ££ = £25-£35; £££ = £35-45; and £LOTS = over £45.

4. Walking codes

Beside each of the many walks in the book is a series of codes, as follows:

3-10KM   CIRC/XCIRC   BIKES/XBIKES/MT BIKES   1-A-1

3-10KM means the walk(s) described may vary in length between the distances shown.
CIRC means the walk can be circular, while **XCIRC** shows the walk is not circular and you must return more or less the way you came.
BIKES indicates the walk has a path which is suitable for ordinary bikes. **XBIKES** means the walk is not suitable for, or does not permit, cycling. **MT BIKES** means the track is suitable for mountain or all-terrain bikes.

The **1-A-1** Code:
First number (1, 2 or 3) indicates how easy the walk is.
1 the walk is easy.
2 medium difficulty, i.e. standard hillwalking, not dangerous nor requiring special knowledge or equipment.
3 difficult: care and preparation and a map are needed.
The letters (**A, B** or **C**) indicate how easy it is to find the path.
A the route is easy to find. The way is either marked or otherwise obvious.
B the route is not very obvious, but you'll get there.
C you will need a map and preparation or a guide.
The last number (1, 2 or 3) indicates what to wear on your feet.
1 ordinary outdoor shoes, including trainers, are probably okay unless the ground is very wet.
2 you will need walking boots.
3 you will need serious walking or hiking boots.
Apart from designated walks, the **1-A-1** code is employed wherever there is more than a short stroll required to get to somewhere, e.g. a waterfall or a monument.

Abbreviations

As well as the codes in the left hand margin, I use abbreviations within the main entries. The most common ones are:

TGP – time of going to print, where available information was correct at the time. The place may not even be fully open but is included on the basis of an informed expectation that it will be good.

AYR – all year round

Other abbreviations include:

N, S, E, W, NE, etc = north, south, east, west, northeast, etc
LO = last orders (for orders from a kitchen)
4/4/4 = in dining, 4 choices for starters, 4 for main course and 4 for pudding
F&C = fish & chips
VG = very good

Wha's Like Us?

Famously Big Attractions

Among the established 'top 10' (paid entry) and the 'top 10' (free) visitor attractions, these are the ones really worth seeing. Find them under their item numbers.

Edinburgh Castle; **Holyrood Palace**; **Edinburgh Zoo**; **The National Museum of Scotland**; **The National Gallery**; **Our Dynamic Earth** 398/402/401/399/406/405/ATTRACTIONS.

The People's Palace, Glasgow; **The Burrell Collection**; **Kelvingrove**; **The Riverside Museum** 678/676/675/674/ATTRACTIONS.

The Glasgow Botanic Gardens; **The Gallery of Modern Art** 682/683/ATTRACTIONS. **The Edinburgh Botanics** 408/ATTRACTIONS.

Culzean Castle; **Stirling Castle**; **Castle of Mey** 1813/1810/1815/CASTLES.

Mount Stuart; **Manderston** 1871/1873/HOUSES.

Skara Brae; **The Callanish Stones** 1850/1852/PREHISTORIC.

Rosslyn Chapel 1898/CHURCHES.

OTHER UNMISSABLES ARE:

1 7/L24   ✓✓✓ **Loch Lomond** Approach via Stirling and A811 to Drymen, or from Glasgow, the A82 Dumbarton road to Balloch. Britain's largest inland waterway and a traditional playground, especially for Glaswegians; jet-skis, show-off boats. **Lomond Shores** at Balloch is the heavily retail gateway to the loch (including Jenners) and the **Loch Lomond National Park** which covers a vast area. Orientate and shop here.

The W bank between Balloch and Tarbet is most developed: marinas, cruises, ferry to Inchmurrin Island. Luss is tweeville, like a movie set (it was used in the Scottish TV soap, *High Road*) but has a good hotel and eaterie (470/HOTELS OUTSIDE GLASGOW). The road is more picturesque beyond Tarbet to Ardlui; see 1312/GOOD PUBS for the less touristy Scots experience of the **Drover's Inn** at Inverarnan. The E is more natural, wooded; good lochside and hill walks (2010/MUNROS). The road is winding but picturesque beyond Balmaha towards Ben Lomond. Hire a rowing boat at Balmaha to Inchcailloch Island: lovely woodland walks (2068/WALKS). Cameron House and **Lodge on the Loch** are excellent accom options (472/ HOTELS). Water taxis: 01301 702356; www.cruiselochlomond.co.uk.

2 5/G19   ✓✓✓ **The Cuillin Mountains** This hugely impressive range in the S of Skye, often shrouded in cloud or rain, is the romantic heartland of the islands. The Red Cuillin are smoother and nearer the Portree–Broadford road; the Black Cuillin gather behind and are best approached from **Glen Brittle** (2030/ WALKS; 1659/WATERFALLS). This classic, untameable mountain scenery has attracted walkers, climbers and artists for centuries. It still claims lives regularly. For best views apart from Glen Brittle, see 1684/SCENIC ROUTES; 1701/VIEWS. Vast range of walks and scrambles (also 1716/SWIMMING). See p. 386–91 for eats/sleep.

3 5/L18   ✓✓✓ **Loch Ness** Most visits start from Inverness at the N end via the Caledonian Canal. Fort Augustus is at the other end, 56km to the south. Loch Ness is part of the still-navigable Caledonian Canal linking to the W coast at Fort William. Small boats line the shores at certain points. The popular way to see the loch is on a cruise from Inverness: Jacobite Cruises 01463 233999, 1-6 hours; or several options from Fort Augustus: Cruise Loch Ness 01320 366277; or the small, friendly Nessie Hunter from Drumnadrochit 01456 450395. Most tourist traffic uses the main A82 N bank road converging on Drumnadrochit, where the Loch Ness Monster industry gobbles up your money. If you must, the official Loch Ness Monster Exhibition is the one to choose. On the A82, you can't miss **Urquhart Castle** (1846/RUINS) but nor does anyone else so it's often hoachin' (a

Scottish word for overcrowded). Two of the best things about Loch Ness are: the south road (B862) from Fort Augustus back to Inverness (1687/SCENIC ROUTES); and the detour from Drumnadrochit to Cannich to Glen Affric (20-30km) (1642/GLENS; 2025/WALKS; 1652/WATERFALLS). Best drop in, eat (and stay) is the **Loch Ness Inn** at Drumnadrochit, or the **Boathouse** 01320 366682. Best pub grub and stay is **Glenmoriston Arms** (1216/INNS). There's also a restaurant – the view is more restoring than the food, so eat outside if possible – the only one on the loch (at Fort Augustus). Abbey (now The Highland Club self-catering accom).

4 8/Q23 ✓✓ **The V&A** Dundee · www.vam.ac.uk/dundee · 01382 411611 The V&A opened amid huge anticipation, excitement and then enthusiastic acclaim in late summer 2018. Japanese architect Kengo Kuma became an honorary Scotsman and not just Dundee but the whole of Scotland fell immediately in love with his consummate design, which makes the most of its riverbank location by the steamship **RRS Discovery** (from 1901), creating a new landmark for Scotland's enterprise and culture. Through a cathedral-sized atrium, up a sweeping staircase to the Galleries: one for changing exhibitions via London's V&A, one an exploration of Scottish design through time, one for community-based work. Restaurant upstairs, café and bookshop in the foyer. The solid but edgy edifice seen in countless photographs is in contrast to its splendid but people-friendly interior, with frequent glimpses of the Tay and its bridge – Dundee's new 'lounge'. The queues may have died down by the time you visit. 7 days 10am-5pm.

5 8/N25 ✓✓ **The Falkirk Wheel and The Kelpies** Falkirk · www.thefalkirkwheel.co.uk; www.thehelix.co.uk Halfway between Edinburgh and Glasgow, signed from the M9, M80 and locally. The splendid wheel and deliberately dramatic massive boat-lift at the convergence of the reinstated Union and Forth & Clyde canals – the world's first coast-to-coast ship canal (to wander or plooter along). The 35-metre lift is impressive to watch and great to go on. Boats leave the visitor centre every 40 mins for the 45-min journey AYR. Great network of paths to walk and cycle from here and it links (though 8km and not so conveniently) to **The Helix** and The Kelpies, dramatically rearing from the canal basin beside the M9. Neither Helix Park (water, walking & family activities), nor the giant horses' heads by Andy Scott are easy to get to (junction 5, then signs; or bus from Grahamstown Station to Falkirk stadium, then walk). Guided tours, including going inside the head-down Kelpie, take 45 mins. Visitor centre and café. Kelpies and the Helix open at all times.

Favourite Scottish Journeys

6 7/K21 ✓✓ **The West Highland Line** 0345 748 4950 One of the most picturesque railway journeys in Europe and quite the best way to get to Skye from the south. Travelling from Glasgow to Fort William, you pass the biggest loch (Lomond), the longest (Awe) and the deepest (Morar), and the highest ben (Nevis), the Bonnie Prince Charlie Country (see p. 329-30) and much that is close to a railwayman's heart by viaducts (including the Harry Potter one) and tunnels over loch and down dale. It's also possible to make the same journey (from Fort William to Mallaig and/or return) by steam train from mid-May to mid-Oct (0844 850 4680; www.westcoastrailways.co.uk) on **The Jacobite** – this is generally regarded as one of the great railway journeys of the world (and it is a very busy wee train). There's a museum in the restored station at Glenfinnan with a tearoom (1447/TEAROOMS) and bunk accom. 3 trains a day leave from Glasgow Queen St for Mallaig (5 hours).

7 5/H19 ✓ **Glenelg-Kylerhea** www.skyeferry.co.uk · 01599 522273 The shorter of the 2 remaining ferry journeys to Skye and definitely the best way to get there

if you're not pushed for time. The drive to Glenelg from the A87 is spectacular (1676/SCENIC ROUTES) and so is this 5-min crossing of the deep Narrows of Kylerhea. Easter-Oct, every 20 mins. The ferry is run by and very much a part of the local community around Glenelg. Cute wee shack to visit before departure. This is a project worth supporting. There's an otter-watch hide at Kylerhea.

8 5/G19 ✓ **Elgol, Isle of Skye** Trips on either the *Bella Jane* (0800 731 3089) or the *Misty Isle* (01471 866288) on Loch Coruisk to see the whales, dolphins, basking sharks and, of course, the famous view (1701/VIEWS).

9 7/K25 **Wemyss Bay-Rothesay Ferry** www.calmac.co.uk · 0800 066 5000 The landmark glass-roofed station at Wemyss Bay, the railhead from Glasgow (60km by road on the A78), is redolent of an age-old terminus (refurbished 2015). The frequent (CalMac) ferry has all the Scottish traits and treats you can handle, and Rothesay (with its period seaside mansions) appears out of blood-smeared sunsets and rain-sodden mornings alike, a gentle watercolour from summer holidays past. Visit the (Victorian) toilet when you get there and especially magnificent **Mount Stuart** (1871/HOUSES) on beautiful Bute.

10 8/L24 **Sailing Loch Katrine** www.lochkatrine.com · 01877 376316 The historic steamship *Sir Walter Scott* (he who put it, and, at the same time, Scottish tourism on the map) and the smaller *Lady of the Lake*. Leave from the 'Trossachs Pier' at the end of large car park 2km off the A821. This journey on Loch Katrine is a classic Trossachs experience, especially in the purple-and-golden-tinted autumn. Both do 1-hour or (to the end of the loch) 2-hour cruises. The Walter Scott café/bar had a revamp 2018. Katrine Wheelz bike hire (01877 376366) in car park. Great cycling round here – you can take bike on board and cycle back (22km).

11 8/P25 **The Maid of the Forth Cruise to Inchcolm Island** www.maidoftheforth. co.uk · 0131 331 5000 The wee boat (though it holds 225 people) which leaves every day at different times (online or phone for details) from Hawes Pier in South Queensferry (30km central Edinburgh via A90) opposite the Hawes Inn, just under the famous railway bridge (400/ATTRACTIONS). 90-min trips under the bridge and on to Inchcolm, an attractive island with walks and an impressive ruined abbey. Much birdlife and also many seals. 1.5 hours ashore. Tickets at pier. Mar-Oct.

12 5/M18 **North & West from Inverness** 0345 748 4950 Two less celebrated (than the West Highland Line above) but mesmerising rail journeys start from Inverness. The journey to Kyle of Lochalsh no longer has an observation car in summer, so get a window seat and take a map; the last section through Glen Carron and around the coast at Loch Carron is especially fine. There are 3 trains a day and it takes 2.5 hours. Inverness to Wick (via Thurso) is a 4.5-hour journey. The section skirting the E coast from Lairg to Helmsdale is full of drama, followed by the transfixing monotony of the Flow Country. 3 trains a day in summer.

13 3/C19 **The Plane to Barra** www.hial.co.uk · 01871 890 212 Most of the island plane journeys pass over many smaller islands (e.g. Glasgow–Tiree, Glasgow–Stornoway, Wick–Orkney) and are fascinating on a clear day, but the daily flight from Glasgow to Barra is doubly special because the island's airport is on Cockleshell Beach in the north (11km from Castlebay) after a splendid approach. The 12-seater Otter leaves and lands according to the tide. Operated by Flybe; you can go on to Benbecula.

14 8/M26 **Paddle Steamer Waverley** www.waverleyexcursions.co.uk Website best for information/bookings. The last seagoing paddle steamer in the world, built on the Clyde and lovingly restored, celebrated 70 years in 2016. Various trips around Western Isles and the west coast during summer months.

The Best Annual Events

15
JAN
Up-Helly-Aa Lerwick · www.uphellyaa.org · 01595 693434 Traditionally the 24th day after Christmas, now the last Tuesday in January. A mid-winter fire festival based on Viking lore; 'the Guizers' haul a galley through the streets of Lerwick and burn it in the park; the night goes on.

16
JAN
Celtic Connections Glasgow · www.celticconnections.com · 0141 353 8000 A huge, 3-week festival of Celtic music from round the world held in the Royal Concert Hall and other city venues. Concerts, ceilidhs, workshops. It's brilliant!

17
25 JAN
Burns Night The National Bard celebrated with supper. Increasing number of local and family celebrations. No single major event, except **The Big Burns Supper Festival** (www.bigburnssupper.com) in Dumfries. It is big. Community focused and over several days and venues. Not just about the Bard. In Edinburgh, the fledging **Red Red Rose Street** is across venues in the city centre around the 25th.

18
FEB
Scottish Snowdrop Festival Cambo, nr Crail · 01333 450054 Yep, a festival to celebrate the carpets of trembling snowdrops in the wondrous woods of **Cambo House** (881/FIFE). For a few weeks in early spring. Popular or what!

19
FEB
Glasgow Film Festival www.glasgowfilm.org · 0141 332 6535 Relatively recent arrival on the FF circuit but hugely popular; imaginatively programmed. Adjunct of and run through Glasgow Film Theatre.

20
MAR
Glasgow International Comedy Festival www.glasgowcomedyfestival.com · 0844 873 7353 In small and large venues, a comedy festival in the city where a comedy festival belongs.

21
MAR
StAnza St Andrews · www.stanzapoetry.org Scotland's only (and rare everywhere) poetry festival with readings, exhibitions, national and international guests. And lovely St Andrews!

22
MID-APR
Glasgow International www.glasgowinternational.org Biennial ('20, '22) festival presenting contemporary visual art in the city's main arts venues and unusual or found spaces; celebrating Glasgow's significance as a source and generator of cutting-edge art.

23
APR
Edinburgh International Science Festival www.sciencefestival.co.uk · 0131 553 0320 Longest established and largest science festival in the UK. Has outreached and branched out even to Abu Dhabi! Fab for kids (especially in NMS and the City Art Centre); fascinating for grown-ups.

24
APR
Melrose Sevens www.melrose7s.com · 01896 822993 This Border town is completely taken over by the tournament in their small-is-beautiful rugby ground. Sevens, now global, were first played here in 1883. Lots of big lads!

25
APR
Aye Write Glasgow · www.ayewrite.com · 0141 353 8000 The city's book festival based at the Mitchell Library. It's good, but!

26
END APR
Shetland Folk Festival www.shetlandfolkfestival.com · 01595 694757 36th anniversary 2016. Britain's most northerly and one of the best folk fests.

27
EARLY MAY
Ten Under The Ben Fort William · www.nofussevents.co.uk · 01397 772899 A 10-hour mountain-bike endurance event around Ben Nevis. Good fun, though. Run by No Fuss Events. 700 riders on average.

28 **Traquair Fayre** Innerleithen · www.traquair.co.uk · 01896 830323 In the
MAY grounds of **Traquair** (1874/HOUSES), a mini-medieval Glastonbury with music,
comedy and crafts. Great café here 1420/TEAROOMS.

29 **Beltane** Edinburgh The gloriously pagan gathering on the city's Calton Hill to
1 MAY celebrate May Day. Full of light, fire, drumming. Wait for the dawn.

30 **Paps of Jura Fell Race** www.jurafellrace.org.uk · 01496 810254 The amazing
MAY hill race up and down the 3 Paps (4 tops in all) on this large, remote island (2231/
ISLANDS). About 200 runners take on the 16-mile challenge from the distillery in
Craighouse, the village. Winner does it in 3 hours!

31 **Tweedlove Bike Festival** Peebles · www.tweedlove.com 2 weeks of cycling
MAY/JUN for all levels, including serious international riders in Tweed Valley. Bike heaven!

32 **Common Ridings** The 11 Borders town festivals. Similar formats over different
MAY-AUG weeks with ride-outs (on horseback to outlying villages, etc), shows, dances and
games, culminating on the Friday and Saturday. Total local involvement. Hawick is
first, then West Linton, Selkirk, Peebles, Melrose, Galashiels, Jedburgh, Duns, Kelso,
Lauder and Coldstream at the beginning of August. All authentic and truly local.

33 **Mhor Festival** www.mhor.net · 01877 384622 The fab farmhouse boutique
MAY hotel (795/CENTRAL) hosts a hoolie and a food feast on its land overlooking the
loch: Scottish chefs and Tom. Cooler than the Cotswolds!

34 **Edinburgh Marathon** www.edinburghmarathon.com The UK's fastest, and
END MAY Scotland's largest and perhaps most picturesque marathon route. Also with 5km
and 10km, junior events, etc.

35 **Knockengorroch World Ceilidh** nr Dalmellington · www.knockengorroch.
END MAY org.uk Much-loved bespoke music festival au naturel on family land in the
Galloway Hills. Small is beautiful.

36 **Moonwalk** Edinburgh · www.walkthewalk.org The big pink and hopefully
EARLY JUN moonlit walk starting at midnight through the streets of Edinburgh in aid of breast
cancer charities. Many, many wimmin (and some guys); euphoric!

37 **Flower Shows** Edinburgh · www.gardeningscotland.com Many Scottish
EARLY JUN towns hold flower shows, mainly in autumn, but the big spring show is Gardening
Scotland at the Royal Highland Centre (Ingliston). The annual **Ayr show** www.
ayranddistrictflowershow.com in August is huge! 30,000 visitors!

38 **Royal Highland Show** Ingliston · www.royalhighlandshow.org ·
JUN 0131 335 6207 The premier agricultural show in Scotland. For the farming world,
the event of the year. Animals, machinery, food, crafts, shopping. > 180,000 attend.

39 **Mountain Bike World Cup** Fort William · www.fortwilliamworldcup.
JUN co.uk Held at Nevis Range 5K run, around the ski gondola. Awesome course with
international competitors over 2 days. Evening events in town. Date varies.

40 **Borders Book Festival** Melrose · www.bordersbookfestival.org ·
JUN 01896 822644 The hugely successful and utterly appropriate (to town and times)
bookfest held in Harmony Gardens. Intimate, friendly: reads well.

41
LATE JUN
Solas Festival nr Tibbermore · www.solasfestival.co.uk Small but beautiful music-based fest held indoors (the steading) and on outdoor stages at the Bield (1285/RETREATS), near Perth, off the A85 to Crieff. Always impressive line-up.

42
LATE JUN
Edinburgh International Film Festival www.edfilmfest.org.uk · 0131 228 4051 Various screens and other locations in Edinburgh city centre. One of the world's oldest film festivals (70th anniversary year 2016). 10 days of film and movie matters. Currently restoring its serious credentials.

43
LATE JUN
St Magnus Festival Kirkwall, Orkney · www.stmagnusfestival.com · 01856 871445 Midsummer celebration of the arts, founded by Sir Peter Maxwell Davies, has attracted big names for almost 40 years. Quite highbrow; the cathedral at its heart. The days are very long.

44
EARLY JUL
Kelburn Garden Party Kelburn Castle, nr Largs · www.kelburngardenparty. com Cool, young, fresh indie music festival, with arty stuff in grounds of crazy graffitied castle on the Clyde coast.

45
EARLY JUL
Scottish Traditional Boat Festival Portsoy · www.stbfportsoy.org · 01261 842951 Perfect little festival in perfect little Moray town over a weekend in early July. Old boats in old and new harbours, open-air ceilidh, good atmos.

46
JUL
Scottish Game Fair Perth · www.scottishfair.com · 01738 554826 Held in the rural and historical setting of Scone Palace, a major Perthshire day out and gathering for the hunting, shooting, fishing and shopping brigade.

47
MID-JUL
Hebcelt Stornoway · www.hebceltfest.com · 01851 621234 Folk-rock format festival under canvas on faraway Lewis. Celebrates 25 years in 2020. Gaelic and notable national names. Music and craic.

48
MID-JUL
Tiree Music Festival Isle of Tiree · www.tireemusicfestival.co.uk Not content with one festival (see Oct), this tiny island proclaims its sand and surf and cultural chutzpah by hosting a home-grown, full-on weekend music festival in a 2,000-capacity tent with great bands.

49
MID-JUL
Great Kindrochit Quadrathlon Loch Tay · www.artemisgreatkindrochit.com The toughest 1-day sporting event: swim 1.3km across the loch, run 24km (incl. 7 Munros), kayak 11km & cycle 54km. Then slice a melon with a sword. Jings!

50
END JUL
Merchant City Festival Glasgow · www.merchantcityfestival.com · 0141 287 8985 A host of free and some ticketed events bringing life to the city's cultural quarter near George Sq. Eclectic programme.

51
EARLY AUG
Black Isle Show Muir of Ord · https://blackisleshow.com · 01463 870870 Notable agricultural show and countryside gathering for the NE Highlands. A big family day out.

52
EARLY AUG
Art Week Pittenweem · www.pittenweemartsfestival.co.uk Remarkable local event where the whole of Pittenweem in Fife becomes a gallery. Over 70 venues show work: public buildings, people's houses. Refreshing!

53
AUG
Belladrum Tartan Heart Festival nr Kiltarlity · www.tartanheartfestival. co.uk · 01463 741366 Off A862 Beauly road W of Inverness. Friendly, 2-day music fest, loyal following – sells out. Beautiful terraced site. Good for families.

54 **The Edinburgh Festivals** Since 1947 (70th anniversary 2017), Edinburgh has
AUG   hosted the biggest arts festival in the world with:
       The International Festival www.eif.co.uk · **0131 473 2000** A major
       programme of music, drama and dance with the **Virgin Money Fireworks** on the
       final Monday.
       The Fringe www.edfringe.com with hundreds of events every night in every
       conceivable venue, especially around the university in the Old Town (daily free
       performances in the Royal Mile) and around George St.
       The **Jazz Festival** www.edinburghjazzfestival.co.uk and (mainly for delegates
       on a bit of a jolly), **The TV Festival**.

55 **Edinburgh International Book Festival** www.edbookfest.co.uk ·
AUG   **0131 718 5666** A tented village in Charlotte Sq Gardens. Same time as the above
       but deserving of another separate entry; uniquely engaging and ever growing – now
       spread down George St.

56 **Royal Edinburgh Military Tattoo** www.edintattoo.co.uk · **0131 225 1188** For
AUG   many the main event of the August festival period and a global attraction. On the
       Castle Esplanade for 3 weeks. Many soldiers and marching. Always stirring stuff.

57 **Fringe by the Sea** **North Berwick** · **www.fringebythesea.com** An alternative
AUG   to the frenetic Fringe in Edinburgh (<50 mins by road, less by train). Mainly music
       in Spiegeltents by the dreamy harbour, and the delights of a gentle E Lothian town.

58 **The World Pipe Band Championships** Glasgow · **www.theworlds.co.uk**
AUG   Since 1930, unbelievable numbers (3,000-4,000) of pipers from all over the world
       competing and seriously attuned on Glasgow Green.

59 **Cowal Highland Gathering** Dunoon · **www.cowalgathering.com** One of
AUG   many Highland games but this, along with **Luss and Loch Lomond Games**,
       Inverness in July, and **Braemar** (below) are the main events in the calendar that
       extends from May to September. Expect heavy events (very big lads only), dancing,
       pipe bands, field and track events, and much drinking and chat.

60 **Braemar Gathering** www.braemargathering.org · **01339 741098** Of many
EARLY SEP Highland games (**Aboyne** early August, **Ballater** mid-August on Deeside), this the
       big attraction. Go ogle the royals.

61 **The Ben Nevis Race** www.bennevisrace.co.uk The race over 100 years old
SEP   up Britain's highest mountain and back. The record is 1 hour 25 mins which seems
       amazing. 600 runners though curiously little national, even local interest. Starts
       2pm at Claggan Park off Glen Nevis roundabout.

62 **Dundee Flower & Food Festival** www.dundeeflowerandfoodfestival.com
SEP   3–6 day food fair and flower fest in the city's **Camperdown Park** (1602/PARKS;
       1757/KIDS). A big Dundee day out.

63 **Skye Live** **Portree** · **www.skyelive.co.uk** The late summer indie music festival
SEP   in the splendorous surroundings of 'The Lump' by Portree. Eclectic, friendly, vibey.
       Very Skye-like.

64 **The Pedal for Scotland Glasgow to Edinburgh Bike Ride** www.cycling.scot Fun
SEP   charity fundraiser and serious annual bike fest. From Glasgow Green to Victoria Park
       with a Pasta Party at the halfway point. 51 miles/100 miles return (or shorter versions).

65 **Wigtown Book Festival** www.wigtownbookfestival.com · 01988 403222
SEP-OCT Small, beautiful bookfest in Scotland's booktown in Galloway. In marquees in and around the square, with great clubrooms above the shop. Edinburgh goes south. See also 1457/1458/1459/TEAROOMS.

66 **Loch Ness Marathon** www.lochnessmarathon.com One of the UK's top
EARLY OCT marathons and a festival of running, starting midway along the SE shore of the loch and finishing in Inverness. Also 10k races and kids' events.

67 **Tiree Wave Classic** www.tireewaveclassic.co.uk Windsurfing heaven on a
EARLY OCT faraway island (2237/ISLANDS) where beaches offer challenging wind conditions and islanders offer warm hospitality.

68 **Tour of Mull Rally** www.mullrally.org The highlight of the national rally
OCT calendar is this racing around Mull weekend. Though drivers enter from all over the world, the overall winner has often been a local man (well, plenty time for practice). Accom tight, but the locals put you up.

69 **The Enchanted Forest** Pitlochry · www.enchantedforest.org.uk ·
OCT 01796 484626 A major month-long son et lumière and performance event in the woodlands outside town.

70 **Perthshire Amber Festival** www.perthshireamber.com · 01350 724281
OCT A music festival all around Perthshire. Started by musician and national treasure Dougie MacLean, based in Dunkeld. Great bakers 1470/ARTISAN BAKERS.

71 **Festival of the Future** Dundee · www.dundee.ac.uk/futurefest A 5-day
OCT celebration of books, reading, ideas, food – everything, really! An initiative of Dundee University and going from strength to strength.

72 **Illuminight** Kilmarnock · www.illuminight.co.uk A full-on lighting experience
OCT/NOV on a trail through Dean Castle Country Park by Unique Events, who did Botanic Lights in Edinburgh when it was good.

73 **St Andrew's Night** Increasingly a bigger deal than before, with government
30 NOV sponsored events. National holiday, anyone?

74 **Edinburgh's Christmas** www.edinburghschristmas.com The city's 6-week
DEC Christmas illuminations, activities, fairground attractions and markets centred in E Princes St Gardens and St Andrew Sq. Take lotsa cash!

75 **Cromarty Film Festival** www.cromartyfilmfestival.org Cromarty on the Black
DEC Isle (1608/VILLAGES). A small but beautiful, mainly local filmfest up north, and a refreshing weekend away.

76 **Stonehaven Fireball Festival** www.stonehavenfireballs.co.uk Celebrated
31 DEC since 1910, a traditional Hogmanay fire festival that probably wouldn't get started nowadays for 'health and safety' reasons. 40 fireballers throw them around in the streets before processing to the harbour and heaving them in. Concert in the square.

77 **Edinburgh's Hogmanay** www.edinburghshogmanay.com · 0131 651 3380
DEC-JAN Scotland's major winter (3 days) festival; a global must-go. It's launched with a **Torchlight Procession** through the city centre. The main event is the **Street Party** on 31st. Be part of a huge, good-natured crowd; it is the Scots at their hospitable best! But I would say that, and false modesty prevents me saying anything else.

What The Scots Gave The Modern World...

Scotland's population is only just over 5 million, yet we discovered, invented or manufactured for the first time the following world-changing things.

3.5 inch hard disc drive
The Advertising Film
The Alpha Chip
Anaesthesia
Ante-Natal Clinics
Antiseptics
Artificial Ice
The Arts Festival
The ATM
Bakelite
The Bank of England
Barr's Irn-Bru
The Bicycle
Bovril
The Bowling Green
The Bus
Colour Photography
The Compass
The Decimal Point
The Documentary
Dolly, the first clone
Electric Light
Electric Toaster
Encyclopaedia Britannica
The Fax Machine
Fingerprinting
The Flushing Toilet
The Fountain Pen
Gardenias
The Gas Mask
Geology
Golf and the Golf Course
Grand Theft Auto
Hallowe'en
Helium
Higgs boson (the 'God Particle')
Hypnotism
The Hypodermic Syringe
Insulin
Interferon
The Kaleidoscope
Kinetic Energy
The Lawnmower
Life Insurance
The Locomotive
Logarithms

The Mackintosh
Marmalade
The Microwave Oven
The Modern Parking Cone
The Modern Road Surface
Morphine
Motor Insurance
The MRI Scanner
Neon
The Oil Refinery
The Overdraft
Paraffin
Penicillin
The Photocopier
The Pneumatic Tyre
Postage Stamps
Postcards
Quinine
Radar
The Refrigerator
Rubber Wellies
The Savings Bank
Sherlock Holmes
Sociology
The Steam Engine
Stocks and Shares
Street Lighting
Streets in blocks (as in US)
The Telegraph
The Telephone
Television
Tennis Courts
The Theory of Combustion
The Thermometer
Thread
The Threshing Machine
Tropical Medicine
Typhoid Vaccine
Ultrasound
Universal Standard Time
The US Navy
The Vacuum (Thermos) Flask
Video
Wave Power
Whisky
Writing Paper

...and Auld Lang Syne

the Best

of Edinburgh

Edinburgh's Unique Hotels

78 8/Q25
168 ROOMS
20 SUITES
LL
£LOTS

✓✓ **The Balmoral** 1 Princes St · www.roccofortehotels.com ·
0131 556 2414 At east end above Waverley Station. Capital landmark, its
clock 3 minutes fast (except at Hogmanay), so you might catch your train. The old
pile dear to owner Sir Rocco Forte's heart. 4 categories of rooms: internals quieter,
all views different; only 'super deluxe' have the castle view. Some top suites. Deluxe
feel to the public spaces: the Palm Court (great afternoon teas; harpist on the
balcony 1464/AFTERNOON TEA). Great concierge service. Pool small (15m) but
beautiful steam room and sauna. ESPA products in the spa. Few hotels anywhere
are so much in the heart of things.
EAT Main restaurant, **Number One** (117/FINE DINING), is below and in formal
brasserie and a top restaurant in the city. **Prince** by Alain Roux is on the Princes St
corner, for breakfast, lunch and dinner. Elegant but casual! And expensive.

79 8/Q25
241 ROOMS
NO PETS
L
£LOTS

£££

✓✓ **Waldorf Astoria – The Caledonian** Princes St · www.waldorfastoria3.
hilton.com · 0131 222 8888 An Edinburgh institution, 'The Caley' – at the
west end of Princes St – a former station hotel built in 1903. Constant refurbishment
under the Waldorf Astoria moniker continues to reinforce the 5-star status of an
Edinburgh landmark hotel. Good business hotel, with all facilities you'd expect of the
brand, including a Guerlain spa with nice pool. Endearing lack of uniformity in the
rooms; castle-view rooms (85) also looking across the graveyard and Princes St are at
a premium. Some very big bathrooms. Main restaurant, **The Pompadour**, for formal
fine dining in an elegant setting does perhaps lack the glamour and gourmet cred of
days gone by. It's run by Galvin's of London, as is the ground-floor Brasserie de Luxe.
Afternoon tea in the adjoining open lounge, **Peacock Alley**. The Caley (whisky) bar is
a famous rendezvous with an impressive whisky selection. Under irrepressible
Canadian General Manager, Dale MacPhee, the Caledonian fulfils all the expectations
of a luxury hotel at the heart of a great city.
EAT While The Pompadour does tend to remain above all that – dinner only Wed-
Sun, **Galvin's Brasserie de Luxe** (0131 222 8988; www.galvinbrasseriedeluxe.
com) is one of the smartest casual dining restaurants in the city, a classic brasserie
menu, some superior signature dishes and cosmopolitan service. 7 days.

80 8/Q25
23 ROOMS
DF
NO KIDS
ATMOS
£LOTS

✓✓ **Prestonfield** off Priestfield Rd · www.prestonfield.com ·
0131 668 3346 3km S of city centre. There's simply nowhere else like
Prestonfield anywhere else; it envelops you. The raucous peacocks in the 20-acre
grounds proclaim that this is not your average urban bed for the night. A romantic,
almost other-worldly 17th-century building with period features still intact. In
2003, James Thomson, Edinburgh's most notable restaurateur of **The Tower** and
The Witchery (120/FINE DINING), turned this old bastion of Edinburgh sensibilities
into Scotland's most sumptuous hotel. He's still collecting fabulous objets for it.
The architecture and the detail are exceptional. All rooms (luxury/named suites
and 'The Owners Suite') are highly individualistic with hand-picked antiques and
artefacts and the usual technologies. Prestonfield probably hosts more awards
dinners and accommodates more celebrity guests than anywhere else in town, and
it itself has won many awards, especially as a 'romantic' or 'individual' hotel. In
summer, the nightly Scottish cabaret (in the stable block) is hugely popular.
EAT House restaurant **Rhubarb**: a memorable experience (121/FINE DINING).

81 8/Q25
9 SUITES
ATMOS
£LOTS

✓✓ **The Witchery** Castlehill · www.thewitchery.com · 0131 225 5613
James Thomson's (Prestonfield, above) much celebrated and awarded
suites at the top of the Royal Mile. The Inner Sanctum, the Old Rectory and 7
others, all highly bespoke, indulgent, theatrical and gorgeous, and consolidated
into a uniquely Edinburgh experience above and around the restaurant and first

venture (120/FINE DINING). At the heart of the Old Town, here at its most atmospheric. 5 apartments are across the street. Join a long, celebrity-studded guest list. Routinely regarded as among the sexiest suites in the world.

82 8/Q25
199 ROOMS
£LOTS

✓✓ **The Edinburgh Charlotte Square** 38 Charlotte Sq · www. phcompany.com · 0131 240 5500 This grand yet discreet Edinburgh hotel of old, on the W End corner of George St, but ranging over a whole block of elegant Charlotte Sq, went through a multi-million, all-encompassing makeover in 2017 and was transformed into a stylish, urban hotel worthy of its location and long veneration. The colour-matched, cosmopolitan look prevails throughout diverse, comfortable lounges and meeting areas, and over several categories and (5) floors of rooms. Breakfast, afternoon tea and drinks are taken in the light inner 'Garden' courtyard. BABA, the casual dining restaurant, has its own entrance on George St. A basement leisure suite of sauna, steam room, 12m pool and spa treatments (the Scottish seaweed-based Oskia and ishga products) opened in 2018. Limited car parking (16 places) should be pre-booked. Surprising and well-thought-out doggie policy.
EAT BABA, 130 George St, 0131 527 4999 Lebanese/Middle Eastern casual meze-style dining. 7 days from noon. See 214/MEDITERRANEAN.

83 8/Q25
249 ROOMS
£££

✓ **The George Hotel** 19-21 George St · www.phcompany.com · 0131 225 1251 Between Hanover St and St Andrew Sq. Designed by Robert Adam and dating back to the late 18th century, this is a classy joint and Edinburgh landmark hotel. Some changes of ownership and names. Recently now in the Intercontinental Group; in Edinburgh we call it 'The George'. Views of the Forth from the deluxe rooms on floors 4 to 7 of the newer 'Forth' wing. Like all the top hotels on this page, it's pricey, but here you pay for the location and the Georgian as well as contemporary niceties. Good Festival and Hogmanay hotel close to the heart of things. The George has successfully shrugged off its once staid, traditional image, fitting into George St's more progressive, more opportunistic present. Great on-street bar/café **Burr & Co.**, with superior snacks, pastries and outdoor seating.
EAT Printing Press Bar & Kitchen (127/BRASSERIES) late 2015. Open to the street, by no means merely a hotel restaurant. Beautiful room. Josper grill.

84 8/Q25
50 APTS
DF
£LOTS

✓ **The Edinburgh Grand** St Andrew Sq · www.chrisstewartgroup.com · 0131 230 0570 Adding to the 'grand' upscaling of St Andrew Sq, this mainly apartment hotel, occupying a magnificent neo-classical, 5-storey building in the southeast corner, opened in summer 2018, along with Hawksmoor, the London-based steakhouse. Very high-spec apartments with kitchen facilities and full concierge service. 4th-floor bar (light food), the Register Club. No dining room or pool. Single bedroom studios (10) to penthouse prime views are expectedly expensive.
EAT Hawksmoor Ground floor with separate entrance on the lane. London's revered steak house, here in a lofty grand room. Lots of non-steak dishes, good wine list and, as expected, smart service.

85 8/Q25
23 CABINS
NO PETS
£LOTS

✓ **Fingal by the Royal Yacht Britannia, Leith** · www.fingal.co.uk · 0131 354 5000 A unique deluxe experience – on a boat, the former Northern Lighthouse MV Fingal. You board up the gangplank, your windows are portholes, you can go on deck. Run by the Royal Yacht (adjacent to the Ocean Terminal, so shopping on land nearby). Not yet open at TGP but presume it's like being on a luxury cruise liner without the pool, the palaver and a new port in the morning.

86 8/Q25
136 ROOMS
£LOTS

✓ **Radisson Collection** 1 George IV Bridge · www.radissoncollection.com · 0131 220 6660 Once a council building and converted '09 into the first Missoni hotel in the UK, the design statement was made from the start. Top of the Radisson range, rooms in a variety of categories determined by size and view. On this busy corner of the Royal Mile with its tourist tide, rooms are quiet and contemporary. **Cucina**, upstairs from the foyer and rather better than the Pizza Express slotted into the same building, and **Ondine** (226/SEAFOOD) complete a strong choice for adjacent dining. The bar, the **Epicurean**, perhaps a little too cool for its own good, does feel like it landed from Glasgow.

EAT Great Italian food and smart dining at a price. Report: 196/ITALIAN.

---

87 8/Q25
47 ROOMS
DF
£££

✓ **Hotel du Vin** 11 Bristo Pl · www.hotelduvin.com · 0131 285 1479 The discreetly tucked-away Edinburgh link in the expanding chain of hotels (451/UNIQUE HOTELS; 877/FIFE) created by imaginative and sympatico conversion of city centre, often historic buildings – in this case, the Lunatic Asylum & Infirmary, where Robert Fergusson, one of Scotland's iconic poets and revered by Robert Burns, died in 1774. This place is old! The hotel, however, enclosing a courtyard (with 'cigar bothy') and making maximum use of the up-and-down labyrinthine space, is comfortable and modern. Rooms in 4 categories are all different but have the same look. Monsoon showers in all but standard rooms. All, including suites, are well priced. Bar (24 hours for guests), a whisky snug (250 to try) and a very bistro bistro. As with other H du Vs, there's much to-do about wine. In a busy quarter near the university and museums; it's at the heart of the Fringe.

---

88 8/Q25
73 ROOMS
NO PETS
ATMOS
£££

✓ **The Scotsman** North Bridge · www.scotsmanhotel.co.uk · 0131 556 5565 Deluxe boutique hotel in landmark building (the old offices of *The Scotsman* newspaper group) converted in 2001 into chic, highly individual accom, and in 2018 refurbished and remodelled by Glasgow's G1 Group. Most of the impressive original features remain – stained glass, panelling and newspaper nostalgia (rooms are Reporter's, Editor's rooms, etc; most have splendid city views). Labyrinthine layout (stairs and fire doors everywhere) and slow lifts apart, this is the convenient 5-star hotel in midtown, though dining is confined to the (nevertheless buzzy) **Grand Café**, an all-purpose guest and public hub: breakfast, afternoon tea (noon-4pm), brasserie and late-night lounge bar (till 3am) with live piano, jazz, etc.

---

89 8/P25
29 ROOMS
£LOTS

✓ **Edinburgh Residence** 7 Rothesay Terrace · www. theedinburghresidence.com · 0131 226 3380 Your 'home in the city' on an extravagant scale. 3 Victorian townhouses have been joined into an elegant apartment hotel, once partly timeshare, so rooms in the 3 categories – Classic, Deluxe and Townhouse – are not always available. No restaurant – breakfast is served in suite, and dinner, if required. 24-hour concierge (snacks & sandwiches). A discreet and distinctive stopover with views of Dean Village. Drawing room if you're feeling lonely in this West End retreat, though nightlife and shops are a stroll away.

---

90 8/Q25
100 ROOMS
££

Malmaison 1 Tower Pl, Leith · www.malmaison.com · 0131 468 5000 At the Leith dock gates. Listed here because of its unique waterfront location and because this was the first Malmaison all those design-led years ago. All facilities that we, who were once smart and young, expect. Rooms have that darkish, masculine, solid yet well-lit look that has been much adopted elsewhere. Some port views. The brasserie and café-bar have stylish ambience too, and there are many very good bistro and other options adjacent, e.g. **Fishers** 227/SEAFOOD and **The Shore** 170/FOOD PUBS. Pity about the flats out front but the outside terrace is pleasant of a summer's evening. Car parking on site. It's a good 20 mins to uptown, where yet another Malmaison opens in 2019 (in St Andrew Sq with 74 rooms).

---

91 8/Q25
77 ROOMS
NO PETS
£££

The Glasshouse 2 Greenside Pl · www.theglasshousehotel.co.uk · 0131 525 8200 Sitting discreetly behind an old church between the Playhouse Theatre and Omni Centre, this Marriott Hotel is built above the multiplex (rooms on 3 floors) and the restaurants in the mall below. Surprisingly large and labyrinthine, and for many a frustrating hike to breakfast or reception. Main feature is the extensive lawned garden on the roof, half of the rooms have access (great views to Calton Hill and perspective on the city). Breakfast in faraway room. No restaurant. The Mall below is a disappointment; the restaurants all high-street staples but guests can use Nuffield Health facilities (including 25m pool) for £10.

92 8/P25
49 ROOMS
DF
£££

The Bonham 35 Drumsheugh Gardens · www.thebonham.com ·
0131 226 6050 Discreet townhouse in quiet West End crescent. Cosmopolitan service and ambience a stroll from Princes St. Much favoured by discerning celebs and Book Festival guests. Independent back in the day, and now managed by the Bespoke Hotel Group. Major refurb 2018/19; rooms are stylish and individual. Great views out back, over Dean Village and New Town. Elegant restaurant.

93 8/Q25
28 ROOMS
NO PETS
£££

Nira Caledonia 6-10 Gloucester Pl · https://niracaledonia.com ·
0131 225 2720 This is the only UK hotel of a small, very particular and understated group (there's one in Mauritius, one in the Alps). Nira is a Sanskrit word for 'pure' and the ethos is to provide a pure experience, in this case of Edinburgh's Georgian New Town. So, although it is neither fancy nor expensive, it is calm, polite and quietly classy. No lift, lounge or leisure facilities, but restaurant for dinner, good concierge service and a key for the adjacent private New Town Gardens.

94 8/Q25
33 ROOMS
NO PETS
£££

Tigerlily 125 George St · www.tigerlilyedinburgh.co.uk · 0131 225 5005
Edinburgh's design-tastic hotel on style boulevard by Montpeliers, who have **Rabble** (previously Rick's) nearby which has cheaper rooms (98/UNIQUE HOTELS). This surprisingly large hotel sits atop the never-other-than-rammed Tigerlily bar and restaurant. Rooms uniquely different but in the contemporary/calm house style. One of the most fashionista hubs in town but you pay to be this close to the pulse. Downstairs in the basement is the nightclub **Lulu**: guests have complimentary admission.

££

EAT Fair to say food ain't the main event – the people are – but it's fun and fast and probably better than it has to be. Big room, big atmos, some quiet corners and a cute, crowded smoking terrace. Ladies do lunch and linger.

95 8/P25
10 ROOMS
££

The Raeburn 112 Raeburn Pl · www.theraeburn.com · 0131 332 7000 At the end of Raeburn Pl, a very Stockbridge watering hole and hotel; it's a slick operation. Rooms are 'deluxe' and upstairs 'standard'; all are individual, with muted colour schemes, tasteful and solid. On the ground floor, a spacious but bustling bar and brasserie-style restaurant with Josper grill and enclosed terraces overlooking the Edinburgh Academicals rugby ground (set for a new stand and controversial shopping block at TGP). Out-front beer garden.

96 8/Q25
18 ROOMS
NO PETS
££

Le Monde 16 George St · https://lemondehotel.co.uk · 0131 270 3900
Central boutique hotel on Edinburgh's designer-dressed street. Part of megabar/restaurant all themed on the world on our doorstep. Individual rooms are named after foreign cities and designed accordingly: L.A., Cairo, Sydney – Dublin one of the quieter ones. Serious attention to detail and very rock 'n' roll. All a tad OTT (the bar not the coolest in town) but the theme does work and beds/bathrooms/facilities would suit young professional thrusting things.

97 8/Q25
31 ROOMS
NO PETS
££

Angels Share Hotel 9-11 Hope St · www.angelssharehotel.com ·
0131 247 7000 Almost on Princes St, this very urban, boutique-style bedbox ain't bad value, with often good walk-in rates. It's a close cousin of Le Monde (above). Taking its name from whisky lore and a film of the same name, it pays homage to notable and honourable Scots (our 'angels') with pics of actors, sportsmen and pop stars on all walls. Rooms have their names and you sleep under an enormous Emeli

Sandé, Rod Stewart, etc. You may not like your bedroom mate, but hey! Restaurant is bold, brassy and chandeliered – best prepare for breakfast!

98 8/Q25
10 ROOMS
NO PETS
NO KIDS
£££

Rabble 55a Frederick St · www.rabbleedinburgh.co.uk · 0131 622 7800 Very city centre hotel and bar/restaurant in a downtown location a stone's throw from George St. By same people who have Indigo (Yard), a buzzing bistro in the West End, and their other stylee hotel, **Tigerlily** (94/UNIQUE HOTELS). Restaurant or 'Taphouse' as they call it (168/BAR FOOD) has (loud) contemporary dining. Rooms through the bar and upstairs are surprisingly quiet (except in the early am with the bottle bin collection). Modern, minimalist feel as standard. Book well in advance – there are lots of people who want to be in this rabble.

99 8/Q25
145 ROOMS
NO PETS
££

Ten Hill Place 10 Hill Pl · www.tenhillplace.com · 0131 662 2080 Address as title on quiet square in southside near the university. Unlikely and surprising departure for the Royal College of Surgeons (410/ATTRACTIONS) who occupy the nearby imposing neoclassical building complex which fronts on to Nicolson St, and who built this unfussy, utilitarian, modern hotel that's probably the best-value boutique hotel in town (a major expansion along the street 2018). Masculine, clean elegance in uniform design with 7 categories of rooms depending on size and view (some of Arthur's Seat). Small, pretty good restaurant and good wine bar. No leisure facilities. Limited parking.

100 8/Q25
208/140
ROOMS
DF
L
££

Motel One: Edinburgh-Royal **18-21 Market St (overlooking Princes St Gardens)** · 0131 220 0730 & **Edinburgh-Princes** **10-15 Princes St** · 0131 550 9220 · www.motel-one.com/en/ The latter at E end of Princes St opposite the Balmoral and above the Apple shop. Part of a German chain but listed here because they are very individual, hip and handy and, here, both occupy very central and convenient locations. They're also well appointed, uber-contemporary and cheap. No restaurant; breakfast in the bar (open 24 hours) for guests is also good for rendezvous. No parking.

Excellent Lodgings

101 8/Q25
4 ROOMS
NO PETS
£££

✓ **21212** 3 Royal Terrace · www.21212restaurant.co.uk · 0131 523 1030 Mainly a restaurant, lavish and urban and Michelin-starred but 4 large rooms up the Georgian staircase (no lift), comfortable and sexy with views to the cruisy gardens opposite and lush, leafy Calton Hill at the back. 2 rooms each floor: 1 front, 1 back; all spacious and loungey. No leisure facilities to work off your gorgeous dinner (119/FINE DINING) but the bedrooms are made for activities not provided for in a gym.

102 8/Q25
7 ROOMS
NO PETS
££

✓ **23 Mayfield** 23 Mayfield Gardens · www.23mayfield.co.uk · 0131 667 5806 On one of the long roads S from the city centre lined with indifferent hotels, 23, a 'boutique guest house', stands out above the rest. Patrons Ross and Kathleen Birnie have aimed for the top, from: underfloor heating, Indonesian and antique furniture, a library and garden, and a Club Room with guest computer, Edinburgh info and Georgian chessboard to – of course – their gourmet breakfast, with a prodigious choice.

103 8/Q25
7 ROOMS
NO PETS
££

✓ **94DR** 94 Dalkeith Rd · www.94dr.com · 0131 662 9265 As with 23 Mayfield (above), this boutique guest house is one of many on a main road south but way better than most. Paul Lightfoot and John MacEwan (and the dug) have created a very calm and contemporary home from home here, with great, no-frills attention to detail and an eye for design in everything. Rooms in 3 'styles' are named after whiskies. Great breakfast (I'm told). Five-star friendly! Some parking.

The Best Hostels

104 8/Q25
71 ROOMS
(200+ BEDS)

✓✓ **Edinburgh Central** 9 Haddington Pl · www.syha.org.uk ·
0131 524 2090 Central it is, in a handy part of town though perhaps unobvious to casual visitors, i.e. it's not in the Old Town area. Haddington Pl is part of Leith Walk (corner of Annandale St) near bars/restaurants and the gay quarter, and on the way to Leith, e.g. **Joseph Pearce's** is across the traffic lights (361/ UNIQUE PUBS). Converted from an office block. Café, internet and every hostel facility. Clean, efficient; rooms from singles to family 4-6 beds. Good for kids.

105 8/Q25
606 BEDS

✓✓ **Safestay Hostel** 50 Blackfriars St · www.safestay.com ·
0131 524 1989 Building is enormous and also opens on to Cowgate. £10 million made this place as hotel-like as you get without completely losing the hostel vibe; part of an international chain. Self-service restaurant, extensive bar, facilities include a roof terrace (with heaters and sometimes BBQ), self-catering kitchens and lots of cool things, such as mobile phone charging boxes, snooker tables and internet zones; and hordes of staying-up/out-late people. Massive number of rooms round the interior courtyard, varying from 2 (though only 7) to 12 occupancy. Good location and superior facilities.

106 8/Q25
38 BEDS

✓ **Royal Mile Backpackers** 105 High St · www.royalmilebackpackers.com ·
0131 557 6120 On the Royal Mile, near the Cowgate with its late-night bars. Ideal central and cheap accom, with all the facilities itinerant youth on a budget might look for. The original hostel in the group (35 years old and *the* first backpacker hostel in Scotland) is the **High Street Hostel**, confusingly at 8 Blackfriars St (0131 557 3984; www.highstreethostel.com), nearby, just across the street. Another, **The Castle Rock** at 15 Johnston Terrace (0131 225 9666; www.castlerockedinburgh.com), at the top of the Royal Mile in the old Council Environmental Health HQ, is huge (190 beds in various dorms; 'private' rooms book up fast) and some great views across the Grassmarket or to the castle across the street. Same folk also have hostels in Fort William, Inverness, Oban, Pitlochry, Loch Ness and Skye, and Mac Backpacker tours; expect to be sold a trip to the Highlands.

107 8/Q25
16 ROOMS

✓ **Argyle Backpackers** 14 Argyle Pl · www.argyle-backpackers.com ·
0131 667 9991 Quiet area and, though in Marchmont, there are great bars and interesting shops nearby. 1km to centre across the Meadows. This is a bit like living in a student flat and there are tenements full of them all around. But it's homely, with 2 kitchens, internet, lounge, conservatory, garden and a piano! 12 rooms are double/twin, 2 singles, 6 small dorms.

108 8/Q25
160 BEDS

✓ **St Christopher Inn** 9-13 Market St · www.st-christophers.co.uk ·
0131 226 1446 Couldn't be handier for the station or city centre. This (with branches in London and other Euro cultural cities) hostel can seem cramped in the bunk rooms, though there are single and double rooms with facilities en suite. As always, price depends on number sharing. Breakfast in buzzing Belushi's café-bar on ground floor open till 1am (food 10.30pm). A very central option.

109 8/Q25
170 BEDS
IN EACH

Budget Backpackers 37-39 Cowgate & 2 West Port · 0131 226 6351 · www. budgetbackpackers.com Two hostels at either end of the Grassmarket; great locations, especially for night life. The first on a corner leading up to the university area is the largest (170 spaces with dorms of all sizes, including double/twins). The other, **Kick Ass**, below the Castle, mainly for larger parties. Both have 24-hour service and great café-bars all day till late. Voted high in hostel world.

The Best Hotels Outside Town

110 8/R25
23 ROOMS
LL · £LOTS
£££

✓✓ **Greywalls** Gullane · www.greywalls.co.uk · 01620 842144 In splendid gardens 36km E of Edinburgh, this is *the* country-house hotel in the region, a mecca for golfers and foodies. Report: 849/LOTHIANS.
EAT An Albert Roux suite of dining rooms. Bar meals and sublime afternoon tea.

111 8/P25
14 ROOMS
NO PETS
££

✓✓ **Champany Inn** nr Linlithgow · www.champany.com · 01506 834532 On A904, 3km Linlithgow on road to Forth Rd Bridge and South Queensferry. Exemplary restaurant with rooms, some overlooking lovely garden. Legendary steaks and seafood; ambience and service. Breakfast in cosy dining-kitchen is excellent (nice bacon, of course!). Extraordinary wine list and cellar shop for take home (7 days noon-10pm). But veggies best not to venture here.
EAT Superb, especially meatier eats. Report: 281/BURGERS & STEAKS.

112 8/P25
132 ROOMS
DF
££

✓✓ **Dakota** South Queensferry · www.dakotahotels.co.uk · 0131 319 3690 Keeping its cool amid an emerging housing scheme, from the people who brought us the Malmaisons and before that, One Devonshire Gardens (now Hotel du Vin 451/UNIQUE HOTELS), a bold concept: the black metropolis-block design statement a homage to travelling theme inside. On the edge of SQ but on main carriageway N from Edinburgh by the Forth Rd Bridge. It's all quite brilliant, a designer (Amanda Rosa) world away from anonymous others of the ilk. Rooms (in 4 categories) are calm and whisper 'understated chic'. The Grill restaurant a destination in itself (guests should book when they make a room reservation). Ken McCulloch's vision and restless energy: unceasing! See also 469/HOTELS OUTSIDE GLASGOW and Glasgow city centre 450/UNIQUE HOTELS.

£££
EAT Brasserie-type, daily-changing menu in signature stylish setting. Journey here!

113 8/P25
83 ROOMS
NO PETS
££

✓ **Norton House** Ingliston · www.handpickedhotels.co.uk · 0131 333 1275 Off A8 near the airport, 10km W of city centre. Victorian country house in 55 acres of greenery, surprisingly woody and pastoral so close to city. Part of reputable Hand Picked Hotel group. 'Executive' rooms have countryside views. Labyrinthine layout with good conference/function facilities. Brasserie and small internal restaurant. Good, contemporary (bedrooms) and traditional (public rooms) mix. Some rooms quite swish. Spa with pool, etc.

114 8/P25
4 ROOMS
££

✓ **The Bridge Inn** Ratho · www.bridgeinn.com · 0131 333 1320 An old pub by an old bridge (over the Union Canal). 4 comfy, quite classy rooms above. Graham and Rachel Bucknall have transformed this waterside watering hole (along with the **Ship Inn** and **The 19th Hole** 1330/1331/FOOD PUBS, both in Elie), into a destination gastropub – less than 30 mins from city centre via the A71 (through Sighthill) or via the A8 and the Newbridge roundabout. Much to-do about boats, i.e. barges and the canal basin, beside the garden. Towpath walks.

££
EAT Gastropub (in an English kind of way) with same menu in bar of canalside dining room with terrace. Carefully sourced, own kitchen garden. Free-range chicken and ducks. Open 7 days. Must book weekends.

115 8/P25
17 ROOMS
NO PETS
££

✓ **Orocco Pier** South Queensferry · www.oroccopier.co.uk · 0131 331 1298 A buzzy restaurant and boutiquey hotel, in often touristy SQ, with great views of the Forth and the **Bridge** (400/ATTRACTIONS). From Edinburgh take first turn-off from dual carriageway. A cool bistro; contemporary rooms above and beside (7 have the view). Food in bar, restaurant or terrace. Privately owned; well run. Parking tricky. A great outside-town option.

The Best Fine-Dining Restaurants

116 8/Q25
£LOTS
✓✓✓ **Restaurant Martin Wishart** 54 Shore · www.
restaurantmartinwishart.co.uk · 0131 553 3557 For many and
me, this remains the top and the most relaxed fine-dining restaurant in town. It
was also the first independent fine-dining restaurant and celebrates 20 years in
2019. The room is designed on simple but swanky lines, like a 1940s' cruise ship,
and calm rather than hushed or rushed; uncomplicated menu and wine list
(though not a lot in lower price ranges). Michelin-star chef Martin; reputation
obviously precedes and raises expectations, but preparation, cooking and
presentation are demonstrably dazzling and especially on show in Martin's **Cook
School & Dining Room** nearby in Bonnington Rd – 4-course dining on Fri/Sat
with inexp. wine. Great vegetarian menus. A la carte and tasting menus all superb.
Also uptown, **The Honours** (123/BRASSERIES). All are a treat. Closed Sun/Mon.
Book well ahead.

117 8/Q25
£LOTS
✓✓ **Number One Princes Street** 1 Princes St · www.roccofortehotels.
com · 0131 557 6727 Though not many Edinburgers venture here for a
night on the town below stairs at the Balmoral, the landmark hotel they pass every
day on Princes St, they're missing one of the best dining experiences in foodtown.
Subterranean opulence with only opaque light from the windows on Waverley
Steps. The calm, cosmopolitan ambience perfectly complements Brian Grigor's
confident cuisine. Long-standing executive chef is Jeff Bland. Michelin starred since
2003. 4/4/4-course, à la carte and tasting menus with vegetarian option, from
canapés to splendid puds with pastry chef Ross Sneddon and petits fours with
many mmm... moments. Attentive, not too fussing-over-you staff: knowledgeable
sommelier and 'cheeselier' can talk you through the impressive list (especially
French) and board (also especially French). 7 days dinner only. **Prince**, the
brasserie at street level by Alain Roux (and lounge), urbane, stylish is the casual
alternative. 7 days lunch & dinner. **The Palm Court** for tea (1464/AFTERNOON TEA).

118 8/Q25
£LOTS
✓✓ **The Kitchin** 78 Commercial Quay, Leith · www.thekitchin.com ·
0131 555 1755 Pre-eminent in the row of restaurants in front of the
Scottish Government offices, you arrive in the chicest restaurant lounge in the land
and proceed to Tom Kitchin's brilliant, busy kitchen looking out on his calm,
urbane restaurant which has received much attention and many awards since it
opened in '06, including an early Michelin star. Though Tom is a TV chef fixture on
the foodfest circuit, admirably he seems omnipresent in the kitchen, keeping an
eye on us as well as what we eat. Good-value lunch menu (set and à la carte),
'surprise', prestige and vegetarian tasting menus, all in an easy-to-follow
ingredient-led menu; so lots of choice all driven by impeccable and serious
sourcing of local and market ingredients. He calls it *From Nature to Plate* (also his
cookbook title). Not a large room; you do get lots of attention. Wine list, as you
would expect, is superb and the sommelier will guide you through it (many
suggestions already on the menu). Tue-Sat lunch & dinner.

119 8/Q25
£LOTS
✓ **21212** 3 Royal Terrace · www.21212restaurant.co.uk · 0131 523 1030
Paul and Katie Kitching's beautiful Michelin-starred restaurant, in an elegant
townhouse backing on to Calton Hill. Name describes the appealing and very
workable format of 3 choices for starters, mains and puds, with a soupçon of soup
(no choice) and a cheese plate in between (the cheese in tip-top condition). Lunch
has same format with 2 choices. Food is playful and innovative, mixing surprise
ingredients prepared by a small army of chefs in the shiny kitchen at the end of the
sexily attired dining room. Good-value wine list. This Michelin is in the right hands.
Closed Sun-Tue. See also 101/LODGINGS.

120 8/Q25 ✓ **The Witchery** Castlehill · www.thewitchery.com · 0131 225 5613 At the
ATMOS   top of the Royal Mile where the tourists throng, maybe unaware that this is
£LOTS   the city's most stylishly atmospheric restaurant, with many awards and famous
names in the guest book. In 2 salons, the upper more 'witchery' and the 'Secret
Garden' downstairs, a converted school playground, James Thomson has created
a more spacious ambience for the (same) elegant Scottish menu. Locals on a
treat, many regulars and visiting celebs pack this place out, and, although the
tables are efficiently turned round, you should book. The Witchery by the Castle
encapsulates this remarkable and indulgent ambience (81/UNIQUE HOTELS). The
wine list is exceptional, the atmos *sans pareil*. 7 days, all day. LO a very civilised
11.30pm. 12 editions ago I wrote these words – reassuringly they are still true.
334/LATE DINING.

121 8/Q25 ✓ **Rhubarb @ Prestonfield** off Priestfield Rd · www.prestonfield.com ·
ATMOS   0131 225 7800 A little out of town but the restaurant of fabulous Prestonfield
£LOTS   (80/UNIQUE HOTELS) is the flagship accomplishment of the maestro, James
Thomson. And as above it's the whole dining experience rather than Michelin-
minded menus that drives their success. Rhubarb is in the gorgeously decadent
and opulent Regency rooms at the heart of the hotel; the public rooms adjacent for
before and après are superb, especially the upstairs drawing rooms. On a recent
visit, we all agreed the food was still as seductive as the surroundings. An evening
of rich romance awaits. And you get your (rhubarb) desserts.

122 8/Q25   **Castle Terrace** 33-35 Castle Terrace · www.castleterracerestaurant.com ·
£LOTS   0131 229 1222 Chef-patron Dominic Jack's smart city restaurant near the Usher
Hall, Lyceum and Traverse Theatres is in partnership with the city's best-known
chef, Tom Kitchin, and his eponymous Michelin-starred restaurant in Leith (see
above). There's a no-nonsense approach and very good dining is to be had here,
though the rooms are perhaps a tad corporate for some (well, me!). All the fine-
dining niceties are observed. A loyal, discerning clientele. Tue-Sat lunch & dinner.

■ The Best Brasseries

123 8/Q25 ✓ **The Honours** 58a Castle St · www.thehonours.co.uk · 0131 220 2513
£LOTS   Informal, calm, urbane, this is the midtown buzzier brasserie version of Martin
Wishart's eponymous brand (116/FINE DINING). All perfectly set and served, sourced
and balanced. Martin's light touch is in evidence. Where to go for smart business
lunch or sophisticated supper; you should book. Tue-Sat lunch & dinner.

124 8/Q25 ✓ **The Ivy** 6 St Andrew Sq · https://theivyedinburgh.com · 0131 526 4777
£££   Possibly Britain's best-known brasserie, now very much a brand, alighted on
the corner of newly urbanised St Andrew Sq in 2017. This, the first of the chain
outside London, was an instant, aspirational hit. Ladies who lunch come from
Glasgow. A prime pitch and perfect pitch, Edinburgh has very much taken to The
Ivy. Ground level and upstairs. Classic brasserie menu, smart service, morning to
night. 7 days.

125 8/Q25 ✓ **The Forth Floor, Harvey Nichols** 30-34 St Andrew Sq · www.
££   harveynichols.com · 0131 524 8350 On the fourth, the foodie floor: the Deli,
and the Chocolate Lounge with champagne and cake on the conveyor. Brasserie
and more expensive (but similar) Mod-Brit menus in the white linen dining area,
which does a 'contemporary afternoon tea'. Chef is Robbie Meldrum. Nice just to
come for cocktails and the view! The terrace (also sectioned) has one of the best
views (of St Andrew Sq) in town – first come first served for tables. 7 days.

126 8/Q25   **Spoon** 6a Nicolson St · www.spoonedinburgh.co.uk · 0131 623 1752 Upstairs
£ opposite the Festival Theatre whose audiences it conveniently and ably serves. The
entrance belies the loft-like apartment: individualist and spacious, with interesting
retro furniture and lighting, and there's just something about Spoon that brings us
back and back (especially on the night of the Film Festival launch). Food is light, not
too meaty, unassuming and good value. A reliable redoubt on the unlovely Bridges.
Mon-Sat 10am-10pm, Sun noon-5pm.

127 8/Q25   **The Printing Press @ The George** 21-25 George St · www.
££ printingpressedinburgh.co.uk · 0131 240 7177 The restaurant and main bar of
The George (83/UNIQUE HOTELS). Intimate though the grand features are discreetly
evident. Bar area and lofty top-end brasserie room, with light filtering in (also used
for breakfast). 'Bites' in the bar and brasserie-style menu are Scottish in context
and cooking. Josper Grill. Fitting, inexpensive wine list. Bar food till 11pm is one of
the tops-in-town late dining choices.

128 8/Q25   **Côte** 51 Frederick St · www.cote.co.uk · 0131 202 6256 Côte is, of course, a
££ chain of restaurants and here at *StB* we avoid recommending chains as a rule, but
the Côtes are particularly good: classic brasserie food at decent prices, open later
than most and though vast (including at weekends, upstairs) you can usually get in
and service is slick. Go for *les plats rapides* and monthly changing specials that are
often better than you find in France. 7 days breakfast till LO 10.45pm.

✓ **Galvin's Brasserie de Luxe** The superior casual dining restaurant of the
Waldorf Astoria Caledonian Hotel. Report: 79/UNIQUE HOTELS.

▉▉▉ The Best Creative Cookery

129 8/Q25   ✓✓ **Edinburgh Food Studio** 158 Dalkeith Rd · www.
£LOTS edinburghfoodstudio.com · 0131 258 0758 An early flag-bearer of the
foodie revolution, this crowdfunded restaurant and 'food research hub' is in
Edinburgh's southside. In a lofty room on 2 long tables they serve a 9-course set
menu (for a very reasonable £60), an à la carte lunch/brunch Thu-Sat and a lazy
Sunday brunch. Other (monthly) events feature international and local guest chefs
and collaborators (there's an impressive list online). Chefs/patrons Sashana Souza
Zanella and Ben Reade with James Murray have eloquent credentials. While dinner
is more like fine-dining without the formalities, it is an adventure in gastronomy –
a unique food/art/science experience. Notify diets ahead.

130 8/Q25   ✓✓ **Timberyard** 10 Lady Lawson St · www.timberyard.co · 0131 221 1222
£LOTS Between Tollcross and the 'theatre district', in a converted timber
warehouse all stone and wood, the city's most stylish food hall, Timberyard was
the first to present a menu around (3–5) stated ingredients and invite diners to
trust the kitchen and go on a journey according to season and circumstance. But
there are lots of options: vegetarian, vegan, 8 courses, lunch in 'bites' and 'small'
and 'large' plates. The award-winning wine list (promoting low intervention
viniculture and British wines) ain't cheap but selectivity, integrity and inventive
cookery are all part of an experience, a mellow but buzzy ambience, smart service,
all c/o the happy Radford family – in the kitchen (Ben), out front (Abi), Lisa
(floating), sommelier Jo and patron Andrew (perhaps somewhere foraging). Best
book. Closed Mon/Sun. Tue-Sat lunch & dinner.

131 8/Q25
£LOTS
✓✓ **The Table** 3a Dundas St · www.thetableedinburgh.com · 0131 281 1689 Sean Clark, his brother, and a sommelier invite you into their open kitchen/dining room to sit along their table (10 only) looking into the kitchen, and have the fixed (no choice, diets or dislikes) – i.e. very fixed – 7-course dinner. It's an intimate foodie experience, best probably with your own party, though you'd have to book well ahead. Dishes are gorgeous to look at and to eat. At £90 a head (plus wine), it is, as they say, no cheap! But it is to adore! Dinner only Tue-Sun.

132 8/Q25
£LOTS
✓✓ **Aizle** 107-109 St. Leonard's St · www.aizle.co.uk · 0131 662 9349 A restaurant in the southside with a great concept and a solid reputation. Ingredients are listed each month, fresh as the day, seasonal and ethical. Chef/proprietor Stuart Ralston, with a Michelin background, creates a fixed dinner menu each calendar month, though basic dietary wishes are accommodated (vegetarian, pescatarian, gluten-free), £55 at TGP, with wines to go with each course £40 (there is a wine list). 2 compact candlelit rooms. Must book. Dinner only Wed-Sun.

133 8/Q25
£££
✓ **The Gardener's Cottage** 1 Royal Terrace Gardens · www. thegardenerscottage.co · 0131 558 1221 It is a cottage – once the gardener's cottage – in a (public) garden, but it's right in the centre of town at the beginning of London Rd near the roundabout on Leith Walk. It is a very particular dining-out experience – you sit at communal tables perhaps talking food with folk you don't know (there is a room for exclusive use). A la carte or 7-course dinner menu, small dishes come at you (with no choice, though diets catered for if notified) from a cottage garden via their bustly wee kitchen. Local, seasonal, grown and found. You have to be in the mood, but when you are it's brilliant. 7 days. They also have **The Lookout** at the top of the hill (141/CASUAL).

134 8/Q25
£££
✓ **Fhior** 36 Broughton St · www.fhior.com · 0131 477 5000 Fhior (an adaption of the Gaelic for 'true'), opening summer 2018, was born out of Norn, the accoladed restaurant that shook up Leith and dining in Edinburgh in 2015 (see below). In Broughton St, chef/patron Scott Smith and partner Laura, with a collective of chefs, suppliers and foragers, have forged a pure food experience. A 4- or 7-course fixed dinner menu (lunch à la carte), with dishes built around 3 stated ingredients, is created daily, chefs taking charge of their own dishes presenting them at the table in 3 minimalist dining rooms (can be noisy). A serious, award-winning foodie experience. Lunch & dinner Wed-Sat.

135 8/Q25
££
✓ **Michael Neave** 21 Old Fishmarket Close · www.michaelneave.co.uk · 0131 226 4747 Halfway down a steep wind between the Cowgate and the Royal Mile, below the Cathedral, where cooking by the eponymous chef is inventive, contemporary and incredibly good value, in a good-choice, Scottish ingredient-led menu. 2-course lunch and pre-theatre menu with brownie and coffee for 10 quid! The room is not big on atmos but it's the food, wine and whisky list that we are here to savour. Swerve off the tourist trudge on the Mile, go downhill below stairs to this cellar of culinary creativity. There's also **Michael's Steak & Seafood** further down the Mile at 15 Jeffrey St, 0131 557 2635. Once again, exceptional value for this level of delivery.

136 8/Q25
££
Borough 50-54 Henderson St · www.boroughrestaurant.com · 0131 629 2525 Formerly Norn (see above), Borough succeeded the landmark Leith restaurant in summer '18, along the same clean lines. At TGP, I hadn't been to Borough on this corner of Leith near the shore, but many good reports suggest that its very reasonably priced à la carte menu is creative cookery easier on the pocket and without the initiation ceremonies of others above. Reports, please.

The Best Casual Dining

CENTRAL/STOCKBRIDGE

137 8/Q25
££
✓✓ **83 Hanover Street** www.83hanoverstreet.com · 0131 225 4862
Attesting to the fact that if you create a good food experience in a good location in Edinburgh, you can succeed immediately. 83 opened late 2018 to rave reviews and packed tables. It is not large, a semi-basement in the restaurant row of Hanover St, but Juan Castro and Vanessa Alfano have given a refreshing twist to small plates, coming when ready, with their Chilean-inspired menu. Expect ceviche, chilli and spice. Some bar seats. It buzzes. Lunch & dinner. Closed Mon.

138 8/Q25
££
✓✓ **Six By Nico** 97 Hanover St · www.sixbynico.co.uk · 0131 225 5050 A rare thing – a restaurant and a concept that has successfully transported from Glasgow, so much so that you couldn't get in for weeks after it opened in summer 2018. 'Six' is the 6 small(ish) courses in a themed menu (a mood, a country) that changes every 6 weeks. 'Nico' is Nico Simeone who came up with a refreshingly different approach to modern eating out that everybody gets, and likes. Fixed menu but can mix/match with vegetarian. Timed slots noon-10pm. 7 days.

139 8/P25
££

8/Q25
✓✓ **Rollo** 108 Raeburn Pl · 0131 332 1232 Lovely Rollo is both a neighbourhood (Stockbridge and Broughton St) and a family affair. Ailsa, front of house (very front of house!), is a fashion designer; Mum and Dad Rollo are a sculptor (works on show) and an architect. Menu follows the bites and bowls for sharing principle, with some decent vegetarian options. Wine list short but to the point. Small converted storefront so a bit of a tight squeeze and you should book even weekdays. **14 Broughton St** · 0131 556 5333 The East Village Rollo. Same format, same squeeze, same smart service and same level of noise, but the soundtrack always spot on. The estimable Ailsa somehow at both helms. Both 7 days noon-10pm.

140 8/Q25
£££
✓✓ **Wedgwood** 267 Canongate · www.wedgwoodtherestaurant.co.uk · 0131 558 8737 Just below St Mary's St. For more than 10 years, the compact, all-present-and-correct Old Town bistro of Paul Wedgwood, where food really does come first. Creative, Modern-Scottish cookery with a big, loyal following and excellent lunch deals. Once included in *The Sunday Times'* Britain's Top 100 Restaurants, this is a real asset to the Royal Mile. 7 days lunch & dinner.

141 8/Q25
££
✓ **The Lookout** Calton Hill · www.thelookoutedinburgh.co · 0131 677 0244 The Lookout was just opening near the end of 2018 as *StB* was going to print, so I speculate, but with every confidence, that by the time you read this, it will be a must-go and probably a must-book (evenings). A great addition to dining in the city, with brilliant views from the top of Calton Hill, beside **The Collective Gallery** (419/GALLERIES). It is by the guys from **The Gardener's Cottage** (133/CREATIVE COOKERY), with chef Graham Baldwin, so expect a contemporary, conscientious approach. More accessible for breakfast (a buffet) and lunch. As I write, I haven't been, so only one tick for now.

142 8/Q25
ATMOS
££
✓ **The Outsider** 15 George IV Bridge · www.theoutsiderrestaurant.com · 0131 226 3131 The long-established but still many folks' favourite contemporary room for casual, social dining from maverick restaurateur Malcolm Innes. Minimalist design with surprising view of the castle; and art! Innovative menu contrasts – the signature beetroot coleslaw in pitta bread is almost compulsory. And the moules frites! Daily specials. Big helpings, pretty people. Good-value lunches and great late! We go here a lot. 7 days lunch & dinner.

143 8/Q25 ✓ **Taisteal** 1-3 Raeburn Pl · www.taisteal.co.uk · 0131 332 9977 The Gaelic
££ name means 'travel', and here there's a Scottish take on an eclectic round-the-world sojourn, chef/proprietor Gordon Craig's creative approach especially welcome in foodie-fashioned Stockbridge. Seasonal sourcing and market menus. Closed Sun/Mon.

144 8/P25 ✓ **First Coast** 99 Dalry Rd · www.first-coast.co.uk · 0131 313 4404 Named
£ after a place in the far north where chef/patron Hector MacRae used to go on his hols, this cool urban restaurant is also on the edge of the visited world – well, Dalry Rd. It is a destination! Superb value and full of integrity. Hector serves food he likes with a light touch and no bamboozling choices. They make everything from scratch, including bread, with a great vegetarian and top vegan choice (they have vegan only evenings). First Coast would grace any neighbourhood. Mon-Sat lunch & dinner.

145 8/Q25 ✓ **Dine** 10 (1F) Cambridge St · https://dineedinburgh.co.uk · 0131 218 1818
££ A metropolitan and handy eaterie in theatreland (adjacent to the Usher Hall and The Lyceum). Stuart Muir has created a sophisticated dining-out experience (under a tree!), and a delicious and approachable Modern-Scottish menu not expensive at this standard (we go for the Market Menu). Food LO 9pm. 7 days (closed Sun eve). The Bar, with a great cocktail list, is open till 1am.

147 8/Q25 ✓ **Urban Angel** 121 Hanover St · www.urban-angel.co.uk · 0131 225 6215
£ In a basement near Queen St, Gilly Macpherson's understated but well-judged café-restaurant perfectly of its time and place. Contemporary, relaxed, great value and, not surprisingly, busy and buzzing in the old flagstoned, worn-wood rooms. Organic where sensible, fairtrade and free-range. Food is wholesome British, with Scottish sourcing, a light touch and great pastry. Takeaway counter offerings of bespoke sandwiches, soup and juices.

148 8/Q25 ✓ **The Scotch Malt Whisky Society** 28 Queen St · www.
££ thediningroomedinburgh.co.uk · 0131 220 2044 'The Dining Room' of this august yet understated private members' club – including the more atmospheric bar upstairs with its separate, more casual menu – now open to all. James Freeman's unfussy, consistently sound menu offers everything a whisky connoisseur would wish for – quality and a dram with your amuse-bouche. An underused oasis in traffic-unceasing Queen St. 7 days lunch & Tue-Sat dinner.

149 8/Q25 **Iris** 47a Thistle St · www.irisedinburgh.co.uk · 0131 220 2111 In a street of
£ many bistros, those that know head for Iris. Not immediately obvious, perhaps, but expect elegant, modern appointments, and a well-judged, light and Mod-Brit menu (not much vegetarian) and excellent service. 7 days lunch & dinner. Dependable Iris!

150 8/Q25 **New Chapter** 18 Eyre Pl · www.newchapterrestaurant.co.uk ·
£ 0131 556 0006 The sort of great-value, buzzy bistro you would be happy to have round your corner, this is in a north New Town residential area between Stockbridge and the East Village. Attracts folk looking for a no-fuss, good-deal dinner. Careful, conscientious cookery, and a well-presented Scottish meets European menu. Reliably good! 7 days lunch & dinner.

EAST CITY AND LEITH

151 8/Q25
££ ✓✓ **The Walnut** 9 Croall Pl · 0131 281 1236 The small, perfectly formed Walnut, halfway down 'The Walk', where chef/proprietor Ben Waumsley, quietly and without fuss or fanfare, turns out some of the best light and contemporary food in town, at decidedly decent prices. Hence a loyal following; you have to book. Seasonal à la carte and blackboard specials. Very reasonable wines by bottle or glass and can BYOB. 7 days lunch & dinner.

152 8/Q25
££ ✓ **The Little Chartroom** 30 Albert Pl (Leith Walk) · www. thelittlechartroom.com · 0131 556 6600 Halfway down Leith Walk as above in a cute neighbourhood bistro, chef Roberta Hall and partner Shaun McCarron (working the tables) have chartered an unobtrusive, inexpensive Mod-Brit menu and an easy-going dining experience. One of the great newcomers 2018. Wed-Sun lunch & dinner.

153 8/Q25
££ ✓ **The Educated Flea** 32b Broughton St · www.educatedflea.co.uk · 0131 556 8092 I'd have to admit this, near where I live, is one of the most convenient and reliable of casual eateries. Always great specials, fish of the day and proper vegetarian choice. By the gals who have The Apiary and Three Birds, both on next page; their zoological family has an easy ambience and a good ethic. 7 days lunch & dinner.

SOUTH CITY/BRUNTSFIELD AND MORNINGSIDE

154 8/P25
££ ✓✓ **Bia Bistrot** 19 Colinton Rd · www.biabistrot.co.uk · 0131 452 8453 In a small strip of shops at the beginning of Colinton Rd near 'Holy Corner', an Edinburgh secret spot where Irish (Roisin) and French (Matthias) Llorentes's combination of Bia (Irish for food) and Bistrot (the authentic French bistro) is an off-Morningside find. The room ain't decor-tastic but it's unpretentious and so is the straight-talking, carefully sourced menu. These guys are cooking for Scotland and they share their love of food with us at exceptional value. Wines très reasonable, ice cream from Chocolate Tree round the corner. Tue-Sat lunch & dinner.

155 8/Q25
££ ✓ **Field** 41 West Nicolson St · www.fieldrestaurant.co.uk · 0131 667 7010 This friendly southside bistro near the university never fails to delight. Small, cosy and invariably packed, it serves 'Scotland's Larder' in winning combinations. The Conways and chef David Lowrens take care over their parlour guests and what they eat, so fads and diets are well catered for. There are many who swear that in this quarter Field is in a field of its own.

156 8/Q25
££ ✓ **The Rabbit Hole** 11 Roseneath St · www.therabbitholerestaurant.com · 0131 229 7953 A mellow Marchmont room is home to a travel-to bistro and neighbourhood redoubt of creative cookery c/o Antonello Exposito and Mo Boulay. Seasonal à la cartes and a lunchtime menu present great-value Mod-Brit dishes in a cosmo style. Wed 'steak nights' (£25 ribeye and trimmings for 2). Lunch & dinner. Closed Sun/Mon.

157 8/Q25
££ ✓ **La Petite Mort** 32 Valleyfield St · www.lapetitemortedinburgh.co.uk · 0131 229 3693 The bistro room behind and beside Bennets Bar (365/UNIQUE PUBS) by the King's Theatre, very handy pre show. Under chef Neil Connor, a classic bistro menu is titivated with creative accompaniments; you can have 3 delicious courses for under £30. Same kitchen does the bar menu next door. 7 days lunch & LO 9.30pm.

158 8/Q25 ✓ **LeftField** 12 Barclay Terrace · www.leftfieldedinburgh.co.uk ·
£ 0131 229 1394 Rachel Chisholm and Phil White's understated bistro is the kind of local, ethical and independent eaterie that folk increasingly like and seek out. On a quiet corner overlooking Bruntsfield Links (over the window boxes) between Tollcross and the Bruntsfield food belt, you feel like you're in their living room: sourcing from local nearby producers, vegetables from the Cyrenians, bread from across the road, organic wine from small producers. Phil has a light touch; clean cuisine.

159 8/Q25 ✓ **Apiary Restaurant** 33 Newington Rd · www.apiaryrestaurant.co.uk ·
£ 0131 668 4999 In southside beyond the Queen's Hall (handy pre & post theatre and for **Summerhall** 417/GALLERIES). A spacious corner building now a rather brilliant bistro by the industrious women – Kath Byrnes and Jo Curtis – who have the **Three Birds** in Bruntsfield and **The Educated Flea** in Broughton St (160/153/CASUAL). A long, eclectic menu from brunch to supper with daily specials is miraculously produced in a tiny kitchen. Inventive surprises and sharing plates – all great value. Perhaps because of its location you can usually get in here despite its high satisfaction rate, so this is a good place to know. 7 days lunch & dinner.

160 8/Q25 ✓ **Three Birds** 3-5 Viewforth · www.threebirds.co.uk · 0131 229 3252 Just
£ off Bruntsfield's main street. This and sister restaurant The Apiary (see above) are hugely popular, great-value bistros with inventive food to love. Always good vegetarian choice and lovely bites that can be starters. Three Birds ain't large so booking probably essential. 7 days lunch & dinner.

160A 8/Q25 ✓ **Sylvesters** 55-57 West Nicolson St · www.sylvestersedinburgh.co.uk ·
£ 0131 662 4493 Kieran Sylvester's quietly brilliant and understated corner bistro near the university and George Sq is a good place to know, especially during Festival time when it is on the fringe of the Fringe's major campus. It remains extraordinary how they can serve food of this quality at those prices. Where in London, or anywhere, could you eat this well for under £25? Cooking with flair and no fuss, artfully presented. Mon-Sat lunch & dinner.

The Good Food Pubs

CENTRAL/STOCKBRIDGE

161A 8/Q25
DF
£

The Scran & Scallie 1 Comely Bank Rd · www.scranandscallie.com · 0131 332 6281 Near the end of the shops etc that make up Stockbridge's main street. This joint venture of Michelin chef Tom Kitchin (118/FINE DINING) and Dominic Jack of **Castle Terrace** (122/FINE DINING) and extended to Bruntsfield in 2018. This is more of a gastropub than most on this page, with the top cooking in a convivial and casual ambience the term suggests. Scottish, seasonal and local throughout the menu (many couthy Scots references: 'Yer starters'). It's no cheap, mind – ham, egg 'n' chips 20 quid or pounds, as they say. Daytime is very child friendly. Mon-Fri lunch & dinner, all day Sat/Sun. Also see **Southside Scran** 178/FOOD PUBS.

161 8/Q25
DF
£

The Bon Vivant 55 Thistle St · www.bonvivantedinburgh.co.uk · 0131 225 3275 It's all about the atmos! Lively BV offers cosy, convivial, contemporary food with great wine (huge by-the-glass list) and cocktail choice. In a busy block of restaurants, the BV is dark, usually candlelit, but always full. A bites and boards menu. The proprietor has fingers in many other foodie pies, so great service and buzz here. 7 days, all day.

162 8/Q25 &
8/P25
DF
£

The Blackbird 37-39 Leven St · www.theblackbirdedinburgh.co.uk · 0131 228 2280 & **Hamilton's Bar & Kitchen** 16-18 Hamilton Pl · www.hamiltonsedinburgh.co.uk · 0131 226 4199 & **Treacle** 39-41 Broughton St · www.treacleedinburgh.co.uk · 0131 557 0627 & **The Voyage of Buck** 29-31 William St · www.thevoyageofbuckedinburgh.co.uk · 0131 225 5748 A local, very personally run chain of great drop-in gastropubs, all in places you want them. Look, food, service and cocktails different but similarly appealing. Hamilton's is especially family and dog friendly. 7 days, all day.

163 8/Q25
££

Indigo Yard 7 Charlotte Lane · www.indigoyardedinburgh.co.uk · 0131 220 5603 Behind Queensferry Street. A great, enduring West End watering hole; consummate, contemporary pubbery by the always on trend Montpelier group (see below). Breakfast, lunch and dinner in several areas, wooden-look, great lighting. A reliable repast, with a huge list of artisan and world beers, 150 whiskies; lots of wine by the glass. 7 days, all day.

164 8/Q25
DF
£

Cambridge Bar 20 Young St · www.thecambridgebar.co.uk · 0131 226 2120 On the W extension of Thistle St. Discreet doorway to an indie-owned Edinburgh institution. Sporty in a rugger kind of way and notable for its big burgers, among the best in town. Huge choice, including vegetarian (bean burgers); Mackie's estimable ice cream to follow. At the quiet end of the street so you can often get a table (there's a spacious upstairs room). Food till 10pm.

165 8/Q25
DF
£

The Fountain 131 Dundee St · www.fountainbar.co.uk · 0131 229 1899 Opposite the soulless Cineworld Mall (though it comes alive during the International Film Festival). At last, a place to eat and hang out in faraway Fountainbridge. Mix 'n' match vibe. Daily menu and à la carte. Home-made grub, some tables on the street. Nice peeps come here. And great with kids (even till 10pm). Lunch & LO 9.20pm.

166 8/Q25
DF
£

The Magnum 1 Albany St · www.themagnumrestaurant.co.uk · 0131 557 4366 Chris Graham's relaxed and reliable gastropub on the corner of Albany and Dublin Sts is the civilised East Village watering hole with eats. It's in my 'hood so it's a personal favourite. Bar and raised dining area. Bar menu available in both has the pub staples (excellent tempura fish 'n' chips) and à la carte. Simple, casual dining, always great staff. Sun-Thu lunch & dinner, all day Fri/Sat.

167 8/Q25 **Hector's** 47-49 Deanhaugh St · www.hectorsstockbridge.co.uk ·
DF **0131 343 1735** On the corner of Stockbridge's main street, Raeburn Pl. A Mitchells
£ & Butlers pub but long a distinctive Stockbridge destination for beers on tap (12), bottled beers (expensive) and all-day decent pub grub (in the back section). Just a lot better than Wetherspoons.

168 8/Q25 **Rabble** 55a Frederick St · www.rabbleedinburgh.co.uk · **0131 622 7800**
££ Basement bar/restaurant or 'Taphouse' along with Rabble hotel rooms (98/UNIQUE HOTELS) by same people as Montpeliers (above) and **Tigerlily** (94/UNIQUE HOTELS). Drinking is the main activity here but they do have a variable – i.e. highs and lows – restaurant menu. Later on maybe too noisy to enjoy food, so choose time and table to suit your mood. Inner courtyard best for dining. Up-for-it crowd (many women) enjoy champagne, cocktails and shouting. 7 days, all day. Also open for breakfast from 7am.

169 8/Q25 **Whighams Wine Cellars** 13 Hope St · www.whighams.com · **0131 225 8674**
££ On corner of Charlotte Sq. First here in 1767, Nicholas Henderson's wine bar-bistro has been discreetly dispensing the wine and the well-tried-and-tested menu (à la carte and the new 'tapas with a Scottish twist') here since 1983. Always an amiable, congenial place to return to. Great for the Book Festival in August. Live band on Sun (and sometimes Tue). A New Town institution. 7 days, all day.

EAST CITY AND LEITH

170 8/Q25 ✓✓ **The Shore** 3 Shore, Leith · www.fishersbistros.co.uk ·
ATMOS **0131 553 5080** A long time on this shore but here is the reassuringly
££ reliable repast of less expensive Leith foodland. Run by people from **Fishers** next door (227/SEAFOOD) with a similar sympatico ambience but more pubby, less fishy. Real fire and large windows looking out to the quayside, strewn with bods on summer nights, coz when it's sunny we head to The Shore. Mod-Brit menu in cosy-in-winter woody bar (selective live music Tue/Thu, Sun) or in the quieter restaurant. 7 days lunch & dinner.

171 8/Q25 ✓ **The King's Wark** 36 Shore · www.kingswark.co.uk · **0131 554 9260** On
££ the corner of Bernard St. Woody, candlelit, stone-walled and comfortable – a classic gastropub, the emphasis on food. Bar and bistro dining room. Pub-food classics and more adventurous evening menu, the rooms traditional and dark rather than pale, light and modern. Scottish slant on the big menu from a small kitchen, with excellent fish, including their famous beer batter haddock and chips. Mellis cheeses. Many gins. 7 days.

172 8/Q25 ✓ **Teuchters Landing** 1c Dock Pl · www.teuchtersbar.co.uk ·
DF **0131 554 7427** Another very good Leith eatery in a former ferry waiting room,
£ with waterside tables spread over adjacent pontoons (they can take a couple of hundred people out there). Mugs of prawns, stovies, etc in half- or full-pint portions. Great wine list – 20 by the glass. Outside open 10.30am-10pm (inside till 1am). See also **A Room in the West End** 249/SCOTTISH.

173 8/Q25 ✓ **Roseleaf** 23/24 Sandport Pl · www.roseleaf.co.uk · **0131 476 5268**
ATMOS Corner of Quayside between The Shore and busy Commercial St. Jonny and
£ Lyn's Roseleaf sees itself as a 'cosy wee hidden treasure' and they're not wrong.

Food definitely the thing here with everything home-made, including an afternoon tea (best pre-order). Small it is and perfectly formed. Kid-friendly. Weekends you'd better book. Food till 9.30pm.

174 8/Q25   **Nobles** 44a Constitution St · www.noblesbarleith.co.uk · 0131 629 7215
DF   Long-standing Nobles has successfully morphed from traditional to contemporary
£   without losing its charm and remains a definitive Leith neighbourhood pub. Now we go there to eat. Still woody, a bit foodie. Comfortably occupying an elegant Victorian room: lofty, beautiful and civilised. It's always busy and full of life! Food served all day (Sat/Sun brunch 10am-4pm).

175 8/Q25   **The Compass** 44 Queen Charlotte St · www.thecompassleith.com ·
£   0131 554 1979 Corner of Constitution St opposite Leith Police Station. This well-run 'bar & grill' is a popular Leith haunt, maybe missed by uptown grazers. Stone and woody look with mix-and-match furniture in bar and adjacent mezzanine with open kitchen. Not as indie as once was – now run by big local barkeeps Caledonian Heritable, but use of space much improved. Some very good deals, e.g. steak and a bottle of wine for 2 for <£30 on Thursdays. Bar kicks in later. Food till 10pm.

176 8/Q25   **The Espy** Portobello · 0131 669 0082 At the foot of Bath St on the said
DF   Esplanade. The original place for pub grub in Porty (the Portobello seaside suburb)
ATMOS   with slouchy couches in the lounge area and a fair few tables (including in the
£   window), with a view of the sea and the surprising beach. Usually full (the pub and these days sometimes the beach). Food cooked to order; good burgers; 4 guest ales. Occasional live music. Some tables outside. Food till 9.30pm.

177 8/Q25   **Guild of Foresters** 40 Portobello High St · www.forestersguild.co.uk ·
DF   0131 669 2750 City end of the main road through Porty – a contemporary bar-
££   bistro in bar and dining room. Selected ales & beers, 'beer garden' with huts – yes, huts! The new Positively Portobello.

SOUTH CITY/BRUNTSFIELD AND MORNINGSIDE

178 8/Q25   ✓✓ **Southside Scran** 14 Bruntsfield Pl · https://southsidescran.com
£££   Southside sis of the long-established destination gastropub in Stockbridge (above), this well-laid-out urban eaterie is not so much a pub, but a major new addition late 2018 to the expanding Kitchin (food) family – and they are very family friendly with a dedicated kids' room and menu. Brasserie-type choices, including from the 'rotisserie'. Good acoustic, light jazz soundtrack. Lunch & dinner, all day weekends.

179 8/Q25   ✓✓ **Canny Man's** 237 Morningside Rd · www.cannymans.co.uk ·
ATMOS   0131 447 1484 Aka The Volunteer Arms on the A702 via Tollcross, 7km
££   from centre. Idiosyncratic renowned eaterie in a labyrinth of snug, atmospheric rooms; a true, original gastropub. Carries a complement of malts as long as your arm and a serious wine list. There is a smørrebrød menu (more than 80 variants), an à la carte, starters, seafood and desserts with Luca's ice cream, a top Sunday lunch and a chintzy afternoon tea. Lunch 7 days & dinner Tue-Sat. Linen table cloths, nice rugs and pictures. This is a very civilised pub of good taste with a lovely patio/garden. See also 385/ALES.

180 8/Q25   ✓ **The Holyrood 9A** 9A Holyrood Rd · www.theholyrood.co.uk ·
DF   0131 556 5044 Round the corner at the bottom of St Mary's St towards the
£   Parliament, a surprisingly bustling beer and burger den, with impressive selections of both. Food is prepared in the tiniest kitchen and somewhere downstairs, and partaken in the packed backroom or bar itself; you might have to put your name

down for a table. Huge range of draught beers but also wines by the glass. An all-round good pub, the first and possibly still the best of local expanding but bespoke chain, e.g. the **Red Squirrel** (338/LATE DINING); all different. 7 days, all day.

181 8/Q25 ✓ **Montpeliers** 159 Bruntsfield Pl · www.montpeliersedinburgh.co.uk ·
££ 0131 229 3115 They call it Montpeliers of Bruntsfield and it is almost an institution south of the Meadows. Same ownership as Rabble above and similar buzz and noise levels; it's a slick operation. From breakfast menu to late supper, they've thought of everything. All the contemporary faves. Sunday roasts. Good people watching from outside tables. 7 days, all day.

182 8/Q25 ✓ **Bennets Bar** 8 Leven St · 0131 229 5143 Next to the King's Theatre. Since
ATMOS 1875, an Edinburgh standby, listed for several reasons (365/UNIQUE PUBS), not
£ least its honest-to-goodness (and inexpensive) pub lunch. A la carte Scottish pub staples, under the enormous mirrors, better since being part of the restaurant **La Petite Mort** round the back, with chef Neil Connor (157/CASUAL).

183 8/Q25 **The Salisbury Arms** 58 Dalkeith St · www.thesalisburyarmsedinburgh.
££ co.uk · 0131 667 4518 Opposite the Commonwealth Swimming Pool, a roadhouse and self-determined gastropub experience perhaps more suburban than *metro urban*, though many boxes are ticked: spacious, great service, well presented. Food on the pub staple side but loads of choice and an impressive vegan menu. Well thought-out and perennially popular. Terrace and garden. 7 days, all day. LO 9pm.

✓ **The Bridge Inn** Ratho Report: 114/HOTELS OUTSIDE EDINBURGH.

The Best French Restaurants

184 8/Q25 ✓✓ **La Garrigue** 31 Jeffrey St · www.lagarrigue.co.uk · 0131 557 3032
££ An airy yet intimate restaurant near the Royal Mile. Chef/proprietor Jean Michel Gauffre brings warm Languedoc to your plate. Expect your cassoulets to be magnifique. A sure foot in the Terroir. Early evening menu du patron is great value. The best artisan bread! Veggies may flounder between the leggy langoustines and les lapins but meat eaters and Francophiles are très content here. Excellent Midi-centric wine list, especially by the glass. 7 days lunch & dinner.

185 8/Q25 ✓✓ **Café Marlayne** 76 Thistle St · www.cafemarlayne.com ·
£ 0131 226 2230 Here a while now but this well-worn wee (we mean wee) gem is reliably one of the best authentic bistros in town. Personal, intimate and very, very French. It's like a place you find in rural France on your hols; you would say 'charmant' and you will go back. Best book! 7 days lunch & dinner.

186 8/Q25 ✓✓ **L'Escargot Bleu** 56 Broughton St · www.lescargotbleu.co.uk ·
££ 0131 557 1600 In a strong French field in this city, another authentic Auld Alliance bistro (and cool wine bar downstairs 390/WINE BARS) – this one un peu upmarket. Very French atmos and menu so tartare means tartare and escargots are snails (from Barra). Well-sourced ingredients (Aberdeen Angus and Orkney beef) mainly écossaise by Monsieur Berkmiller himself, with great French cheese selection. Michelin Bib; always busy. Menu du jour Mon-Sat lunch & dinner.

187 8/Q25 ✓✓ **L'Escargot Blanc** 17 Queensferry St · www.lescargotblanc.co.uk ·
££ 0131 226 1890 Fred Berkmiller's upstairs bistro, à deux with L'Escargot above, though the Blanc is perhaps more bistro-ish. The loyal following love the authentic, lively atmos, the inexpensive food, fine wines, the great steaks and brisk

service. Street-level **Bar à Vin** wine bar has very decent French wine (loads by the glass) and charcuterie all day. Cheery, informed staff both up and down. Report: 391/WINE BARS. Mon-Sat lunch & dinner.

188 8/Q25 ✓✓ **Café Saint Honoré** 34 North West Thistle St Lane · www.
ATMOS   cafesthonore.com · 0131 226 2211 Between Frederick and Hanover Sts
£££ down a lane, a classic bistro with French sensibilities informing an inspired Scottish menu under notable chef/proprietor Neil Forbes. Exudes atmos. Crisp linen tablecloths, tiles and mirrors; at night in candlelight, it twinkles. Sound ethical sourcing and a daily-changing menu. Meat dishes are especially good; minimal vegetarian choice. Deft wine list. 7 days lunch & dinner.

189 8/Q25 ✓ **Petit Paris** 38-40 Grassmarket · www.petitparis-restaurant.co.uk ·
££   0131 226 2442 On busy N side of street below the castle. Tables packed together, upstairs or outside best. Not exactly Montmartre (stags and hens misbehaving) but true, independent and chef/proprietor run, authentic on atmos and ingredients (imported where appropriate). I'd say better than most of what you find in France these days. BYOB (not weekends), corkage £3.50. 7 days lunch & dinner.

190 8/Q25 ✓ **La P'tite Folie** 9 Randolph Pl · www.laptitefolie.co.uk · 0131 225 8678
ATMOS   Virginie Brouard's très sympatico corner of the West End. Mismatched
£ furniture, inexpensive French *plats du jour*. Relaxed dining in a two-floor Tudoresque 'maison' in calm cul-de-sac. Great value. Many old regulars at lunch. Mon-Sat lunch & dinner. **Le Di-Vin** adjacent is a large, lofty wine bar and a surprise find behind the bistro. Great wine list and atmos (and charcuterie-style bar food). Report: 393/WINE BARS. Tue-Sun all day.

191 8/Q25 ✓ **Maison Bleue** 36-38 Victoria St · www.maisonbleuerestaurant.com ·
£   0131 226 1900 And at 372 Morningside Rd. For over 20 years an atmospheric, candlelit, very Edinburgh café-bistro: convivial, hitting all the right notes upstairs and down. Grazing French and tapas/meze approach, building a meal from smallish dishes they call bouchées (and the brochettes!). Morningside (at the end of the) Road has nice corner terrace for watching them (the famous Morningsiders). 7 days. LO 9pm.

193 8/P25 ✓ **Marie Délices** 125 Comiston Rd · www.mariedelices.co.uk ·
£   0131 447 1909 Way up Morningside (Rd) almost into the burbs, an authentic and enthusiastic outpost of La Belle France. Marie Stonys from Bordeaux via Brittany at home in her tearoom/crêperie. Everything handmade (bread from local French bakery), baking (macarons and madeleines, of course), delicious crêpes and galettes worth the extra kilometre, I'd say. 8.30am-5pm, from 10am Sun.

✓✓✓ **Restaurant Martin Wishart** French influence on the city's finest dining. Report: 116/FINE DINING.

The Best Italian Restaurants

194 8/Q25 ££ ✓ **Nonna's Kitchen** 45 Morningside Rd · www.nonnas-kitchen.co.uk · 0131 466 6767 What more can I say, guys – the following is what I wrote in the last edition. It all still holds, you're the top. Nonna's combines friendliness and flair to a degree that repeat custom alone means you probably have to book most evenings. The Stornaiuolo family – dad Mimmo in the kitchen, Gino out front and mama Carmela presiding, with Jimmy their trusty lieutenant (who never falters in reciting the prodigious list of daily, mainly seafood specials) all work damned hard to make this the primo easy-going Italian place in town. Pasta/pizza, long à la carte and specials. Kids' menu. You could come here for a month and not have the same thing twice. Those lucky Morningsiders. Tue-Sun lunch & dinner.

195 8/Q25 ££ ✓ **Tempo Perso** 208 Bruntsfield Pl · www.osteriadeltempoperso.info · 0131 221 1777 On a prominent corner, Marco Iacobelli's buzzy 'osteria', i.e. a tavern, with good local and imported-from-home ingredients. Some but by no means only the usual pastas; no pizzas. A proper daily specials board. A worthy addition to this foodie junction. Good organic wine list. Open later than most. LO 10.30pm.

196 8/Q25 £££ ✓ **Cucina @ The Radisson** 1 George IV Bridge · www.radissoncollection.com · 0131 240 1666 Corner of the Royal Mile. The upstairs spacious Italian kitchen of a Radisson Collection flagship hotel (86/UNIQUE HOTELS), with smart, solicitous service; good sommeliers dispensing a serious Italian wine list. Cheap it ain't. 7 days, all day.

197 8/P25 ££ ✓ **La Bruschetta** 13 Clifton Terrace · www.labruschetta.co.uk · 0131 467 7464 Extension of Shandwick Pl opposite revamped Haymarket station (regulars come by train!). Giovanni Cariello's Italian kitchen and tiny dining room in the West End. A modest ristorante with form and a firm following. The space does not cramp their old-school style or the excellent service. Tue-Sat.

198 8/Q25 £ ✓ **Valvona & Crolla** 19 Elm Row · www.valvonacrolla.co.uk · 0131 556 6066 First caff of the V&C empire (25 years in 2020) behind their world-renowned deli (356/DELIS). An Alexander McCall Smith kind of café much favoured by ladies who lunch. First-class ingredients and great Italian domestic cooking. It hasn't changed much in those years but we love it for that. It was always just right! One of the best and healthiest breakfasts in town (till 11.30am), favoloso lunch and tea and cakes (Fri/Sat till 8.30pm). Can BYOB from shop (with corkage). A venue during the fringe. 7 days, daytime only.

199 8/P25 ATMOS ££ ✓ **Locanda de Gusti** 102 Dalry Rd · www.locandadegusti.com · 0131 346 8800 Rosario Sartore's love letter home to Naples proclaims 3 principles: 'honest, sincere, simple' and they are indeed evident here in this unpretentious neighbourhood restaurant, a rustic Italian parlour 250m from Haymarket station. Excellent home-made pasta and seafood. Hugely popular, so you'll have to book. Lunch Thu-Sat & dinner Mon-Sat. And see 206/PIZZA.

200 8/Q25 ATMOS ££ ✓ **Contini George Street** 103 George St · www.contini.com · 0131 225 1550 Elegant conversion and in 2017 a stunning refresh by Victor and Carina Contini of a lofty, pillared Georgian room, towards the west end of Edinburgh's better boulevard, into the classiest restaurant on the street and easily the most stylish Italian joint in town. Passion for food and good service are always evident. Menu frequently revisited though favourites remain: simple pasta olivia, contadino orecchiette – a seductive carbonara; always top sourcing of Scottish and direct-from-Italy ingredients and wine. Great people watching both inside and from the tables on the street. 7 days, all day, from breakfast Italian-style, to business meets, cocktails and late suppers. They also run **The Scottish Café & Restaurant** in Princes St Gardens (247/SCOTTISH RESTAURANTS) and the **Cannonball Restaurant & Bar** at the very top of the Royal Mile, where there's as much whisky as wine.

Divino Enoteca Neither a tratt nor a ristorante: a superior wine bar with food. Report: 395/WINE BARS.

The Trusty Trattorias

201 8/Q25 ✓ **Vittoria** 113 Brunswick St · www.vittoriagroup.co.uk · 0131 556 6171
£ The original (and for nigh on 50 years) on the corner of Leith Walk, also at 19 George IV Bridge · 0131 225 1740 and the newer **Taste of Italy** by the Playhouse. For aeons Tony Crolla has provided one of the best, least pretentious Scottish-Italian café-restaurants in town. Uptown branch near the university equally full-on, with his son Alberto in charge and chic **Divino Enoteca** downstairs (395/WINE BARS). Tony knows how to work the zeitgeist! Full Italian menu with classic and contemporary pastas. In Leith, outside tables on an interesting corner are great for people watching. Nice for kids (289/KIDS) and for breakfast (porridge, omelettes). **Eatalia** fish 'n' chips adjacent is best on the Walk. And see **La Favorita** above. All 7 days.

202 8/Q25 ✓ **Giuliano's** 18-19 Union Pl · www.giulianos.co.uk · 0131 556 6590
£ Opposite Playhouse Theatre. 'Giuli's' also has the Al Fresco restaurant adjacent after the takeaway counter but it's the original that rocks; it feeds the Playhouse opposite. I've said it (many times) before: it's just pasta and pizza but it's what we like. Surprisingly good wine list and the service from staff – many of whom have been here forever but never seem to age – is top in this town. The food is good, the din is loud and it's always somebody's birthday. 7 days noon-late.

203 8/Q25 **La Favorita** 325 Leith Walk · www.vittoriagroup.co.uk · 0131 554 2430 Tony
£ Crolla's (of **Vittoria** above) upmarket pizzeria halfway down the Walk where the trams may come one day. From the twin, specially imported wood-fired ovens, Tony was determined to produce 'the best pizza in Scotland' (209/PIZZA)! Gluten-free available and a menu of multifarious pastas. Family friendly, especially on Sunday. This is many folks' favorita and good to-go from the takeaway next door, with a fleet of Favorita 500's often outside wanting to bring it to you. 7 days, all day.

204 8/P25 **Mia** 96 Dalry Rd · www.mia-restaurant.co.uk · 0131 629 1750 Same Dalry
£ corner as Locanda de Gusti (above). That Mia is also always full attests to their success as a straight-up neighbourhood tratt where all the staples including pizza are done reliably well. Proprietor Patrick Zace runs a tight ship in very tight trousers; service here is exemplary. You'll wish you had a place like this where you live! 7 days, all day. Morningside's **Mia Italian Kitchen** at 394 Morningside Rd, 0131 629 1019 does the same good Italian job in the southside.

The Best Pizza

205 8/Q25 ✓ **Origano** 236 Leith Walk · www.origano-leith.co.uk · 0131 554 6539 Just
£ down (and opposite) the Walk from the original Origano, Messrs Fletcher,
Blicharski and Ross have expanded into a bigger, more comfortable room, stoking
the oven, plying the wine, working hard to make this our/your perfectly well-
crafted pizzeria. Rather good salads and puds. Takeaway too, as is The Origano
opposite at 227, their home delivery HQ (0131 555 1009). 7 days.

206 8/P25 ✓ **Pizzeria 1926** 85 Dalry Rd · www.pizzeria1926.com · 0131 337 5757
£ Sons of Rosario of **Locanda de Gusti** (199/ITALIAN), Ciro and Santo opened
this neighbourhood Napoli pizza joint on the opposite corner to their dad in Dalry
and brought a new bite to the old oregano. Big crusts, as is the way now (I prefer
Roman myself), but a great streetfood vibe with starters such as arancino and
melanzane, and a load of new pizza variants. 3 beers, red & white wine; no pasta,
no messin'. Lunch Thu-Sat, dinner 7 days.

207 8/Q25 **Ransacked Black Oven** 27-29 Marshall St · www.ransackedblackoven.
£ co.uk · 0131 667 7001 Not strictly speaking a pizza or even an Italian restaurant,
rather they serve Persian streetfood baked in the expensive pizza oven they
inherited. One of their specialities is a crisp flatbread kind of pizza – a welcome
change from the ubiquitous Napoli versions. Lotsa kebabs. A mellow vibe on the
edge of the university campus. 7 days 10am-10pm.

208 8/Q25 **Söderberg** 1 Lister Sq · www.soderberg.uk · 0131 228 1905 In the glass box
£ nearest Laurieston Pl in the campus of blocks of apartments, offices, a hotel, etc,
called Quartermile. Söderberg is now the group name for Peter's Yard; their main
branch is on Meadow Walk (303/TEAROOMS); but the cool Swedish artisan bakers and
coffee shop expanded here in 2015. They're cooking up cool, crisp sourdough pizzas
and salads; bakery upstairs. Not your usual fillings. Scantly Scandic; tables in- and
outside the glass. 7 days till 7pm. There are **Söderberg Bakery Shops**, plenty of
bread but no pizzas in Broughton St and Queensferry St, West End.

209 8/Q25 **La Favorita** 325 Leith Walk · www.vittoriagroup.co.uk · 0131 554 2430
£ They say it's 'the best' and it's certainly the best delivery to your door (from Leith,
Morningside, Blackhall and counting – www.lafavoritadelivered.com). Huge variety,
great mozza and other sound Italian sourcing. You can ask for thin and crispy! This
pizza will travel (often to your office!) in a Fiat 500. Report: 203/TRATTS.

210 8/Q25 **Anima** 11 Henderson Row · www.anima-online.co.uk · 0131 558 2918 The
£ takeaway pizza section of the estimable fish 'n' chip shop **L'Alba D'Oro** (235/FISH
& CHIPS). It's a slice above the rest. 3 sizes (including individual 7-inch) and infinite
toppings to go. Not thin but crispy and crunchy. Also pasta, great wine to go, olive
oils, Luca's ice cream and fresh OJ. This is no ordinary chip (shop) on the block.
Takeaway 349/TAKEAWAYS. Lunch Mon-Fri & dinner 7 days.

211 8/Q25 **Mamma's** 30 Grassmarket · www.mammas.co.uk · 0131 225 6464 Busy,
£ inexpensive American-style pizza. Some alternatives, e.g. nachos, but you come
to mix 'n' match – haggis, calamari and BBQ sauce and 40 other toppings piled
deep within a chunky crust. Good local bottled beer selection: Barney's and Innis
& Gunn. Outside tables. Stag and hen parties are not welcomed here (hurrah!).
Proprietor Paul Duncan also has **o'Oliviero**, the trattoria, and the Mexican
streetfood place **Toro Loco** adjacent. 7 days from noon till 11pm (midnight Fri/Sat).

The Best Mediterranean Restaurants

213 8/Q25 ✓✓ **Le Roi Fou** 1 Forth St · www.leroifou.com · 0131 557 9346 Jérôme
££ Henry's much awarded, regarded and loved, almost neighbourhood
restaurant (and 'salon bar'), serving an à la carte menu of delicious, light
Mediterranean food to the discerning denizens of the East Village and much further
afield. Unpretentious – indeed, not fancy at all – but excellent service and Jérôme's
deft hand in the downstairs kitchen. A dynamic menu that can change every day,
seasonal goes without saying, and appropriate European wine list. Small drop-in
bar at street level and dining up and down. Broughton St area has a lot of good
casual dining now; Le Roi quietly the king. Lunch & dinner Tue-Sat.

214 8/Q25 ✓ **BABA** 130 George St · https://baba.restaurant · 0131 527 4999 On the
££ corner of Charlotte Sq, the restaurant of the Principal Charlotte Square (82/
HOTELS). By the guys from Glasgow's Ox and Finch (479/BRASSERIES), a
Mediterranean/Levant menu, making this probably the most distinctive and
successful of hotel restaurants in town. Food is meze style, all coming when it's
ready on same-size small plates. Easy to get through 6–8 between 2. Cocktails too.
All makes for a good night out. 7 days.

215 8/Q25 ✓ **Radici** 2 Deanhaugh St · 0131 332 1469 In a basement close to the bridge
££ in Stockbridge, 3 Italian guys have made a very neat eaterie here. Giovanni and
chefs Mara and Dario, working out of a tiny kitchen, turn out light, clean, inventive
dishes using organic ingredients (including wine), home-made pasta – you feel not
too full and almost healthy. Then you come back, so they are routinely full. Dinner
only (except Sun lunch). Closed Mon.

216 8/Q25 ✓ **Aurora** 187 Great Junction St · www.auroraedinburgh.co.uk ·
£ 0131 554 5537 At the far end of unlovely Gt Junction St in Leith (near
Edinburgh's exciting venue development – Leith Theatre), Kamil Witek's beautiful
wee café-restaurant, where he almost single-handedly turns out simple but
inventive Mediterranean-style dishes to discerning diners and those that can't
believe their luck – remarkably cheaply. All day, closed Sun eve and Mon.

217 8/Q25 **Eden's Kitchen** 32c Broughton St · www.edens-kitchen.com · 0131 556 6588
£ A discreet and ethical small restaurant/café among many in Broughton St, perhaps
overlooked but don't. Inexpensive meze, pasta, specials and **an excellent pizza**.
Rather good meatballs! Lots organic. BYOB keeps cost of eating here lowest on the
Broughton St strip. Noon-10.30pm. Closed Mon.

218 8/Q25 **Spitaki** 133-135 East Claremont St · www.spitaki.co.uk · 0131 556 9423
£ Corner of a residential street between the East Village (Broughton St area) and
Leith. A properly Greek Greek restaurant, all light and bright, and blue and white.
For some years now, chef/proprietor Christos Babalis quietly and consistently
cooking up the calamari and keftedes to a loyal and growing following. Brought to
you by the twins! Good vegetarian. 7 days dinner, lunch weekends.

219 8/Q25 **Souq** 57-59 South Clerk St · www.souq-edinburgh.com · 0131 667 6801
£ The best and most roomy of Edinburgh's Ahmed family group of Middle Eastern
restaurants (see **Hanam's** below), this on the southside serving the university
campus, The Queen's Hall and Summerhall nearby. All-day meze, chicken, lamb,
fish and lots of vegetarian. Good, cheap sharing and grazing eats. BYOB. 7 days.
LO 10pm.

220 8/Q25 **Serrano Manchego** 297 Leith Walk · www.serranomanchego.co.uk ·
££ 0131 554 0955 Between Dalmeny and Iona Sts, an airy corner 'tapas bar', with the exposed brick, hacked-out stone and bustling open-kitchen look à la mode. Small dishes to share and graze on. The real Bellota ham. Churros for pud! A bueno addition to lower Leith Walk. 7 days, all day.

221 8/Q25 **Cadiz** 77b George St · www.cadizedinburgh.co.uk · 0131 226 3000 Upstairs
££ in mid George St, the smartest Spanish restaurant in town, not your average tapas/small-plate menu. Part of the Di Maggio of Glasgow group, who have the Café Andaluz branches (here, downstairs). This is proper: oysters, jamon, merluza. Paella on Sundays. Light, airy room. Many Spanish people (serving and eating). 7 days lunch through dinner.

222 8/Q25 **Hanedan** 42 West Preston St · www.hanedan.co.uk · 0131 667 4242
£ Small, friendly southside neighbourhood Turkish restaurant. Chef/owner Gursel Bahar a considerate, enthusiastic host. Hot and cold meze to share and shish/kofte/musakka (sic) menu. Daily fish (those charcoal-grilled sardines!) and good vegetarian. Short pud and wine lists complement well. Tue-Sun lunch & dinner.

223 8/Q25 **Tapa** 19 Shore Pl · www.tapaedinburgh.co.uk · 0131 476 6776 Reasonably
£ authentic and great-value tapas. Tucked behind The Shore in Leith. Better and more satisfying by far than high-street tapas chains. Good vino and more Spanish beers than you knew existed. Gambas pil pil and the honey aubergine fritters are the moreish must! 7 days, all day.

224 8/Q25 **Hanam's** 3 Johnston Terrace · www.hanams.com · 0131 225 1329 Near
£ top of the Royal Mile. A not too fancy Kurdish/Middle Eastern restaurant with authentic dishes and a terrace overlooking Victoria St below. Wide-ranging Kurdish, Lebanese, Moroccan and Saudi Arabian soul food. These folk have other restaurants, including **Souq** (see above) and **Pomegranate** opposite the Playhouse Theatre with shisha/hookah terrace. All have good vegetarian choice. 7 days noon-10pm.

225 8/Q25 **Empires** 24 St Mary's St · www.empirescafe.co.uk · 0131 466 0100 Cosy,
ATMOS charming, chaotic, this tiny up-and-down restaurant is an experience – pure
£ Turkish delight. Full of ceramics, rugs and all kinds of people. Usual and unusual meze; great coffee. Good for vegetarians. Mainly just a great atmos. Only 10 tables. BYOB. 7 days from noon.

The Best Seafood Restaurants

226 8/Q25
£LOTS
✓✓ **Ondine** 2 George IV Bridge · www.ondinerestaurant.co.uk · 0131 226 1888 By the Radisson Collection hotel. Shiny, window-surrounded, cosmopolitan destination restaurant upstairs, just off the Royal Mile. Chef/patron Roy Brett runs what's generally regarded as the best seafood restaurant in town, especially for shellfish. Impeccable sourcing, sure hands in the kitchen; they know their oysters; also steak tartare. Little vegetarian. Daily straight-talking menu. Signature is their seafood platter. There is fish 'n' chips. More casual crustaceans at the bar. Mon-Sat lunch & dinner. LO 9.30pm.

227 8/Q25
£££
✓ **Fishers in Leith** 1 Shore, Leith · www.fishersbistros.co.uk · 0131 554 5666 For 30 years in a uniquely special location at the foot of an 18th-century tower in Leith opposite the Malmaison hotel and right on the quay (though no boats come by). Seafood cooking with flair and commitment from small kitchen (how do they keep the constant flow) in boat-like surroundings; traditional Scots dishes get an imaginative twist. Some tables in the bar and outside in summer (can be a windy corner). Often packed, so best book. 7 days, all day.

228 8/Q25
£££
✓ **Fishers In The City** 58 Thistle St · www.fishersbistros.co.uk · 0131 225 5109 Uptown version of Leith eaterie (above); this place works on all its levels (we're talking mezzanine). Fisher fan staples ('features') all here – the fishcakes, soup and blackboard specials; Leith menu but with an uptown edge. Excellent wine list and great service. Some vegetarian and meat (steaks a special). Bar stools for a drop-in bite. 7 days, all day.

229 8/Q25
£££
✓ **White Horse Oyster & Seafood Bar** 266 Canongate · www.whitehorseoysterbar.co.uk · 0131 629 5300 By the people who brought us the **Chop Houses** 282/BURGERS & STEAKS, a smart urban eaterie that brings a bit of elegance to the lower end of Royal Mile. Though there is meat on the menu, this is a straight-up seafood bar specialising in oysters and lobster. Small-plate dishes, delish wines to go with, great home-made straw fries. 7 days noon till 'late'.

230 8/Q25
ATMOS
£££
✓ **Café Royal Oyster Bar** 19 West Register St · www.caferoyaledinburgh.co.uk · 0131 556 1884 On the corner between St Andrew Sq and the Apple shop at the east end of Princes St. Long-standing – and we do mean 'long' – a classic Victorian oyster bar. Decor is unchanged so the marble, dark wood, tiles and glass partition are all major reasons for coming here. Food has been up and down over the years, but keep it simple from the classic seafood menu and you won't go wrong. 7 days, all day. The bar through the partition is more fish 'n' chips but it's also a classic hostelry (367/UNIQUE PUBS).

231 8/Q25
££
✓ **The Ship on the Shore** 24-26 Shore · www.theshipontheshore.co.uk · 0131 555 0409 The Ship has a long reputation as a great quayside bistro/gastropub specialising in seafood. Good ingredient sourcing and wine list (top by-the-glass selection, including fizz). Excellent *fruits de mer*, proper chowder and lemon sole, and a buzzy ambience to enjoy them. A consistently classy joint on a quayside with many options. 7 days, all day. From 9am for (not so fishy) breakfast.

232 8/Q25
££
The Loch Fyne Restaurant 25 Pier Pl, Newhaven Harbour · www.lochfyneseafoodandgrill.co.uk · 0131 559 3900 Large, lofty seafood canteen in excellent location on Edinburgh's secret harbour, though somewhat removed from the Leith restaurant quarter. Outside tables have sunset potential. Exemplary outpost of the UK chain, this, the only one in Scotland, is at least a bit nearer to the

original and its oysters (though it's no longer related 1371/SEAFOOD). Great room, and very on the waterfront.

233 8/Q25   **Mussel Inn** 61-65 Rose St · www.mussel-inn.com · 0131 225 5979 Popular,
££   populist seafood café. In the heart of the city centre where food with integrity can be hard to find, they specialise in mussels and scallops. Also catch of the day, some non-fish options and home-made puds. Their keep it pure and simple formula has stood the test of time – they're also in Glasgow (583/SEAFOOD). Mon-Thu lunch & dinner, all day Fri-Sun.

◼ The Best Fish & Chips

234 8/Q25   ✓✓ **The Fishmarket Newhaven** Newhaven Harbour · www. thefishmarketnewhaven.co.uk · 0131 552 8262 In a Victorian building right on the harbour (with a deck overlooking), right where you'd expect a fish market, a new (2018) café/restaurant and fish 'n' chips takeaway, a collaboration between Edinburgh fishmonger royalty Welch's and Ondine (above). We wouldn't expect anything less than the best here and though the enormous Loch Fyne cafeteria is next door, this was the Edinburger foodie choice from the first fling of the net. Fish without fuss. 7 days 11am-10pm.

235 8/Q25   ✓ **L'Alba D'Oro** 7 Henderson Row · www.lalbadoro.com · 0131 557 2580 Near corner with Dundas St. Large selection of deep-fried goodies, including many vegetarian savouries. Since 1975, Filippo Crolla's chipper has been way above the ordinary – as several plaques on the wall attest (including *StB!*); the pasta/pizza counter **Anima** next door is also a winner (210/PIZZA; 349/TAKEAWAYS). Luca's ice cream. Vegetable oil. 7 days evenings only.

236 8/Q25   **The Deep Sea** 2 Antigua St, off Leith Walk · www.deepseaedinburgh.co. uk · 0131 557 0276 Opposite the Playhouse. Open late. Often has queues though quickly dispatched. The haddock has to be of a certain size and is famously fresh (via Something Fishy in Broughton St nearby). Traditional menu and the deep-fried Mars Bar. There's also kebabs but stick to the fish suppers and feed your impending hangover. Open till 2am-ish (3am Fri-Sat).

237 8/Q25   **Café Piccante** 19 Broughton St · 0131 478 7884 & 7 E Norton Pl · 0131 652 6221 · www.cafepiccante.com The 'Disco Chippie' still rocks. A takeaway and café with tables on the black 'n' white tiles. Near the Playhouse Theatre, this is the clubbers' fuel stop with occasional DJs and unhealthy lads purveying unhealthy food, including kebabs, to the flotsam of the Pink Triangle and demi-monde. There are deep-fried Mars Bars (you'd need to be well out of it). Can sit in. Open till 2am (3am weekends).

The Best Vegetarian & Vegan Restaurants

238 8/Q25 · ££ ✓✓ **David Bann's** 56-58 St Mary's St · www.davidbann.com · 0131 556 5888 Bottom of the street off Royal Mile – slightly off the tourist track – but always a busy restaurant and not only with non-meaters, because this is one of the best 'healthy' restaurants in the city and for vegetarian food in the UK: mood lighting, non-moody staff and no dodgy stodge. A creative take on round-the-world dishes, changing seasonally. Light meal selection; lovely tartlets and 'parcels'. Nice chips! **Vegan** selection, gluten-free, etc, and no ostentatious 'organics' (there are vegan wines), just honest-to-goodness good. David only sometimes chefs, but a great kitchen and out-front team. 7 days.

239 8/Q25 · ££ ✓✓ **Kalpna** 2-3 St Patrick Sq · www.kalpnarestaurant.com · 0131 667 9890 They say 'you do not have to eat meat to be strong and wise' and they are, of course, right. Maxim taken seriously in this lovely Indian restaurant in the southside for 35 years, one of the best vegetarian menus in the UK; ever-dependable, vegetarian or not (and much for **vegans**, especially at lunch). The thali gives a good overview. The butter masala is the definitive dosa. Lovely, light and long may it prevail. 7 days lunch & dinner. See also 264/INDIAN.

240 8/Q25 · ATMOS · £ ✓✓ **Hendersons** 94 Hanover St · www.hendersonsofedinburgh.co.uk · 0131 225 2131 Edinburgh's original and trailblazing basement vegetarian self-serve café-cum-wine bar. A national treasure! Canteen seating to the left, candles and nightly live music down a few stairs to the right (pine interior is retro-perfect). Happy wee wine list and organic real ales. Those salads, hot main dishes and famous puds will go on forever. 7 days.
Drop-in café and takeaway upstairs and, round the corner in Thistle St (25c), their **vegan** bistro. **Hendersons Holyrood** café at 67 Holyrood Rd is less on-brand.

241 8/Q25 · £ ✓ **Thrive Café-Bar** 171 Bruntsfield Pl · www.thrive-edinburgh.co.uk · 0131 623 6885 An on-the-nail vegetarian and **vegan** café-bar and all-round cool place to go, opened in Morningside in late 2018. Charming feel-good room, fresh, vibrant 'burgers, bowls, bites'. Chef Jonathan Neill is on a mission. Special bar/cocktail/music nights (Fridays). BYOB Mondays. 7 days.

242 8/Q25 · ATMOS · £ ✓ **The Mosque Kitchens** There are two Mosque Kitchens; the one on the original site (no website or phone), through an archway in W Nicolson St is the totally stripped-back streetfood version, with some seats upstairs behind the Mosque and a tented section in the lane. You order in the kitchen and can eat for under a fiver. The more substantial 31-33 Nicolson Sq · www.mosquekitchen. com · 0131 667 4035 on a prominent corner is a big, bright canteen with various vegetarian (but also lamb and chicken) curries and naans. Self-serve with paper plates and also incredibly cheap. Downstairs buffet at weekends with plates and cutlery for £10. No frills authentic food, though not much atmos. 7 days 11.30am-10pm. Closed for Friday prayers 12.50-1.50pm.

243 8/Q25 · DF · £ **Harmonium** 60 Henderson St · www.harmoniumbar.co.uk · 0131 555 3160 The bar/café in Leith of Craig Tannock (with partner Iain Baird), proprietors of most of the 100% vegan restaurants in Glasgow (591/594/595/598/VEGAN). Here, a neighbourhood hangout is also **all vegan**: food and drink. It is probably better for you than others hereabouts. 7 days breakfast till late.

244 8/Q25 · £ **Holy Cow** 34 Elder St · www.holycowedinburgh.com · 07733 764616 Below stairs from York Pl leading to the bus station and at TGP the huge building site of the new St James Centre development. A respite (from all that) serving simple

all vegan food. Several kinds of vegan burgers, quiche and soup. Some delicious cakes. 7 days 10am-10pm.

245 8/Q25
£

Pumpkin Brown 16 Grassmarket · www.pumpkinbrown.com · 0131 629 1720 Next to Dance Base, where people are in good shape, but in the midst of the Grassmarket where bad diets abound, is Edinburgh's 'freshest' café. All organic, **all vegan** takeaway and sit-in. Snacks and the best good-for-you smoothies. Coffee with all the plant-based milk variants. Feel clean! 7 days 8.30am-6pm.

246 8/Q25
£LOTS

Restaurant Martin Wishart 54 Shore · www.martin-wishart.co.uk · 0131 553 3557 Not, of course, a vegetarian restaurant, but does have a super vegetarian and **vegan** menu. Food, ingredients and presentation are taken seriously here, so this is where to go for *the best* vegetarian food in Scotland. Report: 116/FINE DINING.

■ The Best Scottish Restaurants

247 8/Q25
L
£

✓ **The Scottish Café & Restaurant** The Mound · www. thescottishcafeandrestaurant.com · 0131 225 1550 Below and very much part of the National Gallery. Victor and Carina (of the **Contini** group 200/ITALIAN) have cast their magic dining dust over the hard-to-get-right gallery caff genre and now this comfort zone of great Scottish cooking is a destination in itself. You enter from Princes St Gardens, which the windows overlook (heart of Christmas in winter). Cullen skink, maccy cheese, Victoria sponge: you can be sure that all the Scottish faves are done properly. 7 days, daytime only (till 7pm Thu). Sun from 10am (343/BRUNCH).

248 8/Q25
ATMOS
££

✓ **The Grain Store** 30 Victoria St · www.grainstore-restaurant.co.uk · 0131 225 7635 For many a long year, this revered restaurant, in an interesting street near the Royal Mile, has regulars and discerning tourists climbing the stairs for a great-value grazing lunch menu or innovative à la carte in the candlelit night. A laid-back, first-floor eaterie in a welcoming stone-walled labyrinth. Good for groups. Perhaps more Modern British than simply Scottish. Chef/proprietor Carlo Coxon and the team are serious about quality and among the most conscientious cooks in town. Hunting/shooting/fishing ingredients like roe deer and woodcock, along with your proper oysters. Mon-Sat lunch & dinner 7 days.

249 8/P25
ATMOS
£

A Room in the West End 26 William St · www.aroomin.co.uk · 0131 226 1036 It is a room in the West End underneath another sprawling space, the pub bit – **Teuchters**, the uptown brother of **Teuchters Landing** in Leith (172/FOOD PUBS). Below stairs the bistro and its many kent faces, but food with Scottish slant all over. Loyal, ruggerish and very Edinburgh crowd. Many whiskies. 7 days.

250 8/Q25
££

Whiski Rooms 4-7 North Bank St · www.whiskirooms.co.uk · 0131 557 0097 Just off the Royal Mile at the top of the Mound. All-round homage to the national drink aimed at both passers-by and aficionados, but all – the shop (0131 225 1532, open daytime only), the bar and the restaurant are sympathetically done. Stone, wood and whisky in the glass (and throughout the menu, e.g. Ardbeg sauce with your steak). Flights and tastings (you might have to book). They're also at 119 High St (www.whiskibar.co.uk) down the hill with **Whiski Bar & Restaurant**, their pub bang on the money and the Mile.

✓ **The Witchery** Top restaurant that really couldn't be anywhere else but Scotland. Report: 120/FINE DINING.

The Best Mexican Restaurants

251 8/Q25 ✓✓ **El Cartel** 64 Thistle St · www.elcartelmexicana.co.uk ·
£ 0131 226 7171 Tiny cantina in mid-Thistle St proclaiming its street and
Mexicana cred. Endorsed by esteemed food critic Joanna Blythman, who extolled
the virtue of their authentic 'pliant' tortillas, the taqueria sauce, and ceviche from
their small-plate and sharing menu. Service rapido so no hanging about, which is
just as well because it's always busy and there's no booking. Put your name down
and they text you. Owned by the Bon Vivant folk across the street so that's where
to wait (161/FOOD PUBS). 7 days, all day.

252 8/Q25 ✓ **Bodega TollX** 36 Leven St · www.ilovebodega.com · 0131 228 9485 A
£ Mexican caff/diner, sister of the original in Leith Walk reopening and
relocating further down in 2019. John Howard's love letter to Mexico. Small plates
to share: tacos, tortillas, tandoori chicken and an Asian twist. They have a way with
avocado. Local and a little loco, we cram in for this. Evening only. Closed Mon.

253 8/Q25 ✓ **Viva Mexico** Anchor Close, Cockburn St · www.viva-mexico.co.uk ·
£ 0131 226 5145 Since 1984, the pre-eminent first-wave Mexican bistro in
town. Judy and Julio's Gonzalez's menu still innovates, although all the expected
dishes are here. Genuine originals, famously good calamares and fajitas; lovely
salad sides. Lots of seafood. Reliable venue for those times when nothing else fits
the mood but proper fajitas and fresh lime margaritas. 2 floors; nice atmos even
downstairs. Lunch Mon-Sat & dinner 7 days.

254 8/Q25 ✓ **The Basement** 10a-12a Broughton St · www.basement-bar-edinburgh.
£ co.uk · 0131 557 0097 Established long before every second doorway in
Broughton St led to a café or bar, this subterranean stalwart joined a bar chain in
2018 but still retains its independent vibe. Tequila central (50 varieties) and
late-night revelries but a surprisingly imaginative, sound and spicy Mexican menu
in restaurant section and bar. The *best* guacamole mixed at your table. Look no
further for your enchiladas! 7 days, all day.

255 8/Q25 ✓ **Mirós Cantina Mexicana** 184 Rose St · www.miroscantinamexicana.
£ com · 0131 225 4376 In the western block of a street of bars and indifferent
dining, a cute, usually crowded Mexican bistro which, though I've never been,
seems a lot like a caff down Mexico way. Seafood stew and big-portion comfort
food. 7 days noon-10.30pm.

The Best Japanese Restaurants

256 8/Q25 ✓✓ **Kanpai** 8-10 Grindlay St · www.kanpaisushi.co.uk · 0131 228 1602
££ Along from the Lyceum Theatre. Probably the smartest Japanese
restaurant in town; staff flow around you, food arrives. Open kitchen where the
magic happens. Choose from the book: numerous nigiri; the dragon rolls. Good
sake list. Hakushu as well as the Yamazaki malt. Tue-Sat lunch & dinner.

257 8/Q25 ✓ **Bonsai** 46 West Richmond St · www.bonsaibarbistro.co.uk ·
£ 0131 668 3847 On a discreet street in the southside, a café/bistro (actually
feels like a Japanese pub) where Andrew and Noriko Ramage show a deft hand in
the kitchen. Unlike the sushi crop that has sprung up in Edinburgh (and
everywhere), this is at least Japanese owned, so the freshly made sushi/yakitori and
teppanyaki are the real McCoy. No conveyor belt in sight, just superb value in
downbeat neighbourhood café setting. The Bento boxes for under a tenner are a
winner. 7 days from noon.

258 8/Q25 ✓ **Yamato** 11 Lochrin Terrace · www.yamatosushiedinburgh.co.uk ·
£ 0131 466 5964 Smart, small bar in Tollcross, little brother of Kanpai (above) beside the Cameo cinema. Surprisingly extensive menu, including paper-thin dumplings; all delicious. Asahi and Sapporo. More drop-in than night out but this place works for aficionados as well as newbies. Tue-Sat lunch & dinner (and takeaway).

259 8/Q25 **Kenji** 42 St Stephen St · www.kenjisushi.co.uk · 0131 226 5111 Up some
£ steps from the street, a tranquil Japanese haven, where the vibe complements simple dishes from a long menu. Great attention to detail, a welcome addition to the Stockbridge, mainly Western food world. Tue-Thu evenings only. Fri-Sun lunch through dinner. Closed Mon.

260 8/Q25 **Harajuku Kitchen** 10 Gillespie Pl · www.harajukukitchen.co.uk ·
£ 0131 281 0526 On the main road between Tollcross and Bruntsfield opposite the Church. Kaori Simpson's delightfully simple, authentic diner with a lengthy menu of all the usuals and many dishes that are not: dumplings, curries, salads with the sushis, rolls and miso. All day Sat, Sun-Fri lunch & dinner.

261 8/Q25 **Hakataya** 120-122 Rose St South Lane · 0131 629 3320 Just off Rose St in the
£ West End section. Small, unassuming Japanese kitchen: sushi, sashimi and loadsa noodles. Asahi/Sapporo beers and sakes. Bento boxes and takeaway. Sun-Fri lunch & all day Sat. It is small.

The Best Indian Restaurants

262 8/Q25 ✓✓ **Mother India Café** 3-5 Infirmary St · www.motherindia.co.uk ·
££ 0131 524 9801 Off South Bridge. That rare thing: a restaurant successfully transferred from Glasgow (537/INDIAN), this the eastern outpost in Monir Mohammed's Indian empire. Has all the things that made it work in Glasgow's West End: neighbourhood feel, great value, small tapas-like dishes to share (40 to choose from), some specials and great service. We always go back to Mum. Mon-Thu lunch dinner, all day Fri-Sun.

263 8/Q25 ✓✓ **Dishoom** 3a St Andrew Sq · www.dishoom.com · 0131 202 6406
££ Dishoom was one of the first of the London chains to set down on the remodelled St Andrew Sq and though we don't do chains at *StB*, we can't ignore this. When it opened in 2017 we, as in London, couldn't get enough of it and joined the queue. Even now you will still wait (in the bar downstairs, with your hand-held remote to order drinks – it tells you when your table is ready on the top floor), but once you're seated, food – small plates and large – come quickly as and when they're ready. Excellent, inventive UK/Indian food. Cosmopolitan atmos. No reservations (except for 6 or more) and allow 30 minutes to an hour in the bar. Food till 10.45pm/11.45pm weekend. Bar later.

264 8/Q25 ✓✓ **Kalpna** 2-3 St Patrick Sq · www.kalpnarestaurant.com ·
££ 0131 667 9890 The original Edinburgh Indian veggie restaurant and still very much the business. Favourites remain on the Gujarati menu and the thalis are famous, but also unique dishes and dosas to die for. Report: 239/VEGETARIAN.

265 8/Q25 ✓ **Kebab Mahal** 7 Nicolson Sq · www.kebab-mahal.co.uk · 0131 667 5214
£ Near Edinburgh University and Festival Theatre. Since 1979, Zahid Khan's slightly misnamed Indian diner (kebabs figure only slightly on a mainly curry menu) has been a word-of-mouth winner. As a no-frills Indo-Pak halal café, it attracts

Asian families, as well as students and others who long for the East. Great takeaway selection of pakoras, samosas, etc. One of Edinburgh's most cosmopolitan restaurants. It's open late! 7 days, all day. Prayers on Fri (1–2pm). A no-alcohol zone.

266 8/Q25
£ **Tanjore** 6-8 Clerk St · www.tanjore.co.uk · 0131 478 6518 In southside near Queen's Hall. Unobtrusive S Indian restaurant, with loyal following for Mrs Boon Ganeshram's inexpensive, authentic and distinctive cuisine, lighter curries and lovely breads (big dosas). BYOB with no corkage. All easy on the pocket and digestion. Good vegetarian choice. 7 days lunch & dinner.

267 8/Q25
£ **Khushi's** 10 Antigua St · www.khushis.com · 0131 558 1947 In the row of restaurants opposite the Playhouse Theatre and feeding its punters. Khushi's, through its various locations, is the city's longest-established Indian diner. There have been a few – now only this one. Many are its loyal clientele. Personally, I'm not an avid fan after some disappointing visits, but it's regularly crammed, so it's lively and it continues to curry favour. BYOB with no corkage is a big attraction. 7 days, all day.

Desi Pakwan Report: 347/TAKEAWAYS.

10 To 10 In Delhi Chai shop. Report: 328/CAFÉS.

Punjabi Junction Report: 321/CAFÉS.

The Best Thai & Asian Restaurants

268 8/Q25
££ ✔✔ **Dusit** 49 Thistle St · www.dusit.co.uk · 0131 220 6846 In the continuing proliferation of Thai restaurants in Edinburgh, this one still gets the gold orchid. Elegant – though a little cramped – interior, excellent service and food that's good in any language but just happens to be exquisite Thai cuisine. Tantalising combinations with atypical, i.e. Scottish ingredients; strong signature dishes with charming names: Two Brothers, A Loving Couple, Fleeing Fish! Decent wine list. 7 days lunch & dinner.

269 8/Q25
£ ✔✔ **Ting Thai Caravan** 8 Teviot Pl · www.tingthai-caravan.com · 0131 225 9801 Bustling like Bangkok, Edinburgh's first Asian streetfood café. Boxes and bowls at long tables, rice noodle dishes and curries. At busy times you might queue for half an hour (but you do; no reservations). Food comes as it's ready; snappy, friendly service. It's Thai without the fat! Alcohol choice similarly stripped down (beers, red & white – 1 choice, and prosecco). You're back on Koh Phangan many full-moon parties ago! 7 days.

270 8/Q25
£ ✔ **Saboteur** 19-20 Teviot Pl · www.saboteurrestaurant.com · 0131 623 0384 The (2018) Vietnamese brother of Ting Thai (above), a few doors down. More roomy, more noodly and Chinesey but similar delivery and drill: boxes and bowls good for sharing and simple alcohol choices. No puds but signature egg coffee. Malcolm Innes's inimitable touch! 7 days lunch & dinner.

271 8/Q25
££ ✔ **Passorn** 23 Brougham Pl · www.passornthai.com · 0131 229 1537 Unpretentious, innovative Thai bistro in Tollcross. Cindy Sirapassorn's enthusiasm and creativity evident in every mouthful (and to Michelin – a Bib year on year). Great tempuras, massaman and panang curries. Lunch Tue-Sat & dinner 7 days.

272 8/Q25
££ ✓ **Nanyang Restaurant** 3-5 Lister Sq · www.nanyangrestaurant.com ·
0131 629 1797 In the middle of the Quartermile (the old Royal Infirmary)
development, on a 'square' (cold as glass, not like Edinburgh, but not unlike
Singapore) with other restaurants; this is the best Asian fusion restaurant in town.
A rich, seductive menu to roam through, with Thai, Malay and Chinese influences.
A ripping rendang! And upstairs, a 'Mini Market', where you can buy the ingredients
to make your own. 7 days lunch & dinner.

273 8/Q25
££ **Nok's Kitchen** 8 Gloucester St · www.nokskitchen.co.uk · 0131 225 4804
Nok's is a newbie compared to many on this page, and though it's tucked away
and a bit of a Stockbridge secret, it's always full. They just hit the sweet Thai basil
spot. A lot of sauce on the plate for some, other Thaiphiles make this a weekly dine
out. Obviously you must book. 7 days.

274 8/Q25
££ **Thai Lemongrass** 40-41 Bruntsfield Pl · www.thailemongrass.net ·
0131 229 2225 Smart but intimate, not too tiddly Thai eaterie. Nice, solid, woody
ambience, charming waitresses (Thai and Chinese) and food that's well loved by
traditional Thai aficionados. Can BYOB (hefty corkage) though has good wine list.
Mon-Thu lunch & dinner, all day Fri-Sun.

275 8/Q25
£ **Phuket Pavilion** 8 Union St · www.phuket-pavilion.co.uk · 0131 556 4323
Near the Playhouse Theatre and Omni Cinemaplex. When other restaurants
in this busy area are full, you can often get a table at Bill Parkinson's roomy,
unpretentious Thai place that is just reliably, saucily good. Decor nothing to write
home from Phuket about but friendly Thai staff and just the right sprinkle of holy
basil. 7 days dinner only.

276 8/P25
£ **Vietnam House** 3 Grove St · www.vietnamhouserestaurant.co.uk ·
0131 228 3383 This tiny, minimalist but charming Vietnamese café is a long way
from its 'parent' in Saigon but is delightful in every way, from proprietor Jodie
Nguyen, its picture menu featuring phos (pronounced 'fuh'), rice-noodle soups,
through its single sticky rice-cake dessert to a small bill at the end. Go west for this
corner of the East. Can BYOB (£1.50). 7 days dinner only.

The Best Chinese Restaurants

277 8/Q25
££ ✓ **Karen's Unicorn** 8b Abercromby Pl · www.karensunicorn.com ·
0131 556 6333 On a very New Town crossroads, a decades-established, fairly
traditional Cantonese restaurant in three calm, grey-toned dining rooms that
nevertheless bustle with loyal customers and many waiters. Decent wine selection.
Predictable but well-presented menu. Tue-Sat lunch & dinner, Sun dinner only.

278 8/Q25
££ ✓ **Edinburgh Rendezvous** 10a Queensferry St · www.edinburghrendezvous.
co.uk · 0131 225 2023 An upstairs restaurant you could walk past for years, but
look up – this is one of the city's best and longest serving: from 1956! Curiously calm
and aesthetic here; old style that's become contemporary. All Cantonese cooking
credentials in place. Mon-Sat lunch & dinner, Sun dinner only. LO 10pm.

279 8/P25
ATMOS
£ **Chop Chop** 248 Morrison St · www.chop-chop.co.uk · 0131 221 1155 Near
Haymarket station. Authenticity and simplicity are the watchwords in Madame
Wang's Chinese diner. Stripped down and bright, and easy on the eye and pocket.
Company makes dumplings wholesale so they're de rigueur here; there's a vast
selection, as with everything else. All come in small dishes when ready. It's a

sharing, daring, dumpling experience; full of people on the go, as in China. 7 days lunch (unlimited for £10) & dinner.

280 8/Q25 **Loon Fung** 2 Warriston Pl, Canonmills · www.loonfungedinburgh.co.uk ·
££ 0131 556 1781 This place has been a destination diner since 1972. Famous lemon chicken and crispy duck signature dishes in a traditional neighbourhood restaurant specialising in Cantonese food. Good dim sum. Closed Tue.

The Best Burgers & Steaks

281 8/P25 ✓✓ **Champany Inn** nr Linlithgow · www.champany.com · 01506 834532
ATMOS On A904, Linlithgow to S Queensferry road (3km Linlithgow) near M9 at
£LOTS/££ junction 3. Accolade-laden restaurant (and **'Chop and Ale House'**) different from others below because it's out of town (and out of some pockets). Candlelit atmos. Superbly surf 'n' turf. The best Aberdeen Angus beef hung 3 weeks and butchered on premises. Good service, huge helpings (Americans may feel at home). Top wine list (and wine cellar shop). The Chop House also has great home-made sausages. C&A: 7 days. Restaurant: closed Sat lunch & Sun. Rooms adjacent (111/HOTELS OUTSIDE EDINBURGH).

282 8/Q25 ✓✓ **Leith Chop House** 102 Constitution St · www.chophousesteak.
£££ co.uk · 0131 629 1919 On the road to Leith. Arrived late 2015, a great addition to eating out in the restaurant quarter, though a bit offshore. Messrs Fraser and Spink have created a smart, very à point, always buzzing bar and eaterie, in which to celebrate or savour steak. The meat is properly hung in the cabinet. All is explained and comes with sides and trimmings. By no means only steak on the menu (fish & burgers), but it is superlative here. 8 cask ales on the bar. 7 days lunch & dinner. Increasing their stake in Edinburgh, the Chop House crew have expanded to **Chop House Market Street** Arch 15, E Market St · 0131 629 1551 and **Chop House Bruntsfield** 88 Bruntsfield Pl · 0131 629 6565 Very similar formula in each. Bruntsfield (on a great corner) is possibly the swankiest. Personally prefer the original (like so much in life). All 7 days.

283 8/Q25 ✓ **Kyloe** 1-3 Rutland St · www.kyloerestaurant.com · 0131 229 3402 Steak
££ place at the corner of the west end of Princes St by the Caledonian Hotel. Through **Huxleys**, the burger/dog sports TV bar, can be blary, and upstairs to the Edinburgh-watching windows. You come here to meet for meat. It's a homage to the cow, including select breeds (at connoisseur prices), and they do know their cuts. Good wine rack. 7 days.

284 8/Q25 **Bells Diner** 7 St Stephen St · 0131 225 8116 Edinburgh's small but celebrated
£ burger joint, the antithesis of the posh nosh. No seasonal/locally sourced/slow food or organic nonsense here. Nothing has changed in 40 years except the annual paint job and (with an unusually low turnover) the Gen X staff. Some people go to Bells *every* week in life and why? For perfect burgers, steaks, shakes and coincidentally, one of the best veggie (nut) burgers in town. Bill ain't running the shop anymore but his presence still looms ... well, large! 7 days.

✓ **The Holyrood 9A** One of many pubs with burgers – this one rather better than most. Report: 180/FOOD PUBS.

Kid-Friendly Places

285 8/P25 ✓ **Luca's** 16 Morningside Rd · www.s-luca.co.uk · 0131 446 0233 The ice-cream kings (1491/ICE CREAM) from Musselburgh brought this modern ice creamery and café to 'Holy Corner' where kids with dads will enjoy their spag and their sundae Sundays. Big cups of capp. Crowded and clamouring upstairs, especially at weekends. Daytime snacks and family evening meals. 'Junior' menu. Food not fab but gorgeous ice cream at all times. BYOB. 7 days, all day.

286 8/Q25 ✓ **Reds** 254 Portobello High St · www.reds4families.com · 0131 669 5558 In main street, along from the shops, a purposefully kid-friendly café with a rear playing/climbing area. Kids' (and baby food) menu, freshly and conscientiously prepared; a no-nugget zone. 7 days, daytime only (till 8pm weekends).

287 8/Q25 ✓ **The Beach House** 57 Bath St, Portobello · www.thebeachhousecafe. co.uk · 0131 657 2636 In the middle of the Prom, a shelter from the storm and those searing hot days on the beach, and confirming 'Porty's' credentials as one of the best parts of town to bring, or bring up, kids. Simple sustenance for buggy-pushing parents and their bairns. Cakes and ice cream. 7 days, daytime only.

288 8/Q25 ✓ **Joseph Pearce's** 23 Elm Row · www.bodabar.com · 0131 556 4140 Leith Walk below London St. Because they've thought of everything that a vibrant and vital pub should (361/UNIQUE PUBS), they've also thought about the kids of their living-the-life clients. A bar but also a delightfully informal café-restaurant (the Swedish meatballs!). Kids are made welcome till 8pm (5pm weekends). There's a toy box.

289 8/Q25 ✓ **Vittoria** 113 Brunswick St · www.vittoriagroup.co.uk · 0131 556 6171 Excellent Italian all-rounder that can seat 200 people, including outside on the pavement on a people-watching corner. On Sundays, kids eat for £1 which is donated to a kids' charity (under 12s till 5.30pm only). Kids' menu at all times. And they get a balloon and crayons and stuff. Report: 201/TRATTS.

290 8/Q25 DF ✓ **Café Tartine** 72 Commercial St · www.cafetartine.co.uk · 0131 554 2588 In 'restaurant row', Leith, facing the Scottish Office off Dock Pl, Michael Graham and Joanne Ramsay's spacious 'family run brasserie' buzzing from breakfast to night. Crêpes, tartines, quite cheffy specials and wine. Family and dog friendly, especially in the loungey conservatory. 7 days, all day.

291 8/P25 ✓ **The Scran & Scallie** 1 Comely Bank Rd · www.scranandscallie.com · 0131 332 6281 At the north end of Stockbridge's main street. Top gastropub that welcomes, feeds and entertains kids. Report: 161A/FOOD PUBS. **Southside Scran** also very family friendly, with separate kids' room. See 178/FOOD PUBS.

292 8/R25 **Goblin Ha' Hotel** Gifford · www.goblinha.com · 01620 810244 35km from town in neat E Lothian village. A restaurant with (6) rooms. Good woodland walking on the **Yester Estate** (435/WALKS). The garden, busy in summer, is nice for kids and there's pizza. 7.

293 8/P25 DF **The Bridge Inn** 27 Baird Rd, Ratho · www.bridgeinn.com · 0131 333 1320 16km W of centre via A71, turning right opposite Dalmahoy Golf Club. Waterside pub by canal basin with walks and barge watching which can be a thrill for kids; occasional canal cruises (must book). Proper food for kids and grown-ups. 7 days.

Skylark Report: 322/CAFÉS.

The Fountain Report: 165/FOOD PUBS.

The Best Coffee

294 8/Q25 ✓✓ **Artisan Roast** 57 Broughton St · www.artisanroast.co.uk · 07858 884756 A honeypot/coffeepot for East Village society, the original AR (also in Stockbridge, Bruntsfield and Glasgow 599/COFFEE), here before the artisan coffee-shop eruption. The Denbys were pioneers of the stand-up service – the guy stands by the machine, there's no counter. Most of the very laid-back seating is in the backroom, like someone's pad (not so cool for private meets). Roastings from selected sources are available wholesale and across Scotland. No panini in sight, though there is cake. 7 days, daytime only.

295 8/Q25 ✓ **Brew Lab** 6-8 South College St · www.brewlabcoffee.co.uk · 0131 662 8963 In a quiet street between 'The Bridges' and the university, they brew. Certainly a lot of calculation and refinement has gone into it, in the 3 designer-distressed rooms where we sample and measure up their caffeinated concoctions. Soup by Union of Genius nearby, cakes by local bakers: it's a good formula (and a great coffee, by the way). 7 days, daytime only.

296 8/Q25 ✓ **Cairngorm Coffee** 41A Frederick St & 1 Melville Pl · www.
& 8/P25 cairngormcoffee.com One midtown, one the corner of Melville Pl in the West End. Down from the Cairngorms, well, Kingussie, 2 spot-on contemporary coffee hangouts, with the beans roasted in Berlin, Denmark and up the road. Lovely, cool avo on toast type snacks. Everyone's on a laptop/pad or phone but some do converse. 7 days, daytime only.

297 8/Q25 ✓ **Castello Coffee** 7a Castle St & 7 Barclay Terrace (in Tollcross/ Bruntsfield overlooking Bruntsfield Links) · 0131 225 9780 Small but cool-as-coffee stop in the New Town (soup and bakes) and the more mellow outpost out on the green (Bruntsfield Links), with an all-day-long brunch menu, from omelettes to churros and French toast. Feed your appetite and your addiction. The hipster's Allpress coffee. Those that know go here. 7.30am-6pm; from 8.30am Sat and 10am Sun.

298 8/Q25 ✓ **Fortitude** 3C York Pl · www.fortitudecoffee.com · 0131 557 3063 A few steps up where the tram turns along from the National Portrait Gallery. Matt Carroll's cool little coffee stop with just the right ingredients and roastings from single origins. Good cake/patisserie and sandwich selection sourced locally, including 12 Triangles, and a cuppa coffee many consider tops. He does change his brews. Guest espressos. Mon-Sat daytime only.

299 8/Q25 **Williams & Johnston** Custom Lane, Leith · www.williamsandjohnson. com A 'micro roastery' and simple café in a tucked-away warehouse behind the Customs House on Commercial St, Leith, also home to a collective studio space and a cool mens' clothes shop, Kestin Hare. You smell the coffee (single-origin select) roasted on the premises (they supply other sympatico caffs in town). Soup and VG toasties. A good place to know (it is beside the Saturday Farmers' Market in Dock Pl). 7 days, daytime only.

300 8/Q25 **Roundsquare Coffee House** 132 Morningside Rd (nr Waitrose) · 0131 603 5818 Roasting their own on a 'snazzy Sanremo'; coffee is king here. Barista Lucas Barraud and partners know their beans. Simple food and bakes to go with. 8am-6pm, from 10am Sun. Till 7pm Sat.

301 8/Q25 **Thomas J Walls** 35 Forrest Rd In a former optometrist's, this probably the most spacious and elegant coffee parlour on this page. There's a John Bellany on the wall and other original art. Great grub of the avo on sourdough variety, so a major brunch venue. Coffee is the business too. 7.30am-7pm (from 8am weekends).

302 8/Q25   **Artisan Coffee** 1 Woleseley Cres & 274 Leith Walk · 07802 353485 First is beyond Meadowbank at 'Jock's Lodge', the other halfway down Leith Walk. Not competing in the barista status stakes (though the coffee is good), these 2 excellent coffee shops (mainly takeaway) have some of the best sweet and savoury snacks in town, with a Greek/Turkish take, e.g. simit and börek. Sicilian pastries. 7 days, daytime only.

The Best Tearooms

303 8/Q25   ✓✓ **Peter's Yard** 27 Simpson Loan · 0131 228 5876 & 3 Deanhaugh St · 0131 332 2901 · www.petersyard.com The first on Middle Meadow Walk, the pedestrian path through the Meadows, part of the Quartermile project that was once the Edinburgh Royal Infirmary. Light, airy bakery/deli/café that feels not like Edinburgh. Soup, salads, artisan bread and non-cream-laden (sometimes a bit heavy) cakes. It gets very busy and the ordering system is a bit annoying, but... you wait! Outside, a nice people-watching patio. Same ambience in Stockbridge: the breads, bakery and other classy and branded stuff (those crispbreads!). Coffee is Johan & Nyström. **Söderberg** (the 'pavilion'), the little brother and drop-in version is next door, and then there's the pizza place (208/PIZZA). There's no stopping these Swedes; their crispbreads are everywhere! Both 7 days 7.30am-7pm.

304 8/Q25   ✓✓ **Twelve Triangles** 90 Brunswick St (the original) & 300 Portobello High St · 0131 629 4664 · www.twelvetriangles.com and **Kitchen Table** 148 Duke St round the corner from the foot of Easter Rd. 3 sympatico coffee shop/tearooms, with more of a menu at Porty and the Table (where mostly you sit round it). Enthusiastic and innovative food cultivists (they ferment!). You can have those casual carbs for breakfast, lunch and tea. 7 days, daytime only.

305 8/Q25   ✓✓ **Lovecrumbs** 155 West Port · www.lovecrumbs.co.uk · 0131 629 0626 We just love Lovecrumbs! In what has endearingly been dubbed the 'Pubic Triangle' – there's a lap-dancing bar opposite. Whilst many on this page may be genteel Edinburgh tearooms, Lovecrumbs positively hums. Boho chic, cables over the ceiling, students from the Art School nearby gorging on their enormous cakes. 'Nice Times' to be had here. 7 days, daytime only. Lovecrumbs also at 22 St Stephen St for cake and tea, Wed-Sun.

306 8/Q26   ✓✓ **The Secret Herb Garden** Old Pentland Rd · www. secretherbgarden.co.uk · 0131 445 5888 On the southern edge of the city beyond the ring road, off the A702 (Morningside) Biggar Rd, signed Old Pentland: a garden/garden centre created around herbs, a shop selling country things and vintage garden implements, and a tearoom in a shed, with mix-and-match furniture on a terrace. Inside the old greenhouses in summer months, there's a full-moon dinner (guest chefs; it's booked weeks ahead). This is Hamish and Liberty Martin's idyllic vision. They make gin from their own botanicals and sell herbs online. Here, you just hang out with great coffee, soup, cake, and take in the country air.

307 8/P25   ✓ **Gallery of Modern Art (Modern 1) Café** Belford Rd · www. nationalgalleries.org · 0131 624 6200 (general enquiries) Unbeatable on a fine day when you can sit out on the patio on the lawn, with sculptures around (411/ATTRACTIONS), wine and a plate of Scottish cheese and oatcakes. Hot dishes are good – always 2 soups, meat/fish and vegetarian baked potatoes. Cakes and stuff! Lunch dishes usually gone by 2.30pm. **Café Newton** at Modern Art Two (412/ATTRACTIONS) across the main road and the gardens is a smaller, more interior café by the same people (Heritage Portfolio much less corporate catering than you might expect). Soup, sandwiches and 2 hot lunch dishes. Paolozzi's *Vulcan* towers above. Both 7 days, daytime only.

308 8/Q25 ✓ **Colonnades @ The Signet Library** Parliament Sq · www. thesignetlibrary.co.uk/colonnades · 0131 226 1064 On the Royal Mile behind the Cathedral. The classiest tearoom in town, in the august, lofty ambience of a classic Georgian library – real books, real colonnades – you are at the heart of Edinburgh: World Heritage site. Lunch 11am-1.30pm, but mainly you come for afternoon tea, which can be booked. The corporate hospitality aspect (by Heritage Portfolio, again) easily tholed in these surroundings. Closed Sat.

309 8/Q25 ✓ **Porto And Fi** 47 Newhaven Main St · www.portofi.com · 0131 551 1900 On the corner of Craighall Rd, Trinity, set back from the busy shoreline road. Light, just right room, where Fi's home cooking and baking hits the spot for the ladies (and others) who lunch. Orkney ice cream. Great cakes and sometimes the sunset over there. A very Edinburgh rendezvous. From early till 8pm (10pm Fri/Sat).

310 8/Q25 ✓ **Leo's Beanery** 23A Howe St · www.leosbeanery.co.uk · 0131 556 8403 Slightly below New Town street level (with patio seating), a much regarded stalwart of New Town/road to Stockbridge society. Good coffee, excellent baking, hot food and takeaway. They also have the café at the **Dovecot** (421/GALLERIES). 7 days, daytime only.

311 8/Q25 ✓ **Mimi's Bakehouse** 63 Shore · www.mimisbakehouse.com · 0131 555 5908 They call it a bakehouse and they do bake, with a big selection of goodies coming out of their small kitchen and into their sprawling, multi-chambered tearooms always packed with cake eaters. 'Award-winning' and from mini to massive, who would think there are so many folk not watching their figures as they work through the tiers. Great for kids and birthdays. Open breakfast till teatime, and though the meals are perhaps less successful than the bakes, at last

8/P25 foodie Leith has a cupcake to call its own. **Mimi's Little Bakehouse** is on the Royal Mile at 250 Canongate (0131 556 6632), and at 277 St John's Rd, Corstorphine, well west of the city centre (0131 334 7474).

312 8/Q25 ✓ **Clarinda's** 69 Canongate · 0131 557 1888 At the bottom of the Royal Mile near Holyrood Palace and the Parliament building. Small but with total tearoom integrity. Hot dishes and snacks worth the sit-down stop on the tourist trail and some of the best home baking in town. Inexpensive; run by good Edinburgh folk (Maggie Hetherington and team) who work that tiny kitchen. Takeaways possible. For 40 years, rock buns, bakewell tart and the best caramel shortcake and apple pie in town. Believe it! No debit/credit cards. 7 days, daytime only.

313 8/P25 ✓ **Henri** 48 Raeburn Pl · www.henriofedinburgh.co.uk · 0131 332 8963 In the midst of a main street, a deli with wine bar/café behind that's just perfect for foodie Stockbridge. Soup with sourdough, home-made quiches, scrumptious salads, charcuterie, great cheese counter, especially French. These guys are enthusiasts. All to take away. 7 days daytime. A wine bar Thu-Sat evenings.

314 8/Q25 **The Pantry** 1-2 North West Circus Pl · www.thepantryedinburgh.co.uk · 0131 629 0206 On the road to Stockbridge. Laid-back, conscientious café-dining, with home-made hot food and proper baking. A hangout and a I'm-writing-a-book kind of place! 7 days, daytime only.

315 8/P25 **Botanic Gardens** Arboretum Pl · www.rbge.org.uk · 0131 248 2909 There are 3 coffee-shop options in these famous and fabulous gardens (408/ATTRACTIONS). Firstly, the small snack-bar/café at the Inverleith Rd entrance. Then the Terrace by 'The House' (where there are regular exhibitions; enter by Arboretum Pl): this self-service food operation though corporate ain't bad but the outside tables and view of the city are why we come here (and the cheeky, not-red squirrels!). And there's the Gateway Restaurant atop the shop in the landmark John Muir Gateway on Arboretum Pl. Waited service for breakfast, lunch and afternoon tea. 7 days, daytime only. The gardens are always to love!

The Best Cafés

CENTRAL

316 8/Q25 ✓ **The Edinburgh Larder** 15 Blackfriars St · www.edinburghlarder.co.uk · 0131 556 6922 Off the middle part of the Royal Mile. Caff and takeaway foodstop. More than a soup 'n' sandwich place, with home-made specials and a foodie approach. A wee Scottish gem, probably missed by tourists trudging around here looking for one. **Larder Go** is the deli and takeaway next door. 7 days, daytime only.

317 8/Q25 ✓ **Fruitmarket Café** 45 Market St · www.fruitmarket.co.uk · 0131 226 1843 Attached to the Fruitmarket Gallery, a cool, spacious place for coffee pastries or a light lunch by the Milk people (350/TAKEAWAYS). Big salads, home cooking, deli plates and 2/3 daily specials. It attracts a mix of tourists, art-baggers and Edinburgers who know that this is where to hang out as well as eat. The rest of the world goes by outside the big windows! 7 days, daytime only.

318 8/P25 **Coates Café and Nomad** 62 Haymarket Terrace · 0131 337 1791 & 2 Haymarket Terrace · 0131 337 3611 2 home-baking, good coffee caffs on corners of the busy street along from Haymarket station by Jacob Philip. The bakery downstairs (at 62) is better, fresher and more inventive than all those with tray bakes across town. Jacob is one hard-working guy (from 6am). Single-batch coffee roasting. Both 8am-4pm (from 9am Sun).

319 8/Q25 **MUM'S Great Comfort Food** 4a Forrest Rd · www.mumsgreatcomfortfood. co.uk · 0131 260 9806 There will always be a place for comfort food in our hearts and in our stomachs. This place does exactly what it declares. It's not a chain so somebody's mum has a lot to do with this. Pies, stews, sausages of the day (including 2 vegetarian), mash and crumble. Maccy cheese in a tin dish, Barney's beer and Beanos on the tables. What exactly is not to like? 7 days, all day.

EAST CITY, LEITH & THE COAST

320 8/Q25 ✓ **The Broughton Deli** 7 Barony St · 0131 558 7111 Just round the corner from Broughton St (and me). Takeaway counter and some deli items (great bread & free-range eggs), but mostly frequented as a caff and takeaway (348/TAKEAWAYS). Soups, tarts, hot dishes and imaginative salads. My local lunch box. 7 days, daytime only.

321A 8/Q25 ✓ **Quay Commons** 92 Commercial St · www.quaycommons.co · 0131 677 0244 Waterside sis of **The Gardener's Cottage** and **The Lookout** (133/CREATIVE COOKERY; 141/CASUAL), their bakery (brill bread), daytime food shop/café/takeaway. Leith's tops for brek 'n' brunch. Good vegetarian. 7 days.

321 8/Q25 ✓ **Punjabi Junction** 122-124 Leith Walk · www.punjabijunction.org · 0131 553 4737 On the Leith Walk block controversially under threat from development but seems likely to survive, a real taste of Punjab in a simple caff run by local women from the diverse ethnic minorities of Leith. Snacks (pakoras, samosas), daals and curries. Excellent, inexpensive thali and genuine sweet desserts. The real deal and great value. They have cookery classes. Closed Sun.

322 8/Q25 **Skylark** 241-243 Portobello High St · www.theskylark.co.uk · 0131 629 3037 E beyond the main traffic lights in the main road through Portobello. All-round café/bistro/bar and neighbourhood hangout, the vibe changing through the day. Great for kids; buggy junction daytime, with soups and salads; candlelit dinner, organic beers and wines at night. Reclaimed furniture and quality time; all easy-going. Food 10am-10pm, bar later Wed-Sun.

323 8/P25 **Boardwalk Café** 50 Marine Dr, Cramond · 07454 936863 300m from Cramond car park and pub. A real seaside café on the grassy foreshore overlooking the islands and the kitesurfers. Taken over with infectious enthusiasm by locals, Eddie and Sarah Tait, it has transformed the Promenade stroll, providing a proper refreshment stop with a huge patio. It's invariably crowded. See **Cramond** 425/WALKS. Wed-Sun till 5pm.

324 8/Q25 **Drill Hall Arts Café** 34 Dalmeny St · www.outoftheblue.org.uk · 0131 555 7100 Off Leith Walk. A drill hall right enough, turned into a vibrant and vital arts centre and neighbourhood social hub by Out of the Blue (an arts & education trust). Flea market (last Saturday of the month and many other events), studios and this eco/fairtrade/creative food kitchen. Soups, sandwiches & big for brunch. Mon-Sat daytime only. The beating heart of Leith.

325 8/Q25 **Word of Mouth** 3A Albert St · 0131 554 4344 Here 12 years, halfway down 'The Walk', missed by me but definitely an *StB* kind of local independent hangout. They roast their own coffee and make the cakes. Hot food; good word of mouth. Daytime only.

326 8/Q25 **Red Kite Café** 7-8 Cadzow Pl · www.redkitecafe.com · 0131 656 9005 On the road from Abbeyhill junction to Meadowbank, a calm, cool caff big on breakfast (the healthy variety) and simple, light lunches. Frittata, pies and avo on sourdough, of course. Loyal locals and maybe you passing by. 7 days 8am-6pm (from 9am Sun).

327 8/Q25 **Café Nom de Plume** 60 Broughton St · 0131 478 1372 Cosy rooms up a few
DF steps on busy Broughton St – local community and LGBT community. Same folk have **The Regent**, which has a similar friendly atmos, yet eclectic, well-made food and drink. Easy to live with. 7 days 11am-11pm.

SOUTH CITY/BRUNTSFIELD AND MORNINGSIDE

328 8/Q25 ✓ **10 To 10 In Delhi** 67 Nicolson St · 07536 757770/0131 510 4746 Near Nicolson Sq and university. A mini maharajah's tent in the southside, a homage to Bollywood (movies on TV) and sweet memories of India. Chai and Pekoe teas (including masala tea), soups and chef Alieu's curries and daal. Chilled vibe, nice people. A no-alcohol zone. 7 days.

329 8/P25 ✓ **Luca's** 16 Morningside Rd · www.s-luca.co.uk · 0131 446 0233 In-town version of legendary ice-cream parlour in Musselburgh (1491/ICE CREAM). Ice cream and snacks downstairs, more family food parlour up. Cheap and cheerful. Great for kids. 7 days 9am-10pm. See also 285/KIDS.

330 8/Q25 ✓ **La Barantine** 202 Bruntsfield Pl · www.labarantine.com ·
0131 229 0267 Also branches in 89 West Bow and 27B Raeburn Pl and the
walk-in bakery at 10 Bruntsfield Pl further down. Best patisserie cafés in town, with
delectable tartes, cakes and quiches baked daily by Vincent Aplincourt and team.
Great coffee and soup & sandwiches. Macarons a must! Daytime only.

331 8/Q25 **Forest Café** 141 Lauriston Pl · 0131 229 4922 At corner of Brougham St at
the main Tollcross crossroads. Busy drop-in café run by volunteers (they're a
registered arts charity) from morning to night. Internet and/or Fringe vibe (which
is where they came from). All food is vegetarian. Hours to some extent depend on
volunteers but 7 days 10am-11pm.

332 8/Q25 **Chocolate Tree** 123 Bruntsfield Pl · www.choctree.co.uk · 0131 228 3144
Crafty chocolatiers are everywhere, but these guys are thought by many to be at
the top of the tree. Their organic products made in E Lothian are widely for sale;
this is the only place you buy on their premises and have a hot choco and churros,
their delicious ice cream, the best selection of chocolate cakes. Always busy but
you can book online! 7 days 10am-7.30pm.

▮▮▮▮ The Best Late-Night Restaurants

333 8/Q25 ✓✓ **Dishoom** 3a St Andrew Sq · www.dishoom.com · 0131 202 6406
The London chain Indian restaurant here running a very slick operation.
You always have to wait in the bar downstairs. 7 days, all day till 10.45pm
weekdays, 11.45pm weekends. Bar till 1am. See also 263/INDIAN.

334 8/Q26 ✓ **The Witchery** Castlehill · www.thewitchery.com · 0131 225 5613 Top of
ATMOS Royal Mile near the Castle. Excellent late-night dining and atmos in one of the
city's best restaurants; somewhere civilised to eat late. Worth it for the atmos
alone. See also 120/FINE DINING. 7 days lunch & LO **11.30pm**.

335 8/Q25 ✓ **Giuliano's** 18-19 Union Pl · www.giulianos.co.uk · 0131 556 6590 Leith
Walk opposite Playhouse Theatre. Buzzing Italian tratt day and night. Report:
202/TRATTS. Till **11.30pm/1am** weekends.

336 8/Q25 ✓ **El Cartel** 64 Thistle St · www.elcartelmexicana.co.uk · 0131 226 7171
Really good Mexican streetfood. No booking. Till **11.30pm weekends** (10pm
during the week). Report: 251/MEXICAN.

337 8/Q25 ✓ **The Holyrood 9A** 9A Holyrood Rd · www.theholyrood.co.uk ·
DF 0131 556 5044 Round the corner from the bottom of St Mary's St. Like other
Fuller Thomson bar/restaurants (The Red Squirrel below), this, their original, serves
its burger based menu all day till **11pm**. Report: 180/FOOD PUBS.

338 8/Q25 **Red Squirrel** 21 Lothian Rd · www.redsquirreledinburgh.co.uk ·
0131 229 9933 Best in the West End. Burgers and beers done well, with great
ambience. Only place hereabouts to eat after theatre or film. Well-managed all-day
watering hole till **11.15pm**.

Mamma's Open till **midnight on Fri/Sat**. Report: 211/PIZZA.

Good Places For Brunch

339 8/Q25 ✓ **Peter's Yard** 27 Simpson Loan · www.petersyard.com · 0131 228 5876
One of the best places in town for the civilised non-fry breakfast and people
watching on Middle Meadow Walk; they're the real cinnamon bun. From **7.30am**
weekdays and **9am** Sat/Sun. Report: 303/TEAROOMS.

340 8/Q25 ✓ **Joseph Pearce's** 23 Elm Row · www.bodabar.com · 0131 556 4140 Near
the top of Leith Walk. Up-and-down corner bar, good for many reasons and in
the way they know what people want, a top Sunday breakfast/brunch till 4pm,
including Swedish/classic healthy versions and every way with eggs. 7 days from
11am. Report: 361/UNIQUE PUBS.

341 8/Q25 ✓ **Edinburgh Larder Café** 15 Blackfriars St · www.edinburghlarder.co.uk ·
0131 556 6922 This is where to go for Sunday brekkie near the Royal Mile – as
the queue will attest. 7 days from **8.30am**. Report: 316/CAFÉS.

342 8/Q25 ✓ **The Broughton Deli** 7 Barony St · 0131 558 7111 Neighbourhood café/deli.
Daily bread and other fresh baking. Breakfast from **8am** (Sun **10am**). Report:
320/CAFÉS.

343 8/Q25 ✓ **The Scottish Café & Restaurant** The Mound · www.
thescottishcafeandrestaurant.com · 0131 225 1550 Below the National
Gallery; enter via Princes St Gardens. The definitive Scottish breakfast of course,
but many variations. Great location for easing into the day, and upstairs there's
very good art. From **9am** (Sun **10am**). Report: 247/SCOTTISH.

344 8/Q25 **King's Wark** 36 Shore · http://kingswark.co.uk · 0131 554 9260 On busy
corner for traffic, but calm and comforting inside. Dining room or bar. A civilised
brunch on the waterfront. From **10am**.

345 8/Q25 **The Broughton Street Breakfast** There's lots of choice in the main street of
Edinburgh's East Village. From the top down: Lovely-looking **Treacle** kicks in from
10am with upmarket gastropub choices. **Artisan Roast** has the best coffee from
9am. **The Basement** also does Tex-Mex brex from **noon** and regulars attest to its
ability to hit the spot. Further down, on the corner, with people-watching windows,
is **The Barony** with breakfast **12.30-3.30pm**, the papers and live music; **The New
Town Deli** on the corner of Barony St is neither a deli nor a café but has a few
seats, the papers and is open from **9am**. The NTD is also at 23 Henderson Row
(355/TAKEAWAYS). And special mention for:

346 8/Q25 **The Olive Branch** 91 Broughton St · www.theolivebranchscotland.co.uk ·
0131 557 8589 At the weekend, the definitive **Broughton Street Breakfast**: big
windows, outside tables. Med menu and breakfast fry-ups. This place is routinely
packed. On Sundays you pray for a table. From **11.45am** during the week and from
10am Sat/Sun.

The Best Takeaway Places

347 8/Q25 ✓ **Desi Pakwan** 61 Leith Walk · www.desipakwanonline.com · 0131 555 3333 On the right, near the bottom of Leith Walk, Leithers and those in the know come here to sit in the stripped-back café that could be in Delhi Old Town, and to get in the queue of their roaring takeaway trade. The 'pure taste of Punjab' is all made to order; the kitchen fast 'n' furious. 7 days noon-11pm.

348 8/Q25 ✓ **The Broughton Deli** 7 Barony St · 0131 558 7111 Neighbourhood café/deli with daily fresh bread and baking, including cakes. Soup, tart, frittata and a hot dish all to go. See 320/CAFÉS.

349 8/Q25 ✓ **Anima** 11 Henderson Row · www.anima-online.co.uk · 0131 558 2918 Adjacent to and part of **L'Alba D'Oro** (235/FISH & CHIPS). Smart, busy Italian hot 'n' cold takeaway. 'Italian soul food' includes great pizza and freshly prepared pastas made to order. Excellent wine selection. Some desserts. A welcome expansion from chips – our soul food – to theirs. Lunch Mon-Fri & 7 days evenings.

350 8/P25 ✓ **Milk Café** 232 Morrison St · www.cafemilk.co.uk · 0131 629 6022 Here, the original home of Milk caff and takeaway that has now gone on to provide sustenance for visitors to two cool art venues – the **Fruitmarket Gallery** 416/GALLERIES and **Edinburgh Sculpture Workshop**. Far from bland, Milk's menu includes world food from all over: Brazil, Morocco, Thailand. Great brunch menu, including burritos. Creative cuisine unusual in a takeaway, and a pale, calm place to graze. 7 days 8am-4pm.

351 8/Q25 ✓ **Social Bite** 131 Rose St · www.social-bite.co.uk · 0131 220 8206 In the heart of the consumer throng, this is a foodstop with heart. All the profits go to charity (the homeless). This, 1 of 5 of Josh Littlejohn's pioneering 'social enterprise cafés', where the menu is created by a Michelin chef. Expect innovative bespoke sandwiches and comforting hot dishes. George Clooney was here. 'I can do stew', he said, and we swooned. Mon-Fri 7am-3pm.

352 8/Q25 ✓ **The Edinburgh Larder and Larder Go** 15 Blackfriars St · www.edinburghlarder.co.uk · 0131 556 6922 Off the Royal Mile. The café and takeaway next to each other. High-quality home cooking here, in the tiny kitchen. Simple and seasonal soups, salads, cakes 'n' all and deli delights. 7 days, daytime only.

353 8/Q25 ✓ **Kebab Mahal** 7 Nicolson Sq · www.kebab-mahal.co.uk · 0131 667 5214 For 30 years this unassuming but cosmopolitan Indian diner and takeaway has occupied a fond place on the edge of the university quarter for snacks, curries, babas, kulfi and lassis. 7 days from noon till late (2am Fri/Sat).

354 8/Q25 **Embo** 29 Haddington Pl · 0131 652 3880 Halfway down Leith Walk, Mike Marshall's neighbourhood hangout and takeaway is a step up from the rest. Bespoke sandwiches, wraps, etc. Excellent coffee and smoothies. Few seats in and a couple of tables on the step. Nice cakes. Local sourcing. They do festivals. Closed Sun.

355 8/Q25 **The New Town Deli** 42 Broughton St & 23 Henderson Row · 0800 073 1211 · www.thenewtowndeli.com These slightly misleadingly named soup 'n' sandwich places are not delis but great local takeaways (and breakfasts in Henderson Row). Open daytime with big windows for people watching. There's another coffee shop branch at 33 Deanhaugh St, the main street of Stockbridge.

The Best Delis

356 8/Q25
ATMOS

✓✓✓ **Valvona & Crolla** 19 Elm Row · www.valvonacrolla.co.uk · 0131 556 6066 Near top of Leith Walk. An Edinburgh institution since 1934 and the perfect provisioner for the good things in life. Full of smells, genial, knowledgeable staff and a floor-to-ceiling range of cheese, meats, oils, wines and artisan bread. Superlative fresh produce, irresistible cheese counter, their own bakery, great café-bar (198/ITALIAN). Buy Mary Contini's evocative trilogy of how the family left the mountains of South Italy on foot, finding their way to Edinburgh. Demos, tastings and a Fringe venue – V&C is a national treasure, they did define the word delicatessen for Scotland. 7 days, daytime only.

357 8/Q25

✓✓ **I.J. Mellis** 30a Victoria St · www.mellischeese.co.uk · 0131 226 6215 Cheesemonger extraordinaire and very select deli for food that's good and 'slow'. Coffees, hams, sausages, olives and seasonal stuff, e.g. apples and mushrooms (branches vary); smells mingle. Eyesome and toothsome. Branches in Glasgow (631/DELIS) and St Andrews. He's still the cheese guy. Times vary. See also 1527/CHEESES.

358 8/P25

✓✓ **George Mewes** 3 Dean Park St · www.georgemewescheese.co.uk · 0131 332 5900 At end of Raeburn Pl. Further extending Stockbridge's food quarter, George arrived from Glasgow's West End where he's long been the Cheese King (632/DELIS). This temperature controlled, bespoke shop is both chilled and chilled. New Town dinner parties wouldn't be the same without GM's prime selection of English cheeses and the gorgonzola. 7 days, daytime only.

359 8/Q25

✓✓ **181 Delicatessen** 181 Bruntsfield Pl · 0131 229 4554 On the foodie strip near 'Holy Corner', a deli that takes a lot of care to get it right, with conscientious sourcing from local producers (pies, bread, even butter) and shelves of trusted labels. Mike and Charlotte Billinghurst there for chat on their good foods. Couple of tables for soups, platters and scones. Licence on the way at TGP. Mon-Sat, daytime.

360 8/P25

✓ **Herbie of Edinburgh** 66 Raeburn Pl · www.herbieofedinburgh.co.uk · 0131 332 9888 Notable originally for cheese (that Brie!) and other cold-counter irresistibles (1529/CHEESES). There's always a queue in their packed-from-floor-to-ceiling emporium of good things. Excellent artisan bread and home-made quiches, pâtés and cakes. Mon-Sat daytime only.

Unique Edinburgh Pubs

361 8/Q25
DF
✓ **Sofi's/Boda/Joseph Pearce's/Victoria** Leith · www.bodabar.com 4 pubs all in the Leith area where the Christophersons have built a very particular little empire that could only happen in Edinburgh. All have been transformed from old, defunct pubs and are fresh, quirky, laid-back, mix 'n' match and full of individual touches. Sofi's is the smallest, in a Leith backstreet (Henderson St); JP's is the largest on a busy corner (Elm Row) at the top of Leith Walk (good pub-grub menu, outside tables), there's a jogging club (Tue nights); the others are on corners on the Walk and dogs are welcome in all. There's also **Hemma** in Holyrood Rd, near the Parliament, and then the super Swedes opened super **Akva**, a huge 2-floor and canalside bar in Fountainbridge.

362 8/Q25
DF
✓ **The Royal Dick at Summerhall** 1 Summerhall · www.summerhall.co.uk · 0131 560 1572 Very close to the Meadows, a bar in the corner of the central courtyard of the extraordinary independent art and cultural centre, Summerhall, a huge complex of creative types, where anything is possible. Formerly the Royal Dick Veterinary College, the bar maintains the theme. They say it's a bar-bistro and though the food is a bit hit and miss, it's always good to hang out here, indoors or in the yard, whether you're at a gig, exhibition, festival or the Fringe, where it is a major venue. Unique! Food from noon till 10pm.

363 8/Q25
✓ **Leith Depot** 138-140 Leith Walk · www.leithdepot.com · 0131 555 4738 An important independent Edinburgh, Leith and music community bar on a limited lifespan at TGP, due to an imminent and controversial development of this block of the Walk. A vociferous campaign in progress (it will still be here till late 2019). A people place with an upstairs music/arts venue, great food, beers and craic!

364 8/Q25
✓ **Bramble Bar** 16A Queen St · www.bramblebar.co.uk · 0131 226 6343 A discreet, unprepossessing basement doorway; cool, comfy and big (internationally big) on cocktails. Mike Aikman and Jas Scott have made a discerning drinkers' haven on the leading edge of what we're drinking now and next. Nice Gen X and millennials in the mix(ology) and non-compromising soundtrack (not fluffy lounge music). They get through a lotta limes!

365 8/Q25
ATMOS
✓ **Bennets Bar** 8 Leven St · 0131 229 5143 By King's Theatre. Stand at the back and don't watch the sports – watch light stream through the stained glass like it always did. Same era as Café Royal and similar ambience, mirrors and tiles. Food much improved of late. Lunch and early evening (182/FOOD PUBS).

366 8/Q25
ATMOS
✓ **Sandy Bell's** 25 Forrest Rd · www.sandybellsedinburgh.co.uk · 0131 225 2751 Near the university and Greyfriars Kirk; it seems like it's been there as long. Mainly known as a folky/traditional music haven (live 7 nights), it reeks (though the smoke has gone) of atmos (it should be given a dispensation). Soup 'n' pies and the fiddle.

367 8/Q25
ATMOS
✓ **Café Royal** 19 West Register St · www.caferoyaledinburgh.co.uk · 0131 556 1884 Behind the Apple shop at the east end of Princes Street, one of Edinburgh's longest-celebrated pubs. Unrelated to the London version, though there is a similar Victorian/Baroque elegance. Through the partition is the **Oyster Bar** (with perfect atmos for oysters and all 230/SEAFOOD). Central counter and often standing room only. Bar food till 10pm.

368 8/Q25   **Barony Bar** 81-85 Broughton St · 0131 558 2874   East Village venue with a mixed clientele and always a good vibe. With new ownership, a refresh and a rebooted food menu, the Barony is on a roll. Mix-and-match furniture, woody and convivial. Wine is, for some reason, expensive. Newspapers to browse over a Sunday brunch. Bert's band and others on early Sunday evenings one of the best pub-music nights in town, though only till 8pm.

369 8/Q25   **The Basement** 10a-12a Broughton St · www.basement-bar-edinburgh. co.uk · 0131 557 0097   Years down the line, The Basement is still a happening sort of, er, basement bar, with perennially popular Mex-style food served by smiley staff (254/MEXICAN). At night, the punters are well up for it – late, loud and still alive.

370 8/Q25   **Kay's Bar** 39 Jamaica St · www.kaysbar.co.uk · 0131 225 1858   Tucked away in
DF   a corner of the New Town, a true original: the oak casks, Kay's Bar jugs, a real fire.
ATMOS   They care for the beer and do a bit of grub at lunchtime (anything that goes with HP Sauce). 4 screens for the rugby only – no footie here.

371 8/Q25   **The Stockbridge Tap** 2 Raeburn Pl · 0131 343 3000   On a corner. A definitive
DF   local – i.e. Stockbridge – pub in understated Edinburgh style. Up to 17 ales on the taps, many whiskies, very decent grub, including Sun lunch. By the people who have **The Bow Bar** and **Cloisters** (383/384/REAL-ALE PUBS). Lunch & dinner.

372 8/Q25   **The Regent** 2 Montrose Terrace · 0131 661 8198   On prominent Abbeyhill corner near Calton Gardens, an all-round friendly and especially gay-friendly bar; a place for Edinburgers perhaps more than the tourists milling down the hill at the Palace and the Parliament. Food noon-10pm. Notable ale selection (9).

373 8/Q25   **Port o' Leith** 58 Constitution St · 0131 554 3568   The legendary Leith bar on the
DF   busy road to what used to be the docks is perhaps not what it once was when Mary
ATMOS   Moriarty was Madame, but some aura still remains. Always good music. It's still a port in the storm for a' sorts.

374 8/Q25   **The Safari Lounge** 21 Cadzow Pl · www.thesafarilounge.co.uk ·
ATMOS   0131 661 4741   Don't know why it took me so long to cotton on to this vibey bar except its location – just beyond the pale: down from the Abbeyhill junction and the Regent Bar on the road to Meadowbank. Darkish bar at the front, light lounge at the back – both safarified. Mixed crowd of locals and hipsters. Great soundtrack. Surprisingly eclectic food menu. They say 'Quality Provisions & Libations'. This is more or less correct. 7 days noon-midnight; food till 9pm.

375 8/Q25   **The Sheep Heid Inn** 43-45 The Causeway, Duddingston · www.
ATMOS   thesheepheidedinburgh.co.uk · 0131 661 7974   18th-century inn 6km from city centre behind Arthur's Seat and reached most easily through the Queen's Park. Village and nearby wildfowl loch should be strolled around if you have time. Food gets mixed reviews but can be al fresco; also comfy upstairs room. Atmos and history is why we come. Food served all day (book weekends).

376 8/Q25   **The Dome** 14 George St · www.thedomeedinburgh.com · 0131 624 8624 Edinburgh's first megabar (and not a Wetherspoon) in truly impressive former bank, and grandiose in a way that only a converted temple to Mammon could be. The main part sits 15m under an elegant domed roof with an island bar and raised platform at back (**The Grill Room**) for determined diners. Big chandeliers, big, big flower arrangements: you come for the surroundings more than the victuals, perhaps. Adjacent and separate **Club Room** is more intimate, more clubby, better for a blether. 'Garden' patio bar at back (in good weather) – enter via Rose St. Final bit downstairs: **Why Not?** – a nightclub for late millennials lookin' for lurve.

The Best Original Pubs

377 8/P25 · DF   ✓ **The Diggers** 1-3 Angle Park Terrace · 0131 337 3822 Officially the Athletic Arms, a Jambo pub *par excellence*, stowed with the Tynecastle faithful before and after games. Still keeps a great pint of locally brewed 'The Diggers' 80/- and 6 guest ales. Pies and pies. A great snug.

378 8/Q25 · ATMOS   ✓ **The Royal Oak** 1 Infirmary St · www.royal-oak-folk.com · 0131 557 2976 Tiny upstairs and not much bigger down. During the day, pensioners sip their pints (couple of real ales), downstairs 'lounge' from 9pm (Thu-Sun). Has surprisingly survived the smoking ban. Mainly known as a folk-music stronghold (live music every night for 50 years!) and home of Sunday's 'Wee Folk Club', they definitely don't make 'em like this anymore. Gold-carat pubness. 7 days till 2am.

379 8/P25   ✓ **Roseburn Bar** 1 Roseburn Terrace · www.roseburnbar.co.uk · 0131 337 1067 On main Glasgow road out W from Haymarket and one of the nearest pubs to Murrayfield Stadium. Wood and grandeur and red leather; bonnie wee snug. A fine pint, and wall-to-wall rugby, of course. Heaving and heaven before internationals. It is a man's bar.

380 8/Q25   **Oxford Bar** 8 Young St · www.oxfordbar.co.uk · 0131 539 7119 Downhill from George St. No time machine needed – just step in the door and find one of Edinburgh's most celebrated non-reconstructed bars. Inspector Rebus wuz here. Be prepared to be scrutinised when you come in. Some real ales but they're beside the point. No accoutrements – food menu is crisps or nuts.

381 8/Q25   **Mathers Bar** 1 Queensferry St · 0131 225 3549 Worth visiting just to look at the ornate fixtures and fittings – frieze and bar especially. Unreconstructed in every sense since 1903. Men quietly drinking. Pies all day. 50 malts. Alongside many smart bars in the West End, it caters for men with ties and few domestic ties. A stand-up, stand-alone place for old-fashioned pubbery, slack coiffeur and idle banter.

Bennets Bar Report: 365/UNIQUE PUBS.

Sandy Bell's Report: 366/UNIQUE PUBS.

The Best Real-Ale & Craft-Beer Pubs

382 8/Q25 ✓ **The Cumberland Bar** 1-3 Cumberland St · www.cumberlandbar.co.uk ·
DF 0131 558 3134 Corner of Dundonald St. After work, this New Town bar
attracts its share of suits, but later the locals (and droves of posh students) claim it
too. Long a CAMRA (Campaign for Real Ale) redoubt but now, as well as 8 real-ale
taps, an impressive selection of lagers and ciders on tap and bottles aplenty. Nicely
appointed, very decent pub food (including the Sunday roast), unexpected beer
garden (noon-evening Sat/Sun).

383 8/Q25 ✓ **The Bow Bar** 80 West Bow · www.thebowbar.co.uk · 0131 226 7667
DF Halfway down Victoria St. They know how to treat drink in this excellent,
award-winning wee bar. Traditional selection of 6 keg ales, 8 casks, many bottles and
top for whiskies (over 270 malts) – no cocktails! One of the few places in the
Grassmarket area an over-30-year-old might not feel out of place. Pie 'n' pint at lunch.

384 8/Q25 ✓ **Cloisters** 26 Brougham St, Tollcross · www.cloistersbar.com ·
DF 0131 221 9997 This is a drinker's paradise: 19 taps and dozens of whiskies and
many wines by the glass in this simple and unfussy bar with wooden floors and
laid-back approach. Good, pragmatic pub grub – many burgers. Food Tue-Sat,
lunch & dinner, Sun 12.30pm-4pm. 5 kegs, 9 casks, 8 on rotation. Bar closes
midnight (1am Fri/Sat). Both pubby and clubby; girls go too! The same people own
the Bow Bar (above) and **The Stockbridge Tap** (371/UNIQUE PUBS) on the corner
of busy Raeburn Pl. All good neighbourhood spots.

385 8/Q25 ✓ **Canny Man's** 237 Morningside Rd · www.cannymans.co.uk ·
ATMOS 0131 447 1484 Officially the Volunteer Arms but everybody calls it the Canny
Man's. Many smørrebrøds at lunch (7 days) and evenings (Tue-Sat). Report: 179/
FOOD PUBS. A wide range of real ales and myriad malts. Clubby and civilised, this
much-loved family fiefdom is one of the city's most convivial pubs.

386 8/Q25 ✓ **The Guildford Arms** 1 West Register St · www.guildfordarms.com ·
 0131 556 4312 Behind the Apple shop at east end of Princes St on same block
as the **Café Royal** (367/UNIQUE PUBS). Forever in the same family. Lofty, ornate
Victorian hostelry with loadsa good ales, typically 7 Scottish, 3 English (and 16
wines by the glass). There are some you won't find anywhere else in the city. Pub
grub available on 'gallery' floor as well as bar. Tourists and locals mingle.

387 8/Q25 ✓ **Blue Blazer** 2 Spittal St · 0131 229 5030 Opposite Doubletree Hilton. No
 frills, no pretensions, just wooden fixtures and fittings and all sorts in this fine
howff that carries a huge range of real ales (8 on tap). Regularly a 'Pub of the Year'.
Extraordinary rum and gin list and then the malts. Much more soul than its
competitors nearby.

388 8/Q25 ✓ **Brewdog** 143 Cowgate · www.brewdog.com · 0131 220 6517 The
 Edinburgh Brewdog barking louder for craft beers than the others. All their
estimable strong, very strong and pale and interesting are here, served with their
signature strut and spirit and Punk IPA. It's come a long way from Fraserburgh (and
their crowdfunded brewery up north in Ellon); they're now even at the airport.

389 8/Q25 **Cask & Barrel** 115 Broughton St & 24-26 W Preston St · 0131 556 3132 A real
pub with a great selection of ales (8) and a couldn't-care-less crowd at the foot of
gay and groovy Broughton St. Here they prefer a good pint and the football. Outside
tables on a windy corner. Southside version has many ales too (8) and integrity (and
sport on the TV all around you).

The Best Wine Bars

390 8/Q25
DF
✓✓ **Pickles** 56a Broughton St · www.getpickled.co.uk · 0131 557 5005
Though this sympatico parlour set discreetly below stairs in Broughton St, near where I live, gets plenty of likes on social media, it's still a find and I'm not the only one who'd prefer it if you didn't. But like their charcuterie platters, it's to share. Jonny Bristow and a coterie of capable cheerful lassies dispense banter and distinctive wines to the discerning likes of you and me. Tables packed in but somehow you can usually get a seat (till now, anyway). Food till late and 10pm outside on the below-street patio. 4-11pm, later weekends.

391 8/Q25
✓ **Bar à Vin** 17a Queensferry St · www.lescargotblanc.co.uk · 0131 226 1890
The most sympathetically French of Bars à Vins in town, the on-street hostelry you go through to reach the ambiente **L'Escargot Blanc** bistro upstairs (187/FRENCH). The bar has perfect atmos and pitch, and a top selection of only French wines, by bottle or glass. Snacks and cheese/charcuterie plats into the evening. 7 days.

392A 8/Q25
✓ **The Fat Pony** 47 Bread St · www.thefatpony.com · 0131 229 5770 Wine bar in the Tollcross/Theatre District by the irrepressible Dave Ramsden. Fresh approach, 'clean' and organic wines, probably the coolest collection in town with frequent change of choice. 4-11pm. Closed Sun.

392 8/Q25
✓ **One 20 Wine Café** 120 Dundas St · www.one-20.co.uk · 0131 556 1911
The wine bar/café/restaurant of wine importers Kyle (and his dad) Ronnie Reid at the bottom of Dundas St, near Hamilton Pl. Decidedly Italian spin to the food menu with hot dishes, lunch & dinner. As you'd expect, a selective wine list. 7 days.

393 8/Q25
✓ **Le Di-Vin** 9 Randolph Pl · www.ledivin.co.uk · 0131 538 1815 In quiet cul-de-sac off busy Queensferry St, a lofty wine bar in a church-like Tudor mansion adjacent to **La P'tite Folie** (190/FRENCH). Great non-cosy ambience with loyal following for French wine and the right food to go with. Noon till 11pm/midnight. Closed Sun.

394 8/Q25
✓ **The Good Brothers** 4-6 Dean St · www.goodbrothers.co.uk · 0131 315 3311 The good brothers, Rory and Graeme Sutherland, have 120 wines on their list and, not surprisingly, a good by-the-glass selection. The woody, foodie, wine-supping ambience here is very Stockbridge (100m from Raeburn Pl). Closed Mon.

395 8/Q25
✓ **Divino Enoteca** 5 Merchant St · www.divinoedinburgh.com · 0131 225 1770 This is the downstairs of **Vittoria** (201/TRATTS), and is the wine and food bar of maestro Tony Crolla. You can descend through the restaurant from George IV Bridge but you usually enter at ground level off the Cowgate. Atmosphere of dark materials and fairy-lit garden, designed to make you love Italian wine. Small-plate/grazing menu and more substantial dishes. The fancy machinery keeps the wines pristine (16 white, 16 red). Closed Sun.

396 8/Q25
Toast 65 The Shore, Leith · http://toastleith.co.uk · 0131 467 6984 Corner site by the Water of Leith, a wine bar-café from breakfast (at 8am) till late with a patisserie counter, a light Med menu and an impressive wine collection, with loads available by the glass, including many organics. 7 days.

397 8/Q25
Smith & Gertrude 26 Hamilton Pl · www.smithandgertrude.com · 0131 629 6280 A room in Stockbridge, a couple of hospitable patrons (though not Smith or Gertrude – these are streets in Melbourne where the Findlaters used to live). Well-selected wines (and music soundtrack) and cheeses – on wine flight nights the cheese is free. Tasting events downstairs. Closed Mon.

The Main Attractions

398 8/Q25
LLL
ADMISSION
HES

✓✓✓ **Edinburgh Castle** www.edinburghcastle.gov.uk · 0131 225 9846
Go to Princes St and look up! Extremely busy AYR and yet the city's
must-see main attraction does not disappoint. St Margaret's 12th-century chapel is
simple and beautiful; the rolling history lesson that leads up to the display of
Scotland's crown jewels is fascinating; the Stone of Destiny is a big deal to the
Scots (though others may not see why). And, ultimately, the Scottish National War
Memorial is one of the most genuinely affecting places in the country – a simple,
dignified testament to shared pain and loss. The Esplanade is a major concert
venue in July, just before the International Tattoo, the largest nightly event of the
Festival in August. Last entry 1 hour before closing. 9.30am-5/6pm.

399 8/Q25

✓✓✓ **The National Museum of Scotland** Chambers St · www.nms.
ac.uk · 0300 123 6789 After a £50-million refit and further external
works, the fully integrated and effectively reinvented NMS is one of the UK's most
successful and visited attractions. The restored-to-former-Victorian-grandeur
atrium, thousands of objects in state-of-the-art displays and interactivity, and
integration with the adjacent Museum of Scotland (opened in 1999), make this a
uniquely special homage to and celebration of the ingenuity, industry and
influence of a small country that changed the world. Not to forget the big animals
and all that went before! With the Riverside Museum in Glasgow, Scotland has
2 paeans to its proud cultural and entrepreneurial past that are in themselves
everything to be proud of. 7 days 10am-5pm. A roof terrace reveals the city skyline.
3 café areas. The independently run rooftop Tower Restaurant is rather good.

400 8/P25

✓✓✓ **The Forth Bridge** www.forth-bridges.co.uk 20km W of
Edinburgh via A90. First turning for S Queensferry from dual
carriageway; don't confuse with signs for road bridges. Or train from Waverley to
Dalmeny, and walk 1km. The mighty bridge was 100 in 1990. The Road Bridge – 50
years old in 2014 and celebrated with a spectacular firework displays – was followed
by the similarly impressive and much-loved **Queensferry Crossing**, opened by the
Queen in 2017 (I had a hand in that!). So now there are uniquely **Three Bridges**.
The Forth Bridge, however, is an international symbol of Scotland and it should
certainly be seen, but go to the N side: S Queensferry often crowded can seem a bit
tacky though improving these days. Shame that Tesco spoiled the view from the
road bridge approach and well done the **Dakota** for dramatising it (112/HOTELS
OUTSIDE EDINBURGH). There is also a good hotel-restaurant in S Queensferry (115/
HOTELS OUTSIDE EDINBURGH) with views of the bridge. You can walk across the
Road Bridge but not the QC (it's a motorway).

401 8/P25
ADMISSION

✓✓✓ **Edinburgh Zoo** Corstorphine Rd · www.edinburghzoo.org.uk ·
0131 334 9171 4km W of Princes St; buses from Princes St Gardens
side. Opened in 1909, this is no ordinary zoo. Apart from being fun and educational
and all that, its conservation work and serious zoology is highly respected (hence The
Giant Pandas). Penguins parade at 2.15pm daily in summer months and there are
many other old friends and favourites, as well as new ones: the Sumatran tigers, the
only UK koalas and the beavers – there are many animals here to love and cherish.
Though Tian Tian's much anticipated baby did not arrive in 2017, the pandas remain
a major attraction (you hope you see one). Timed tickets. Check the website. Open
AYR 7 days. Apr-Sep 9am-6pm, reduced hours in winter. See also 1737/KIDS.

402 8/Q25 ✓✓ **Palace of Holyroodhouse** Canongate · www.rct.uk · 0131 556 5100
ADMISSION 🖥 Foot of the Royal Mile, the Queen's North British timeshare – she's here
for a wee while late June/early July. Large parts of the palace are a bit dull and only
a dozen or so rooms are open, most dating from the 17th century, with a couple
from the earlier 16th. Lovely cornices abound. Anomalous Stuart features, adjacent
12th-century abbey ruins quite interesting. Courtyard and conservatory café
spacious and a bit soulless. Apr-Oct: 9.30am-6pm (last ticket 4.30pm) daily.
Nov-Mar: 9.30am-4.30pm (last ticket 3.15pm) daily. Also... **The Queen's Gallery**
0131 556 5100. Visually appealing addition opposite the Parliament building with
separate entrance. By architect Ben Tindall (who also did The Hub at the top of the
Royal Mile, though this is better). Beautiful, contemporary setting for changing
exhibits from Royal Collection every 6 months, which include art, ceramics,
tapestries, etc. Shop stuffed with monarchist mementoes. Apr-Oct 9.30am-5pm
(last ticket), reduced hours in winter.

403 8/Q25 ✓✓ **The Royal Mile** www.edinburgh-royalmile.com The High Street, the
medieval main thoroughfare of the capital follows the trail from the volcanic
crag of Castle Rock and connects the castle and palace (above). Heaving during the
Festival and actually AYR now, but if on a winter's night you chance by with a frost
settling on the cobbles and no one is around, it's magical. Always interesting with its
wynds and closes (Whitehorse Close, Dunbar's Close, the secret garden opposite
Huntly House), but lots of ghastly, opportunistic, made-in-China tartan shops too.
Central block closed to traffic and during the Festival Fringe it's the best street-
performance space in UK. See the Mile on a walking tour: there are several, especially
at night (ghost/ghouls/witches, etc). Mercat Tours (0131 225 5445), Cadies & Witchery
Tours (0131 225 6745) and City of the Dead (0131 225 9044) are pretty good.
The Real Mary King's Close 0131 225 0672 Part of a medieval street under the
Royal Mile. Daily tours. Enter by Warriston's Close near City Chambers. **Scottish
Poetry Library** is in Crichton's Close on right between St Mary's St and the
Parliament. Great collections, lovely contemplative space. Endorses Edinburgh's
status as City of Literature. www.scottishpoetrylibrary.org.

404 8/Q25 ✓✓ **The Scottish Parliament** Royal Mile · www.scottish.parliament.uk ·
ADMISSION 0131 348 5200 Adjacent to Holyroodhouse (above) and Our Dynamic
Earth (below). Designed by Catalan architect Enric Miralles who died long before it
opened, this building was mired in controversy after first First Minister, the late
Donald Dewar, laid the first stone. We got over it though and we're rather proud of
it now. It's used publicly a lot and is the finest modern building in the city (it won
the 2005 Stirling Prize, the UK's premier architectural award). Tour (including a visit
to the Debating Chamber) times vary; best book in advance. We gather around it
whenever we've got big things to celebrate or protest against (as we should).

405 8/Q25 ✓✓ **Our Dynamic Earth** Holyrood Rd, Edinburgh · www.dynamicearth.
ADMISSION co.uk · 0131 550 7800 Edinburgh's Dome, an interactive museum/visitor
attraction, made with Millennium money. For kids really; good for a family outing.
Now within the orbit and campus of the Parliament building. Salisbury Crags rise
above. Vast restaurant and outside, an amphitheatre. Underused and inexpensive
car park underneath from which to explore the area.

406 8/Q25 ✓✓ **Scottish National Gallery** The Mound · www.nationalgalleries.org ·
0131 624 6200 Neoclassical buildings housing a superb collection of Old
Masters in a series of hushed salons. Many are world famous but you don't emerge
goggle-eyed as from the National in London. The building in front, the **Royal**

Scottish Academy, often has blockbuster exhibitions. Daily 10am-5pm, Thu 7pm. Extended hours during Festival. Very good caff, **The Scottish Café & Restaurant** (247/SCOTTISH) offers high-quality nosh with views.

407 8/Q25
ADMISSION

✓✓ **Royal Yacht Britannia** Ocean Dr, Leith · www.royalyachtbritannia. co.uk · 0131 555 5566 In the docks, enter by Commercial St at end of Great Junction St. Berthed outside Conran's shopping mall, the Ocean Terminal. Done with ruling the waves, the royal yacht has found a permanent home as a tourist attraction (and prestigious corporate night out). Check out the Royal Deck Tea Room. Close up, the Art Deco lines are surprisingly attractive, while the interior was one of the sets for our best ever soap opera. Booking advised.

✓✓✓ **Rosslyn Chapel** Roslin Famous, infamous, fabulous. Report: 1898/ CHURCHES.

The Other Attractions

408 8/P25
ADMISSION
FOR
GLASSHOUSES;
OTHERWISE
FREE
🖃

✓✓✓ **Royal Botanic Garden** Inverleith Row · www.rbge.org.uk · 0131 248 2909/0131 552 7171 3km Princes Street. Enter from Inverleith Row or the landmark John Muir gateway in Arboretum Place. 70 acres of ornamental gardens, trees and walkways; a joy in every season. Tropical Palm House, landscaped rock and heath garden, the more recent 'Chinese Garden' and Queen Mother's Garden and space just to wander. Precocious squirrels everywhere. The Botanics have talks, guided tours, and events. They also look after other important outstanding gardens in Scotland. Gallery with occasional exhibitions and 3 separate cafés, one with an outdoor terrace for afternoon teas (315/TEAROOMS), and views. Total integrity and the natural high. Houses the National Biodiversity Interpretation Centre and garden. Open 7 days AYR.

409 8/Q25
ATMOS
🖃

✓✓ **Scottish National Portrait Gallery** 1 Queen St · www. nationalgalleries.org · 0131 624 6200 Sir Robert Rowand Anderson's fabulous, custom-built neo-Gothic pile holds paintings and photos of the good, great and merely famous. Alex Ferguson hangs out next to the Queen Mum, and Nasmyth's familiar Burns pic is here. Good venue for photo exhibitions, beautiful atrium with star-flecked ceiling and frieze of (mainly) men in Scottish history, from a Stone Age chief to Carlyle. The caff does a good cheese scone! 7 days 10am-5pm (7pm Thu). Extended hours during Festival.

410 8/Q25
ADMISSION

✓✓ **Surgeons' Hall Museum** Nicolson St · www.museum.rcsed.ac.uk · 0131 527 1649 Housed in the landmark Playfair building (1832) this museum is the real deal, integrity writ large and full of fascinating stuff. With recent major renovations, for over 500 years the Royal College of Surgeons has set and tested the standards of their craft and this museum records the growth of scientific medicine and Edinburgh's extraordinary contribution to it. Some key collections and changing exhibitions but wonder and wince through the Wohl Pathology Hall, the History of Surgery Museum, including a reconstruction of the first dissection, and get your teeth into the Dentistry Collection, all the finest in the UK. 7 days 10am-5pm (4.30pm last entry).

411 8/P25
🖃

✓ **Scottish National Gallery of Modern Art One** 75 Belford Rd · www. nationalgalleries.org · 0131 624 6200 Between Queensferry Rd and Dean Village (nice to walk through). Best to start from Palmerston Pl and keep left; or see below (Modern Two). Former school with permanent collection from

Impressionism to Emin; the Scottish painters alongside and a growing collection of the conceptual art in which Scotland is notably strong (see the Douglas Gordon on the staircase and see if you can find a name you know). All in all, an intimate space where you can fall in love (with paintings or each other). Around 3 major temporary exhibitions annually. Excellent café (307/TEAROOMS). Charles Jencks' landscape piece outside is elevating and nice for kids. 7 days.

412 8/P25 ✓ **Scottish National Gallery of Modern Art Two** 73 Belford Terrace ·
www.nationalgalleries.org · 0131 624 6200 Across the road from Modern One (above). Originally built as a grand orphan hospital, with high windows children cannot see out of, there is plenty of light but no distractions in this mansion of intimate spaces. Cool coffee shop, large gardens to wander. Superb 20th-century collection; many surreal moments. Great way to approach both galleries is by Water of Leith walkway (423/WALKS). No miracles here but there is magic. 7 days.

413 8/Q25 **Museum of Childhood** 42 High St · www.edinburghmuseums.org.uk ·
0131 529 4142 Shrine to the dreamstuff of tender days, where you'll find everything from tin soldiers to Lady Penelope on video. Full of adults saying, 'I had one of them!' Child-size mannequins in upper gallery can be very spooky if you're up there alone. 7 days 10am-5pm.

414 8/Q25 **St Giles' Cathedral** Royal Mile · www.stgilescathedral.org.uk · 0131 225 9442
Not really a cathedral anymore, though it was once: the High Kirk of Edinburgh, Church of Scotland central since the 16th century and heart of the city since the 9th. The building is mainly medieval with Norman fragments encased in a Georgian exterior. Lorimer's oddly ornate chapel and the 'big organ' are impressive. Simple, austere design and bronze of John Knox set the tone historically. Holy Communion daily; short worship service at noon Mon-Sat and services on Sun. Cathedral open 7 days, daytime only.

Arthur's Seat Report: 424/WALKS.

The Pentlands Report: 427/WALKS.

The Scott Monument/Calton Hill Report: 447/443/VIEWS.

Newhailes House Report: 1875/HOUSES.

Dr Neil's (Secret) Garden Report: 1570/GARDENS.

The Best Independent Galleries

415 8/Q25 ✓✓ **Ingleby Gallery** 33 Barony St · www.inglebygallery.com · 0131 556 4441 Surely one of the most beautiful private galleries in the land, the former Glasite Meeting House, a magnificent glass-domed main space and upstairs smaller room, both showing contemporary Scottish and international work to great effect. Closed Sun-Tue.

416 8/Q25 ✓✓ **The Fruitmarket Gallery** Market St · www.fruitmarket.co.uk · 0131 225 2383 Behind Waverley Station and opposite City Art Centre. A 2-floor, warehousey gallery showing international work, retrospectives, installations; the city's most contemporary public art space. Excellent bookshop. Always interesting. 7 days 11am-6pm. Café (317/TEAROOMS) highly recommended for meeting, eating and watching the world (and the art world) go by. 7 days 10am-6pm.

417 8/Q25 ✓✓ **Summerhall** 1 Summerhall · www.summerhall.co.uk · 0131 560 1581 By SE corner of the Meadows. Unlike anywhere else in the UK, with little or no public funding, a multi-arts centre with several non-conventional gallery spaces and a prodigious number of (free) exhibitions. Especially vibrant during August. Open all hours. Café and 362/UNIQUE PUBS (The Royal Dick).

418 8/Q25 ✓ **Edinburgh Printmakers** 23 Union St · www.edinburghprintmakers.co. uk · 0131 557 2479 Workshop-studio and gallery with exhibitions of work by contemporary printmakers and shop where prints from many of the notable names in Scotland are on sale at reasonable prices. Good courses. A local treasure moving to major new art complex in Fountainbridge 2019.

419 8/Q25 ✓ **The Collective Gallery** City Observatory & City Dome, 38 Calton Hill · www.collectivegallery.net · 0131 556 1264 Installations and exhibitions of Scottish and other young contemporary trailblazers. Installed here on top of the hill with panoramic views of the city, embedded in the Edinburgh World Heritage site, an airy location for art. **The Lookout** café/restaurant (by the guys at **The Gardener's Cottage** at the foot of the hill 133/CREATIVE COOKERY) is adjacent, with spectacular views while you snack or dine.

420 8/Q25 ✓ **The Scottish Gallery** 16 Dundas St · www.scottish-gallery.co.uk · 0131 558 1200 Guy Peploe's influential New Town gallery. Excellent exhibitions. Where to go to buy something painted, sculpted or crafted by up-and-comers or established names – from affordable jewellery to Joan Eardleys. Or just look.

421 8/Q25 ✓ **Dovecot Studios** 10 Infirmary St · www.dovecotstudios.com · 0131 550 3660 Altogether fascinating centre for contemporary art and craft, built around a functioning tapestry studio of international repute. In a former swimming baths you can look down from an all-round gallery to watch work in progress. The ground-floor gallery programmed with high-quality changing exhibitions. Good café by the esteemed **Leo's** (310/TEAROOMS). Closed Sun.

422 8/Q25 ✓ **Stills** 23 Cockburn St · www.stills.org · 0131 622 6200 Bang in the city centre and 40 years old in 2017, this is Scotland's original photography gallery with facilities, courses and year-round exhibitions. 7 days.

The Best Walks In The City

See p.12 for walk codes.

423 8/P25
1-15KM
XCIRC
BIKES
1-A-1

Water of Leith www.waterofleith.org.uk The indefatigable wee river that runs from the Pentlands through the city and into the docks at Leith can be walked for most of its length. The longest section is from Balerno, 12km outside the city, through Colinton Dell to what was the old Blue Goose on Lanark Rd (4km from city centre). The dell itself is a popular glen walk (1-2km). All in all, a superb urban diversion. The Water of Leith Visitor Centre is worth a look (0131 455 7367). Open 7 days 10am-4pm AYR.
STARTS (A) A70 to Currie, Juniper Green, Balerno; park by the high school.
(B) Dean Village to Stockbridge: enter through a marked gate opposite the hotel on Belford Rd (combine with a visit to the art galleries 411/412/ATTRACTIONS).
(C) Warriston, past the spooky old graveyard to The Shore in Leith (plenty of pubs to repair to). Enter by going to the end of the cul-de-sac at Warriston Cres in Canonmills; climb up the bank and turn left. Most of the Walkway (A, B and C) is cinder track and good for cycling.

424 8/Q25
1-8KM
CIRC
MT BIKES
(RESTRICTED
ACCESS)
2-B-2

Arthur's Seat Edinburgh's landmark mountain and playground. Of many walks, a good circular one taking in the wilder bits, the lochs and great views (444/VIEWS) starts from **St Margaret's Loch** at the far end of the park from Holyrood Palace. Leaving the car park, skirt the loch and head for the ruined chapel. After 250m, in a dry valley, the buttress of the main summit rears above you on the right. Keeping it to the right, ascend over a saddle joining the main route from Dunsapie Loch, which appears below on the left. Crow Hill is the other peak crowned by a triangular cairn – both can be slippery when wet. From Arthur's Seat head for and traverse the long, steep incline of Salisbury Crags. Paths parallel to the edge lead back to the chapel. Or just cross the road by **Holyrood Palace** and head up. No mountain bikes. For info on the Ranger service and special events through the year, call 0131 652 8150.
START Usually, enter park at Palace by the Parliament. Cross the main road or follow it and find your path or from St Margaret's Loch (above) via the ruined chapel.
PARK Car parks beside the loch and in front of the Palace.

425 8/P25
1/3/8KM
XCIRC
BIKES
1-A-1

Cramond The charming village (though not so the suburb) on the Forth at the mouth of the Almond with a variety of great walks. (A) To the right along the prom; the traditional seaside stroll. (B) Across the causeway at low tide to Cramond Island (1km). Best to follow the tide out; this allows 4 hours (tides are posted). People have been known to stay the night in summer (oh yes they have!). (C) Past the boathouse, up the River Almond Heritage Trail, which goes eventually to the Cramond Brig restaurant on the A90 and thence to the old airport (3-8km). Though it goes through suburbs and seems to be on the flight path of the London shuttle, the Almond is a real river with a charm and ecosystem of its own.
The bustling **Boardwalk Café** is on the foreshore 300m east (323/CAFÉS). 500m upriver is the **Cramond Falls Café** (0131 312 8408) for hot food and cakes till 5pm (Closed Wed in winter). The **Cramond Gallery Bistro** (0131 312 6555) at the start is a pleasant quayside caff (open 7 days) and The **Cramond Inn** (0131 336 2035) is a proper inn with grub all day till 8.30pm (Sun 6pm).
START Leave centre by Queensferry Rd (A90), then right following signs for Cramond. Cramond Rd North leads to Cramond Glebe Rd; go to end.
PARK Off Cramond Glebe Rd to right, behind Cramond Inn. Walk 100m to the sea.

426 8/P25 **Corstorphine Hill** www.corstorphinehill.org.uk W of centre, a knobbly,
1-7KM hilly area of birch, beech and oak, criss-crossed by trails. A perfect place for the
CIRC contemplation of life's little mysteries and mistakes. Or walking the dog. It has a
XBIKES radio mast, a ruined tower, a boundary with the wild plains of Africa (at the zoo)
1-A-1 and a vast redundant nuclear shelter that nobody's supposed to know about. If it
had a tearoom in an old pavilion, it would be perfect.
START Leave centre by Queensferry Rd and 8km out, turn left at lights, signed
Clermiston. The hill is on your left for the next 2km.
PARK Park where safe, on or near this road (Clermiston Rd).

Easy Walks Outside The City

427 8/P26 ✓ **The Pentlands** nr Edinburgh · www.pentlandhills.org · 0131 445 3383 A
1-20KM serious range of hills rising to almost 600m, remote in parts and offering some
CAN BE CIRC fine walking. Many paths up the various tops and round the lochs and reservoirs.
MT BIKES (A) A good start in town is made by going off the bypass at Colinton, follow signs for
2-B-2 Colinton Village, then the left fork up Woodhall Rd. Go left (signed Pentland Hills
Regional Park). Go as far as you can (2km) and park by the gate leading to the hill
proper where there is a map showing routes. The path to Glencorse is one of the
classic Pentland walks. (B) Most walks start from signposted gateways on the A702.
There are starts at Boghall (5km after Hillend ski slope); on the long, straight
stretch before Silverburn (a 10km path to Balerno); from Habbie's Howe about
18km from town; and from the village of Carlops, 22km from town. (C) The most
popular start is probably from the visitor centre behind **Flotterstone Inn**, also on
the A702, 14km from town (decent pub grub); trailboard and ranger service. The
more remote tops around Loganlea Reservoir are worth the extra mile. (D) Lower
slopes can be enjoyed from Swanston village (with R.L. Stevenson connections
1968/LITERARY PLACES) where quaint thatched cottages are passed en route to the
'T' wood and a relatively easy climb to a great city view to the north. Car park next
to **Swanston Golf Club** – good tea and scones.

428 8/Q25 **Hermitage of Braid** www.edinburgh.gov.uk Strictly speaking, still in town, but
1-4KM a real sense of being in a country glen. Main track along the burn is easy to follow
CAN BE CIRC and you eventually come to Hermitage House Visitor Centre; any paths ascending
XBIKES to the right take you to the ridge of Blackford Hill. From the windy tops of the Braid
1-A-1 Hills there are some marvellous views back over the city. In snowy winters there's
a great sledging place over the first bridge up to the left across the main road.
Nearest caffs are in Morningside.
START Entrance on Braid Rd, just yards beyond junction with Hermitage Dr.

429 8/Q26 **Roslin Glen** www.midlothian.gov.uk Spiritual, historical, enchanting and
1-8KM famous with the chapel **Rosslyn** (1898/CHURCHES), a ruined castle and woodland
XCIRC walks along the River Esk. The map at the visitor centre isn't that helpful (and
BIKES there's little waymarking) but the people are.
1-A-1 **START** A701 from Mayfield, Newington or bypass: turn-off Penicuik, A702 then left
at Gowkley roundabout and other signed roads. Park near chapel 500m from Main
St/Manse Rd corner, or follow B7003 to Rosewell (also marked Rosslynlee Hospital)
and 1km from village the main car park is to the left.

430 8/N25 **Beecraigs & Cockleroy Hill** nr Linlithgow · www.beecraigs.com ·
2-8KM 01506 284516 Country park S of Linlithgow, with trails and clearings in mixed
CIRC woods, a deer farm and a fishing loch. Great adventure playground for kids. Best is
MT BIKES the climb and extraordinary view from Cockleroy Hill, far better than you'd expect
1-A-1 for the effort – from Ben Lomond to the Bass Rock; and the gunge of Grangemouth

in the sky to the east. Visitor centre and café. The hill never closes.
START M90 to Linlithgow (26km), through town and left on Preston Rd. Go on 4km, park is signed, but for hill you don't need to take the left turn. The hill, and nearest car park to it, is on the right. 7 days. Summer 9am-8pm, winter 10am-4pm.

431 8/Q26
7KM
XCIRC
XBIKES
1-B-1

Borthwick & Crichton Castles nr Gorebridge · www.borthwickcastle.com · **01875 820514** Takes in 2 impressive castles, the first a fancy wedding hotel, the other an imposing ruin on a ridge overlooking the Tyne. Walk through dramatic Border country steeped in lore. From Borthwick follow the old railway line. From Crichton, start behind the ruined chapel. In summer, vegetation can be high and may defeat you.
START From Borthwick: A7 S for 16km, past Gorebridge, left at North Middleton; signed. From Crichton: A68 almost to Pathhead, signed then 3km past church. Park and walk 250m.

Woodland Walks Near Edinburgh

432 8/Q25
ADMISSION

✓ **Dalkeith Country Park** Dalkeith · www.dalkeithcountrypark.co.uk · **0131 654 1666** 15km SE by A68. Part of the Buccleuch Estates, these wooded policies of Dalkeith House (enter at end of Main St) just got a whole lot more interesting. Along the river banks and under these stately deciduous trees are, according to season, carpets of bluebells, daffs and snowdrops, primroses and wild garlic. Most extensive preserved ancient oak forest in southern Scotland. Now a major leisure destination, with café, deli/shop, picnic tables and an adventure playground. You won't have much of it to yourself. 7 days.

433 8/Q25

✓ **Gosford House Estate** nr Aberlady On the A198, where the road comes down to the shore after Longniddry Bents. From Edinburgh direction, turn into the farm road signed for the **Bothy** farm shop and park there (the gate closes at 5pm). Paths in the park and woodland of **Gosford House** (1878/HOUSES) wind round a beautiful lake (lots of birds) and a pond. There's an old, spidery boathouse and an ice house. The house itself is elegant and grand but don't intrude. Tea, cake and provisions, especially meats, at the Bothy, 7 days.

434 8/P27
ADMISSION

✓ **Dawyck Gardens** nr Stobo · www.rbge.org.uk · **01721 760254** 10km W of Peebles on B712 Moffat road. Outstation of the Edinburgh Botanics. Tree planting here goes back 300 years. Sloping grounds around the Scrape Burn, which trickles into the Tweed. Landscaped woody pathways for meditative walks. Famous for shrubs, fungi and Himalayan blue poppies. Visitor centre, café, studio and shop. Last entry 1 hour before gardens close. 7 days. Apr-Sep 10am-6pm. Winter hours vary. Closed Dec-Jan.

435 8/R25

✓ **The Yester Estate** Gifford Large estate, in which there are some beautiful woodland walks. Hard to find (and I won't tell you how) is the legendary Goblin Ha', the bad-fairy place (the hotel in the village takes its name 855/LOTHIANS). Access from the village: 100m beyond Tweeddale Arms, turn left; various lanes lead to Park Rd. Go to end (500m), small car park and a gate in the wall, or 4km along the B6365 road, foot of steep tree-lined hill, on bend. Park by house, Danskine Lodge, and go through marked gate. 3km back to village, it's 2km to Goblin Ha' itself.

436 8/R25

Smeaton Nursery Gardens East Linton · www.smeatonnurserygardens. co.uk · **01620 860501** 2km from village on North Berwick road (signed Smeaton). Up a drive in an old estate is this early 19th-century walled garden. An additional pleasure is the **Lake Walk** halfway down the drive through a small gate in the woods. A 1km stroll round a secret finger lake in magnificent woodland. Garden Centre hours Mon-Sat 9.30am-4.30pm, Sun from 10.30am; phone for winter hours. Tearoom OK (2229/GARDEN CENTRES). Lake Walk 10am-dusk.

437 8/Q26 **Vogrie Country Park** nr Gorebridge · www.midlothian.gov.uk · 01875 821716 25km S by A7, then B6372 6km from Gorebridge. Small country park well organised for 'recreational pursuits'. 9-hole golf course, tearoom and country-ranger staff. 01875 821716 for events and opening times. Busy on Sundays, but a spacious corral of countryside on the very edge of town. Open 7.30am-sunset.

438 8/Q27 **Cardrona Forest/Glentress** nr Peebles · www.7stanesmountainbiking.com · 01721 721180 40km S to Peebles, 8km E on B7062 and similar distance on A72. Cardrona on same road as **Kailzie Gardens** (1578/GARDENS). Forestry Commission woodlands so mostly regimented firs, but Scots pine and deciduous trees up the burn. Glentress (on A72 to Innerleithen) has become a major destination for mountain bikers, but tracks also to walk. Consult at the visitor centre. See 2132/CYCLING. The **Gypsy Glen** walk from Glen Rd via Springhill Rd, across the Tweed Bridge from the High St in Peebles, is signed and a very decent amble with a wee climb at the end.

▬▬▬ The Best Beaches

439 8/Q25 ✓ **Portobello** Edinburgh's town beach, 8km from centre by London Rd. Resurgent of late; came to a boil in the summer of 2018. Buskers (there's a fest in September), barbies, the Rowing Club on the water, mad swimmers and the **Little Green Van** for excellent coffee, etc. **The Espy** 176/FOOD PUBS, **Miro's** www. mirosportobello.co.uk; 0131 669 9996 (all day, best food), **The Beach House** café (287/KIDS) best for baking and ice cream – all together on the Promenade. **Guild of Foresters** (177/FOOD PUBS) on the main street. Portobello is back!

The East Lothian Beaches: Edinburgh's golden coast.

440 8/R25 ✓ **Yellowcraigs** nr Dirleton A sandy splendour 35km from town. A1 or bypass, then A198 coast road. Left outside Dirleton for 2km, park and walk 100m across links to fairly clean strand and sea. Gets busy, but big enough to share. Hardly anyone swims, but you can. Many a barbie has braved the indifferent breeze, but on summer evenings, the sea slips ashore like liquid gold. See also 1748/KIDS. Scenic. **Gullane Bents**, a sweep of beach, is nearby and reached from village main street. Connects westwards with **Aberlady Reserve** and its dunes.

441 8/R25 ✓ **Tyninghame Beach** Also off A198. Going towards North Berwick from the A1, it's the first (unmarked) turning on the right after Tyninghame village. 1km then park, walk to left through gate 1km, past a log cabin on clifftop that you can hire for parties (as I have); great wild camping and the beach magnificent. **Smithy** tearoom in Tyninghame village has courtyard seating and good cake. And 2km S of Tesco in North Berwick off the A198 near Tantallon is the **Drift** tearoom and a nearby path to **Quarrelly Beach**.

442 8/R25 ✓ **Seacliff** North Berwick The best: least crowded/littered, perfect for picnics, beachcombing and rock-pool gazing. Old harbour good for swimming. Off the A198 to or from N Berwick, 3km from **Tantallon Castle** (1845/RUINS). At a bend in the road and a farm (Auldhame) is an unsigned road to the left. 2km on there's a barrier, costing £3 (3 x £1 coins) for cars. Car park 1km then walk. From A1, take East Linton turn-off, go past Whitekirk towards N Berwick, then it's on the right, at a corner.

The Best Views Of The City

443 8/Q25 ✓✓ **Calton Hill** www.edinburgh.gov.uk Great view of the city easily gained by walking up from east end of Princes St by Waterloo Pl to the end of the buildings and then up the stairs on the left. The City Observatory and Greek-style folly lend an elegant backdrop to a panorama (unfolding as you walk round) where the view up Princes St and the sweep of the Forth estuary are particularly fine. At night the city twinkles. Popular cruising area for gays; take care if you do. The **Beltane Fire Festival** (30 Apr) is very atmospheric 29/EVENTS. CH now home of the **Collective Gallery** 419/GALLERIES and **The Lookout** (141/CASUAL). Calton Hill Observatory was where the word **panorama** was coined.

444 8/Q25 ✓✓ **Arthur's Seat** E of city centre. Best approach through Holyrood Park from the foot of Canongate by Holyrood Palace. The igneous core of an extinct volcano with the precipitous sill of Salisbury Crags presiding over the city and offering fine views for the fit. Top is 251m; on a clear day you can see 100km. Surprisingly wild, considering proximity to city. Report: 424/WALKS.

445 8/Q25 **Penthouse of the Hilton Doubletree** 34 Bread St · www. doubletreeedinburghcity.co.uk · 0131 221 5555 Unadvertised spot but the penthouse function space of the Hilton Doubletree hotel offers a unique perspective of the city. They may allow you up if there's nothing booked in but it opens as a public bar on the first Thursday of the month.

446 8/Q25 **The National Museum of Scotland Terrace** Chambers St · www.nms.ac.uk · 0300 123 6789 6th floor of the fabulous recreated museum (399/ATTRACTIONS) has a beautiful terrace planted all round and offering revealing city skyline views and a great castle perspective. Andy Goldsworthy sculptures.

447 8/Q25 **Scott Monument** Princes St · www.edinburghmuseums.org.uk · 0131 529 4068
ADMISSION This 1844 Gothic memorial to one of Scotland's best-kent literary sons (1967/LITERARY PLACES) rises 61.5m above the main drag and provides scope for the vertiginous to come to terms with their affliction. 287 steps mean it's no cakewalk; narrow stairwells weed out claustrophobics too. 4 landings to catch the breath and view. Those who make it to the top are rewarded with fine views. Underneath, a statue of the mournful Sir Walter gazes across at the shops! 7 days AYR.

448 8/Q25 **Camera Obscura & World of Illusions** 549 Castlehill · www.camera-
ADMISSION obscura.co.uk · 0131 226 3709 At very top of the Royal Mile near the castle entrance, a tourist attraction that, surprisingly, has been there for over a century. You ascend through a shop, photography exhibitions and interactive gallery to the viewing area where a continuous stream of small groups are shown the effect of the giant revolving periscope thingy. An Alice in Wonderland room, a revolving tunnel of light, hall of mirrors: plenty to distort your view of reality! 7 days.

449 8/R25 **North Berwick Law** www.eastlothian.gov.uk The conical volcanic hill, a
1-A-1 170m-high beacon in the E Lothian landscape easily reached from downtown N Berwick. **Traprain Law** nearby (signed from the A1 S of Haddington) is higher, more frequented by rock climbers but has major prehistoric hill-fort citadel of the Goddodin and a definite aura. Both are good family climbs. Allow 2-3 hours. For refreshments – Steampunk – brilliant coffee shop, restaurant and fish 'n' chips in N Berwick (860/LOTHIANS).

Edinburgh Castle Ramparts Report: 398/ATTRACTIONS.

the
Best
of Glasgow

Glasgow's Unique Hotels

450 8/M26
83 ROOMS
(11 SUITES)
NO PETS
££

✓✓ **Dakota Deluxe** 179 West Regent St · http://glasgow.dakotahotels. co.uk · 0141 404 3680 The signature clean-cut block of Glasgow's very stylish Dakota Hotel. Ken McCulloch, once the pioneer behind One Devonshire Gardens, and leaving the Malmaison far behind, did it again, when the Dakota opened its discreet doors on the corner of W Regent St and Pitt St in 2016. Now with others in Leeds and Manchester, Ken is no longer the patron but his vision and eye for design remains. Solicitous but friendly and not overbearing service – they're there when you need them. The characteristic atmospheric lighting, solid, dark furnishings, muted palate and evocative photography designed by Amanda Rosa (they are a winning team) make us feel as stylish and relaxed as the surroundings. Understated opulence perfectly pitched. I love the Library. Parking a fair walk away.

£££ **EAT** The Bar & Grill downstairs from the foyer, but with its own entrance, has a brasserie ambience and good service. Urban, urbane, but not too fancy.

451 8/L25
49 ROOMS
DF
ATMOS
££–£££

✓✓ **Hotel du Vin** 1 Devonshire Gardens, off Great Western Rd · www. hotelduvin.com · 0141 378 0385 Long Glasgow's no. 1 boutique hotel (as One Devonshire Gardens, one of the first in the UK, by Ken McCulloch – see above), now part of the small but selective Hotel/Bistro du Vin chain. This hotel probably offers the most individual experience, and some of the smartest service in town. Five townhouses, the whole of a West End terrace, integrated into an elegant and sumptuous retreat a world away from Glasgow's wilder West End (centred on Byres Rd, a 12-min walk). Even parking is easy. House 1 has the bistro, bar, etc, and House 5 the function rooms, but each retains character with fabulous stained glass, staircases and own doors to the street (though enter by reception in House 3). Cosy sitting rooms everywhere. Rooms large, as are beds, bathrooms, drapes, etc, all being refurbished with a lighter look. Great bar (especially late) with malt list and, as you'd expect, well-chosen wines. No spa or pool; there is a treatment room. Long after its original conception, this is an enduring oasis of style.
EAT Chic dining under chef Gary Townsend in elegant salons with fastidious service and excellent wine list. See also 478/HIGH-END RESTAURANTS. Also a great upscale pub food menu in **The Bar**.

452 8/M26
114 ROOMS
£££

✓✓ **Blythswood Square** 11 Blythswood Sq · www.blythswoodsquare. com · 0141 248 8888 Along one side of a serene square (one of Glasgow's dear green places) in the city centre. An ambitious and sympathetic conversion of the historic building that was home to the Royal Scottish Automobile Club; the motoring theme is everywhere. The restaurant buzzes, the upstairs Salon is a civilised rendezvous for cocktails and afternoon tea, and the seductive, state-of-the-art, chilled-out spa is almost too busy to keep its calm (1293/SPAS). Original classic features (that lobby floor) and contemporary furnishings (acres of marble in the rooms and Harris Tweed big lamps) throughout. Rooms, all in house style, vary in size and amount of light – larger in the original 'old' section, 'deluxe' rooms in the new, while others round an internal courtyard can be dark but are quiet. Parking a bit of a pain but, all in all, a great urban hotel.

££ **EAT** Restaurant/brasserie menu covers all classic and contemporary themes – à la carte, small plates, 'tasting'. Always busy with non-res guests, indeed the most buzzing hotel dining in town.

453 8/M26
250 ROOMS
NO PETS
£££

✓✓ **Radisson Blu** 301 Argyle St · www.radissonblu.com/hotel-glasgow · 0141 204 3333 Probably the best of the big city centre hotels, which is why there's nearly always a 'do' on upstairs on the mezzanine – awards ceremonies, etc. Frontage makes major modernist statement; lifts the coolest in town. Leaning to minimalism but rooms have all you need. Poster art from Glasgow's cultural events, though no great views; some face the internal 'garden'. All in all, a sexy urban bed for the night. Good rendezvous bar in lofty atrium foyer. Collage, the only restaurant, is curiously small. Fitness facilities by direct lift in basement include a small pool (15m). No parking.

454 8/M26
230 ROOMS
NO PETS
L
££-£££

✓ **Grand Central** 99 Gordon St · www.thegrandcentralhotel.co.uk · 0141 240 3700 Beside and very much on Central Station. Extensively (£20 million) refurbished in 2010, restored its position as an iconic hotel and gathering place for the city; more rooms added 2019. The famously long corridors still go on forever but rooms are all that they should be (at this price). Champagne bar à la Grand Central NYC overlooks the station concourse. You could miss your train! Tempus so-so for food, the Deli caff ditto. Out there, the station and the full-on Saturday night. Parking a pain but you'd arrive by train, wouldn't you? You're in the beating heart of Glasgow!

455 8/M26
198 ROOMS
£

✓ **Citizen M** 60 Renfrew St · www.citizenm.com · 0141 404 9485 Between the Theatre Royal and the Pavilion Theatre, this is a very superior bed (or identical pod) box; a very good value boutique hotel. Part of an international chain and its first in the UK – spot-on for Glasgow. Rooms solid, sexy and for once not just ergonomic but also well designed. No restaurant, but café/bar (till 3am) and 24-hour tuck shop. Online check in, EasyJet-style: you can only pay by card. Public space extensive (ground/first floor) and relaxing. Great breakfast. Room controls (temperature, blackout, TV) by iPad. TV films (including adult) free. Ubiquitous exhortations to 'Get Together' and other slogans surround you. Total brand immersion not to all tastes, but this is way ahead of Ibis/Yotel and a host of urban-chic arrivistes. Parking 250m.

456 8/M26
59 ROOMS
NO PETS
£

Abode Glasgow 129 Bath St · www.abodeglasgow.co.uk · 0141 221 6789 Smart, contemporary Edwardian townhouse hotel, with wide, tiled stairwell and funky lift to 3 floors of individual rooms (so size, views and noise levels vary a lot). Fab gold-embossed wallpaper in the hallways, notable stained glass and some OK art. Part of the Andrew Brownsword Hotel Group, which specialises in sympathetic conversions of notable old buildings. Heart of Bath St, so very downtown location, with many good restaurants adjacent and nearby. The hotel's Pie & Brew bar in the basement has, well, pies and craft beers, and occasional live music.

457 8/M26
174 ROOMS
££

Radisson Red 25 Tunnel St · www.radissonred.com · 0141 471 1700 Big refurb 2018 and now possibly the hotel is the destination that Finnieston (for foodies) and the Hydro (concert-goers) has been waiting for. Not high end as the Blu is (above) but contemporary boutique-hotel standard. Ground-floor restaurant and feature **Sky Bar** on the 9th floor, with views to the river and the skyline of the West End. Not in itself a great location but not expensive (except on concert nights). Adjacent parking.

458 8/M26
94 ROOMS
££

Hotel Indigo 75 Waterloo St · www.hotelindigoglasgow.com · 0141 226 7700 Smart, mid-price, very urban boutique hotel in a UK chain by Intercontinental (another in Edinburgh), which embeds sympathetically into locale – here, a classy, sympathetic conversion of a historic building in a former power station in Glasgow's downtown financial district. The city is referenced throughout: themed floors (theatre, Clyde, etc). Uniformity but high design values. Well priced.

£££   **EAT** Marco Pierre White's presence looms large in 'sophisticated' street-level restaurant with good steaks (484/BRASSERIES).

459 8/M26   **The Millennium Hotel**   50 George Sq · www.millenniumhotels.co.uk ·
61 ROOMS   **0141 332 6711**   Modest landmark hotel situated on the square, which is the
NO PETS   municipal heart of the city, and next to Queen St Station (trains to Edinburgh and
££   points north). Glasgow will be going on all about you and there's a conservatory
terrace, serving breakfast and afternoon tea, from which to watch. Bedrooms vary
(ask for a front room overlooking square). Major redevelopment of adjacent site and
station should be completed 2020. No parking or leisure facilities. Restaurant so-so
but there are many nearby.

460 8/M26   **The Brunswick Hotel**   106-108 Brunswick St · www.brunswickhotel.co.uk ·
18 ROOMS   **0141 552 0001**   Contemporary, minimalist hotel that emerged back in the 90s as
£   part of the new Merchant City. New ownership and refurb 2018, rooms making use
of tight space; prices swing a lot as it fills up. Bold colours. Good base for nocturnal
forays into pub- and clubland. Restaurant **Brutti Ma Buoni** (499/CASUAL)
enduringly and rightly popular. Pleasant breakfast, especially Sundays. Penthouse
suite is a – and the – top room. No parking.

461 8/M26   **Z Hotel**   36 North Frederick St · www.thezhotels.com · 0141 212 4550   The
104 ROOMS   Scottish outpost of the emerging cool, urban budget hotel chain that started as the
£   cheapest decent stopover in Covent Garden. Stripped to basics (some rooms have
no windows) but all you need for a short stay. Good breakfast, complimentary (very
decent) cheese and wine in the foyer café early evening, helpful staff and handy
location 100m from George Sq, close to Queen St Station.

462 8/M26   **Babbity Bowster**   16-18 Blackfriars St · www.babbitybowster.com ·
5 ROOMS   **0141 552 5055**   This much-loved 18th-century townhouse was pivotal in the
NO TV   redevelopment of the Merchant City and is famous for its bar (673/ALES), where
£   you get breakfast, and for its beer garden. Schottische restaurant upstairs
(weekends only); rooms are above, with pleasing, simple facilities. No TV. A very
authentic hostelry and, though only 5 rooms, a unique Glasgow hotel.

463 8/M26   **Alamo Guest House**   46 Gray St · www.alamoguesthouse.com ·
12 ROOMS   **0141 339 2395**   By Kelvingrove Park. A Victorian (1880s) grand house in a
£   quiet residential area overlooking the tennis courts of the park and beyond to
Kelvingrove Art Gallery & Museum (675/ATTRACTIONS). The Benzies run a very
individual and hospitable house. No evening meal, but many good restaurants
nearby. Only 5 rooms en suite but aesthetics intact (Grade A listed).

464 8/M26   **Grasshoppers**   87 Union St · www.grasshoppersglasgow.com ·
29 ROOMS   **0141 222 2666**   Right next to and on Central Station, a surprisingly mellow, simply
NO PETS   stylish and inexpensive urban hotel on the 6th floor of a historic office building.
££   More of a quiet bed for the night than a place to hang out in – small dining/
breakfast room and tiny lounge. But independently and personally run.

465 8/M26   **Artto**   37-39 Hope St · www.arttohotel.com · 0141 248 2480   Beside Central
50 ROOMS   Station, a pleasingly appointed budget hotel with a Punjabi Indian restaurant
NO PETS   – Bombay Blues – at street level. Rooms are good value; all standard price.
£   Independently owned.

466 8/M26   **The Pipers' Tryst Hotel**   30-34 McPhater St · www.thepipingcentre.co.uk ·
8 ROOMS   **0141 353 5551**   Opposite the top of Hope St and visible from dual carriageway near
££   *The Herald* HQ at Cowcaddens. Circuitous route to the street by car. Hotel upstairs
from café-bar of the adjacent piping centre and whole complex a nice conversion
of an old church and manse. Centre has courses, conferences and a museum, so
staying here is to get close to Highland culture. Small restaurant.

The Best Hostels

467 8/M26
108 BEDS

✓ **Glasgow SYH** 8 Park Terrace · www.syha.org.uk · 0141 332 3004 Oddly quiet and upmarket location, in an elegant terrace in posh West End, overlooking Kelvingrove Park. Was, until 1992, the Beacons Hotel, which was where rock 'n' roll bands used to stay in the 80s. Dorms for 4-6 (some larger), some singles and doubles, all en suite. Public rooms with TV, games, etc.

468 8/M26
365 BEDS

Euro Hostel Glasgow 318 Clyde St · www.eurohostels.co.uk · 0141 222 2828 A very central (2 mins Central Station), independent hostel block (one other in Liverpool) at the bottom of Jamaica St, almost overlooking the river. Mix of single, twin or dorm accom, but all en suite. Breakfast included in price. Kitchen and laundry. Games and TV room. The ground-floor bar, **Mint & Lime** is good to hang out in and is open to the public. A good all-round spot; very good value. 24-hour desk.

The Best Hotels Outside Town

469 8/M26
92 ROOMS
DF
££

✓✓ **Dakota** EuroCentral · www.dakotahotels.co.uk · 01698 835444 24km from centre on the M8. Like the South Queensferry version (112/ HOTELS OUTSIDE EDINBURGH) this is a chip off the new (black granite, smoked glass) block and similarly situated overlooking the highway, in the spot of regenerating Lanarkshire they call EuroCentral. Behind the severe exterior is a design-driven roadhouse that is a paean to travel. Come off the thrashing M8 into an oasis of subdued colour, wood and brick – a perfect antidote. The Dakota Deluxe is in the city centre 450/UNIQUE HOTELS. **The Bar & Grill** is excellent.

470 7/L24
15 ROOMS +
6 COTTS
DF
££

✓✓ **Loch Lomond Arms Hotel** Luss · www.lochlomondarmshotel.com · 01436 860420 Well smart and empathetic hotel in a village sometimes thought to be on the twee side of cute. This (main) roadside inn does not reach to the loch or overreach itself; rooms are tastefully done. Run by Luss Estates. Many birds on the walls! Restaurant, cosy pub-like pub and beer garden. Loch Lomond tourist trail is the better for this.

471 8/L25
53 ROOMS
NO PETS
££

✓ **Mar Hall** Bishopton · www.marhall.com · 0141 812 9999 M8 junction 28A/29, A726 then A8 into Bishopton. 5-star luxury a convenient 10 mins from the airport and 25 mins from central Glasgow, in 240 acres of wooded estate. Impressive conversion of imposing baronial house with grand though gloomy public spaces – the central hall where you congregate. Rooms vary (some huge), but all with 5-star niceties. Spa/leisure club adjacent, with 15m pool, gym and fitness programme: it's a lift and a wee walk away. The Cristal, with long windows on to the gardens, is the fine-dining restaurant. 18-hole golf course.

472 7/L24
47 ROOMS
££

✓ **The Lodge on Loch Lomond** nr Luss · www.loch-lomond.co.uk · 01436 860201 Edge of Luss on A82 N from Balloch; 40 mins to Glasgow's West End. In a linear arrangement that makes the most of a great lochside setting. This unpretentious, family-run hotel, ignored by the posher guides, is a good prospect. Wood-lined rooms (the Corbetts), with balconies and saunas, overlook the bonnie banks; then there's the Grahams; and in the adjacent, newer, higher block, the Munros and suites – it's a Scottish hill thing. Spa, nice pool, weddings; and once, Bill Clinton. Colquhoun's restaurant has the view and the terrace and is rather good; book weekends. Get close to Loch Lomond here.

✓✓ **Cameron House on Loch Lomond** nr Luss A long-standing premier lochside resort hotel reopening 2020 after a tragic fire.

The Best Of The High-End Restaurants

473 8/M25 ✓✓ **Cail Bruich** 725 Great Western Rd · www.cailbruich.co.uk · £££ 0141 334 6265 The name means 'Eat Well' and after a 2018 well-thought-out reboot, Cail Bruich looks and feels ever more in good fettle: more light, more space (with a sit-round bar) and a revitalised menu that wouldn't be out of place in Michelin territory (it would be Glasgow's first). But it isn't stuffy or starry at all, with seasonal 4×4 options and a tasting menu for <£60. Well-informed, friendly service (there are 2 sommeliers), and guest chefs on their 'Madklubben' nights. Moving on Up for Chris Charalambous and a top team.

474 8/M25 ✓✓ **Ubiquitous Chip** 12 Ashton Lane · www.ubiquitouschip.co.uk · ATMOS 0141 334 5007 The pioneering creation of legendary Ronnie Clydesdale, £££ now in the hands of son Colin and his wife Carol, is an assembly of top food and drink options. Its essential characteristics – smart and friendly service and unpretentious fine dining, with conscientiously sourced ingredients under the skylights and vines – are much in evidence. Almost 50 years on, The Chip remains the destination restaurant in the West End. The upstairs Brasserie has a lighter, less expensive menu. Beyond that, a rare-in-Glasgow rooftop terrace (not usually dining), and in the Lane, on the corner, the **Wee Bar**, with its windows on the world and library of whiskies. See also **Stravaigin** (490/CASUAL) and **Hanoi Bike Shop** (551/VIETNAMESE): all these chips off the old block are open later than most. 7 days. Bar till 1am.

475 8/M26 ✓ **Two Fat Ladies At The Buttery** 652-654 Argyle St · www. ATMOS twofatladiesrestaurant.com · 0141 221 8188 In an unlikely but historic £££ spot, just W of the M8, for decades and for now, 'The Buttery' remains Glasgow's quintessential fine-dining experience – though delightfully non-precious. Under Ryan James and his team, The Buttery is forever *the* posh night out. There is a smaller Two Fat Ladies City Centre in the … city centre 580/SEAFOOD. Mahogany-dark, discreetly sumptuous surroundings, gorgeous period tableware in a calm Victorian salon. Chef's table in a glass box in the kitchen where Stephen Johnson still leads a well-oiled team. Top for seafood, some vegetarian. The Grand Dessert! **Shandon Belles**, the Ladies' thinner sister round the corner, is the below-stairs parlour and bistro; cosier and less costly – in fact, very well priced. And some careful attention to detail (the side plates!); the wine!

476 8/M26 ✓ **Le Chardon D'Or** 176 West Regent St · www.brianmaule.com · £££ 0141 248 3801 Brian Maule's midtown eaterie. Meaning 'Golden Thistle' in English, with contemporary spin on Auld Alliance as far as the food's concerned: impeccable ingredients, French influence in the prep. With a delightfully simple, unpretentious menu, this tranquil room remains one of Glasgow's temples to culinary excellence and you're in good hands. Before it became de rigueur, Brian put cooking ingredients and seasonality first. This is honest, fine-in-the-right-way dining. Smart, not too solicitous service. Vegetarian (and vegan) menu and very good deal pre-theatre menus. An exemplary, easy-to-follow wine list. After almost 20 years, Le Chardon D'Or is still the business. Events programme; gin tastings, demos. Lunch (Mon-Fri) & LO 9.30pm. Closed Sun/Mon.

477 8/L25 ✓ **111 By Nico** 111 Cleveden Rd · www.111bynico.co.uk · 0141 334 0111 N of ££ Gt Western Rd beyond the Botanic Gardens, in an almost suburban setting, the original restaurant of one of Scotland's most creative chef/proprietors, Nico Simeone. Exponent of concept cookery (see 488/CASUAL), here customers are invited to 'trust' the chefs (under Modou Diagme) to create a bespoke dish for you over 5 courses using 12 stated ingredients (which change by the month). Unlike some 'tasting menus' there is, therefore, no choice. The whole meal, with or without wine pairing, is incredibly cheap. So must book! Lunch & dinner. Closed Mon.

478 8/L25 ✓ **Bistro du Vin** 1 Devonshire Gardens, off Great Western Rd · **www.**
£££ **hotelduvin.com** · **0141 339 2001** Glasgow's oldest and original boutique hotel (451/UNIQUE HOTELS) has, since it opened, had one of the city's classiest dining rooms. The salons in House 5 like dining in your club. Presentation and service has always been exemplary under chef Gary Townsend. Also a great bar menu next door.

◼◼◼ The Best Brasseries

479 8/M26 ✓✓ **Ox and Finch** 920 Sauchiehall St · **www.oxandfinch.com** ·
££ **0141 339 8627** In the heart of Glasgow's eating-out quarter between Kelvingrove Park and Finnieston's restaurant row, Jonathan MacDonald's hugely popular, airy corner diner. In 2014 O&F pioneered the small-plate menu in Glasgow (good helpings, usually 2 or 3 per person). Global and local and seasonal; dishes emerging from the bustling open kitchen come as and when they're ready. Chef Aurélien Mourez leads the team. Good service turns the tables. Urbane atmos. Faultless Ox and Finch is still the one. 7 days from noon.

480 8/M26 ✓✓ **Rogano** 11 Exchange Pl · **www.roganoglasgow.com** · **0141 248 4055**
ATMOS Between Buchanan and Queen Sts, a Glasgow institution since the 1930s.
£££/££ Decor replicating a Cunard ship, the *Queen Mary*, is the major attraction. An independently owned flagship restaurant for the city, serving contemporary surf (those oysters) and turf (that steak) brasserie-style menu, with classic dishes of reassuringly high quality. Spacious and perennially fashionable, the buzzing old-style glamour still holds. Downstairs, **Café Rogano** is the less expensive bistro. Outdoor heated 'terrace' is pure dead Glasgow, though the surrounding 'hedges', being plastic, never actually die. Restaurant: 7 days lunch & LO 10.30pm. Café Rogano: 7 days noon till LO 11pm.

481 8/M26 ✓✓ **Guy's Restaurant & Bar** 24 Candleriggs · **www.guysrestaurant.co.**
ATMOS **uk** · **0141 552 1114** This intimate and busy Merchant City restaurant does
££ 'real food' really well; unquestionably one of the best restaurants in the quarter. It's a long-time favourite of mine. The menu is long and diverse and never disappoints. In a welcoming, convivial, old-style room, the eponymous Guy and family serve you Scottish staples like mince 'n' tatties and prawn cocktail (and sushi), their signature 'Glasgow Tapas' with a bit of everything, and particularly good pasta. It's all home-made. Wines vary from good house to Cristal Rosé at £600 a bottle. Live but sympatico music Thu-Sat and Sun afternoons. 7 days, all day.

482 8/M26 ✓✓ **Hutchesons** 158 Ingram St · **www.hutchesonsglasgow.com** ·
£££ **0141 552 4050** Landmark building near George Sq, looking down Hutcheson St. Converted by James Rusk to very high spec into a 2-storey (and private dining up top) café-bar and first-floor brasserie. Clubby, though with high ceilings, it feels elegant and spacious. Open 7 days early till late. Excellent rep though some say pricey. Great steaks and cocktails, as in other Rusk restaurants (572/574/STEAKS).

483 8/M26 ✓ **Urban Bar & Brasserie** 23-25 St Vincent Pl · **www.urbanbrasserie.**
££ **co.uk** · **0141 248 5636** Very central (off George Sq), urban, as they say, and very Glasgow. Great brasserie atmos; it just works, as you might expect from

notable Glasgow restaurateur Alan Tomkins. Clubby atmos and linen tablecloths, etc, in different seating areas; outside terrace for people watching. Bar and congenial à la carte and market menu. Many ladies lunch. 7 days lunch & dinner.

484 8/M26 ✓ **Marco Pierre White** 75 Waterloo St · www.mpwsteakhouseglasgow.
£££ co.uk · 0141 226 7726 The restaurant of the **Hotel Indigo** (458/UNIQUE HOTELS). They call it a steak house and there's plenty of meat on the menu (28-day dry-aged, etc) but it's a mixed brasserie offering (with vegetarian). The governor looms large over this urban, sophisticated room that doesn't feel too much like being in a hotel, and we know that MPW only comes once a year. Stick to the 'Market Menu' if you're not set on steak and can dine 'pre-theatre'. Urbane atmos. 7 days lunch & dinner.

The Best Casual Dining

485 8/M26 ✓✓ **Five March** 140 Elderslie St · www.fivemarch.co.uk · 0141 573 1400
££ Arrived 2018 at the top end of Elderslie St (above Sauchiehall St), a spacious, uncluttered, easy-going eaterie that slipped quietly and mainly by word of mouth into the top end of Glasgow's emergent and stellar casual-dining club – and it's not in Finnieston. Joanna Nethery and Kevin Small lead a team committed to conscientiously prepped and presented contemporary food in small-plate style. I don't know what but there's something about it – it's just damned good. Around 30 nibbly/starter things and more main-size dishes to choose from and a couple of puds. Independent, integrated and with integrity – all eyes are on Five March. 7 days.

486 8/L25 ✓✓ **Gather by Zique** 70-72 Hyndland St · 0141 339 2000 2 doors up from
££ Cafezique, in 2018 Delizique turned into Gather. Zique, the brand, moves on. It's a Hyndland thing, and very Scottish. As you sit (as we have in the window, or upstairs in the comfy mezzanine banquettes, or in the airy back room), you may reflect on how empathetically and somehow effortlessly Mhairi Taylor creates spaces to feel at home with and to graze on, serving foodie's food without faff. Lots of flavour and spice in the veg/fish/meat small plates – the aubergine caponata, the semifreddo and the naughty coffee martinis. All is understated, including solid sourcing (our chanterelles were picked that morning up the glen, beyond Balquhidder, where the family's top boutique hotel is) though sourcing is not referred to in the menu. The brill bakery is along the road (644/BAKERS). Another palpable, life-affirming hit from the Mhor team. Closed Sun evening/ Mon/Tue.

487 8/L25 ✓✓ **Cafezique** 66 Hyndland St · www.delizique.com · 0141 339 7180
ATMOS The original launch pad for Mhairi Taylor's food project – cool casual
£ dining for Glasgow. It's still the definitive West End grazing spot and see **Gather by Zique** above. Convivial is the word and though cramped, the ground floor and mezzanine hum along nicely day and night. Light, easy food with top sourced ingredients; Mediterranean with apple crumble. From the best (all-day) breakfast, including home-made potato scones, to later than most (last orders at 10.30pm), you can only wish you had an eaterie like this in your neighbourhood. Perfect pitch! 7 days 9am-midnight (day menu till 5pm).

488 8/M26 ✓✓ **Six By Nico** 1132 Argyle St, Finnieston · www.sixbynico.co.uk ·
££ 0141 334 5661 Middle of the 'Finnieston Strip', one of Scotland's most alluring and innovative restaurants. Here, the concept of chef/proprietor Nico Simeone is central to the immersive dining experience: 6 courses (all small plates)

on a theme that changes every 6 weeks – the Chippie, Picnic, New York, Mexico. No choice but a vegetarian menu and you can mix and match. Like Nico's 111 (477/ HIGH-END RESTAURANTS), it's remarkably good value. Seems always full; 2-hour turnarounds. All great fun but also efficiency; kitchen genius at work here. 7 days.

489 8/M26 ✓✓ **Alchemilla** 1126 Argyle St · www.thisisalchemilla.com ·
££ 0141 337 6060 The 2016 arrival of Alchemilla on the already crowded Finnieston food strip nevertheless caused a stir in the melting pot; it remains many a Glasgow foodie's favourite fix. It's not large; tables packed in (with small, not-so-comfy chairs and a couple of tables on a mezz), so booking essential. It's the small plates as they come from the galley kitchen across the bar by chef Rosie Healy, cooking up a light Mediterranean menu Yotam Ottolenghi-style that we have come to adore. Ceviche is a signature dish; menu changes frequently according to ingredients. It's small-plate heaven! And it's all great value. Finnieston rocks on! 7 days 12-10pm.

490 8/M26 ✓✓ **Stravaigin** 28 Gibson St · www.stravaigin.co.uk · 0141 334 2665 This
ATMOS indispensable bar/restaurant, along with **Ubiquitous Chip** (474/
££ HIGH-END RESTAURANTS), exemplifies the feel-good attitude to food (and where/ how to eat it) of Colin and Carol Clydesdale. The original restaurant (refreshed 2018) is downstairs – food served in both bar areas (no apologies for flagging it up also in 503/FOOD PUBS). In standards, Stravaigin sets – a high bar. Mixes cuisines, especially Asian and Pacific Rim: the mantra 'think global, eat local'. Stravaigin is still very Scottish (a little more so under new head chef James Macrae). Excellent, affordable food without the formalities and open later than most. All areas can be cramped but it buzzes brilliantly. Open 7 days, all day (till 1am). The Clydesdales also have the excellent **Hanoi Bike Shop** nearby in Ruthven Lane (551/VIETNAMESE).

491 8/M26 ✓✓ **The Gannet** 1155 Argyle St · www.thegannetgla.com ·
££ 0141 204 2081 An earlier arrival to this part of Argyle St (in 2013), the 'Finnieston Strip', which put Glasgow on the foodie map. Its look (wood and metal), its atmos (casual and buzzy), its clientele and its Mod-Scot menu set the tone. Chef/proprietors Ivan Stein and Peter McKenna leave their well-sourced Scottish ingredients to speak for themselves (salad leaves from the maître d's nearby garden). Narrow bar-like front section leads to raised dining room through the back, with a good acoustic so you can talk. A very Glasgow dinner destination. Lunch & dinner (Sun 1-7.30pm). Closed Mon.

492 8/L25 ✓ **Epicures of Hyndland** 157 Hyndland Rd · www.epicuresofhyndland.co.
£ uk · 0141 334 3599 This very Hyndland coffee shop/bistro in the heart of the territory is simply a great place to hang out, graze or just eat. Breakfast, lunch, snacks and dinner on the airy ground floor, more intimate mezzanine or outside terrace. 7 days, all day.

493 8/M26 ✓ **The Western Club** 32 Royal Exchange Sq · www.theclubrestaurant.co.
££ uk · 0141 248 2214 Behind the Gallery of Modern Art in a corner close to George Sq. Stylish first-floor restaurant, part of the long-established private members' Western Club (on top floor), but open to the public, by estimable restaurateur Alan Tomkins. Formalities are observed by the slightly older clientele. Well-sourced classic dishes in a reassuringly comfortable and stylish setting. Closed Sun.

494 8/M26 ✓ **The Left Bank** 33-35 Gibson St · www.theleftbank.co.uk ·
£ 0141 339 5969 Laid-back, stylish, all-round and all-day eaterie. For 12 years a

West End sanctum near the university. Catherine Hardy and Jacqueline Fennessy got it right from the start; no need to change much, not even the basics of the menu. From healthy, imaginative brunch (that granola!) to great-value snack and main meal menu, this is a grown-up Glasgow place to hang out and graze with your cooler friends. Good vegetarian. Southside sister is **The Bungo** at 17 Nithsdale Rd (a bit jumpier).

495 8/M26 ✓ **Ian Brown Food & Drink** 55 Eastwoodmains Rd · www.
££ ianbrownrestaurant.co.uk · 0141 638 8422 A neighbourhood restaurant (albeit an affluent one): it's a long way from town but this is probably the best meal in the southside; discriminating southsiders know this! Unpretentious, well-judged and confident cooking at excellent value ensures packed houses. Notably, Ian's always there, visible in the kitchen and talks round the tables: you can see that he cares. Lunch & dinner. Sunday roast 12.30-9.30pm. Closed Mon.

496 8/M26 ✓ **Fanny Trollopes** 1066 Argyle St · www.fannytrollopes.co.uk ·
£ 0141 564 6464 Discreet presence on this once unloved but now booming boulevard, and a narrow, sometimes candlelit room, but Fanny's has always been a dining and much-loved destination. Unpretentious, and great value and flair in the kitchen from chef/patron Gary Bayless make this is a Glasgow fave. Franco-Scottish menu with lovely puds. An all-round good vibe! Lunch & dinner; all day Fri-Sun. Closed Mon.

497 8/L26 ✓ **Art Lover's Café** 10 Dumbreck Rd, Bellahouston Park · www.
£ houseforanartlover.co.uk · 0141 353 4779 Near the artificial ski slope and the walled garden, on the ground floor of House for an Art Lover, a building based on drawings left by Mackintosh. Bright room, crisp presentation and a counterpoint to wrought iron, purply, swirly Mockintosh caffs elsewhere. This is unfussy and elegant. Soup 'n' sandwiches and light à la carte, all beautifully presented; a serious and aesthetically pleasing lunch spot. Great terrace looks on the Park. 7 days, daytime only.

498 8/L25 **Monadh Kitchen** 19 New Kirk Rd, Bearsden · www.monadhkitchen.co.uk ·
££ 0141 258 6420 This modern Scottish restaurant nestles in the north of Glasgow in residential Bearsden. I've never been but it gets very good reports, including from my long-suffering editor, whom I must keep happy with this inclusion. Let us know how it was for you. Lunch & dinner. Closed Sun eve & Mon.

499 8/M26 **Brutti Ma Buoni at The Brunswick Hotel** (460/UNIQUE HOTELS) **& Brutti**
£ **Compadres** 3 Virginia Ct · 0141 552 1777 · www.brutticompadres.com The latter at 43 Virginia St through the arch. Two sympatico Mediterranean-menu (brutti, a light pizza) joints by Stephen Flannery and Michael Johnson who just slice it right. Grazing food, good vibe. Both have well-located outside tables.

500 8/M26 **Tibo** 443 Duke St, Dennistoun · www.cafetibo.com · 0141 550 2050 An East
£ End i.e. Dennistoun neighbourhood cool caff/bistro, now many years down the lived-in line. Kinda funky and kinda rustic-in-the-city. Full-on menu but can graze and great for all-day brunch. Tibo takeaway on the opposite corner for sandwiches, lunch, boxes, 'pour over coffee'. Takeaway 7 days, daytime only.

501 8/L25 **Wee Lochan** 340 Crow Rd · www.an-lochan.com · 0141 338 6606 A
££ neighbourhood café, just a short diversion from the West End food belt, Aisla and Rupert Staniforth's wee lochan is worth diving into. A Mod-Brit menu, affable staff. Loyal followers rave about the unpretentious food. Art on the walls is for sale. It's an a'body eaterie! 7 days lunch & dinner.

The Good Food Pubs

502 8/M26
££
✓✓ **The Finnieston** 1125 Argyle St · www.thefinniestonbar.com ·
0141 222 2884 In the West End restaurant mile of Argyle St, a seafood gastropub famed for its oysters. Cosy and low-ceilinged, always busy, and excellent service. Fish freshly picked: mackerel, halibut, cod, one meat dish. Generally classy menu in a classy, comfortable joint. You should book! 7 days, all day.

503 8/M26
ATMOS
££
✓✓ **Stravaigin** 28 Gibson St · www.stravaigin.co.uk · 0141 334 2665
Excellent pub food on the ground floor (doors open on to sunny Gibson St) above the restaurant (490/CASUAL). Mezzanine gallery above. Often packed. Superior grub; no pretence. Must have the busiest, most exercised waiters in town. Nice wines. One of the happiest hostelries in the West End. 7 days till late.

504 8/M26
£
✓ **The Butterfly and The Pig** 153 Bath St · 0141 221 7711 & **The Butterfly and The Pig South @ The Corona** 1039 Pollokshaws Rd · 0141 632 6230 · www.thebutterflyandthepig.com Two very different spaces, though same look and feel. Among many come-and-go, style-heavy bars and eateries, the original B&P in Bath St is here to stay. Kitschy and cosy but more real than just recherché and cooler than merely contrived. Colloquial food descriptions but what comes is imaginative and fun to eat. They do proper afternoon tea upstairs in the proper Tearooms (609/TEAROOMS). The southside venture is bigger and newer but still mix-and-match everything (lights, crockery, furniture), with restaurant area through the back, slouching out front (plus a proper bar). Derived from the makers of the legendary Buff Club (they have The Shed venue next door). Many events at the B&P. It is a great, socially engaging concept and very Glasgow.

505 8/M26
£
✓ **Bar Gandolfi** 64 Albion St · www.cafegandolfi.com · 0141 552 4462
Above Merchant City landmark **Café Gandolfi** (605/TEAROOMS) in a light, airy upstairs garret, with a congenial atmos and classy comfort food served till 10pm. Bar 11.45pm. Good veggie choice (same menu) and pizzas. Great rendezvous spot.

506 8/M26
£
✓ **The Vintage at Drygate** 85 Drygate · www.drygate.com · 0141 212 8815
In East End below the Necropolis, adjacent to Tennent's Brewery. The Drygate site itself is rambling and impressive: a relatively large-scale microbrewery you see into (with tours 2/5pm Sundays), an outdoor terrace, an event hall (comedy, music, festival programmes), a bottle shop with an extraordinary selection of bottled craft beers, knowledgeable and enthusiastic advice on what to drink. The Vintage part (bar/restaurant), in a great beerhall restaurant, has staples but some gastropubbery using the right ingredients. If you like beer or casual good food or just a great place to hang out, Drygate covers it all. 7 days, all day.

The Best Italian Restaurants

507 8/M26 ✓ **La Lanterna** 35 Hope St · www.lalanterna-glasgow.co.uk ·
££ 0141 221 9160 A basement restaurant near Central Station, surprisingly spacious and busy with a loyal clientele – well, it has been here almost 50 years. Tightly yet informally run, with meticulous attention to detail and service, it strikes a comfortable balance between a tratt and a ristorante, traditional and contemporary: friendly service but linen tablecloths and sparkling glasses. Closed Sun. Then Chris Martinolli and Luca Conreno moved uptown to:

508 8/M25 ✓ **La Lanterna West End** 447 Great Western Rd · www.
££ lalanternawestend.co.uk · 0141 334 0686 Long-established top ristorante in Kelvinbridge by the Giovanazzi brothers, La Parmigiana turned into the West End, fresher and brighter La Lanterna West End in 2017. Smart and contemporary, and continuing the Italian posher nosh for the discerning diner that characterised this site for decades. 7 days.

509 8/M26 ✓ **The Italian Caffe** 92 Albion St · www.theitaliancaffe.co.uk ·
££ 0141 552 3186 Modelled on an enoteca (a wine bar serving small tapas-like plates of food), it's a long way from tratt territory. Well located opposite the City Halls, well smart and lit, and usually packed. Flair and attention in the kitchen. Diverse menu; a lotta risotto, cute pizzas, frittatas. Good wine selection. 7 days.

510 8/M26 ✓ **Tarantino** 914-916 Sauchiehall St · 0141 237 3902 In the Finnieston food
££ quarter (next to Ox and Finch), this is good-to-go-to Italian. Title the name of the proprietor, not a Hollywood director. Together with chef Giovanni Giglio, they have created a genuinely top slice of the Italian pie (not pizzas, you understand). Genuine faves from Puglia and Sicily. Good Italian wines. Not large; book!

511 8/M26 **Piccolo Mondo** 344 Argyle St · www.piccolomondo.co.uk · 0141 248 2481
££ In midtown, along from the Radisson Blu. A proper, quite classy Italian joint with a long, loyal following. Despite being a wee bit out of the restaurant zones, it's invariably packed. Classic fare from Tuscan origins and ingredients. An intimate or celebratory choice. Closed Sun.

The Trusty Trattorias

512 8/M26 ✓✓ **Battlefield Rest** 55 Battlefield Rd · www.battlefieldrest.co.uk ·
££ 0141 636 6955 In southside opposite the old Victoria Infirmary, in a landmark pavilion building, a former tram station on a traffic island. 25 years on, this is just possibly still the best tratt in Glasgow Italia. Huge menu, from solid staples to surprising specials, using sourced north Tuscan produce, including the real prosciutto. Wines especially good value. 'Event' express menu when there's something on at Hampden up the road. Marco Giannasi at the helm. Family-run, lovingly home-made, great Italian atmos. Small, with good daylight, this place unquestionably is one of the most convivial places to eat in the southside. Closed Sun.

513 8/M26 ✓✓ **Eusebi Deli** 152 Park Rd · www.eusebideli.com · 0141 648 9999 On
££ a prominent Woodlands corner opposite the park, by Gibson St. The West End deli of the industrious Eusebi family, a takeaway, traiteur but also a perfect and popular Italian eaterie. After 35 years in Shettleston (the East End original, now the bakery), Edmund and Giovanna opened this demonstrably authentic and heartfelt aria to Italian food. The tomatoes are from Calabria, the passata from a farmer they know

back 'home'. An impressive range of food made on the premises; the pasta made for all to see; the pizza or pinsa dough (ancient Rome version) rises for 72 hours. The Sicilian pastry chefs start very early in Shettleston. Not a lot of tables, so waiting merges with the counter queue – it's all worth the wait. 7 days 8am-10/11pm.

514 8/L26 & 8/M26 £ ✓✓ **Celino's** 235 Dumbarton Rd · 0141 341 0311 & 620 Alexandra Parade · 0141 554 0523 · www.celinos.com The original, way out E on the long Parade, a brilliant, very neighbourhood deli counter and tratt that's always busy. Their winning formula has been turned into a celebration of all things Italian at their upscaled uber Celino's on a prominent corner in Partick in 2018 (New York style). Cheeses, meats galore, chilled whites on tap. Both 7 days, early till late.

515 8/M26 ATMOS ££ ✓ **Fratelli Sarti** 133 Wellington St · 0141 248 2228 & 121 Bath St · 0141 204 0440 & 42 Renfield St · 0141 572 7000 · www.fratelli-sarti. co.uk For over 25 years Glasgow's famed *Impero d'Italia* combining a deli/wine shop in Wellington St, wine shop in Bath St and bistro in each. Great, bustling atmos (eating upstairs in the bottle-lined old deli has more atmos). The restaurant in Renfield St (corner of W George St) is more like dining; an elegant room with exceptional marble tiling and wine list. All have the same extensive menu of all the staples – pasta list of mare, terra and vegetariano. Specials vary according to the chefs in each. 7 days till 10pm.

516 8/M25 £ ✓ **Te Seba** 393 Great Western Rd · www.teseba.co.uk · 0141 334 6622 Well, I love pasta: simple, pure, silky pasta with classic and inventive sauces. And that's what you get in this airy Kelvinbridge room; you just feel better for coming here. And for dinner it is cheap. Straight-forward but selective and inexpensive wine list and fizz – Prosecco and bellinis. A modern paean to pasta; lo adoro. 7 days noon-10pm.

517 8/M26 ££ ✓ **Michaelangelo's** 9 Helena Pl · www.michaelangelosglasgow.co.uk · 0141 638 7772 In Clarkston, in the southside, at the roundabout on Busby Rd. For years they had Roma Mia nearer town, then dad Massimo Onorati handed the pasta tongs to son Michaelangelo who's set up a simple, contemporary and delightful restaurant/tratt; folk travel across the burbs and from town to visit. Some beautiful, imaginative cooking. 7 days, all day.

518 8/M26 £ ✓ **Oro** 83 Kilmarnock Rd · www.oro.restaurant · 0141 632 4222 Once the fabulously full-on family tratt on main road through the southside, chef/proprietor Domenico Crolla gave it a major makeover 2017, turning it into a blingier, full-on tratt and ristorante, with pretty much the same pasta/pizza we always wanted. Wins awards. It's a Glasgow thing. 7 days.

519 8/M26 £ **Mora** 1170 Argyle St · https://morabarandkitchen.com · 0141 560 2070 At the E end of the Finnieston strip of restaurants. Luciano Mora took over from dad and contemporised this family-run tratt to fit into the Finnieston vibe. But he keeps it (mainly) inventive pasta/pizza (with Mora favourites: veal, sea bass, risotto), in a menu that changes a bit every 2/3 weeks. Friendly with it. Noon till late. Closed Tue.

520 8/M26 £ **Panevino** 1075 Argyle St · www.panevino.co.uk · 0141 221 1136 Wine bar/enoteca kind of tratt with big windows looking out on Finnieston's restaurant row. Sister of Little Italy, a Byres Rd staple, this is the upscale Sardinian version, with decent regional wine list and fastidious, friendly service. 7 days, noon onwards.

Coia's Café Report: 620/CAFÉS.

The Best Pizza

521 8/M26 **Firebird** 1321 Argyle St · www.firebirdglasgow.com · 0141 334 0594
£   Big-windowed, spacious bistro at the far west end of Argyle St. Mixed modern menu and everything covered, but notable for their light, imaginative Neapolitan pizzas and pastas (big on gluten-free). Firebird is a perennially popular West End hangout and still a key spirit-of-Glasgow spot. 7 days, all day.

522 8/M26 **Brutti Ma Buoni at The Brunswick Hotel** 106-108 Brunswick St · www.
£   brunswickhotel.co.uk · 0141 552 0001 The not-large, usually bustling bar and restaurant of this hip-ish hotel in the Merchant City (460/UNIQUE HOTELS) has a big reputation for its brutti bread, a delicious, thin pizza – the star on a grazing/ sharing menu turned out from a gantry kitchen. 7 days. Sister restaurant **Brutti Compadres** in a courtyard in Virginia St does the same good stuff in an enticingly convivial room, with outdoor terrace.

523 8/M26 **Republic Bier Halle** 9 Gordon St · www.republicbierhalle.com ·
£   0141 204 0706 Near Buchanan St. Notable for its mind-boggling and presumably mind-altering selection of beers from all over the world (670/CRAFT BEERS), they also do a great pizza. 2-for-1 'offers' (though they are around £15 a pop). Noon-midnight; pizza till 10pm (there are other things on the menu).

524 8/M26 **Paesano Pizza** 94 Miller St · 0141 258 5565 & 471 Great Western Rd
& 8/M25 0141 370 0534 · www.paesanopizza.co.uk Probably Glasgow's most popular
£   pizzeria in a stripped-down menu (only pizza) and a cool-looking room that's always full-on. It's cheap (as pizza should be). Some hoo-ha about the ovens, imported from Italy and costing a fortune, turning out the classic sourdough Neapolitan with the ridge around ... they still ain't thin and crispy enough for me! 7 days. West End Paesano opened 2018 – the same formula packing 'em in.

525 8/M26 **Fratelli Sarti** 133 Wellington St, 121 Bath St & 42 Renfield St · www.
££   fratelli-sarti.co.uk Excellent, thin-crust pie, buffalo mozzarella and freshly made *pomodoro*. 7 days, hours vary. It's the ingredients that count here. The pizza dough can be on the chunky side. Report: 515/TRATTS.

526 8/M26 **CC's Pizzas** 685 Clarkston Rd · www.ccspizza.co.uk · 0141 637 8883 They
£   take their several awards seriously here – as you would to draw both attention and the pizza nuts this far into the south lands. It is the real-deal wood-fired pizza (Napoli, thick crust). It's simple, straight-up and straight out of the oven. Takeaway and delivery only (to these burbs) 7 days 5-10pm.

527 8/M26 **Baked** 120 Duke St, opposite Tennent's brewery A pizza-to-go place with a
£   pop-up feel on the way to Dennistoun. They say 'pizza al taglio', i.e. by the 'cut' or slice, Rome-style (all for £3 or less). Vegetarian, vegan, with meat. Good reports. Noon-9pm (10pm weekends). Closed Mon/Tue.

528 8/M26 **A'Challtainn Pizza** 54 Calton Entry (off Moncur St) · www.achalltainn.com
£   · 0141 237 9220 Part of the A'Challtainn food, music and arts venue/project (582/ SEAFOOD), with its own entry and counter. A 7 by 7 pizza: 7", 7 combinations, 7 quid to eat in (the indoor ground floor) or take away. Open 7 days, I guess?

    The Clutha Great pub, great pizza. Report: 658/UNIQUE PUBS.

The Best French Restaurants

529 8/M26 ✓✓ **Le Chardon D'Or** 176 West Regent St Not a French restaurant *per se*
£££ but Monsieur Maule worked with the Roux brothers (a while back now) and the French gastronomy prevails here more than most. Report: 476/HIGH-END RESTAURANTS.

530 8/M26 ✓ **Côte** 41-43 West Nile St · www.cote-restaurants.co.uk · 0141 248 1022
££ Downtown Glasgow edition of the Côte story, expanding across the UK. Though *StB* doesn't champion chains, Glasgow has precious few French restaurants and this well-laid-out and presented contemporary brasserie is à la mode and tout va bien. From breakfast till late, it's very Parisien and very on trend. Côte also at 51 Frederick St, Edinburgh (where there is plenty of French competition).

531 8/L25 **Beaumartin The Cottage** 156 Milngavie Rd, Bearsden · www.
££ beaumartinthecottage.co.uk · 0141 258 1881 These Beaumartin guys are a determined lot. In a city hardly oversupplied (this short list), they moved their authentic la belle France corner of Glasgow from midtown to Chalet Beaumartin by Kelvinbridge, and now out to the burbs. Francophiles and foodphiles will not be disappointed. Scottish ingredients. French sensibilities. Fondues and 'posh tartes'. Closed Mon.

The Best Scottish Restaurants

532 8/L26 ✓ **Roastit Bubbly Jocks** 450 Dumbarton Rd · www.roastitbubblyjocks.
£ com · 0141 339 3355 Far up in the West End but for over 15 years we have beaten our way to this Partick dining room, where Mo Abdulla runs a seriously good kitchen at admirably good value. Wines under £20. Comforting, creative, unpretentious Scottish fare make for one of the best dinners (or 'teas' as we may call them) in the West End. Scottish breakfasts Fri-Sun – don't get better. You'll have to book at weekends. It's very Scottish, by the way! Closed Mon.

533 8/M26 ✓ **Babbity Bowster** 16-18 Blackfriars St · www.babbitybowster.com ·
£/££ 0141 552 5055 Listed as a pub for real ale and as a hotel (there are rooms upstairs), their all home-made food is mentioned mainly for its authentic Scottishness (haggis and stovies) and all-day availability. It's pleasant to eat outside on the patio/garden in summer. **Schottische** is their upstairs dining room. Reports: 673/ALES; 462/UNIQUE HOTELS.

534 8/M26 ✓ **Ardnamurchan** 325 Hope St · www.ardnamurchan.biz · 0141 353 1500
££ Top end of Hope St opposite the Theatre Royal. Owner has family connection with the eponymous wild and enigmatic far west peninsula. Here, in a large, light and spacious brasserie setting, a contemporary bar and restaurant celebrating Scottish flavour without too much fervour and with some style. Soundly sourced produce, including from Ardnamurchan. 7 days. LO 9.30pm, bar later.

535 8/M26 ✓ **The Horseshoe** 17-19 Drury St · www.thehorseshoebarglasgow.co.uk ·
ATMOS 0141 248 6368 A classic pub to be recommended for all kinds of reasons, and
£ on this page because it serves the epitome of the Scottish pub 'bar lunch'. There is a particularly good deal upstairs in the lounge, with 3 courses for £5 at TGP: old favourites on the menu, like mince pie, gammon & pineapple. Food till 10pm. And every night their famous ... karaoke. Other report: 655/UNIQUE PUBS.

536 8/M26   ✓ **The Black Sheep Bistro** 10 Clarendon St · www.blacksheepbistro.co.uk ·
£   **0141 333 1435** Off the start (eastern end) of Great Western Rd, a little off the (foodie) map. Not proclaiming itself as a particularly Scottish restaurant, but it is. A neighbourhood diner where Angela Loftus with nae bother prepares an extensive menu that includes all the faves your ma made: lentil soup, traditional prawn cocktail, haggis, steak pie. Honest scran with all the trimmings. Tue-Thu dinner only; Fri-Sat lunch & dinner; Sun 12.30-8.30pm.

■ The Best Indian Restaurants

537 8/M26   ✓✓ **Mother India** 28 Westminster Terrace · www.motherindia.co.uk ·
ATMOS   **0141 221 1663** Monir Mohammed's mothership restaurant; it's *sans*
££   *pareil*! The story is told in his book *Mother India at Home*. Different dining experiences on each of 3 floors, though the straightforward, not absurdly long menu is the same in each. Ground floor more clubby with panelling and leather benches, the larger (more asked for) upstairs room intimate, candlelit, and downstairs a more contemporary ambience (Fri/Sat only). It's all stylish, solid and quite the best Indian restaurant in town (also in Edinburgh 262/INDIAN). House wine and Kingfisher beer, but for £3.50 corkage you can BYOB. Best book. Lots of vegetarian choice. 7 days. Takeaway too. **The Bungalow Café** adjacent does coffee, ice cream, including mango kulfi and great lussis (i.e. lassis).

538 8/M26   ✓✓ **Madha** 42 Albion St · www.madha.co.uk · 0141 552 6000 Better
££   informed pundits than me (Scotland's Big Three food critics – you'll have to guess) all gave Joseph Joseph's (it starts with a very appealing name) homage to Indian home (and his mother Madha's) cooking when it opened in the less appealing end of Albion St in the Merchant City in late 2017. 4 chefs from different regions of N & S India preside over their own dishes. Lots of vegetarian and a proper vegan menu. Loved it – so high marks from me too. JJ and team are effortlessly obliging. 7 days till late.

539 8/M26   ✓✓ **Balbir's** 7 Church St · www.balbirs.co.uk · 0141 339 7711 Round the
££   corner at the bottom end of Byres Rd, the elegant low-lit dining rooms of the grandee Glasgow proprietor, Balbir Singh Sumal, in the careful hands of his son, Neki. Great use of space with a pre-dinner cocktail area and after-dinner bar upstairs. Private dining sections. Conversation-friendly. Both regular and innovative dishes from the subcontinent that Glasgow has taken to its heart and stomach (though low-cholesterol rapeseed oil is used instead of ghee). Good vegetarian, with some recipes from Balbir's wife Paramjit. 7 days.

540 8/M26   ✓ **Mother India Café** 1355 Argyle St · www.motherindia.co.uk ·
£   **0141 339 9145** Opposite **Kelvingrove Art Gallery & Museum** (675/ ATTRACTIONS). Rudely healthy progeny of Mother (above) and cousin to Wee Curry Shop (below); a distinctive twist here ensures another packed house at all times. Menu made up of 40 thali or tapas-like dishes (4/5 for a party of 2), so just as we always did, we get tastes of each other's choices – only it's cheaper! Fastidious waiters (do turn round the tables). Miraculous tiny kitchen. Can't book – you may wait! 7 days.

541 8/M26   ✓ **Dining In With Mother India** 1347 Argyle St · www.motherindia.co.uk ·
£   **0141 334 3815** Right next door to Mother India Café, a more intimate dining in option. Somewhere between Mother herself and the tapas-driven caff (above) is this more laid-back place also known as The Den, with hot (i.e. temperature) and cold dishes. You can dine here or take it home. The usual signature irresistible curries and breads. Closed Mon/Tue. Can BYOB and exclusive hire.

542 8/M26 ✓ **Ranjit's Kitchen** 607 Pollokshaws Rd · www.ranjitskitchen.com ·
£ 0141 423 8222 They say 'homemade Panjabi food' ('Pan' not 'Pun'), in this southside vegetarian caff high on ethnic integrity, which was a hit from the weekend it opened in 2015. Ranjit in the kitchen, friendly young staff on the counter. Great value. Squeeze up on the benches or take away. No alcohol; superb lassis. Closed Mon. Noon-8.30pm.

543 8/M26 ✓ **Nakodar Grill** 13 Annfield Pl · www.nakodargrill.com · 0141 556 4430
££ On the little park on Duke St, this N Indian diner wins awards and has a far-and-wide loyal following but is still a bit of a Dennistoun secret. Great tandoori menu and the 'Golden Oldies' and vegetarian. Very cheap lunch. 7 days.

544 8/M26 ✓ **The Wee Curry Shop** 7 Buccleuch St · 0141 353 0777 & 29 Ashton Lane
& 8/M25 · 0141 357 5280 · www.weecurryshopglasgow.co.uk Wee franchises of
£ Mother India above, 2 neighbourhood home-style-cooking curry shops, just as they say. Cheap, always cheerful. Stripped-down menu in small – if not micro – rooms. Buccleuch St: 7 tables; Ashton Lane the bigger, with 2 sittings (7 & 9pm) at weekends. House red and white and Kingfisher but can BYOB (1 bottle wine max. £3.50). Lunch & dinner. Sun lunch Ashton Lane only. No credit cards.

545 8/L26 ✓ **The Little Curry House** 41 Byres Rd · www.littlecurryhouse.co.uk ·
£ 0141 339 1339 Little it is and all the better for it, with banquettes at the back and the mezzanine overlooking the gantry kitchen and its aromas. This is close to real streetfood. A former head chef from Mother India; compact menu all enticing. Must book weekends. Sun-Thu 4-10.30pm & Fri/Sat noon-11pm.

546 8/M26 ✓ **Shish Mahal** 60-68 Park Rd · www.shishmahal.co.uk · 0141 334 7899
££ First-generation Indian restaurant that still, after (unbelievably) over 50 years, remains one of the city's faves. Modernised some years back but not compromised and still feels like it's been here forever. Menu of epic size. Many different influences in the cooking, and total commitment to the Glasgow curry (and chips). The Shish Mahal's great claim to fame is that it invented the chicken tikka masala, the UK's most popular Asian dish. Though son Asif now runs the restaurant, Mr Ali, the pioneer, still presides with grace and elegance. 7 days.

547 8/M26 **Banana Leaf** 76 Old Dumbarton Rd · 0141 334 4445 Across Argyle St from
ATMOS Kelvingrove Art Gallery, up Regent Moray St, turn left. Discreet doorway into 2 tiny
£ S Indian living rooms in a Glasgow tenement. Some chicken and lamb dishes but mostly vegetarian and loadsa dosas. Disarmingly real, cheap as chapatis; even the slightly chaotic service and mad kitchen is reminiscent of downtown Cochin. 7 days.

548 8/M26 **Dakhin** 89 Candleriggs · www.dakhin.com · 0141 553 2585 Up somewhat
££ tired stairs, out of sight and a find for lovers of southern Indian food. Same owners as The Dhabba (below) but menu is a subcontinent away. Lighter and saucier with coconut, ginger and chilli and light-as-a-feather dosas make essential difference to the tandoori/tikka-driven menus of most other restaurants in this category. Signature dish: the paper-thin dosa. 7 days lunch & dinner.

549 8/M26 **The Dhabba** 44 Candleriggs · www.thedhabba.com · 0141 553 1249 Mid-
££ Merchant City curry house serving slow-cooked N Indian cuisine in big-window diner. Complemented by sister restaurant Dakhin (above); often busy. I still reckon it's not as good as it thinks it is, but is a decent Merchant City choice. 7 days.

550 8/M26 **Bukharah @ The Lorne Hotel** 923 Sauchiehall St · www.lornehotelglasgow.
££ com · 0141 330 1550 Big and buzzing but also a wee Glasgow secret. A hotel restaurant that works. It's in Finnieston; has a great rep for Indian food.

The Best Thai & Vietnamese Restaurants

551 8/M25 ✓ **The Hanoi Bike Shop** 8 Ruthven Lane · www.hanoibikeshop.co.uk ·
££ 0141 334 7165 From the makers of the **Ubiquitous Chip** (474/HIGH-END RESTAURANTS) and **Stravaigin** (490/CASUAL), a different proposition but still the same innovative, contemporary approach, with appropriate well-sourced ingredients, subtle flavours and authentic combos: phos and banh mi, home-made tofu and salads. Fish sauce used instead of seasoning. A refreshing offshoot of the Clydesdales' eclectic approach to food. Like their other restaurants, you can eat here late. 7 days.

552 8/M26 ✓ **Thairiffic** 303 Sauchiehall St · www.thairifficrestaurant.com ·
£ 0141 332 3000 Upstairs on the corner with Pitt St, above Antipasti. Thai restaurants often have daft names, this one is little difficult to live up to, perhaps, but actually it comes close. At last Glasgow has a Thai place with good food in a great room. Though not big on atmos, it overlooks Sauchiehall St, which took such a beating in 2018, when it closed after the School of Art (and ABC venue opposite) fire. But these tenacious Thais have soldiered on. Support them! 7 days.

553 8/M25 **Non Viet Hai** 609 Great Western Rd · www.nonviet.co.uk · 0141 334 3090
£ Between Kelvinbridge and Byres Rd, a main street location for a fresh, 'authentic' Vietnamese restaurant with Vietnamese owners and cooks. Extensive menu: chicken, pork, in betel leaf 'shaking' beef, noodles, tofu, peanuts and peanuts. Original branch at 536 Sauchiehall St; I prefer the West End. 7 days lunch & LO 10.30pm.

554 8/M26 **Thai Siam** 1191 Argyle St · www.thaisiamglasgow.com · 0141 229 1191
££ Traditional, low-lit atmos but a discerning clientele forgive the decor and get their heads down into fragrant curries et al. All-Thai staff maintain authenticity (same chef for years). Vegetarian menu. What it lacks in style up front it makes up for in the kitchen. 7 days (closed Sun lunch).

The Best Chinese Restaurants

555 8/M26 ✓ **Loon Fung** 417-419 Sauchiehall St · 0141 332 1240 Through a long hall off
££ the night-time (western) end of the legendary street, a legendary Cantonese restaurant (for 40 years) risen from the ashes of a fire in 2010. Remade in a lovely, spacious interior room that feels like China, this is the real deal – as the regular Chinese clientele attest. 7 days.

556 8/M26 ✓ **Ho Wong** 82 York St · www.ho-wong.com · 0141 221 3550 Inconspicuous
££ location (just along from the Radisson Blu) for a discreet, urbane Pekinese/ Cantonese restaurant that relies on its reputation (for over 30 years) and makes few compromises. Calm backroom with mainly upmarket clientele; an ambience you either love (a lot) or hate. Good champagne list. Reassuringly expensive. Notable for seafood and duck. 7 days.

557 8/M26 ✓ **Sichuan House** 345-349 Sauchiehall St · www.sichuanhouse.co.uk ·
£ 0141 333 1788 A good choice in the city's Chinese (and Malay) menu. May seem a bit chain-like and it's big, but it's a Glasgow one-off. It's spicy; a lavish picture menu offers exotic choices. This very-good-value place is just a little 'hotter' than the rest of the pack. 7 days, all day.

558 8/M26 ✓ **Amber Regent** 50 West Regent St · www.amberregent.com · £ £ 0141 331 1655 Elegant Cantonese restaurant that prides itself on courteous service and the quality of its cuisine, especially seafood. Chung family here over 30 years. The menu is traditional, as is the atmos. Influences from Mongolia to Malaysia. Creditable wine list, quite romantic at night and a good biz lunch spot. The only Glasgow Chinese restaurant regularly featured in both AA and Michelin. Lunch & dinner Mon-Sat, Sun dinner only.

559 8/M26 ✓ **Banana Leaf** 67 Cambridge St · www.bananaleafglasgow.com · £ 0300 124 5099 Near the Concert Hall and Buchanan Bus Station, below the Easy Hotel. Perhaps in accord with the digs upstairs, this is an excellent, on-a-budget cosmopolitan diner. Big Malaysian more than Chinese/Singaporean-style menu; everything you could want with rice or noodles. Chef Kong presides and is family run. 7 days, all day. No relation to Banana Leaf (Indian).

The Best Fusion & Japanese Restaurants

560 8/M26 ✓✓ **Nonya** 10 Claremont St · www.nonyaglasgow.co.uk · 0141 221 6200 £ £ Small street just off Argyle St and the Finnieston strip (bar opposite is called Strip Joint), a fusion restaurant that became a destination as soon as it opened in 2018 (and critics gave it 10/10). Gina Hopkins and Andy Kelly brought lots of experience and love of Thai/Malay/Chinese food and a very different home-cooking approach to Glasgow's eastern dining. Small plates, unusual combos and ingredients. Not expensive. Downstairs a cool cocktail rendezvous. Keeping Glasgow on the (foods) up! 7 days noon-midnight.

561 8/M26 ✓✓ **So L.A.** 43 Mitchell St · www.solaglasgow.com · 0141 473 7333 Only £ £ Glasgow could get away with a restaurant called So L.A., bringing some Californian dreaming and heat to dark Merchant City streets. By the Rusk & Rusk Collection (also **Hutchesons** and **The Spanish Butcher** nearby). Opening late 2018, it is clearly another well-thought-out, cool and casual and kinda groovy dining experience. Expect light, summery fusion food in a menu you won't find anywhere else in Scotland. Lots of vegetarian choice. 7 days.

562 8/M26 ✓ **Rumours** 21 Bath St · 0141 353 0678 From an elevated first-floor position £ £ at the corner of W Nile and Bath Sts, this Malaysian caff (or kopitiam) eschews the style dictates of the restaurant/bar culture further along Bath St and is the better for it. Odd name but it refers to the word on the street and by the way the word is good. Many Chinese/Asian folk come here for fusion/Malaysian cooking that is fresh and authentic. A long, unusual, non-alcoholic drinks list (though also Tiger, Singha and wine). 7 days.

563 8/M26 ✓ **Opium** 191 Hope St · www.opiumrestaurant.co.uk · 0141 332 6668 City £ £ centre corner location for this Hong Kong-style fusion restaurant regularly lauded for its dim sum. But chef Kwan Yu Lee's mainly Chinese menu ranges aromatically over the continent and is much to our taste: good fish and prawn choices, decor is Malaysian minimalist with calm lighting. Alluringly Asian. 7 days lunch & dinner.

564 8/M26 ✓ **Dragon-i** 311-313 Hope St · www.dragon-i.co.uk · 0141 332 7728 £ £ Refreshingly contemporary Chinese/Pan-Asian opposite Theatre Royal. Thai/Malaysia and rice/noodle/tempura dishes with sound non-MSG. Often unlikely Scottish ingredients make for fusion at its best. Proper puds. Chilled-out room, creative cuisine, smart service and handy for theatre. 7 days.

565 8/M26 **Pickled Ginger** 512 St Vincent St · www.pickledgingerfinnieston.co.uk ·
£ 0141 328 8941 Out west, just before the Finnieston strip, the sushi bar of choice in this foodie quarter, a clean-cut Japanese diner and takeaway. They show you how to eat it. Wide choice of ingredients, including octopus, clams, sizzling beef and all the usuals. Beers to go with. I think there is a Japanese chef. 7 days, all day.

566 8/M26 **Ichiban Noodle Bar** 50 Queen St · www.ichiban.co.uk · 0141 204 4200
£ Steven Tsang's noodle bar, based loosely on the Wagamama formula. Fundamental food, egalitarian presentation. Ramen, udon, soba noodle dishes; also chow meins, tempuras and other Japanese snacks. Long tables, eat-as-it-comes 'methodology'. Loyal team; loyal customers climb the stairs coz it's good! 7 days.

567 8/M26 **Yen** 28 Tunnel St · https://glasgowrotunda.com/yen · 0141 847 0220 In
££ the landmark Rotunda building near the SEC/Hydro, so often busy with pre- or après-concert audiences. First-floor 'oriental' i.e. Cantonese/Japanese/Thai noodle restaurant (the ground floor La Rotunda is Italian). Location and convenience the thing here. 7 days.

The Best Mediterranean Restaurants

568 8/M26 ✓ **Rioja** 1116 Argyle St · www.riojafinnieston.co.uk · 0141 334 0761 In
£ heart of Finnieston food quarter, this avowedly Spanish vinoteca doesn't let the side down, i.e. contemporary Spanish cuisine which, despite its renaissance, is not so well represented in this or any UK city. Classic and reconstructed tapas, an appealing example of small-plate sharing/grazing. In Barcelona/Madrid style, it's open unusually late – the Finnieston crowd come in for their rioja. 7 days till 1am.

569 8/M26 ✓ **Gnom** 758 Pollokshaws Rd · www.gnomfood.com · 0141 258 2949 New
£ 2018, in the long sweep of Pollokshaws Rd, Felicity Day's daytime and very different café, with a menu not done justice by describing it as merely 'eclectic'. Breakfast bao (rice buns) is not Mediterranean at all, but there were Turkish eggs, freekeh dishes and Parmesan polenta when I was there, and the French Toast ice-cream sandwiches were so popular that they're probably still on her evolving menu. This food is anywhere, anytime. It is refreshingly different! 7 days 9am-4pm (may change).

570 8/M26 **Elena's Spanish Bar & Restaurant** 90 Old Dumbarton Rd · www.
£ elenastapas.com · 0141 237 4730 Near Kelvingrove Museum, Elena Xavier's homage to Cantabria actually feels like a Spanish bar and restaurant. Compadres tell me they like it mucho here but I haven't eaten at TGP. Reports, please. 7 days.

571 8/M25 **Bay Tree** 403 Great Western Rd · www.thebaytreewestend.co.uk ·
£ 0141 334 5898 Mediterranean and Levant caff/diner at Kelvinbridge, here for aeons but the real deal. Meze and falafel, BBQ chicken, lots of vegetarian and couscous, of course. Food all day till 9.30pm. Closed Mon.

The Best Burgers & Steaks

572 8/M26 ✓✓ **The Butchershop Bar & Grill** 1055 Sauchiehall St, Kelvingrove ·
£££ www.butchershopglasgow.com · 0141 339 2999 Near the Art Gallery
& Museum (675/ATTRACTIONS), this high-end, very well-conceived and presented
restaurant is in some ways as it says, a shop. It sells the cow, the animal: its parts
and cuts frame the menu. Of the other places on this page and all over the city, this
is where you can be sure the meat is hung, quartered and cooked to the modern
taste – actually the NYC style, as is envisioned by proprietor James Rusk, who's also
behind **Hutchesons** (482/BRASSERIES). There are other meaty options (pork, lamb)
and a decent fish curry, but it's the cow the regular clientele really come for, in two
smart, urban dining rooms, always buzzing and with personal, attentive servers.
There are burgers at lunch and a Sunday roast till 5pm. 7 days lunch & dinner.

573 8/M26 ✓✓ **Porter & Rye** 1131 Argyle St · www.porterandrye.com ·
£££ 0141 572 1212 By the guys with The Finnieston next door, both
restaurants that have blazed a trail on Glasgow's foodie map, this has the meatier
métier. Carcasses from the cabinet next to the kitchen counter, from which
perfectly cooked steaks emerge (any stray vegetarians should eat upstairs). Nice
touches; amuse-bouche, sauces, toppings, butters. Beef from related
Gaindykehead Farm. Booths, bar stools and mezzanine. There is also a reduced but
great late menu Fri/Sat 11pm-midnight.

574 8/M26 ✓✓ **The Spanish Butcher** 80 Miller St · www.spanishbutcher.com ·
£££ 0141 406 9880 After the Butchershop (above) which proclaims Scottish
beef and produce, Rusk & Rusk touched down in the Merchant City, 100m from
George Sq, to do the same for Spain. A large, dramatically dark brasserie divided
into intimate chambers and with seats at the bar, this paean to all things Iberian is
big on steak and hams (and a whole roast suckling pig you can pre-order), but
there's lots of non-meat choices. Great Spanish wine list by bottle and glass, as
you'd expect. 7 days.

575 8/M26 ✓ **Ad Lib** 111 Hope St · www.adlibglasgow.com · 0141 248 6645 American-
££ style diner since 1998 ('the first burger joint in the city') still pumping it out;
the soul music, soul food and a burger hard to beat (and long before there were
'gourmet' burgers). Steaks very reasonably priced. DJs and dancin' Fri/Sat. Owner
Billy McAneney has opened an Ad Lib on the other side – of the globe – in Malawi,
southern Africa, a country kind of adopted by Scotland. A good guy, Billy!

576 8/M26 ✓ **Alston Bar & Beef** 79 Gordon St, Central Station · www.alstonglasgow.
£££ co.uk · 0141 221 7627 In left corner of main entrance, also on Gordon St. A
great diner/bar to have in a station... well, underneath it. Best makeover of any
basement in the city – it's light and bright, individual, innovative and smart.
Apparently this was once Alston Street. Great tiled floor; there's stylish life under
the archways. A departure board reminds you where you are. Good gin and wine
selection, for the road or rail. Very good steaks, cool starters and imaginative
burgers. Eat here – you don't even need to go into Glasgow! Food till 10pm.

The Best Seafood Restaurants

577 8/M26
££
✓✓ **The Fish People Café** 350 Scotland St · www.thefishpeoplecafe. co.uk · **0141 429 8787** Next to Shields Rd subway station, opposite **Scotland Street School Museum** (719/MACKINTOSH). In fact, you walk out the station on to their 'terrace'. This is S of the river (about 1km) near the junction of the M8 and M74, and not that easy to find so best to go by train. 'Fish People' because the fishmonger is right next door – the wholesaler of choice to many of Glasgow's top-end restaurants. Here in the caff, head chef John Gillespie has the pick of the daily (sustainable) catch; expect simple but innovative cookery. This place is a real treat for fish people. Closed Sun eve/Mon.

578 8/M26
££
✓✓ **Gamba** 225a West George St · www.gamba.co.uk · **0141 572 0899** In basement, at corner of W Campbell St, a seafood bistro that for a long time now has been one of the best restaurants of any in the city. Low light, a sea of calm lounge for pre drinks, an understated, grown-up kind of ambience. A great maître d' and the service to follow. Simplicity and sourcing are the touchstones here and chef/proprietor Derek Marshall doesn't put a finger wrong. His signature fish soup with prawn dumplings is always there but menu changes around every 8 weeks. One meat, one vegetarian choice and the good-value 'Market Menu'. Exemplary wine list includes halves. Gamba, unlike many, opens on Mondays. They take the sustainable fishing code seriously, like we should. Lunch (not Sun) & dinner.

579 8/M26
££
✓✓ **Gandolfi Fish** 84-86 Albion St · www.cafegandolfi.com · **0141 552 9475** Adjacent to the much-loved caff and bar, this big-windowed Merchant City diner has a good location, stylish look, good proprietorship (Seumas MacInnes) and a direct link to the West Coast, Skye and Hebridean fishing grounds (Seumas is from Barra) through the estimable Fish People (above). Brilliant fish 'n' chip shop adjacent (584/FISH & CHIPS). Always busy and buzzing, even midweek (a good sign in Glasgow). Mon-Sat from noon till late, Sun 10am-9pm.

580 8/M26
ATMOS
££
✓✓ **Two Fat Ladies City Centre** 118 Blythswood Sq · www. twofatladiesrestaurant.com · **0141 847 0088** The city extension of the finer-dining Ladies at the Buttery (475/HIGH-END RESTAURANTS). The original in Dumbarton Rd was closed at TGP. Everything selectively sourced; tiny kitchen produces delicious dishes with a light touch for packed-in discerning diners. Splendid puds. Best seafood midtown. 7 days lunch & dinner.

581 8/M26
ATMOS
££
✓✓ **Crabshakk** 1114 Argyle St · www.crabshakk.com · **0141 334 6127** John Macleod's tiny, 2-floor caffshakk, pioneering straight-up seafood since 2009, once *the* destination foodstop hereabouts. Now there are many good options in this humming section of Argyle St, but CS really was the first to put Finnieston food on the map. Expect squid, moules marinière and fab fish 'n' chips, though most notably the meat of shell and claw, in a drop-in, grab-a-seat kind of atmos. 7 days noon-midnight.

582 8/M26
££
✓✓ **A'Challtainn** 54 Calton Entry · www.achalltainn.com ·
0141 237 9220 A'Challtainn (pronounced 'A-cawl-tane') means 'The Calton' after the area of Glasgow it's in, which to most of us means the East End; it's behind the Barrowlands Ballroom (Scotland's legendary concert venue). Part of the Barras Art and Design Centre, the hub of an emerging food and arts quarter, Ricky Scoular and Brian Traynor moved on from their pop-up fish café interventions and opened this cool, contemporary permanent restaurant in a big, glassed-over kind of courtyard in late 2016. Airy mezzanine overlooking the space – a 300-capacity venue for all sorts of events, including a Sunday market, cookery classes, proper big gigs – a complete lifestyle experience. Menu *au courant* and of the season changes every 3 months; great light, imaginative seafood (and vegetarian), well presented with hipster service. Then there's the pizza (528/PIZZA) and a bakery opening at TGP. Go east. Closed Mon.

583 8/M26
££
✓ **Mussel Inn** 157 Hope St · www.mussel-inn.com · 0141 572 1405
Downtown location for light, bright bistro (big windows) where seafood is serious but fun. From cold waters up north (such as Shetland). Mussels, scallops, oysters, catch-of-the-day-type blackboard specials; also vegetarian options. Mussels in variant concoctions; kilo pots are the thing, of course. As in Edinburgh (233/SEAFOOD), this formula is sound; the owners are to be commended for keeping it real. Mon-Fri lunch & dinner. All day Sat/Sun.

 Rogano Report: 480/BRASSERIES.

 The Finnieston West End bar and seafood restaurant with great ambience and attention to detail. Report: 502/FOOD PUBS.

The Best Fish & Chips

584 8/M26
✓ **Gandolfi Fish To Go** 84-86 Albion St · www.gandolfifish.com ·
0141 552 9475 The takeaway (and a few tables) bit of Gandolfi Fish in 'Gandolfi World' at this Merchant City crossroads. Same quality and conscientious approach. Haddock (breaded or battered), cod, salmon, sea bass, as well as Stornoway black pudding and proper Cullen skink. Best in the zone. 7 days from noon.

585 8/L26
✓ **Catch** 186 Fenwick Rd · www.catchfishandchips.co.uk · 0141 638 9169
In the deep south but you might want to sail over here for the smartest, most thought-through F&C shop/café in town. Seasoned restaurateurs behind this 2015 venture on a suburban strip (you could see it spreading). Starters from Cullen skink to salt & chilli squid, through to proper puds, via all the fish in the sea (maccy cheese with lobster, anyone?). They pride themselves on the batter; they're not wrong! Good for the family tea. Use rapeseed oil. 7 days from noon. There is another Catch at 570 Clarkston Rd, Netherlee.

586 8/M26
Merchant Chippie 155 High St · www.amoreglasgow.co.uk · 0141 552 5789
At corner of High & Ingram Sts. A chippie that does try harder and wins awards. Long seafood list, including whiting and calamari, together with 'chip-shop classics', pizza and haggis. Unusually, they use palm oil. 7 days (Fri/Sat till 1am).

587 8/M25   **Old Salty's** 337 Byres Rd · www.oldsaltys.co.uk · 0141 334 3334
Reconstructed new-style, big-scale chippie, designer-distressed but traditional fare
nevertheless. Range of fish (veg oil used) and 'old school suppers': mince and peas,
macaroni pies. Open early (8.30am) should you not be able to face the day without
a fry-up. Tables and takeaway. 7 days till late.

588 8/M26   **Salt & Vinegar** 1044 Pollokshaws Rd · http://saltandvinegarglasgow.co.
uk · 0141 649 9159 In southside, but central, near Queen's Park, another
new-style chippie (from the same shoal as the Merchant Chippie above), with
café seating and fishy dishes from lemon sole to linguini vongole (some more
successful than others). 7 days noon-10pm.

589 8/M25   **Philadelphia** 445 Great Western Rd · 0141 339 2372 Adjacent to **La Lanterna
West End** (508/ITALIAN). Since 1930, a Glasgow fixture and a fresher fryer than
most. Open 7 days (Fri till 1.30am; Sat till 2.30am).

The Best Vegetarian & Vegan Restaurants

590 8/M26
£   ✓ **Saramago Café Bar** 350 Sauchiehall St · www.cca-glasgow.com/
saramago-caf · 0141 352 4920 The café-bar of the CCA arts & exhibition
centre. In the midst of the west end of Sauchiehall St and so decimated by the Art
School fire, a calm, laid-back restaurant which takes its foodie and vegan
credentials seriously. A lofty atrium space and nice people either side of the
counter. Small plates, great soups and salads. May seem samey over time.

591 8/M26
ATMOS
£   ✓ **Stereo** 22-28 Renfield Lane · www.stereocafebar.com · 0141 222 2254
Unobtrusive (some might say scruffy) in this lane off Renfield St near Central
Station, Iain Baird and Craig Tannock's **all vegan** Stereo nevertheless happily
occupies a notable building, the former *Daily Record* printing works, designed by
Charles Rennie Mackintosh (see p. 127), and built in 1900. Sits above street level
with a music venue downstairs and is crowded at weekends. Vegan wines. Much to
graze; daily specials. Handmade and more delicious than the somewhat grungy
surroundings may suggest. 7 days. Opposite, the **Old Hairdresser's**, is a cool bar,
exhibition and event space evenings & weekends.

592 8/M26
£   ✓ **Ranjit's Kitchen** 607 Pollokshaws Rd · www.ranjitskitchen.com ·
0141 423 8222 Minimalist, stripped-back southside caff, with home-cooking
Panjabi streetfood vibe. Takeaway and benches. Lovely lassis, breads and daily daal.
Noon-8.30pm. Closed Mon. See 542/INDIAN.

593 8/M26
£   ✓ **Grassroots Café** 20 Woodlands Rd · 0141 237 4646 Spacious self-service
café and deli, conscientiously and carefully run by an Indian crew, but with an
eclectic menu from curry to tofu dishes, veggie meatballs and burgers to delicious
thin pizza. Not in the hipster veggie family, perhaps, but some of the best
vegetarian and vegan dishes in town. Not licensed. 7 days till 7.30pm.

594 8/M26
£   ✓ **Mono** Kings Court · www.monocafebar.com · 0141 553 2400 In odd
no-man's land between the Merchant City and East End behind Parnie St, a
cool hangout in an alternative world! PC in a 'people's collective' kind of way; the
antithesis of Glasgow's manufactured style. Great space with art, music (and a
vinyl & CD store, Monorail), occasional performance and interesting **all vegan**
menu served with few frills by friendly staff. Organic ales/wines. 7 days.

595 8/M26 ✓ **The 78** 10-14 Kelvinhaugh St · www.the78barandkitchen.com ·
£ **0141 576 5018** Round the corner from (and preceding) the 'Finnieston Strip'.
Mix 'n' match laid-back bar/café from the same Tannock/Baird **all vegan** stable as
Stereo and Mono above. Legendary Vic Henderson the chef here. Great daily
specials adding to the veggie burgers, wraps, nachos of the à la carte. Some
organic. Lived-in pub-like atmos. Some outside tables. 7 days.

596 8/M26 ✓ **The Cran** 994 Argyle St · www.thecran.co.uk · **0141 237 3435** Just edging
DF into the Finnieston foodie mile, Aziz's vegetarian and vegan café with excellent
£ coffee. Seems to be a kind of seminal hipster Cranily thing, involved in foodie
pop-ups and events, yet below the mainstream radar. Bread from the estimable
Bavarian Bakery. Very good cakes and vegan pies. Breakfast porridge and granola.
Avo, of course. And toasties. 7 days, daytime only.

597 8/M26 **The 13th Note** 50-60 King St · www.13thnote.co.uk · **0141 553 1638** Old-
£ style veggie hangout – a good attitude/good vibes café-bar; live music downstairs
most nights. Menu unexceptional but honest, from veggie burgers to Indian and
Greek meze dishes. Some dairy, otherwise vegan. Organic booze and Glasgow
bevvy. 7 days.

598 8/M26 **The Flying Duck** 142 Renfield St · www.theflyingduck.org · **0141 564 1450**
£ Enter from the top of Renfrew St leading to the Herald building, downstairs to an
underground bar/restaurant very much in the mould of Tannock and Baird's all-
vegan venues on this page, but, if anything, raunchier. Food American-diner style,
including dogs and subs, but is **100% vegan**. 7 days 11am-late; food till 10pm.

VEGETARIAN/VEGAN FRIENDLY

Tchai-Ovna Old-style vegetarian caff; truly boho. Report: 613/TEAROOMS.

Madha Report: 538/INDIAN.

Mother India Reports: 537/540/INDIAN.

Café Gandolfi Report: 605/TEAROOMS.

Banana Leaf Report: 547/INDIAN.

Balbir's Report: 539/INDIAN.

Alchemilla Report: 489/CASUAL.

The Hanoi Bike Shop Report: 551/VIETNAMESE.

Project Café Report: 623/CAFÉS. **All vegan**.

So L.A. Report: 561/FUSION.

The Best Coffee

599 8/M26 ✓ **Artisan Roast** 15-17 Gibson St · www.artisanroast.co.uk · 07864 984253
Follow that aroma that blew over from Edinburgh where they dispense the same indispensable coffee in a similar neighbourhood (294/COFFEE). A bit fancier and snackier here, with more tables and a mezzanine, but the same blend and stripped-back offering. Once the pioneers – the best coffee in the West (End) – now there are so many (see here). 8am-8pm (till 6.30pm weekends).

600 8/L26 ✓ **Kaf** 5 Hyndland St · www.kafcoffee.co.uk Leonora Belcher's tiny coffee and chow room behind the big window at the Partick end of Hyndland St is very indie, sources from small roasters and has an eclectic and decidedly different selection of food plates and cakes. There's probably a queue. 7 days 8am-5pm.

601 8/M25 ✓ **Papercup** 603 Great Western Rd · www.papercupcoffeecompany.bigcartel.com · 0141 339 7822 Heart of artisan coffee culture, frequently said to be 'the best flat white'. Much ado about beans and individual brewing. Unusual snacks, good chat. They roast but not here – at 11 Belmont Lane nearby. All aficionados welcome (and those who just love ... coffee). 7 days, daytime only.

602 8/M26 **Coffee, Chocolate & Tea** 944 Argyle St · 0141 204 3161 Among many others, this stands out: they make the chocolates, they blend and roast their own coffee (different beans), both in the shop, and there's 40 teas and unquestionably good cuppas of C, C & T, though limited munchies. 8am-4pm. Closed Sun.

603 8/M26 **The Steamie** 1024 Argyle St · www.thesteamie.co.uk · 07821 544449 A People's Palace (678/ATTRACTIONS) retro/nostalgia vibe but, yes, homely. Your coffee made at the sideboard, à la Artisan Roast. Stephen Meek has put this together well, though it might be a bit open-plan for some. They roast (not in the premises) and sell the beans. Lots of eggs on the menu, sandwiches and soup.

604 8/M26 **It All Started Here** 75 Deanston Dr, Shawlands · 07743 069632 These guys came from pop-up land (bakeries, markets, beer festivals) and settled on the southside. They're serious about coffee, sourcing, rotating, batch-brewing the beans. Bakes, cakes and sandwiches. Indie through and through, they are coffee evangelists. Daytime only. Closed Mon.

The Best Tearooms

605 8/M26 ✓✓ **Café Gandolfi** 64 Albion St · www.cafegandolfi.com · 0141 552 6813
ATMOS For even more decades now, Seumas MacInnes's definitive and landmark meeting/eating place (not only a tearoom) has occupied a pivotal corner of the Merchant City. A bistro menu, and the casual, boho ambience. 40 years ago, the stained glass and heavy, over-sized wooden furniture created an ideal ambience that has withstood the vagaries of Glasgow style. The food is light and imaginative and served all day. You may have to queue. Mon-Sat 8am till late, Sun from 9am (637/BRUNCH). The **Bar** upstairs (505/FOOD PUBS), **Fish** restaurant (579/SEAFOOD) and takeaway next door (584/FISH & CHIPS) contribute to a unique and exemplary Glasgow experience. Don't change a thing, Seumas!

606 8/M25 ✓✓ **Kember & Jones** 134 Byres Rd · www.kemberandjones.co.uk · 0141 337 3851 A tearoom/bakery, café with the foodstuff of the good life. Of all those places with piles of pies and meringues, this is the real deal. They roast the coffee, they bake the bread. Tables outside and on the mezzanine. Great sandwiches, honey-toasted granola, and the best tartes and tortes in town. How they get all those plates out from their small kitchen is a triumph of cookability (their bakery is elsewhere). 7 days.

607 8/M26 ✓✓ **Hidden Lane Tearoom** 1103 Argyle St · www. thehiddenlanetearoom.com · 0141 237 4391 The lane next to Tesco leads to a courtyard of studio craft shops and, at the end, as it says, the Hidden Tearoom. This was one of the first of the tearoom new wave, Kirsty Webb paying proper retro respect to the tradition of afternoon tea (1461/AFTERNOON TEA). Small downstairs and upstairs parlour quiet and civilised. Sandwiches, soup and top cakes (new ones every month) especially combined in the tier for the afternoon tea. Good gluten-free selection. Mon-Sat 10am-6pm (Sun from noon).

608 8/M25 ✓ **Sonny & Vito's** 52 Park Rd · 0141 357 0640 On a West End corner between Great Western Rd and Gibson St, a daytime deli-caff with excellent home baking, light menus and tartelettes to eat in or take away. Sonny and Vito the kids of the Pelosis – they'll be quite grown-up now! Not many tables, always busy; those outside have interesting urban aspects. Nice for breakfast. 7 days.

609 8/M26 **The Tearooms** 151 Bath St · www.thebutterflyandthepig.com · 0141 243 2459 Upstairs and part of The Butterfly and The Pig, this really is a Tearoom, fully embracing the T-comeback. But it's on the go from breakfast (traditional with twists) through soup and super 'sanner' lunch (with home-made bread) to the all-important tier of afternoon tea, then, of course, high tea. All very much in-period, and in the vibe of **The Butterfly & the Pig** (504/FOOD PUBS).

610 8/M26 **The Willow (aka The Mackintosh) Tearooms** 217 Sauchiehall St · www. mackintoshatthewillow.com · 0141 332 7696 It is confusing but there are 2 other Willow Tearooms in Buchanan St and in the Watt Brothers department store in Hope St, but this one has the marvellous original interior and the official Mackintosh shop. All tell the story of Catherine Cranston, who commissioned Mackintosh and opened her tearoom in 1903. Here, there's hot food and, as you'd expect, a perfectly tiered afternoon tea. 7 days 9am-5pm.

611 8/M26 **Cup Tea Lounge** 71 Renfield St · www.cupglasgow.co.uk · 0141 353 2959 Corner of W Regent St, in a stunning lofty, ornate room, once the Bank of India (a listed building), an urban, calm place to take tea, cake and snacks. After 5pm it turns into **Gin 71** 661/UNIQUE PUBS. **Cup Merchant City**, in Virginia Ct, behind Glassford St has a similar civilised ambience, and outdoor seating.

612 8/M26 **Once Upon A Tart** 45 King St · www.onceuponatart.co.uk · 0141 552 0305 At art end of Merchant City, big on cakes but also ciabattas, soups and the apple tart. Very pink, shabby kitsch with mix 'n' match furniture and laid-back lassies. Great daily selection of cakes under the domes. Ladies who lunch and laugh off the calories. Mon-Fri 8am-5pm, Sat/Sun from 9.30am.

613 8/M26 **Tchai-Ovna** 42 Otago Lane · www.tchaiovna.com · 0141 357 4524 For almost 20 years now, a 'house of tea' hidden away off Otago St on the banks of the Kelvin. A decidedly gap-year tearoom which could be Eastern Europe, North Africa or Kathmandu but the vibe mainly Middle Eastern. 70 kinds of tea, soup, organic sandwiches and cakes from the tiny kitchen. A good place to read a book (perhaps from the second-hand bookshop next door, or the one in the next lane). A real find but suits and ladies who lunch may not be quite so chilled out here. 7 days, all day from 11am.

The Best Cafés

614 8/M26 ✓✓ **Singl-end** 265 Renfrew St · 0141 353 1277 & 15 John St · 0141 552 4433 · www.thesingl-end.co.uk Michele and Jo Pagliocca's brilliant boho below-street café/restaurant along from Glasgow School of Art opened its Merchant City branch in 2018. The original, named after the Glasgow vernacular for a tiny tenement living space, set a new standard in garage-style urban chic, with ethical, home-made dining, especially baking. Though subterranean, the space is bright and comfortable. John St has a terrace spilling over the pedestrian street and 2 floors. 7 days, daytime only.

615 8/M26 ✓✓ **The Glad Café** 1006A Pollokshaws Rd · www.thegladcafe.co.uk · 0141 636 6119 Door in a wall of shops and restaurants (including Glad Rags, the vintage clothes bit) opposite the park in arterial Pollokshaws Rd. You enter a different, more civilised world and an arterial route for the life blood of the southside's (and the city's) roots cultural scene. There are books (and they have their own newspaper), music, gigs, theatre and performance, and home-made and properly outsourced café food and drink for more corporeal sustenance. Rachel Smillie has done a very good thing here. The event space is through another door.

616 8/M26 ATMOS ✓✓ **University Café** 87 Byres Rd · 0141 339 5217 People have been coming here for generations to sit at the 'kneesy' tables and share the salt and vinegar. Here nothing much changes. Run by the Verecchia family who administer advice, sympathy and pie, beans and chips with equal aplomb. And have done so for 100 years! 6 booths only; it resists all change. BYOB (no corkage). Sometimes there's trifle! 9am-10pm.

617 8/M26 ✓ **Trans Europe Café** 25 Parnie St · www.transeuropecafe.co.uk · 0141 552 7999 Easy-going classic caff near Glasgow Cross off Trongate, with neighbourhood atmos and home-made food individually prepared in Tony Sinclair's mad gantry kitchen. Light food, especially bespoke sandwiches, and more meal-like at night (Fri/Sat only). Could be Europe? Naw, this could only be Glasgow! 7 days.

618 8/M25 ✓ **William Café** 94 Queen Margaret Dr · www.william.cafe · 07968 857161 Small, celebrated and much-loved home-cooking café between Kelvinbridge and Maryhill, where Sandy and Sandra dispense breakfast (all day), top cake, avo toast, friendly chat and their quite famous sausage rolls. 7 days.

619 8/M26 ✓ **Wilson Street Pantry** 6 Wilson St · www.wilsonstreetpantry.com · 0141 552 0606 Heart of the Merchant City, probably the best hangout for snack and chat and all-day brunch. An avo-on-sourdough kind of vibe but lots of other stuff on the toast too. Specials and cake. 7 days till 5pm (kitchen closes 4pm).

620 8/M26 ✓ **Coia's Café** 473 Duke St · www.coiascafe.co.uk · 0141 554 3822 Since 1928, and now in its fourth generation, Coia's has been supplying this East End high street with ice cream, great-deal breakfasts and the kind of comforting lunch that any neighbourhood needs: a full-blown food operation with deli counter, takeaway and restaurant. It's traditional grub and ice cream along with the olive-oil niceties. Do they still do the Havana cigars? 7 days.

621 8/M26 ✓ **Fylkir of Copenhagen** 134 Newlands Rd · 0141 633 1722 Deep in suburban southside, opposite a beautiful big white building – actually an engineering works – a unique and surprising corner of Denmark. Caroline Carlsen turns out her authentic rye bread smørrebrøds, with all the toppings you find as soon as you arrive at Copenhagen airport, but not until now in Glasgow or Scotland. Big Bear Bakery provides the cinnamon buns. The rye bread's from Sweden. It's an even healthier way to get your avo. Daytime only. Closed Tue.

622 8/M26   **Lagom Kitchen** 76 Victoria Rd · 0141 237 2424 Kevin Brolly's civilised southside bakery and café, where you can breakfast on beans on toast or a Loch Fyne kipper, lunch on toasties and spiced lamb, and snack on cakes on a lazy afternoon. The delicious bread is from Freedom Bakery. Daytime only. Closed Tue.

623 8/M26   **Project Café** 134 Renfrew St · www.theprojectcafe.weebly.com · 0141 332 9520 A local (behind Sauchiehall St near the ruined School of Art) café/deli, community project and focal point. Food to eat in and take away is of consistently tasty high standard, and 100% vegetarian. A sunny terrace, from where to watch the Art School being rebuilt.

624 8/M26   **McCune Smith** 3-5 Duke St · www.mccunesmith.co.uk · 0141 548 1114 The very beginning of Duke St, heading E off the High St and the Merchant City. There's a Scottish Enlightenment thing going on here: it's named after the 19th-century African-American abolitionist 'as somebody who embodies both Glasgow's complicity in slavery and the fortunes its merchants made and the abolitionist movement which sprang from Enlightenment'. A fascinating connection that runs through the look and the menu of this very cool caff, with imaginative sandwiches and salads. And an 'enlightened' breakfast. Daytime only.

625 8/L26   **Acid Bar @ SWG3** 100 Eastvale Pl · www.swg3.tv · 0141 337 1731 At first and for non-Glaswegians, a surprising find between Finnieston and the river, an arts/exhibition/TV studio and substantial music and club venue with a daytime caff and at weekends a pop-up restaurant (Thai inspired at TGP). Daytime menu from granola to daal, baked potato and hot dogs with chilli in the mix. An essential hipster watering hole. 7 days.

626 8/M26   **Chaiwallah** 55 Eldon St · 0141 334 9559 At the entrance to Kelvingrove Park at the bottom of Gibson St, with a terrace on the roof among the trees, a social enterprise café that arranges and puts profits back into a mobility scooter scheme for folk to access the steep entrance and paths of the park. Good works and a lovely wee caff. Cakes & sandwiches. 7 days, daytime only.

627 8/M26   **Brooklyn Café** 21 Minard Rd · 0141 632 3427 Here since 1931, the kind of all-purpose caff any neighbourhood would be proud to have. More tratt perhaps than caff, with pasta, salads and the ice cream (the Pelosi family still make it from their own vanilla recipe). It will, of course, never die, like their Empire biscuits. Since 2018, everything, including the biscuits, is gluten free. BYOB.

628 8/M25   **North Star** 108 Queen Margaret Dr · 0141 946 5365 Up from the Botanic Gardens, long a fave caff in the West End. New owners, same team 2018, still a happy hangout. Only a few tables and when, as often, it's busy, it's a bit chaotic at the counter. Soup, hot specials, their great 'hot rolls' and a big gluten-free choice. This really is the tiniest kitchen but they do get on. 7 days, daytime only.

629 8/M26   **Where The Monkey Sleeps** 182 West Regent St · www.monkeysleeps.com · 0141 226 3406 Lo-fi, below stairs, Gen X caff and takeaway. 2 soups, 2 stews, mean panini and bagels. It's a vibe! Mon-Fri 7am-3pm. A new bigger, loftier, more aspirational but nonetheless funky Monkey is at 340 Argyle St (0141 204 5260). Food's big too.

The Best Delis

630 8/M25 ✓✓ **Roots & Fruits** 451-457 Great Western Rd · www.
rootsfruitsandflowers.com · **0141 339 3077** Main branch (see 648/
TAKEAWAYS) of the all-round, all-good-things-in-life provisioner of the West End:
the flower shop, the deli and the fruit & veg together offering a superlative service.
Excellent traiteur/takeaway counter and café seating inside and out. 7 days.

631 8/M25 ✓✓ **I.J. Mellis** 492 Great Western Rd · www.mellischeese.net ·
0141 339 8998 Started out as *the cheese guy*, now more of a very select
deli for food that's good and 'slow'. Coffees, Iberico hams, sausages, olives and
seasonal stuff like apples and mushrooms (branches vary), so smells mingle.
Irresistible! Branches also in Edinburgh (357/DELIS) and St Andrews. See also 1527/
CHEESES. Supplies many restaurants. He *is* the cheese guy!

632 8/M25 ✓✓ **George Mewes** 106 Byres Rd · www.georgemewescheese.co.uk ·
0141 334 5900 Well, there was Ian Mellis (above, since 1993), then there
was a George Mewes (2009) and his beautifully chilled (hence the woolly-hatted
staff) and fragrantly smelly shop in Byres Rd, giving Mellis a run, well, a runny
cheese, for his money. Great presentation and range (Scottish selection seasonal),
Poilâne bread, top organic eggs. 7 days. George also in Edinburgh and on many
restaurant cheeseboards. See 358/DELIS.

633 8/L26 &
8/M26 ✓ **Celino's** 235 Dumbarton Rd · www.celinos.com · **0141 341 0311** And the
original at 620 Alexandra Parade, 0141 554 0523. Recently expanded into
Partick, with an uber trattoria/deli. Both with big selection of the Italian stuff of life
and open till 10pm, 7 days. Report: 514/TRATTS.

Good Places For Brunch

634 8/L25
ATMOS ✓✓ **Cafezique** 66 Hyndland St · www.delizique.com · **0141 339 7180**
This award-winning and hard-to-fault 2-level bistro/caff (487/CASUAL)
opens at **9am** every day for snacking or more ambitious breakfast. A very civilised
start to the day: from **9am** 7 days.

635 8/M26 ✓✓ **Stravaigin** 28 Gibson St · www.stravaigin.co.uk · **0141 334 2665** Same
care and flair given to their famous brunch menu as the rest (490/CASUAL).
Cramped maybe, but reflects appetite for Sunday breakfast, from home-made
granola to French toast and the Ayrshire bacon. Served till 5pm. From **11am**.

636 8/M26 ✓ **The Left Bank** 33-35 Gibson St · www.theleftbank.co.uk ·
0141 339 5969 Classy and popular café-bar-restaurant in student and
luvvyland. From great granola to eggs mornay and beans on toast. See also 494/
CASUAL. From 9am weekdays, Sat/Sun from **10am**.

637 8/M26
ATMOS ✓ **Café Gandolfi** 64 Albion St · www.cafegandolfi.com · **0141 552 6813**
Breakfast here an institution in itself, in an atmospheric room with daylight
filtering through stained glass, and comforting, oversized wooden furniture. See
also 605/TEAROOMS. All breakfast variants are here, including eggs Florentine,
Benedict or 'Hebridean'. With the chat, the coffee and the papers, what better start
to a lazy Sunday? From **8am** (**9am** Sun).

638 8/M25 ✓ **Sonny & Vito's** 52 Park Rd · 0141 357 0640 Much-loved West End brunch rendezvous. A deli-caff with home baking: scones, muffins, Mediterranean platefuls. Outside tables; takeaway. See 608/TEAROOMS. From **9am** (**10am** Sun).

639 8/M26 ✓ **Coia's Café** 473 Duke St They've been doing breakfast here for over 85 years. Goes like a fair and still damned good. The full-fry monty lasts all day (vegetarian too). The East End choice. From **10am**. Report: 620/CAFÉS.

640 8/L25 ✓ **Epicures of Hyndland** 157 Hyndland Rd · www.epicuresofhyndland.co. uk · 0141 334 3599 This definitive West End coffee house and more is perfect for a buzzing brunch any day. On Sundays you may need to wait to join this congregation. From **9am** (brunch till noon Mon-Sat, 3pm Sun). Report: 492/ CASUAL.

641 8/M26 ✓ **Wilson Street Pantry** 6 Wilson St · www.wilsonstreetpantry.com · 0141 552 0606 Merchant City brunch central. From 8am, Sun **9am**. Report: 619/CAFÉS.

642 8/M25 ✓ **William Café** 94 Queen Margaret Dr · www.william.cafe · 07968 857161 Cosy North Kelvinside café. Homespun and many folks' favourite Glasgow caff. Report: 618/CAFÉS.

The Best Bakeries & Takeaways

643 8/M25 ✓✓ **Cottonrake Bakery** 497 Great Western Rd · www.cottonrake.com · 07910 282040 Stefan Spicknell's superlative bakery ('the donut repair shop') brings proper patisserie and top takeaway tarts, real croissants and the sausage roll extraordinaire to Glasgow's West End. He was the first to light the oven. The crusty baguette sandwich! You better be quick! 7 days.

644 8/L25 ✓✓ **The Bakery by Zique** 76 Lauderdale Gdns, Hyndland · http:// byzique.com · 0141 339 6824 The bakehouse that supplies Mhairi Taylor's Zique brand – Cafezique 487/CASUAL. Open as a neighbourhood bakery; some indoor and outdoor seating. Great bread, of course, but also scrumptious cakes, pastries and savouries à la mode. And the scones! Go brunch. 7 days.

645 8/M26 ✓✓ **Social Bite** 103 St Vincent St & 5 Bothwell St · http://social-bite. co.uk Both in midtown near Central Station, the Glasgow outlets of the Edinburgh social project to involve, help and support the homeless. Soup, salad, sandwiches all not for profit, all to sustain us. Mon-Fri 7am-3pm.

646 8/L26 ✓ **Cherry and Heather** 7 North Gower St, Cessnock · www. cherryandheather.co.uk · 0141 427 0272 Just off Paisley Rd West, next to Bellahouston Post Office. A perfect wee takeaway, with food of (Asian) integrity and a great range of soups, casseroles in winter and truly gourmet sandwiches in unusual combos. A few stools. Cherry is for Japan (where the cook comes from) and Heather is for Scotland, where she and her Indonesian partner, Iwan, have settled; a happy combination. Dear Green coffee. Closed Sat/Sun.

647 8/M26 ✓ **Wild Flours Bakery** 526 Kilmarnock Rd · www.wildflours.co.uk · 0141 811 0441 Way down the Kilmarnock Rd, set back a little (with terrace in summer) Calum Bryce (and his mum's) bakery and takeaway. You'd never know it was all gluten free. Soup, toasties and their selection of trad and on trend cakes.

They supply many places in town – Glad Café, Bier Halle – with **gluten-free** options. 'Beignet' brunch on Sundays. Closed Mon/Tue.

648 8/M25 & 8/M26 ✓ **Roots & Fruits** 451-457 Great Western Rd · 0141 339 3077 & 1137 Argyle St · 0141 229 0838 · www.rootsfruitsandflowers.com In Great Western Rd, a row of wholefood shops near Kelvinbridge, famously where to go for fruit & veg in the West End (and a lovely flower shop). A traiteur section, with some seats, but the delicious home-made food (paellas, tortillas, salads) and bakery is mainly to take home. Argyle St is mainly a deli. Opening hours vary.

649 8/M26 ✓ **Riverhill** 24 Gordon St · 0141 204 4762 One of the best fuel stops in midtown (near Central Station). Narrow room, with queue often out the door. Home-made food to go, including their pies. 7 days.

650 8/M26 ✓ **Piece** 1056 Argyle St · www.pieceglasgow.com · 0141 221 7975 Neat and nifty, hard-working sandwich bar that started here and has proliferated piece by piece. Bespoke fillings (all better than most), daily soup and rather good tartes. More Pieces in Waterloo St, Miller St, W Regent St, Albion St and Dawson Rd. All good to go. 8am-5pm (some branches close earlier).

651 8/L26 **My Home Bakery** 59 Hyndland St Corner-shop counter, and bakery in the back where two real baker guys turn out the daily rolls, bread and big range of savoury (4 kinds of big sausage rolls) and big cakes. Some stools. The goodies do get snaffled up and they are made daily, so less choice later on. Closed Mon.

652 8/L25 **The Kitchen Window** 187 Hyndland Rd · 0141 339 3303 Small but brilliant. Minerva Harkins' baking skills in evidence. Soups, salads and other irresistibles. Closed Sun/Mon.

653 8/M26 **A'Challtainn Bakery** 54 Calton Entry · www.achalltainn.com · 0141 237 9220 Opening at TGP as part of the restaurant and venue hub and, as with all things A'Challtainn, it will be an asset and destination for the East End.

Unique Glasgow Pubs

654 8/M25
ATMOS
✓✓ **Òran Mór** 731 Great Western Rd · www.oran-mor.co.uk ·
0141 357 6200 This is the epitome of all the things you can do with a
pub; you could spend your (Glasgow) life here. A hugely popular emporium of drink
and divertissements in a converted church on a prominent West End corner, the
always evolving vision of Colin Beattie. Drinking on all levels (and outside) but also
decent pub food and separate brasserie, the only bit that seems less to set the
heather alight. Big entertainment programme from DJs to comedy in the club, and
is home of the brilliant 'A Play, a Pie and a Pint'. From lunch till very late, this is a
hostelry of happiness and hope. 7 days till midnight (club later). This encomium
unchanged, coz it hasn't.

655 8/M26
ATMOS
✓✓ **The Horseshoe** 17-19 Drury St · www.thehorseshoebarglasgow.
co.uk · 0141 248 6368 A mighty pub since the 19th century in a small
street between W Nile and Renfield Sts near Central Station. Early example of this
style of pub dubbed 'gin palaces'. Island rather than horseshoe bar ('longest in the
UK'), impressive range of alcohols and an upstairs lounge where they serve lunch
and dinner and karaoke till midnight (no, really!). Food is amazing value (535/
SCOTTISH). All kinds of folk. Daily till midnight up and down.

656 8/M26
ATMOS
✓✓ **Scotia Bar** 112 Stockwell St · www.scotiabar.net · 0141 552 8681
Probably Scotland's oldest continuously running pub – established 1792.
Tudor-style with a low, beamed ceiling and intimate, woody snugs. Long the haunt
of folk musicians, writers and raconteurs. Music and poetry sessions, folk and blues
Thu-Sun. A must-visit for true pub lovers though it will never be the same now the
smoke and mirrors have gone. Great photo record.

657 8/M26
✓✓ **The Pot Still** 154 Hope St · www.thepotstill.co.uk · 0141 333 0980
Pub of legend, mainly their whisky collection (750 and counting) on every
shelf and ledge, nook and cranny. For 35 years a mecca for the buffs and the
dram-atists. Snacks and pies till 5pm; the lovely, dark whisky womb till midnight.

658 8/M26
✓ **The Clutha & Victoria Bar** 167-169 Stockwell St · 0141 552 7400 Corner
with Broomielaw opposite bridge to the Gorbals. These historic riverside pubs
merged after the tragic helicopter crash in November 2013. Reopened (though
memorial part will remain closed) by owner Alan Crossan in 2015. A pub of
memories but great live music 7 nights in the 'beer garden' (Alex Harvey looks on)
and very good pizzas.

659 8/M26
✓ **The Winged Ox @ St Luke's** 17 Bain St · www.stlukesglasgow.com ·
0141 552 8378 Round the corner from the Barrowlands, heart of an emerging
East End quarter. In an impressively no-expense-spared conversion of Glasgow's
third oldest church (1836), a bar/restaurant and venue for all kinds of gigs,
receptions, launches and weddings. Michael and Tony Woods took a bold step East.
Music, food and drink for the soul (of Glasgow).

660 8/M26
✓ **Corinthian** 191 Ingram St · www.thecorinthianclub.co.uk · 0141 552 1101
Mega makeover of impressive listed building to form a restaurant and comfy
lounges/bar, The Gaming Room casino and a nightclub downstairs, all in glorious
surroundings. Awesome ceiling in main room – Tellers Brasserie. The flagship unit
of the mighty (Glasgow-based) G1 Group, this in both senses mirrors Glasgow
perfectly (see me!). More or less all of the day and all of the night.

661 8/M26 ✓ **Gin 71** 71 Renfield St · www.gin71.com · 0141 353 2959 Glasgow's first specialist gin lounge in the spectacularly appropriate surroundings of the marbled and lofty former Bank of India building, presided over by the young Queen Victoria. During the day it's **Cup Tea Lounge** (611/TEAROOMS) and from 5pm it's a gin lover's sample room – they have 71 (changing varieties) arranged by origin and flavour. Who'd have thought gin would make this impact? 7 days.

662 8/M26 **The Saracen Head (aka the 'Sarry Heid')** 209 Gallowgate · www.
ATMOS saracenhead.com · 0141 552 1660 Close to Barrowland. If ever the word 'legendary' could be legitimately used for a pub this might be it! At one time across the road, the SH dates from 1755. Often said to be haunted, it's home to the skull of the last witch to be executed in Scotland. It's featured in films (most recently in *The Legend of Barney Thomson*, directed by and starring Robert Carlyle, his homage to the East End of Glasgow, where he grew up). But it's whenever Celtic play at home that it comes into its own (sea of green); you're better to be with them than against! Low on gentrification, high on Glasgow! Craft beers, naw!

663 8/M26 **The Baby Grand** 3 Elmbank Gardens · www.babygrandglasgow.com · 0141 248 4942 By Charing Cross station in the shadow of a high-rise Premier Inn. One of the first and fully conceived operations of serial restaurateur Billy McAneney. Piano player, food, a new brunchy extension and a window at the back looking over the motorway to the august Mitchell Library. This bar could only be Glasgow. Sun-Wed till midnight, Thu-Sat till 1am.

664 8/M26 **Vroni's** 47 West Nile St · www.vronis.co.uk · 0141 221 4677 One of Glasgow's first wine bars (since 1995) – even today there are very few (compared with Edinburgh) – but dark and welcoming from the days when wine bars were where we went after work. A great list, champagne and other fizz and 8 wines by the glass. Interesting 'small plates' to snack and graze. Food daytime only. From men in suits to ladies sipping Sancerre.

665 8/L26 **The Lismore** 206 Dumbarton Rd · 0141 576 0102 Named after the long island
ATMOS off Oban. Great neighbourhood (Partick) bar that welcomes all sorts. There's just something about this place – from the stained glass to the floor and walls – that's good to be in. Good atmos, succour and malts. Often live (trad and jazz) music.

666 8/M26 **Ben Nevis** 1147 Argyle St · 0141 576 5204 Owned by the same people as Lismore and Òran Mór (above) but run by others. A great look and feel to this bar in contemporary but not faux-Scottish style. Small and pubby, the Glasgow beers (WEST, Drygate) and great malt list. A calm and civilised corner of the West End. 'Killie pies' (from Kilmarnock daily). And a lot of whisky to choose from.

The Best Real-Ale & Craft-Beer Pubs

667 8/M26 ✓ **Bon Accord** 153 North St · 0141 248 4427 Since 1971 on the road above the motorway near the Mitchell Library. One of the first real-ale pubs in Glasgow. Good selection of malts and up to 12 beers; always Deuchars IPA plus many guest ales on hand pump. Food from 11am till 7.45pm (LO). Light, civilised atmos but they do take their ale to heart. Quiz night on Wed; live band on Sat.

668 8/M26 ✓ **WEST on the Green** 4 Binnie Pl, Templeton Building, Glasgow Green ·
DF www.westonthegreen.com · 0141 550 0135 First find the **People's Palace** (678/ATTRACTIONS) then gaze at the fabulous exterior of the Templeton edifice, where on the bottom corner, the UK's first German brewery brews its award-winning beers (4 ingredients only: water, malt, hops and yeast). 8 in total in a beerhall setting and garden overlooking the Green. St Mungo for starters and a massive selection of imports. 'Simple, hearty' food with a German slant till 9pm. Decent wine list. WEST beers are found in many other craft-beer pubs.

669 8/M26 ✓ **Brewdog** 1397 Argyle St · www.brewdog.com · 0141 334 7175 Opposite Kelvingrove Art Gallery & Museum in a prominent corner site. The Glasgow Brewdog of the fast proliferating pack unleashed on a sober public in 2007 from Fraserburgh, the flag-bearers of the craft-beer revolution. All their cute and trashily named beers present, including their not-so-strong ones. Food, games, music. Martin and James have their hands on the pump. 7 days till midnight.
The Doghouse Corner of Hutcheson and Garth Sts in the Merchant City, a Brewdog with a focus on food, self-service select, BBQ/smoked meats. Interesting but methinks the beer is best. Draughts here from 0.5% to 9.2%, including their signature Punk IPA. And there's a bottleshop.

670 8/M26 ✓ **Republic Bier Halle** 9 Gordon St · www.republicbierhalle.com ·
0141 204 0706 Street between Buchanan St and Central Station, a basement and summer street terrace for about half a block. One of the first with a long (very long) beer list: 92 when I last looked (12 on draught), listed by country. Good pizzas 523/PIZZA till 10pm. 7 days noon-midnight.

671 8/M26 ✓ **The State Bar** 148-148A Holland St · www.comedyatthestate.co.uk ·
ATMOS 0141 332 2159 Off west end of Sauchiehall St. Uncompromising, old-style pub, all wood and old pictures. 7 guest ales. No fancy extras. Will probably outlive the many makeovers around here. Food at lunchtime. Some music and stand-up.

672 8/M25 **Inn Deep** 445 Great Western Rd · www.inndeep.com · 0141 357 1075 A
DF destination Kelvinbridge bar for two reasons: its location and terrace/balcony overlooking the Kelvin (you enter on Gt Western Rd and go down deep); and its eclectic, extensive collection of craft beers (70+), a bank of taps and 25 on draught. It's a very Glasgow hangout. Some pub grub. Noon-midnight (1am at weekends).

673 8/M26 **Babbity Bowster** 16-18 Blackfriars St · www.babbitybowster.com ·
0141 552 5055 In a pedestrianised part of the Merchant City and just off the High St, a now classic Glasgow pub/restaurant/hotel (462/UNIQUE HOTELS); but the pub comes first. Caledonian, Deuchars IPA and well-chosen guests. Many malts and cask cider. Food all day (533/SCOTTISH), occasional music, and outside.

✓ ✓ **Drygate** Mega microbrewery with own bottle shop, bar/café. Bottled beers from next door and all over, and draught. 2 ticks for the beers, for which it is a mecca and a mover in the craft-ale tsunami. Less pre-eminent for food but main report 506/FOOD PUBS.

The Main Attractions

674 8/L26 ✓ ✓ ✓ **Riverside Museum** 100 Pointhouse Rd, by Clydeside Expressway · www.glasgowlife.org.uk · 0141 287 2720 Across the Clyde from Govan, Glasgow's most recent big attraction, the Zaha Hadid-designed Museum of Transport and Travel. Entirely at home here, with the 'Tall Ship' berthed beside it. 3,000 objects, from trains and trams to paddle steamers and prams, are skilfully and imaginatively arranged and displayed in the big, battleship-grey wavy shed, with the New Glasgow and Glasgow Harbour emerging in the distance and getting closer. Given Scotland's and in particular Glasgow's pre-eminence in the invention and manufacture of so many forms of transport, it's heartening that this museum is such an impressive showcase. Like much of its contents, it's world class! Not just for boys! 7 days.

675 8/M26 ✓ ✓ **Kelvingrove Art Gallery & Museum** Argyle St · www.glasgowlife.
ATMOS org.uk · 0141 276 9599 Huge Victorian sandstone edifice with awesome atrium. On the ground floor is a natural history/Scottish history museum. The upper salons contain the city's superb British and European art collection. Temporary exhibition space (admission fee) downstairs. A prodigious success, with literally millions of visitors since it reopened '06 after major refurb. Endless interest and people-friendly presentations. Dali's *Christ of St John on the Cross* is a focal point. Excellent online and digital pre- and post-visit extras. See the world from a Glasgow point of view! (You go through 'Glasgow Stories' to get to 'Ancient Egypt'). And it's free! 7 days.

676 8/L26 ✓ ✓ **The Burrell Collection** 2060 Pollokshaws Rd · www.glasgowlife.
org.uk · 0141 287 2550 S of the river via A77 Kilmarnock Rd (over Jamaica St Bridge from the city centre), or M77, well signed. Set in rural parkland, this award-winning modern gallery was built to house the eclectic acquisitions of Sir William Burrell. It is expected to reopen in all its finery after a major refurb in 2020. **Pollok House/Park** www.nts.org.uk · 0141 616 6410 (with works by Goya, El Greco, William Blake) is worth a detour. Since 2018 the top floor is a new interesting temporary exhibition gallery and it has, below stairs, the better tearooms (Edwardian Kitchen). Gardens to the river. 10am-5pm. See also 693/WALKS.

677 8/M26 ✓ **Glasgow Cathedral** www.historicenvironment.scot · 0141 552 8198 & **Provand's Lordship** www.glasgowlife.org.uk · 0141 276 1625 Both on **Castle St** Across the road from one another, they represent what remains of the oldest part of the city, which (as can be seen in the People's Palace below) was, as late as the early 18th century, merely a ribbon of streets from here to the river. The present cathedral, though established by St Mungo in AD 543, dates from the 12th century and is a fine example of very real, if gloomy, Gothic. The house, built in 1471, is a museum which strives to convey a sense of late medieval life. Don't get run over when you re-emerge into the 21st century and try to cross the street. In the background, the **Necropolis** (1928/GRAVEYARDS) piled on the hill invites inspection and offers a viewpoint and the full Gothic perspective (maybe don't go alone). Part of a precinct, it's easy to do these and **St Mungo's Museum** (below) together; allow half a day. **Vintage at Drygate** nearby for food and drink for the soul (506/FOOD PUBS). Cathedral 7 days; Provand's Lordship Tue-Sun.

678 8/M26
ATMOS

✓ **The People's Palace** Glasgow Green · www.glasgowlife.org.uk ·
0141 276 0788 Approach via Glasgow Cross and London Rd, then turn right
into Glasgow Green. This has long been a folk museum *par excellence* wherein,
since 1898, the history, folklore and artefacts of a proud and working-class city
have been gathered, cherished and displayed. But this is much more than a mere
museum; it is part of the heart and soul of the city and, together with the Winter
Gardens adjacent, shouldn't be missed if you want to know what Glasgow's about
(especially 'The Steamie' on the first floor and the 'Single End' on the top). At TGP
the Winter Gardens were closed for repairs. Check website.

679 8/M26
ADMISSION

✓ **Glasgow Science Centre** 50 Pacific Quay · www.glasgowsciencecentre.
org · 0141 420 5000 On south side of the Clyde by the BBC and opposite the
SEC. Built with Millennium dosh. Approach via the Clyde Arc ('Squinty') Bridge or
walk from SEC complex by Bell's Bridge. Impressive, titanium-clad mall, IMAX
cinema and 127m-high tower. 4 floors of interactive exhibitions, planetarium and
theatre. Separate tickets or combos. Book slot for the on-again, off-again tower
(closed on windy days). 7 days 10am-5pm. Check website for winter opening hours.

680 8/M26

St Mungo Museum of Religious Life & Art 2 Castle St · www.glasgowlife.
org.uk · 0141 276 1625 Part of the lovely, perhaps not-cherished-enough
cathedral precinct (see above), this houses art and artefacts representing the
world's 6 major religions arranged tactfully in an attractive stone building with a
Zen garden in the courtyard. 3 floors, 4 exhibition areas. The assemblage seems
like a good and worthwhile vision in a time and place where sectarianism can still
be an issue and a problem. Telling and informative displays. Closed Mon.

681 8/M26

Hunterian Museum & Art Gallery University Avenue · www.gla.ac.uk/
hunterian · 0141 330 4221 On one side of the street, Scotland's oldest public
museum with geological, archaeological and social history displayed in a venerable
building. The **University Chapel** and cloisters are an immersive experience. Across
the street, a modern block holds part of Glasgow's exceptional civic collection:
Rembrandt to the Colourists and the Glasgow Boys, as well as one of the most
complete collections of any artist's work and personal effects to be found anywhere,
viz. that of Whistler. Fascinating stuff, even if you're not a fan. There's also a print
gallery and superb **Mackintosh House** (718/MACKINTOSH). Closed Mon.

The Other Attractions

682 8/M25

✓✓ **Botanic Gardens & Kibble Palace** 730 Great Western Rd · www.
glasgowbotanicgardens.com · 0141 276 1614 Smallish park close to
River Kelvin with riverside walks (691/WALKS), and pretty much the 'Dear Green
Place'. Kibble Palace (built 1873; renovation 2006, reassessment 2018) is the
distinctive domed glasshouse, with statues set among lush ferns and shrubbery
from around the (mostly temperate) world. Carnivorous Plant House especially
popular. Main range arranged through smell and colour and seasonality. A
wonderful place to muse and wander. Heritage Trail. Tearoom with outside tables.
Gardens open from 7am till dusk. Check website for Palace opening times.

683 8/M26 ✓✓ **Gallery of Modern Art** Royal Exchange Sq · www.glasgowlife.org.
uk · 0141 287 3050 Central, accessible and housed in former Stirling's Library, Glasgow's big visual arts attraction opened in a hail of art-world bickering in 1996, though it now more reflects Glasgow's eminence as a provenance of cutting-edge or conceptual work (all those Turner Prize nominees and winners? – the 'Glasgow Miracle'). It should be on your Glasgow hit list. 7 days, late opening Thu.

684 8/M26 ✓ **The Barras** Gallowgate The sprawling street and indoor market area around the Gallowgate. Over 20 years ago when I first wrote this book, the Barras was pure dead brilliant, a real slab of Glasgow life, and across the street the legendary **Sarry Heid** (662/UNIQUE PUBS). Its glory days are over but, as with all great markets, it's full of character and characters and it's still just about possible to find bargains, if not collectables. Everything from clairvoyants to the latest scam. Now part of a major cultural regeneration area, with **A'Challtainn** 582/SEAFOOD at its centre. Sat/Sun 10am-5pm.

685 8/M26
ADMISSION
NTS

The Tenement House 145 Buccleuch St · www.nts.org.uk · 0141 333 0183 Near Charing Cross but can approach from near the end of Sauchiehall St and over the hill. Typical 'respectable' Glasgow tenement, kept under a bell jar since 'Our Agnes' moved out in 1965. She had lived there with her mother since 1911 and wasn't one for new-fangled things. It's a touch claustrophobic when busy and is distinctly voyeuristic, but, well... your house would be interesting, too, in 50 years if the clock were stopped. Reception on ground floor. **Singl-End** 614/CAFÉS nearby for superb sustenance. 7 days.

686 8/M26
ADMISSION

Sharmanka Kinetic Theatre 103 Trongate · www.sharmanka.com · 0141 552 7080 A small and intimate experience like most others on this page, but a fascinating one. The gallery/theatre of Russian émigré Eduard Bersudsky shows his meticulous and amazing mechanical sculptures. Short performance (40 mins) Wed-Sun. Full performances Thu/Sun. Unique!

687 8/L26
ADMISSION
NTS

Greenbank Garden Flenders Rd, Clarkston · www.nts.org.uk · 0141 616 5126 10km SW of centre via Kilmarnock Rd, Eastwood Toll, Clarkston Toll and Mearns Rd, then signposted (3km). A spacious oasis in the suburbs; formal gardens and 'working' walled garden, parterre and woodland walks around elegant Georgian house. Very Scottish. Gardens open AYR 9.30am-dusk; shop/tearoom. Closed Jan/Feb. Number 4 bus from Union St by Central Station takes you here directly.

688 8/M26 **City Chambers** George Sq · www.glasgow.gov.uk · 0141 287 4018 The hugely impressive building along the whole east side of Glasgow's municipal central square. This is a wonderfully evocative monument of the days when Glasgow was the Second City of the Empire. Guided tours Mon-Fri, 10.30am and 2.30pm (subject to availability).

689 7/L25
ADMISSION
⌨

Finlaystone Country Estate Langbank · www.finlaystone.co.uk · 01475 540505 Signed off the dual carriageway just before Port Glasgow. Delightful gardens and woods around mansion house, with many pottering places and longer trails (and ranger service). Estate open AYR 10am-5pm. Visitor centre and the Finlaystone tearoom. Spectacular bluebells and voluptuous peonies in May, colour therapy in autumn. Visitor Centre & shop 11am-5pm (till 4pm Oct-Mar). Tearoom 10am-5pm weekends and during school holidays.

690 8/M26 **The Waverley** www.waverleyexcursions.co.uk · 0845 130 4647 'The World's
ADMISSION Last Seagoing Paddle Steamer' which plied the Clyde in the glorious 'Doon the
Watter' days had a £7-million lottery-funded refit. Definitely the way to see the
West Coast. Sailings from Glasgow's Science Centre to Rothesay, Kyles of Bute,
Arran. Other days, leaves from Ayr or Greenock, many destinations. Call for
complex timetable of late June to August. Bar, restaurants, live bands: it's a party!

Paisley Abbey Reports: 707/VIEWS; 1922/ABBEYS.

The Lighthouse Report: 720/MACKINTOSH.

The Best Walks In The City

See p.12 for walk codes.

691 8/M26
2-13+KM
XCIRC
BIKES
1-A-1

Kelvin Walkway A path along the banks of Glasgow's other river, the Kelvin, which enters the Clyde unobtrusively at Yorkhill, but first meanders through some of the most interesting parts and parks of the NW city. Walk starts at Kelvingrove Park through the university and Hillhead district under Kelvin Bridge and on to the celebrated **Botanic Gardens** (682/ATTRACTIONS). The trail then goes N, under the Forth & Clyde Canal (see below) to the Arcadian fields of Dawsholm Park (5km), Killermont (posh golf course) and Kirkintilloch (13km from start). Since the river and the canal shadow each other for much of their routes, it's possible, with a map, to go out by one waterway and return by the other (e.g. start at Great Western Rd, return Maryhill Rd).
START Usual start at the Eildon St (off Woodlands Rd) gate of Kelvingrove Park or Kelvin Bridge. Street parking only.

692 8
ANY KM
XCIRC
BIKES
1-A-1

Forth & Clyde Canal Towpath www.scottishcanals.co.uk The canal, opened in 1790, reopened 2002 as the Millennium Link. Once a major short-cut for fishing boats and trade between Europe and America, it provides a fascinating look round the back of the city from a pathway that stretches on a spur from Port Dundas just N of the M8 to the main canal at the end of Lochburn Rd off Maryhill Rd, and then E all the way to Kirkintilloch and Falkirk (**Falkirk Wheel** 01324 619888 5/ATTRACTIONS), and W through Maryhill and Drumchapel to Bowling and the Clyde (60km). A good option is to go as far as Croy and take the very regular train service back. Much of the route is through the forsaken or redeveloped industrial heart of the city, past waste ground, warehouses and high flats, but there are open stretches and curious corners and, by Bishopbriggs, it's a rural waterway. More info from Scottish Canals (0141 332 6936).
START (1) Top of Firhill Rd (great view of city from **Ruchill Park**, 100m further on 704/VIEWS). (2) Lochburn Rd (see above) at the confluence from which to go E or W to the Clyde. (3) Top of Crow Rd, Anniesland where there is a canalside pub, Lock 27, with tables outside, real ale and food (noon-evening). (4) Bishopbriggs Sports Centre, Balmuildy Rd. From here it is 6km to Maryhill and 1km in other direction to the country churchyard of Cadder or 3km to Kirkintilloch. All starts have some parking.

693 8/L26

Pollok Country Park www.glasgow.gov.uk · 0141 276 0924 The park that (apart from the area around the gallery and the house 676/ATTRACTIONS) most feels like a real country park. Numerous trails through woods and meadows. The leisurely guided walks with the park rangers can be educative and more fun than you would think (0141 276 0924 for details). The **Burrell Collection** and **Pollok House & Gardens** are obvious highlights. The Edwardian Kitchen tearoom, in the basement of the latter, serves an excellent range of hot home-made dishes, as well as the usual cakes and tea things. 7 days 10am-5pm. Enter by Haggs Rd or by Haggs Castle Golf Course. Well signed for cars, including from Pollokshaws Rd and then to car park by the Burrell or the House.

694 8/L25
5-20KM
CAN BE CIRC
BIKES
1-A-2

Mugdock Country Park **Craigallian Rd, near Milngavie** · www.mugdock-country-park.org.uk · 0141 956 6100 Not technically within the city, but one of the nearest and easiest escapes. Park, which includes Mugdock Woods (an SSSI) and a castle, is NW of Milngavie. Regular train from Queen St Station takes 20 mins, then follow route of the West Highland Way for 4km across Drumclog Moor to S edge of the park. By car to Milngavie by A81, park is 5km N. Well signed.

5 car parks – the main one includes Craigend Visitor Centre, Stables Tearoom, craft gallery and theatre, garden centre and farm shop. Many trails marked out, including the nearby reservoirs. It is a godsend between Glasgow and the Highland hills.

Cathkin Braes S edge of city with views. Report: 702/VIEWS.

Easy Walks Outside The City

See p.12 for walk codes.

695 8/M25
10+KM
CAN BE CIRC
MT BIKES
2-B-2

Campsie Fells nr Glasgow 25km N of city best reached via Kirkintilloch or Cumbernauld/Kilsyth. Encompasses area that includes the Kilsyth Hills and Fintry Hills, and the Carron Valley between. **START** (1) Good approach from A803, Kilsyth main street up the Tak-me-Doon (sic) road. Park by golf club and follow path by the burn. It's possible to take in the two hills to left, as well as Tomtain (453m), the most easterly of the tops, in a good afternoon; views to the E. (2) Car park on the S side of the B818 to Fintry, at the W end of the Carron Valley reservoir, opposite the access road to Todholes Farm and the wind farm. Follow tracks along reservoir to ascend Meikle Bin (570m) to the right. (3) The bonnie village of Fintry is a good start/base for the Fintry Hills and Earl's Seat (578m). (4) Campsie Glen – a sliver of glen in the hills. Approach via Clachan of Campsie on A81 (**Campsie Glen Tea Room** 01360 313049 for food stop) or from viewpoint high on the hill on B822 from Lennoxtown to Fintry; the easy Campsie introduction.

696 8/L26
2-10KM
CAN BE CIRC
MT BIKES
1-A-2

Gleniffer Braes Paisley · www.renfrewshire.gov.uk Ridge to the S of Paisley (15km from Glasgow) has been a favourite walking-place for centuries. M8 or Paisley Rd West to town centre then S via B774/B775 (Causeyside St then Neilston Rd) and sharp right after 3km to Glenfield Rd. Park/start at Robertson Park (signed). Here there are superb views and walks marked to E and W. 500m along Glenfield Rd is a car park/ranger centre (0141 884 3794). Walk up through gardens and formal parkland and then W along marked paths and trails.

697 7/K25
15/16KM
CIRC
MT BIKES
1-B-2

Greenock Cut www.clydemuirshiel.co.uk 45km W of Glasgow. Can approach via Port Glasgow but simplest route is from A78 road to Largs. Travelling S from Greenock take first left after IBM, brown-signed Loch Thom. Lochside 5km up winding road. Park at Greenock Cut Centre (01475 521458). Walk left along lochside road to Overton (5km) then path is signed. The Cut – an aqueduct built in 1827 to supply water to Greenock and its 31 mills – is now a historic monument. Great views from the mast along the Cut, though it is a detour. Another route to the right from the centre leads through a glen of birch, rowan and oak to the Kelly Cut. Both trails described on board at the car park.

698 7/L26

Clyde Muirshiel www.clydemuirshiel.co.uk General name for vast area of Inverclyde W of city, including Greenock Cut (see above), Lochwinnoch, Castle Semple Country Park and Lunderston Bay, a stretch of coastline near the Cloch Lighthouse, S of Gourock on the A770, for littoral amblings. Best wildish bit is around Muirshiel Centre itself, Muirshiel Country Park (01505 842803), with trails, a waterfall and Windy Hill (350m). Nothing arduous, but a breath of air. The hen harrier hunts here. From M8 junction 29, take A737 Lochwinnoch, then B786 to top of Calder Glen Rd. Follow brown signs.

699 8/L25 **Dumgoyne** nr Blanefield Close to Glasgow and almost a mountain, so a popular
2-A-2 non-strenuous hike. Huge presence, sits above A81 and Glengoyne Distillery (open
to public). Approach from Strathblane War Memorial via Campsie Dene Road.
7km track, allow 3-4 hours (or take the steep way up from the distillery). Refresh/
replenish in Killearn (1341/FOOD PUBS) or **The Beech Tree Inn** in Dumgoyne, with
family menu and play area for kids.

700 8/L25 **The Whangie** On A809 N from Bearsden, about 8km after last roundabout and
5KM 2km after the Carbeth Inn, is the car park for the **Queen's View** (703/VIEWS). Once
CIRC you get to the summit of Auchineden Hill, take the path that drops down to the
XBIKES west (a half right angle) and look for crags on your right. This is the 'back door' of
NO DOGS The Whangie. Carry on and you'll suddenly find yourself in a deep cleft in the rock
1-A-1 face with sheer walls rising over 10m on either side. The Whangie is more than
100m long and at one point the walls narrow to less than 1m. Local mythology has
it that The Whangie was made by the Devil, who lashed his tail in anticipation of
a witchy rendezvous somewhere in the north, and carved a slice through the rock,
where the path now goes.

701 8/M26 **Chatelherault** nr Hamilton · www.slleisureandculture.co.uk · 01698 426213
2-8KM Junction 6 off M74, well signposted into Hamilton, follow road into centre,
CIRC then bear left away from main road where it's signed for A723. The gates to the
BIKES 'château' are about 3km outside town. A drive leads to the William Adam-designed
1-A-2 hunting lodge of the Dukes of Hamilton, set amid ornamental gardens with a
notable parterre and extensive grounds. Tracks along the deep, wooded gorge of
the Avon (ruins of Cadzow Castle) lead to distant glades. Good walks and ranger
service (01698 426213). House open 10am-4.30pm 7 days (except when there's
events); walks at all times. Café, gift shop, visitor centre. The longest circular walk
from the visitor centre is about 8km.

The Best Views Of The City & Beyond

702 8/M26 **Cathkin Braes** The southern ridge of the city on the B759 from Carmunnock to
Cambuslang, about 12km from centre. Go S of river by Albert Bridge to Aikenhead
Rd which continues S as Carmunnock Rd. Follow to Carmunnock, a delightfully
rural village, and pick up the Cathkin Rd. 2km along on the right is the Cathkin
Braes Golf Club and 100m further on the left is the park. Marvellous views to N of
the Campsies, Kilpatrick Hills, Ben Lomond and as far as Ben Ledi. Walks on the
Braes on both sides of the road. Refresh in **Laura's** in Carmunnock (15 Busby Rd,
0141 644 5657).

703 8/L25 **Queen's View** Auchineden Not so much a view of the city, more a perspective
1-A-1 on Glasgow's Highland hinterland, this short walk and sweeping vista to the north
has been a Glaswegian pilgrimage for generations. On A809 N from Bearsden
about 8km after last roundabout and 2km after the old Carbeth Inn. Busy car
park attests to popularity. The walk, along a path cut into ridgeside, takes 40-50
mins to the cairn, from which you can see **The Cobbler** (1986/HILLS), that other
Glasgow favourite, Ben Ledi and sometimes as far as Ben Chonzie 50km away. The
fine views of Loch Lomond are what Queen Victoria came for. Further on is **The
Whangie** (700/WALKS).

704 8/M25   **Ruchill Park** **Firhill Rd** An unlikely but splendid panorama from this overlooked but well-kept park to the N of the city near Possilpark housing estate. Go to top of Firhill Rd (past Partick Thistle football ground) over **Forth & Clyde Canal** (692/ WALKS) off Garscube Rd where it becomes Maryhill Rd. Best view is from around the flagpole; the whole city among its surrounding hills, from the Campsies to Gleniffer and Cathkin Braes (see above), becomes clear.

705 8/M25   **Bar Hill** **Twechar, nr Kirkintilloch** 22km N of city, taking A803 Kirkintilloch
1-A-2   turn-off from M8, then the low road to Kilsyth, the B8023, bearing left at the black-and-white bridge. Next to the old Twechar Quarry Inn (closed), a path is signed for Barhill Fort and the Antonine Wall. Steepish climb for 2km; ignore the strange dome of grass. Over to left in copse of trees are the remains of one of the forts on the Roman wall which was built across Scotland in the 2nd century AD. Ground plan explained on a board. This is a special place with strong history vibes and airy views over the plain to the city which came a long time after.

706 8/N27   **Black Hill** **nr Lesmahagow** 28km S of city. Another marvellous outlook, but in the
1-A-2   opposite direction from above. Take junction 10/11 on M74, then off the B7078 signed Lanark, take the B7018. 4km along past Clarkston Farm, head uphill for 1km and park by Water Board mound. Walk uphill through fields to right for about 1km. Unprepossessing hill that unexpectedly reveals a vast vista of most of east-central Scotland.

707 8/L26   **Paisley Abbey** **Paisley** · **www.paisleyabbey.org.uk** · **0141 889 7654** M8 to Paisley; frequent trains from Central Station. Abbey Mon-Sat 10am-3.30pm. Every so often on Abbey 'open days', the tower of this amazing edifice can be climbed. The tower (restored 1926) is 50m high and from the top there's a grand view of the Clyde. This is a rare experience, but phone the tourist information centre (0141 889 0711) or abbey itself (mornings) for details; it could be your lucky day. Guided tours Tue & Thu. Regular events. Café. See also 1922/ABBEYS.

708 7/K25   **Lyle Hill** **Gourock** Via M8 W to Greenock, then round the coast to relatively genteel old resort of Gourock where the Free French worked in the yards during the war. A monument has been erected to their memory on the top of Lyle Hill above the town, from where you get one of the most dramatic views of the great crossroads of the Clyde (Holy Loch, Gare Loch and Loch Long). Best vantage point is further along the road on other side by trig point. Follow station signs, then Lyle Hill. There's another great view of the Clyde further down the water at **Haylie, Largs**, the hill 3km from town reached via the A760 road to Kilbirnie and Paisley. The Isle of Cumbrae lies in the sound and the sunset.

709 8/M26   **Top of the Lighthouse** **11 Mitchell Lane** · **www.thelighthouse.co.uk** · **0141 276 5365** Off Buchanan St. Viewing platform atop the six-floor Mackintosh and Design Centre, reached by 136 steps or lift for views across a great city. See also 720/MACKINTOSH.

Campsie Fells & Gleniffer Braes Reports: 695/696/WALKS.

The Best Independent Galleries

The Merchant City hub of contemporary arts, all with work for sale, in changing exhibitions. All closed Sun/Mon.

710 8/M26 ✓✓ **Glasgow Print Studio** Trongate 103 · www.glasgowprintstudio.co. uk · 0141 552 0704 Influential and accessible gallery in Glasgow's contemporary-art centre, with print work from many of Scotland's leading and rising artists.

711 8/M26 ✓✓ **Transmission Gallery** 18 King St · www.transmissiongallery.org · 0141 552 2540 Cutting-edge and often off-the-wall work from contemporary Scottish and international artists. Reflects Glasgow's importance as a hotspot of conceptual art. Stuff you might disagree with and stuff you'll love!

712 8/M26 ✓✓ **Street Level Photoworks** Trongate 103 · www. streetlevelphotoworks.org · 0141 552 2151 Provides 'encounters in photography'. Gallery production facility. Changing exhibitions of Scottish and international work, invariably of high quality and interest.

• •

713 8/M26 ✓✓ **The Modern Institute** 14-20 Osborne St · www. themoderninstitute.com · 0141 248 3711 The original gallery and exhibition space at 3 Aird's Lane nearby. Scotland's leading gallery/art space for commercial and conceptual contemporary art. International reputation for cutting-edge art ideas and occasional events. MI shows at London's pre-eminent, highly selective Frieze Art Fair. Closed Sun.

714 8/M26 ✓ **Mary Mary** 51 Oswald St · www.marymarygallery.co.uk · 0141 226 2257 Cool, always interesting gallery showing the kind of work that keeps Glasgow pre-eminent as a UK centre of edgy, contemporary work. Closed Mon.

715 8/M26 ✓ **Compass Gallery** 178 West Regent St · www.compassgallery.co.uk · 0141 221 6370 Glasgow's oldest established independent, contemporary art gallery. Their New Generation exhibition in Jul-Aug shows work from new graduates of the art colleges and has heralded many a career. Closed Sun. **Cyril Gerber Fine Art** www.gerberfineart.co.uk is at the same address but has a separate raison d'être: British 'contemporary' paintings, prints and sculpture (not living), and especially the Scottish Colourists and 'name' contemporaries. Gerber and the Compass were created by the late Cyril Gerber, who probably did more for young Scottish artists than anyone else; now run by his similarly informed and enthusiastic daughter Jill. They have summer and Christmas exhibitions with small, accessible work. Closed Sun.

The Mackintosh Trail

Architect and designer Charles Rennie Mackintosh (1868-1928) had an extraordinary influence, 150 years of it celebrated in 2018. www.crmsociety.com

716 8/M26 ✓✓✓ **Glasgow School of Art** 167 Renfrew St · www.gsa.ac.uk · 0141 353 4500 Mackintosh's supreme architectural triumph and one of Europe's favourite buildings as evinced by the response to the fires that engulfed it and decimated its priceless library in 2014 and again in 2018. The second conflagration especially was a tragedy for Glasgow, for Scotland and for art students, Sauchiehall St and the west city centre. The complementary 2014 Reid building by US architect Steven Holl, though also full of students, has a superb permanent exhibition of the workings and influence of the Art School, temporary exhibitions, and a great café-bar open to all. The future of one of the world's most revered working buildings and Mackintosh's triumph is uncertain at TGP.

717 8/M25 ✓✓ **Queen's Cross Church** 870 Garscube Rd · www.mackintoshchurch.
ADMISSION com · 0141 946 6600 Built 1896-99. Calm and simple, the antithesis of Victorian Gothic. If all churches had been built like this, we'd go more often. The HQ of the Charles Rennie Mackintosh Society which was founded in 1973.

718 8/M26 ✓✓ **The Mackintosh House** 82 Hillhead St, off University Avenue ·
ADMISSION www.gla.ac.uk/hunterian · 0141 330 4221 Opposite and part of the **Hunterian Museum & Art Gallery** (681/ATTRACTIONS) within the university campus. The master's house has been transplanted and methodically reconstructed from the next street (they say even the light is the same). If you've ever wondered what the fuss is about, go and see how innovative and complete an artist, designer and architect he was, in this inspiring yet habitable set of rooms. Last admission 4.15pm. Closed Mon. Maximum of 12 people at a time.

719 8/M26 ✓✓ **Scotland Street School Museum** 225 Scotland St · www.
ATMOS glasgowlife.org.uk · 0141 287 0500 Opposite Shields Rd underground station; best approach by car from Eglinton St (A77 Kilmarnock Rd over Jamaica St Bridge). Entire school (from 1906) preserved as museum of education through Victorian/Edwardian and war times. Original, exquisite Mackintosh features, especially tiling, and powerfully redolent of happy school days; a uniquely evocative time capsule. Café and temporary exhibitions. Closed Mon. Brilliant café **The Fish People** over the road (577/SEAFOOD).

720 8/M26 ✓✓ **The Lighthouse** 11 Mitchell Lane · www.thelighthouse.co.uk ·
ADMISSION 0141 276 5360 Glasgow's legacy from its year as UK City of Architecture & Design. Changing exhibitions in Mackintosh's 1893-95 building for *The Herald* newspaper. It houses, over 6 floors, a shop and books, a café-bar, an interpretation centre and exhibition space. Fantastic rooftop views 709/VIEWS.

721 7/K25 ✓✓ **The Hill House** Upper Colquhoun St, Helensburgh · www.nts.org.
ATMOS uk · 01436 673900 Take Sinclair St off Princes St (at Romanesque tower
ADMISSION and tourist information centre) and go 2km uphill, taking left into Kennedy Dr and
NTS follow signs. A complete house incorporating Mackintosh's typical total unity of design, built for publisher Walter Blackie in 1902-04. Much to marvel over and wish that everybody else would go away and you could stay for the night (in that fabulous bedroom). There's a library full of books (though not to touch).

722 8/M26 **The Willow Tearooms** 217 Sauchiehall St Original interior in a working tearoom, with retail shop next door. Report: 610/TEAROOMS.

the Best

of Regional Hotels & Restaurants

The Best Hotels & Restaurants In Argyll

723 7/J22
11 ROOMS +
COTTAGE
DF
£LOTS

Airds Hotel Port Appin · www.airds-hotel.com ·
01631 730236 32km N of Oban, 4km off A828. For a reassuringly long time, Airds has been one of the foremost hotels in the north and a legendary gourmet experience. Shaun and Jenny McKivragan, with great attention to the details of a comfortable experience lead a great team; Airds remains a 'civilised escape in a hectic world'. Contemporary-cosy might describe bedrooms and lounges. A lovely, light conservatory dining room; dinner is the culmination of a hard day on the croquet lawn or just gazing over the bay. Unobtrusive service and the creativity of chef Chris Stanley. Tasting menu and à la carte. 2 elegant suites: one with patio, one with balcony. Port Appin is one of Scotland's most charming places. The **Lismore** passenger ferry is 2km away (2242/ISLANDS). Then walk.

£££ **EAT** Has always been one of the best meals in the North, a destination in itself.

724 7/H24
20 ROOMS
DF
LL
£££

Crinan Hotel Crinan · www.crinanhotel.com · 01546 830261 8km off A816. On coast, 60km S of Oban (Lochgilphead 12km) at head of the Crinan Canal which joins Loch Fyne with the sea. The Ryan family's landmark hotel in a stunning setting and some of the best sea views in the UK. Rooms do vary. This hotel has long housed one of the great seafood restaurants. Nick Ryan, sailor and consummate patron passed away 2018, the hotel continuing under his wife, the notable artist Frances Macdonald. Pictures of these shorelines and those by son, Ross (who does boat trips in the classic *Sgarbh* motor boat 07766 277818), are hung around you and are for sale; the rooftop lounge regularly shows other curated pictures from significant Scottish artists and there's the piano famously first played by Dave Brubeck. The perfect sunset setting for your aperitif. Flowers, art, the ineffable boho chic.

£££ **EAT** Choice of Westward dining room, Lock 16 up top with 'the view' (Fri/Sat), or perfect pub grub in Seafood Bar.

725 7/J24
25 ROOMS
DF
ATMOS
££

George Hotel Inveraray · www.thegeorgehotel.co.uk ·
01499 302111 On the main street of a historic town on Loch Fyne with credible attractions both here (castle) and nearby, The George gets 2 ticks because this ancient inn (1770), still in the capable and friendly hands of the Clark family (since the 1860s), has fantastic atmos, especially in the bars. Rooms recherché in a Highland-chic kind of way. Downstairs open fire, great grub; all Scottish towns on the visitors' map should have a place like this. The First House adjacent (actually the first house in the town) has 8 (recently refurbished) of the 25 rooms, with some great loch views. Very much part of the local community, the main bar is surprisingly cosmopolitan: memories of Scotland are made of this!

££ **EAT** Gastropub grub in multi-chambered stone and wood setting and conservatory. Good ales, wines and staple/classic-led menu. Music Fri/Sat.

726 7/H26
5 ROOMS
DF
MAR-OCT
££

The Kilberry Inn nr Tarbert · www.kilberryinn.com ·
01880 770223 The small Knapdale roadside inn with the famously good food. Simple, stylish cottage-courtyard rooms. Beautiful drive out on B8024 off the Tarbert–Lochgilphead coast road. 2-tick gastropub food as good as it gets. Michelin agree. David out front, Clare in the kitchen. The very reasonable hotel deal includes dinner. Secret beaches nearby to wander. Opens every year on March 16th! Closed Mon. Report: 1206/INNS.

727 7/J25
16 ROOMS +
BY THE NIGHT
££

Portavadie Marina Portavadie · www.portavadie.com ·
01700 811075 Off the B8000. The surprisingly shiny sheltered marina that's popped up at the mouth of Loch Fyne opposite Tarbert, with a steel and glass restaurant and yachty complex with rooms and also in the separate 'Lodge' and cottages; leisure centre with Scotland's largest infinity pool and outdoor tubs – the

sunset! All with a yachty theme and clearly shipshape, the juxtaposition of wild Argyll all around is splendidly surreal. Brilliant beach nearby (1628/BEACHES) and walks in woods or coves, or go boating!

££ **EAT** A marina-side café-bar with mezzanine restaurant, a café-bar in the lodge and a pizza caff in the leisure centre. All-day dining.

728 7/H24 ✓ **Loch Melfort Hotel** Arduaine · www.lochmelfort.co.uk ·
30 ROOMS **01852 200233** 30km S of Oban on the beautiful road between Oban and
DF Campbeltown. Landmark hotel, which owners Calum and Rachel Ross take
FEB-DEC conscientious care of. You get the view of Loch Shuna from most rooms, including
££ all those in the extension that come with either balcony or patio, and 4 newly added rooms in the main mansion, which are pleasantly large; 2 suites. Same view dominates the dining room and **The Bistro** with pub-food menu (seafood specials). Hotel has the same access road as **Arduaine**, an extraordinary back garden in which to wander (1571/GARDENS).

729 7/H23 ✓ **The Manor House** Oban · www.manorhouseoban.com ·
11 ROOMS **01631 562087** On S coast road out of town towards Kerrera ferry, overlooking
££ bay where the big ferries come and go. Understated elegance in restored intimate Georgian lounge and dining room, the restaurant serving probably the most fine-dining dinner in town. Daily-changing menu. Bedrooms small but cosy; it is a civilised lodging. More delightful than deluxe. Nice bar.

730 7/H25 ✓ **The Anchor Hotel** Tarbert · www.lochfyne-scotland.co.uk ·
12 ROOMS **01880 820577** A fine wee town much favoured by messers-about-on-boats.
(4 AFLOAT) The Anchor is not only on the harbour, it is also in the harbour – 4 of the
NO PETS · L contemporary, well-appointed rooms are on a boat. Here you really do wake up at
££ sea level. You definitely feel at one with this town on the water.
££ **EAT** The Sea Bed Restaurant, the best bet in Tarbert. Its slant is seaward.

731 7/H23 ✓ **Glenburnie Hotel** Oban · www.glenburnie.co.uk · 01631 562089 In the
12 ROOMS middle of a broad sweep of hotels overlooking the bay, this is the most notable.
MAR-NOV Amiable Graeme Strachan's a natural innkeeper so everything in his seaside
££ mansion is welcoming and easy on the eye. Great detail: home-made muesli and fruit for breakfast; nice furnishings. No dinner but the best advice for where to go.

732 7/J24 ✓ **Brambles** Inveraray · www.inverarayhotel.com · 01499 302252 Main
12 ROOMS street of quiet Argyll epicentre, adding well-priced contemporary rooms above
££ the shops, including Stuart and Victoria Campbell's buzzy coffee shop/restaurant (1412/TEAROOMS), where you have breakfast. Some rooms (and 2 apartments) are opposite. All friendly and very Inveraray.

733 7/G28 ✓ **Machrihanish Dunes** nr Campbeltown · www.machrihanishdunes.com ·
22 ROOMS **01586 810000** Over the wide ocean across from America came a new golf
L course and resort adjacent to the time-honoured and Old Tom Morris-designed
££ Machrihanish; same dunes, same strand. Here we are talking about **The Ugadale Hotel** by the first tee of the Machrihanish Golf Club (the actual Dunes course is 5km away), with rooms, cottages and a spa. Part of the same group, the refurbished **Royal Hotel** in Campbeltown (23 rooms) is tops in town at the end of the road.

734 7/H21 ✓ **Kilcamb** nr Strontian · www.kilcamblodge.co.uk · 01967 402257 A
11 ROOMS country-house hotel just outside the hamlet of Strontian. A comfortable,
DF welcoming place and base from which to explore glorious Ardnamurchan and
££ Morvern. Good outlook with lawns to Loch Sunart, great woodland walking nearby (2067/WALKS). The brasserie restaurant is strong on seafood. It is calm!

735 7/J25
11 ROOMS
FEB-DEC
££

The Royal Hotel Tighnabruaich · www.theroyalanlochan.co.uk · 01700 811239 New owners 2018 finding feet in dreamy Tighnabruaich at TGP. Spacious rooms (and bathrooms), many looking over to Bute, comfy furnishings and a plethora of pictures in their 'Gallery'. Lots of public space and the lovely wee Shinty Bar with pics of decades of the team. Food in bar or conservatory. Time moves slowly in Tighnabruaich!

THE BEST RESTAURANTS IN ARGYLL

736 7/J24
££

✓✓ **Inver Restaurant** Strathlachlan, Loch Fyne · www.inverrestaurant. co.uk · 01369 860537 S of Strachur on scenic B8000, a cottage bar/restaurant overlooking loch and ruins of Castle Lachlan (nice 15-min walk along the shore). Rob Latimer and Pam Brunton (in the kitchen) transformed the old Inver Cottage and, well, ... eating out in Argyll. This truly is *the* destination restaurant in the region (if not the west). Food is foraged, found, grown and sourced locally and made into something simple; beautiful to look at and to eat. Bar (a cosy fire) menu or à la carte in the dining room. Many awards, all deserved. Pam has a hearty laugh. That pleasure is on the plate too. Inver also has 4 adjacent luxury **Bothies** – delightfully comfy. A scrumptious Scottish breakfast delivered to your door.

737 7/J25
££

✓ **Portavadie Marina** Portavadie · www.portavadie.com · 01700 811075 On the edge of Loch Fyne and the known world, the surprising super-yachty and all-round leisure complex with restaurant and accom options. Report: 727/ARGYLL.

738 7/K23
££

✓ **Loch Fyne Oysters** Clachan · www.lochfyne.com · 01499 600264 On the A83 near Arrochar, the one that started it all and still a fine place to stop for seafood and sustenance. Report: 1371/SEAFOOD.

739 7/J22
££

✓ **The Deck @ Isle of Eriska** Ledaig · www.eriska-hotel.co.uk · 01631 720371 Isle of Eriska Hotel has its notable fine-ish dining room but The Deck is the light and casual alternative café/restaurant in the spa overby. Possibly overlooked for a drop-in lunch or high tea but definitely a good option between Oban and Ballachulish. The spa has treatment rooms and a pool (ask to dip; well, I did!). The restaurant overlooks the golf course with a wide terrace/deck and has serene views over the greens to the loch. Familiar food done well; a pleasant detour. See also 1161/COUNTRY-HOUSE HOTELS.

740 7/J24
CLOSED JAN
££

✓ **Samphire** Inveraray · www.samphireseafood.com · 01499 302321 Andrew Maclugash came home to Inveraray, that most beguiling of Argyll towns, crafting his skills in some top kitchens to open this seafood restaurant in the main street that leads to Loch Fyne. An intimate bistro where ethical supply and simple presentation has proven to be a winning fishy formula – fennel-infused fish stew, chowder and fish pie. Closed Nov-Mar. Best book!

741 7/J25
££

✓ **Botanica** Tighnabruaich · www.botanicafood.co.uk · 01700 811186 The eat-well destination restaurant in this Kyles of Bute county, on the corner of Main St, with outside and sunny garden seating. Chef/proprietor Michal Pasiecznik and Leoma's perfectly pitched daily-changing menu of locally sourced and foraged produce and an impressive organic wine list. 4 sweet rooms upstairs (inexpensive). Make time for timeless Tighnabruaich! 8.30am-4pm (till 11pm Fri/Sat). Closed Mon/Tue.

✓✓ **The Kilberry Inn** nr Tarbert A destination inn. Report: 1327/FOOD PUBS.

✓ **The Oystercatcher** Otter Ferry Report: 1344/FOOD PUBS.

If You're In Oban...

WHERE TO STAY

742 7/H23
5 ROOMS
NO PETS
NO KIDS
££

✓ **Greystones** www.greystonesoban.co.uk · 01631 358653 At the end of a cul-de-sac, an imposing house with splendid views over the town out front, and below **McCaig's Folly** (1894/MONUMENTS) behind (lit at night). Mark and Suzanne McPhillips have created a superb, calm, aesthetic luxury B&B. Makes Oban all the nicer if you can get one of their spacious, airy rooms (with the view!).

743 7/H23
££

✓ **The Manor House** Gallanach Rd · www.manorhouseoban.com · 01631 562087 S of centre and ferry terminal. Quietly posh. Report: 729/ARGYLL.

744 7/H23
££

✓ **Glenburnie Hotel** Corran Esplanade · www.glenburnie.co.uk · 01631 562089 From tea and shortbread on arrival and lovely rooms, it's clear this is a superior bed for the night. Report: 731/ARGYLL.

745 7/H23

Oban Youth Hostel Corran Esplanade · www.syha.org.uk · 01631 562025 Good location on the front.

Oban Backpackers & Backpackers Plus Report: 1194/HOSTELS.

WHERE TO EAT

746 7/H23
££

✓ **Coast** 104 George St · www.coastoban.co.uk · 01631 569900 Main street on corner of John St. Richard (in the kitchen) and Nicola (out front) Fowler have since 2004 run the best (with or without seafood) restaurant in Oban. Mod-Brit menu by a proper chef in contemporary, laid-back room. Excellent value for this quality, especially their 'Light Bites' menu, and no fuss. Seasonal menu. Independence rules. Closed Jan.

747 7/H23
££

✓ **Etive** 43 Stevenson St · www.etiverestaurant.co.uk · 01631 564899 Through Argyll Square heading south. Chef John and sommelier David from the well-thought-of **Taynuilt Guest House** (1080/ARGYLL) moved into town in 2018 and this former Indian restaurant space (still some echoes) became Etive. Quickly it was the place to eat and drink good wine. Nothing too fancy, just fine cooking. Try and get a table. Dinner only. Closed Mon/Tue.

748 7/H23
£££

✓ **The Manor House** Gallanach Rd · www.manorhouseoban.com · 01631 562087 The best hotel dining room in town. Creative cuisines and fresh seafood in an elevated location. Book. Report: 729/ARGYLL.

749 7/H23
£

✓ **The Green Shack @ The Port** Calmac Pier The shack with the green roof at the port where the ferries come and go, almost the first place you come to when you arrive from the islands (beside but a world away from Wetherspoons). No fish (except their own hot-smoked salmon) but all locally sourced oysters, whelks, scallops in an al fresco/pop-up and takeaway set up. A capital spot in the 'seafood capital'. Mar-Oct 10am-6pm.

750 7/H23
L
££

✓ **Ee-Usk** North Pier · www.eeusk.com · 01631 565666 & **Piazza** North Pier · www.piazzaoban.com · 01631 563628 These 2 adjacent contemporary steel-and-glass restaurants on the corner of the bay are both the once-ambitious creation and abiding passion of the Macleod family; Calum presides. They epitomise the open and up-for-it Oban; a new hotel is (still) planned nearby. Ee-Usk is a bright, modern seafood café with great views. Shellfish, though not fish, is sourced locally; hand-cut chips; home-made starters and puds. Piazza purveys standard though rather a good standard of Italian fare. Both pack 'em in. You need look no further out to sea. Open AYR. 7 days lunch & dinner.

751 7/H23 ✓ **Fish & Chips In Oban** Oban has called itself the 'seafood capital of Scotland'
£ and for good reason. Not only is there a choice of seafood restaurants, there are also 4 good fish 'n' chip shops, 3 with cafés: **Nories**, the related **Oban Bay Fish Bar**, the **Oban Fish & Chip Shop** and the **George Street Fish & Chip Shop**. See 1380/FISH & CHIPS and see who tops the list.

752 7/H23 **Waterfront Fishouse** No 1 Railway Pier · www.waterfrontfishouse.co.uk ·
££ **01631 563110** In the port, by the station, in the midst of it all. Blackboard (well, TV screen) menu and the usuals à la carte. Big on oysters and scallops. An airy upstairs diner whose busyness attests to popularity.

753 7/H23 **Kerrera Tea Garden (& Bunkhouse)** Isle of Kerrera · www.
L kerrerabunkhouse.co.uk · **01631 566367** An Oban secret and an open secret,
APR-SEP this tea garden rather than tea room comes at the end of a wee adventure i.e.
£ the 3-min ferry from Gallanach pier (2km along the coast beyond the big ferry terminal) and then a 2km (signed – with teapots!) walk (or from the quay by the Piazza restaurant in the bay then a lovely though longer walk). A garden and a cosy, decorated barn. Martin and Aideen have made a cool retreat; it's somewhere to head to. Home cooking, including bread. Apr-Sep: 7 days 10.30am-4.30pm.

754 7/H23 **Oban Chocolate Coffee Shop** Corran Esplanade · www.obanchocolate.
£ co.uk · **01631 566099** The place to go for coffee, cake and, of course, chocolate. And they do go; it's usually packed. Chocs are made on the premises (you can see in through the window Mon-Fri). You can have the hot variety. Croissants for breakfast. Waffles whenever. 7 days. Closed Jan.

755 7/H23 **Cuan Mor** 60 George St · www.cuanmor.co.uk · **01631 565078** On the bay,
£ very central and busy bar-bistro attached to Oban Brewery. They say 'contemporary Scottish' and that's right, up to a point. It is an adequate pit stop. 7 days, all day.

756 7/H23 **Waypoint Bar & Grill** Isle of Kerrera · www.obanmarina.com/restaurant ·
MAY-SEP **01631 565888** Another caff on Kerrera (see above), this one just over there at
££ the (Oban) marina on the island, 8 mins away by a free ferry from the North Pier (by Piazza, online or call for times). Casual dining, seafood and sandwiches, and evening meals in summer (last ferry 10pm). Closed Mon.

757 7/H23 **Julie's Coffee House** 33 Stafford St · www.juliescoffeehouse.co.uk ·
£ **01631 565952** Opposite Oban Whisky Visitor Centre. No Julie, rather Karen and Katie, who bake and make it probably Oban's best home-style coffee shop. Only 10 tables, so fills up. Nice approach to food (excellent home baking, soups and snacks) and customers. Good Elektra coffee machine. Closed Sun.

758 7/H23 **The Oban Inn** 1 Stafford St · **01631 567441** On the corner of the bay, a
£ prominent site by the Columba Hotel. Not a place to eat as such (though they have a decent bar menu, some home-made) but an all-round, independent, good pub (since 1790) where an Obanite can be found of an evening. Great on-street/on-quay terrace. Breakfast till 11.45am; then noon-LO 8.45pm.

The Best Hotels & Restaurants In Ayrshire

759 7/L27
32 ROOMS
NO PETS
£££

✓✓ **Lochgreen House** Troon · www.lochgreenhouse.com ·
01292 313343 Top hotel of the Bill Costley group which is so pre-eminent in this neck of the Ayrshire woods. Lochgreen (adjacent to and overlooking Royal Troon Golf Course) is a comfortable, spacious yet homely country house, with big bedrooms looking out to the green. Andrew, the younger Costley, is in executive charge (and all those below) of the smart brasserie-type menu in chandeliered but clubbable dining room; many lounges to lounge in (famous people have lounged here too). The **Brig o' Doon** at Alloway is the romance-and-Rabbie Burns hotel (01292 442466), with a fabulous self-catering house, **Doonbrae**, opposite (1304/HOUSE PARTIES) in gorgeous gardens, while **Highgrove** (01292 312511), more intimate and with great coastal views, is just outside Troon. All operate at a high standard. The Costleys also have the **Ellisland Hotel** in Ayr (767/AYR).

£££ **EAT** Lochgreen: The top restaurant here but consistently high quality throughout the group. The consummate Costleys cater for all.

760 8/L28
22 ROOMS +
2 COTTS
DF
L
££

✓✓ **Dumfries House Lodge** nr Ochiltree · www.dumfrieshouselodge. co.uk · 01290 429920 On the A70 25km E of Ayr. The conservation and spectacular transformation of the House and extensive grounds is in no small part due to Prince Charles, much done in the name of the Prince's Foundation. Around a courtyard near the House, the Lodge is a luxury GH and self-catering cottages. As with all else, rooms are in excellent taste. There is a breakfast room and, nearby, the Woodlands Restaurant in the sawmill, both social and educational projects (Thu-Sat from 5pm & Sun lunch); the **Coach House Café** is open 7 days from 10am. Wonderful walks await 1558/GARDENS.

761 7/K28
6 SUITES +
LODGES
NO PETS
LL
APR-OCT
£LOTS

✓✓ **Eisenhower Hotel @ Culzean Castle** nr Maybole · www.culzean-eisenhower.com · 01655 884455 18km S of Ayr, this accom on the upper floors of Culzean (1813/CASTLES), includes the famous and lavishly refurbished actual Eisenhower apartment. Though not a conventional hotel, a bed for the night rarely comes as historically posh. The second floor (you enter by the original 1920s lift and there's a very grand staircase) has some fabulous views. Rates are expensive but include afternoon tea. Dinner is available Wed-Sun. Bookable for individual or exclusive use (where you won't find strangers in the drawing room) 1302/HOUSE PARTIES. The clifftop setting, the gardens and the vast grounds are superb. No better demesne than this.

762 8/L27
4 ROOMS
DF
££

✓ **The Sorn Inn** Sorn · www.sorninn.com · 01290 551305 8km E of Mauchline on the B743 off the A76. Traditional inn in rural setting and pleasant village in deepest Ayrshire. The Grant family have established a big reputation for food with a continuing clutch of awards, including consecutive Michelin Bib Gourmands. There are 4 simple, great-value rooms with Wi-Fi, etc.

££ **EAT** People travel from miles around to eat here. Restaurant and pub meals. Craig Grant a good man in the kitchen. See 1328/FOOD PUBS.

763 7/K28
11 ROOMS
NO PETS
££

✓ **Wildings Hotel & Restaurant** Maidens · www.wildingshotel.com · 01655 331401 The family of the late legendary restaurateur Brian Sage run this 'restaurant with rooms' with love and respect for him and their legions of loyal customers. Contemporary and comfortable rooms overlook a serene harbour in this coastal village near Turnberry (and a fraction of the cost of that hotel up the road).

££ **EAT** A beautiful spot and excellent gastropub-style menu in 2 large, buzzing rooms. They come from all over the county for the best casual dining.

764 **7/K27**
37 ROOMS
DF
££

Piersland Hotel Troon · www.piersland.co.uk · 01292 314747 Opposite Portland Golf Course, which is next to Royal Troon. Privately owned mansion-house hotel of character and ambience much favoured for weddings. Wood-panelling, open fires, lovely gardens and only a 'drive' away from the courses (no preferential booking on Royal, but Portland usually possible); lots of great golf nearby. 15 rooms in the house, 14 in 'cottages' around the building and 9 lodges. Eat in the Red Bowl Restaurant. Local reputation also for bar meals.

✓✓ **Glenapp Castle** nr Ballantrae Discreet and distinguished. A jewel in the Scottish crown in fabulous grounds and gardens in deepest Southeast Ayrshire. Report: 1162/COUNTRY-HOUSE HOTELS.

THE BEST RESTAURANTS IN AYRSHIRE & THE CLYDE VALLEY

765 **7/K26**
£££

✓✓ **Braidwoods** nr Dalry · www.braidwoods.co.uk · 01294 833544 Simplest approach is from the section of A78 N of Irvine; take B714 for Dalry. Cottage restaurant discreetly signed 5km on left. Michelin-star dining doesn't get more casually accomplished and they've had that star for longer than anyone else in Scotland. Keith and Nicola Braidwood here since 1994 with their impeccable sourcing (long before it was de rigueur); they use selected local suppliers and naturally everything is made on the premises (bread, chocolates). With its own quiet dignity, Braidwoods remains the best meal in the shire and; you'll go a long way to find this quality at these prices. Michelin without liturgy. Lunch Wed-Sat & dinner Tue-Sat. Sun lunch in winter.

766 **7/K26**
£

Nardini's Largs · www.nardinis.co.uk · 01475 675000 On the Esplanade. This legendary seaside salon came back after a million-dollar refit, trading somewhat on its glory days. Still, in a town now hoaching with ice creameries, I'm with the new Nardini, though it has nowt to do with the original family. The cafeteria – and it is a cafeteria, not just a café – is usually packed; waiter service. Up back there's a Tony Macaroni trattoria. Approach through snowdrifts of ice cream.

MacCallums of Troon Oyster Bar Report: 1363/SEAFOOD.

The Catch @ Fins Fairlie, nr Largs Report: 1374/SEAFOOD.

GRO Coffee Irvine Report: 1451/TEAROOMS.

If You're In Ayr...

WHERE TO STAY IN AYR

767 7/K28 ✓ **The Ellisland** 19 Racecourse Rd · www.ellislandhouse.com ·
9 ROOMS **01292 260111** On road to Alloway. Another success story by the Costley group
££ who have Lochgreen and other restaurant options (see above). Rooms vary but
mostly large and well appointed. Very decent restaurant for their irresistible
comfort food.

768 7/K28 **Savoy Park** 16 Racecourse Road, Ayr · www.savoypark.com · 01292 266112
15 ROOMS On same road out of town as Ellisland, above, a traditional but charming, friendly
DF and somehow peaceful (except when there's a wedding on) hotel; an informed
££ choice! See also 1240/SCOTTISH HOTELS.

769 7/K27 **Fairfield House Hotel** 12 Fairfield Rd · www.fairfieldhotel.co.uk ·
44 ROOMS **01292 267461** 1km from centre, on the front. Solid, decent, suburban. 'Deluxe'
££ facilities include pool/sauna/steam, and conservatory brasserie. 5 rooms have sea view.

WHERE TO EAT IN AYR & TROON

770 7/L27 **Saffy's** 2 Dalbair Rd, Ayr · www.saffys-ayr.com · 01292 288598 Opposite the
£ Mercure Hotel. An honest, home-made, indie restaurant: seafood, meat, game and
good vegetarian. Ayr is the better for the earnest endeavours of the splendid Smith
family. Lunch & dinner. Closed Mon.

771 7/K27 **The Lido** 11 West Portland St, Troon · www.lido-troon.co.uk · 01292 310088
££ Contemporary Italo-American café-bar that buzzes from breakfast to supper.
Massive-choice menu and a stylish spot. 7 days from 8.30am. They also have:

772 7/K27 **Scott's** Harbour Rd, Troon · www.scotts-troon.co.uk · 01292 315315 In the
££ marina about 2km from Troon centre. A self-consciously stylish but seriously well-
thought-out contemporary bar/restaurant upstairs overlooking the surprisingly
packed marina. Owners, the Buzzworks Group, have another Scott's in Largs and
The Lido (above), **Elliots** in Prestwick, and the less interesting **Treehouse** in Ayr.
Food OK, bling in evidence. A local collection of great eateries, all spot on. 7 days
from 8.30am.

773 7/K27 **Cecchini's** 72 Fort St, Ayr · 01292 263607 & Prestwick & Clyde Marina,
££ **Ardrossan** · www.cecchinis.com Decent Italian and Med restaurants run by the
estimable Cecchinis. It's dependable! In Ardrossan where the Arran ferry comes in.
Mon-Sat lunch & dinner.

✓ **The Wee Hurrie** Harbour Rd, Troon The best fish 'n' chips on the coast.
Report: 1382/FISH & CHIPS.

The Best Hotels & Restaurants In The South West

774 9/J31
10 ROOMS
DF
LL
£LOTS

✓✓ **Knockinaam Lodge** Portpatrick · www.knockinaamlodge.com · 01776 810471 Tucked away on a dream cove, a historic country house full of fresh flowers, great food, sea air and sympatico service. Sian and David Ibbotson balance a family home and a top-class get-away-from-it-all hotel. Rooms traditional but contemporary and with a calm ambience, especially the famous Churchill suite. See 1165/COUNTRY-HOUSE HOTELS.

£LOTS **EAT** Best meal in the South from an outstanding and long-established chef, Tony Pierce. Fixed menu – lots of unexpected treats.

775 9/N30
6 ROOMS
DF
££

✓ **Cavens** Kirkbean · www.cavens.com · 01387 880234 20km S Dumfries via A710, Cavens is signed from Kirkbean. This elegant mansion in 20 landscaped acres has been converted by Angus and Jane Fordyce into a homely, informal Caven-haven of peace and quiet – a great base for touring the SW and Angus is your personal tour guide. Ask about 'the beach'. Lots of public space so you can even get away from each other. Honest, good cooking using locally sourced ingredients: lots from **Loch Arthur** (1512/FARM SHOPS), including the excellent granola for breakfast. A cottage garden supplies your fixed, inexpensive dinner. Sideboard of drinks/honesty bar. Gardens to wander, possibly with the family dogs, and see 1306/HOUSE PARTIES.

££ **EAT** Best food in area; very reasonably priced. Simple daily-changing menu. Like a dinner party though you don't necessarily have to get on with the guests.

776 9/N29
14 ROOMS
DF
££

✓ **Buccleuch & Queensberry Arms Hotel** Thornhill · www.bqahotel.com · 01848 323101 At the crossroads of charming Thornhill 25km N of Dumfries on the A76. A very civilised billet operating in partnership with **Drumlanrig Castle** 6km N (1585/PARKS). Tasteful, contemporary bedrooms. Bar and dining room. Great for the hunting/shooting/fishing crowd and the rest of us.

777 9/M29
6 ROOMS
DF
£

✓ **The Clachan Inn** St John's Town of Dalry · www.theclachaninn.co.uk · 01644 430241 Main street of this wee town N of New Galloway on the A702 to Moniaive and Thornhill (and on the A713 to Ayr), also a major stop on the **Southern Upland Way** (2026/WALKS), so geared to walkers, cyclists and outdoorists generally; and drinkers. Open fires, cheery folk, a haven on the way as you'd hope. Good food, big on ales, and simple, inexpensive rooms above.

778 9/N31
20 ROOMS
DF
LL
FEB-NOV
£££

✓ **Balcary Bay** nr Auchencairn · www.balcary-bay-hotel.co.uk · 01556 640217 15km S of Dalbeattie. Off A711 at end of shore road and as close to the shimmering Solway as you can get. The Lamb family run a well-cared-for and well-loved hideaway and romantic retreat (as weekend magazines might call it). Ideal for walking, bird-watching, outdoor pursuits (dogs welcome). Kitchen continues a strong commitment to local produce. Strong wine list. Cream tea by the sea in lounge. Half the rooms have the Solway view. Location, location!

779 9/M31
16 ROOMS
££

✓ **Selkirk Arms** Kirkcudbright · www.selkirkarmshotel.co.uk · 01557 330402 By popular accord, the best hotel in Kirkcudbright (pronounced 'Cur-coo-bree'), in the very good private hands of Chris Walker. They set out to turn this townhouse into the best accom and dining in the district; they did! 16 comfortable, medium-expensive rooms in this most interesting of SW towns.

££ **EAT** Dining with strong local menu; informal bar-bistro and, in summer, the garden.

780 **9/J30** **Corsewall Lighthouse Hotel** nr Stranraer · www.lighthousehotel.co.uk ·
11 ROOMS 01776 853220 A718 to Kirkcolm 3km, B738 to Corsewall 6km (follow signs). Wild
DF · LL location on clifftop. Cosily furnished, clever but snug – don't say cramped, just
ATMOS go with someone you like. The adjacent fully functioning lighthouse (since 1817)
££ makes for surreal evenings and room lighting. 3 suites are by the lighthouse and 2
are further away. All suites have the sea and sky views (though only half the hotel
rooms do). Small dining room. Food OK, it's a long way to the chipper.

781 **9/M30** **The Ship Inn** Gatehouse of Fleet · www.theshipinngatehouse.com ·
££ 01557 814217 On main street, the best accom of a few more traditional hostelries,
the Ship's sails reset by new proprietors 2018. Pub food in restaurant. Good base
for expeditions 1492/ICE CREAM; 1641/BEACHES; 1681/SCENIC ROUTES.

782 **9/N30** **Holiday Inn** Dumfries · www.hidumfries.com · 01387 272410 Edge of town
71 ROOMS in the Crichton Estate (signposted from centre; 20-min walk), a surprising 100-acre
££ campus of listed sandstone buildings. We don't do chain hotels as a rule in *StB*
but this is quite the best stay in Dumfries. Contemporary-furnished hotel with
brasserie. Modern facilities and OK food. Use of pool 100m adjacent.

Cally Palace Gatehouse of Fleet Report: 1179/KIDS.

THE BEST RESTAURANTS IN THE SOUTH WEST

783 **8/M28** ✓ **Blackaddie Hotel** Sanquhar · www.blackaddiehotel.co.uk · 01659
£££ 50270 This foodie destination hotel is as far-flung as it's sensible to be; first
find Sanquhar then left at gas station (Glasgow end of village), through a small
industrial estate; surprisingly, it's on a river (the Nith). Notable once-Michelin chef/
patron Ian McAndrew (a mentor to many others) carries the cook's blowtorch here
with dogged determination. Hotel itself very adequate if not quite in the league of
the cooking but this is a bold bothy in unforgiving hills (Wanlockhead and Leadhills
are also worth discovering). Hail to the chef! Amazing **Crawick** nearby (2179/ART).

784 **9/M30** ✓ **Mr Pook's Kitchen** Castle Douglas · www.mrpooks.co.uk ·
££ 01556 504000 At the top of the main street in red sandstone former Clydesdale
Bank building, a restaurant that finally adds credence to Castle Douglas's claim to be
the 'Food Town' in the South West (along with the **Earth's Crust Bakery** 1473/
ARTISAN BAKERS). At TGP I hadn't made it to Mr Pook's table but this new restaurant
2018 seems set to justify its claim to be the gateway to Dumfries and Galloway's best
produce. They have foraging days out. Reports, please. Closed Sun/Mon.

785 **9/M30** ✓ **Galloway Lodge Preserves** Gatehouse of Fleet · www.gallowaylodge.
£ co.uk · 01557 814001 On a corner of the main street. A shop for pressies,
ceramics and stuff in jars but also a great self-service comfort-food and home-
baking station – I mean café. It's better than the rest for some miles. 7 days.

786 **9/N29** **Home** Dumfries · 01387 262296 Above the Coach & Horses, on corner of Bank
££ St and White Sands, on the river. Small upstairs restaurant still a Dumfries secret
when I found it (closed that day, a Monday), hopefully no longer. A much needed
Italian-flavoured, imaginatively home-cooked menu. Reports, please.

787 **9/J30** **The Old Colfin Creamery** by Portpatrick · 01776 820622 5km before
£ Portpatrick on the A77, 150m from the road, a cool café/restaurant in ... an old
farm creamery. Emma Pyatt and Nick Cramsie-Smith's retreat to the country. A
Mod-Brit menu, a wood stove and a funky bar (The Moo Bar) that goes on the road.
Lunch or dinner (all day at weekends). Closed Mon/Tue.

788 9/M30 **Carlo's Castle Douglas · www.carlosrestaurant.co.uk · 01556 503977** Here
££ nearly 30 years, the Bignami family restaurant with Carlo in the kitchen is your
absolute safe bet in this self-designated 'food town'. Bustling tratt atmos –
probably the best Italian food in the far South West. Tue-Sat dinner only.

789 9/J30 **Campbell's Portpatrick · www.campbellsrestaurant.co.uk · 01776 810314**
££ Robert and Diane Campbell's quayside restaurant since 1998. Unpretentious fishy
fare with something for everyone, including vegetarians. Crab and lobster from their
boat a good, fresh bet. Best in town and invariably gets a Michelin mention. Tue-Sun
lunch & dinner.

790 9/N29 **Bruno's Dumfries · www.brunosrestaurant.co.uk · 01387 255757** Off Annan
££ Rd. Very long-established, through 4 generations of the Torriani family, old-style
Italian eaterie. Many folks attest to this being the most reliable albeit old-style
eating out in town. Wed-Mon dinner only.

791 9/N29 **Balmoral Dumfries · 01387 252583** Chippie adjacent Bruno's (family related);
£ the best in or out choices are next to one another. Interior room (and blinds closed)
but home cooking and real. Wed-Mon dinner only. See 1390/FISH & CHIPS.

792 9/J30 **The Crown Portpatrick · www.crownportpatrick.com · 01776 810261**
L Harbourside hotel and pub with better-than-average grub. Goes like a fair in
£ summer. 7 days. Competition from the Waterfront next door. The Crown has better
atmos and decidedly better seafood. The **Chip Ahoy** chip van on the opposite side
of the harbour does what it says on the van.

793 9/M29 **Piccola Italia Moniaive · 01848 200400** High St of lovely village N of Dumfries
£ and E of New Galloway. Surprisingly good Italian menu and wood-fired pizza from
Serbian chef/proprietor. Summer: 7 days dinner only. Closed Mon/Tue winter.

794 9/L31 **The Pheasant Sorbie · www.thepheasantsorbie.com · 01988 850270** The
old Pheasant in tiny Sorbie, 15 mins from Wigtown in the midst of bucolic
Galloway, given a new Italian lease of life, and now a destination rural food pub.
3 adjoining rooms. Home-made Mediterranean food, including pizza (also as
takeaway). Lunch & dinner. Closed Mon/Tue.

Thomas Tosh Thornhill Great selective shopping. Lovely caff. Report: 2216/SHOPS.

The Schoolhouse Ringford Caroline Lawrie's excellent, here-forever roadside
(A75) café/bistro. Report: 1456/TEAROOMS.

Caffs in Wigtown 3 to choose from in the Book Town. Report: 1457/1458/1459/
TEAROOMS.

The Best Hotels & Restaurants
In Central Scotland

795 8/L23
16 ROOMS
DF · LL
ATMOS
£LOTS

✓✓ **Monachyle Mhor** nr Balquhidder · www.mhor.net · 01877 384622
Along the ribbon of road that skirts Loch Voil, 7km beyond the village (which is 4km) from the A84 Callander–Crianlarich road. Relatively remote (1220/GET-AWAY HOTELS), the Braes a splendid backdrop for this now long-established informal and pink farmhouse hotel that has famously fab food, sexy, contemporary rooms and altogether good vibes. An urbane back of beyond. Tom, Lisa and the gang just take you in. MM is the mothership in a constellation of Mhors, the word connotes everything they are (look it up in your Gaelic dictionary!). In May, there is a Mhor festival for 5,000 people like us 33/EVENTS.

£LOTS
EAT It's a long way for dinner but some of the best informal fine-dining in Scotland is to be had here. The wee bar before for the craic, dinner in the conservatory and a drawing-room dram after.

796 8/L23
7 ROOMS
DF
ATMOS
££

✓✓ **Mhor 84** nr Balquhidder · www.mhor.net · 01877 384646 On the A84 near Strathyre and Balquhidder. After MM above, came another idiosyncratically cool hotel – actually and really, a motel – which you see from the road on the right as you hurtle for Oban, Fort William and the North West. You should stop, and, if you're lucky, stay (there are only 7 mix-and-match furnished rooms and 4 more uniformly decked-out cottage rooms 'out back'). Purposefully a budget stopover, with few frills, it's the whole friendly bar/restaurant – where locals become fellow travellers – that makes this as rock 'n' roll as Scotland gets to Route 66. And there's a shop where you can buy the lifestyle. See 2213/SHOPS.

797 8/M24
15 ROOMS
DF
ATMOS
£££

✓✓ **Roman Camp Hotel** Callander · www.romancamphotel.co.uk · 01877 330003 Through a chink in Callander's main street to a more refined world, nothing much changes – or needs to – in Eric and Marion Brown's top-of-the-Trossachs hotel, away from the tourists. Set in extensive gardens on the Teith, with Roman ruins nearby. The house, built for the Dukes of Perth, has been a hotel since the war. Highly individual rooms; some snug. Magnificent period furnishings. Candlelight and log fires! In the old building corridors do creak. Delightful drawing room and conservatory. Oval dining room very sympatico. This is what chandeliers can do! Private chapel should a prayer come on and, of course, some weddings. Rods for fishing – the river swishes past the lawn.

£££
EAT Dining room effortlessly the best food in town with a great and long-standing chef – Ian McNaught. Nice for Sunday lunch. New 2018, the **Potting Shed Bistro**, in the surprisingly huge walled garden. It's where to go for the best casual food.

798 8/M24
15 ROOMS
DF
L
£LOTS

✓✓ **Cromlix House** nr Dunblane · www.cromlix.com · 01786 822125
3km from A9 and 4km from town on B8033; follow signs for Perth, then Kinbuck. A leisurely drive through the old estate with splendid mature woods to this spacious mansion, with comfortable but a bit soulless public rooms. Since 2014 and a major revamp, 'Andy Murray's hotel', managed by ICMI. No leisure facilities – except, of course, tennis – but woods to walk and 3,000 acres of meadows and fishing lochs. House Loch is serenity itself. Private chapel. Cromlix adding 30+ new rooms at TGP.

£££
EAT As with other ICMI hotels, the menu is under the Albert Roux brand (brasserie-style); the signature soufflé. All light and delicious. The room, with an open kitchen that lends little to the aesthetic, is somewhat Premier Inn (gosh, how could I say that!) but service is good. Lovely terrace.

799 8/M24 ✓✓ **Lake Hotel** Port of Menteith · www.lake-hotel.com · **01877 385258**

17 ROOMS   A very lakeside hotel on the Lake of Menteith in the Trossachs' purple

LL   heart. A good centre for touring, walking and especially fishing (adjacent;

££   01877 385664): the lake swarms with fishermen in floaty boats. The **Inchmahome** ferry leaves from nearby (1950/MARY). A kind of New England feel pervades (they also have a hotel on Chesapeake Bay; stylish wooden floors throughout). All rooms are light and quiet. 5 rooms have the mesmerising lake view and 2 upstairs rooms are enormous. Conservatory restaurant for sunset supper or lazy lunch; also bar menu. A great hotel if you're in love with Scotland or each other.

££   **EAT** Best informal dining in the shire.

800 8/M24 ✓ **The Cross Keys** Kippen · www.kippencrosskeys.com · **01786 870293**

3 ROOMS   Main St of loved little village 15km from Stirling. 3 pleasant, airy rooms above a

DF   homely pub with a great reputation for a warm welcome and excellent food.

£   Everything a pub stopover should be (1329/FOOD PUBS).

801 8/M24 ✓ **Doubletree Dunblane** Dunblane · www.doubletreedunblane.com ·

200+ ROOMS   **01786 825800** One of the huge hydro hotels left over from the last health

DF   and holiday-at-home boom, refurbished at vast expense (£12m) in 2009 by Hilton

££   to create a massive urban edifice on the edge of a small town. Smart public rooms, including vast restaurant. Nice views for some and a long walk down corridors for most. 'Living Well' leisure facilities include a pool.

££   **EAT** Celebrity chef Nick Nairn has created a contemporary menu in the **Kailyard Restaurant**. His 'signature dishes', though mainly standard fare, are reasonably priced under executive chef Steven Campbell.

THE BEST RESTAURANTS IN CENTRAL SCOTLAND

802 8/N24 ✓ **Jam Jar** Bridge of Allan · www.jamjarcafe.co.uk · **01786 831616** Bustling

££   all-day café-bistro where they've thought of you and what you like to eat. Various eating areas including terraces on the street and out back with a stove. From ingredients to trimmings to the wine list, it's all good. Home-made cakes, excellent breakfasts. Definitely worth coming over the bridge from Stirling.

803 8/M24 ✓ **Venachar Lochside** nr Callander · www.venachar-lochside.com ·

££   **01877 330011** On the banks of the very water's edge of Loch Venachar on the A821 about 7km from Callander. A great roadside/lochside restaurant (rather than merely café) in the watery heart of the Trossachs. Meghan Haste and chef Andrew Barrowcliffe at the helm. They won the Scottish Thistle Award for Casual Dining in 2018, which yours truly presented to them. This is well-sourced food with a view. 7 days 10am-5pm & dinner Thu-Sun.

804 8/N24 **Allan Water Café** Bridge of Allan · www.allanwatercafe.co.uk ·

£   **01786 833060** Caff that's been here forever at end of the main street in BoA with big glassy extension. Original attitude and clientele still remain – everybody has the fish 'n' chips and the ice cream (Bechelli's) 1500/ICE CREAM. 7 days.

✓ **The Cross Keys** Kippen Report: 1329/FOOD PUBS.

✓ **Lion & Unicorn** Thornhill Report: 1332/FOOD PUBS.

If You're In Stirling or Bridge of Allan...

WHERE TO STAY

805 8/N24
10 ROOMS
££
✓ **Victoria Square** 12 Victoria Sq, Stirling · www.victoriasquareguesthouse.com · **01786 473920** Corner of elegant, wide, open square, short walk to centre. Victorian townhouse guesthouse with individually decorated and furnished rooms. An airy orangery for afternoon tea and lunch. May do evening meals. Your solicitous hosts: Kari and Phil Couser.

806 8/N24
10 ROOMS
££
✓ **Friars Wynd Hotel** 17 Friars St, Stirling · www.friarswynd.co.uk · **01786 447501** Friendly, contemporary town centre hotel near station. Nice bar/bistro on street; rooms over 3 floors (mainly doubles). Excellent urban but cosy ambience.

807 8/N24
36 ROOMS
NO PETS
££
Colessio 33 Spittal St, Stirling · www.hotelcolessio.com · **01786 448880** On the road to Stirling Castle (250m), therefore historic (actually Victorian) and in a central location. A trying-very-hard (to be boutiquey) hotel, too blingy for my taste and it might date rather quickly but populist and popular. The restaurant, the bar, afternoon tea. Bedrooms exude 'opulence'. Certainly, it is Stirling's most contemporary hotel; service is good. Part of the local Aurora chain, who also have the on-brand revamped **Royal Hotel** in Bridge of Allan (see below).

808 8/N24
30 ROOMS
££
The Royal Hotel 55 Henderson St, Bridge of Allan · www.royalhotelstirling.com · **01786 832284** On main road of BoA, sister hotel of Colessio in Stirling (807/STIRLING), poshed up 2017, bright and showy restaurant has Josper grill; bar **The Fifty Five** has an impressive drinks list.

809 8/N24
9 ROOMS
££
Park Lodge 32 Park Terrace, Stirling · www.parklodge.net · **01786 474862** The Manquetty's Victorian/Georgian town (they say country) house near King's Park and golf course is resolutely old style. Objets and lawns. Med-influenced menu in restaurant. In the *Good Hotel Guide*. Some weddings.

810 8/N24
4 ROOMS
£
Portcullis Hotel Castle Wynd, Stirling · www.theportcullishotel.com · **01786 472290** Jim and Lynne Walker's pub with rooms in one of the best locations in town, no more than a cannonball's throw from the castle. Unpretentious, uncompromising basic accom on upper floors – 3 with the stunning view – near the tourist magnet. Pub and pub food. Good courtyard terrace.

811 8/N24
100 ROOMS
NO PETS
£
Stirling Court Hotel University of Stirling · www.stirlingcourthotel.co.uk · **01786 466000** On main road between Stirling and Bridge of Allan, 7km town centre. Part of the university campus, near the National Swimming Academy, and in the shadow of the Wallace Monument (some views). No atmos but a good business-like option on a budget.

812 8/N24
SLEEPS 92
Stirling Youth Hostel St. John St · www.syha.org.uk · **01786 473442** On road up to the castle in a great location is this well-appointed hostel (1187/HOSTELS). **Willy Wallace Hostel** 77 Murray Pl, Stirling · **01786 446773** is more funky. Upstairs in busy centre. Caffs and pubs nearby. Bunk rooms for 54.

813 8/N24 ✓ **The Hideaway** Fountain Rd, Bridge of Allan Find this truly hidden-away
£ gem: Fountain Rd to the left of the main street as you come in from Stirling
(opposite the Royal Hotel). 80m on left, 25m down Fountain Mews, in an old
telephone exchange, a permanent pop-up kind of café with great people, baking,
breakfast and delicious gelato. Daytime only. Closed Sun.

814 8/N24 ✓ **The Greengrocer** 81 Port St, Stirling · 01786 479159 Through a pend in
£ town centre, boxes of fruit & veg outside. For well over 20 years, the Carter
family's Stirling secret. Intimate, friendly, efficient and great home-made,
deli-driven food – soups, salads, home-made cakes. Daytime only. Closed Sun.

815 8/N24 ✓ **Hermann's** 58 Broad St, Stirling · www.hermanns-restaurant.co.uk ·
££ 01786 450632 After many a year (since 1995), still Stirling's best bet for
dinner. A townhouse very close to the castle. Hermann Aschaber's corner of
Austria, where schnitzels and strudels figure along with Scottish fare. 2-floor,
ambient, well-run rooms (conservatory best). 7 days lunch & dinner.

816 8/N24 ✓ **Corrieri's** 7 Alloa Rd, Stirling · www.corrieris.co.uk · 01786 472089 On
£ the road to Bridge of Allan at Causewayhead. Since 1934, this excellent café
near busy corner below the Wallace Monument has been serving pasta/pizza and
ice cream properly, as it should be. A genuine family caff. Closed Tue.

817 8/N24 ✓ **Sable & Flea** 12 Friars St, Stirling · 01786 475597 Opposite Friars Wynd
£ (hotel, above). Cool little caff for cakes and snacks, with vintage furniture,
showroom upstairs and a great terrace out the back door. Closed Sun/Mon.

818 8/N24 ✓ **The Inn at Torbrex** 62 Torbrex Lane, Stirling · www.torbrexinn.co.uk ·
£ 01786 461832 10 mins from town centre via Torbrex Rd in the burbs, and the
sister inn of the Birds & Bees (the original) below. An 18th-century inn, now a
contemporary and hugely popular gastropub. Must book. 7 days.

819 8/N24 **La Cucina** 64 Henderson St, Bridge of Allan · www.lacucinabridgeofallan.
£ co.uk · 01786 834679 On the main (Henderson) street. Contemporary, reasonably
authentic Italian place. Once again, BoA is where to eat! 7 days.

820 8/N24 **Birds & Bees** Easter Cornton Rd, Causewayhead · www.thebirdsandthebees-
£ stirling.com · 01786 473663 Between Stirling and Bridge of Allan at Causewayhead.
Going towards Stirling from BoA it's first on the right (Easter Cornton Rd). A local
secret and a hugely popular pub-grub destination in the burbs. This unlikely
roadhouse occasionally hosts *pétanque* (boules to you!). Good for kids. Terrace. 7 days.

821 8/N24 **Gabe's Diner** Forthside Waterfront, Stirling · 07513 742211 200m from
£ bridge by railway station (or bus station). In emerging quarter on the riverside, by a
car park surrounded by Nando's, Frankie & Benny's, etc – this is the antithesis of a
chain restaurant; a great, intimate home-cooking bistro. Eclectic menu; loyal fans.
7 days breakfast, lunch & dinner.

822 8/N24 **Bite East** 52 Port St, Stirling · www.biteeaststirling.wordpress.com ·
£ 01786 479799 Much frequented by Chinese students from the university, a
genuine Chinese and Japanese restaurant and takeaway; large airy room. 7 days.

The Best Hotels & Restaurants In The Borders

824 8/S27
22 ROOMS
£LOTS

✓ **Roxburghe Hotel** nr Kelso · www.roxburghe-hotel.net ·
01573 450331 *The* consummate country-house hotel in the Borders has undergone a major refurbishment and, at TGP, there is more to come. Keeping the comfortable elegance of the main house – the dining rooms, the Library Bar – 60 more contemporary rooms will be added behind (2020), with a casual dining restaurant and a 25m pool. Hopefully, the rural ambience and the encompassing countryside will not be disturbed. Owls hoot at night and once – no, twice, a crow fell down my chimney (the Bowmont Suite). This was good luck! The 18-hole golf course has major appeal – it's challenging, championship-standard and in a beautiful riverside setting. Non-res can play. Fairways at the golf clubhouse open for dining (till 6pm). The Roxburghe seems set to be the major hotel and 5-star resort of the region (so 2 ticks likely next edition).

825 8/Q27
6 ROOMS
DF
££

✓ **Windlestraw** Walkerburn · www.windlestraw.co.uk ·
01896 870636 On A72, up discreet driveway and overlooking the Tweed Valley, a beautiful historic house and garden; more a restaurant with rooms than merely a boutique B&B. In the Borders it is the only one. Wood panelling, comfortable lounge and destination dining (non-res if space – must book).

£££ **EAT** Chef/proprietor John Matthews, with Sylvia and chef Stuart Waterston, with great attention to detail, make this the most urbane dining experience in the valley and beyond (prix fixe menu). Borders sourcing and from the greenhouse and garden.

826 8/R27
20 ROOMS
DF
££

✓ **Burt's** Melrose · www.burtshotel.co.uk · 01896 822285 In Market Sq/ main street; some (double-glazed) rooms overlook. Busy bars, especially for food; it's easy to see why. The dining room is where to fine dine in this part of the Borders. Cosy in winter, it looks out to the garden and is summery in summer. Traditional but comfortably modernised small-town hotel, though some rooms also feel small (there are 7 singles). Convenient location for Borders roving (1926/ ABBEYS; 2004/HILL WALKS; 1577/GARDENS). Where to stay for the **Sevens** or the **Book Festival** (if you can get in) 24/40/EVENTS.

££/£££ **EAT** The bar routinely wins awards for gastropub food and craft ales. It and the main restaurant together are, in a good way, an institution!

827 8/R27
11 ROOMS
££

✓ **The Townhouse** Melrose · www.thetownhousemelrose.co.uk ·
01896 822645 The long-standing (i.e. 4 decades) Burt's (above) spawned a stylish little sister across the street some years back. Charming and boutique-ish with a coherent, elegant look by Michael Vee Decor (from down the street); it's very Melrose! Dining room and busy brasserie confidently positioned between the fine dining of Burt's and its gastrogrub bar. The Hendersons (James) here and over the road (Nick) have always put their town on the Borders map.

828 8/P26
13 ROOMS
DF
£LOTS

✓ **Cringletie House** Peebles · www.cringletie.com · 01721 725750 Privately owned and carefully tended country-house hotel 5km from town just off A703 Edinburgh road (35km). Late-19th-century Scottish baronial house in 28 acres. Quintessential Peeblesshire: comfortable and civilised with an imperturbable air of calm. Well-loved local art. Restful garden view from every room. Top disabled facilities, including a lift! Conservatory, lounges up and downstairs; gracious dining room.

829 8/R27
19 ROOMS
DF
££

✓ **Buccleuch Arms** St Boswells · www.buccleucharms.com · **01835 822243** Here forever on the A68 where the road turns into St B – as a Borders lad from Jedburgh, I've passed it all my life. Under Rachael (the local MSP) and Billy Hamilton, it's become a stylish, convivial roadstop, local inn and destination place to eat – in extensive bar area and separate Blue Coo Bistrot (similar but more gastrofied menu) – all at once. And it so works! Garden tables in summer. Comfortable, contemporary rooms are inexpensive. A coaching inn for today's roads of life.

£ **EAT** Informal dining in bistro and bar favoured by Bordering locals, like me!

830 8/S27
3 ROOMS
NO PETS
L · APR-DEC
££

✓ **Edenwater House** Ednam, nr Kelso · www.edenwaterhouse.co.uk · **01573 224070** Find Ednam on Swinton road B6461 from Kelso, 4km. Discreet manse-type house beside old kirk and graveyard overlooking Eden Water, the lovely garden and tranquil green countryside. Bucolic is the word. You have the run of the home of Jeff and Jacqui Kelly. Jacqui's flair in the kitchen and Jeff's carefully wrought wine list (he has a wine shed in the old coach house and he will suggest) make this the secret Borders dinner destination. B&B, dinner Fri/Sat.

831 8/P26
8 ROOMS
NO PETS
££

Horseshoe Inn Eddleston, nr Peebles · www.horseshoeinn.co.uk · **01721 730225** On the A703 (8km Peebles, 35km Edinburgh), a recreated reconstructed coaching inn and a convivial and contemporary stopover with destination decent food in 2 dining areas. Rooms in the old village school behind are peaceful and, well, plain, but you can stumble back there replete after dinner.

832 8/Q27
14 ROOMS +
3 LODGES
DF
££

Philipburn Selkirk · www.bw-philipburnhousehotel.co.uk · **01750 720747** 1km from town centre. Serviceable, privately owned Best Western 'Plus' hotel for families, walkers, a weekend away from it all; Selkirk a good Borders base. Bar with great malt selection and decent bistro. Comfy rooms, some more 'luxurious' than others. Garden.

833 8/S27
33 ROOMS
££

Ednam House Kelso · www.ednamhouse.com · **01573 224168** Overlooking River Tweed; a majestic Georgian mansion with very old original features, including some of the guests, who quietly get on with the main business of fishing and dozing in an old armchair. After being owned by the same family for 70 years, the august Ednam is now with the bespoke Robert Parker 'Collection'. Half the bedrooms have the river view. The Garden Restaurant conservatory is the main attraction: a stunning setting. Food not a strong point but the days-gone-by ambience and the River Tweed running by confer a comforting serenity many modern hotels can only dream of (and not in an old armchair).

 The Wheatsheaf Swinton Report: 1335/FOOD PUBS.

 Traquair Arms Innerleithen Report: 1214/INNS.

THE BEST RESTAURANTS IN THE BORDERS

834 8/R27
£
✓✓ **Main Street Trading Company** St Boswells · www. mainstreetbooks.co.uk · **01835 824087** Main Street, as they say, and an all-round affirmation of life emporium, bookshop and caff. Eat before/after browsing/walking, etc. Great home baking. Hot dishes noon-3pm. Closed Mon. Report: 2211/SHOPS.

835 8/R27
££
✓ **Seasons** Gattonside, nr Melrose · www.seasonsborders.co.uk · **01896 823217** Over the River Tweed (you could walk by footbridge as quickly as going round by car). A bistro highly regarded by locals, very much worth finding by you, by estimable and conscientious restaurateurs Roger (chef) and Bea (out front) McKie. Working closely with local producers and suppliers (portraits of many of them grace the walls), the menu is accessible, with seasonal à la carte and daily-changing specials. Good chargrill meats, home-made pasta, cheeseboard. Roger reliably presides. Loved everything I ate on a recent visit. Lunch Fri-Sun & dinner Wed-Sun.

836 8/R27
££
✓ **The Hoebridge Inn** Gattonside · www.thehoebridge.com · **01896 823082** At Earlston end of village, signed towards the river from tiny Gattonside's main street (or from Melrose by footbridge). A surprising oasis of contemporary dining. Discreet and understated, yet can be lively in dining room, conservatory bar (and pre drinks in the garden). Kyle Pidd and Hamish Carruthers (on the stoves) have created probably the Borders' most stylish eaterie. Menu changes first Wed of the month. Everything made from scratch, from bread and preserves to ice cream; naturally all sourced locally. They also do the daytime café at **Mellerstain** 1880/HOUSES Wed-Sat dinner only.

837 8/Q27
££
✓ **Coltman's** Peebles · www.coltmans.co.uk · **01721 720405** Bridge end of main street. A light, contemporary deli and café, with restaurant through the back and bar upstairs with cocktails. Karen and Kenny Coltman have created Peebles' most contemporary eaterie. Exudes confidence and class. Weekly changing menus. Dining area small, so book. Lovely breakfasts and puds. Deli counter out front with café tables. Sun-Wed 10am-5pm & Thu-Sat 10am-10pm.

838 8/Q27
££
✓ **Osso** Peebles · www.ossorestaurant.com · **01721 724477** 10 years on, Ally McGrath's perfectly judged and effective bistro/tearoom/restaurant changes through the day from lightsome lunch to scones and cakes and then to a superb comfort-food dining-out experience at night. With local staff and no city prices or pretensions, this is the eat-out place for many of Peebles' peoples. Lunch 7 days, dinner Thu-Sat.

839 8/R26
££
✓ **Firebrick Brasserie** Lauder · www.firebrickbrasserie.co.uk · **01578 718915** In the market place, the main street. Chef David Haetzman and pastry chef Amanda Jordan cooking up 'simply special food' and, well, great pastry and puddings in the northern gateway to the Borders (only 30 mins from Edinburgh bypass on the A68). Local sourcing, top ingredients but nothing too fancy. 45-day hung meat and the *best* chips. Light lunches and the desserts! Closed all Mon & Tue eve.

840 8/S27
£
✓ **The Cobbles Inn** Kelso · www.thecobbleskelso.co.uk · **01573 223548** Off the main square behind the Cross Keys. Popular local pub-grub (more grub than pub) restaurant. Luca and Stuart run a tight, friendly ship and care about their (mostly local) suppliers. Everything here is home-made: the bread, the chips, even the beer (Tempest Ales, 7 varieties). Bar and restaurant menu (evenings). This is without doubt where to casually eat in Kelso. 7 days.

841 8/P26 ✓ **The Old Bakehouse** West Linton · www.theoldbakehouserestaurant.
££ com · 01968 660830 Main street of village on A702, 12km S of Penicuik, 30km S of Edinburgh. Steve and Fiona are back at the Bakehouse, with Gareth and Scott in the kitchen, a top team in a country inn. Locals happy that this surprisingly roomy (3) restaurant, cosy throughout, with old bakehouse features and with a light conservatory type section at the back, is in their midst. Great comfort and gastropub menu. Evenings only (all day Sun). Closed Mon/Tue.

842 8/P26 **Whitmuir, the Organic Place** nr West Linton · www.
£ whitmuirtheorganicplace.co.uk · 01968 661908 Off A701, 15 mins from Peebles. Ambitious farm shop (1516/FARM SHOPS), food hall, gallery and café/restaurant in contemporary build on a real farm in the best kind of middle of nowhere. Food is taken seriously on a light, largely organic menu with fish, meat and vegetarian. Making things better; we need more farms like this! 7 days.

843 8/R28 **Damascus Drum Café & Books** Hawick · www.damascusdrum.co.uk ·
ATMOS 0786 7530709 Near tourist office, Chris and Frances Ryan's laid-back second-
£ hand bookshop and caff nestling discreetly in a Hawick backstreet. A love letter to (old) Damascus (Chris wrote a book, on sale here). Comfy seats. Home-made soups, meze and bagels ... and rugs. Closed Sun.

844 8/R27 **Monte Cassino** Melrose · www.montecassinomelrose.co.uk · 01896 820082
£ Up from the main square in the old station and station master's house, Melrose's biggest and buzziest restaurant. Cheerful, non-pretentious and popular Italian – i.e. Neapolitan – with pasta/pizza staples and the odd OK special. The place is packed; as always, that tells you something! Tue-Sun lunch & dinner.

845 8/Q27 **Saffron** Innerleithen · www.saffronauthenticindianrestaurant.co.uk ·
£ 01896 833466 The food here is authentic and surprising at that, on this street of traffic and bikes such a long way from, well, India. Smallish room, longish menu. Some say this is the best ethnic food in the Borders. 7 days 4-11pm.

846 8/R27 **Hunters Stables** St Boswells · www.huntersstables.co.uk · 01835 822710
££ Off Main Street from the A68 (the B6404), narrow road between the church and the town hall, a real surprise – a wine bar and Italian restaurant in the old Legion Clubroom, all spruced up, glass roof, light and roomy. Who'd expect it? Well, locals do and it's often lively. Salvatore de Martino and family work away turning out pasta and stone-baked pizzas. They're pretty good! Lunch & dinner. Closed Tue.

847 8/R28 **The Denholm Meet** Denholm · www.denholmmeet.com · 01450 870999 To
££ be honest, I didn't meet the Denholm Meet when I last whizzed through Denholm but I'm told I missed a great coffee shop and, at weekends, Italian restaurant run by Antonio Caterino, who has Monte Cassino (above). This must be true! There's an antique emporium upstairs. They say they have 'the best coffee in the Borders'. Tue-Sun 10am-4pm, Fri/Sat dinner.

848 8/R27 **Greenhouse Café** Melrose · www.greenhousecafemelrose.com ·
£ 01896 800360 By the road to the Abbey and the car park, usually thronged with people in and out, you can't miss The Greenhouse. Breakfast/lunch/tea. A Scottish café made for now. It grows people. 8am-6pm (5pm in winter).

✓ **Woodside** nr Ancrum Report: 1452/TEAROOMS.

✓ **Cross Keys** Ancrum Report: 1339/FOOD PUBS.

The Best Hotels & Restaurants
In The Lothians

See p. 30 in Section 2 for Edinburgh hotels/restaurants near the city.

849 8/R25
23 ROOMS
NO PETS
LL · **ATMOS**
£LOTS

✓✓ **Greywalls** Gullane · www.greywalls.co.uk · 01620 842144 Outside the village on the North Berwick road 36km E of Edinburgh, a classic country-house hotel in 6 superb acres of garden. Especially convenient for golfing: there are 12 courses nearby, including 3 championship and the hotel overlooks Muirfield (though no right of access). No grey walls here but warm sandstone and light, summery (cosy in winter) rooms: a manor house designed by Lutyens, the garden by Gertrude Jekyll – a rather winning combination. The roses are legendary and what could be nicer than afternoon tea ... well, dinner probably, in the Albert Roux-managed (and very branded) restaurant. Unsurprisingly expensive, the hotel and adjacent Colonel's House can be taken for exclusive use. There's a tennis court and croquet. 5 garden rooms look seaward. The evening light from the western sky over Muirfield is, in every way, priceless.

£LOTS **EAT** Dining rooms, drawing rooms and conservatory for bar and à la carte menu; both it and the wine list characteristically (of Roux outstations) well priced. And a classic afternoon tea pre/post the garden.

850 8/P25
14 ROOMS
NO PETS
££

✓✓ **Champany Inn** nr Linlithgow · www.champany.com · 01506 834532 Excellent restaurant with rooms near M9 junction 3, 30 mins from Edinburgh city centre, 15 mins from the airport. Long-established roadhouse hotel, and, across the courtyard, their famed restaurant (111/HOTELS OUTSIDE EDINBURGH), especially for those who want their meat properly hung (3 weeks, butchered on the premises) and presented. Superlative wine list, especially South African vintages also available to buy from The Cellar. Excellent breakfast.

£LOTS/££ **EAT** Accolades confirm the best meaty meal in West Lothian. More casual dining in the Chop 'n' Ale House. Angus beef, home-made sausages, the right oysters.

851 8/R25
12 ROOMS
£££

✓✓ **The Bonnie Badger** Gullane A major new East Lothian restaurant with rooms is opening after *StB* goes to print and no details are at hand. By Tom Kitchin and partners (118/FINE-DINING; 178/FOOD PUBS), it seems likely that this will be the new destination place to eat in the county and a stylish stopover (especially for golfers). 2 ticks here in anticipation! Search for website. **Eat** here.

852 8/R25
12 ROOMS
DF
££

✓ **Open Arms** Dirleton · www.openarmshotel.com · 01620 850241 Under careful and conscientious private ownership for a long time, the OA is a cosy and countrified hotel in this quintessentially East Lothian village opposite ancient ruins. If this were in France it might be a Hôtel de Charme. Location means it's a golfers' haven. Nice public rooms and lounging space. Deveau's Brasserie.

853 8/R25
12 ROOMS
££

✓ **Nether Abbey** North Berwick · www.netherabbey.co.uk · 01620 892802 On the Coastal Trail. Long-established, well-managed family (the Stewarts for 50 years) seaside hotel and a major drop-in bar/restaurant operation – the Fly-Half Bar and Grill (locally and well-sourced dishes). They also have the **Lobster Shack** (1365/SEAFOOD) and the Rocketeer Restaurant by the harbour. Busy downstairs, comfy bedrooms.

854 8/R25   **The Linton Hotel** East Linton · www.thelintonhotel.co.uk · 01620 860202
6 ROOMS   Family-run (the Cairneys) small country village hotel; friendly and welcoming.
£   Simple, quiet rooms and notable locally for bar meals and dining. Surprising
upstairs walled garden. A cosy corner of the county; unusually good value.
£   **EAT** Honest pub food (especially steaks) and 'small portion' menu in the bar and
upstairs in the restaurant opening to the garden.

855 8/R25   **Goblin Ha' Hotel** Gifford · www.goblinha.com · 01620 810244 A restaurant
7 ROOMS   with rooms in a much-loved village 7km from Haddington on the road to
££   Lammermuirs (good walking and on the village's **Yester Estate** 435/WALKS).
Always busy dining areas especially good for families, with a big beer garden. Very
personally run.
££   **EAT** Extensive menu. Exemplary village pub grub in an exemplary village.

856 8/R25   **Marine Hotel** North Berwick · www.macdonaldhotels.co.uk ·
83 ROOMS   01620 897300 The old seaside hotel of North Berwick extensively remodelled by
££   the Macdonald Group into a corporate hotel, spa and conference centre. Done in the
sombre/elegant style à la mode with lots of public space, and everywhere (except
the leisure area) the great views of the links and the sea. There are 20 golf courses on
your doorstep. Fine-ish dining in the purplish restaurant. Links bar less formal. And
there's afternoon tea. Pool and other vital facilities. It's all very North Berwick sitting
there with your tea or your G&T, the lawn, the links and mesmerising sea!

857 8/R25   **The Rocks** Dunbar · www.therockshoteldunbar.co.uk · 01368 862287 Not
11 ROOMS   signed but at the E end of Dunbar (take a right at Marine Rd), with great views
££   across the rocky harbour area (and at the start of a surprisingly scenic clifftop
walk past the Winterfield Golf Course (2k return), a hotel with big local reputation
for food. Rooms vary but about half have a view.
££   **EAT** They come from across the county to the gastropub but it's very much a
Dunbar thing. Old-style food & service.

858 8/P25   **The Hawes Inn** South Queensferry · www.innkeeperslodge.com ·
14 ROOMS   0131 331 1990 On the front by the pier in SQ, a historic inn (R. L. Stevenson
DF · L   connection) and a world-class view of the iconic Forth Bridge (7 rooms river facing).
££   This and the fact that it's inexpensive merit inclusion, though it's fairly basic
accom. Refreshingly, it doesn't try too hard. OK bar.

  Dakota South Queensferry Designed for travellers. Report: 112/HOTELS
OUTSIDE EDINBURGH.

Orocco Pier South Queensferry Boutique on the water. And the bridge.
Report: 115/HOTELS OUTSIDE EDINBURGH.

THE BEST RESTAURANTS IN EAST LOTHIAN

859 8/R25 ✓✓ **La Potinière** Gullane · www.lapotiniere.co.uk · 01620 843214 On
£££ the main street of a golfing mecca, this small, discreet restaurant has
been the East Lothian destination restaurant for decades. Keith Marley and Mary
Runciman, who share the cooking, have guarded its reputation since 2003. The
simple room is not bustling, but is just right for genteel Gullane and appreciation of
their effortlessly excellent 2-choice, locally sourced menu. By far the best casual
fine dining in East Lothian. Lunch Wed-Sun & dinner Wed-Sat. Closed Jan.

860 8/R25 ✓✓ **Steampunk** North Berwick · www.steampunkcoffee.co.uk ·
£ 01620 893030 Parallel small road to main street (Kirk Ports, opposite
church ruins). It is only a coffee shop, but two ticks because it's a perfect wee
coffee shop permanently established but with a pop-up (as in hipster) atmos. Great
coffee is roasted, blended and brewed here in an old joinery warehouse, with comfy
seats upstairs and some outside. Superior cheese toasties, brownies and the like.
People do come from Edinburgh. 7 days, daytime only.

861 8/R25 ✓ **Carlyle House** Haddington · www.carlylehousecafe.com ·
£ 01620 282201 Ambitious, aesthetically pleasing, architecturally sound and all
foodie credentials in order, opened late 2018, by Mhairi and Roy of Fenton Barns
below. Prominent Haddington location on Main St, in a historic building, a
ground-floor daytime café and beautiful upstairs room for exclusive use and regular
'Supper Club'. Chef Robin Campbell formerly of Edinburgh's Fruitmarket Gallery. An
eclectic, contemporary menu. Cool furniture and prints. 7 days 10am-5pm.

862 8/R25 ✓ **Fenton Barns Farm Shop** nr Drem · www.fentonbarnsfarmshop.com ·
£ 01620 850294 Farm shop/deli but also a great café (the original East Lothian
foray of the people with Carlyle House, above), with delicious food home-made
from the mainly local produce they sell; hot dishes till 3.30pm include their famous
stovies, then scrumptious cake. Not licensed. 7 days. See 1522/FARM SHOPS.

863 8/R25 ✓ **The Loft** Haddington · www.loftcafebakery.co.uk · 01620 824456 A
£ converted loft, find it down a non-traffic street 100m from the main street by
the council car park. Downstairs shop/takeaway, upstairs spacious, buzzing café/
restaurant featuring all of their bakings, bread, cakes, quiche, soups, all à la mode.
Charlotte and Anita come from the outskirts of Haddington, the crowd come by
word of mouth. Daytime only. Closed Sun.

864 8/R25 ✓ **Creel** Dunbar · www.creelrestaurant.co.uk · 01368 863279 Logan
££ Thorburn's meticulously run but informal bistro on a corner of old Dunbar
near the harbour; from a tiny kitchen he produces sound and simple, almost rustic
menus. Local, of course (crab and Eyemouth-landed haddock & whiting); but not
only seafood. Close-up and personal. Lunch Thu-Sun & dinner Wed-Sat.

865 8/R25 ✓ **Osteria** North Berwick · www.osteria-no1.co.uk · 01620 890589 A classic
££ Italian restaurant in main street of North Berwick, which has a growing
reputation as a foodtown, this out of Edinburgh's legendary restaurant Cosmo.
Angelo and family run it with old-fashioned values yet it is comfortably urbane in
both menu and service. Veal escalopes and proper posh pasta. Probably still North
Berwick's most consistently good restaurant. Good Italian wine list. Closed all day
Sun & Mon lunch.

866 8/R25
£
✓ **The Old Clubhouse** Gullane · www.oldclubhouse.com · 01620 842008
Behind main street, on corner of Green. Large, woody clubhouse; a bar/bistro serving a long menu (of the burgers/pasta/nachos variety) and daily specials all day till 9.30pm. Obliging, reliable. Great busy atmos. Surprising wine selection.

867 8/R25
DF
L
££
✓ **Waterside Bistro** Haddington · www.thewatersidebistro.co.uk · 01620 825674 Long a food find on the Tyne (over the bridge by St Mary's – the big church), it has had mixed fortunes but the Findlay brothers of the family who made the Waterside's reputation years ago have re-found the mojo. It is a classic waterside bistro. Separate chambers and ambience options (including long upstairs room), same menu throughout. Perfect on a summer's eve with the ducks plashing.

868 8/R25
££
The Herringbone North Berwick · www.theherringbone.co.uk · 01620 890501 Arrived on trend and perfectly formed in 2014, a bar (great by-the-glass wine list and all the right bottled and draught beers) and restaurant on the cool Edinburgh side of casual dining.

✓ **Falko** Haddington Report: 1476/ARTISAN BAKERS.

THE BEST RESTAURANTS IN WEST LOTHIAN

869 8/P25
££
✓ **The Boathouse** South Queensferry · www.theboathouse-sq.co.uk · 0131 331 5429 Enter from main street or down steps to terrace overlooking shingly beach and excellent views of the Bridge (400/ATTRACTIONS). Bistro serving all day from noon and a restaurant room in evenings. Nothing too fancy, mainly seafood in a lucky location. Best in SQ.

870 8/P25
££
✓ **Scott's At South Queensferry** Shore Rd · www.scotts-southqueensferry. co.uk · 0131 370 8166 Opened 2018 at Port Edgar, the SQ marina/boatyard and sea activity centre between the Forth Road Bridge and new Queensferry Crossing. Big shed transformation to make the most of the views and the attraction of Scotland's new landmark bridge. All the contemporary hospitalities by Buzzworks, who have Scott's (and other restaurants) in Troon 772/AYR and are all things to all drinkers and diners from breakfast to dinner. 7 days 8.30am-10pm.

871 8/Q26
££
✓ **The Radhuni** Loanhead · www.theradhuni.co.uk · 0131 440 3566 Centre of this small Midlothian town 8km S of Edinburgh city centre. This very good Indian restaurant, recommended by loads of readers, is a real surprise. Not much appears to be happening in downtown Loanhead till you go through their door and a huge restaurant (and outside terrace) opens up. Standard fare in an extensive menu, but all well done. Lunch & LO 10.30pm. Closed Mon.

872 8/N25
DF
£
Granary Café Linlithgow · www.granary.scot · 01506 253408 On High St near the Palace. Sweet coffee shop with great home baking, including hot dishes. Better than the brasher Cafebar 1807 adjacent. Closed Mon. 9am-4pm (Sat till 5pm).

✓✓ **Dakota** South Queensferry Report: 112/HOTELS OUTSIDE EDINBURGH.

✓ **Orocco Pier** South Queensferry Report: 115/HOTELS OUTSIDE EDINBURGH.

The Best Hotels & Restaurants In Fife

873 8/R23
109 ROOMS
35 SUITES
DF · LL
£LOTS

✓✓ **Old Course Hotel** St Andrews · www.oldcoursehotel.co.uk ·
01334 474371 Arriving in St Andrews on the A91, you come to the Old
Course and this world-renowned hotel first. An elegant presence on the hallowed
greens, it's full of golfers coming and going. It was designed by NY architects with
Americans in mind. American owner Herb Kohler and top manager Stephen Carter
at the helm of continuing upgrading, including a recent leisure centre extension to
the spa, with a lap pool in 2017. Rooms, most overlooking the famous course and
sea, are immaculate and tastefully done, with no facility or expense spared, as with
the **Sands Grill** and fine-dining **Road Hole Restaurant** up top. Bar here also for
lingering views and a big choice of drams. Truly great for golf, but anyone could
unwind here, towelled in luxury. Excellent Kohler Waters Spa with own pool,
thermal suite and some top treatments (1291/SPAS). No preferential deal on the Old
Course adjacent but there are 11 courses nearby; hotel has its own course, Dukes,
5km away.

£££ **EAT** Road Hole Restaurant for spectacular dinner, especially on late, light summer
nights. Sands is a grill, but an all-round casual dining menu. Nice afternoon tea.

874 8/Q24
8 ROOMS
NO PETS
£LOTS

✓✓ **The Peat Inn** nr St Andrews · www.thepeatinn.co.uk ·
01334 840206 A luxurious restaurant with rooms at a historic crossroads
20 mins from St Andrews (by Leven road or Strathkinness Rd). Long a foodie
destination. Geoffrey and Katherine Smeddle have upgraded the rooms and
transformed **The Residence** into a comfortable, very contemporary and above all
quiet retreat, rather than just a place to kip so you don't have to drive anywhere
after dinner. 7 of the rooms over 2 floors, pre-ordered breakfast discreetly delivered
to your upstairs dining room so you start your day relaxed. Llamas in the field
outside the hedge and woolly sheep in the garden when I was last there.
EAT Very special. This is Fife's top dining experience. Report below.

875 8/R23
24 ROOMS +
3 LODGES
DF
L
£LOTS

✓✓ **Rufflets** St Andrews · www.rufflets.co.uk · 01334 472594 4km from
centre along Strathkinness Low Rd. The Murray-Smiths' calm, elegant
country-house hotel on edge of town is the epitome of comfort and I once again
have to declare that I love it for its tranquillity and simple good taste. The
celebrated topiary gardens, tended by Phil and Grant, that lead down to the burn
(you can walk to St A in half an hour) are not just a joy, they're among the most
beautiful hotel grounds in the land. The redesigned restaurant, under chef David
Kinnes, makes the most of its verdant aspect, as do the comfy lounges, where
afternoon tea can be taken in peace. Cosy rooms, half overlook garden: 3 lodges in the
grounds and a conference/wedding suite in a separate building (so serenity remains
intact). The whisky bar with French windows to the lawn demonstrates the pleasing
balance of traditional and contemporary that a superb management team achieve
here. Emerging from the short drive on the road to downtown St A (10 mins), a field
opens before you – ploughed earth in winter, rippling wheat in summer. Sublime!

876 8/R24
4 ROOMS
DF
L
££

✓ **The Ship Inn** Elie · www.shipinn.scot · 01333 330246 On the famously
fine and quiet bay and beach, the destination Ship Inn has
4 superbly appointed rooms above (3 look out to sea). Bar and restaurant on
2 floors (1330/FOOD PUBS). The Ship has its own cricket team; there are frequent
fixtures on the beach (and boules). Graham and Rachel Bucknall have made
The Good Life here.

877 8/R23
37 ROOMS
DF
£LOTS

Hotel du Vin St Andrews · www.hotelduvin.com · 0844 748 9269
Overlooking sea to W of the West Sands. It's a measure of the seemingly
unstoppable sophisticating of hotels and restaurants in St A that H du V set up
shop here after Glasgow and Edinburgh (451/87/UNIQUE HOTELS), before anywhere
else in Scotland. As with the 11 others in the UK, in historic buildings, this is a
sympathetic conversion. Understated opulence. Corporate, golfy and masculine
style. 9 premium rooms have the sea view. No leisure facilities.

£££ **EAT** Bistro du Vin out front, al fresco terrace out back.

878 8/R23
212 ROOMS +
2 LODGES
L
£LOTS

Fairmont St Andrews (aka St Andrews Bay) nr St Andrews · www.
standrewsbay.com · 01334 837000 8km E on A917 to Crail overlooking
eponymous bay. Smart modern edifice in rolling greens taken over in 2017 by Accor,
with every facility a golfing family could need. Much more convivial than formerly. It
does have 2 notable courses and service is top. The St Andrews Bar & Grill, with the
Clubhouse 250m away and views to St Andrews and the bay, looks into an enormous
atrium, bars and **La Cucina** (their Italian restaurant). Indoor pool.

879 8/R23
8 ROOMS
££

The Old Station nr St Andrews · www.theoldstation.co.uk ·
01334 880505 On B9131 (Anstruther road) off A917 from St Andrews. Colin and
Fiona Wiseman's individualist contemporary makeover of a Victorian station with
themed rooms; they are most hospitable hosts! Library, putting green, snooker,
ping-pong. Conservatory breakfast room, comfy lounge. 2 garden suites in a railway
carriage are curiously comfy! Nice for kids. B&B only.

880 8/P25
141 ROOMS
LL
££

Doubletree by the Queensferry Crossing North Queensferry · www.
doubletree-queensferry.co.uk · 01383 410000 Only just in Fife. From
Edinburgh, take first turn-off after Queensferry Crossing and it's just before the
village. Superior bedbox in Hilton-land, recommended because of its location
between both road bridges; peerless view (from the Shore Grill and some rooms).

881 8/R24
45 BEDS
L
££

Cambo Estate nr Crail · www.camboestate.com · 01333 450054 2km E of Crail
on A917. Huge country pile in glorious gardens on the St Andrews–Crail coastal road.
Individual, even quirky self-catering, B&B (communal-style breakfast in enormous
morning room). Rooms arranged in apartments (and 3 cottages). This home-stay in
the grand manner, especially for groups (1305/HOUSE PARTIES), is not so expensive.
Grounds are superb, especially in early spring – the snowdrops! (18/EVENTS).
The walled garden 150m from house is a joy and a massive work in progress, with a
great tearoom and shop in the adjacent stable block. Great walks and **Kingsbarns**
golf (2104/GOLF), distillery (1548/GIN) and beach adjacent. Cambo is becoming a dear
green place: as house guests, there are many grounds for loving it.

For accommodation in St Andrews, see p. 155.

THE BEST RESTAURANTS IN FIFE

882 8/Q24
ATMOS
£LOTS

The Peat Inn nr St Andrews · www.thepeatinn.co.uk ·
01334 840206 Legendary restaurant (with 8 suites; see above) at the
eponymous crossroads. Geoffrey and Katherine Smeddle have made it one of the
great Scots dining-out experiences. Tables spread over 3 separate cottage dining
rooms. A tasting menu, seasonal à la carte and good-value menu du jour offer
loads of food for thought. Unlike some top chefs, Michelin-starred chef-patron
Geoffrey Smeddle is always there. Handily close to St Andrews, it is still the most
sophisticated and accomplished dining spot in an area not short of foodie options.
Superb wine list, especially French. Sommelier on hand. Tue-Sat lunch & dinner.

883 8/R24
££
✓✓ **East Pier** St Monans · www.eastpier.co.uk · 01333 405030 Arrive at the front in St Monans and look left, by the harbour: the big weatherworn shed. Inside, and on the roof in summer, still Fife's most effortlessly cool place to eat. Shellfish and fish from the sea that laps (or crashes) below. Superbly matched wines and home-made cakes. Upstairs tables in and out. A rosé on the terrace on a summer's eve, dolphins over there is not the Fife we used to know. We do now! Apr-Oct.

884 8/R24
ATMOS
£££
✓✓ **The Cellar** Anstruther · www.thecellaranstruther.co.uk · 01333 310378 Off a courtyard behind the Fisheries Museum in this busy East Neuk town (1613/VILLAGES). Discreet entrance to a comforting oasis of epicurean delight, one that has put Anstruther on the foodie map for 40 years. Now under chef/patron Billy Boyter, a new chapter is being written. Billy brings a deft touch to masterful dishes that so invoke the seasons, but this is Michelin-starred cooking (and a seductive wine list) at infeasibly reasonable prices. 5-course set lunch and 7-course dinner (inform of diets ahead). I was very glad I made the journey from Edinburgh on a wild winter's day for food that would soothe the soul in any season. Lunch Thu-Sun & dinner Wed-Sun.

885 8/Q23
£££
✓ **Ostler's Close** Cupar · www.ostlersclose.co.uk · 01334 655574 Down a close off the main street, Amanda and Jimmy Graham quietly and conscientiously run a bistro/restaurant that has been on the gastronomic map and a reason for coming to Cupar since 1981; it's so reassuring they're still such consummate restaurateurs. Intimate, cottagey rooms. Amanda out front also does puds, Jimmy a star in the kitchen. Long before it was de rigueur they pioneered local and personal sourcing. Often organic and from their garden, big on mushrooms and other wild things, and lots of fish choice – the handwritten menu sums up their approach. Cupar is only 20 mins from St Andrews. Go to it! Must book.

886 8/P25
££
✓ **The Wee Restaurant** North Queensferry · www.theweerestaurant.co. uk · 01383 616263 Just over the Road Bridge from Edinburgh and in the shadow of the **Rail Bridge** (400/ATTRACTIONS). It's a wee restaurant (in a quiet wee town) with only a few tables up a few stairs from the street, but it is a gem. Award-winning owner/chef Craig Wood and missus, Vikki, live through the back, bake the bread in the morning and prepare their no-fuss menu with commitment (to good food) and aplomb (and awards!). There's no bistro as good as this nearby except in Edinburgh. Neat wine list. Tue-Sat lunch & dinner and Sun lunch.

887 8/Q23
££
✓ **The Newport Restaurant** Newport-on-Tay · www. thenewportrestaurant.co.uk · 01382 541449 Sharing with the Tatha Gallery, a prominent building with a fabulous view over the (seldom silvery) Tay to Dundee, Jamie Scott's (a Professional MasterChef winner) 2-floor contemporary restaurant created a stir when it opened in 2017. Small plates at lunch and a 6-course tasting menu for dinner, this is a special treat and foodie experience that I haven't had myself at TGP; all reports effusively good. Closed Mon.

888 8/Q23
££
The View Wormit · www.view-restaurant.co.uk · 01382 542287 On the main road in or out of Wormit next to the PO, it has a great view right enough (of the Tay Bridge and bonnie Dundee). Steve and Karen Robertson's cool, calm restaurant over the water, though not in the city, is urbane dining. All-day menu from breakfast through lunch and tea/cake/light bites to dinner; Steve's unpretentious contemporary cooking is worth coming over the Bridge for. Closed Mon.

Fish & Chips In Fife: Valente's, Anstruther Fish Bar, Pittenweem Fish & Chip Bar 3 great fish 'n' chip shops; queues every day. All very good and a change from the fancier foodie places. Reports: 1392/1396/1383/FISH & CHIPS.

If You're In St Andrews...

Many of the places below are also listed in Scotland- or Fife-wide categories.

WHERE TO STAY

✓✓ **Old Course Hotel** Old Station Rd Report: 873/FIFE.

✓✓ **Rufflets** Strathkinness Low Rd Report: 875/FIFE.

✓ **Fairmont (St Andrews Bay)** nr St Andrews Report: 878/FIFE.

✓ **Hotel du Vin** 40 The Scores Report: 877/FIFE.

The Old Station nr St Andrews Report: 879/FIFE.

889 8/R23 **Rusacks Hotel** The Links · www.macdonaldhotels.co.uk · 0344 879 9136
68 ROOMS Long-standing, golfy hotel near all courses and overlooking the 1st and 18th of
DF the Old. You're at the heart of the matter here. Nice sun lounge and breakfast
£LOTS overlooking the greens. Jack Nicklaus looms large. Reliable and relatively classy
Macdonald Hotel. Fine-ish dining and gastropub The One Under.

890 8/R23 **Ardgowan Hotel** 2 Playfair Terrace · www.ardgowanhotel.co.uk ·
36 ROOMS 01334 472970 Highly regarded but modest hotel (incorporating the Pilmour
££ adjacent) and restaurant, **Playfair's**, with chef Duncan McLachlan (does a very
good steak). Simple, serviceable rooms the best in these blocks.

891 8/R23 **Albany Hotel** 56 North St · www.albanyhotelstandrews.co.uk ·
22 ROOMS 01334 477737 Townhouse hotel with surprising number of rooms and secret back
NO PETS garden. All rooms are individually (though not in a boutique sense) done; 3 suites.
££ Bar and basement breakfast room, The Garden. A very St Andrews kind of a hostelry.

892 8/R23 **Kinnettles Hotel** 127 North St · www.kinnettleshotel.com ·
9 ROOMS 01334 473387 Corner of Murray Park where there are numerous guest-house
££ options. Boutique-ish rooms above restaurant and civilised café-bar. Comfy,
contemporary rooms, much improved from previous Ogstons.

893 8/R23 **Five Pilmour Place** 5 Pilmour Pl · www.5pilmourplace.com ·
7 ROOMS 01334 478665 Adjacent 18th green of Old Course. Contemporary-style and well-
NO PETS TripAdvised guest house with lounge. The Wrights have got it, well, ... right, and are
££ notably obliging. Great breakfast choice.

894 8/R23
££ ✓✓ **The Adamson** 127 South St · www.theadamson.com ·
01334 479191 Could be Glasgow, could be NYC: together with its cocktail bar adjacent, The Adamson brought a truly urban-contemporary look and feel to St Andrews dining and drinking. Always busy but smart, sympatico service. And the food, Modern British, seasonal and locally sourced is somehow even better than you'd expect from this level of turnover (and noise). Along with The Vine Leaf next door (and almost the polar opposite), this is probably the most fine, though not *fine* dine in town. 7 days.

895 8/R23
££ ✓ **The Vine Leaf** 131 South St · www.vineleafstandrews.co.uk ·
01334 477497 Not the most enticing entrance belies what has been for a very long time St A's best all-round restaurant. Unapologetically old style, the incredibly long and varied eclectic menu covers all bases, including not just token vegetarian. Morag and Ian Hamilton look after you and kinda know what you like (especially for pud). How they manage to turn out such consistently high-quality food of this variety remains a mystery; they pick the leaves in their garden, they bake many breads. The wine is good! David Joy's calming pictures around the walls are for sale. Tue-Sat dinner only.

896 8/R23
£ ✓ **Little Italy** 2 Logies Lane · 01334 472595 Behind the church in South St, down the lane from Pizza Express. Here the pizzas, pastas and all things tratt are better. Hidden from view it is perhaps surprising that this is one of St A's busiest restaurants. 7 days noon-10.30pm (open later than most). Best book.

897 8/R23
££ ✓ **Steak Barn @ Balgove Larder** Strathtyrum, nr St Andrews · www.balgove.com · 01334 898145 2km from town on the A91 beyond the Old Course Hotel. Beside the excellent emporium (1518/FARM SHOPS), one of the most innovative and interesting diners in the land – a lofty barn with crates for walls, serving great steaks and burgers. Al fresco but undercover, it's a bit like a great long B&Q. Luvians ice cream. Rough, ready and rather good. 7 days noon-9pm.

898 8/R23
£ **The Tailend Restaurant & Fish Bar** 130 Market St · www.thetailend.co.uk · 01334 474070 The original of the Tailends (they're also in Dundee) and demonstrably a commitment to good F&C served sizzlingly fresh. Contemporary design (fresh fish on ice), takeaway out front, surprisingly spacious caff through the back and outside terrace. Many choices but it's haddock/cod 'n' chips, ain't it?

899 8/R23
£ **Cromars 'Classic' Fish & Chips** 1 Union St · www.cromars.co.uk ·
01334 475555 Corner at the top of Market St. Café/takeaway and delivery (winter only). 'Classic', so they use lard but everything fresh and, yes, so tasty. They also do Cullen skink, maccy cheese and Jannetta's ice cream. St A has two, not one, great chippies. One of the partners opened **The Fish Hoose** in Main St, Thornton. 7 days.

900 8/R23
£ **Mitchell's** 110-112 Market St · www.mitchellsstandrews.co.uk ·
01334 441396 A deli and, along with **Forgan's** 110 Market St · www.forgans.co.uk · 01334 466973 adjacent, a café-bar with all the right contemporary civilities. These are, I'd say, the best of a number of eateries run by the G1 Group aimed at the lucrative student market (and their parents). Modern, modish menu and great atmos. Breakfast right through to late suppers. 7 days.

901 8/R23 **Northpoint** 24 North St · 01334 473997 Top of North St. Great little caff.

£ Coffee, salads, home-made stuff – soup, scones, hot dishes; good vibe. Notably inexpensive in this town. Open daytime.

 **Taste** 148 North St By common consent, I believe, the best coffee in a caffeinated town. Report: 1429/COFFEE.

✓ **The Seafood Ristorante** Bruce Embankment Top seafood, top view (Old Course and the sea). Report: 1366/SEAFOOD.

✓ **Jannetta's** 31 South St Famous popular caff. Extremely good ice cream, et cetera. 7 days till 10pm. Report: 1493/ICE CREAM.

✓ **Balgove Larder** nr St Andrews The always busy café in the farm shop. Report: 1518/FARM SHOPS, and see **Steak Barn** above.

The Best Hotels & Restaurants In Perthshire & Tayside

902 8/N22
42 ROOMS
DF
£LOTS

✓✓ **Fonab Castle Hotel** Pitlochry · www.fonabcastlehotel.com ·
01796 470140 Above town and Loch (Faskally), grounds edged by A9 but reached via road behind Festival Theatre. Joanne and Jed Clark spent a lot of money and a lot of love on this extraordinary contemporary hotel, unique in the county. Rooms in the 'Castle' itself and two more contemporary extensions all to very high spec; spacious and comfortable. Some balconies. Brasserie or fine-dining restaurants, spa overby, with 4 treatment rooms and 15m pool. None of this is cheap but it is a well-shorn cut above the rest.

£LOTS/£££ **EAT** Paul Burns oversees fine-dining **Sandemans** (dinner only Tue-Sat), and the **Brasserie**; views and terrace. Hotel picks up and taxis back to Pitlochry if you're staying elsewhere.

903 8/P21
17 ROOMS
DF
L
££

✓✓ **Dalmunzie Castle** Spittal of Glenshee · www.dalmunzie.com ·
01250 885224 3km from Perth–Braemar road close to Glenshee ski slopes and good base for Royal Deeside without Deeside prices. 9-hole golf course for fun and the air. Highland hunting-lodge feel: tasteful, comfortable, great attention to detail; a semi-chic retreat! Hills all around and burn beside; a truly peaceful outlook. Regular mention in Michelin, and many loyal returnees, notable wine list, bar-billiards room, great whisky bar. A fire in the hall! Roger Aston and Vietnamese Trong Aston your solicitous hosts. It's pronounced 'Dalmungee', BTW.

904 8/M23
11 ROOMS
DF
££

✓ **The Royal Hotel** Comrie · www.royalhotel.co.uk · 01764 679200 Central square of cosy town, and a surprisingly stylish small-town hotel in the capable hands of the Milsom family. Good restaurant with light comfy lounge and a bar and also a pub out back with ale and atmos. Lovely gardens for both hotel and pub. Bar food menu available all over and à la carte and specials in the dining room. Nice rugs and pictures. Rooms vary. A pleasing touch of understated class in the country bit of the county. Both restaurant and bar food till 9pm.

905 8/N21
10 ROOMS
DF · L
MAR–NOV
££

££

✓ **Killiecrankie Hotel** Killiecrankie · www.killiecrankiehotel.co.uk ·
01796 473220 5km N of Pitlochry off A9 on B8079 signed Killiecrankie; near Blair Castle. Roadside inn long loved for food and cosy rooms. Delightful garden supplying kitchen. Conscientiously run with a simple good taste. Henrietta Fergusson's cottage home from home will also be yours. As Henrietta well knows, I have never stayed here – I just know with audacious certainty that it's good.

EAT Bar and conservatory seasonal menus and dining room with daily à la carte menu. Proper good food from chef Mark Easton.

906 8/N22
4 ROOMS
£££

£££

✓ **Errichel** Aberfeldy · www.errichelhouseandrestaurant.co.uk ·
01887 829562 4km from Aberfeldy in the hills overlooking the valley, including Schiehallion on a good day, a farm homestead with self-catering cottages and boutique-type rooms in the farmhouse. Great location and rural setting with a duck pond and a notable restaurant open for dinner (they also run a cook school). If I regret anything in these Perthshire hills, it's that I haven't (at TGP) made it yet to Errichel to stay and eat.

EAT **Thyme at Errichel**: food with views and very good reviews. Thu-Sat dinner only. Paul Newman is your award-winning chef.

907 8/N23 ✓ **Yann's** Crieff · www.yannsatglenearnhouse.com · 01764 650111
4 ROOMS   Yannick and Shari Grospellier's splendid restaurant with rooms: a bistro and a
DF   small mansion-house hotel on the Perth road out of town. This really is where to
££   eat around here. Very French (Yann from Chamonix). A la carte, specials, grill menu
           and Savoyard specials, raclette and fondue and, well, ... steak frites. Dining very
           family friendly. The so comfy rooms are not expensive. Don't ever stop, guys!
           Dinner Wed-Sun & Sun lunch. Best book!

908 8/P22 ✓ **Ballathie House** Kinclaven, nr Perth · www.ballathiehousehotel.com ·
25+ 16   01250 883268 A true country-house hotel on the Tay that you can fall in love
+ 11 ROOMS with, especially if you hunt, shoot, fish, or just love rivers. Comfortingly old-style,
DF · L   the river and the astonishing trees are the thing. Great fishing – they have rights
££   Jan-Apr; good for a weekend away. 'Riverside' rooms are across the lawn (150m
           walk for breakfast) and uniform but you taste the Tay. Also cheaper, motel-like
           Sportsman's Lodge adjacent main house. Always enjoy the approach: red squirrels,
           copper beeches, sometimes the golden corn.
££   **EAT** Chef Scott Scorer. Local and estate produce, especially beef/lamb.

909 8/M22 **Fortingall Hotel** nr Aberfeldy · www.fortingall.com · 01887 830367 Historic
10 ROOMS   roadhouse hotel on the road to gorgeous Glen Lyon, 8km from Aberfeldy, one of
££   the most beautiful Arts and Crafts villages in Scotland. Refurbished to a boutique-
           style standard. Adjacent the kirkyard and famous Fortingall Yew, the oldest tree in
           Europe. It has long had a reputation for food (in 2 dining rooms and bar) under chef
           David Dunn and conscientious local (and very local) sourcing. **The Ewe Bar** at the
           side is a sympatico spot. Sunday lunch.

910 8/Q21 **Glen Clova Hotel** Clova · www.clova.com · 01575 550350 Near end of Glen
18 ROOMS   Clova, one of the great Angus glens (1647/GLENS) on B955 25km N of Kirriemuir.
DF · L   The Nivens' walk/climb/country-retreat hotel; very comfy. Superb walking nearby.
££   Often full. 9 luxury lodges out back have hot tubs and fluffy duvets. This place is a
           very civilised Scottish inn in the hills and great value.

911 8/P22 **Atholl Arms Hotel** Dunkeld · www.athollarmshotel.com · 01350 727219 On
17 ROOMS   main street by the bridge. Decent hotel in a great Perthshire town with great
DF   walking, fishing, etc. Good that there's somewhere to stay to recommend here.
££   Simple rooms of different sizes (2 with river view). Food so-so, perhaps, but
           splendid garden and river terrace by the bridge overby.

✓✓✓ **Gleneagles** Auchterarder Report: 1160/COUNTRY-HOUSE HOTELS.

✓✓✓ **Crieff Hydro** Superb. These ticks especially for family holidays.
Quintessentially Scottish. Report: 1166/KIDS.

✓✓ **Kinloch House** nr Blairgowrie Quintessential Perthshire comfort and
joy. Report: 1163/COUNTRY-HOUSE HOTELS.

✓ **The Barley Bree** Muthill, nr Crieff Report: 1205/INNS.

✓ **The Inn on the Tay** Grandtully Report: 1212/INNS.

For restaurants in Pitlochry, see p. 163.

912 8/N24
£LOTS

✓✓✓ **Andrew Fairlie at Gleneagles** Auchterarder · www.gleneagles.com · **01764 694267** A rare 3 tick restaurant in *StB* and the only one in Scotland with 2 Michelin stars. Gleneagles is obviously a world-class destination and Andrew's international accolades, unassuming dedication to food, to good cooking and to Scotland all place it in a class of its own. Deep in the hotel's interior, well laid out and lit, a room where we come to experience as well as eat ingredients that seem both effortlessly and masterfully matched, dish after dish. Tasting menus and à la carte. Many perfectly judged, mouth-watering morsels, pre and après. The kitchen garden supplies superb salad and veg. Though Andrew is no longer in the kitchen, he will always be here in spirit and on the wall in a portrait among the Archie Forrests, and in his influence across the menu. Hotel guests and international visitors may frequent these tables; we Scots are proud of this restaurant and go there for that special food experience. Dinner only. Closed Sun and Jan.

913 8/P23
££

✓✓ **North Port** Perth · www.thenorthport.co.uk · **01738 580867** Beside Perth Theatre. Karen Milne and acclaimed chef Andrew Moss preside over Perth's 'Scottish Restaurant' *par excellence*, seasonal menu sourced and found locally. Kind to vegetarians and vegans. Great pre-theatre menu served all night Tue-Thu. Integrity on the plate. Lunch & dinner. Closed Sun/Mon.

914 8/P23
£LOTS

✓✓ **63 Tay Street** Perth · www.63taystreet.com · **01738 441451** On the riverside road and walk. Graeme Pallister from Parklands hotel (see Perth), where there is another 63, presides over a premier Perthshire food destination; well sourced, seasonal and, as they say, 'local, honest, simple'. Tasting menu, à la carte fine dining. Well priced. Book weekends. Tue-Sat lunch & dinner.

915 8/R22
£££

✓✓ **Gordon's** Inverkeilor · www.gordonsrestaurant.co.uk · **01241 830364** Halfway between Arbroath and Montrose on the main street. A restaurant with rooms (5) which has won loadsa accolades for the Watson family, Garry in the kitchen, a Scottish Chef of the Year. It's been here for 33 seriously good years! Splendid people doing good Franco-Scot cooking. Seasonal menu. It is the best meal for miles. Closed Mon (except for residents). **Lunan Bay** to work up an appetite 1629/BEACHES.

916 8/P23
£££

✓ **The Roost** Bridge of Earn · www.theroostrestaurant.co.uk · **01738 812111** About 5km from Perth and 5 mins from the M9, Bridge of Earn turn-off (signed) and at the gates of Kilgraston School, a superb little cottage bistro. Chef Tim Dover and wife Anna have created a secret food oasis in the Perth hinterland. Great local sourcing: Josper grill, meat from cows on the hills over there. A small, informal, usually full parlour. Go book! Lunch through to LO 8pm, Wed-Sat (LO 4pm Sun).

917 8/R22
LL
££

✓ **The But 'n' Ben** Auchmithie · www.thebutnben.com · **01241 877223** 2km off A92 N from Arbroath, 8km to town, or 4km by clifftop walk. Village on that clifftop where a ravine leads to a cove and quay. Adjacent cottages converted into a cosy restaurant. All very Scottish and informal, emphasising fresh fish, seafood and the smokies. The brilliant couthy creation of Margaret Horn; after nearly 40 years, still in the family – Angus (in kitchen) and Margo out front, assuring a warm welcome and consistency for a huge loyal following. Lunch & dinner. Famous Sunday high tea, sittings at 4pm and 5.30pm. Closed Tue. Book!

918 8/M23 ✓ **Deil's Cauldron** Comrie · www.deilscauldron.co.uk · 01764 670352 On
££ bend of the A85 main road through town, corner of the Glen Lednock road. For
15 years, Katy and Brian Healy have run their cottage restaurant quietly and
consistently. A much-loved destination for lunch, dinner (especially steaks) and the
eclectic tapas menu in the wine bar. Seriously good wine list; cosy ambience and
just possibly a summer garden out back. Tue-Sun lunch & Tue-Sat dinner.

919 8/N23 ✓ **Delivino** Crieff · 01764 655665 & Auchterarder · 01764 660033 · www.
£ delivino.co.uk The original branch (Crieff) is just off the main street. Jamie
Stewart's perfectly judged, comfy bistro, where ladies may lunch. Great thin, crispy,
wood-oven pizza. On Auchterarder's High St, an all-day café/restaurant, and
takeaway too. Opening times vary.

920 8/Q22 **88°** Kirriemuir · 07449 345089 On main square. Johanna and Philip
£ Woodhead's labour-of-love deli-café is a welcome find hereabouts. Artisan food,
chocolates, handmade specials and great coffee. The hot food and deli platters are
conscientiously done. 8.30am-5pm (10am-4pm Sun). Closed Mon/Tue.

921 8/N23 **Lounge (aka Wee Yann's)** Crieff · www.loungeincrieff.co.uk ·
£ 01764 654407 West end of main street. As it says, a lounge, an uptown extension
of Yann's (see Hotels, above) – his sister Delphine keeping even more Perthshire
people happy and well fed. Here you come to graze and sup, not pig out. Has the
comfy wine-bar look. Another good thing about Crieff. Closed Sun/Mon.

922 8/P22 **Little's** Blairgowrie · 01250 875358 On the A93 after the square on the Braemar
££ road N, in the church on the corner. Willie Little's mainly fish bistro may be a
long way from the sea but it's among the best upriver in the shire. Casual dining,
no airs, a bit of a find on your way to the Glenshee slopes or Royal Deeside, and
definitely where to eat in Blairgowrie. Tue-Sat lunch & dinner, Sun noon-8pm.

923 8/N22 **Three Lemons** Aberfeldy · www.threelemons.co.uk · 01887 820057 East end
££ of main street. An all-round bar/restaurant, pizzas-to-go place. Surprisingly urban
atmos and original features, good contemporary dining, whiskies and cocktails.
Closed Mon.

The Best of Pitlochry

WHERE TO STAY

924 8/N21
14 ROOMS
££

✓ **Craigatin House** 165 Atholl Rd · www.craigatinhouse.co.uk · 01796 472478 Gorgeous boutique B&B in, as they say, Highland Perthshire, on main street (but the road N) of this tourist town. The house and courtyard (1820s) transformed into a smart contemporary and comfortable retreat from Pitlochry's more tourist-driven hostelries. Martin and Andrea Anderson are your obliging and constantly upgrading hosts. Rooms in both mansion and courtyard; great bathrooms. Breakfast and guest lounge built around a wood-burning stove. Serene garden. **Derrybeg** 18 Lower Oakfield · www.derrybeg.co.uk · 01796 472070 is their other B&B in, but above, the town. 8 less expensive rooms; same hospitality.

925 8/N21
14 ROOMS
NO PETS
££

✓ **Knockendarroch** Higher Oakfield · www.knockendarroch.co.uk · 01796 473473 Find via E Moulin Rd. The Lothian family moved from Torrdarach (see below) to this larger mansion also overlooking the town and transformed it into a contemporary top stay with a destination dining room. Comfortable, friendly Perthshire accom. For food see below.

926 8/N21
7 ROOMS
NO PETS
££

✓ **Torrdarach House** Golf Course Rd · www.torrdarach.co.uk · 01796 472136 The big pink house above town (via Larchwood Rd off N main street) and almost in the country: they have their own wee woody glen. Complete contemporary makeover of old established B&B: light, modern rooms; lots of pictures. Free-range hens in garden and their eggs for breakfast in beautiful room overlooking garden and gorge with scampering squirrels. Golfy guy Graeme Fish your enthusiastic host.

927 8/N21
29 ROOMS
DF
££

✓ **Pine Trees Hotel** Strathview Terrace · www.pinetreeshotel.co.uk · 01796 472121 A safe and sophisticated haven in visitor-ville – it's above the town and above all that (there are many mansions here). Take Larchwood Rd off N end of main street. Woody gardens, woody interior. Valerie and Robert Kerr the careful owners. Very traditional but with taste (nice rugs). Annex and Coach House have added more standardised but high-spec rooms (a short walk).

928 8/N21
12 ROOMS
££

✓ **The Old Mill Inn** Mill Lane · www.theoldmillpitlochry.co.uk · 01796 474020 Behind the main bus stop on the main street (opposite Fishers Hotel). Extraordinary conversion to create this restaurant with rooms, done to a high spec. There is an old mill wheel and a busy bar/restaurant around it, with OK contemporary food. Rooms are surprisingly fresh, urban and relaxing. Good value and right in the centre of town.

929 8/N22
13 ROOMS
DF
££

✓ **East Haugh House** by Pitlochry · www.easthaugh.co.uk · 01796 473121 On S approach to Pitlochry from A9, a mansion house built in the 18th century; part of the Atholl estate. Notable for hunting/shooting and especially fishing breaks, and for very decent food in dining room or in the cosy Fisherman's Bar. Family-run with chef/proprietor Neil McGowan. Nice fly-fishing themed rooms, some are romantic with it (3 rooms have four-posters). A top retreat and restaurant near the Tay.

930 8/N21
17 ROOMS
DF
££

McKays Hotel 113 Atholl Rd · www.mckayshotel.co.uk · 01796 473888 An all-round smart operation – they've thought of everything. Extensive bar, bistro with sports TV, live music, even dancing on Saturdays. Black-kilted waiters; over 100 whiskies. Contemporary rooms. It all presents well (to both tourists and locals).

WHERE TO EAT IN PITLOCHRY

931 8/N22
£LOTS
✓ **Fonab Castle Hotel** Foss Rd Only 'fine dining' in town, and brasserie with a view. Will pick up from other accom and taxi back. See 902/PERTHSHIRE.

932 8/N22
££
✓ **East Haugh House** by Pitlochry 10 mins by car/taxi from main street. Top dining in bar and conservatory restaurant under chef Neil McGowan. Lunch & LO 8.30pm. See above.

933 8/N21
££
✓ **Knockendarroch** Higher Oakfield A suburban dining room above the town. Everyone I know in Pitlochry says eat here. Chef Graeme Stewart excels. Dinner only. See above.

934 8/N21
£
The Auld Smiddy Inn 154 Atholl Rd · www.auldsmiddyinn.co.uk · 01796 472356 A long time here, and great of late, the Auld Smiddy dispenses reliable grub that remarkably is all (the chips, the bread, the ice cream) home-made. If in downtown Pitlochry, look no further. 7 days lunch & LO 8.30pm.

935 8/N21
££
McKays Hotel 113 Atholl Rd & **The Old Mill Inn** Mill Lane Somewhat similar contemporary casual dining. Locals seem to prefer The Old Mill but maybe that's just the ones I've met. McKays has a good F&C café and takeaway adjacent. See above.

936 8/N21
££
Victoria's 45 Atholl Rd · www.victorias-pitlochry.co.uk · 01796 472670 For 20 years the local bistro/brasserie of choice. By the folk who have The Old Mill, above. Lunch & LO 9pm.

937 8/N21
££
Fern Cottage Ferry Rd · www.ferncottagepitlochry.co.uk · 01796 473840 Just off main street, by Victoria's, above. Another long-standing, highly regarded Pitlochry pit stop. They say 'where Scotland meets the Mediterranean', some sun needed in the darkish interior, perhaps, to believe this, but consistently good fare.

938 8/N21
££
Prince of India 5 Station Rd · 01796 472275 50m from junction with the main street. This standard but good Indian restaurant has also stood the time test (25 years). It still thrives. When you long for a change from avocado on sourdough, or chips. 7 days lunch & LO 10.30pm (the latest in town).

The Best Places To Stay In & Around Dundee

939 8/Q23
151 ROOMS
NO PETS
££

✓ **The Apex** West Victoria Dock Rd, Dundee · www.apexhotels.co.uk · 01382 202404 There are 4 Apex hotels in Edinburgh, 3 in London, and one in Glasgow, and they're all good 4/5-star business and leisure options. Here in Dundee, this glassy waterfront edifice, overlooking both bridge and dock has for years been the contemporary hotel of choice. Now there's some competition, but it's good value; there's a pool and the Yu Spa. Restaurant serviceable but now many choices in the emerging waterfront quarter. Rooms facing the firth and out to sea are best. Big waterfront developments are in progress; and the V&A is changing everything. The beauty of the Apex location is its urban serenity, with dreamy views of a non-bustling waterfront and with the Foxlake frolics down below.

940 8/Q23
91 ROOMS
L
££

✓ **Malmaison** 44 Whitehall Crescent, Dundee · www.malmaison.com · 0844 693 0661 On the roadways bordering the waterfront and the recent public space developments, including the V&A. So, a great location near the station and downtown Dundee. No expense spared in the 2014 'Mal-ing' up of this old hotel building, though the plush purple and grey drapes and decoration may feel a tad OTT (or dare we suggest ... already passé). Rooms kind of look to the river or the city. Original windows so not a lot of light. First-floor brasserie, with classic brazz menu, does overlook the developments. Breakfast not a strong point. Malbar (the bar) is cool, but no leisure facilities or parking (though car park adjacent). Rooms are often surprisingly good value.

941 8/Q23
12 ROOMS
ATMOS
£

✓ **Fisherman's Tavern** Fort St, Broughty Ferry · www.fishermanstavern-broughtyferry.co.uk · 01382 775941 Not a hotel, it's a pub but an old and interesting one at that, down by the river and the sea. These modest 17th-century fishermen's cottages were converted into a pub in 1827. Rooms above and the adjacent cottages are contemporary and exceptionally good value, hence 'the tick'. Excellent real ales and pub menu, but also near **The Ship Inn** (952/DUNDEE RESTAURANTS) and many other eats.

942 8/Q23
102 ROOMS
££

✓ **Hotel Indigo Dundee** Constable St, Dundee · www.ihg.com · 0330 331 1750 At TGP, Dundee's latest contemporary chain hotel (Indigos are part of the Intercontinental Group), as the V&A helps to revitalise the city's attraction to visitors. Remodelling of a historic mill building, so many references to 'Jam, Jute & Journalism'. Spacious, light brasserie/bar (the Daisy Tasker – who's she?). All the expected urban hotel niceties.

943 8/Q23
26 ROOMS
NO PETS
££

The Fort Hotel Fort St, Broughty Ferry · www.fort-hotel.com · 01382 737999 On street leading to the waterfront, 'The Ferry' is 20 mins from downtown Dundee but it's just possibly where you want to be: low rise, low noise and the village boasts a lovely riverfront and esplanade, lots of good restaurant/café choices, and is rather genteel. This hotel has a good bar, a new wine bar and a very good Italian dining room (see below). Rooms either above or along the street are pleasant, contemporary and quiet.

The Best Places To Eat In & Around Dundee

944 8/Q23
£££
✓ **Castlehill Restaurant** 22-26 Exchange St, Dundee · www.
castlehillrestaurant.co.uk · **01382 220008** Not on a hill at all (there is an explanation) but since 2014 this has been Dundee's downtown fine diner. Paul McMillan and Graham Campbell's straight-talking 4 starters/4 mains, or a monthly changing tasting menu plays to an enthusiastic audience. Best to book (I couldn't get in myself but I take the word of foodie friends who eat here regularly). Intimate and nicely unpretentious. Tue-Sat lunch & dinner.

945 8/Q23
£££
✓ **The Tayberry** 594 Brook St, Broughty Ferry · www.tayberryrestaurant.
com · **01382 698280** On the front, the best-located restaurant in and around Dundee, a corner at the very end of Brook St (Broughty Ferry's main drag) overlooking the dunes and the estuary. Can walk along 'The Esplanade' (2099/WALKS), 300m from 'The Castle'. Adam Newth opened The Tayberry to great local acclaim 2015. Mod-Scot menu, upstairs has the sea views and afternoon tea. 'Steak Club' on Tue. Closed Sun/Mon.

946 8/Q23
££
✓ **Jute at Dundee Contemporary Arts** 152 Nethergate · www.jutecafebar.
co.uk · **01382 909246** Jute, the downstairs bar/restaurant of Dundee's acclaimed arts centre, DCA, is the most convivial place in town to eat – no contest. A menu superior to any old arts venue, especially one that here is all things to all people. Bar and restaurant: your rendezvous in Dundee. A good kids' menu. Very pleasant outdoor terraces on warmer days. Book weekends.

947 8/Q23
£
✓ **The Agacan** 113 Perth Rd, Dundee · www.agacan.co.uk · **01382 644227** Since 1983 Dundee's fabled bistro for Turkish eats and wine (and beer). Brilliantly boho with much (rotated) art, chosen by Zeki Agacan and his once art lecturer wife, on the walls. You smell the meat (veggies go meze). Tue-Sat dinner only.

948 8/Q23
£
✓ **Jessie's Kitchen** 3 Albert Rd, Broughty Ferry · **01382 778488** 20 mins direct from city centre via Dundee Rd or Victoria Rd. Part of **Turriff's** (2228/GARDEN CENTRES) which has been in the grounds of this suburban Victorian house for decades. Jessie's, which takes up the ground floor of the very lived-in mansion is ticked because of what it does so very well – a brilliantly couthy and comforting café, with good home baking and cooking, all very Dundonian. All rooms on the go at once. Excellent cakes, of course. Local lassies. Granny Jessie not there now, but the family still live upstairs. Sometimes the old record player is on, with Ross's eclectic collection of pop classics. 7 days.

949 8/Q23
£
✓ **Sol y Sombra** 27 Gray St, Broughty Ferry · **01382 776941** On corner with King St. An upstairs authentic and decidedly good tapas bar; yes, probably one of the best in Scotland. Fixed, daily-changing selection of hot and cold dishes: 15 for lunch and 18 for dinner (you will eat them!). Very good value (£24.50 dinner at TGP). *Postres* – Santiago almond or Turron cake – yum! 3 tapas for £10 in downstairs bar at lunch. This place definitely worth the 20 mins from city centre. 7 days lunch & dinner.

950 8/Q23
£

✓ **Manchurian** 15A Gellatly St, Dundee · www.manchuriandundee.com · 01382 228822 In an unprepossessing street between the waterfront and main street and above an Oriental supermarket, one of the best restaurants for dim sum in any Scottish downtown. Huge menu. Spacious room; from both outside and in, this feels like Chinatown. 7 days lunch & dinner.

951 8/Q23
££

✓ **Piccolo** 210 Perth Rd, Dundee · www.piccolodundee.co.uk · 01382 201419 An intimate dining experience (only a dozen tables) with chef/patron Athol Shepherd in the hot kitchen, cramped but civilised out front. Many regulars attest to the abiding assertion that this is Dundee's best Italian. Definitely more ristorante than mere tratt. Well-priced wine list. Tue-Sun dinner only.

952 8/Q23
L
ATMOS
££

✓ **The Ship Inn** 121 Fisher St, Broughty Ferry · www.theshipinn-broughtyferry.co.uk · 01382 779176 There's nowt nicer than heading down 'The Ferry' and on the front, weathered by the River Tay since the 1800s; this cosy pub that has sustained smugglers, fishermen and foodie folk alike. Bar and upstairs restaurant; no-nonsense Scottish menu and a fabulous picture window overlooking the Tay. Bar food and upstairs restaurant (best book). 7 days. See 1338/FOOD PUBS.

953 8/Q23
££

✓ **Collinsons Restaurant** 122 Brown St, Broughty Ferry · www.collinsonsrestaurant.com · 01382 776000 Stephen Collinson's well-established, dependable, good-food eaterie off main street of Broughty Ferry. Quietly, almost suburbanly contemporary, and confidently so. Mod-Scot menu. 5/5/5 (starter, mains etc). Lunch & dinner. Closed Sun/Mon.

954 8/Q23
££

✓ **Kobee** 42 Dock St, Dundee · www.kobee.co.uk · 01382 221811 Overlooks the waterfront area (though not the water itself). The new Dundee had to have a Japanese restaurant and this one (with token Thai and an Indonesian rendang curry) is a pretty good go at the genre. Teppanyaki (especially good for steak), a roomy though rather atmos-less room and a welcome break from Italy and India in midtown. 7 days lunch & dinner.

955 8/Q23
£

✓ **Fisher & Donaldson** 12 Whitehall St, Dundee · www.fisheranddonaldson.com · 01382 223488 The best traditional bakers in Scotland (1479/BAKERS) with busy tearoom; 2 other Dundee branches. Snacks and all their fine fare from maccy cheese to chocolates. Mon-Sat, daytime only.

956 8/Q23
££

Borgotaro Fort St, Broughty Ferry · www.fort-hotel.com · 01382 737999 Part of the Fort Hotel, an interior tratt and most probably the best of the pasta/pizza parlours. A top spot in 'The Ferry'! New wine bar adjacent 2018. 7 days from 5pm till late.

957 8/Q23
£

Visocchi's 40 Gray St, Broughty Ferry · www.visocchis.co.uk · 01382 779297 A busy destination Broughty Ferry tratt and ice-cream parlour. Over 3 generations they've made mouth-watering Italian ice creams (amaretto, cassata, etc) and ice-cream cakes, alongside home-made pasta (and only a little less impressive pizza) and snacks. Hard work and integrity evident here. Lovely prints on the walls by Leon Morrocco, and dad Alberto. Closed Mon.

958 8/Q23
£

The Parlour West Port, Dundee · 01382 203588 At the top end of S Tay St, Gill Veal's wee caff in a row of shops and caffs, including the arriviste Gallery 48 next door, is easily missed but loyal locals and students pack it for home-made light food, tortes/tortillas, soups, salads, slabs of cake. Good vegetarian; and ... they have their own cookbook. Breads from Wild Hearth Bakery. Daytime only. Closed Sun.

959 8/R23
L
£
The Glass Pavilion Broughty Ferry · 01382 732738 Along and overlooking the Tay from centre, can walk east from the castle and harbour, about 1km. Food so-so but the glass pavilion is a modern reconstruction of an Art Deco gem. Pictures of old Broughty Ferry beach and Esplanade are worth the trip alone (2099/WALKS). Nice coffee and terrace. 7 days 9am-9pm.

960 8/Q23
££
Italian Grill City Sq · www.italiangrill.net · 01382 690600 Brasserie-style contemporary spacious room and terrace on Dundee's classy central square. Grills and pasta and pizza. 7 days lunch & dinner.

961 8/Q23
£
Pacamara Perth Rd · 01382 527666 Quite far up Perth Rd, a convivial coffee shop and great cuppa, soups, grilled sandwiches, burgers and proper chips. Has Bean Coffee (cool name). 7 days, daytime only.

962 8/Q23
£
The White Goose 44 Dock St · 01382 221504 Fronting on to the hotel/V&A quarter, a lofty café/diner with all the contemporary grace and grazing notes. All day till mid-evening.

963 8/Q23
£
Tailend 81 Nethergate · www.thetailend.co.uk · 01382 229990 Very central and probably the best F&C in Dundee (I'd say). Made to order, fish best, beef dripping – like it or not. See also 898/ST ANDREWS. 7 days 11.30am-10pm.

964 8/Q23
£
The Flame Tree Café 20 Exchange St & 75 Perth Rd · 01382 204200 (The latter is the smaller and more recent student-quarter outpost.) Dundee hipster coffee shop (Matthew Algie coffee), avocado toast, brownies, vegetarian/vegan vibe. 7 days, daytime only.

965 8/Q23
£
The Palais Union St · 07842 155730 Downtown, off Nethergate. Cosy, retro tearoom where Tania and Tania's mum bake top cakes and serve a top downtown Dundee breakfast, soups and stuff. Nice soundtrack. Daytime.

If You're In Perth...

WHERE TO STAY

966 8/P23
15 ROOMS
DF · ££

££
✓ **Parklands** 2 St Leonard's Bank · www.theparklandshotel.com · 01738 622451 Near station overlooking expansive green parkland of South Inch. Privately owned, personally run mansion hotel with a reputation for food under Graeme Pallister who also cooks at **63 Tay Street** (914/PERTHSHIRE). **EAT** Smaller **63 @ Parklands** for fine dining. Closed Tue/Wed. The bistro has eclectic menu; nice conservatory. Garden terrace. Top hotel dining in this town.

967 8/P23
34 ROOMS
NO PETS
££
Huntingtower Hotel nr Perth · www.huntingtowerhotel.co.uk · 01738 583771 Crieff road (1km off A85, 3km W of ring route A9 signed). Modernised mansion-house hotel outside town, now in the Leonardo Boutique chain. Good gardens (that copper beech!). Subdued, panelled restaurant; decent menu and wine list. Business-like service (and weddings!).

968 8/P23
46 ROOMS
DF
££
The Royal George Tay St · www.theroyalgeorgehotel.co.uk · 01738 624455 By Perth Bridge over the Tay to the A93 to Blairgowrie. Georgian proportions and nostalgic niceties, all unapologetically old style. Log fire and piano in the bar. Big on high tea, especially on Sundays. Weddings and functions. Rooms vary, 18 have the river view. Perthshire does gather here.

WHERE TO EAT IN PERTH

969 8/P23 ✓ **Cardo** 38 South St · https://cardo.restaurant · 01738 248784 Paula and
££/£ Herve Tabourel's very French bistro; c'est formidable! Poisson du jour, trotters
in filo. Good service and wine list. Best downtown choice in a town well served by
la cuisine française. Delicious macarons. Closed Mon. The Tabourels also have
Wee Cardo just round the corner – they share the same kitchen. The Italian
version, with takeaway pizza. Small but sympatico.

970 8/P23 ✓ **Effie's** 202 High St · www.effiesofperth.co.uk · 01738 634770 A
£ tearoom, proudly traditional (no website, lots of word of mouth). Renamed
after mum, who's actually baking in the kitchen. A top spot to eat during the day
but you'll have to wait or book. 7 days, daytime only. Report: 1421/TEAROOMS.

971 8/P23 ✓ **Grand' Italia** 33 George St · www.granditaliaperth.co.uk ·
£ 01738 626016 Iris and Mario's excellent ristorante in the town centre does all
that it says on the tin, i.e. on the menu outside. Better than the place opposite and
possibly the best Italian food in the shire. 7 days noon-9.30/10pm.

972 8/P23 ✓ **Tabla** 173 South St · www.tablarestaurant.co.uk · 01738 444630 Very
£ credible Indian by the Kumar family. North and south cuisine. Farm-grown
spices from family in India. Open kitchen. A big plus for ethnic eating in Perth. The
Kumars also run an Indian cookery school. Lunch (not Sun) & dinner.

973 8/P23 **Café Tabou** 4 St John's Pl · www.cafetabou.co.uk · 01738 446698 Central
££ corner of a pedestrianised square (one day they'll get City Hall sorted); from outside
and in, it feels like an unassuming *café de la place*; locals go. French staff, French
wine and a reasonable pass at French country food. 7 days lunch & dinner.

974 8/P23 **Breizh** 28-30 High St · www.breizhrestaurant.com · 01738 444427 Breizh
££ (pronounced 'Brez'), the Breton name for Brittany, is a buzzy eaterie: galettes
galore, salads, grillades, good pizza, chips and home-made puds. Good food
all round. 7 days from 9am till 9/9.30pm.

975 8/P23 **Reids** 32-34 High St · www.reidscafe.com · 01738 636310 Next to Breizh,
£ another good café/restaurant but with a Scottish – and unlike others in this town,
an authentic Scottish – flavour. Food though is eclectic, including Italian, and all
home-made, including the bread (which is for sale). Great casual dining! 7 days.

976 8/P23 **Willows** 14 St John's Pl · www.willowscoffeeshop.co.uk · 01738 441175 Been
£ here nigh on 30 years but not mentioned by me till now. Basically, an honest-to-
goodness café/restaurant with – as it happens – possibly the best scones in Scotland.
That did it for me! Also soups, hot dishes; many lassies lunching. Daytime only.

977 8/P23 **Holdgate's Fish & Chips** 146 South St · 01738 636922 Here since 1901! A
classic, with reconstructed caff through the back. Well-sourced haddock; their
fritters! Not veg oil. Noon-8.30pm (Sun 3-7pm).

  63 Tay Street Report: 914/PERTHSHIRE.

✓✓ **North Port** Report: 913/PERTHSHIRE.

The Best Hotels & Restaurants In The North East

Excludes Aberdeen (except Marcliffe at Pitfodels and Chester Hotel); see p. 173. Speyside listings on p. 178.

978 7/G22
46 ROOMS
15 SUITES
DF
£LOTS

✓✓ **The Fife Arms** Mar Rd, Braemar · www.thefifearms.com · 01339 720200 This, the most exciting hotel development in the north, opened late 2018. The venerable Victorian facade remains, but behind an exceptional but sympathetic transformation has taken (with great pride of) place. Its distinctive decorative features have been incorporated by architect Ben Addy and team of designers led by Russell Sage into an elegant, uber-contemporary hotel, with a heather-roofed courtyard and state-of-the-art features. Art and design are watchwords here, since the hotel's recreation is the vision of owners Iwan and Manuela Wirth of international art dealers Hauser & Wirth. The art on the walls is *sans pareil* but the detail in bar, restaurant, cinema and spa, working with Scottish and local artists and artisans, is also first class. Head chef is Robert Cameron, the ghillie is local woman Ros Evans (there are boot/drying/rod and gun rooms should you shoot or fish). The Fife Arms, though way down the world-famous valley (at its most romantic and dramatic part), is Scotland's new smart destination.

979 6/S19
40 ROOMS
DF
£££

✓✓ **Marcliffe at Pitfodels** Pitfodels, by Aberdeen · www.marcliffe.com · 01224 861000 En route to Royal Deeside, 5km from Union St. On the edge of town, an exemplary mix of intimate and spacious, the old (mansion house) and the newer wing are still personally run by the Spence family: Stewart Spence the consummate hotelier; his son Ross is head chef. All staff greet you with genuine warmth. Many pics on the piano with the famous (both Margarets – the princess and Mrs Thatcher; and that other T, The Trump) attest to this hotel's enduring primacy. Excellent restaurant and breakfast in light conservatory with nice courtyard and terrace overlooking gardens. Spa treatment rooms (no pool). Honeymoon suites are fab; there are many weddings and rollicking Aberdonian functions (hotel has a big reputation for corporate dining), so this understated hotel caters for all. When in Aberdeen, I wouldn't go anywhere else. Mr Spence generous not just to guests but with a rare insight into hospitality in the city generally: collaboration, not competition, making Aberdeen a better place to visit.

980 6/S19
50 ROOMS
££

✓✓ **The Chester Hotel** 59-63 Queen's Rd, Aberdeen · www.chester-hotel.com · 01224 327777 A smart, deluxe hotel in the heart and mind of Aberdeen, with one of the city's top restaurants. Report: 997/ABERDEEN.

981 6/S18
51 ROOMS
DF
££

✓✓ **Meldrum House** Oldmeldrum · www.meldrumhouse.com · 01651 872294 1km from village, 30km N of Aberdeen via A947 Banff road. Immediately impressive chunk of Scottish baronial set amid top-notch 18-hole golf course (private membership, but guests can use) and a lake with swans. Suites in the mansion itself (10), traditional and capacious; in the new wing, more corporate-contemporary (28 standard/'Club') and executive rooms in 'The Stables' overby. Main house has atmos and nice furnishings; original antiques and period pictures. A lot of effort has gone into restoring this landmark Aberdeenshire hotel to its former glory: the deluxe choice for business (especially for the whisky industry – a great whisky bar) and the golfing fraternity. Expect weddings – increasingly big weddings. Nice afternoon tea. Chef Paul Grant in the kitchen.

982 6/R20
8 ROOMS
DF
££

✓✓ **The Boat Inn** Aboyne · www.theboatinnaboyne.co.uk ·
01339 886137 Beyond the prominent green, off the road connecting to the South Dee road. Eileen and David Haywood have transformed this long-serving riverside inn, with comfy, contemporary, inexpensive rooms, and a great bar and food operation downstairs; the boat floated into a Deeside destination for good gastropub food and known for its great fish & chips. Same menu in bar and restaurant (and with outside tables). There is simply nowhere else to eat of an eve; thankfully it's as good as it is. 8 new rooms to be added 2019.

983 6/P17
15 ROOMS
DF
££

✓ **Knockomie** nr Forres · www.knockomie.co.uk · 01309 673146 Well placed for the Moray Coast, Inverness and your golfing and Speyside meanderings. Gavin and Penny Ellis are discreet, fastidious hosts in this comfortable but contemporary mansion house, which is more gastro inn with rooms than stuffy manor with manners. Informal dining, nice whisky-oriented bar. Comfortable in its tree-surrounded self, the suburbs have arrived and Knockomie is on the very edge of Forres looking out to country.

984 6/R20
25 ROOMS
££

✓ **Tor-Na-Coille Hotel** Banchory · www.tornacoille.com · 01330 822242 On the A93, on the way into Banchory from Ballater, a solid granite manor-house hotel, contemporised and made smart and homely by master chef/proprietor David Littlewood and, of course, with a night-out menu (under head chef Colin Lyall). 3 categories of rooms, inexpensive for these appointments, which include the adjacent high-spec gym, 'The Unit'. Weddings, as you'd expect, and a good corporate choice.

985 6/R19
27 ROOMS
L
£££

✓ **Pittodrie House** nr Inverurie · www.macdonaldhotels.co.uk ·
01467 681444 A large family mansion house on an estate in some of the best rural acres of Aberdeenshire with **Bennachie** above (2000/HILLS). 30km Aberdeen; well signed. Comfortable rooms look out on verdant lawns and topping trees. Exquisite walled garden 500m from house and many walks around. A Macdonald hotel (possibly their best) with very individual rooms in old house and a newer extension out back. Period pictures, great whisky bar. Afternoon tea a treat. Many weddings (not surprising in this epic setting)!

986 6/S20
28 ROOMS
DF
££

✓ **Banchory Lodge** Banchory · www.banchorylodge.co.uk ·
01330 822625 Downhill from the main town crossroads, the B974 to Strachan, S Deeside and the Falls of Heugh. Makeover of riverside hotel in suburban Banchory (well, it's all suburban, really, and caravans lurk behind the hedge on the long driveway) transformed it into a major food (though not foodie) spot: a restaurant, in the bar, a dining room and outside deck (same menu). Rooms fine (in main house and in the separate Cobbleheugh building behind, away from the fray). The river setting here is superb.

987 6/S18
6 ROOMS
££

✓ **The Redgarth** Oldmeldrum · www.redgarth.com · 01651 872353 This family-run (the Singers) inn (signed from main road system) has only 6 rooms but it's great value; food is very popular locally. Stuart does everything, including the garden. View of Bennachie. Nice flowers. Very Aberdeenshire lodgings.

988 6/P17
10 ROOMS
££

✓ **Blervie House** Forres · https://blervie.com · 01309 674629 At Rafford, 3km S of Forres, on the B9010. Handsome, quite grand house in rural setting (300 acres), personally run with great attention to detail and to guests by Graham and Sheena Thompson. Commodious bedrooms, cosy downies. Billiard room. Lovely terrace overlooking the policies to faraway hills.

989 6/T17 **Tufted Duck Hotel** St Combs, nr Fraserburgh · **www.tuftedduckhotel.co.uk**
20 ROOMS   · **01346 582481** Here's a surprise, though only 40 mins from Aberdeen and 8km
L   S of Fraserburgh by the B9033. Not the most beautiful, but functional and locally
££   loved. Its best feature is the location adjacent to the **Loch of Strathbeg Nature Reserve** (1790/BIRDS). Incongruously, the owners' rather OTT art and architecture house is next door, and the St Fergus gas plant that supplies one-third of the UK with power is 4km away. However, what you see is a sand-dune coast on the serene or wild North Sea and lighthouse at Rattray Head. No frills in accom or dining, but it's inexpensive, with friendly staff and locals in the bar.

THE BEST RESTAURANTS IN THE NORTH EAST

990 6/S18   ✓✓ **Eat On The Green** Udny Green · **www.eatonthegreen.co.uk** ·
£££   **01651 842337** Former pub, now a restaurant on a cute village green. Folk come from miles for this celebratory, unpretentious food that's great value. Chef/proprietor Craig Wilson has built it into a Treat to Eat venue and one of Scotland's premier country restaurants. 2 private dining rooms upstairs, a working garden, and in 2018 a gin bar and terrace. Metropolitan decor is a long way from publand. Food elegant and simple but ambitions undimmed on the distant green (only 30 mins from Aberdeen); you'll be pushed to get in at weekends. Wed-Sun lunch & dinner.

991 6/Q20   ✓ **Rothesay Rooms** Ballater · **www.rothesay-rooms.co.uk** ·
£££   **01339 753816** Just off the main road (the A93) through Ballater, a discreet building, where the Prince of Wales Foundation (as at **Dumfries House** 760/AYRSHIRE) has set up a rather spiffing restaurant. All the hallmarks of their support for rural communities are evident: tasteful interior and lighting (candlelit at night), excellent and ethically produced food, great service. Not cheap but not at all pretentious or grand. Chef is Ross Cochrane; the top menu in these Deeside parts. Closed Mon/Tue.

992 6/R17   ✓ **Rockpool** Cullen · **www.rockpool-cullen.co.uk** · **01542 841397** On a corner of
£   the square in the long main street (A98) through Cullen, a café that has everything a good caff should have: location, great baking and coffee and imaginative hot dishes – Barra asparagus with Tain cheese brûlée when I was there – at lunchtime, windows on the street. Stephen McDonald and Carrie Anderson have created the best casual diner on the Moray coast. Great 'ice cream shop' next door. Closed Mon. Daytime only.

993 6/S20   ✓ **Buchanan's Bistro** Banchory · **www.buchananfood.com** ·
£   **01330 826530** Turn right at Tesco as you enter town from Aberdeen; 1km signed. Adjacent Woodend Barn arts centre (home to an eclectic, high-quality mix of music, theatre and film), the bistro in the barn is a contemporary, urbane, informed eaterie on the edge of Banchory, the prospering heart of Royal Deeside. Val and Calum Buchanan have an enlightened grow-your-own approach (there are allotments out back and Calum brews beer) and this airy bistro demonstrates the best kind of rural re-creation – consider from the terrace! Their daily breads are fantastic. 7 days.

994 6/S20   **Milton Brasserie** Crathes · **www.miltonbrasserie.com** · **01330 844566** On
£   A93, 4km E of Banchory, opposite the entrance to **Crathes** (1555/GARDENS; 1883/HOUSES). Contemporary restaurant in old steading. A light and pleasant space. Long known for its good cookin' using local produce. Adjacent craft village, river walks and 'The Royal Deeside Railway' offer many diversions. Daytime only.

995 6/S19 **Echt Tandoori** Echt · **www.echttandoori.co.uk** · **01330 860601** On the B9119 N of
£ Banchory and 24km W of Aberdeen via Westhill. An unlikely outpost, perhaps, but here
is where to find what many consider to be the best Indian food in the city or shire. Crisp
linen, candlelight, roses. Extensive menu, big portions; tandoori dishes best. Krishna
Gurung a modest (and much-loved locally) chef/proprietor. Tue-Sun lunch & dinner.

996 6/T19 **Cock & Bull** Balmedie · **www.thecockandbull.co.uk** · **01358 743249** On A90,
DF 20km N of Aberdeen, near Trumpland. Atmospheric roadside pub long a fixture
L here but increasing reputation for grub and winning awards; a strong team in the
£ kitchen. A lot of Aberdeen Angus. Very pubby and intimate, oak beams, etc. Always
busy. Kids' menu. 7 days.

 **The Tolbooth** Stonehaven Report: 1370/SEAFOOD.

✓ **The Creel Inn** Catterline, nr Stonehaven Report: 1337/FOOD PUBS.

✓✓ **Marcliffe at Pitfodels** My favourite hotel in Aberdeen: nothing is close for old-style comfort and service. Report: 979/NE HOTELS.

997 6/S19
50 ROOMS
NO PETS
££

✓✓ **The Chester Hotel** Queen's Rd · www.chester-hotel.com · 01224 327777 The high-end hotel in the West End, 2km from Union St (adjacent to Malmaison below). 'Luxurious' but often inexpensive for this standard and spec. Corporate feel but nicely done. Scottish artist John Byrne in evidence in all public spaces and most bedrooms (an informed and tasteful choice). 6 categories of rooms, even 'standards' are good. More being added at TGP. Restaurant and bar in adjoining building; both are night-out destinations. Small gym & spa.

£££ **EAT** Well-laid-out bar (casual food menu) with banquettes and extensive restaurant, **IX Restaurant** – the city's most flash. Kevin Dalgleish executive chef; Josper oven. Top-notch nosh. Lunch & dinner. Bar food noon-9pm.

998 6/T19
185 ROOMS
NO PETS
££

✓ **Park Inn By Radisson** Justice Mill Lane · www.parkinn.co.uk/ hotel-aberdeen · 01224 592999 Though we don't do chains in the main, for location, style and convenience, this has to get a mention. Just behind the west end of Union Street, in an area of some of the city's best bars and restaurants. Contemporary and efficient. No pool, small gym, parking adjacent.

999 6/S19
79 ROOMS
££

✓ **Malmaison** Queen's Rd · www.malmaison.com · 01224 327370 2km from centre. Once the only contemporary hotel in Aberdeen (though see above), being refurbished at TGP. Usual design values of the brand here put to notably good use. Ambient, accessible. ESPA spa, no pool. Rooms cosy and cool. Good bar and other spaces for corporate meets.

££ **EAT** Large, well-laid-out brasserie: you dine surrounded by wine; meat in the larder and animals on the walls, so veggies pass by. They do like their Aberdeen Angus!

1000 6/T19
7 ROOMS
NO PETS
NO KIDS
£

✓ **The Globe Inn** 13 N Silver St · www.theglobeinn-aberdeen.co.uk · 01224 624258 Rooms above the Globe, the civilised pub in a street off Golden Sq. Pub has good reputation for ales, food (and live music Tuesday and weekends, so no early to bed). Accom is reasonably priced. Since decent value and individuality are hard to find in Aberdeen, book ahead. Parking is cheap in nearby square. Hope the makeover at TGP keeps the wood and the stained glass.

1001 6/T19
39 ROOMS
NO PETS
££

Bauhaus Hotel Langstane Place · www.thebauhaus.co.uk · 01224 212122 Excellent downtown location for a *soi-disant* boutique hotel. Not exactly a homage to Le Corbusier and the Modernists but good quality, no fuss and nice furniture. 3 standards of room all good value. B&B only; good bars and restaurants adjacent (see below). Parking 100m.

1002 6/S20
40 ROOMS
NO PETS
L · ££

Maryculter House Hotel Maryculter · www.maryculterhousehotel.com · 01224 732124 Superb setting on banks of Dee: riverside walks and an old graveyard and ruined chapel in the priory. The hotel is on the site of a 13th-century preceptory. Newer annex; rooms overlook river. **Poachers Bar** is special, dining room not so much (weekends only); same menu in both. At weekends this hotel can be a wedding factory! Fishing rights on Dee not expensive for guests.

1003 6/S19
9 ROOMS
£

Dutch Mill Hotel 7 Queen's Rd · www.dutchmill.co.uk · 01224 322555 A classic, one might say an Aberdeen institution; here forever. Not large or expensive. Original wood and echoes of travellers past. Enormously popular bar for drinking, OK pub food and rugby on TV. The genuine article.

The Best Places To Eat In Aberdeen

1004 6/T19 ✓ **Café 52** The Green · www.cafe52onthegreen.co.uk · 01224 590094
ATMOS   Below the east end of Union St in the 'Merchant Quarter': go down the steps
£ or approach via Market St. A sliver of a cosy bistro with outside terrace. It has the
boho chic. For 25 years, chef/owner Steve Bothwell has kept customers happy with
unusual dishes and comforting combinations. Mum does the puds and supplies
herbs and leaves from her organic garden (she's over 80 and is a force of nature)
and Café 52 is still the biz! Busy at (good-value) lunch and dinner. LO 9.30pm (4pm
Sun). Bar till midnight.

1005 6/T19 ✓ **Moonfish** Connection Wynd · www.moonfishcafe.co.uk ·
££ 01224 644166 Down steps from east end of Union St. Discreet location in
'Merchant Quarter' and still a bit of an insider secret. Aberdeen foodies have been
flocking here for 15 years. An easy-on-the-eye, informal caff/restaurant, with chef
Brian McLeish cooking up simple good food with panache. Usually 4 starters/
mains/puds, each with 4 listed ingredients. Tue-Sat.

1006 6/T19 ✓ **Yatai Izakaya** Langstane Place · www.yatai.co.uk · 01224 592355 West
£ end of Union St opposite Bauhaus Hotel (above), adjacent to **Orchid** (1024/
ABERDEEN BARS) and Dusk bars, neither of which is a chain, this is a cool
Aberdonian corner. Any city would relish this Japanese eaterie with tapas-style
eating (Omakase) in ambient rooms up and down (not the usual Japanese
minimal/clinical), with superior sakes, beers and wine list. And credible edibles.
Closed Sun/Mon.

1007 6/T19 ✓ **Le Café Bohème** Windmill Brae · www.cafebohemerestaurant.co.uk ·
ATMOS 01224 210677 Authentic French bistro, atmos and food in an area that gets
££ drunk at weekends. Here, all is calm with style and good service. Food proper
French from chef John Pattillo, à la carte and plats du jour (especially seafood) and
a très charmante madame du comptoir, Maxine Mancellon. Mainly French wine list
(many by the glass) and good Bios (organics). Best place to eat by far in this side of
the city centre. Closed Sun/Mon.

1008 6/T19 ✓ **The Silver Darling** Pocra Quay · www.thesilverdarling.co.uk ·
LLL 01224 576229 The once exemplary seafood bistro in a perfect spot, after a
ATMOS less loved patch is back 2018 under the people from **No 10** (below). Not so easy to
££ find: head for Beach Esplanade, the lighthouse and harbour mouth (Pocra Quay).
The light winks and ghostly boats glide past. Upstairs dining room not large and
you so want to be by the window. Menus vary with catch and season, but under
esteemed chef, Craig Somers, are not so fish focused as before. It's a sharp
operation, usually packed (and noisy) but one of the best locations in the north.
Mon-Fri lunch & dinner; all day from noon Sat/Sun.

1009 6/T19 ✓ **No. 10 Bar & Restaurant** 10 Queen's Terrace · www.no10aberdeen.co.
££ uk · 01224 631928 Est. 1986, No. 10 has long been a smart West End
watering hole since the oil first surfaced; a destination restaurant more recently.
Same people took over **Silver Darling** (above) 2018. Great for drinks after work, but
you could take your mum here for dinner. Moderne menu. Food LO 9.15pm, Sun
7.30pm. Bar till late.

1010 6/S19 ✓ **The Cognitos** First there was the **Café** 39 St Swithin St · www.
£ cafecognito.co.uk · 01224 209727 Unlikely sharing of premises with a nail
bar, where ladies have their nails done in a kind of pod at the side. Doesn't detract

though from this buzzy, popular café from breakfast through lunch to supper. So busy that sometimes it is a tad cramped through the back. Then, on a nearby corner, the **Deli** 245 Union Grove · www.cognitodeli.co.uk · 01224 379299 Not really a deli, I'd say, but a great café with more room and more of a food menu. Moving across town, to the Beechwood area (near the BBC) came **On The Corner** 1 Mid Stocket Rd · www.cognitoonthecorner.co.uk · 01224 977896 On a prominent corner, right enough, the most cognito Cognito, a bar and restaurant with a wide-ranging menu from breakfast to dinner. And, in 2018, **At The Cross** 38 Albyn Pl · www.cognitoatthecross.co.uk At the Queen's Cross Church near the first two, an art venue type set-up, with coffee/snax. Daytime only. Nicky Turnbull's Cognitos are a big Aberdeen success story. Love them all!

1011 6/T19 ✓ **Parx Café** 19 Rubislaw Terrace · www.cafeparx.co.uk · 01224 632960 In
£ the street that's the extension of Queen's Terrace – as No. 1 (below) and No. 10 (above) – so a central if discreet basement location. Here, Kirsty Moncrieff has created a cool, ethical café: home-made food of the moment, salads, blackboard specials. The best soda bread and bakes by Alice of Bakery Lane. Outside seats out front and in the garden. Go find this easy easily good eaterie. 7.30am-4pm. Closed Sun.

1012 6/T19 **No. 1 Bar & Grill** Queen's Terrace · www.number1restaurant.co.uk ·
££ 01224 611909 Other corner of the same block as No 10 (above). Basement bar and grill, highly regarded hereabouts because quite simply it's a classy joint with good, contemporary food and smart, friendly service. Nice conservatory at the back. It's an Aberdonian thing. Mon-Sat lunch & dinner.

1013 6/T19 **Café Harmony** 21 Bon-Accord Terrace · www.cafeharmony.co.uk ·
£ 01224 580590 In the street behind Union St at the West End, an area of many indifferent restaurants, this small corner, a contemporary haven is, well, … harmonious. A Mediterranean lightness to a menu, which includes a well-priced local steak and a good, easy-drinking wine list. LO 10pm. Closed Sun.

1014 6/T19 **Howies** Chapel St · www.howies.uk.com · 01224 639500 Follows successful
£ formula once made in Edinburgh in classic/contemporary Scottish bistro style, this discreetly fronted restaurant presses all the right Aberdonian buttons (including the price!). A reliable redoubt. Mon-Sat lunch & dinner.

1015 6/T19 **Rustico** Union Row · www.rustico-restaurant.co.uk · 01224 658444 If this
££ were French I'd say it had the *je ne sais quoi*, but it is most definitely Italian (Sicilian actually). Tony and Nikos' love for Sicily evident (their brill photos on the walls), though Nikos is Greek. And the food is well above the tratt average: everything home-made, including the puds. A happy crew here (always a good sign). 7 days.

1016 6/T19 **Yorokobi by CJ** Huntly St · www.yorokobibycj.co.uk ·
£ 01224 566002 Authentic Japanese/Korean restaurant by chef/proprietor Jang – that's (the shyly modest) Chef Jang to you and me. Sushi, sashimi and maki rolls, this is a share-and-savour kind of place but there are teriyakis, even curry. Setting perhaps less inspired than the food. Much Michelin mentioned. Closed Sun/Mon.

1017 6/T19 **Jewel In The Crown** Crown St · www.thejewelaberdeen.com ·
£ 01224 210288 Way down the street on corner with Affleck St. The Ahmeds have been serving up great N Indian food for over 30 years, home-made and authentic. Recent new makeover; some say the best curry in town (this is where Jay Rayner had his). The friendly family of Farooq Ahmed works like a football team to make this a top spot. Mon-Sat lunch & LO 11pm, and Sun 2.30pm-10.30pm.

1018 6/T19 **Madame Mews** Aberdeen Market · www.madamemews.com ·
£ **01224 460211** There's not a lot in Aberdeen Market (corner of Union & Market Sts) to rave about, but this straight-up, genuine Thai streetfood caff near the back is fabulously incongruous and real. You could be in any (old-style) Asian mall. Big, authentic menu made to order there and then. Cheap as (not) chips. Daytime only. Closed Sun.

 IX Restaurant at The Chester Hotel Queens Rd Report: See above.

 Hammerton Store Great Western Rd Report: 2210/SHOPS.

 The Tippling House Belmont St Report: See below.

 The Craftsman Company Guild St Report: See below.

Food Story Thistle St Report: 1353/VEGETARIAN.

The Best Bars In Aberdeen

1019 6/T19 **The Prince of Wales** St Nicholas Lane · www.princeofwales-aberdeen.
ATMOS co.uk · **01224 640597** Just off Union St at George St. An all-round great pub (by Belhaven) always mentioned in beer guides and one of the best places in the city for (rotating guest) ales (and 150 whiskies). Very cheap self-service food till 9pm. Wood, flagstones, booths. Large and very pub-like; gets very crowded.

1020 6/T19 **Ma Cameron's** Little Belmont St · www.macamerons-aberdeen.co.uk ·
ATMOS **01224 644487** Labyrinthine old pub (dating back 300 years, the oldest in the city), named after the wife who took it over in 1937. Plenty of different spaces to eat and sup: intimate snugs and the busy main bar; there is even a 'beer garden' on the roof. Big menu of pub-grub classics till 9pm.

1021 6/T19 **The Grill** Union St · www.thegrillaberdeen.co.uk · **01224 573530** Here
ATMOS in the middle of the main street, i.e. Union St, since 1870. Historic, atmospheric, solid, and a great place to drink. Mahogany gantry of superb whisky range (served in a Glencairn Glass) from a definitive bible of a list, and ales and craft beers. Integrity is intact and evident. No ladies served here until 1973; their other principles have endured.

1022 6/T19 **Under the Hammer** N Silver St Time-served basement bar. Forever and a day favourite (and certainly mine) in Aberdeen. No snooker, no sports, no food. Candlelight, ales and the mellow vibe.

The first four pubs above are old style. These are contemporary:

1023 6/T19 **The Craftsman Company** Guild St · www.thecraftsmancompany.com ·
01224 945600 A roomy corner room in a good spot, immediately a good vibe when you come in. Here, they are seriously into their beer (16 on draught), but also coffee and cake and a proper food menu (served till 6pm). An all-round top 'coffee & ale house' in the modern manner.

1024 6/T19 ✓ **Orchid** **Langstane Place** · **www.orchidaberdeen.com** · **01224 516126** In West End behind Union St. Stylish bar for hipsters and discerning drinkers in a relaxed, low-lit, contemporary ambience. Big on cocktails, served by knowledgeable mixologist types. A gin bar downstairs. Open late so a good crowd after 11pm. 7 days 6pm (Fri 5pm) till 2am (3am Fri/Sat).

1025 6/T19 ✓ **The Tippling House** **Belmont St** · **www.thetipplinghouse.com** Through a door by an interesting window and down a few stairs in busy-with-riff-raff Belmont St into a more calm and sure of itself world. More of a restaurant/cocktail bar than mere pubbery here. Small plates, platters, starters and (5) mains. Food served until 1 hour before bar closes so this is the place in Aberdeen to eat late. Bar 4pm-2am (3am Fri/Sat). From 1pm Sat.

✓ **The Globe Inn** **N Silver St** Report: 1000/ABERDEEN HOTELS.

The Best Hotels In Speyside

1026 6/Q18
26 ROOMS
DF
L
££

✓ **The Craigellachie Hotel** Craigellachie · www.craigellachiehotel.co.uk · 01340 881204 The quintessential Speyside hotel, off A941 Elgin to Perth, in a pre-eminent (actually overlooking the Spey) location. Good for fishing, walking (**Speyside Way** at the bottom of the garden 2027/WALKS) and distillery visits (1539/WHISKY) – several nearby. Piers Adam, of celebrity-studded (Prince Harry's wild oat days) Mahiki, in London, took over Craigellachie but kept it trad. Service and style are a long way from Mayfair (though also prices). The **Copper Dog Grill** below serves public-school grub - cottage pie/Eton mess and steaks. The whisky room/bar is the smartest part. It all has a lived-in and local feel; management laid-back, but they don't need to try too much.

1027 6/P18
11 ROOMS
L
££

✓ **Archiestown Hotel** Archiestown · www.archiestownhotel.co.uk · 01340 810218 Main street of village in the heart of Speyside near **Cardhu Distillery** (1541/WHISKY). Now in the hands of the Dowans folk (see below), a village hotel with comfortable rooms and bistro, with a long-standing reputation for good food. Hopefully it will keep its lived-in (especially by fisherfolk) charm. A plethora of armchairs to lounge in and take a dram (with many to choose from).

1028 6/Q18
16 ROOMS
££

Dowans Hotel Aberlour · www.dowanshotel.com · 01340 871488 Above river and v. Speyside town signed off the A95 to/from Grantown-on-Spey. Solid mansion, solid Speyside hospitality, smart rooms and service. Bedrooms to good standard. 2 dining options – posh and less posh (haven't tried either). Bar and whisky lounge (500+, a ladder for higher shelves). Corporate friendly.

1029 6/Q17
14 ROOMS
££

The Station Hotel Rothes · www.stationhotelspeyside.com · 01340 832200 In the middle of the gateway-to-Speyside (from the north) town, the home of **Glen Grant** (1540/WHISKY) and within a dozen miles of many of the biggies. Recent refurbishments have transformed this into the most boutiquey in the region. Small 'Pagoda' dining room, **Toots** café-bistro more a drop-in and the **Spirit Safe** bar. Haven't stayed or sampled but looks good. Reports, please.

1030 6/Q18
5 ROOMS
££

The Mash Tun Aberlour · www.mashtun-aberlour.com · 01340 881771 Off main street behind the church by a lovely river meadow park. A restaurant/pub with rooms above (all named after whiskies). This is a very Malt Trail destination that's boutique standard, informal and better value than most. 2 of the 5 rooms are higher spec. Pub has nice ambience, good grub and a big whisky selection.

1031 6/P17
23 ROOMS
NO PETS
££

Mansion House Elgin · www.mansionhousehotel.co.uk · 01343 548811 This mansion house in grounds below the monument to the last Duke of Gordon is also overshadowed by a 24-hour Tesco, in a suburb somewhat encroaching on its serenity. Comfy enough. Recent refurbishment under new owners. Still best in Elgin?

1032 6/P18
50 ROOMS
DF
£

The Grant Arms Grantown-on-Spey · www.grantarmshotel.com · 01479 872526 In very heart of peaceful Speyside town and here a long time (well, 1765), proudly traditional in its essence, part of the history of the town and river, and increasingly specialising in accom and facilities for lovers of wildlife/outdoor pursuits: walking, birdwatching, as well as fishing. An interior corridor is lined with maps, literature and things to do. Family-owned, very independently run, fairly standard rooms but nice with it. Bar and dining room.

Blervie House nr Forres Impressive mansion and grounds. Report: 988/NE HOTELS.

The Best Hotels In The Highlands

1033 6/N17
9 ROOMS
£LOTS

✓✓ **Boath House** Auldearn, nr Nairn · www.boath-house.com · 01667 454896 Signed from A96 3km E of Nairn. A small country-house hotel in a classic, immaculately restored mansion: Don and Wendy Matheson's family home with superb landscaped grounds, including their long TLC project, the Walled Garden. Comfy public rooms with local artists' pics. Bedrooms, with their own conservatory and Apple Cottage in the aforementioned gorgeous garden, where I stayed last time. I've been coming to Boath for 20 years and, unlike many others, it never fades or tires – Don and Wendy and now son, Sam, continue to redesign, refresh and renew with the same passion for detail and good taste. Wendy's home and garden shop has been converted from the potting shed. The bathrooms are all fabulous. Afternoon tea in one of the lounges, then the dining room looking down to the lake, where deer come to drink and a heron sits motionless waiting for its dinner, or in the bistro. **Brodie** is nearby (1812/CASTLES). The good life in a nutshell.

£££/££   **EAT** 2 great options. Eschewing the stuffy country-house dining 'experience', Boath has opted for something lighter, less Michelin-driven. As an alternative, the **Kale Yard Bistro**, with casual eating and proper pizza, in sublime surroundings. Chef Stefano Agostini. Closed Mon/Tue.

1034 7/J21
14 ROOMS
5 LODGES
DF
LL
£LOTS

✓✓ **Glencoe House Hotel** Glencoe · www.glencoe-house.com · 01855 811179 By Glencoe village, a Victorian estate house and once the local maternity hospital, a welcoming, splendid yet homely house and the 'Bell Tower' overby, in big scenery surroundings. Roger Niemeyer and Judy Pate have made an exemplary project of creating deluxe suites to a very high standard, without losing intimacy and the comforting niceties: open fires and Highland views (some have private terraces and hot tubs). In the newer building, the suites have tubs in their own courtyards, Agas in the kitchen and upstairs bedrooms. While the hotel works on an apartment basis, with cooking facilities, freezers (with Cook's meals), inexpensive selected wine and honesty bars, there is a small dining room in the main house. Set in woodlands, with a lily pond, the secret Glencoe Lochan 250m away, and Glen Coe's Aonach Eagach Ridge in the distance, there are endless strolls and hikes on the doorstep. The legendary Glen now has a resplendent refuge.

1035 5/H20
14 ROOMS
3 COTTAGES
DF
L
ATMOS
££

✓✓ **Arisaig House** Beasdale, Arisaig · www.arisaighouse.co.uk · 01687 450730 On the Road to the Isles, 12km from Mallaig, Arisaig House under Sarah Winnington-Ingram and family and a largely local team welcome you here as if you were arriving at a house party. With spacious comfy lounges and a terrace with spectacular views, woodlands, fields, a walled garden and a resurfaced tennis court, there is opportunity aplenty for privacy and to get lost. For what you have (and eat) and compared with many on these pages, this home from home is very good value. Sarah and Colin Nicholson create a menu of light, local produce but without fine-dining formalities. Unwind in the gardens, croquet lawn and on walks; 8km away are some of Scotland's sandiest beaches (1632/BEACHES) and from Arisaig (2km) boats to the small isles. Comfort and joy!

1036 5/H16
3 ROOMS
DF · NO KIDS
L · ATMOS
NC500
£LOTS

✓✓ **Pool House Hotel** Poolewe · www.pool-house.co.uk · 01445 781272 Once owned by Osgood MacKenzie who founded the nearby gardens (1553/GARDENS). With taste and determination the Harrisons have transformed this Highland home into one of Scotland's most stylish stopovers. Rooms, now only 3 in use, due to bonkers business rate regulations are 2-room suites, with enormous bathrooms all fastidiously themed to reflect the history of the house, its original and current occupants. You are reminded that during WWII, it was an HQ for combined forces – once there were 1,000 boats in the bay. This artistic creation and curation is a family project, memorabilia is meticulously assembled and decorated by Pop and Mum Harrison and daughters Lizzie and Mhairi. There's a library, massage room, billiards room and Chinese bedroom, great 4-course dinner, windows to the sea and sunset and really comfy beds, all for a fraction of what others (though this is *sans pareil*) boutique hotels cost. It's a mystery but good for us that one of Scotland's most uniquely special hotels is still a secret. Go luxuriate in their remarkable achievement. Not open Mon.

1037 7/K21
17 ROOMS +
LODGE
DF · LL
ATMOS
£LOTS

✓✓ **Inverlochy Castle** Torlundy · www.inverlochycastlehotel.com · 01397 702177 5km from Fort William on A82. One of Scotland's long-established flagship castle hotels is filled with sumptuous furnishings and elegant decor. Old-style hospitality prevails in this, the anchor hotel of the ICMI hotel management group, which includes **Inver Lodge** (below) and **Isle of Eriska** nearby. All you might expect of a castle and, they like to think, the epitome of grandeur and service. Huge comfortable bedrooms, acres of rhododendrons, trout in the lake, tennis and a lovely terrace; though no spa or pool. The big Ben is over there.

1038 5/M18
28 ROOMS
DF
LL
£LOTS

✓✓ **Culloden House** Inverness · www.cullodenhouse.co.uk · 01463 790461 5km E of town near A9, follow signs for Culloden village not the battlefield. Easiest approach from A96 Nairn road, turn right at first roundabout after the mall (3km, look for the stone rotunda). Hugely impressive Georgian mansion and lawn a big green duvet on edge of suburbia and, of course, history (the last redoubt of the Jacobites before the Battle). Near town and airport. Demonstrates that sometimes old style is the best style. Lovely big bedrooms overlooking the policies. Some fab suites in main and separate garden house. Elegant dining in beautifully conserved room under long-serving chef Michael Simpson. Garden Mansion House, with 5 recently refurbished rooms, is adjacent to an immaculately restored 4-acre walled garden, yours to wander. Fabulous trees include redwoods. Tennis courts. A true country house (but close to town) courtesy of its discreet and caring American owners.

1039 5/M18
11 ROOMS
NO PETS
£LOTS

✓ **Rocpool Reserve** Inverness · www.rocpool.com · 01463 240089 Above the town, a determinedly urbane hotel by the ICMI people who have several very different smart hotels in Scotland, including Inverlochy, above. Though look and feel are poles apart from the others' more traditional style, service is similarly top. Room categories somewhat off-putting ('extra decadent', for example, which has a Jacuzzi on an outside deck. See 1108/INVERNESS). They do expect expectations.

£££

EAT Albert Roux's no-nonsense French food brilliantly done for a fraction of what you'd pay in London.

1040 4/J14
5 ROOMS
NO PETS
NO KIDS
LL · MAR-DEC
NC500
£LOTS

✓ **The Albannach** Lochinver · www.thealbannach.co.uk · 01571 844407 2km up road to Baddidarach as you enter Lochinver on the A837. Lesley Crosfield and Colin Craig's uniquely special boutique hotel in the north: ancient splendid landscape around you, contemporary comfort to return to. The Byre suite overlooks the Croft from its own conservatory and hot tub. The Loft has its own terrace. Colin has put these immaculate rooms together with admirable DIY determination. In 2018, they changed the format and the emphasis. Guests are now invited to eat at their dining pub **The Caberfeidh** in the village 1089/HIGHLAND RESTAURANTS, a 20-min (beautiful) walk away (or they can arrange transport), where you can partake of Lesley and Colin's long-held Michelin-star cookery without the Michelin formalities and foodie reverence. Back at the house, Suilven is the big mountain over there as you linger in the conservatory or on a relatively midge-free terrace, contemplating its grandeur.

1041 5/M18
30 ROOMS
£LOTS

✓ **Glenmoriston Townhouse** Inverness · www.glenmoristontownhouse.
com · **01463 223777** Along the riverside opposite Eden Court Theatre. No
expense was spared in the conversion of 2 adjacent buildings into a chic boutique
and urban hotel in the early 21st-century ascendance of Inverness (though that
was then). Rooms split 50/50 between main hotel and adjacent Windsor House,
the latter more contemporary, with rooms overlooking the river. Piano bar and
bistro/brasserie, **Contrast**, where breakfast is served. Overall stylish operation.

1042 5/M20
8 ROOMS
FEB-DEC
££
£££

✓ **The Cross** Kingussie · www.thecross.co.uk · **01540 661166** Off main
street at traffic lights 200m uphill then left. Tasteful hotel and long-regarded
restaurant in converted tweed mill by the river which gurgles outside most
windows. Comfy rooms. Derek and Celia Kitchingman continue the reputation of
this discreet, slightly out-of-the-way riverside retreat.
EAT Deal probably includes dinner (3-course table d'hôte). Or there's a 6-course
tasting menu. Open to non-res. Imaginative, signature dining.

1043 5/L17
4 ROOMS
APR-OCT
NC500
££

✓ **The Dower House** nr Muir of Ord · www.thedowerhouse.co.uk ·
01463 870090 On A862 between Beauly and Dingwall, 18km NW of
Inverness and 2km N of village after the railway bridge. Charming, personal and
luxury B&B; you are the house guest of Robyn (in the kitchen) and Mena Aitchison,
your empathetic hosts. Cottagey-style, lived-in, small country house, with comfy
public rooms and lovely garden with pond for G&T moments. Packed lunch for
those fishing. Lovely dinner (residents only).

1044 5/N16
6 ROOMS +
3 COTTS
NO PETS
NC500
£LOTS

✓ **Glenmorangie House** Cadboll, nr Fearn · www.theglenmorangiehouse.
com · **01862 871671** S of Tain 10km E of A9. Old mansion in open grounds
overlooking a distant sea. Owned, like the distillery, by Moët Hennessy-Louis
Vuitton (LVMH) so expect some luxury (understated in public areas but all-
embracing in bedrooms). No leisure facilities but no shortage of distractions
around (the 'seaboard villages', the dolphins, **Anta Factory** and **Tain Pottery**
2193/2195/SCOTTISH SHOPS). Open fires and communal, house-party atmos.
Afternoon tea; fixed dinner round one table, honesty bar; great service.

1045 4/J15
12 ROOMS
DF · LL
APR-OCT
£LOTS

✓ **The Summer Isles Hotel** Achiltibuie · www.summerisleshotel.com ·
01854 622282 40km from Ullapool with extraordinary views over the isles;
Stac Polly and Suilven are within range. A long-established romantic retreat on the
strand at Achiltibuie, with a range of comfortable rooms in the main hotel and
adjacent cottage conversions. The iconic Summer Isles had new owners again in
2018 and I haven't stayed or eaten so reports, please. Adjacent pub offers similar
more casual dining at half the price. Lots to do outdoors, including boat trips and
don't miss some of the best views of Scotland nearby (1698/VIEWS).

1046 4/N15
21 ROOMS +
APARTS
DF · NC500
· ££

✓ **Royal Marine Hotel** Brora · www.royalmarinebrora.com ·
01408 621252 Turn-of-century mansion house by Robert Lorimer, (kind of)
overlooking the harbour, with self-catering apartment block newly built,
overlooking the golf course. Great for golfers; a civilised stopover for the rest of us.
Comfy public rooms; bedrooms vary. Decent pool in spa. Bistro and dining room.

1047 4/N16 ·
22 ROOMS
· DF
NC500 · ££

✓ **Royal Golf Hotel** The First Tee, Dornoch · www.royalgolfhoteldornoch.
co.uk · **01862 810283** Comfy, not-too-golfy golf hotel beside Dornoch's
famously fabulous golf course. On a much more human scale than others of the ilk
further south, though the new expansive apartment block adjacent does take from
the aesthetic. Casual dining, whisky bar and conservatory restaurant overlooking
course and distant waves. An excellent seafood curry courtesy of their Sri Lankan
chef.

1048 4/J14
21 ROOMS
DF · LL
MAR-OCT
NC500 · £££

✓ **Inver Lodge** Lochinver · www.inverlodge.com · 01571 844496 Here a long time on the hill overlooking the bay and the harbour, in recent years run by the never less than excellent ICMI group, who have **Inverlochy Castle** and **Rocpool Reserve** (above) in the region. House is somewhat austere though comfortable, but it's dinner and that view that you probably come for. Albert Roux's classic menu. No leisure facilities.

1049 5/M18
11 ROOMS +
2 COTTS
DF · £££

✓ **Loch Ness Country House Hotel** Inverness · www. lochnesscountryhousehotel.co.uk · 01463 230512 6km SW of town on A82. The old-style mansion-house hotel, refurbished to a fairly high standard is a good alternative to hotels in town. Gorgeous gardens; real countryside beyond. **The Park** restaurant in various (3) cosy dining rooms with sound Scottish menu. Excellent wine and malt list. Enviro-friendly garden (where the cottages are) and a great deck/terrace for a warmer evening. Weddings at weekends in adjacent suite (many, but kept largely separate).

1050 4/P12
14 ROOMS
COTTS
NC500
££

✓ **Forss House Hotel** Forss, nr Thurso · www.forsshousehotel.co.uk · 01847 861201 Georgian mansion house set in 20 woodland acres (rare in these parts) by the meandering River Forss. This stretch of the river and the foot of the lawn with its perfect pool and waterfall is yours to contemplate and (if fortunate) to fish. It's quite exceptional and the main reason for the *StB* tick. Rooms are spacious and comfortable (4 in separate River House, 2 in cottages), conservatory is nice and the bar has an impressive malt list. Though long the only decent hotel in the NE corner, it is a bit set in its ways: dinner (LO 8.30pm), bar no later than 11pm. But fishermen will always throw a line into this river and if you, passing-through tourist, toe theirs, you can enjoy their well-located, well-honed hospitality. The unforgettable Anne very much in charge.

1051 5/M18
16 ROOMS
DF · NC500
£££

Bunchrew House Hotel nr Inverness · www.bunchrewhousehotel.com · 01463 234917 On A862 Beauly road only 5km from Inverness yet completely removed from town; on the wooded shore of the Beauly Firth. A historic and atmospheric billet that often functions as a wedding hotel (so midweek stays are easier to book). Lovely dark public rooms and the light on the water.

1052 7/J21
20 ROOMS +
8 LODGES
DF · ££

Holly Tree Hotel Kentallen · www.hollytreehotel.co.uk · 01631 740292 On A828 Fort William (Ballachulish)–Oban road, 8km S of Ballachulish Bridge. On road and sea and once the railway; it was formerly a station. Convenient location and superb setting on Loch Linnhe with views from all bedrooms (some balconies) and dining room. Appropriate location for surf 'n' turf menu. Nice for kids. Surprising pool and the jetty on the sea outside. Also see 1176 /KIDS.

✓✓ **The Torridon** nr Kinlochewe At the end of Glen Torridon and **Torridon Inn** (inexpensive). Report: 1221/GET-AWAY HOTELS.

✓✓ **Eilean Iarmain** Skye Report: 2279/SKYE.

✓✓ **Kinloch Lodge** Skye Report: 2278/SKYE.

✓✓ **Scarista House** South Harris Report: 2261/ISLAND HOTELS.

✓✓ **House Over-By at The Three Chimneys** Skye Report: 2277/SKYE.

The Best Less Expensive Highland Hotels

1053 4/K15
13 ROOMS +
20 BUNKS
NO TV
ATMOS
NC500
££/£

The Ceilidh Place Ullapool · www.ceilidhplace.com ·
01854 612103 'Books, Music, Art' and Life: the original oasis of
hospitality, craic and culture in the Highlands. Rebecca and Jock in charge, their
mither Jean Urquhart moved on from a lifetime of keeping other folk happy. What
started out in the 1970s as a coffee/exhibition shop in a boat shed, spread along
the row of cottages, now comprises a restaurant, bookshop, café/bar (and
performance) area with bedrooms upstairs. Bar and restaurant go all day from
famously good breakfast to dinner menu from 6.30pm (LO 9pm). Though it's hardly
changed a bit, it's still on the button. Bunkhouse across the road offers cheaper
accom: stay 'luxuriously rough' (13 bunks). Live music and events through the year
(check the website) or you can simply sit in the cosy downstairs parlour or, if you're
a hotel guest, in the lounge upstairs with honesty bar or on the terrace overlooking
Ullapool where the boats come in.

££ **EAT** Bar and restaurant areas in one big, people-friendly room. All-day menu then
supper. Puts the craic into casual dining.

1054 4/K13
23 ROOMS
DF
NC500
££

Scourie Hotel Scourie · www.scouriehotel.com · 01971 502396 In
Scourie, on Scourie Bay, in the far North West on the A894 and 'the 500',
Fiona and Richard Campbell and daughter Charlotte have transformed this village
coaching inn into a calm, comfortable, modern stopover and a fishing hotel *par
excellence*. They have 25,000 acres of loch and river estate at your pleasure, a ghillie
to advise and an allocation of 46 beats each evening after dinner (the dinner gong
sounds at 7.30pm). Great public areas, real fire. Whether you fish or not, this is a
hotel with a strong sense of purpose – a civilised billet in wildly beautiful country.

1055 4/L12
7 ROOMS
DF · L
MAY–OCT
NC500
££

Mackay's Durness · www.visitdurness.com · 01971 511202 In the centre
and at the heart of a straggled-out township. Small but perfectly conceived
and formed hotel at the corner of NW Scotland (literally where the road turns S
again). In the Mackay family for generations. Fiona and Robbie have transformed
this solid old house into a cool spot in this northern hemisphere where in summer
the light lingers forever. Wood and slate. Discreet but efficient service. Comfy beds
in calm, stylish rooms. No bar/restaurant; eat at **The Café @ Balnakeil** (2196/
SCOTTISH SHOPS). Many interesting distractions nearby (1618/BEACHES; 2120/GOLF;
1891/MONUMENTS, Smoo Cave, etc). As well as the adjacent bunkhouse (1198/
HOSTELS), they now have 2 fabulous state-of-play new-build eco-cottages at Lade,
9km E, overlooking **Loch Eriboll** (1672/LOCHS).

1056 7/J20
14 ROOMS
DF · LL
NO TV
MAR–OCT
ATMOS
££

Glenfinnan House Hotel Glenfinnan · www.glenfinnanhouse.com ·
01397 722235 Victorian mansion with lawns down to Loch Shiel and the
Glenfinnan Monument over the water (1957/CHARLIE). No shortbread-tin twee or
tartan carpet here; instead a warm welcome from the Gibsons. Everything is just
right. Bar with atmos, craic and music (Thu); eat in bar or dining room (Duncan
Gibson was Highland Chef of the Year 2018). Cruise on the stunning loch
(07946 842732), great church (1918/CHURCHES) next door and the Viaduct walk.
Great for kids and quintessentially Scottish. Also see 1239/SCOTTISH HOTELS.

1057 5/L19
28 ROOMS
££

The Lovat Fort Augustus · www.thelovat.com · 01456 490000 On edge
of town, on the road to Fort William. Refurbished and very effectively run by
the family of the people who brought us **The Torridon** (1221/GET-AWAY HOTELS). A
contemporary, comfortable, wood-panelled hotel, unquestionably the best of the
Loch Ness options. Brasserie popular with non-res. Good looks and smart service in
the heart of the Great Glen. I reckon you'll love it, the Lovat.

1058 4/K14 ✓ **Kylesku Hotel** nr Kylestrome · www.kyleskuhotel.co.uk ·
11 ROOMS **01971 502231** Off A894 between Scourie and Lochinver. A hotel and bistro
DF · LL with a great quayside location on Loch Glencoul, where boats leave for trips to see
FEB–NOV the highest waterfall in the UK (1660/WATERFALLS). Tanja Lister and Sonia
NC500 · ££ Virechauveix's contemporary lochside inn project, with rooms merging old and new
buildings, ranging from Willie's Hoose with balconies to inexpensive attic rooms up
top. The bar and restaurant area has been completely reconfigured and there's an
outside deck. Book well ahead.

££ **EAT** Mixed menu with local fish and seafood, including interesting specials, e.g.
'spineys' (the tails of squat lobsters), and their signature seafood platter. Lunch &
dinner (food from noon all day in summer). Cool spot!

1059 4/P13 ✓ **Ulbster Arms Hotel** Halkirk · www.ulbsterarmshotel.co.uk ·
13 ROOMS **01847 831641** In middle of village off A9 10km S of Thurso. By the river which
££ is there to be fished (the hotel has 13 beats). Refurbished to comfy and country-
stylish standard, unusually contemporary up Caithness way. Dining more
traditional in atmospheric bar or dining room.

1060 7/K22 ✓ **Kingshouse Hotel** Glen Coe · www.kingshousehotel.co.uk In the heart
60 ROOMS of the Glen, the historic Kingshouse Hotel opens 2019 after an extensive (and
££ expensive) makeover. At TGP, I wasn't able to experience this ambitious total
transformation by the people who have Crieff Hydro, and the Ballachulish Hotel nearby,
but great expectations from all those who know this landmark hostelry for walkers,
climbers and what will now be many more independent tourists. Very different
standards from days of yore; the amazing view of Buachaille Etive Mòr remains.

1061 7/K20 ✓ **Corriechoille Lodge** Spean Bridge · www.corriechoille.com ·
4 ROOMS + **01397 712002** 4 (riverside) km out of Spean Bridge on the small road by the
2 CABINS station. Justin and Lucy Swabey's hideaway house facing the mountains. Beautiful
NO PETS · L corner of the country with spectacular views to the Grey Corries and Aonach Mòr.
APR–OCT · £ Lovely set dinner, simple cosy rooms. (No kids under 7 years.) 2 turf-roofed
self-catering chalets. Great walks begin here. Closed Sun/Mon. Also 1230/
GET-AWAY HOTELS.

1062 7/J21 ✓ **The Lime Tree** Fort William · www.limetreefortwilliam.co.uk ·
9 ROOMS **01397 701806** At the roundabout as you come from the south. Regional and
££ local art gallery (owner David Wilson's work for sale, and some great visiting
exhibitions) with rooms above and a good restaurant that's one of the best in Fort
William. Simple, convivial, contemporary atmos in the usually buzzing restaurant
and the 2 comfy lounges of this Old Manse.

1063 7/K20 ✓ **Old Pines** nr Spean Bridge · www.oldpines.co.uk · 01397 712324 3km
8 ROOMS from Spean Bridge via B8004 for Garlochy at **Commando Monument** (1893/
££ MONUMENTS). Open-plan pine cabin with wood stove, neat bedrooms and a bright,
conservatory-type dining room looking out to the woods. A very comfy,
unpretentious hotel with great food; à la carte menu open to non-res for lunch and
dinner. Chickens run, the pines are old! And see 1174 KIDS.

1064 5/K20 ✓ **Glengarry Castle** Invergarry · www.glengarry.net · 01809 501254 A
26 ROOMS · L family-run hotel for over 50 years, in the charge of the younger MacCallums
APR–OCT (mum still does the flowers and the scones!); they're sticking with tradition.
££ Rhoddies, honeysuckle as you walk to the loch. Magnificent trees, and a newly
restored castle in the grounds, the stronghold of the MacDonells: you may remember
the famous portrait by Raeburn – the epitome of the fashionable Highland chief. 2
rowing boats at your disposal (and the brown trout). Romantic! Big rooms.

1065 5/H17 ✓ **Tigh an Eilean** Shieldaig · www.tighaneilean.co.uk · 01520 755251 This
11 ROOMS roadside, cosily furnished hotel on the waterfront overlooks a Scots pine island
DF · LL on loch (sea eagles swoop). **Coastal Kitchen** pub, transformed with upstairs bistro
CLOSED JAN and deck overlooking the loch, is adjacent. Live music weekends. Dining room and
NC500 · ££ the Kitchen busy with people, pizzas and specials. A good spot at the heart of a
Highland village.

1066 5/M20 ✓ **Coig na Shee** Newtonmore · www.coignashee.co.uk ·
5 ROOMS 01540 670109 Road out of Newtonmore (which is just off the A9) for Fort
£ William. Mansion house with light, contemporary feel and furnishings. Nice
breakfast (they have free-range hens) and evening meals on request. **The
Letterbox** (01540 673231) in the village also has good food. Back at CNS, the
Broads are friendly and will tell you where else you can go. Exceptional value.

1067 4/K14 ✓ **Glencanisp Lodge** Lochinver · www.glencanisp-lodge.co.uk ·
7 ROOMS 01571 844100 Signed from the Shore road near the turn-off for Achiltibuie,
DF · L 3km up the road into the glen and hills to an old mansion, with young proprietors,
NC500 Rachael and Sam Hawkins, and staff making the most of the outdoors around
££ them, the loch, the lovely woods. Comfy, lived-in rooms, inexpensive for country-
house comforts, including delicious dinner.

1068 4/Q12 **Castle Arms Hotel** Mey, nr Thurso · www.castlearmshotel.co.uk ·
9 ROOMS 01847 851244 An old, tastefully presented roadside inn adjacent to the **Castle
APR-SEP of Mey** (1815/CASTLES), very much in a similar aesthetic though of course ...
NC500 simplified. Nice bathrooms and bar/restaurant (Caithness/Orkney produce). Good
££ stopover before Orkney and on the North Coast 500.

1069 4/K13 **Eddrachilles Hotel** nr Scourie · www.eddrachilles.com ·
10 ROOMS 01971 502080 Between Scourie and Kylesku (and their hotels, see above),
DF · LL Eddrachilles is undoubtedly all about – the view. Overlooking the bay, a classic
NC500 · ££ Assynt vista of mountains and seascape with islands thrown in, you could sit in the
conservatory (on their very long chairs) for wistful hours on end (and have
afternoon tea). There's a tree stump (sic) trail to the foreshore. Rooms at front (6)
clearly best. Scandic twist to the menu.

1070 4/H16 **Aultbea Hotel** Aultbea · www.aultbeahotel.co.uk · 01445 731201 Seafront
8 ROOMS hotel as you come into Aultbea from the A832 Ullapool to Gairloch road, revitalised
FEB-NOV 2018 by bright and bold French couple with culinary and photographic background
NC500 · ££ (nice pictures). An inexpensive tavern and simple, contemporary rooms on a great
coast to explore. Whatever happens on your venture here, courage, mes braves!

1071 5/M17 **The Anderson** Fortrose · www.theanderson.co.uk · 01381 620236 Main
9 ROOMS street of town in the middle of the Black Isle. Restaurant, bar and reasonable
ATMOS rooms in very individual hotel notable for its extraordinary bottled ales and whisky
££ collection and then the food. Rooms have a certain and well-chosen charm; in fact
this place exudes boho-chic with a tartan trim. US owners diligent in their pursuit
of approvals. Accolades over the years, including mine.
££ **EAT** Anne Anderson remarkably manages an ambitious long daily-changing menu
(smokes the venison, makes the black pudding and just about everything else) in
atmospheric bar and dining room. It's 'creative cuisine'.

1072 5/L18 **The Loch Ness Inn** nr Drumnadrochit · www.staylochness.co.uk ·
12 ROOMS 01456 450991 1km from the monster mash of Drumnadrochit. A functional
NO PETS · ££ roadhouse hotel, quite the best in the area and with a notable restaurant that's

invariably full. The estimable Judy Fish from the **Applecross Inn** (1229/GET-AWAY HOTELS) has a hand in this.

££ **EAT** The best casual meal between Inverness and Fort Augustus – may have to book; separate bar menu; beer garden is out the back. By arrangement, a minibus can get you home.

1073 5/H18 **The Plockton Inn** www.plocktoninn.co.uk · 01599 544222 & **The Plockton**
14/15 ROOMS **Hotel** · www.plocktonhotel.co.uk · 01599 544274 Two stays in perfect
££ Plockton (1605/VILLAGES) though the village is why we come. The Inn is away from the front. Some good cask ales in bar. Very basic rooms – 7 in hotel and 7 in more contemporary annex over the street. Bistro in labyrinth of rooms: mainly seafood. Tables on terrace in summer, back garden for kids; the pub is the locals' choice. The Plockton Hotel is by the water's edge and is busier and buzzier, with better bedrooms. Pub and pub meals; it's always packed.

1074 6/N19 **Boat Hotel** Boat of Garten · www.boathotel.co.uk · 01479 831258 Centre
34 ROOMS of village overlooking the steam-train line and near golf course (2112/GOLF). Great
££ old-style (Victorian/1920s) hotel, with a variety of rooms. There are also 6 chalet-type 'garden' rooms: OK and quiet. Decent food in very pleasant bar, bistro and dining room: woody, tasteful and timeless.

1075 4/N16 **Dornoch Castle Hotel** Dornoch · www.dornochcastlehotel.com ·
24 ROOMS 01862 810216 Main street of delightful Sutherland town with nice beaches, great
NC500 golf and a cathedral made famous by Madonna who once got married here. Very
££ castle-like (from 15th century), up-and-down building where rooms vary hugely, as do prices (The Tower Room, Cathedral View). Garden Restaurant (yes, on the garden) is up and down (for food) too. Great lounge bar for whisky and ales. Overall there is charm, and locals do go, especially to the Beer Garden (it has a gin distillery in the corner).

1076 5/N17 **Hotels in Nairn: The Golf View** www.crerarhotels.com · 01667 452301 &
42/14 ROOMS **The Clubhouse** www.clubhousenairn.co.uk · 01667 453321 Both in suburban
NO PETS Seabank Rd, off the A96. Comfy, refurbished Golf View, often busy, has 'The View'
££ (of the sea). Clubhouse is the brasher arriviste with slightly lurid decor that may date quickly – inexpensive though, and the restaurant gets good local reports.

1077 5/L18 **Lovat Arms** Beauly · www.lovatarms.com · 01463 782313 In lovely wee priory
33 ROOMS town 20 mins from Inverness. They say 'home away from home' and this old-style
DF · NC500 hotel run by the Fraser family for over 25 years is definitely that kind of thing.
££ Rooms in hotel and 22 in separate townhouse behind. Good pub. All very Highland.

1078 5/K18 **Tomich Hotel** Tomich · www.tomichhotel.co.uk · 01456 415399 The inn of
8 ROOMS a quiet conservation village, part of an old estate on the edge of Guisachan Forest.
DF · L Odd fact: the Golden Retriever breed was invented here! Near fantastic **Plodda**
££ **Falls** (1652/WATERFALLS) and **Glen Affric** (1642/GLENS). Rooms pleasant and cosy. Use of pool nearby in farm steading (key in the Post Office caff opposite); especially good for fishing holidays. 25km from Drumnadrochit by A831. New owners at TGP. Reports, please.

1079 4/K16 **The Arch Inn** Ullapool · www.thearchinn.co.uk · 01854 612454 On the shore
10 ROOMS of Loch Broom along from the ferry, heart of the town and especially its music
DF scene and festivals (Loopallu and Fèis). Most rooms have a view and may be on the
NC500 · £ street. An all-round good base and you sleep by the sea.
£ **EAT** Long-established, locally popular pub for food, fish 'n' chips, seafood specials. Busy at weekends – put your name down and wait.

1080 7/J23   **The Taynuilt Guest House** Taynuilt · www.thetaynuilt.co.uk · 01866 822437
10 ROOMS Main road (A85 to Oban, 18km) of village on Loch Etive. A traditional roadhouse
DF · **ATMOS** hotel restructured as a guest house, with a lounge and dining room for lovely
£ breakfast (recently a notable restaurant run by the chef/proprietors now also have
Etive in Oban 747/OBAN). Upstairs, individual (some spacious) rooms with period
furniture and atmos. Great value.

HOTELS ON THE NORTH COAST (all on NORTH COAST 500)

1081 4/M13   **Tongue Hotel** Tongue · www.tonguehotel.co.uk · 01847 611206 One
19 ROOMS of 2 hotels in Tongue at the centre of the N coast where Ben Loyal rises. The
££ Hooks' hotel on the main road, an excellent-value 4 star with nicely turned-out
rooms. Lounge bar and candlelit dining room. Very Highland. The **Brass Tap** pub
downstairs has atmos and many locals.

1082 4/M13   **Ben Loyal Hotel** Tongue · www.benloyal.co.uk · 01847 611216 Just off the
13 ROOMS main road, the A836. Cheaper than above and with some views of the Big Ben
£ around here.

1083 4/M13   **Bettyhill Hotel** Bettyhill · www.bettyhillhotel.com · 01641 521202 An old
20 ROOMS hotel (well, 200 years), recently revitalised c/o the NC500, in a superb location
DF · L bang on the road and overlooking the vast stress-relieving strand of **Torrisdale**
£ **Beach**. Inexpensive rooms undergoing a rolling refurbishment (they're very
pleased with their Simba mattresses). Public bar and a dining room in the sunset.

1084 4/Q12   **Natural Retreats** John o' Groats · www.naturalretreats.co.uk ·
££ 0844 384 3166 Top-of-the-North/end-of-the-road inn of apartments and lodges,
café and store. Self-catering but night stays are possible in the brightly coloured,
shed-like structures built on the shoreline facing the sea, the sea. Well-appointed
and not expensive. For surfers and those who just want to be north.

The Best Restaurants In The Highlands

1085 7/H22

L

MAR-OCT

£££

✓✓ **The Whitehouse Restaurant** Lochaline, Ardnamurchan · www. thewhitehouserestaurant.co.uk · 01967 421777 Sits above the ferry port as the Mull boats come in, a restaurant adjacent the village shop with all the right/best principles: local produce, organic, imaginative cooking. Ingredients from Mull and Lochaber – bay, woods and hedgerow. Sarah and Jane's award-winning, back-of-beyond bistro under chef Michael Burgoyne is a true destination in itself; often fully booked. Quiet days in Ardnamurchan begin here. Home-made everything and Scottish cheeses. Tue-Sat, 11am-afternoon tea-dinner.

1086 6/P17

£

✓✓ **The Bakehouse** Findhorn · www.bakehousecafe.co.uk · 01309 691826 Follow the one-way system round the village – you can't and mustn't miss it. Jan Boultbee and David Hoyle run this brilliant coffee shop/ restaurant where you eat ethically and well. Home-made/home-grown/organic, naturally, part of the slow-food movement; all individually prepared. Mostly vegetarian though they do great burgers and breakfasts. 7 days 10am-4pm. Famous locally for David's bread (1485/BAKERS) and their Fri/Sat pizza nights (book!). On a recent visit, all the above from a previous edition was still all true.

1087 6/N17

££

✓✓ **Kale Yard Bistro @ The Boath House** Auldearn, nr Nairn · www. boath-house.com · 01667 454896 30 mins Inverness, 10 mins Nairn. The bistro/café, eating-in-the-garden experience – the conversion of potting sheds and glasshouses in the magnificent walled garden of the best hotel in the region (1033/HIGHLANDS). Chef Stefano Agostini. Closed Mon/Tue.

1088 5/H18

L

MAR-OCT

NC500

£

✓ **Walled Garden Restaurant** Applecross · www.applecrossgarden.co.uk · 01520 744440 In N Applecross along the strand, 'The Potting Shed', at the back of a gorgeous walled garden, Jon Glover's ongoing project. Enter via a pergola of roses (in summer). A destination coffee shop/restaurant like the **Applecross Inn** (1229/GET-AWAY HOTELS), making that harrowing drive worthwhile. Everything home-made and often from the garden or the sea over there. Breakfast, full-menu lunch and dinner. 7 days 'early till evening'.

1089 4/J14

NC500

££

✓ **The Caberfeidh** Lochinver · www.thecaberfeidh.co.uk · 01571 844321 Main St as you come into the village. An old, now dining pub on the sea (actually, at the river mouth) run by the Michelin-starred Lesley Crosfield and Colin Craig, from the landmark Highland hotel, the **Albannach**, up the road (1040/HIGHLANDS). Here, a pub (on the street) and a dining room overlooking the water, with perfect gastropub ambience and a daily-changing blackboard menu, with their impeccable seasonal sourcing policy. In Lochinver, this is the must eat. Check website for opening times.

1090 4/M12

MAY-SEP

NC500

£££

✓ **Côte du Nord** nr Bettyhill · www.cotedunord.co.uk · 01641 521773 5km E of Bettyhill, signed for Kirtomy, 2km from A838. This small (very small, 8–10 covers) Highland croft bistro (i.e. French-influenced cooking) has something of a legendary status among foodies. Ingredients for the 10-course, no-choice menu really are sourced mostly locally on the far N coast. For Chris Duckham, also the local GP, cooking is a hobby. Incredible value, including from the selective French and Spanish wine list. May-Sep: dinner only on Wed/Fri/Sat. Obviously, you must book.

1091 5/H18

L

££

✓ **Plockton Shores** Plockton · www.plocktonshoresrestaurant.com · 01599 544263 Shores and village stores! On the foreshore of lovely Plockton, Ian and Anne James' all-purpose eaterie with fine home cooking that makes the most of location and hinterland (for ingredients). Some vegetarian choice.

1092 5/M17 ✓ **Sutor Creek** Cromarty · www.sutorcreek.co.uk · 01381 600855 Near the
L seafront. An end-of-the-road (across the Black Isle) diner in Cromarty (1608/
££ VILLAGES). Both a destination and a neighbourhood caff, conscientiously run by the
Foxes, with focus on seasonal- and local-produce specials. Wood-fired oven
turning out their locally famous crispy pizza. Tapas and tasting nights. Noon-9pm.
Winter hours vary. See **Couper's Creek** 1436/TEAROOMS.

1093 5/H18 ✓ **Waterside Seafood Restaurant** Kyle of Lochalsh · www.
LL watersideseafoodrestaurant.co.uk · 01599 534813 Not quayside, more
ATMOS platform-side by the busy port, off the road to Skye, that bridge in the distance.
££ *Brief Encounter* location; being actually on the platform at the end of the line lends
distinction to Jann and Neil MacRae's long-standing destination. Seafood from
Kyle/Mallaig/Skye, i.e. very local. A la carte and blackboard. Dinner Mon-Sat.

1094 7/K20 ✓ **The Smiddy House** Spean Bridge · www.smiddyhouse.com ·
L 01397 712335 Near junction of A82 for Skye on A86 for Laggan, Messrs
£££ Bryson and Russell's conscientiously run restaurant with (4) rooms (and cottage
apartment). Excellent, unpretentious fare, all home-made. Fish selection and great
chargrill steaks. Especially good for vegetarian food and diets. This is a destination
place to eat (including from Fort William). Afternoon tea (must book) in light lounge
with great choice of teas and tier of tea things (1465/AFTERNOON TEA).

1095 5/N17 ✓ **Café One One Two** Nairn · 01667 457135 At the harbour end of High St, a
£ refreshingly contemporary wine bar/bistro. Excellent wine selection, mains,
small plates. Closed Mon.

1096A 5/N17 ✓ **Sun Dancer** Nairn · www.sun-dancer.co.uk · 01667 370037 Upstairs
££ bistro on the promenade, with astonishing sea view (and dolphins!). I enjoyed
everything I ate here. Closed Mon.

1096 4/K14 ✓ **Kylesku Hotel** nr Kylestrome · www.kyleskuhotel.co.uk · 01971 502231
LL Just off the A894, on the shore overlooking Loch Glencoul. Tanja and Sonia's
FEB-NOV small quayside pub/hotel (1058/HIGHLANDS) serves, among other seasonal dishes,
NC500 langoustines, crab, lobster and 'spineys' (c/o Hamish's boat from the quay) in a
££ fabulous setting with mighty **Quinag** behind (1984/HILLS). Same menu in bar and
dining room. Check website for opening times.

1097 5/N19 ✓ **Mountain Café** Aviemore · www.mountaincafe-aviemore.co.uk ·
£ 01479 812473 On the main street above an outdoor shop, the best bet for
food in this activity hub town. Great for breakfast and home baking (especially
bread). Good vegetarian: they make everything and have their own-branded deli.
Kirsten Gilmour even has her own cookbook. Big, big helpings for hungry outdoorsy
types. But they ain't open for dinner. 7 days.

1098 5/J18 **Carron Restaurant** Strathcarron · 01520 722488 On A890 round Loch Carron
NC500 (joins A87 Kyle of Lochalsh road) near Strathcarron. A long-standing roadside diner.
£ The McGales have worked hard to make this a welcome destination on a long road
through big scenery. Home cooking, from caff in the day to proper dinner in the
evening. Focus on whisky (and sherry) and special food events. 2km to **Attadale
Gardens** (1582/GARDENS).

1099 5/H17 **Gille Brighde** Diabaig, Torridon · www.gille-brighde.com · 01445 790245
£ Far away in/through the marvellous Torridon mountains to the end of the road (30
mins from Torridon village and the A896) to where Loch Torridon comes out to the

sea 1678/SCENIC ROUTES. Brave, determined but laid-back in their endeavour, Aart and Amanda Lastdrager have made a great wee café/bistro in the Old Schoolhouse, with local seafood, steaks and vegetarian in daytime and evening menus. It's great to eat outside here.

1100 6/N19   **Anderson's Boat of Garten** · www.andersonsrestaurant.co.uk ·
££   **01479 831466** On the main road to/from Aviemore and Carrbridge. The Andersons' family-run restaurant, a welcome dine-out around here where there are lots of visitors and not much good food on the go. Laudably, all home-made, including bread and many ice creams. Nothing fancy but an eclectic choice. Lunch & dinner. Great Sun lunch. Closed Mon/Tue in winter.

1101 4/N16   **Luigi Dornoch** · www.luigidornoch.com · 01862 810893 On the way into
NC500   town. Smart-looking café/restaurant, a welcome find in dreamy Dornoch. Drop-in
£   snack place by day with good Lavazza coffee; Euro-Scottish menu and pizza in evenings. Open AYR from 10am. Dinner 7 days in summer.

1102 4/M16   **Crannag Bistro Bonar Bridge** · www.crannag.com · 01863 766111 Brill bistro,
££   where you might least expect one in faraway Sutherland. Scottish, local – as usual these days – but with more than a soupçon of spice: Ian and Kathy Smith run what some say is a 'culinary oasis'; in this quarter there's not much else and this is a worthwhile detour from the NC500. Tue-Sat dinner only.

1103 5/M17   **The Storehouse nr Evanton** · www.thestorehouse.scot · 01349 830038
NC500   Roadside farm shop/deli and destination diner on A9 N of Inverness, overlooking
£   the firth. Locally sourced meats and various olives/haggis/and mugs! (you get the picture). The self-service restaurant goes like a fair and reads its clientele well. Often queues. Not as many lashings of cream as before (as I regretted on a recent visit). 7 days, daytime only.

1104 5/N17   **The Classroom Nairn** · www.theclassroombistro.com · 01667 455999 At
££   top end of main shopping street in Cawdor St, a continuation. Contemporary makeover (though some time ago now) in this conservative, golfy town. An airy bar/restaurant; like a real brasserie. Good for kids, for afternoon tea and grown-up dinner. 7 days, morning to night.

1105 4/J14   **Riverside Bistro Lochinver** · www.lochinverlarder.co.uk · 01571 844356 On the
NC500   way into town on A837. This Lochinver larder is notable mainly for the vast array of Ian
£   Stewart's superb home-made pies (www.piesbypost.co.uk) and calorific cakes (1481/ BAKERS). The banoffee pie here is truly wicked. You can eat in or take away. LO 7.45pm.

1106 5/N16   **The Oystercatcher Portmahomack** · www.the-oystercatcher.co.uk ·
L   **01862 871560** On promontory of the Dornoch Firth (Tain 15km), this hidden
APR-OCT   seaside village (the only east-coast village that faces west) may bring back beach-
£££   plootering memories. The restaurant (there are also 3 B&B rooms) is a destination in itself, the wine list and malt choice truly extraordinary. Food is inventive, multi-ingredient and always interesting, but you must book.

1107 4/P15   **La Mirage Helmsdale** · www.lamirage.org · 01431 821615 A bright little gem
NC500   up Sutherland way and once a homage to Barbara Cartland, the romantic novelist, who
£   lived nearby in this gorgeous wee village by the sea and strath. Snacks of every kind all day, great home cooking and baking from Don, son-in-law of Nancy Sinclair, who famously put this caff on the map. Great fish & chips (can takeaway). Open AYR, 11am-8.45pm. Also in Helmsdale, opposite La Mirage: **Thyme & Plaice** 01431 821598 for home cooking, good atmos and not chips with everything. Closed Mon.

The Best Places To Stay In & Around Inverness

1108 5/M18
11 ROOMS
NO PETS
£LOTS

Rocpool Reserve **Culduthel Rd** · www.rocpool.com · **01463 240089**
Looking down on the centre from above (great view from terrace), this self-consciously presented boutique hotel is owned by the expanding superlative ICMI group who have **Inverlochy Castle** (1037/HIGHLANDS) and manage several other highly individual Scottish hotels. Each room a design statement, divided into Hip, Chic or Decadent, and, er, ... Extra Decadent. You may feel you have to live up to the titles. 2 rooms have hot tubs on outdoor decks. Probably best to have someone to share these demanding surroundings with you.

· £££ **EAT** As with others in the group, an Albert Roux restaurant; the menu has some of his signature dishes. Prix fixe and à la carte. A top dining room in town.

1109 5/M18
8 ROOMS
££

The Heathmount **Kingsmill Rd** · www.heathmounthotel.com · **01463 235877** Uphill from Eastgate Mall. Fiona Newton's stylish boutique-style hotel – a hipsterish stopover – with popular, and at weekends very busy, bar/restaurant with outside deck on the corner. High standard of mod con; rich, individual boudoir decor with personal attention to detail. Good value; friendly service.

1110 5/M18
84 ROOMS
DF · L
££

Royal Highland Hotel **18 Academy St** · www.royalhighlandhotel.co.uk · **01463 231926** Literally on top of the station. Nice staircase and a recherché charm but rooms rather average. A surreal start to the day in the very interior breakfast room. For lunch/dinner, just 'Ask' (the chain restaurant beside). Very much in the centre of things; definitely more functional than flash. Many of the old bods in the central foyer seem like they've been waiting for that train forever! A Rubens behind the desk sets a higher tone (no, not a real one!).

**Culloden House** **Culloden Rd** 5km E, near (but not adjacent to) the battlefield. Gracious living, splendid grounds. Report: 1038/HIGHLANDS.

Black Isle Bar & Rooms **68 Church St** Bunks and dorm accom – some singles/doubles. Report: See below.

Glenmoriston Townhouse **Ness Bank** Smart riverside hotel. Brasserie. Independently owned; good service. Report: 1041/HIGHLANDS.

Loch Ness Country House Hotel **Loch Ness Rd** 6km SW on A82. Comfy country house just outside town. Weddings. Report: 1049/HIGHLANDS.

Bunchrew House Hotel **nr Inverness** 4km N on the road to Beauly on firth shore. Atmospheric and refined. Weddings. Report: 1051/HIGHLANDS.

The Best Places To Eat In & Around Inverness

1111 6/N17
£££/££

Boath House **Auldearn, nr Nairn** · www.boath-house.com · **01667 454896** Well out of town off A96, 3km E of Nairn, 30km E of Inverness. In the dining room in beautiful surroundings both within or without, or more casually in the **Kale Yard Bistro**, in the wonderful walled garden – pizza and such. Reports: 1033/1087/HIGHLANDS.

1112 5/M18 ✓✓ **Rocpool** Ness Walk · www.rocpoolrestaurant.com · 01463 717274
£££ Corner of main bridge over river. Steven Devlin is a consummate host in this stylish, bright, buzzy restaurant with daytime and eclectic evening menus. Still the consistently good place to eat in the centre of Inverness. Look no further – if you can get in! Mon-Sat.

1113 5/M18 ✓✓ **Café One** Castle St · www.cafe1.net · 01463 226200 For a few years
££ now, Norman MacDonald has been running and working the floor of one of the most in-tune-with-its-clientele restaurants in Scotland. With wine bar out front and 2 happily crowded rooms, it's quite apparent that this is Inverness's number one choice for an affordable dinner out. Norman seems to speak to every table and there's a lot of them. Seasonally changing menu, superb well-informed wine list (with huge by-the-glass choice) at good prices. Café One and Rocpool are the *par excellence* urban eateries in this ville. Closed Sun.

1114 5/M18 ✓ **Contrast** Ness Bank · www.glenmoristontownhouse.com ·
££ 01463 223777 Part of the Glenmoriston Townhouse (above), this bistro/brasserie is quite French, informal but smart. Piano bar adjacent for pre and après. 7 days lunch & dinner.

1115 5/M18 ✓ **The Mustard Seed** Fraser St · www.mustardseedrestaurant.co.uk ·
££ 01463 220220 Inverness's long-standing urbane restaurant by Messrs Bisset and Littlejohn, in architectural riverside room with good attitude and buzz. Contemporary menu, OK wine. Downstairs and up, with a balcony overlooking the river. Great service. 7 days lunch & dinner.

1116 5/M18 ✓ **Girvans** Stephens Brae · www.girvansrestaurant.co.uk · 01463 711900
£ Behind M&S. Fast-turnover food for all folks. Home-made and on the button. All towns should have an easy drop-in, reliable eaterie like this. 7 days. Report: 1401/CAFÉS.

1117 5/M18 ✓ **Black Isle Bar & Rooms** 68 Church St · www.blackislebrewery.com ·
DF 01463 229920 First there was a microbrewery at Munlochy on the Cromarty
£ Peninsula in the Black Isle, then they popped up at festivals, and in 2017 opened this large bar/restaurant with (bunk)rooms above (and in a separate block nearby), which has been going like a fair ever since. Over 100 craft beers, including their own, and food all day, mainly wood-fired (thin) pizzas and salads, cheeseboard and chocolate truffles. A simple, largely organic menu that demonstrably works. 7 days. Food till 11pm, bar later.

1118 5/M18 ✓ **Fig & Thistle** Stephens Brae · 01463 712422 The F&T is a 2-floor,
£ contemporary wee bistro opposite the Eastgate shopping centre. By lovely Karen Smith and chef partner Steven Dewart, who once had a Pig & Whistle in Portugal. Light and bright it is; Mod-Brit/Scot menu. Lunch Wed-Sat & dinner Tue-Sat.

1119 5/M18 ✓ **The Kitchen Brasserie** Huntly St · www.kitchenrestaurant.co.uk ·
££ 01463 259119 In a glassy building on the river almost opposite its parent, The Mustard Seed (see above). On 3 floors of an 'architectural' building, so waiters work hard up and down those staircases, as does the kitchen which you can watch on screen. Often all floors (though small) are packed. Good value. Though tiny, they have best terrace in town. 7 days lunch & dinner.

1120 5/M18 ✓ **MacGregor's** 109-113 Academy St · www.macgregorsbars.com ·
££   **01463 719629** At the end of Academy St, on the corner of Church St.
Founded by Bruce MacGregor of folk royalty Blazin' Fiddles, this is a pub and bistro
that takes both food and music seriously. Not many tables and often a live act but
never intrusive. Simple, folksy food in contemporary style. Great Sunday roast. Food
till 9pm. 7 days.

1121 5/M18 ✓ **Riverhouse Restaurant** Greig St · www.riverhouseinverness.co.uk ·
£££   **01463 222033** Over the pedestrian bridge. Intimate seafood restaurant by Allan
Little, who knows his oysters, in an open kitchen. A 'cicchetti menu' of small plates
3-5.30pm. Mussels, oysters and daily/seasonal specials. Gets busy so can feel cramped
but big local reputation. Lunch Tue-Sat & dinner Tue-Sun. Closed Sun in winter.

1122 5/M18 **The White House** 50 Union St · www.thewhitehouse.uk.com ·
£££   **01463 226767** A 'cocktail bar & bistro' that hits all the contemporary notes for a
good food-night out. Mod-Brit/Scot menu, brasserie-type room. Very good service.
Lunch & LO 9/9.30pm; bar all day. 7 days.

1123 5/M18 **La Tortilla Asesina** 99 Castle St · www.latortillaasesina.co.uk ·
£   **01463 709809** Top of street, near castle and hostels. For a lot of years now,
an Inverness fave spot for good vibes and reasonably authentic Spanish, i.e. UK
version, of tapas – 2/3 portions as a meal. All the expected and some variants are
here with lots of *platos del día*. Rioja and the beers. 7 days.

1124 5/M18 **Little Italy** Stephens Brae · **01463 712963** Up the brae from the Eastgate
£   Centre end of main street. Small, we do mean small, family-run (the De Vitas) tratt
that Inverness folk like. Authentic menu of everything you'd want that ends in a
vowel. Outside tables. Closed Sun.

1125 5/M18 **Rajah** www.rajahinverness.com · **01463 237190** Downstairs in the lane
£   (between Church and Academy Sts, behind Queensgate), one of the best of several
curry houses. Here since 1982 and usually packed. Says it all! Will probably see off
all the nouveau Indians.

1126 5/M18 **Sam's** Church St (next to Hootananny) · www.samsindian.com ·
£   **01463 713111** And this is the other (more recent) one opposite. Invernessians
swear by one or the other.

1127 5/M18 **The Malt Room** 34 Church St · www.themaltroom.co.uk · **01463 221888**
£   Down a lane by the Victorian Market. Not so much a foodstop, but most definitely
a cool bar to partake of whisky, gin, cocktails, with snacks to go with. A great
hangout. Noon till late (Sun from 3pm). 7 days.

 Castle Restaurant Castle St Legendary caff of the Highlands. Hardest-
working kitchen in the north? Report: 1404/CAFÉS.

✓ **Café One One Two** Nairn 28km Inverness. Worth the journey for this
outpost of hipster foodland in the north. Report: 1095/HIGHLANDS.

If You're In Fort William...

WHERE TO STAY

1128 7/J21
9 ROOMS
££

✓ **The Lime Tree** Achintore Rd · www.limetreefortwilliam.co.uk · 01397 701806 As you come in from S, the last hotel of many. By the roundabout, the start of the main street. Combines regional art-gallery space in the old manse, with (Victorian) rooms above and a (modern/rustic) newer extension. Bar/restaurant with open kitchen and terrace. David Wilson (his art on the walls) and Charlotte Wright run Fort William's convivial, cosmopolitan inn.

1129 7/J21
20 ROOMS
NO PETS · ££

✓ **Nevis Bank Inn** Belford Rd · www.nevisbankinn.co.uk · 01397 705721 On the main A82 to Inverness near the roundabout and road into Glen Nevis. Extensively refurbished hotel in contemporary style: neutrals, browns, stone and wood. Busy bistro **Browns** better than several very dated stopovers in this town.

1130 7/K21

Glen Nevis Youth Hostel Glen Nevis · www.syha.org.uk · 01397 702336 5km from Fort William by picturesque but busy Glen Nevis road. The Ben is above. Grade 1. Many other hostels in area, especially **Fort William Backpackers** Alma Rd · www.fortwilliambackpackers.com · 01397 700711.

1131 7/K21

Achintee Farm Glen Nevis · www.achinteefarm.com · 01397 702240 On approach to Ben Nevis main route and adjacent Ben Nevis Inn (see below). Guest house/self-catering and bunkhouse in walkers' haven.

WHERE TO EAT

1132 7/J21
L · MID–
MAR–OCT
££

✓ **Lochleven Seafood Café** North Ballachulish · www.lochlevenseafoodcafe.co.uk · 01855 821048 From the A82 15km S at Ballachulish, take the lochside road to this award-winning seafood caff. Simply worth the drive. Report: 1361/SEAFOOD.

1133 7/J21
££

✓ **Blas** 147 High St · www.blasfortwilliam.co.uk · 01397 702726 On main street, near the S end. Described as a bistro, bar, brewery (and the home of Lochaber Gin), this at once ticked all the contemporary boxes when it opened in 2018. Open kitchen, à la carte and specials. Lunch and dinner with coffee and cake in between. Same folk have **Delicraft**, a takeaway and sit-in café further along the street. Closed Sun/Mon.

1134 7/K20
L · £££

✓ **The Smiddy House** Spean Bridge · www.smiddyhouse.com · 01397 712335 Acclaimed restaurant at a busy Highland junction 10km N. Good vegetarian. Reports: 1465/AFTERNOON TEA; 1094/HIGHLANDS.

1135 7/J21
££

✓ **The Lime Tree** Achintore Rd · www.limetreefortwilliam.co.uk · 01397 701806 At roundabout as you arrive from S or the S end of the main street. Restaurant of boutiquey hotel (above) with good atmos, open kitchen and terrace. 4 starters/mains/desserts. Local sourcing; Scottish cheeses; neat wine list.

1136 7/K21
LL
£LOTS

✓ **Inverlochy Castle** Torlundy · www.inverlochycastlehotel.com · 01397 702177 5km out on A82. Victorian elegance, classically stylish; impeccable service. Restaurant open to non-res but this is not casual dining. Jacket and tie required.

1137 7/J21 ✓ **The Wildcat** 21 High St On main street, the new vegan café for the
£ Highlands has good food for all. Report: 1352/VEGETARIAN.

1138 7/J21 **Crannog Restaurant** Town Pier · www.crannog.net · 01397 705589 Finlay
L Finlayson's long-established landmark restaurant on the waterfront. Freshly caught
££ seafood mainly (one meat/one vegetarian) in informal bistro setting. Good wine
list. Open AYR. 7 days lunch & dinner.

1139 7/J21 **Garrison West** 4 Cameron Sq · www.garrisonwest.co.uk · 01397 701873 By
££ the same folk who have **Crannog**, above, a very different but on-the-zeitgeist, pub-
like eaterie that's as busy as the A82 – possibly Fort William's most popular haunt.
Ales, gins, small and big plates. Live music. 7 days.

1140 7/K21 **Ben Nevis Inn** Achintee · www.ben-nevis-inn.co.uk · 01397 701227 On
ATMOS main approach to the Ben itself. Reach across river by new footbridge from visitor
£ centre or by road on right after Inverlochy/Glen Nevis roundabout on A82 (marked
Claggan and Achintee; 3km). Excellent atmospheric inn in converted farm building.
Good grub/ale and walking chat. LO 9pm; bar 10.45pm. Thu-Sun in winter.

1141 7/J21 **The Grog & Gruel** 66 High St · www.grogandgruel.co.uk · 01397 705078 In
£ downtown Fort William, a long-established pub known for its ales and atmos, but
also Scottish pub grub. Upstairs restaurant. 7 days.

Gay Scotland the Best

EDINBURGH

1142 8/Q25 ✓ **The Street** **2b Picardy Place** · **www.thestreetbaredinburgh.co.uk** · **0131 556 4272** Corner of Broughton St and Picardy Pl on the big roundabout by the Playhouse Theatre, a crossroads, as it were, of the gay village. Great people watching, i.e. all kinds of people, with outside tables and big windows. Trendy Wendy made this over 16 years ago and it is still the spot to gather and gossip, and later, downstairs, dance (3am Fri/Sat). Quizzes, cabaret and food till 9pm.

1143 8/Q25 ✓ **CC Bloom's** **Greenside Lane** · **https://ccblooms.co.uk** · **0131 556 9331** CC's is the city's longest-enduring gay nightspot. Once described as wonderfully cheesy, it's now more likely to serve wonderful cheese on its food menu. Only becomes proper gay later on; till 9/10pm it's a pre-theatre rendezvous (it's next to the Playhouse). There's even an all-day breakfast. Late night, however, it's fun and frolics and deafening disco. 2 floors. Cruisy, of course. Queue weekends. 7 days. Bar 11pm-3am.

1144 8/Q25 ✓ **The Regent** **2 Montrose Terrace** · **0131 661 8198** A great neighbourhood bar for many reasons (372/UNIQUE PUBS), gay but not so much. Adjacent well-known cruising gardens. Friendly locals, relaxed, straight-friendly. They have many ales and food all day. 7 days till 1am.

1145 8/Q25 **Planet** **6 Baxter's Place** · **0131 556 5551** A happy, clappy place on the gay strip. Clubby and pre-club crowd dominate later but an unthreatening vibe in this long bar below the Playhouse. Karaoke and gals out to play. 7 days till 1am.

1146 8/Q25 **Café Habana** **22 Greenside Lane** · **0131 558 1270** Adjacent CC's above and Playhouse Theatre. Banging music. Young crowd. Quite tiny really, so usually rammed. Line-up on the mezzanine so coming in is like arriving on the beach at Mykonos (i.e. you are immediately checked out, probably dismissed, then you can relax). Outside tables. 7 days noon-1am.

1147 8/Q25 **Café Nom de Plume** **60 Broughton St** · **0131 478 1372** Very gay-friendly proper café-bistro with changing à la carte home-made food and nice people sitting around at the heart of the village! Related to The Regent, above. 7 days noon-9.30/10pm food, bar later. See 327/CAFÉS.

1148 8/Q25 **Steamworks** **Broughton Market** · **0131 477 3567** At the end of Barony St, off Broughton St. Modern, Euro-style wet and dry areas. Cubies and lockers. Café. Dark room and cruise area. Mixed crowd. 7 days 11am-10pm.

1149 8/Q25 **No. 18** **18 Albert Place** · **0131 553 3222** Sauna for gentlemen (mainly older). Discreet doorway halfway down Leith Walk. Dark room. 7 days noon-10pm.

GLASGOW

1150 8/M26 ✓ **Delmonica's** **68 Virginia St** · **www.delmonicas.co.uk** · **0141 552 4803** Del's has been in this quiet lane at the heart of the Merchant City gay quarter for nearly 30 years (can it be that long?). Glasgow-stylish pub with long bar and open plan. Pleasant and airy by day but busy and sceney at night, especially weekends. It's nice if your face fits. Themed nights, loads of karaoke, quizzes, etc 7 days till midnight (then the PL, below).

1151 8/M26 ✓ **Polo Lounge** 84 Wilson St · www.pologlasgow.co.uk · 0845 659 5905
Similarly long-established late-night venue with stylish decor. Smart service, themed nights downstairs. Gents' club meets Euro-lounge ambience. From 11pm, 3am licence; otherwise till 1am. Downstairs disco (with admission).

1152 8/M26 ✓ **Waterloo Bar** 306 Argyle St · 0141 248 7216 Scotland's oldest gay bar and it tells. But an unpretentious down-to-earth vibe, refreshing in its way. Long-in-the-tooth, like its clientele, very LGBT friendly. Good soundtrack, at times dancin'! You might not fancy anybody but they're a friendly old bunch. 7 days noon-midnight.

1153 8/M26 ✓ **Underground** 6a John St · 0141 553 2456 In basement of a pedestrian street, in the heart of the Merchant City. Civilised subterranea. Free juke box, pool, ale. Some uniform nights. Big on karaoke, or 'queeraoke' but most of the men will be men. 7 days all day to midnight.

1154 8/M26 ✓ **The Pipeworks** 5 Metropole Lane · www.thepipeworks.com · 0141 552 5502 E of St Enoch Centre, near Slater Menswear, down an unlikely lane. Scotland's most full-on (and contemporary) sauna labyrinth on 3 floors. 7 days noon-11pm, all night Fri/Sat.

1155 8/M26 **The Lane** 60 Robertson St · 0141 221 1802 Near Waterloo (above), across Argyle St, lane on right. You look for the green light. Sauna, private club with dark room. You wouldn't call it upmarket. 7 days, afternoons till 7/8pm.

ABERDEEN

1156 6/T19 **Cheerz** 2 Exchange St · www.cheerzbar.co.uk · 01224 582648 Evening gay bar and (next door) club later on. A cheeky z but a cheery kind of (local) gay as gay bar. Aberdeen's only LGBT (how can that be?). 6pm-midnight. Club till 2/3am.

DUNDEE

1157 8/Q23 **Liberty Nightclub** 124 Seagate · 01382 200660 Bar and dance floor. Everybody knows everybody else, maybe not you. This may have its advantages. Wed-Sun, till 2.30am.

1158 8/Q23 **The Klozet** 73 Seagate · www.klozetdundee.co.uk · 01382 226840 Mixed, mainly gay bar close to Liberty Nightclub (above). Make a night of it.

1159 8/Q23 **Salty Dog** 9 Crichton St, nr Nethergate · 07580 171426 Cosy (very cosy), good fun pub. Mixed but very gay-friendly. 2pm-midnight.

the
Best
of Places to Eat & Stay

Superlative Country-House Hotels

1160 8/N24
232 ROOMS
DF
L
£LOTS

✓✓✓ **Gleneagles** Auchterarder · www.gleneagles.com ·
01764 662231 Off A9 Perth-Stirling road, signed. Scotland's truly
luxurious resort hotel. For facilities on the grand scale; others pale into insignificance.
This is an international destination. In 2015, Gleneagles became part of the
ambitious Ennismore Group, who have London's Hoxton hotels. Many changes
have followed, all a contemporary celebration of a grand tradition: of a hotel in the
country with its own railway station – since 1924: **The American Bar**; **The
Birnam Brasserie**; **Auchterarder 70**, the bar in the Clubhouse; the new **Dormy**
restaurant; the complete upgrading of Braid House, the newer wing, new suites.
Much still ongoing (incl. a townhouse hotel in Edinburgh). Rooms from the Royal
Suite to standard deluxe envelop you in an understated and calm elegance. Though
it runs like a well-oiled and beautiful machine, it is surprisingly human and
welcoming – they make you feel special from arrival (I'm sure this is not just me).
Sport and leisure activities include: shooting, riding, fishing, gun-dog school,
off-roading (even kids' jeeps), and in my view Scotland's best suite of swimming
pools (one for lengths) with outdoor tub, and for inactivity the gorgeous spa (1294/
SPAS). Gleneagles golf (3 courses and a 9-hole) is world-renowned; the Ryder Cup
was here 2014 and the Solheim Cup 2019. **Strathearn Restaurant** is a foodie (if
formal) heaven, though still has a bustling cosmopolitan ambience; breakfast to
look forward to.
EAT Casual dining in the classic Birnam Brasserie. The Clubhouse (200m) has 2
informal options and **Andrew Fairlie's** intimate dining room is Scotland's only
2-Michelin-star restaurant (912/PERTHSHIRE). Gleneagles is world-class throughout
but quintessentially Scottish. It has airs and graces but it's still a friendly old place,
the essence of good service.

1161 7/J22
25 ROOMS +
2 COTTS
DF
LL
£LOTS

✓✓ **Isle of Eriska** Ledaig · www.eriska-hotel.co.uk · 01631 720371 20km
N of Oban (signed from A85 N of Benderloch). Hotel, spa and, as they do
say, island! As you drive over the Victorian iron bridge, you enter a more tranquil
and gracious world. Its 300 acres are a sanctuary for wildlife; you are not the only
guests. The famous badgers come to the door of the conservatory bar for their milk
and peanuts. In 2017, this comfortable baronial house, for decades in the capable
and empathetic hands of the Buchanan-Smiths, was sold. Little doubt, one
thought, that its reputation for food, fastidious service, and gracious tranquillity
would prevail. At TGP, this does remain to be seen and I haven't stayed. Two
2-bedroom and five 1-bedroom suites in spa outbuilding are more contemporary,
with private terraces and hot tubs. 8 hilltop lodges and 'Reserves' are above all
that; comfy and private. Picturesque 9-hole golf, great 17m pool and gym excellent
in summer when it opens on to the garden. In the spa, ishga and ESPA treatment
rooms. Dining in formal rooms or in the **Deck Restaurant**, overlooking the golf
course, is casual, with open kitchen and nice terrace (739/ARGYLL).

1162 9/J29
17 ROOMS
DF
APR-DEC
£LOTS

✓✓ **Glenapp Castle** nr Ballantrae · www.glenappcastle.com ·
01465 831212 Relais & Châteaux luxury in South Ayrshire S of Ballantrae.
Very discreet entrance (first right turn after village): no sign, and with entryphone
system. From the oak-lined cloakrooms on either side of the main entrance, even
before you go up the staircase to the lounges, you sense a soft enveloping
opulence. Home of Inchcape family for most of 20th century; opened as a hotel in
first year of 21st. Excellent and considerate service, top-notch food, impeccable
interiors. The rooms are all individually beautiful, the suites enormous. Plans at
TGP to create a lavish penthouse suite. Quality costs but the price includes just

about everything, so relax and join this effortless house party. Kids can have separate high tea. Recently resurfaced tennis court, lovely walks in superb grounds (especially May and September) kept by almost as many gardeners (5) as there are chefs. Get their illustrated map and go explore. A southern secret, though with many accolades and more to come, I suspect.

£LOTS **EAT** Dinner commensurate with surroundings in 2 elegant dining rooms. Outside, the verdant policies and a serene terrace for aperitifs. Afternoon tea also for non-res by appointment. Teahouse in the garden.

1163 8/P22 ✓✓ **Kinloch House** nr Blairgowrie · www.kinlochhouse.com ·
15 ROOMS   01250 884237 5km W on A923 to Dunkeld. Quintessential rural Scottish
£LOTS comfort and joy. Beautiful mansion among the green fields and woods of Perthshire, home to exemplary, welcoming hosts and consummate hoteliers, the Allen family. Gumboots in the hall. Open fires, oak-panelled hall and portrait gallery. Comfy rooms and informal but sure service. Nice conservatory. Those bucolic south-facing views!

£££ **EAT** Excellent food: Graeme Allen and Steven MacCallum in the kitchen. Top wine list (especially French). This is classy dining.

1164 8/M24 ✓✓ **Cromlix House** Dunblane · www.cromlix.com · 01786 822125 5km
15 ROOMS   from Dunblane following signs and just through Kinbuck on the B8033. A
£LOTS long-established and favourite country-house hotel, taken over by Andy Murray's family (who famously hail from Dunblane), discreetly modernised, managed by the premier ICMI Group and reopened in 2014. Many more rooms underway at TGP. All mod cons, as you'd expect, with some fittings and fixtures from before, though a rather corporate feel overall. No spa/leisure but 2 tennis courts, fishing lochs and 3,000 acres of a beautiful wooded estate to wander. Private chapel, open fires, nice terrace.

£££ **EAT** Brasserie-style restaurant in conservatory by Albert Roux, who does, as with the other Scottish franchises, take a close interest. Light, contemporary cuisine.

1165 9/J31 ✓✓ **Knockinaam Lodge** Portpatrick · www.knockinaamlodge.com ·
10 ROOMS   01776 810471 An ideal place to lie low; a historic Victorian house nestled
DF on a cove. The Irish coastline is the only thing (maybe) on the horizon, apart from
LL discreet service and excellent food. Winston Churchill was once very comfortable
£LOTS here, too! (His room the top suite and there have been recent refinements.) Superb wine (especially French) and whisky list. 15km S of Stranraer, off A77 near Lochans but get directions. See also: 774/SW HOTELS.

£LOTS **EAT** Tony Pierce – one of Scotland's great chefs. Tasting set menu (advise requirements). Understated foodie fabulousness.

✓✓ **Monachyle Mhor** nr Balquhidder More farmhouse than country house; certainly more laid-back than many of the above. A top rural relax. Report: 1220/GET-AWAY HOTELS.

✓✓ **Glencoe House Hotel** Glencoe Luxe loveliness in magnificent surroundings. Report: 1034/HIGHLANDS.

✓✓ **Arisaig House** Beasdale, Arisaig Laid-back, quietly elegant, tasteful and good value. Report: 1035/HIGHLANDS.

✓ **Ballathie House** Kinclaven, nr Perth Superb situation on River Tay. Handy for Perth. Report: 908/PERTHSHIRE.

Hotels That Welcome Kids

1166 8/N23
250 ROOMS +
55 LODGES
££

✓✓✓ **Crieff Hydro** Crieff · www.crieffhydro.com · 01764 655555 A national institution, still a family business and a truly great family hotel that moves with the times. They strike the perfect balance between relaxation and activity (of which there is a staggering range of choice). In every way they do Scotland proud. Welcoming from arrival, this vast Victorian pile is still run by the Leckies from historic hydropathic beginnings. The continuous refurbishments ongoing at the fabulous winter gardens, the sports hall (the Hub), café and kids' centre and in the rooms keep up with more informal, more demanding times. Formal chandeliered dining room **(Meikle's)** and the Brasserie (best for food Med-style; open all day). There are 5 dining choices. Gentle and exhilarating activities all day and all around: great tennis courts, riding school, **Action Glen** in nearby woods has segways, zip lines. 2 pools including the Victorian pool (and spa) for adults only (in sessions). Tiny cinema shows family movies; nature talks, donkey rides. Kids' entertainment and kids' menus to go with yours. Chalets in the grounds are among the best in Scotland. Great for family get-togethers. Despite the many bairns, it's also brilliant for adults on their own. Populism with probity and no preciousness.

1167 7/J27
28 ROOMS
(HOUSE) +
36 (SPA) +
LODGES
££

✓✓ **Auchrannie Spa Hotel** Brodick, Arran · www.auchrannie.co.uk · 01770 302234 Much expanded from the original house, the Spa block especially is perfect for a family holiday. You may have the run of both. Loadsa activities on tap and out back, including the 'Playbarn', 2 pools, racquet court, spa and outdoor stuff (c/o Arran Adventures) on rivers, trails and hills. Many rooms for 2 adults and 2 kids. Main restaurant is a bit motorway services but 2 other options in the original hotel, including decent dining in **eighteen69** (phone-monitoring service; hotel can arrange babysitting). Kids will begin their lifelong love of Arran here. See also Arran p. 392–3.

1168 7/J25
16 ROOMS
££

✓✓ **Portavadie Marina** Portavadie · www.portavadie.com · 01700 811075 End of the road, very contemporary, very yachty leisure and activity complex on Loch Fyne, across from Tarbert. Rooms (16) by the night, others in cottages, the main building apartments or nearby lodge have 2-night or week minimums. Much ado about boats but lots of other activities inside and out. Pool complex and spa with outside infinity pool and tubs. Great walks and a legendary beach 5km (1628/BEACHES). Report: 727/ARGYLL.

1169 3/E16
6 ROOMS
DF · LL · NO TV
MAR-DEC
£££

✓✓ **Scarista House** South Harris · www.scaristahouse.com · 01859 550238 20km S of Tarbert on W coast of South Harris, an hour to Stornoway. Big, comfortable former manse overlooking amazing beach (1619/BEACHES); and golf course (2108/GOLF). Lots of other great countryside around. The Martins having had 3 kids of their own will welcome yours and are happy to do a separate supper at 6pm. And a famously good dinner for grown-ups. All in all, a precious and memorable escape. See also 2261/ISLAND HOTELS.

1170 3/E14
7 ROOMS
DF · LLL
MAY-SEP
££

✓ **Baile-Na-Cille** Timsgarry, West Lewis · www.bailenacille.co.uk · 01851 672242 Far, far into the sunset on the W of Lewis. 60km Stornoway so a plane/ferry and drive to somewhere you and the kids can leave all your other baggage behind. Exquisite, vast beach and many others nearby; garden, tennis, games room. Limited Wi-Fi in the lounges. Plenty of books. Rooms refurbished recently, I'm told. Good places nearby for lunch (2371/HEBRIDES). 4-course set dinner (closes one night a week) is excellent value, with help-yourself wine. Your kids will keep this place in their hearts.

1171 7/F23
17/27 ROOMS
APR-OCT
£

Argyll Hotel www.argyllhoteliona.co.uk · 01681 700334 & **St Columba Hotel** www.stcolumba-hotel.co.uk · 01681 700304 · **Iona** The 2 Iona hotels owned by local people on this charmed and blessed isle. Holidays here are remembered forever. Argyll has more atmos, St Columba is basic but more spacious, both child and people in general friendly (especially older folk). Unhurried, hassle-free; beautiful organic gardens, though seem less tended of late; kids run free. Food in both depends on staff, of course, here perhaps more so; usually good vegetarian. Both Apr-Oct.

1172 7/J20
14 ROOMS
DF · LL
NO TV
MAR-OCT
ATMOS · ££

Glenfinnan House Hotel Glenfinnan · www.glenfinnanhouse.com · 01397 722235 Just off the Road to the Isles (the A830 from Fort William to Mallaig 1689/SCENIC ROUTES). Very large Highland hoose with so many rooms and such big gardens you can let them loose (or stick them in front of a DVD in the mini-playroom – no, let them loose). Great introduction to the Highland heartland; music, scenery and local characters. Comfy rooms: no phone or TV but fresh flowers. The loch's at the foot of the lawn. Harry Potter viaduct (1km), the famous monument (500m), and an outdoor education. Report: 1056/HIGHLANDS.

1173 8/Q27
132 ROOMS
DF
££

Peebles Hydro Peebles · www.peebleshydro.co.uk · 01721 720602 One of the first Victorian hydros (1881, rebuilt 1907) and a complete resort for families; it has that well-worn look but it doesn't matter too much if they run amok. Huge grounds, corridors (you get lost) and floors of rooms. Run by the Crieff Hydro folk (above), who know a thing or two about family breaks; they keep it traditionally wholesome and refreshingly untrendy. Dining room is vast and, well, hotel-like. Conservatory tables look over the valley. Many family rooms (35), self-service high tea for the kids. Pool and spa. Peebles area is great for active kids!

1174 7/K20
8 ROOMS
££

Old Pines nr Spean Bridge · www.oldpines.co.uk · 01397 712324 3km Spean Bridge via B8004 for Gairlochy at Commando Monument. A ranch-like hotel in a good spot N of Fort William. This hotel has long had a big rep, not only for food, but also for welcoming kids. The Dalleys had 2 kids too and welcome yours. Separate mealtimes with Imogen's proper family-food menu, then a great dinner for the adults. Very safe, easy environment with chickens, goats and geese and woods (those pines!) to run. Nice stroll to the old High Bridge (1km).

1175 5/N19
175 ROOMS
££

Hilton Coylumbridge nr Aviemore · www.hiltonaviemore.com · 01479 810661 8km from Aviemore Centre on B970 to ski slopes and nearest hotel to them. 2 pools of decent size, sauna, flume, etc. Plenty to do in summer and winter (1766/KIDS) and enough to do when it rains. Best of the often criticised Aviemore concrete blocks. Huge shed with kids' play area (the Funhouse). Majority are family rooms. Whole hotel a playground in school hols.

1176 7/J21
20 ROOMS +
8 LODGES
DF
££

Holly Tree Hotel Kentallen · www.hollytreehotel.co.uk · 01631 740292 On A828 Fort William–Oban road S of Ballachulish. Long-established roadside and seaside hotel in great setting. All rooms have the view. Garden on the shore with pier. Former railway station. Surf 'n' turf restaurant with children's menu, bar and surprising swimming pool (though not shallow) and sauna.

1177 8/N22
6 ROOMS
DF
££

The Inn on the Tay Grandtully · www.theinnonthetay.co.uk · 01887 840760 Road and riverside inn in small village near Aberfeldy. This stretch of river famous for its rapids so usually plenty of raft and canoe action. Josie and Geoff ensure this place is family friendly. Some rooms have 3 beds (kids £20 at TGP). 4 overlooking the river which soothes you to sleep. Nice lounge and café/bar with river deck. The brilliant chocolate shop is opposite (1426/TEAROOMS).

1178 7/J21
59 ROOMS
DF
L
££

Isles of Glencoe Hotel Ballachulish · www.islesofglencoe.com ·
01855 811602 Beside the A82 Crianlarich to Fort William: a modern hotel and
leisure centre jutting out on to Loch Leven. Adventure playground outside and
nature trails. Conservatory restaurant overlooks the water. Hotel has small pool.
Almost half are family rooms. Snacks in the restaurant all day. Glen Coe and 2 ski
areas nearby. Across the way, SeaXplorer do short, speedy cruises. The loch is the
thing!

1179 9/M30
56 ROOMS
DF
££

Cally Palace Gatehouse of Fleet · www.mcmillanhotels.co.uk ·
01557 814341 The big, all-round family and golf hotel in the SW, in charming
village with safe, woody walks in the grounds. Old-style ambience (let's not say
tired); a piano is played at dinner. Leisure facilities include pool. 500 acres of forest
good for cycling. There are allegedly red squirrels. Kids' tea at 5pm. Nice beach
nearby at **Sandgreen** (1641/BEACHES) and, of course, **Cream o' Galloway** (1492/
ICE CREAM) with loads of activities. See also 1572/GARDENS.

Comrie Croft Hostel accom on working farm with basic/quite posh camping in
the woods in beautiful Perthshire setting. See below.

Lazy Duck nr Nethy Bridge See below.

The Best Hostels

1180 8/N23

✔✔ **Comrie Croft** nr Comrie · www.comriecroft.com · 01764 670140 On
A85 Comrie–Crieff/Perth road, Andrew Donaldson and 50 shareholders'
Perthshire landmark stopover. 2 self-contained buildings: the Farmhouse, and the
steading and courtyard of a working farm in beautiful countryside, which includes a
millpond and a 'mountain'. Excellent facilities: shop, bike shop (and workshop),
kitchen, lounges. Mountain bikes for hire/sale. Bike trails, 'squirrel trails' and a wee
hike up the road. Eco-friendly camping in the woods, including 7 Swedish kata
tents for hire, with wood-burning stoves. Cool for kids, great for grown-ups!
Laid-back tea garden does cakes and snacks (Easter-Oct).

1181 6/P19
L

✔✔ **Lazy Duck** nr Nethy Bridge · www.lazyduck.co.uk · 0131 618 6198
'Tiny hostel' (8 beds), eco-hut for 2, facing across the moor to Cairngorm,
'The Duck's Nest', a beautifully elemental lodge on the waterfowl pond, and the
Lambing Bothy. Also a 4-pitch camping ground. 2km from Nethy Bridge off the
B970 towards the A939 to Tomintoul. Idyllic, romantic; all that and not expensive.
In same family, in both senses, as **The Dell of Abernethy** www.holiday-
cairngorm.co.uk · 01479 821643, a Georgian lodge for 8, and 5 self-catering
cottages in another part of the woods. All so sylvan.

1182 3/E13
LL

✔✔ **The Blackhouse Village** Gearrannan, Lewis · www.gearrannan.
com · 01851 643416 At the road end (3km) from A858, the W coast of
Lewis, an extraordinary reconstruction of several blackhouses, the traditional
thatched dwelling of the Hebrides, now several self-catering cottages and a hostel.
Authentic and atmospheric, basic but far from spartan. Township on a cove with
beach, so sunsets and the wild Atlantic foam. Sleeping 2/14 and 2 for 4/5. No
Sunday arrivals. Café open Mon-Sat 9.30am-5.30pm. See also 2161/HISTORY.

1183 5/H18
L
NC500

✔ **Hartfield House** Applecross · www.hartfieldhouse.org.uk ·
01520 744333 Exceptional hostel in lovely, very big house (50 beds) in
glorious Applecross. Remote, grand scenery but lots to do here (1677/SCENIC
ROUTES; 2088/WALKS); the famous **Applecross Inn** 2km (1207/INNS) and **Walled**

Garden café (1088/HIGHLANDS). Very well-appointed rooms, kitchens. There are doubles.

1184 7/F23 ✓ **Iona Hostel** Iona · www.ionahostel.co.uk · 01681 700781 Bunkhouse in N, 2km hike from ferry on John Maclean's farm. Feels like the edge of the world looking over to Staffa and beyond; beach beside. Beautiful open-plan space with wood stove. Open AYR. 5 rooms, sleeps 20, and Shepherd's Hut more secluded, for 2. Also the **Iona Pods** self-catering, www.ionapods.com. **Iona**, you must know, is very special (2232/ISLANDS).

1185 5/H20 ✓ **Knoydart Bunkhouse** Inverie · www.knoydart-foundation.com · 01687 462163 Run by the community/Knoydart Foundation, 500m from the quay and the ferry from Mallaig in a farmyard setting at the side of the village, Inverie, which has a pub (with food), the **Tearoom**, a campsite (1252/WILD CAMPING) and even an off-licence at the Foundation office, with all the maps and info you need to explore this extraordinary corner of Scotland. All power supply on Knoydart is renewable. This is a complete eco-holiday. See also 2072/WALKS.

1186 5/J17 ✓ **Torridon** by Achnasheen · www.syha.org.uk · 01445 791284 A hostel at NC500 the heart of the matter: the mountains, the walking, climbing and the love thereof. HQ also of Torridon Mountain Rescue. At the foot of Liathach, Beinn Eighe and many tops and easier walks within reach. Café, laundry, terrace. The Torridon/ Torridon Inn 1km (1222/GET-AWAY HOTELS).

1187 8/N24 ✓ **Stirling** St. John St · www.syha.org.uk · 01786 473442 Modern conversion in great part of town, close to castle, adjacent ancient graveyard and with fine views from some rooms. One of SYHA's hotel-like hostels with student-hall standard and facilities. Many oldies and international tourists. Breakfast included or self-catering. Sleeps 92. Open AYR.

1188 4/K14 ✓ **Inchnadamph Lodge** Assynt · www.inch-lodge.co.uk · 01571 822218 LL 25km N of Ullapool on A837 road to Lochinver and Sutherland. Well-appointed NC500 mansion house for individuals or groups in geology-gazing, hill-walking, mountain-rearing Assynt. Kitchen, canteen (dinner not provided but 'continental' breakfast). Games room, real fires. Commune with nature, then with each other. Some private rooms. Easter-Oct.

1189 5/G17 ✓ **Dun Flodigarry** nr Staffin, Skye · www.flodigarry-hostel.scot · LL 01470 552212 In far N, 32km from Portree in big, big scenery beside APR-OCT Flodigarry Country House Hotel, which has a bistro/pub with a great view. Overlooks sea. Bunk rooms for 4-6 and 3 doubles (holds up to 30), and very pleasing kitchen and refectory. Very green credentials; sometimes runs entirely on wind power.

1190 8/Q21 ✓ **Glen Prosen Hostel** Glen Prosen · www.prosenhostel.co.uk · LL 01575 540238 Glen Prosen, the gentlest, most beautiful and wooded of the Angus glens (1647/GLENS). 10km from start of glen at Dykehead and part of Prosen village (well, church) at the end of the road. An SYHA 'green' hostel; wood-burning stove, internet. Rooms for 4/6; 18 beds. Grassy sward, lovely terrace and the red squirrels. Open AYR.

1191 5/M20 **Pottery Bunkhouse** Laggan Bridge · www.potterybunkhouse.co.uk · 01528 544231 On A889 near Loch Laggan. Homely bunkhouse: 3 'dorms' for 6, 2 family rooms (group basis only), great home-bakes caff (1437/TEAROOMS). Lounge overlooks hills and has TV; wood stove. Open AYR.

1192 3/E16
L

Am Bothan Harris · www.ambothan.com · 01859 520251 At Leverburgh in the S of South Harris, a bunkhouse hand-built and personally run – a bright, cool building with well-lived-in feel. Good disabled facilities. 18 beds. Caff & shop nearby. Eat at the pier 2385/HEBRIDES.

1193 5
LL
ATMOS

Hostelling in the Hebrides www.syha.org.uk Simple hostelling in the crofting communities of Lewis, Harris and the Uists. Run by a trust to maintain standards of Highland hospitality; local crofters act as wardens. The Blackhouse cottages on Lewis at Gearrannan (above) are exceptional.

1194 7/H23

Hostels in Oban As well as a relatively grand SYHA House & Lodge (sleeps 79, good facilities) on the seafront www.syha.org.uk, there are 2 cosy independent hostels in Oban. One of them, **Backpackers Plus** Breadalbane St · www.backpackersplus.com · 01631 567189 has 3 separate dorm areas – the main one was the United Free Church. They have the most private rooms. Continental breakfast. **Oban Backpackers** www.obanbackpackers.com · 01631 562107 across the street is probably the more chilled. All close to the main street and the port.

1195 5/L19

Morag's Lodge Fort Augustus · www.moragslodge.com · 01320 366289 A mansion house up the brae off the road (the A82) as you come into Fort Augustus from the Inverness direction. Not on the loch (Ness) side but the loch is probably why you're here. Good facilities, including bar, café and garden. Various room types, including doubles. Minibus backpacker tours come here.

1196 1/Q9
L

Bis Geos Hostel & Cottages Westray, Orkney · www.bisgeos.co.uk · 01857 677420 Remote and fabulous: this is how this traditionally rebuilt croft is described, because I still haven't been. Sounds like it may warrant a tick or two. Exceptional standard with nautical theme. Conservatory overlooks the wild ocean. Minibus from the ferry. Sleeps 12. 2 cottages.

1197 5/G20
L

The Glebe Barn Eigg · www.glebebarn.co.uk · 01687 482417 On fabulously good Eigg, a haven in a haven (sailings from Mallaig and Arisaig 2234/ISLANDS). Civilised, comfy, wood-burning, well-furnished; duvets and linen provided. Sleeps 22; also 'an apartment' (for 2/3). Just what you and the island needs. Mar-Oct. Exclusive use possible.

1198 4/L12
NC500

Lazy Crofter Bunkhouse Durness · www.durnesshostel.com · 07803 927642 Adjacent (and with the same owners as) **Mackay's Hotel** (1055/HIGHLANDS). A small, laid-back woody chalet (sleeps 12 in 4 rooms) in good location for exploring Durness, Cape Wrath, etc (2084/WALKS; 1618/BEACHES); caff at **Balnakeil** nearby (1403/CAFÉS). No pub/dining in the hotel. Kitchen and outdoor terrace. Open AYR.

1199 5/M18

Inverness Student Hostel 8 Culduthel Rd · www.invernessstudenthotel. com · 01463 236556 Best independent hostel in town uphill from town centre. Run by same folk who have the great Edinburgh one (106/HOSTELS), with similar laid-back atmos and camaraderie. **Bazpackers** 4 Culduthel Rd · www.bazpackershostel.co.uk · 01463 717663 100m downhill, similar vibe.

1200 7/L24

Rowardennan Loch Lomond · www.syha.org.uk · 01360 870259 The hostel at the end of the road up the E (less touristy) side of Loch Lomond from Balmaha and Drymen. Large, well managed and modernised, and on a waterside site. On West Highland Way and an obvious base for climbing **Ben Lomond** (2010/MUNROS). Good all-round activity centre and lawns to the loch of your dreams. Rowardennan Hotel boozer nearby. 57 beds; some private rooms. Open AYR.

1201 7/G22 **Tobermory** Mull · www.syha.org.uk · 01688 302481 Looks out to Tobermory Bay. Central, very pink, highly rated hostel; very busy in summer. 5/6 bunks in 7 rooms (4 on front). Kitchen. Internet. Sweet garden terrace. Near ferry to Ardnamurchan; main Oban ferry 35km away (1610/VILLAGES). Mar-Oct. The newer **Craignure Bunkhouse** www.craignure-bunkhouse.co.uk · 01680 812043 is handy for the main Mull ferry. Rooms for 4 or 6 only.

1202 7/J26 **Lochranza** Arran · www.syha.org.uk · 01770 830631 On left coming from south. Refurbished Victorian house overlooking fab bay, castle ruins. Swans dip at dawn. Full self-catering. Sleeps 53. Comfortable sitting room. Mar-Oct. Nice bistro, **Stags Pavilion**, nearby (2317/ARRAN).

1203 7/K21 **Glencoe** Glencoe village · www.syha.org.uk · 01855 811219 Heart of the glen,
L 3km off A82, 4km by back road from Glencoe village and 33km from Fort William. Modern timber house near river; especially handy for climbers and walkers. Laundry, good drying room. **Clachaig** pub 2km, for good food and craic. Open AYR. See 1675/SCENIC ROUTES; 1971/ENCHANTING PLACES; 1946/BATTLEGROUNDS; 1313/GOOD PUBS; 2032/WALKS.

The Best Roadside, Seaside & Countryside Inns

1204 5/F17 ✓✓ **The Three Chimneys** Colbost, Skye · www.threechimneys.co.uk ·
6 ROOMS 01470 511258 7km W of Dunvegan on B884 to Glendale. The Chimneys:
£LOTS smokin' now and forever! 6 comfy, 2-level rooms in **The House Over-By** across yard from the much-loved, much-awarded Three Chimneys restaurant (2296/SKYE). Roadside, yes, but only the traffic of local life and you, and there's the smell of the sea. Calm and contemporary rooms, with own doors to the sward. Little treats and nice touches. Breakfast room doubles as a pre-dinner lounge in the evening. Many destination inns up north now – this the first. Book for dinner!

1205 8/N23 ✓✓ **The Barley Bree** Muthill, nr Crieff · www.barleybree.com ·
6 ROOMS 01764 681451 On main road through village, a stylish, excellent-value
ATMOS restaurant with rooms above. Great food; tasteful, comfortable rooms. Fabrice
££ Bouteloup a great chef/patron and all-round nice guy. Bar/restaurant open Wed-Sun for lunch & dinner. A top Sunday lunch. Not much to do in Muthill itself but the amazing **Drummond Castle Gardens** are nearby (1559/GARDENS) and an easy walk along the **Earn** (2048/RIVER WALKS). Everyone I've sent here has loved this inn.

1206 7/H26 ✓✓ **The Kilberry Inn** nr Tarbert, Argyll · www.kilberryinn.com ·
5 ROOMS 01880 770223 Halfway round the Knapdale peninsula on the single-track
DF B8024 (1691/SCENIC ROUTES), the long and breathtaking way to Lochgilphead.
MAR-OCT Homely roadside inn with simple, classy rooms and excellent cooking (1327/FOOD
££ PUBS) that comes fresh and local. Michelin Bib Gourmand. Dinner Tue-Sun. Breakfast, beach, walk, relax. Repeat!

1207 5/H18 ✓✓ **Applecross Inn** Applecross · www.applecross.uk.com/inn ·
7 ROOMS 01520 744262 The end of the legendary road to a definitive seaside inn
DF · LL · NO TV on the Applecross strand. Spectacular journey to get here (1677/SCENIC ROUTES)
NC500 · ££ and not for the faint-hearted driver; hit the shoreline and settle in (though only 7 small rooms). They all face the sea, which is what you want here. Then have a

pint from the Applecross microbrewery, eat at Judy Fish's seafood table or from the Airstream caravan/food truck outside (fish & chips, ice cream, coffee) and get forever Applecrossed. Report: 1229/GET-AWAY HOTELS.

1208 5/H19 ✓✓ **Glenelg Inn** Glenelg · www.glenelg-inn.com · 01599 522273 At the
7 ROOMS   end of that great road over the hill from Shiel Bridge on the A87 (1676/
DF · L   SCENIC ROUTES) ... well, not quite the end because you can drive further round to
APR-OCT   ethereal Loch Hourn. This halt has always been a civilised hostelry and often a
ATMOS · ££   whole lot of fun. Great home-cooked food in warm, cosy bar. Good drinking, snug
             lounge. Garden with tables and views. Sheila Condie and a great team keep this
             quintessential village pub at the heart of a thriving community that makes you
             very welcome. From Glenelg, take the best route to Skye (7/JOURNEYS). Winter:
             bar only.

1209 8/P22 ✓✓ **Meikleour Arms** Meikleour · www.meikleourarms.co.uk ·
11 ROOMS   01250 883206 1km A93 Perth–Blairgowrie road (on B984) by and behind
DF   famously high beech hedge (a Perthshire landmark), the Mercer Nairne's hugely
££   improved but quietly and tastefully made-over roadside inn in sweet village with
             quiet accom and 5 cottages; food in dining room or (more convivially) the bar. The
             new civilised destination restaurant in this neck of the Perth shires. Woody, not
             too foodie. Fishing on the Tay. Could it be any better?

1210 7/F23 ✓ **Argyll Hotel** Iona · www.argyllhoteliona.co.uk · 01681 700334 On
17 ROOMS   beautiful turquoise bay between Iona and Mull on road between ferry and
LL · NO TV   abbey. Day-trippers come and go; you should stay! A charming hotel on a
APR-OCT   remarkable island. Cosy rooms (1 suite and singles in the 'annex'). All home-made
££   food (especially vegetarian) from organic garden, though depends on seasonal staff.
             Real peace and quiet and that's just sitting in the sun lounge or on the bench
             outside. It's Colourist country and this is where they would have hung out too. Nice
             for kids (1171/KIDS).

1211 7/K22 ✓ **Bridge of Orchy Hotel** Bridge of Orchy · www.bridgeoforchy.co.uk ·
32 ROOMS   01838 400208 Unmissable on the A82 (the road to Glen Coe, Fort William
££   and Skye) 11km N of Tyndrum. A great stopover for motorists and walkers; it's on
             the **West Highland Way** (2024/WALKS). 10 rooms in hotel and 3 new blocks, with
             smart, contemporary motel-like rooms – 3 price structures, depending on the
             'view'; good à la carte menu and specials in pub/conservatory. Good spot for the
             malt or a munch on the Way.

1212 8/N22 ✓ **The Inn on the Tay** Grandtully · www.theinnonthetay.co.uk ·
6 ROOMS   01887 840760 Contemporary conversion of roadside inn that also has a
DF   commanding position on the riverbank where rapids tax legions of helmeted rafters
££   and canoeists; so constant entertainment. Café/bar with good food, residents'
             lounge, outside deck and comfortable modern bedrooms – some with 3 beds.

1213 8/R26 ✓ **Black Bull Hotel** Lauder · www.blackbull-lauder.com · 01578 722208
13 ROOMS   On Market Pl, main street of town strung along the A68, a gateway to the
DF   Borders. Over the years of varying quality in accom and food but now firmly
££   re-established as a comfortable, welcoming roadside inn, with lots of wood, wood
             stoves, friendly bar, good pub food, and inexpensive, tastefully individual bedrooms
             above. Stay here for a third of the price of this standard in Edinburgh (40 mins
             away).

1214 8/Q27
16 ROOMS +
2 COTTS
DF
££

✓ **Traquair Arms Hotel** Innerleithen · www.traquairarmshotel.co.uk · 01896 830229 100m from the A72 Galashiels–Peebles road towards Traquair. An old roadside inn, deep in Border and biking country. Notable for bar meals (Scottish emphasis), real ale and family facilities. Rooms refurbished to a decent standard. David, Jane and young Jamie Rogers making a good go of it here. Lovely beer garden out back. New sports bar with tapas at TGP. Much cycling nearby; and the Tweed.

1215 7/J22
12 ROOMS +
COTTAGE
DF
LL
££

✓ **The Pierhouse Hotel** Port Appin · www.pierhousehotel.co.uk · 01631 730302 Inn at the end of the road (minor road that leads off A828 Oban–Fort William) and at end of the pier where the tiny Lismore passenger ferry leaves (2242/ISLANDS). A mainly seafood restaurant (1372/SEAFOOD) in a great setting. Comfy adjacent rooms (more expensive overlook the sea and island). Sauna and showers. Good place to take kids and a great yachty stop.

1216 5/L19
10 ROOMS
FEB–NOV
££

✓ **Glenmoriston Arms Hotel** Invermoriston, Loch Ness · www. glenmoristonarms.co.uk · 01320 351206 On main A82 between Inverness (45km) and Fort Augustus (10km) at the Glen Moriston corner, a worthwhile corner of Scotland to explore (river walk). Busy local bar, fishermen's tales. Food by a real chef and the owner Ailsa McInnes. Extensive malt list – this is certainly a good place to drink them. Inn-like bedrooms with 3 cottagey rooms overby. Some antlers but not too much tartan.

1217 5/J19
13 ROOMS +
BUNKHOUSE
DF
L
£

✓ **Cluanie Inn** Glenmoriston · www.cluanieinn.com · 01320 340238 On road to Skye 15km before Shiel Bridge, a traditional, redesigned but not poshed-up inn surrounded by mountain summits (they say 21 Munros within reach) that attract walkers and travellers: Five Sisters, Ridge and Saddle (2034/ WALKS). Clubhouse adjacent has some group accom while inn rooms vary (one has a sauna, one a Jacuzzi). Dining room and bar food all wholesome. Friendly staff.

1218 5/H16
18 ROOMS
DF
NC500
££

The Old Inn Gairloch · www.theoldinn.net · 01445 712006 Southern approach on A832, tucked away by river and old bridge. Decent pub for food in bar, lounge and restaurant and tables by the river; above are simple rooms. The pub goes like a fair; **Solas Gallery** overby has interesting art, mainly of local landscapes (take home the memory).

1219 7/K21
23 ROOMS
DF · L
ATMOS · ££

Clachaig Inn Glencoe · www.clachaig.com · 01855 811252 Basic accom in main building and lodges; you will sleep well, especially after walking/climbing/ drinking, which is what most people are doing here. Great atmos both inside and out; wood stoves. Food available in bar/lounge and dining room till 9pm. Ales · aplenty 1313/GOOD PUBS. An all-round Glencoe/outdoors/Scottish experience.

The Best Restaurants With Rooms

The following all have 2 ticks:

The Peat Inn nr St Andrews Brilliant restaurant under Michelin chef Geoffrey Smeddle. Swish suites. Report: 874/FIFE.

The Three Chimneys Colbost, Skye State-of-the-art dining and contemporary rooms far away in the west. Report: 2296/SKYE.

The Barley Bree Muthill, nr Crieff French guy in the kitchen, Scots partner on design have put sleepy village on the map. Report: 1205/INNS.

Windlestraw Walkerburn Very special house discreetly overlooking Tweed Valley. Excellent dining. Report: 825/BORDERS.

The Cross Kingussie Rooms upstairs in converted tweed mill. Best restaurant and wine list in the region. Report: 1042/HIGHLANDS.

The Cross Keys Kippen Long-established gastropub with rooms in foodie village main street. Report: 1329/FOOD PUBS.

The Kilberry Inn nr Tarbert, Argyll Report: 1206/INNS.

The Ship Inn Elie On the bay, on the money. Report: 1330/FOOD PUBS.

The Boat Inn Aboyne Perfect Deeside stopover. Report: 982/NE HOTELS.

Gordon's Inverkeilor Smart rooms; food with flair. Report: 915/TAYSIDE.

The following all have 1 tick:

The Sorn Inn Sorn 8km E of Mauchline on the B743, 30 mins from Ayr. Report: 762/AYRSHIRE.

Buccleuch & Queensberry Arms Hotel Thornhill Great bar and smart rooms in drive-through village N of Dumfries. Report: 776/SW HOTELS.

Yann's Crieff Victorian mansion with 5 rooms above best bistro in the county. Report: 907/PERTHSHIRE.

The Mash Tun Aberlour Boutique-style rooms above pub in whisky country. Report: 1030/SPEYSIDE.

The Inn on the Tay Grandtully A made-over inn on the banks of the rushing River Tay. Great for kids. Report: 1212/INNS.

The Smiddy House Spean Bridge Comfy roadside inn; best casual food in Fort William area. Report: 1094/HIGHLANDS.

Wildings Hotel & Restaurant Maidens Huge local reputation for food; refurbished rooms overlook the sea. Report: 763/AYRSHIRE.

The Wheatsheaf Swinton, Berwickshire 12 all-different bedrooms above gastropub of long standing. Report: 1335/FOOD PUBS.

Edinbane Inn Skye Centre of the big island with big prices – but not here. Report: 2308/SKYE.

The Great Get-Away-From-It-All Hotels

1220 8/L23
16 ROOMS
DF
LL
ATMOS
£LOTS

Monachyle Mhor nr Balquhidder · www.mhor.net · **01877 384622**
Though only 11km from the A84 Callander–Crianlarich road as you follow a thread of road along Loch Voilside, you know you're leaving those urban blues behind. Many years later, MM is still the urbanite's get-away choice, though it's the Balquhidder Braes, not the Cotswolds. Once you're inside the old pink farmhouse you could be in a boutique hotel in smart downtown anywhere, except your window looks over the farm to big, beautiful countryside. Contemporary, calm and sexy. 9 rooms around the courtyard, 5 (a bit smaller) in main building, 1 out back. All completely gorgeous, especially the baths and bathrooms. A bar that locals and visitors use. Tom Lewis still exec-chefs the kitchen. Marysia and Graham on the stoves! Lisa keeps the vibe going. Very family and dog friendly; altogether cosy. Almost inexpensive for this standard; a place to relax summer or winter. MM is the HQ, perhaps, of what Tom, Dick and Madeleine have turned into the Mhor brand, which includes **Mhor 84**, the 'motel' on the A84 20 mins away and a less expensive get-away (796/CENTRAL), the bakers and café in Callander (1480/BAKERS) and Mhor Fest in May, the best rural boutique fest in Scotland (33/EVENTS). See also 1279/GLAMPING. There's always Mhor to come!

1221 5/J17
18 ROOMS
LL
CLOSED JAN
NC500
£LOTS

The Torridon Glen Torridon, nr Kinlochewe · www.thetorridon.com · **01445 791242** Impressive former hunting lodge on lochside, surrounded by the pick of the peaks of the Scottish mountains. Deluxe comfort and taste in this family-run (the Rose-Bristows) baronial house with relaxed atmos: an all-round Highland experience. Probably Scotland's most successful and committed to getting you out there, it focuses on outdoor activities: clay-pigeon shoots, kayaking, gorge-scrambling, mountain biking or fishing, with 2 full-time guides/instructors (book before arrival). Lots of walking possibilities nearby including the Torridon big 3: **Beinn Alligin** (2015/MUNROS), **Liathach** right in front of the hotel and the easier **Beinn Eighe**. This great hotel spawned some years ago a less expensive roadside option: **The Torridon Inn** in adjacent block (12 rooms, DF) with own bar and bistro. An excellent budget choice (live music on Fridays). Main hotel has elegant dining room under 3-rosette chef Ross Stovold, who presents a table d'hôte and a tasting menu. Fruit & veg from their splendid Kitchen Garden. Nice afternoon tea after the exertions and a fantastic malts bar for a dram in the dwindling day (see Whisky, p. 260). The Torridon is far from being just a country-house hotel – you will have their personal attention and go to bed in rooms with world-class views to wake up to.

1222 7/G23
7 ROOMS +
5 COTTS ·
DF · L
EASTER-OCT
£LOTS

£££

Tiroran House Mull · www.tiroran.com · **01681 705232** SW corner on road to Iona from Craignure then B8035 round Loch na Keal (they say 35 mins, but good luck), or more scenic and sometimes scary via Salen. 1 hour Tobermory. Small, family-friendly country house in fabulous gardens by the sea, under conscientious owners Laurence and Katie Mackay. Near Iona and Ulva ferry; you won't miss Tobermory. Excellent food from sea and organic kitchen garden. Traditional rooms. Sea eagles fly over, otters flop in the bay.

EAT Though tucked away, this is top dining on Mull. Well-priced, locally sourced à la carte menu in refined surroundings (the garden, the sea) and afternoon tea. Also the **Whitetail Coffee Shop** adjacent for lunch and all-day food Sun 11am-8pm (dining room closed).

1223 8/P21
17 ROOMS
· DF
L · ££

Dalmunzie Castle Spittal of Glenshee · www.dalmunzie.com · **01250 885224** 3km off Blairgowrie–Braemar road and near Glenshee skiing. By a Highland riverside and surrounded by bare hills, this laird's house is warm and welcoming but splendidly remote. Some great rooms, Michelin-mentioned dining, bar and 9-hole golf course. Good aesthetic, comfy yet stylish. You wanna be here! See also 903/PERTHSHIRE.

1224 7/L21
5 ROOMS
DF · LL
NO TV
MID FEB-OCT
££

✓ **Moor of Rannoch Hotel** Rannoch Station · www.moorofrannoch.co.uk · 01882 633238 Beyond Pitlochry and the Trossachs and far W via Loch Tummel and Loch Rannoch (B8019 and B8846), a classic Scots journey to the edge of Rannoch Moor and adjacent station (you could get the sleeper from London and be here for breakfast. 4 trains either way each day via Glasgow, where there's a cool tearoom 1425/TEAROOMS. Literally the end of the road, they make much of their perfect isolation (no phone reception or Wi-Fi). Cosy, wood-panelled rooms. A lovely wee restaurant with locally sourced suppliers and a great-value, quintessential Highland inn. Superb walking (esp. Loch Ossian, train back) and they hire bikes.

1225 7/F23
17 ROOMS
LL · NO TV
APR-OCT · ££

✓ **Argyll Hotel** Iona · www.argyllhoteliona.co.uk · 01681 700334 Quintessential island hotel on the best of small islands just large enough to get away for walks and explore (2232/ISLANDS). You can hire bikes (or bring). Abbey is nearby (1920/ABBEYS). 3 lounges (1 with TV, 1 with sun) and 1 lovely suite (with wood-burning stove). Decent home-grown/made food from their organic garden.

1226 5/H20
4 ROOMS +
LODGE
NO PETS
APR-SEP
£

✓ **Doune Stone Lodge** Knoydart · www.doune-knoydart.co.uk · 01687 462667 On the wonderful and wild and remote peninsula of Knoydart, this great spot on the W tip overlooking the Sound of Sleat to Skye. They have boats, so will pick you up from Mallaig and drop you round the inlets and islands for walking, photography, etc. 10km from Inverie, the village and pub. The Bay Lodge mainly for groups (shared bathroom area), spectacular location on its own cove, 200m from the 4 individual Stone Lodge rooms and the dining room. Fixed menu, home-made dinner, with chef Liz Tibbetts, to a high standard; convivial and communal; wine list. Breakfast and packed lunch. An edge of the wilderness labour of love for Martin and Jane Davies, and Liz and Andy Tibbetts, and an edge-of-Scotland experience for you.

1227 8/Q21
18 ROOMS
DF
L
££

✓ **Glen Clova Hotel** nr Kirriemuir · www.clova.com · 01575 550350 Well, not that near Kirriemuir: 25km N up the glen on B955 from Dykehead. Rooms surprisingly well appointed. Climbers' bar (till all hours). Superb walking (e.g. Loch Brandy and classic path to Loch Muick). A laid-back get-away though lots of families drive up on Sunday for lunch. Also has a bunkhouse (cheap) and 3 'luxury lodges' with hot tubs. Great value, great craic! Calmer, greener and much more basic is **Glen Prosen Hostel** at the head of Glen Prosen, probably the most beautiful and unspoiled of the glens. No pub, no interference (1190/HOSTELS).

1228 9/J30
11 ROOMS
DF · LL
ATMOS · ££

✓ **Corsewall Lighthouse Hotel** nr Stranraer · www.lighthousehotel.co.uk · 01776 853220 20 mins from Stranraer (via A718 to Kirkcolm) and follow signs, but way up on the peninsula and, as it suggests, a hotel made out of a working lighthouse. Romantic and offbeat, but only OK food. Local attractions include Portpatrick, 30 mins by quiet back roads. Report: 780/SW HOTELS.

1229 5/H18
7 ROOMS
DF
LL
NO TV
NC500
££

✓ **Applecross Inn** Applecross · www.applecross.uk.com/inn · 01520 744262 At the end of the road (the Pass of the Cattle which is often snowed up in winter), you can really disappear here, N of Kyle of Lochalsh and W of Strathcarron. After a spectacular journey, this waterside inn is a haven of hospitality. Buzzes all seasons. Rooms small and not so cheap but Judy Fish, a great team and chef, Robert Macrae, will look after you. Famously good fish 'n' chips in the pub and outside from the Airstream. Poignant visitor centre (2168/HISTORY), walled garden with café 2km and lovely walks (2088/WALKS) are easily enough to keep you happy in faraway Applecross for days.

1230 7/K20
4 ROOMS +
2 CABINS
L · APR–OCT
£

✓ **Corriechoille Lodge** Spean Bridge · www.corriechoille.com · 01397 712002 3km from Spean Bridge via road by station. Lovely road and spectacularly situated; it's great to arrive. Justin and Lucy share their perfect retreat with you in house and 2 turf-covered chalets out back. Rooms simple. Set-menu dinner. All round serenity! Closed Sun/Mon. Report: 1061/HIGHLANDS.

1231 3/D17
12 ROOMS
DF
APR–OCT
££

Langass Lodge North Uist · www.langasslodge.co.uk · 01876 580285 On the A867, which runs through the middle of the Uists, 8km S of Lochmaddy, 500m from the road. Small, hideaway hotel with garden and island outlook. Half of rooms in extension; others in hotel to stylish standard. Nice bar and decent dining on the garden, from where your veg and salads may come. Kid-friendly and you can bring the dog. Uists are wonderful to explore and there's prehistoric stuff nearby and a great short (2.5km) walk. See 1866/PREHISTORIC; 1624/BEACHES.

1232 5/H18
SLEEPS 50
DF · L
NC500
£

Hartfield House Applecross · www.hartfieldhouse.org.uk · 01520 744333 Big, old house round a courtyard, 1km from the strand in dreamy Applecross – see Inn (above) – this incomparably cheaper. Hostel dorms and private rooms. Bit rough and ready but has atmos. Kitchen and dining room; **Walled Garden** café nearby (1088/HIGHLANDS). Gorgeous location for an Applecross sojourn. Also see 1183/HOSTELS.

1233 5/K18
8 ROOMS
DF
L
££

Tomich Hotel Tomich, nr Drumnadrochit · www.tomichhotel.co.uk · 01456 415399 25km from Drumnadrochit. Fabulous **Plodda Falls** nearby (1652/WATERFALLS). Cosy, well-run (though new ownership 2019) country inn in conservation village with faraway feel, surprising bar round the back, where locals do linger, and good base for outdoorsy weekend (Glen Affric across the way). This is the nearest good place to stay. Ebullient Joyce's café in the old post office opposite; you can get keys here for the swimming pool up the hill in the steading.

✓✓ **Glenapp Castle** nr Ballantrae Report: 1162/COUNTRY-HOUSE HOTELS.

✓✓ **The Fife Arms** Braemar Report: 978/NE HOTELS.

✓✓ **The Three Chimneys** Skye Reports: 1204/INNS; 2277/SKYE.

✓✓ **Knockinaam Lodge** Portpatrick Report: 774/SW HOTELS.

✓ **Broad Bay House** Lewis Report: 2367/HEBRIDES.

✓ **Balcary Bay** Auchencairn Report: 778/SW HOTELS.

The Best Very Scottish Hotels

1234 4/K15
13 ROOMS +
20 BUNKS
NO TV
ATMOS
NC500
£/££

✓✓ **The Ceilidh Place** Ullapool · www.ceilidhplace.com · 01854 612103 Off main street near port for the Hebrides. Inimitable Jean Urquhart's and now daughter Rebecca and son Jock's hostelry which, more than any other in the Highlands, encapsulates Scottish traditional culture and hospitality. Caters for all sorts: hotel rooms are above (with a truly comfortable lounge – you help yourself to drinks) and a bistro/bar below, often with live music and performance (ceilidh-style). A bunkhouse across the way with cheap and cheerful accom (11 bunk rooms) and a bookshop where you can browse through the best of Scottish literature. There's nowt like coming back from a walk and sitting down with a book and a dram in the downstairs lounge. Though it was long ago that the Ceilidh Place put Ullapool on the must-visit map of Scotland, it has moved effortlessly with the times. Long may its lums reek! See also 1053/HIGHLANDS.

1235 8/L23
7 ROOMS
DF
ATMOS
££

Mhor 84 nr Balquhidder · www.mhor.net · 01877 384646
Determinably a motel on the busy A84 between Callander and the NW, and in the heart of the Trossachs, and what you might call a joint venture of the Lewis family's Mhorification of the country life hereabouts (1220/GET-AWAY HOTELS; 1480/BAKERS). Their places all feed off each other. But this is the perfect realisation of friendly, sympatico, old-fashioned yet cool contemporary Scottish hospitality. Locals use the bar, school-room-type bistro – excellent food includes Scottish staples; a brazier burns on the road outside. Best to know that the accom is relatively basic, mix-and-match retro. 4 cottages out back are more uniform. There's a shop **Mhor In Store** adjacent (2213/SHOPS); Thu-Sun 10am-5pm. Welcome to Mhor country! Also see 796/CENTRAL.

1236 5/H19
12 ROOMS
4 SUITES
LL
ATMOS
££

Eilean Iarmain Sleat, Skye · www.eileaniarmain.co.uk · 01471 833332 Sleat area in S of Skye, this snug and seminal Gaelic inn nestles in the bay and is the classic island hostelry: the word 'location' comes very much to mind. Bedrooms in hotel and across the road are tastefully traditional; no TVs. The 2-floor suites in adjacent steading are more expensive, like being in your own Highland cottage. Food decent in dining room and with immersing atmos in the brilliant **Praban** bar. Mystic shore walks. Gallery with selected exhibitions and shop by the quay. Very Highland and very Scottish, its voice is Gaelic, its charm subtly friendly - all totally engaging. Begun by Sir Iain, the Eilean Iarmain torch is now carried with much panache and commitment by Lady Lucilla Noble. See also 2279/SKYE.

1237 4/J14
5 ROOMS
NO PETS/KIDS
LL
MAR-DEC
NC500
£LOTS

The Albannach Lochinver · www.thealbannach.co.uk · 01571 844407 2km up road to Baddidarach as you come from S into Lochinver on A837, at the bridge. Lovely 18th-century house in one of Scotland's most scenic areas, Assynt, where the mountains take your breath away (1982/1984/HILLS). The **Byre** overlooks the croft, and 3 suites: bespoke rooms handcrafted by the irrepressible owners. The Penthouse and the Loft, with outside cliff-enclosed terrace. Great walk behind house to Achmelvich beach – otters on the way – and the 'secret' beach nearby (1630/BEACHES). Colin and Lesley also have the **Caberfeidh** in the village, a 20-min walk away (1089/HIGHLANDS), which is where to go for dinner. Top-notch cookery (Michelin starred when they made with the niceties, now just nicely informal), with impeccable sourcing. Hotel and the pub – all in all, a highly individual urban-boutique-hotel and gastropub experience in a glorious landscape.

1238 6/Q19
16 ROOMS
LL
£££

Kildrummy Castle Hotel nr Alford · 01975 571288 60km W of Aberdeen via A944 through some fine bucolic scenery and the green Don valley to this spectacular location with real Highlands aura. Well placed on the Castle Trail, this comfy chunk of Scottish Baronial has the redolent ruins of Kildrummy Castle on the opposite bluff and a gorgeful of gardens between. Some rooms small; all very Scottish and a bit old style. Romantic in autumn when the gardens are good.

1239 7/J20
14 ROOMS
DF · LL
NO TV
MAR-OCT
ATMOS · ££

Glenfinnan House Hotel Glenfinnan · www.glenfinnanhouse.com · 01397 722235 Off the Road to the Isles (A830 Fort William to Mallaig 1689/SCENIC ROUTES). The Gibsons are the amiable, careful curators of this historic, much-loved house owned by the MacFarlane family for almost 50 years. Ongoing refurbishments retain its charm; the huge rooms remain yet are intimate and cosy; there are fresh flowers everywhere. Impromptu sessions and ceilidhs in the bar, especially on Thursdays. Eat in the bar or dining room. Fishing or dreaming on Loch Shiel at foot of the lawn. Day trips to Skye and the small islands. Scotland the best!

1240 7/K28
15 ROOMS

Savoy Park 16 Racecourse Road, Ayr · www.savoypark.com · 01292 266112
In a street and area of indifferent hotels, this one, owned and run by the Henderson

DF   family for over 50 years, is a real Scottish gem. Many wedding guests will agree.

££   Period features, much oak, lovely garden; not too much tartan. The antithesis of a chain hotel and a warm, cosy, homespun atmos.

1241 4/Q13   **Ackergill Tower** nr Wick · www.ackergilltower.com · 01955 603556 Deluxe

34 ROOMS   retreat once geared for parties and groups, now also accommodating individual

DF   guests. A 15th-century castle with a lot of history and a bit of mystery – what's it

L   doing there so far north of everything? It stands sentinel on the wild coast, the sea

ATMOS   and the wind outside your windows. Quite an estate (3,000 acres), with cottages,

NC500   event spaces and the **Smugglers Inn** (Fri/Sat/Sun) for public and guests. Castle-

££   like stone interiors with some big rooms, panelling, portraits, antlers, a whispery dining room, 4 lounges and a snooker room. Activities on request: archery, shooting, games. More corporate methinks than convivial but that would depend on whom you're with. Outside in all weathers, the sea, the sea!

■■■ Luxurious Isolation

In StB there's no category for self-catering accommodation – too much to choose from and not possible to try them out and then select the best, but these cottages for 2/4 in exceptional locations are too special to go unmentioned.

1242 5/H20   ✓ **Knoydart Hide** nr Inverie · www.knoydarthide.co.uk · 01687 460278 Near the village, in the woods, this is a high-spec, architect-designed cabin with deck, tub, sauna, fab views and perfect privacy, and all of Knoydart is on your doorstep (get your boots on) and check the *StB* index for many Knoydart references (and page opposite). You could call it a romantic retreat. A comfy, single-room **Studio** is also available (with exclusive hot tub access). Pub and tearoom 5 mins away. Self-catering, or a cooked-meal package possible. Water taxi or ferry from Mallaig, then Jackie picks you up by Land Rover.

1243 3/E15   ✓ **Borve Lodge Estate** South Harris · www.borvelodge.com ·

LL   01859 550358 Off the A859 on the W of South Harris by the amazing beaches, 4 self-catering options, 2 traditional and comfortable, and 2 newly built to exceptional standards – 'The Rock House' (along the lines of Blue Reef, below, who established luxe-remote first), and the landmark 'Broch', a glass and stone tower of contemporary living and luxury. None of this was cheap to build or is cheap to rent but provided you're getting on quite well, it will be unforgettable!

1244 3/E16   ✓ **Blue Reef Cottages** South Harris · www.stay-hebrides.com ·

LL   01859 550370 1km from **Scarista House** (2261/ISLAND HOTELS) and overlooking the same idyllic beach (1619/BEACHES). 2 exceptional turf-roofed cottages, the first of the new wave of luxury-in-good-location lodges. For couples only, though the study could be another bedroom at a pinch. Stylish, good facilities, amazing view. Gourmet meals from lady nearby, eat at Scarista House or stock up from **Croft 36** at Northton.

1245 8/S25   ✓ **Blue Cabin by the Sea** Cove · www.bluecabinbythesea.co.uk ·

LL   07849 058493/07768 990998 It's blue and it's on its own little beach and perfect little Cove harbour S of Dunbar. You reach the cottage through a rock-cut smuggling tunnel and across the strand. Owned by remarkable architect Ben Tindall; you can expect a uniquely, even quirkily comfortable abode and perfect isolation. Crabs and lobsters from the boats in the harbour. It's only 2km from the A1. I once spent a very special day here on Ben's Cove. Sleeps 4.

1246 4/L13

L

NC500

✓ **Croft 103** nr Durness · www.croft103.com · 01971 511202 2 state-of-the-eco-art lochside cottages by the people who have Mackay's in Durness (10km along beautiful coast 1617/1618/BEACHES). Hill and sea cottages overlooking **Loch Eriboll** (1672/LOCHS), with their own wind turbine and solar panels, so carbon negative. Merging into the rocky, watery landscape with big, big windows, underfloor heating, outside tubs and high-tech appliances. Well … you'll never want to leave. One bedroom. Open AYR.

1247 7/J23

Achnacarron (aka Loch Awe) Boathouse nr Taynuilt · www.lochawe.co.uk · 07850 722721 Modern-build, 2-bedroom house with deck on the quiet, woody western shore of mysterious and magnificent Loch Awe. Oban nearest town for restaurants, bars and fish & chips. Here, glorious garden, water's edge and many woodland walks. Like most on this page, it does get booked months ahead.

1248 3/E14

LL

Beach Bay Cottage Carnish, nr Uig, Lewis · www.beachbaycottage.co.uk · 07768 711881 Way out W to the Atlantic and the sunset, a new build – stone, glass, turf roof – nestling into the hillside 150m above a truly spectacular beach (1626/BEACHES). 180° windows, sauna, totally mod con. 2 bedrooms. Though you're in seemingly splendid isolation, there are stores and a new café at Uig.

Great Wild Camping Up North

1249 3/E16

& 3/E15

✓ **South Harris West Coast** S of Tarbert, where the boat comes in. 35km to Stornoway. Follow road and you reach some truly splendid beaches (e.g. **Scarista** 1619/BEACHES). Camp here or **Luskentyre**, or **Horgabost**, between them, which is an official site. Treat yourself to dinner at **Scarista House** (2261/ISLAND HOTELS). Gaze on your own private sunset and swim in a turquoise sea.

1250 3/E16

✓ **Lickisto Blackhouse Camping** South Harris · 01859 530485 On **East Coast** (see 1683/SCENIC ROUTES), a beautiful natural campsite in landscaped rough garden, not so wild because there are showers and a 180-year-old blackhouse for warmth and wash-up facilities. Terraced pitches; also a couple of yurts for hire. Unlikely as it may seem, there's a great caff nearby. For sale at TGP, so check.

1251 7/F22

✓ **Calgary Beach** Mull 10km from Dervaig, where there are toilets, picnic tables and BBQs but no other facilities – this is classic wild camping but you won't be alone. Sculpture trail, art gallery and a great café nearby (2188/ART SPACES). Also on Mull, S of Killiechronan on the gentle shore of **Loch na Keal**, there is nothing but the sky and the sea and you have it all to yourself. **Ben More** is in the background (2016/MUNROS). Both sublime!

1252 5/H20

✓ **Knoydart** Idyllic camping on the Knoydart peninsula (ferries from Mallaig) in woods or shore, near or away from Inverie (the village), but look no further than the 'official campsite', 1km along the coast past Inverie House by the river, where there are compost toilets, no campervans and you can build a fire. Pub, tearoom and off-licence in the village. It's perfect!

1253 7/K22

✓ **Glen Etive** nr Ballachulish & Glen Coe One of Scotland's great unofficial camping grounds. Along the road/riverside in a classic glen (1645/GLENS), guarded where it joins the pass into Glen Coe by the awesome Buachaille Etive Mòr. Innumerable grassy terraces and small meadows on which climbers and walkers have camped for generations, and pools to bathe in (1717/SWIMMING).

Repair, perhaps, to the completely reconstructed **Kingshouse Hotel**, 2km from the foot of the glen, reopening in 2019 (1060/HIGHLANDS).

1254 7/J27 ✓ **Glen Rosa** Arran · 07985 566004 4km N from Brodick Pier via Blackwaterfoot road, then by the 'cart track', 500m past the pretty village, a serene meadow by the lazy river (choose pitch carefully), with very basic facilities, i.e. toilets and water. Wood for fires. Goat Fell above. Bliss but for the midges.

1255 5/K20 ✓ **Faichemard Farm** Invergarry · **www.faichemard-caravancamping.co.**
18 YEARS+ **uk · 01809 501314** OK, it's not wild camping and they do allow campervans
ONLY (discreetly, out of the way) but this campsite through Invergarry village on the A87 to Kyle of Lochalsh (turn right at the shinty pitch and then 3km) is special. Here in the Grant family since 1935, it provides 35 carefully located pitches, each with its own picnic table and loads of space between, 2 toilet blocks with dreamy hills and woods all around. And a pond. Perfect family camping.

1256 7/F26 **Kintra** Islay Bowmore–Port Ellen road, take Oa turn-off, then look for sign on the right 7km. A long beach one way, a wild coastal walk the other. Camping (and room for a few campervans) on grassy strand looking out to sea; basic facilities in farmyard – shower, toilet, washing machine.

1257 7/H20 **Lochailort** A 12km stretch S from Lochailort on the A861, along the southern shore of the sea loch itself. A flat, rocky and grassy foreshore with a splendid seascape and backed by brooding mountains. Nearby is **Loch nan Uamh** where Bonnie Prince Charlie left Scotland for the last time (1956/CHARLIE). Once past the salmon farm laboratories, you're in calendar scenery; the excellent **Glenuig Inn** at the southern end is the pub to repair to. No facilities except the sea.

1258 5/H19 **Glenelg** Near Glenelg village which is over the amazing hill from Shiel Bridge (1676/SCENIC ROUTES). Village has great pub, the **Glenelg Inn** (1208/INNS) and a shop. Best spots to camp are 2km from village on road to Skye ferry on the strand.

1259 4/K13 **Oldshoremore** nr Kinlochbervie 3km from village and supplies. Gorgeous beach (1623/BEACHES) and **Polin**, next cove. On the way to **Sandwood Bay** where the camping is legendary (but you have to carry everything 7km).

1260 4/J14 **Achmelvich** nr Lochinver Signed off the mythical Lochinver–Drumbeg road
NC500 (1679/SCENIC ROUTES) or walk from village 3km via Ardroe (a great spot to watch otters that have been there for generations). There is an official campsite adjacent unattractive caravan park, but walk further N towards Stoer following coast path and on to the fabulous beach at **Altanabradhan** with the ruins of the old mill. Best sea-swimming on this coast. Directions: 1630/BEACHES.

Camping With The Kids

Caravan sites and camp grounds that are especially kid-friendly, with good facilities and a range of things to do (mostly including a good pub).

1261 8/R28 ✓✓ **Ruberslaw Wild Woods** Denholm · www.ruberslaw.co.uk · 01450 870092 Halfway along the A698 between Hawick and Jedburgh, 3km to Bedrule in woods under Ruberslaw, the big hill (well, not that big) of the Borders. It's not often on my travels that I come across somewhere that so wholly embraces its sense of place and is so perfectly realised. A gentle, sheltered campsite set around a walled garden with spaciously laid out pitches (30), a 'hub' with roofed eating and gathering area (wood brazier), kitchen, showers, phone charging. 4 safari tents with beds, etc, a little further away. Fire pits (logs provided). Trees, privacy, quiet. The hill to climb. Family-run for yours!

1262 6/N19 ✓ **Glenmore Campsite** nr Aviemore · www.campingintheforest.co.uk · 01479 861271 9km Aviemore on the road to the ski slopes, B970. Across the road from Glenmore Visitor Centre and adjacent to **Loch Morlich Watersports Centre** (2148/WATERSPORTS). Extensive grassy site on lochside with trees and mountain views. Loads of activities include watery ones, reindeer (1766/KIDS) and at the **Coylumbridge Hotel** (1175/KIDS). There's a pool and the Fun House, a separate building full of stuff to amuse kids of all ages. Shop at site entrance; café and bar.

1263 5/H18
APR-OCT
NC500 ✓ **Applecross Campsite** Applecross · www.applecross.uk.com/campsite · 01520 744268 First thing you come to as you approach the coast after a hair-raising drive over the *bealach*, the mountain pass. Grassy meadow in farm setting, 1km sea. Some wishbone wooden cabins (and trailers further in). Usual facilities. Famous Applecross Inn 1km (with Airstream food-truck takeaway) and a great café/restaurant along the bay (1088/HIGHLANDS). A green, grassy, safe landing.

1264 4/J15 ✓ **Port A Bhaigh Campsite** Altandhu, nr Achiltibuie · www.portabhaigh. co.uk · 01854 622339 Wild yet civilised camping on grassy sward gently sloping to a wee beach on one of Scotland's secretly celebrated foreshores, with an immense and forever memorable view of the Summer Isles. Add the toilet/shower/laundry block, and the pub (who run the site), the **Am Fuaran**, with its great grub, and it would be hard to find a more perfect spot. Cruise to the isles, climb something, gaze at the sunset.

1265 4/L12
APR-OCT
NC500 ✓ **Sango Sands** Durness · www.sangosands.com · 07838 381065 Great location overlooking sea in downtown Durness with most things you would want, including a pub (The Oasis), though food is average, so go to **The Café @ Balnakeil** (2km) 1403/CAFÉS. View only obstructed by campervans. Plenty to do round here (1617/1618/BEACHES), Smoo Cave, Balnakeil Craft Village, etc. Well run and very friendly.

1266 5/G18
LL
JAN-DEC ✓ **Sligachan** Skye · www.sligachan.co.uk · 01478 650204 The campsite you see at the major bend in the road on the A87 going N to Portree from the bridge and the ferries. Sligachan is major hotel landmark (2284/SKYE), as is the all-day bistro-**Seamus' Bar** (famous whisky list). Lovely site by river with many walks from here. Free choice. Just pitch up and they'll come round. Laundry. Adventure playground by hotel, adventure playground of Skye all around.

1267 7/H22
APR-MID OCT
✓ **Shieling Holidays** Craignure, Mull · www.shielingholidays.co.uk ·
01680 812496 35km from Tobermory right where the Oban ferry docks. Great views and a no-nonsense, thought-of-everything camp park. Self-catering shielings (carpeted cottage tents with heaters and en-suite facilities) or hostel beds. Loads to do and see (though mainly by car), including nearby **Duart Castle** (1820/CASTLES); and a pool at the Isle of Mull Hotel (1km). Eat here too or at the Craignure Inn.

1268 7/J28
APR-OCT
✓ **Seal Shore** Kildonan, Arran · www.campingarran.com · 01770 820320
In the S of the island, the emerging fun place to be, **Kildonan** (2315/ARRAN) with a long littoral to wander and open views to Pladda Island. Smallish, intimate greenfield site (40+) for campers and caravans. BBQ, day room and hotel adjacent for grub and pub. 'We're always in the UK top 20,' says Mr D, who will brook no nonsense from naughty kids or naughty parents. Sleep with the seals! Bus stop nearby. And beaches (1639/BEACHES) and walks (1654/WATERFALLS).

1269 7/H21
MAR-OCT
✓ **Resipole Farm** Loch Sunart, Ardnamurchan · www.resipole.co.uk ·
01967 431235 Arrive via Corran Ferry or from Mallaig or Fort William route via Lochailort (1690/SCENIC ROUTES). Extensive grassy landing on lochside with all mod cons, including shop, dishwashers, washing machines. A bit caravan-cluttered, but quiet days in Ardnamurchan are all around you. Adventurous may kayak on the loch.

1270 5/H16
APR-OCT
✓ **Sands Holiday Centre** nr Gairloch · www.sandsholidaycentre.co.uk ·
01445 712152 4km Gairloch (road to Melvaig) with island views, a large grassy park with dunes and its own long, sandy beach (1631/BEACHES). Separate camping area. 10 wooden wigwams named after islands. Kids' play area. Lots to do and see in Gairloch: a good pub, the **Old Inn** (1218/INNS); well-equipped shop, mountain bikes for hire; great camping in dunes plus walking, fishing, etc.

1271 4/J14
APR-SEP
NC500
Clachtoll Beach Campsite nr Lochinver · www.clachtollbeachcampsite. co.uk · 01571 855377 Friendly, grassy beach site in spectacular scenery (1680/ SCENIC ROUTES). The caravan part is a blot on the landscape but the beach is the thing. Camping, caravan hook-ups and chalets: all usual facilities in a great wild area.

1272 7/H23
MAR-OCT
Roseview Caravan Park Oban · www.roseviewoban.co.uk · 01631 562755 3km out of Oban. Quiet, clean and friendly ground with stream running through. All sorts of extras such as undercover cooking area, BBQ, play park. No bar. No dogs. The **Oban Caravan & Camping Park** www.obancaravanpark.com · 01631 562425 is adjacent at Gallanachmore overlooking the sea and easier to find. Well-run C&C Club family site with shop and ducks! Both near the Kerrera ferry, the walks and the **Tea Garden** (753/OBAN).

1273 7/L24
MAR-OCT
Cashel Caravan & Campsite Rowardennan · www.campingintheforest. co.uk · 01360 870234 Forestry Commission site on the quieter shores of Loch Lomond in Queen Elizabeth Forest Park. Jumbo pitches and pre-pitched tents. Excellent facilities, including shop, takeaway and play area, and tons to do in the surrounding area, which includes Ben Lomond and plootering on or by the loch.

1274 5/F18
APR-OCT
Kinloch Campsite Dunvegan, Skye · www.kinloch-campsite.co.uk ·
01470 521531 Friendly, family-run grassy campsite on Glendale road by Dunvegan. Not so caravan heavy; choose your own pitch from many. Good location for NW Skye wanderings and eating-out options in Dunvegan, especially **Jann's Cakes** and **The Old School Restaurant** (2305/2303/SKYE).

Glorious Glamping

1275 8/R25 · NO PETS · L ✓✓ **Lochhouses Farm** nr North Berwick · **www.harvestmoonholidays. com** · **07960 782246/07914 013621/07817 968985** From A1 S of Haddington, A198 to North Berwick past Tyninghame; Lochhouses signed on right. 1km to farmyard. 7 well-appointed safari tents (can take 8) under trees and 7 treehouses (all with wood-burning stoves and en-suite toilets) in beautiful farmland near beach. Fabulous light and a microclimate one of the driest places in Scotland. Shop, BBQ. All mod glamping cons. Can be exclusive use. Also available through Canopy & Stars.

1276 5/N19 ✓✓ **Inshriach** Rothiemurchus, nr Aviemore · **www.inshriachhouse. com** · **01540 651341** In the grounds of this quirky Edwardian country house (1298/HOUSE PARTIES) by the Spey, a range of wonderful woodland retreats: a 16-foot yurt (by Red Kite), a converted (1954 Commer) lorry, an 'isolated' bothy and a Shepherd's Hut by the river. All are highly individual, comfy and quite beautiful, especially the bothy (part of a project funded by the Royal Scottish Academy), a mile away, and the Hut by the March Pool, by Tim Westman. Wood-burning stoves, sauna/hot tub, compost loos; it's eco-heaven and 'achingly romantic'.

1277 6/P19 ✓✓ **Lazy Duck** nr Nethy Bridge · **www.lazyduck.co.uk** · **0131 618 6198** Beautiful setting and eco-accom in heart of the Cairngorms National Park. A hut, a lodge, wee hostel and camping by the River Nethy. Report: 1181/HOSTELS.

1278 8/N23 ✓ **Comrie Croft** nr Comrie · **www.comriecroft.com** · **01764 670140** On A85 Comrie–Crieff road, essentially a hostel (1180/HOSTELS) and camp ground, but 7 Swedish katas, canvas yurts up the hill in the woods. Stoves, platform to sleep, picnic tables. Millpond nearby, superb walking. Bike hire (and sales) on premises. Shop, tearoom, trails; good eating-out options in Comrie and Crieff (918/907/921/ PERTHSHIRE).

1279 8/L23 · L ✓ **Lovestruck & The Ferry Cabin @ Monachyle Mhor** nr Balquhidder · **www.mhor.net** · **01877 384622** 11km from Balquhidder along Loch Voil. Mhor got on the glamping bandwagon – in this case a (horse) wagon, overlooking the loch, a discreet distance from their fab hotel (1220/GET-AWAY HOTELS), where you eat and hang out in bar or lounge. Veranda and wood stove. Also, stroke of genius, the old waiting room from the Port Appin ferry has been transplanted here, and the adjoining reclaimed Bothy. Both romantic, recycled hideaways.

1280 8/Q27 **Glentress Forest Lodges** nr Innerleithen · **www.glentressforestlodges. co.uk** · **01721 721007** In Glentress Forest cycling hub, so this is mainly a bikey/ walker thing. Lodges and pods form a community that looks like it just landed from outer space. On a gentle slope opposite the café, bike shop for all the cyclists who converge in the Tweed Valley. Timber frames, light, spacious, a deck, BBQ, campfire. Communal facilities.

1281 7/F26 **Storm-Pods** Lagavulin, Islay · **www.islay-pods.co.uk** · **01496 300129** Road W of Port Ellen in the S of Islay, where the distilleries – Ardbeg, Laphroaig and Lagavulin – sit by the sea, these (currently 5) 'pods' are lodged discreetly into the bank overlooking the cove on a farm. Apart and private. The delights of Port Ellen – pub, and food at the **Islay Hotel**, and 3km in the other direction, the **Ardbeg Distillery Café** (2340/ISLAY).

✓✓ **Ruberslaw Wild Woods** Denholm · **www.ruberslaw.co.uk** · **01450 870092** Superb safari tents, woods. Report: 1261/CAMPING.

Real Retreats

1282 9/Q28
LL
NO TV
ATMOS

✓✓✓ **Samye Ling** nr Eskdalemuir · www.samyeling.org ·
01387 373232 Bus or train to Lockerbie/Carlisle then bus (Mon-Sat
0871 200 2233) or taxi (01576 470480). Community consists of an extraordinary
and inspiring temple not so incongruous in these Border wilds. The complex
comprises main house (with some accom), dorm and guest-house blocks (many
single rooms), Tibetan Tearooms and shop. Further up the hill, longer retreats in
annexes. Samye Ling, a world centre for Tibetan Buddhism, is always under
construction under the supervision of Tibetan masters, but they offer daily and
longer stays and courses in all aspects of Buddhism, meditation, t'ai chi, yoga, etc.
Daily timetable from prayers at 6am and work period. Breakfast/lunch; light supper
at 6pm, all vegetarian. Busy, thriving community atmos. This is Buddhism, pure
and simple. See also World Peace Centre (below).

1283 6/P17

✓✓✓ **Findhorn Community & Park** nr Forres · www.findhorn.org ·
01309 690311 The world-famous and world-class spiritual
community and foundation begun by Peter and Eileen Caddy and Dorothy Maclean
in 1962, a village of caravans, cabins and brilliant houses on the way into Findhorn
on B9011. Visitors can join the community as short-term guests, eating and
working on-site but probably staying at recommended B&Bs. This sprawling,
always-growing eco-village is fascinating and a joy just to pass through.
Programme of courses and residential workshops in spiritual growth/dance/
healing, etc. Many other aspects and facilities available in a cosmopolitan and
well-organised community. Excellent shop (1502/DELIS), pottery (2205/SCOTTISH
SHOPS) and **The Phoenix Café** (1350/VEGETARIAN); the Universal Hall has a great
music and performance programme featuring many of Scotland's finest.

1284 6/P17
ATMOS

✓✓ **Pluscarden Abbey** nr Forres & Elgin · www.pluscardenabbey.org
Signed from the main A96 (11km from Elgin) in a sheltered south-facing
glen, with a background of wooded hillside, this is the only medieval monastery in
the UK still inhabited by monks. It's a deeply calming place. The Benedictine
community keep walled gardens and bees. 8 services a day in the glorious chapel
(1921/ABBEYS), which visitors can attend. Retreat for men (10 rooms, meals shared
with monks) and women (12 separate rooms, self-catering) with 2-week maximum
and no obligatory charge. Write to the Guest Master, Pluscarden Abbey, by Elgin,
IV30 8VA; no telephone bookings. Mobile signal not good (there are telephone
boxes). Restoration/building work always in progress (of the abbey and of the spirit).

1285 8/P23

✓✓ **The Bield at Blackruthven** Tibbermore, nr Perth · www.
bieldatblackruthven.org.uk · 01738 583238 Take Crieff road (A85)
from Perth and A9/ring road past Huntingtower then left for Tibbermore. 2km.
Bield is an old Scottish word for a place of refuge and shelter; also means to
nurture, succour, encourage. All are possible here in this superbly well-managed,
tasteful Christian retreat. A Georgian home with outbuildings containing accom,
lounges and meeting rooms in 30 gorgeous garden acres, which have a
swimming pool, chapel (in old carpenter's workshop) and a surprisingly spacious
barn laid out for events; they're always open. More like a country-house hotel but
there are prayers, courses and support if you want it. No guests on Monday, so
6 days max. Very cheap for this level of comfort. It is beautiful, peaceful and
contemporary. The estimable **Solas Festival** is in mid-June (41/EVENTS); there are
open days, concerts. Yet this is possibly Perthshire's best-kept secret. Meals and
self-catering. Serenity!

1286 8/L24 ✓ **Lendrick Lodge** Brig o' Turk · www.lendricklodge.com · 01877 376263
On A821 scenic road through the Trossachs. Near road but in idyllic grounds with beautiful (though imported from the river that gurgles below) standing stones. An organised retreat and get-away-from-it-all yoga and healing centre. Yoga, reiki and shamanic teaching throughout year (they even do fire walking!). Can take up to 50 people and run 2 courses at the same time. Individual rooms and full board if required. 'River Retreat' in separate building overlooking the river has a pool and 2 en-suite rooms.

1287 8/L23 ✓ **Dhanakosa** Balquhidder · www.dhanakosa.com · 01877 384213 3km village on Loch Voilside, 9km from A84 Callander–Crianlarich road. Gentle Buddhist place with ongoing retreat programmes (Introductory or Regular; 1 week or weekends in winter). Guidance and group sessions. Yoga and t'ai chi. Meditation room. Rooms hold 2–4 and are en suite. Vegetarian food. Beautiful serene setting on Balquhidder Braes: you will 'radiate love'. Open day in June.

1288 7/J27 ✓ **The World Peace Centre** Holy Isle · www.holyisle.org · 01770 601100
LL Take a ferry from Lamlash on Arran (ferry 01770 700463) to find yourself part of a Tibetan (albeit contemporary) mystery. Escape from the madding crowd on the mainland and compose your spirit or just refresh. Built by Samye Ling abbots, this tiny Celtic refuge centre offers a range of activities to help purge the soul or restore the faith. Day-trippers, holiday-breakers and all faiths welcome. Can accommodate 60. Conference/gathering centre. Must phone ahead. And there's a hill to climb (2251/ISLAND WALKS). Ferries very limited in winter.

1289 7/K26 **College of the Holy Spirit** Millport, Cumbrae · www.cathedraloftheisles.org · 01475 530353 Continuous ferry service from Largs (every 15 mins, and 30 mins in winter) then 6km bus journey to Millport. Off main street through a gate in the wall, into grounds of the **Cathedral of the Isles** (1903/CHURCHES) and another, more peaceful world. A retreat for the Episcopal Church since 1884. Available for groups but there are 16 comfortable rooms (5 en suite), with B&B. Also half/full board. Morning and night prayer each day, Eucharist on Sunday and delightful Sunday afternoon concerts in summer. An uplifting 'Open Programme'. Fine library. Bike hire available on island. See also 1406/CAFÉS.

1290 7/H24 **EcoYoga Centre** Ford, Argyll · www.ecoyoga.org · 01546 810259 In a sylvan, almost lochside setting, deep in glorious Argyll, reached by an unnumbered road from Ford off the A816, 20km N of Lochgilphead. On booking you'll get directions but, suffice to say, it's discreetly delightful here – when you find it. Off-grid electricity, wild swimming in the gorge, room to roam and superb food. I haven't stayed or sampled but Dana M, a regular retreater, world traveller and a bit of a foodie recommends their yoga courses highly. I'm going to go with that and one day I'll go there (to stay rather than visit).

The Best Spas

1291 8/R23 ✓✓ **The Kohler Waters Spa** The Old Course Hotel, St Andrews · www. oldcoursehotel.co.uk · 01334 468067 In the mega Old Course resort (873/FIFE), this beautifully designed leisure/treatment suite, though small, is another reason for staying. The spa was designed by the team who created the original Cowshed at Babington House. Owners of the hotel, the Kohler Company, produce iconic kitchens and bathrooms in the US and own a slew of luxury resorts. In the main suite there's a 20m pool, monsoon showers, saunas, crystal steam rooms and treatment rooms; you will be perfectly pampered. Non-res welcome. A new, adjacent leisure centre with lap pool and gym 2017.

1292 8/P27 ✓✓ **Stobo Castle** Stobo, nr Peebles · www.stobocastle.co.uk · 01721 725300 Border baronial mansion 10km S of Peebles in beautiful countryside of towering trees and trickling burns. **Dawyck Gardens** nearby (1563/ GARDENS) and there are Japanese Water Gardens in the grounds. Mainly a hotel (51 rooms) but day visits possible; the spa is the heart of the pampering experience. Over 70 treatments. Not too much emphasis on exercise though a lovely pool. Different categories of rooms and suites; also lodges. Bespoke and every conceivable and currently fashionable treatment for men and women; all medical peculiarities accounted for. Decent dining: 'healthy', of course, but no denial of carbs or cream. Coffee shop/juice bar. White-towelled ladies lounge all over. Deals often available for days and half days.

1293 8/M26 ✓✓ **The Spa at Blythswood Square** Glasgow · www.blythswoodsquare. com · 0141 240 1662 In the basement of Glasgow's fab city centre hotel, a top spa and destination in itself. Hugely popular with Glasgow lasses for individual treatments and day packages using, among others, ishga products (natural, organic, Scottish). Great lighting, steam, sauna, Jacuzzi-tastic; seductive and indulgent, as they say. Pure (as well as purifying) Glasgow.

1294 8/N24 ✓✓ **The Spa at Gleneagles** Gleneagles Hotel, Auchterarder · www. gleneagles.com/spa · 01764 694332 Naturally, the leisure suites here have always offered one of the best spa experiences. 20 treatment rooms, a plethora of therapists and built-in soothing atmos, it's practically irresistible with or without golf fatigue. Suites for men and women, vitality pool, heated beds and a long menu of tantalising treatments.

1295 7/L25 ✓✓ **The Carrick Spa at Cameron House** www.cameronhouse.co.uk · 01389 727647 The spa of Cameron House (which is being rebuilt after a fire in late 2017) is 4km along the road and lochside at the Carrick, the 18-hole golf course (shuttle service). New building complex incorporates golf clubhouse facilities, shop and recommended Claret Jug bar/restaurant. Very professional service. Many treatment rooms and therapists; 3 different spa products in use. There's a pool, a rooftop infinity pool, an outside (sheltered) deck, bar and restaurant. When you've made enough dosh to afford this (or somebody treats you), just relax.

1296 8/Q25 ✓ **One Spa** Sheraton Grand Hotel, Edinburgh · www.onespa.com · 0131 221 7777 Considered the best spa in the city and on many lists, it's also one of the best things about the hotel, which is centrally situated on Festival Sq opposite the Usher Hall. As well as the usual (reasonably spacious) pool, there's another that extends outdoors, dangling infinity-style over Conference Sq behind the hotel. Decent gym. Exotic hydrotherapy and a host of treatments, with all the right unguents. Range of day and half-day tickets and gift vouchers available.

For The Best House Parties

Rent these for families or friends, and have to yourselves: exclusive use.

1297 8/P20 · LL · NTS ✓✓ **Mar Lodge Estate** nr Braemar · www.ntsholidays.com · 0844 493 2173 There are several remarkable properties in the NTS-run, extensive 72,000-acre estate 15km from Braemar. Classic Highland scenery superb in any season; the upper waters of the Dee. Apartments in main mansion (takes 4–15) and 2 other houses. Library, billiard room; ballroom can be hired separately. Expensive, of course, but not when divided between mates. And big wow factor. Live like the royals down the road, without the servants (unless you bring with). Somewhat dated interiors, otherwise, it's all sorted!

1298 5/N19 ✓✓ **Inshriach House** nr Aviemore · www.inshriachhouse.com · 01540 651341 On B970 back road between Inverdruie and Feshiebridge, 8km S of Aviemore. Atmospheric, comfy Edwardian country house with lived-in boho public rooms, highly individual bedrooms, gardens and small estate. Close to spectacular **Loch an Eilean** (1667/LOCHS). Self-catering or food from the **Old Bridge Inn** (1333/FOOD PUBS) nearby. Up to 17 can stay and there is uniquely fabulous eco-accom in the woody grounds (1276/GLAMPING). One of the most laid-back options on this page. They have fishing and red squirrels. Walter is a very fine host (he may ply you with his limited edition gins).

1299 8/R25 ✓✓ **Lochhouses Farm** nr North Berwick · www.harvestmoonholidays. com Not a house-party venue but a cool, canopied campsite by a beach, with separate, well-appointed tents, common gathering areas (treehouses nearby). Exquisitely outdoors. 1275/GLAMPING (with contact numbers).

1300 5/N17 ✓ **Drynachan Lodge** nr Nairn · www.cawdor.com · 01667 402402 This fab 19th-century hunting lodge is on the Cawdor Estate, S of Nairn. The castle is signed from all over (1816/CASTLES). While there are many cottages for let, this is the big house (12 bedrooms) and was personally decked out by Lady Isabella Cawdor. Like all things on the estate it's done with great taste. Fully staffed and catered, it's like a hip shooting lodge. It'll cost ya.

1301 7/H24 ✓ **Lunga House** Ardfern, Argyll · www.lungahouse.co.uk · 01852 500237 Take Craobh Haven (marina) turn-off on A816. Once had a boho-chic, Lunga-time rep among those who know, this rambling big hoose is less crumbly of late and, though still old style, is perfect for parties, gatherings and mainly weddings. Great public space includes ballroom. 18 bedrooms and many cottages. You really can call it your own! Catering provided (there are suppliers for all needs).

1302 7/K28 · LL · NTS ✓ **Culzean Castle: Eisenhower Hotel** nr Maybole · www.culzean-eisenhower.com · 01655 884455 The upper-floor apartments once stayed in by the wartime Supreme Allied Commander in Europe and later president of the US. 6 suites and public rooms available singly or for exclusive use. Spectacular both in and out. Dinner can be provided; the grounds are superb (1813/CASTLES).

1303 3/E15 · ATMOS ✓ **Amhuinnsuidhe Castle** Harris · www.amhuinnsuidhe.com · 01859 560200 N from Tarbert then W to faraway strand (directions: 2246/ISLAND WALKS). Staffed, fab food and gothic Victorian castle/shooting and fishing lodge (salmon arrive in a foaming mass at the river mouth). 12 bedrooms; mainly sporting and fishing weeks but individuals can book (like a mixed house party). Grand interiors and top fishing on 9 lochs and rivers. Very expensive for exclusive use but everything – from ghillies to afternoon tea – is thrown in.

1304 7/K28 ✓ **Doonbrae House** Alloway · www.doonbrae.com · 01292 442466 In heart of unspoiled, well-kept village still evocative of Burns, whose birthplace, gardens and Tam o' Shanter graveyard are nearby. Opposite and part of Brig o' Doon Hotel, much favoured for weddings. This refurbished mansion is separate and you have it to yourself (group bookings only). Also 2 cottages. On Doon banks (to amble) in delightful gardens. Self-catering or eat at hotel. 5 suites.

1305 8/R24 ✓ **Cambo Estate** nr Crail · www.camboestate.com · 01333 450054 On Fife
 L coast route, 14km from St Andrews. Rambling house, fabulous au naturel grounds, woods famous for snowdrops and bulbs in spring (18/EVENTS). Walled Garden and café/shop in lovely stable block. 5 B&B rooms, 4 apartments, 3 cottages. A very special country-house experience awaits here; you make it what you will. Great walking, golfing and garden-loving opportunities. See also 881/FIFE.

1306 9/N30 ✓ **Cavens** Kirkbean · www.cavens.com · 01387 880234 Off A710 Solway Coast road 20km S Dumfries. Informal and well-appointed mansion in gorgeous grounds near beach. Sleeps up to 22 in house (16) and lodges. Great value compared to other grand manors. Angus's dinner-party cooking. See 775/SW HOTELS. Some famous people have partied here – no names from me.

1307 7/J24 **Castle Lachlan** Loch Fyne · www.castlelachlan.com · 01369 860669 For
 L directions see **Inver**, the fab restaurant on the estate (736/ARGYLL). Stunning setting in heart of Scotland scenery, the 18th-century ancestral home of the Clan Maclachlan. Snooker room; all-weather tennis. Self-catering but dining can be arranged. Sleeps '15 people comfortably' (more for dinner) in 7 bedrooms and 2 cottages. Sumptuous surroundings for rock stars and weddings and the like.

1308 8/Q22 **Kinnettles Castle** Kinnettles, Forfar · www.kinnettlescastle.com · 01307 820354 I can't say much about this august pile in Angus because I haven't been, but if you're thinking of an exclusive-use get-together in a real castle with all the trimmings, then I'm told it's grand both inside and out. 11 rooms. Reports, please. There are weddings and more weddings!

1309 7/H27 **Saddell Castle** nr Campbeltown · www.landmarktrust.org.uk · 01628 825925 According to mates, this castle and adjacent properties are 'marvellous'. A drive from Glasgow/Edinburgh to the E coast of the peninsula, 15km N of Campbeltown, there's a great beach looking over to Arran and a real sense of away from it all. Very good golf at Machrihanish 20km SW. Castle sleeps 8.

1310 8/S25 **Barns Ness Lighthouse** nr Dunbar · www.coast-properties.co.uk · 01620 671966 On the A1 south of Dunbar, turn left before the formidable cement works. At first this coastal location doesn't seem promising, but taking the road to Whitesands, you quickly reach one of East Lothian's secret littorals and the road that leads straight to the Stevenson Barns Ness Lighthouse. Sleeping 12 in a comfy cottage below, a garden and beach over the wall, nobody will know you're here. Uninterrupted sea views. 40 mins from Edinburgh.

1311 **National Trust for Scotland** has many interesting properties they rent out for weekends or longer. www.nts.org.uk or 0131 243 9331 for details. **The Landmark Trust** also has 20 mostly fabulous properties in Scotland, including **The Pineapple** (1890/MONUMENTS), **Auchenleck House** in Ayrshire, which sleeps 13, and the wonderful **Ascog House** or **Meikle House** on the Isle of Bute which sleep 9 and 10 respectively. Phone 01628 825925 to get their beautiful handbook (properties throughout the UK) or see www.landmarktrust.org.uk.

the Best
of Good Food & Drink

Bloody Good Pubs

Pubs in Edinburgh and Glasgow are listed in their own sections. See also Real Ale/Craft Beers and Good Food Pubs in following pages.

1312 7/K23
L
ATMOS
✓ **The Drover's Inn** Inverarnan · www.thedroversinn.co.uk · 01301 704234 A famously Scottish drinking den/hotel, just N of Ardlui at the head of Loch Lomond and 12km S of Crianlarich on the A82. Much the same as it was when it won 'Pub of the Year 1705'. Smoky, low-ceilinged rooms, open ranges, whisky in the jar, stuffed animals in the hall and kilted barmen; slack though it sometimes seems, this is nevertheless the antithesis of the contrived Scottish tourist pub. Hotel rooms above and over the road are inexpensive (definitely not deluxe).

1313 7/K21
DF
L
ATMOS
✓ **Clachaig Inn** nr Glencoe · www.clachaig.com · 01855 811252 300 years deep in the glen itself, down the road signed off the A82, 5km from Glencoe village. Both the pub (the Boots Bar), with its wood-burning stoves, and the lounge are woody and welcoming. Back door best for muddy footwear or those averse to sofas. Many real ales and many real climbers and walkers. Handy if you're in the hostel 2km down road or camping. Walking fuel food in bar/lounge and good, inexpensive accom, including lodges. Impressive plethora of ales and beer fests in May and October.

1314 8/S20
L
✓ **Marine Hotel** Stonehaven · www.marinehotelstonehaven.co.uk · 01569 762155 Popular local on a great harbour with seats outside and always a crowd. 6 guest ales, big Belgian and wheat-beer selection, and their own brew – 6°N. Food till 9pm. Upstairs dining room overlooks the boat-bobbing bay. Same menu; local fish specials. Lunch & dinner.

1315 7/G22
✓ **Mishnish** Tobermory, Mull · www.themishnish.co.uk · 01688 302500 Though perhaps no longer the iconic island pub for craic and music culture, still a great bar (groomed up a bit). On the bay and on the money. Report: 2348/MULL.

1316 3/C20
LL
ATMOS
Castlebay Bar Castlebay, Barra · www.castlebay-hotel.co.uk · 01871 810223 Adjacent to Castlebay Hotel. A deceptively average-seeming but brilliant bar. All human life is here. More Irish than all the Irish makeovers on the mainland. Occasional live music including the – legend in their own lifetime – Vatersay Boys; the comfort of craic with strangers. Report: 2274/ISLAND HOTELS.

1317 5/J19
DF
L
Cluanie Inn Glenmoriston · www.cluanieinn.com · 01320 340238 On A87 at head of Loch Cluanie, 15km before Shiel Bridge on the long road to Kyle of Lochalsh (and Skye). A wayside walkers' inn, with pub food, a restaurant and the (both bunkhouse and hotel) accom outdoorists want (1217/INNS). Good base for climbing/walking (especially **Five Sisters of Kintail** 2034/WALKS). A cosy refuge.

1318 9/L31
LL
ATMOS
The Steampacket Inn Isle of Whithorn · www.thesteampacketinn.biz · 01988 500334 The hub of this atmospheric wee village at the end of the road south (1615/VILLAGES). On harbour (with picture windows) that fills and empties with the tide. Great for ales and food. 7 inexpensive rooms upstairs. An all-round happy hostelry.

1319 6/R17 **The Shore Inn** Portsoy · 01261 842831 In cute Moray Coast village, at a corner of the old harbour, this is the old inn. Strong community pub, seats outside are with the village not the pub, darts are played, food during the day actually comes from the café in the other corner (they bring it over). Always locals and brimming over the walls at the annual **Boat Festival** (45/EVENTS). 7 days 11am–11pm.

✓✓ **Glenelg Inn** Glenelg A pub for the village and those who make it over the Pass. A classic. Report: 1208/INNS.

✓✓ **Applecross Inn** Applecross Like the Glenelg above, it serves its community and folk who come from everywhere to eat. Report: 1207/INNS.

▮ Great Pubs For Real Ale/Craft Beers

Real-Ale & Craft-Beer pubs in Edinburgh, p. 71; in Glasgow, p. 117.

1320 6/T19 ✓ **The Craftsman Company** Aberdeen · www.thecraftsmancompany.com · 01224 945600 In Guild St, near harbour. An exemplary craft-beer alehouse/café/restaurant. Selection of beers changes weekly – Scottish/English craft breweries, 15 at any one time on tap, huge range of bottled or canned. Excellent, wholesome food from breakfast to supper. 7 days. See also 1023/ABERDEEN.

1321 8/Q23
ATMOS ✓ **Fisherman's Tavern** Broughty Ferry · www.fishermanstavern-broughtyferry.co.uk · 01382 775941 In 'The Ferry', but not too far to go from Dundee centre for great atmos and great collection of ales (6), though not so crafty. In Fort St near the seafront. Regular IPAs and many guests. Low-ceilinged and friendly. Inexpensive accom upstairs and pub grub as you like (941/DUNDEE).

1322 8/N21
ATMOS ✓ **Moulin Inn/Hotel** Pitlochry · www.moulinhotel.co.uk · 01796 472196 4km uphill from main street on road to Bridge of Cally, an inn at a picturesque crossroads since 1695. Some rooms and some rep for pub grub but loved for cosy bar and brewery out back, from which comes Moulin Light, Ale of Atholl and 2 others (one of Scotland's first microbreweries). Food noon-9.30pm.

1323 8/N25 **The Four Marys** Linlithgow · www.fourmarys-linlithgow.co.uk · 01506 842171 Main street near road up to Palace (1830/RUINS), so handy for a pint after schlepping around the historical attractions. Mentioned in most beer guides. 8 ales, Deuchars, St Andrews and guests. Notable malt whisky collection and popular locally for lunches (daily) and evening meals.

1324 8/M24 **The Lade Inn** Callander · www.theladeinn.com · 01877 330152 At Kilmahog, western approach to town, at the start of road into the Trossachs; a good place to stop. Inn brews its own (Waylade, Ladeback, Ladeout). Ale shop adjacent with well over 200 of Scotland's finest (noon-6pm). Big pub food operation (reports vary).

1325 8/Q23 **Duke's Corner** Dundee · www.dukescorner.co.uk · 01382 205052 All that the current out-and-about consumer wants is covered here, including food, music, and also a strong beer list on the taps and on the shelf – selected Scottish, Tempest, Fyne ales; many Belgians.

1326 8/Q25 **The Volunteer Arms (aka Staggs)** Musselburgh · www.staggsbar.com · 0131 665 9654 The CAMRA Scottish Pub of the Year 2018.

The Best Good Food Pubs

Pubs serving particularly good food in Edinburgh and Glasgow are listed in their own sections.

1327 7/H26
MAR–OCT
£££

✓✓ **The Kilberry Inn** nr Tarbert, Argyll · www.kilberryinn.com · 01880 770223 On the single-track B8024 that follows the coast of the Knapdale peninsula between Lochgilphead and Tarbert, halfway round, this is out on its own. For almost 15 years, one of Argyll's foodie destinations. Everything made from scratch, like Knapdale itself. Clare Johnson is a great cook, all her ingredients purposefully sourced; the lounges have a smart, pubby ambience with relaxed, unobtrusive service led by Clare's bloke David. Make that journey (1691/ SCENIC ROUTES) and see Knapdale, see wild Scotland. Closed Mon.

1328 8/L27
DF
ATMOS
££

✓✓ **The Sorn Inn** Sorn · www.sorninn.com · 01290 551305 Village main street, 8km E of Mauchline, 25km Ayr. Pub with rooms and regional rep for food. Restaurants and tables in bar. Family-run (the Grants, with chef Craig Grant). Consistently classic, comforting food and steaks rarely come better than this – a homey rural gastropub experience and great value. 7 days.

1329 8/M24
DF
£

✓✓ **The Cross Keys** Kippen · www.kippencrosskeys.com · 01786 870293 Here forever, we hope, in this quiet town off A811 15km W of Stirling. A cheery, welcoming local, folk passing through pub and for family lunch (not just on Sundays). 3 bedrooms upstairs, open fires, great food in bar or lounge. Seriously thought-over and sourced, and tempting (ambitious even) gastropub food. Some live music. Beer garden. Local Fallen Brewery ales. Mon-Fri lunch & dinner. All day Sat & Sunday roast till 8pm.

1330 8/R24
L
ATMOS
££

✓✓ **The Ship Inn** Elie · www.shipinn.scot · 01333 330246 Legendary pub on the bay at Elie, the perfect toon in the picturesque East Neuk (1613/ VILLAGES), the Bucknalls transforming it with meticulous attention to detail into an exemplary and contemporary restaurant with rooms. In summer a huge food operation upstairs and down (the former has good views). Same menu throughout; all is home-made; blackboard specials. On warm days the Beach Bar terrace overlooking the strand goes like Bondi. 7 days.

1331 8/R24
££

✓✓ **The 19th Hole** Earlsferry · www.19thhole.scot · 01333 330610 At the furthest point of Earlsferry from Elie on the Links Rd facing the golf course (follow the one-way system round). Sister restaurant of The Ship Inn above (it's a where-to-eat decision). Classy, contemporary menu and presentation. Very gastro-pubby. Must book weekends. Cottage layout makes for intimate dining. 7 days.

1332 8/M24
££

✓✓ **Lion & Unicorn** Thornhill · www.lion-unicorn.co.uk · 01786 850204 Since 1635! On A873 off A84 road between M9 and Callander, near Lake of Menteith in the Trossachs. On main road through the village. They come from miles around for pub grub and sizzling steaks. 3 cosy dining areas, open fires, flowers and a real garden. Changing menu (including a gluten-free one), not too fancy, just nice. 7 days noon-9pm.

1333 5/N19
££

✓ **Old Bridge Inn** Aviemore · www.oldbridgeinn.co.uk · 01479 811137 Off Coylumbridge road at S end of Aviemore as you come in from A9 or Kincraig. 100m from main street by the river. Old like it says but one of those homely inn-like inns that completely takes you in! Excellent eclectic menu under chef Chris McCall. Cask ales, artisan beers; kids, skiers, walkers. Very much part of the local music scene, so it also rocks. Kids' menu. 7 days lunch & dinner. In summer, tables over road by the river. Hostel adjacent.

1334 4/J15
LL
£
✓ **Am Fuaran Althandu** · www.amfuaran.co.uk · **01854 622339** Along from Achiltibuie, this pub has an elevated, elevating view of the Summer Isles from its terrace. Inside is dark and pub-like and welcoming. Classic pub-grub menu. Home-made, locally sourced (especially lobster, crab and salad leaves). How do they do this so well so far from, well, anywhere? They also have a cute campsite on the foreshore (1264/CAMPING WITH KIDS). 7 days.

1335 8/S26
££
✓ **The Wheatsheaf Swinton** · www.eatdrinkstaywheatsheaf.com · **01890 860257** A village hotel pub about halfway between Kelso and Berwick (18km) on B6461. In deepest Berwickshire, owners Chris and Jan Winson serve up the best pub grub you've had since England. Rooms in main building and in cottages with great dinner, B&B deals. An all-round good hostelry. 7 days.

1336 4/J15
LL
APR-OCT
££
✓ **The Summer Isles Hotel Bar Achiltibuie** · www.summerisleshotel.com · **01854 622449** The adjacent bar of this romantic hotel on the foreshore faces the isles and the sunset (1045/HIGHLANDS), under new ownership 2018. All the superior qualities of their famed food operation available at less than half the price in the cosy bistro-like bar with tiny terrace; occasional traditional music. Great seafood and vegetarian. Apr-Oct lunch & dinner.

1337 8/S21
L
££
✓ **The Creel Inn Catterline, nr Stonehaven** · www.thecreelinn.co.uk · **01569 750254** 8km S Stonehaven, perching above the bay from where the lobsters come. Lots of other seafood. Good wine; huge speciality beer selection. Cove itself has a haunting beauty. Catterline is Joan Eardley (notable artist) territory. It's also famous for this great atmospheric pub and its grub. 7 days lunch & dinner.

1338 8/Q23
L
ATMOS
££
✓ **The Ship Inn Broughty Ferry** · www.theshipinn-broughtyferry.co.uk · **01382 779176** Excellent seafront pub with food upstairs and down (look out the picture window upstairs). Famous for clootie dumpling at Christmas, other classic pub fare, not so very gastro but good for Arbroath-landed fish. Occasionally dolphins in the estuary (binoculars are available). 7 days lunch & dinner. See also 952/DUNDEE.

1339 8/R27
£
✓ **Cross Keys Ancrum** · www.ancrumcrosskeys.com · **01835 830242** On the green in tiny Ancrum, 2km from the A68. Lovely local gastropub with bar (own brews), woody restaurant and outside tables. Pub classics and some imaginative variations. Strong local connection and reputation. Related to **Born in the Borders** (2208/SCOTTISH SHOPS) across the Teviot.

1340 7/J26
££
✓ **Smiddy Bar at the Kingarth Hotel Isle of Bute** · www.kingarthhotel. co.uk · **01700 831662** 13km Rothesay, 4km after **Mount Stuart** (1871/ HOUSES). Good, friendly old inn serving probably the best pub food on the island. Blackboard menu and à la carte. Covered terrace; good for family feeding. The atmos is just right. Open AYR. 7 days from noon.

1341 8/L25
££
✓ **Old Mill Killearn** · www.theoldmillkillearn.co.uk · **01360 550068** More than one inn in this village but this on the main street is the cosy, friendly one and all that an old pub should be (old here is from 1774). Pub and restaurant. Log fires, brilliant for kids. Garden. 7 days.

1342 8/R25
££ ✓ **Goblin Ha' Hotel** Gifford · www.goblinha.com · 01620 810244 In twee village in East Lothian heartland, it is named after a faery place in the nearby woods, and serves a very decent pub lunch and supper (7 days) in lounge and pub, conservatory, terrace and beer garden. Nice rooms above. Very family friendly. See also 855/LOTHIANS.

1343 8/R25
DF
L
££ ✓ **Waterside Bistro** Haddington · www.watersidebistro.co.uk · 01620 825674 On the banks of the River Tyne near **Lamp of the Lothians** (1916/CHURCHES). This great multi-chambered gastropub – back with its original owners – makes the most of a great riverside location. Report: 867/LOTHIANS.

1344 7/J25
££ **The Oystercatcher** Otter Ferry · www.theoystercatcher.co.uk · 01700 821229 Halfway down Loch Fyne, a seaside, roadside pub with local produce, especially seafood and home baking. Haven't revisited at TGP but reliably informed by local foodies that it's a must if you are along this way.

1345 8/L24
££ **The Byre Inn** Brig o' Turk · www.byreinn.co.uk · 01877 376292 Off A821 at Callander end of the village by Loch Achray. C/o Messrs Allardyce and Hunter, a country inn in deepest Trossachs. Pub grub in cosy, firelit rooms with outside decks in summer. Pizza oven. Inexpensive wine list. Can walk from here to **Duke's Pass** (1688/SCENIC ROUTES).

1346 8/M24
££ **The Riverside** Dunblane · www.theriversidedunblane.co.uk · 01786 823318 Stirling Rd, near the river and station. Family-friendly pub based around food, just where you need it in downtown Dunblane. Wide menu with good choice for vegetarians and vegans. Big Sunday lunch. Contemporary efficiencies and choices. Breakfast, lunch through dinner. 7 days.

1347 9/J30
L
££ **The Crown** Portpatrick · www.crownportpatrick.com · 01776 810261 Popular, busy pub on harbour with tables outside in summer and everywhere else (it's huge!). Light, airy conservatory. Freshly caught fish their speciality. 12 simple rooms above. Locals and Irish who sail over. Very Portpatrick. Lunch & LO 9.30pm.

1348 9/N30
LL
££ **The Anchor Hotel** Kippford · www.anchorhotelkippford.co.uk · 01556 620205 A defining pub of this popular coastal village on the 'Scottish Riviera'. The bowl of sauce sachets lets you know this ain't gastro territory but it's hearty and old style, with a huge throughput in bar and lounges and especially outside tables. Overlooking a tranquil cove and maybe a sunset. 7 days.

1349 8/S26
££ **The Craw Inn** Auchencrow · www.thecrawinn.co.uk · 01890 761253 Off A1 near Reston and Eyemouth – actually 5km off the A1 and further than they sign but near enough for a swift detour and the best place to eat between Berwick and the Lothians: a real destination for great food (lovely pies) and decent wine in classic pub atmos. A great deck out the back. 7 days.

Cock & Bull Balmedie 20km N of Aberdeen by A90. Very popular roadside gastropub near Trumpland. Report: 996/NE RESTAURANTS.

The Best Vegetarian & Vegan Restaurants

For vegetarian restaurants in Edinburgh, see p. 51-2; for Glasgow, see p. 106-7.

1350 6/P17
£
✓ **The Phoenix Café at Findhorn Community** nr Forres · 01309 690110
You will go a long way in the north lands to find real vegetarian food, so it may be worth the detour from the main A96 Inverness–Elgin road to Findhorn and the famous community (1283/RETREATS), a village with streets of brilliant architectural buildings and houses. There is a great deli (1502/DELIS) and this vibrant caff by the 'Universal Hall'. Very pleasant garden terrace. 7 days till 5pm and evenings if event in the hall (hot food till 3pm). **La Bohème**, by the gate on the road in, also serves vegetarian pizzas, crêpes, juices, etc, with outside tables under the big tree.

1351 6/P17
£
✓ **The Bakehouse** Findhorn · www.bakehousecafe.co.uk · 01309 691826
Same neck of the woods as Findhorn Community (above); its owners loosely connected. Not strictly vegetarian but lots of vegetarian choice; all ethical and 'slow'. Bread and cakes from the bakery behind. Lovely, conscientious cookery. 7 days 10am-4pm (open longer in summer).

1352 7/J21
£
✓ **The Wildcat** Fort William 21 High St, near Cameron Sq. A great asset to Fort William, an only **vegan** café with great coffee, teas and home-made hot and cold food. Locally sourced (sourdough from local microbakery) and largely organic with a small wholefoods shop. A buzzing, busy place full of locals, walkers and cyclists and tourists happily going vegan because the food is great. Sustainable approach to everything, including the loo rolls. 7 days, daytime only.

1353 6/T19
£
✓ **Food Story** Aberdeen · http://foodstorycafe.co.uk Food Story's story is a great Aberdeen story. From small takeaway beginnings they expanded into larger premises nearby, knocked them into what is a spacious, always ambient café to hang out in and eat ethically and heartily, and then they added upstairs studios for yoga, life-drawing classes, etc. Basically, it's a (holistic) lifestyle thing. Vegetarian and vegan. Creative approach to lounging, living and lunch. Lara and Sandy have done a good thing here. 8am-9/10pm. Pancake Sundays 11am-3pm.

1354 7/J26
£
✓ **Musicker** Rothesay · www.musicker.co.uk · 01700 502287 Beside the castle, 200m up from the ferry. Great pastries, panini and soup. Best coffee in town. And the ginger cake! Totally vegetarian! Nice books, old juke box, newspapers, bluesy, jazz CDs for sale. Friendly, relaxed. Loyal clientele. Mon-Sat 10am-5pm.

1355 6/T19
£
Bonobo Café Aberdeen · www.bonobotribe.co.uk · 01224 636777 A true workers' co-operative purveying **only vegan** food to a committed and growing following. Breakfast (not Mon) and lunch. Unique dishes and replicates, for example, the full Scottish breakfast and the maccy cheese. Small downstairs counter, café room upstairs, and Aberdeen's best roof-terrace garden, which was built from scratch – a tranquil spot, the ingredients are to hand. Website for hours.

The Best Vegetarian-Friendly Places

Excludes Edinburgh and Glasgow.

NORTH

The Ceilidh Place Ullapool Report: 1053/HIGHLANDS.
Café One Inverness Report: 1113/INVERNESS.
The Three Chimneys Colbost, Skye Report: 2296/SKYE.
Café Arriba Portree, Skye Report: 2302/SKYE.
Mountain Café Aviemore Report: 1097/HIGHLANDS.
Riverside Bistro Lochinver Report: 1105/HIGHLANDS.
Old Pines nr Spean Bridge Report: 1063/HIGHLANDS.
The Smiddy House Spean Bridge Report: 1094/HIGHLANDS.
Buchanan's Banchory Report: 993/NE RESTAURANTS.

ARGYLL & THE ISLES

St Columba Hotel Iona Report: 2353/MULL.
Inver Restaurant Strathlachlan, Loch Fyne Report: 736/ARGYLL.
The Green Welly Stop Tyndrum Report: 1418/TEAROOMS.
Kilmartin House Café Kilmartin, nr Lochgilphead Report: 1414/TEAROOMS.
Kerrera Tea Garden Isle of Kerrera Report: 753/OBAN.

CENTRAL

Monachyle Mhor nr Balquhidder Report: 1220/GET-AWAY HOTELS.
Mhor 84 nr Balquhidder Report: 796/CENTRAL.
Jute at Dundee Contemporary Arts Dundee Report: 946/DUNDEE.
The Parlour Dundee Report: 958/DUNDEE.
Jam Jar Bridge of Allan Report: 802/CENTRAL.
The Hideaway Bridge of Allan Report: 813/STIRLING.
Pillars of Hercules nr Falkland Report: 1424/TEAROOMS.
Ostler's Close Cupar Report: 885/FIFE.
The Vine Leaf St Andrews Report: 895/ST ANDREWS.
The Riverside Dunblane Report: 1346/FOOD PUBS.

SOUTH

Osso Peebles Report: 838/BORDERS.
Whitmuir, the Organic Place Lamancha, nr Peebles Report: 842/BORDERS.
Saffy's Ayr Report: 770/AYR.
Thomas Tosh Thornhill Report: 2216/SHOPS.
Woodside nr Ancrum Report: 1452/TEAROOMS.
Damascus Drum Hawick Report: 843/BORDERS.

The Best Seafood Restaurants

1356 4/P12
LL
NC500
££

✓✓ **Captain's Galley and Scrabster Seafood Bar** Scrabster · www.captainsgalley.co.uk · 01847 894999 In the Galley there is a very firm and sure hand on the tiller. This is the place to eat on the N coast, a reputation built on total integrity and with a conservation, sustainability and slow-food ethos throughout. Chef/proprietor Jim Cowie and his missus Mary know exactly where everything comes from: salad from their polytunnel and daily-landed fish from the boat *The Deeside* – it's berthed over there. Last time, I saw it going out and what it brought in (on ice in Jim's van). Menu short (usually 4/4/4 choices or you can push the boat out with intermediates). Closed Mon-Wed. And opened 2018 on the side, a wee conservatory café/bar (www.scrabsterseafoodbar.co.uk; 07470 004625), with same ethos but even simpler: mussels, fish 'n' chips, crab. Open daytime. 'From sea to plate' never got truer than this. Japanese folk come here from afar for Jim's sashimi. Seafood Bar daytime only, closed Mon/Tue.

1357 8/R24
££

✓✓ **East Pier** East Shore, St Monans · www.eastpier.co.uk · 01333 405030 James Robb's converted shed by the slipway in sleepy St Monans, where East Neuk shellfish (some smoked on the premises) is served box-fresh upstairs in the café or out on the roof overlooking the ever-changing sea. Easter and Apr-Oct: Wed-Sun. Real plates; great little wine list. Fortunate for Fife that James and Kilp have fetched up on this shore.

1358 7/G22
L
££

✓✓ **Café Fish** Tobermory, Mull · www.thecafefish.com · 01688 301253 The upstairs café/restaurant on the corner of the famously picturesque bay, one of the best and least assuming in the land. Here, seafood really does come straight off the boat (*The Highland*) and into the tiny kitchen. Absurdly good value; laid-back, sympatico service. Definitely best to book. Report: 2354/MULL.

1359 5/F17
LL
ATMOS
£££

✓✓ **Lochbay Restaurant** Stein, Skye · www.lochbay-restaurant.co.uk · 01470 592235 12km N Dunvegan; A850 to Portree, B886 Waternish peninsula coastal route. A scenic Skye drive leads you to this small cottage at end of the village row, where Michelin-starred chef Michael Smith and an incredibly small team and spinning three plates at once produce mouth-watering pure and simple seafood with no bother or pretence. There are chips and clootie dumpling. Make an intimate date with good food. Mar-Dec. See website for days and times.

1360 4/K15
NC500
£

✓✓ **Seafood Shack** Ullapool · www.seafoodshack.co.uk · 07876 142623/07596 722846 In an open courtyard space behind the ferry car park, Kirsty and Fenella's seasonal pop-up seafood caravan/shack, winner of awards, a destination diner. Menu changes daily depending on what's landed from yon sea. Graze at the wooden spool tables and come back for more. Apr-Oct. 7 days noon-6pm (till 8pm summer).

1361 7/J21
L
MID-MAR-OCT
££

✓✓ **Lochleven Seafood Café** North Ballachulish · www.lochlevenseafoodcafe.co.uk · 01855 821048 Leave the A82 at N Ballachulish, 15km S of Fort William, then 7km on B863 down the side of gentle Loch Leven to the Grieve family's shellfish tankery, shop and bright, airy restaurant. A la carte of scallops, mussels, clams, lobster, crab from their 3 boats (and they export internationally); specials on the board. Katie Macfarlane in the kitchen. Excellent wine list. Best food in the area. No chips are served!

1362 5/F18
£

✓ **The Oyster Shed** Carbost, Skye · 01478 640383 Find the Talisker Distillery, the shed (and it really is a shed) is behind it, well signed. From an oyster farm in Loch Harport, established 1981, Paul McGlynn has created a pop-up style seafood takeaway and eaterie; a seafood destination and the whole foodie experience in season, with daily specials and local and home-made pâtés, smoked food, etc. AYR. Daytime only. See also 2300/SKYE.

1363 7/K27
L
££

✓ **MacCallums of Troon Oyster Bar** Troon · www.maccallumsoftroon.co.uk · 01292 319339 On the quayside 3km from centre. Follow signs for ferry, past the woodpiles and fish market. Red-brick building with discreet sign, so eyes peeled. MacCallums here on their home quay, in the back, where langoustines lurk. Lovely fish (big on oysters and catch of the day), great atmos, unpretentious. They keep it admirably simple. Wed-Sun lunch & Wed-Sat dinner. John's adjacent fish 'n' chip shop is the best in the west (1382/FISH & CHIPS).

1364 4/J15
££

✓ **Salt Seafood Kitchen** Achiltibuie · www.saltseafood.com · 01854 622380 On the long road that follows the Achiltibuie shoreline (actually you're in Polglass), a seafood cabin and deck that's built a big rep hereabouts in a short time. Seasonal (Apr-Oct) and seasonal in what they serve. Phone ahead for evening reservations. Closed Sun/Mon.

1365 8/R25
L
£

✓ **Lobster Shack** North Berwick · www.lobstershack.co.uk · 07910 620480 It is a shack, it is on the quayside; takeaway and outside tables, by the people with **Nether Abbey** (853/LOTHIANS). Box-fresh, wok-fresh. Lobster and the like. Day-tripping Edinburgers love it. Jun-Sep.

1366 8/R23
LL
££

✓ **The Seafood Ristorante** St Andrews · www.theseafoodristorante.com · 01334 479475 In a landmark position overlooking the Old Course and bay, this glass-walled pavilion is a top spot in the town and for a sunset supper. Italianised under the Pieraccinis, there's home-made pasta with their fresher-than-fresh fish – their dedicated boat lands lobster, crab and mackerel. Scallops dived for every day. Great wines, their own beers, nice puds but mainly fish, pure and simple (usually 1 meat option). 7 days lunch & dinner.

1367 7/H23
£

✓ **The Green Shack @ The Port** Calmac Pier, Oban Yep, a green shack (aka Oban Seafood Hut) at the port where the ferry comes in, in Scotland's 'Seafood Capital'. Daytime only. See 749/OBAN.

1368 8/R24
L
££

✓ **Craig Millar @ 16 West End** St Monans · www.16westend.com · 01333 730327 Title sounds like a cosmopolitan upmarket bistro in a city somewhere but this is a street up from the harbour in a quiet East Neuk Village. It is smart, though, and a destination dinner. Conservatory and terrace overlooks sea, waves lap, gulls mew, etc. Superb, out-of-the-way setting. Chef/proprietor Craig Millar rattles the pans. Seasonal menu; lunch Wed-Sun & dinner Wed-Sat. Savoury soufflés and the panna cotta: creative cookery. Complementing East Pier (above), St Monans is seafood central.

1369 7/H23
L
££

✓ **Ee-Usk** Oban · www.eeusk.com · 01631 565666 Landmark new-build on the N pier by the hospitable Macleods (adjacent to Italian restaurant in a similar building which they also run – the Piazza). A full-on seafront caff with urban-bistro feel, great views and fish from that sea. Goes like a ferry; deft service. Good wee wine list. 7 days lunch & dinner.

1370 8/S20
LL
££

✓ **The Tolbooth** Stonehaven · www.tolbooth-restaurant.co.uk · 01569 762287 On a corner of the harbour, long one of the best restaurants in the area, in a great setting (reputedly the oldest building in town) under chef Tyron Ellul. Upstairs bistro, a light room with windows overlooking the beach. Harbour no longer landing much fish but fishermen from here and Gourdon do supply crab, langoustine, great lobster and the odd halibut. In summer, this sea still hoaches with mackerel. Fresh, simple and decent value. Closed Mon.

1371 7/K23 ✓ **Loch Fyne Oysters** Loch Fyne · www.lochfyne.com · 01499 600482 On
££ A83, the Loch Lomond to Inveraray road, 20km Inveraray/11km Rest and Be Thankful. Landmark roadside restaurant and all-round seafood experience on the way out west. Though Loch Fyne Seafood is a huge UK chain, this in 1978 was home to the original aquaculture (and is not actually in the chain after a management buy-out). People come from afar for the oysters and the smokery fare, especially the kippers. Spacious and with many banquettes though somewhat refectory-ish! Well-chosen wine and whisky. Same menu all day. Shop sells every conceivable packaging of salmon and other Scots produce. Loch Fyne often pop up at festivals and events. Daytime only (till early evening in summer).

1372 7/J22 ✓ **The Pierhouse Hotel** Port Appin · www.pierhousehotel.co.uk ·
LL 01631 730302 At the end of the minor road and 3km from the A828 Oban–
££ Fort William road in Port Appin village, right by the tiny pier where the passenger ferry leaves for Lismore; the setting is everything. A hotel and restaurant with bar. Ingredients from local suppliers: oysters, mussels, crab. The Cullen skink and the platters! Lively atmos, wine and the view of the island. Report: 1215/INNS.

1373 7/J26 ✓ **The Seafood Cabin** Skipness · www.skipnessseafoodcabin.co.uk ·
LL 01880 760207 Adjacent Skipness Castle, signed from Claonaig where the
£ CalMac ferry from Lochranza arrives. Sophie James's famous wee cabin with outdoor seating and indoor options in perfect spot for their fresh and local seafood, snacks and cakes. Mussels come a little further (Loch Etive). Smoked stuff from the estate. Jun-Sep 11am-7pm. Closed Sat.

1374 7/K26 **The Catch @ Fins** Fairlie, nr Largs · www.fencebay.co.uk · 01475 568989
££ On main A78 south of Fairlie, a seafood bistro and smokery, and probably the best place to eat for miles in either direction. Simple, straightforward good cookin' (with head chef Richard Finlay), the wine list similarly to the point. Nice conservatory; and geraniums. Thu-Sun lunch & Thu-Sat dinner. Farmers' market here last Sunday of the month.

1375 9/J30 **Campbell's** Portpatrick · www.campbellsrestaurant.co.uk · 01776 810314
££ Friendly harbourside restaurant in much visited Portpatrick. Some meat dishes, but mainly seafood. Every day their own boat brings back crab and lobster (and sea bass and pollock). Tue-Sun lunch & dinner. Closed Jan & Mon.

1376 7/J21 **Crannog Restaurant** Fort William · www.crannog.net · 01397 705589
L Long-established landmark and destination restaurant. Nice, bright contemporary
££ setting, not only good seafood but also a real sense of place in this rainy town. They do cruises from adjacent pier. 7 days lunch & dinner.

1377 4/K13 **Shorehouse Restaurant** Tarbet, nr Scourie · www.shorehousetarbet.co.uk
DF · 01971 502251 Charming conservatory restaurant on cove where boats leave for
LL **Handa Island** reserve (1773/BIRDS). Julian catches your seafood from his boat
££ and Jackie cooks it; they have the Rick Stein seal of approval. Home-made puds. Located at end of beautiful unclassified road off the A894 between Laxford Bridge and Scourie (5km); best phone to check openings. Apr-Sep: Mon-Sat noon-7pm. Closed Sun.

1378 5/H18
MAR–NOV
NC500
££

Kishorn Seafood Bar Kishorn · www.kishornseafoodbar.co.uk ·
01520 733240 Conveniently located and long-established on A896 at Kishorn, on the road between Lochcarron and Shieldaig, near the road over the hill to Applecross (1677/SCENIC ROUTES). Fresh local seafood in a roadside diner: Kishorn oysters, hand-dived scallops, squat lobsters. Applecross crab; lobsters live in a tank out back. Light and bright. Lucy Kerr, the good fishwife. Daytime and supper weekends in summer. Busy, so book.

✓✓ **Applecross Inn Applecross** At the end of the road. Seafood and classic fish 'n' chips. Report: 1229/GET-AWAY HOTELS.

✓ **The Silver Darling Aberdeen** On the harbour in an ethereal location. Best in the NE. Report: 1008/ABERDEEN.

The Best Fish & Chip Shops

For Edinburgh listings see p. 50; for Glasgow see p. 105–6.

1379 8/S20 ✓✓ **The Bay Stonehaven · www.thebayfishandchips.co.uk ·**
01569 762000 On the prom towards the pool (2138/OPEN-AIR POOLS), just look for the queue almost always there. They really do come from miles away (and to Aunty Betty's next door 1497/ICE CREAM). All is cooked to order. You wait and walk on the front – perfect! The Bay wins many awards. 7 days noon–10pm.

1380 7/H23 ✓✓ **Fish & Chips in Oban** Oban has declared itself the 'Seafood Capital of Scotland', with good seafood restaurants but also these 4 great chip shops. All are in George St near the bay, with sit-in caffs adjacent. **Nories** at 86 has been here over 50 years. They are uncompromising about the lard but they do great F&C (noon–10.30pm). They've recently opened a shiny newcomer, the **Oban Bay Fish Bar** at 34, right on the bay itself; same deal and lard again but a bigger caff (11.30am–9.30pm). **Oban Fish & Chip Shop** is the fancy newcomer at 116 with coley, hake and home-made fishcakes, along with sustainable haddock and cod. They do use vegetable oil (11.30am–11pm). A poll of Obanites and the longer queues suggest this is *the* top takeaway. The **George Street Fish & Chip Shop** (number 15) behind the Caledonian Hotel is bright and fresh, with the smartest sit-in. They use beef dripping and keep the menu small (it's for sale at TGP). 7 days 10.30am–11pm. Wherever you go, Oban's waterfront is the perfect place to scoff 'em.

1381 8/Q25 ✓✓ **Alandas Prestonpans · www.alandas.co.uk · 01875 815999** Here almost 30 years and I'd have to admit I didn't notice and only became a big fan of Alandas when they came as a pop-up to George Sq, Edinburgh, during the Fringe – and became the best F&C in the city. Never mind the dozens of other temporary takeaways in this heart of the Fringe quarter, Alandas is simply the best for festival food on the go. In Prestonpans there's also pizza. 7 days 4–10pm. Alandas supreme ice cream in North Berwick (1496/ICE CREAM).

1382 7/K27
L

✓✓ **The Wee Hurrie Troon · www.maccallumsoftroon.co.uk ·**
01292 319340 Famed, fabulous and stripped-down, on Troon harbour with its boats, the Wee Hurrie is part of MacCallums oyster and fish restaurant (see 1363/SEAFOOD for directions because it's a fair walk from the town centre). Big range of fresh daily fish. Light tempuras. Tue-Sun noon-8pm (9pm Fri/Sat). Best in the west. You smell the sea.

1383 8/Q24
& 8/R24 ✓ **Fish & Chips in Fife** Apart from the estimable **Valente's** in Kirkcaldy, the much vaunted **Anstruther Fish Bar** (in the Lard section; see below), and **The Tailend** and **Cromars** in St Andrews (898/899/ST ANDREWS), Fife has other less celebrated but damned good fish 'n' chip shops. The better-kept secret is the **Pittenweem Fish & Chip Bar**, a door in the wall at the end of the High St next to the clock tower. Resolutely old style. 6-10pm. Closed Mon.

1384 8/Q23 ✓ **The Silvery Tay** Newport-on-Tay · 01382 540300 54 High St, on the corner. Legendary in the locale since 1978. What would Newport do without it? Join the queue. 7 days 4.30-10pm.

1385 7/K26 ✓ **The Fish Works** Largs · www.thefishworks.co.uk · 01475 674111 On the prom by the Cumbrae ferry in a town of much ice cream and F&C, this is the best of the latter and the batter. It wins awards and the local consensus. 7 days noon-9pm.

1386 7/J26 ✓ **West End Café** Rothesay, Bute · www.westendcafebute.co.uk · 01700 503596 Remains a Rothesay must-do and always a queue. Huge range of fry-ups and fresh pizza. Haddock fish supper, as always, best! 7 days. Till 2am Fri/Sat.

1387 6/T19
& 6/P17
6/S19 &
6/T18
6/R20 &
8/R21 ✓ **The Ashvale** Aberdeen, Elgin, Inverurie, Ellon, Banchory, Brechin · www.theashvale.co.uk Original restaurant (1979) in Aberdeen at 42-48 Great Western Rd (always rammed); 3 other city branches. Restaurant/takeaway à la Harry Ramsden (stuck to dripping for long enough but changed to vegetable oil in '09). Various sizes of haddock, sole, plaice. Home-made stovies, etc, all served fresh so you do wait. From noon but hours vary. The Ashvale is an institution.

1388 4/K16
NC500 **Deli-Ca-Sea** Ullapool · www.delicasea.co.uk · 01854 612141 By many accounts, the best F&C in the NW is here on Shore St at the amusingly named Deli-Ca-Sea. Owned by the local fish merchant, the fish is flapping all the way to the fryer. Choose your haddock or cod, but line-caught and sustainable fish also available. Rapeseed oil. Note the hours: noon-2pm and 4-8pm.

1389 5/N19 **Harkai's** Aviemore · www.harkai.co.uk · 01479 810430 On main street at S end as you come in from A9. Aka **The Happy Haggis**. Here for decades with a big local reputation. A long way from the sea but this a chipper (and café) that takes itself seriously (although no obvious sustainable fish policy, local sourcing or any of that malarkey). 7 days till 9pm.

1390 9/N29 **Balmoral** Dumfries · 01387 252583 Seems as old and essential as the Bard himself (actually 100 years!). Adjacent is the equally legendary **Bruno's** (790/SW RESTAURANTS) Italian restaurant (same family). Using rapeseed oil, it's the best chip in the south. Out the Annan road heading E, 1km from centre.

1391 7/G22
L **The Fish & Chip Van aka The Fishermen's Pier** Tobermory, Mull · www.tobermoryfishandchipvan.co.uk By the clock on Fisherman's Pier, this van has almost achieved destination-restaurant status. Always a queue. Fresh and al fresco. Summer 12.30-9pm. Closed Sun in winter.

AND THESE THAT STICK TO LARD:

1392 8/Q24 ✓✓ **Valente's** Kirkcaldy · www.valentes.co.uk Ask directions or satnav to this superb chippie in E of town; worth the detour and the queue when you get there. They also make ice cream. At 73 Hendry Rd (01592 203600) and also at 73 Overton Rd (01592 651991). Both closed Wed.

1393 6/T18 ✓ **The Dolphin Café** Peterhead · www.dolphincafe.co.uk · 01779 478595
By the harbour, where the fish come from, so you don't get closer to the source than this. Serving the fishermen (from yon time), as well as us; it's a community thing. The cold North Sea outside (no, we wouldn't want to go there). 4.45am-7pm. Closed Sun.

1394 6/T19 ✓ **Herdy's Dolphin Fish & Chips** Aberdeen · 01224 644555 Despite the pre-eminence of the Ashvale in Aberdeen, many swear by this small, always busy chippie just off Union St. Stave off your hangover. Till 1am (4am Fri/Sat).

1395 8/R22 ✓ **Peppo's Harbour Chip Bar** Arbroath · 01241 872373 By the harbour where those fish come in. Fresh as that and chips in dripping. Peppo was here in 1951; John and Frank Orsi carry on the family tradition of feeding the hordes. Closed Mon/Tue.

1396 8/Q24 ✓ **The Anstruther Fish Bar** Anstruther · www.anstrutherfishbar.co.uk · 01592 261215 On the front (1613/VILLAGES). Often listed as the best F&C in Scotland/UK/Universe and the continuous queue suggests that either: a) we want to believe that; or b) they may be right. Sit in (paper plates) or walk round the harbour and decide for yourself. There's also the ice cream. 7 days 11.30am- 10pm.

1397 8/T26 ✓ **Giacopazzi's** Eyemouth · www.giacopazzis.co.uk · 01890 750317 By the big wooden boat in this real working harbour. A caff and takeaway with the catch on its doorstep. For nigh on 120 years, the home of the now oft-cited Eyemouth-landed haddock and their award-winning ice cream. Takeaways eaten on boat-filled harbour, probably attended by scary gulls. 7 days 9am-8pm (till 9pm Fri/Sat). Upstairs to flashier **Oblò's Bistro** (01890 752527), a bar, restaurant and deli. 7 days.

1398 8/R25 **North Berwick Fry** North Berwick · 01620 893246 At the E end of town. As they say, 'it's East Lothian's original fish bar' (about 50 years). Old style, hard-working family business, no reason to change the format or the flow. Take to harbour or the garden overby, or sit in. 7 days, 11am-11pm, they fry.

1399 8/Q27 **Jim Jacks** Peebles · 01721 721497 Off main street. Here a while, hereabouts, Jim Jacks is the one. Sit in adjacent and small front shop, you probably queue. All the usuals, chips with cheese, gravy, curry sauce. No question of the beef dripping.

Great Cafés

For Edinburgh listings, see p. 62-4; for Glasgow, see p. 110-11.

1400 7/K23 ✓✓ **The Real Food Café** Tyndrum · www.therealfoodcafe.com · 01838 400235 On the main A82 just before the junction Oban/Fort William. May initially appear to be a chip shop but this is Real good food for the road, conscientiously prepared and seriously sourced. Fish 'n' chips probably best but burgers, breakfasts – all home-made. Vegware sustainable plates. Lounge with wood-burning stove. Birds to watch. Café, takeaway and newer coffee, cake and sandwich stop. 7 days 7.30am-8/9pm.

1401 5/M18 ✓✓ **Girvans** Inverness · www.girvansrestaurant.co.uk · 01463 711900 A different proposition to the Castle (below), more of the moment – more perhaps a restaurant, but the atmos is of a good, unpretentious caff serving everything from omelettes to full-blown comfort meals. Great all-day Sunday breakfast. Tempting cream-laden cakes. Always busy but no need to book. I never go to Inverness without coming here. 7 days.

1402 5/G19 ✓ **The Blue Shed** Torrin, Skye · www.theBlueShedCafe.co.uk · 01471 822847 8km from Broadford, down the sublime single-track road (depending on campervans) to Elgol, this blue shed owned by the John Muir Trust is where the Davies's share their home cooking and the most spectacular view of Blà Bheinn (2020/MUNROS) and Loch Salpin with you while you travel through. Mar-Oct. 7 days noon-5pm.

1403 4/L12 ✓ **The Café @ Balnakeil** Balnakeil Craft Village · 01971 511473 Somewhere
NC500 among the craft studios and workshops at Balnakeil, 2km W of Durness. At last a decent place to eat in the far NW corner; home-made, imaginative, on trend. Bagels, soups, sandwiches and at night a 4/4/4/ menu with vegetarian and fish options. Simple set-up. BYOB. LO 8.30pm. Closed Mon.

1404 5/M18 ✓ **Castle Restaurant** Inverness · 01463 230925 On road that winds up to the castle from the main street, near the tourist office and the hostels. No pandering to tourists here, but this great caff has been serving chips (home-made from local potatoes) with everything for over 40 years. Pork chops, perfect fried eggs, prawn cocktail to crumbles. They work damned hard (Rab's in at 2am – can this be right? – to start the prep). In Inverness or anywhere nearby, you'll be pushed to find better-value grub than this (but see below). New owners, the MacKinnons, but all is well – no change. 10am-8.15pm (Sun 11am-4pm).

1405 8/N24 ✓ **Allan Water Café** Bridge of Allan · www.allanwatercafe.co.uk · 01786 833060 The main street, beside the eponymous bridge. Worth coming over from Stirling (8km) for a takeaway or a seat in the caff (a steel-and-glass extension somewhat lacking in charm but not in buzz) for great fish 'n' chips and the ice cream (1500/ICE CREAM). Practically an institution. 7 days 8am-8.30pm.

1406 7/K26 ✓ **The Ritz Café** Millport · 01475 530459 See Millport, see the Ritz. Since
L 1906 (though pure 1960s) and now new owners, after 4 generations of the
ATMOS same family, the largely unchanged café on the Clyde. A short ferry journey away (from Largs, continuous; then 6km), an essential part of any visit to this part of the coast, and Millport is not entirely without charm. Toasties, rolls, the famous hot peas. Excellent ice cream (especially with melted marshmallow). Something of 'things past'. 7 days 10am-9pm (in season). The **Round Island Café**, same main street, has a 'no fry' policy and outside tables.

1407 7/J26 ✓ **Ettrick Bay Café** Bute · 01700 500223 End of the road from Port
L Bannatyne near Rothesay. In the middle of the bay and the beach looking over to Arran/Kintyre – this is the caff with the view. Here forever, a family fixture from seaside days gone by. Honest, home-made, 'North American' menu (owner is Canadian), including their famous chowder at weekends and Alec's rather large cakes. 7 days 10am-5pm. Cash only.

1408 8/Q23 **KitschnBake** Newport-on-Tay · 01382 542704 Mary-Jane Duncan's very personal home baking and cooking café across the road from the Tay and the bridge from Dundee. Always busy with all kinds of folk. Kinda kitschy but awfy good. 7 days 8.30am-4.30pm (Sun from 10am).

Rockpool Cullen Top on the Moray Coast. Report: 992/NE RESTAURANTS.

The Best Tearooms & Coffee Shops

For Edinburgh listings, see p. 59-62; for Glasgow, see p. 108-9.

ARGYLL & THE ISLES

1409 7/G22
EASTER-OCT

✓✓ **Glengorm Farm Coffee Shop** nr Tobermory, Mull · www. glengormcastle.co.uk · **01688 302321** First right on Tobermory–Dervaig road (7km). Organic food served in well-refurbished stable block. Soups, cakes, staples (maccy cheese, steak pie), specials and delicious salads from their famous garden (they supply other Mull restaurants). All you need after a walk in the grounds of this great estate (2347/MULL; 2249/ISLAND WALKS) ... and the *best* cappuccino on Mull. 7 days.

1410 7/G22

✓ **The Glass Barn at Sgriob-Ruadh Farm** nr Tobermory, Mull · www. isleofmullcheese.co.uk · **01688 302627** On the road to Dervaig 2km from town, a boho barn at the heart of the farmyard-smelling farm and dairy, where they turn thousands of litres of milk into the famous Mull cheddar. Hard to be precise about what's on offer here or when, but drop by for something unique and authentic, even on your way to/from Glengorm (above). See 1530/CHEESES.

1411 7/K25

✓ **Riverhill Courtyard Restaurant & Bar** Helensburgh · **01436 676730** By no means a simple tearoom but a 'courtyard' restaurant. It does Helensburgh proud. In a converted boxing gym, a great place to eat, drink and hang out. All-day menus and lunch till 6pm. Steak frites, maccy cheese. Also proper evening dining. Great room, great formula. 7 days.

1412 7/J24

✓ **Brambles** Inveraray · www.inverarayhotel.com · **01499 302252** A busy, gorgeous, unpretentious tearoom there where you want it, in the main street of Argyll's historic town on Loch Fyne. Home baking, 'butties', light meals; friendly locals hang out here. 7 days, daytime only.

1413 7/H27

✓ **Glenbarr** Glenbarr, south of Tarbert · www.glenbarrstores.com · **01583 421200** Halfway down the peninsula, 16km N of Campbeltown. A letter from a reader (thank you, Heather Paterson) sent me to this garden centre/ village stores/post office and tearoom in Glenbarr, just off the main A83 from Tarbert. An extraordinary local provisioner with great Kintyre supplier list for all home-made food in café and in the garden's tended rows. Lots of good things to buy, things you need. Discreetly, uniquely here on its own. 7 days, daytime only.

1414 7/H24
MAR-DEC

✓ **Kilmartin House Café** Kilmartin, nr Lochgilphead · www.kilmartin.org · **01546 510278** Attached to early peoples' museum (2172/HISTORY) in Kilmartin Glen and on main road N of Lochgilphead. Worth swinging in here from road or glen walk for home-made, conscientiously prepared light food. Down steps to bright conservatory with pastoral outlook. Organic garden produce. Good vegetarian choices and creative cooking. 7 days. Hot food till 3pm, cakes till 5pm. Closing for extensive refurbishment Sep '19 to 2021.

1415 3/E14
L

✓ **Loch Croistean Coffee Shop** nr Uig, Lewis · **01851 672772** Further W than all the rest but a great road c/o the EC (30 mins from Stornoway by A8110), Marianne Campbell's homely oasis in an unforgiving landscape. She works hard but keeps it simple. Further on, the amazing beaches and the sunset; here, home-made, lovely food (the soda bread and the stovies). Noon-8pm. Closed Sun/Mon.

1416 7/H24
LL
Crinan Coffee Shop Crinan · www.crinanhotel.com · 01546 830261 Run by the hotel people (724/ARGYLL) in this fascinating village for yachties and anyone with time to while away. The café overlooks canal basin with boats always going through. Excellent cakes, bread and scones. Easter-Oct daytime only.

1417 7/H24
Crafty Kitchen Ardfern · 01852 500303 Down the Ardfern B8002 road (4km) from A816 Oban–Lochgilphead road, the classier yachty haven of the Craignish peninsula. More kitchen craft than crafty craft: great home-made cakes and special hot dishes emerge, along with superior salads. Tue-Sun daytime only. Weekends only Nov/Dec. Closed Jan-Mar.

CENTRAL

1418 7/K23
L
✓✓ **The Green Welly Stop** Tyndrum · www.thegreenwellystop.co.uk · 01838 400271 On A82, a strategically placed natural pit stop and all-round super services on the drive to Oban or Fort William (just before the road divides), with a Scottish produce shop, a gas station, a snack stop which does pizzas, and a self-service restaurant: great home-made comfort food prepared to order, excellent cakes and puds, fresh OJ and fast, friendly service. Shops stuffed with every kind of Scottishness. Opening hours vary.

1419 8/N22
✓✓ **The Watermill** Aberfeldy · www.aberfeldywatermill.com · 01887 822896 Off Main St direction Kenmore near the **Birks** (2069/WALKS). Downstairs caff on riverside in a conserved mill. Much more than this, though: the top independent bookshop in the Highlands, a remarkable art gallery upstairs, with Scottish artists and photographers, and international print work for sale, and **Homer**, a selective, always interesting home and garden shop both upstairs and on Aberfeldy's main street (they have opened another Homer in Howe St, Edinburgh). Waiter service in busy caff with inside and terrace seating. Soups, quiches, home baking. 10am-5pm (Sun from 11am). Signed from all over. The Watermill still at the heart of the Aberfeldy revival!

1420 8/Q27
✓✓ **Garden Café at Traquair** Traquair House · www.traquair.co.uk · 01896 830777 The grounds around historic Traquair House (1874/HOUSES) are one of the great escapes of the central Borders – walks, events, cycling. The Garden Café, made great again by Mary Shields and David Shearer, is where to refresh and reboot (and boots are welcome). Hot and cold dishes, top baking (many cakes), Glen Lyon coffee, sheltered garden, Mary's polytunnel. Closed Dec-Mar. 7 days till 5pm.

1421 8/P23
✓✓ **Effie's** Perth · 01738 634770 Unobtrusive online (no website) and on the street but this is the best kind of a 'traditional' tearoom (hence 2 ticks). All home-made and to order: maccy cheese (same recipe for 22 years), mince & tatties, stovies, great scones and cakes, signature cheesy 'Dutch' eggs. Lovely and twee, meticulously managed (proprietor George Sinclair), and his mum, the remarkable 'Effie', ever making the old-style puds (roly-poly, rice puddin') and the ice cream. May have to book. The best carrot cake! 7 days 9.30am-5.30pm.

1422 7/L25
& 8/L25
✓ **Three Sisters Bake** Quarrier's Village, nr Bridge of Weir & Killearn · www.threesistersbake.co.uk · 0333 3447344 The original in the truly remarkable and always uplifting Quarrier's Village (quarriers.org.uk) and in the village hall in Killearn; both villages great to walk in/around. The sisters Gillian, Nichola and Linsey are all involved in the purveying of lovely food from 'brekkie' to tea. Quiche, tartlets, soda bread sandwiches. Both 7 days, daytime only.

1423 8/M24 ✓ **Buttercup Café** Doune · www.buttercupcafe.co.uk · 01786 842511
Great wee-town tearoom in Doune main street, where home-made means home-made. From the best breakfast hereabouts through hot and salad lunches to afternoon tea, this is worth the short detour from the A84 Callander–Stirling road. 7 days 9am-4pm (5pm Sat).

1424 8/P24 ✓ **Pillars of Hercules** nr Falkland · www.pillars.co.uk · 01337 857749
Rambling, rustic tearoom on organic farm on A912 2km from village towards Strathmiglo and the M90. Excellent, homely place and fare; and ethical. Home-made cakes, soup, hot dishes, etc. They also have a bothy and you can camp. See also 1517/FARM SHOPS. Very wholefoodie ambience. 7 days.

1425 7/L21 ✓ **Rannoch Station Tearoom** www.rannochstationtearoom.co.uk ·
DF   01882 633247 Probably the remotest tearoom in Scotland, at the end of the B846, an hour from Pitlochry but also on the West Highland Line from Glasgow Queen Street to Mallaig. The cosy **Moor of Rannoch Hotel** is 200m away (1224/ GET-AWAY HOTELS). Open for breakfast, lunch and afternoon tea; top cakes. It can honestly claim to be a wee gem. Apr-Oct. Closed Fri.

1426 8/N22 ✓ **Legends & The Highland Chocolatier** Grandtully · www. highlandchocolatier.com · 01887 840775 Main street of village on the Tay, where the river's as busy with rafters as the road is with traffic. Gifts and, in the now crowded chocolate-making world, Iain Burnett's famously good artisan and recognisable celestial chocolates, in their butter paper surface graphics. Through the back, a loungey tearoom for light snacks, home-made stuff, great tea list and, of course, hot chocolate with double chocolate cake. 7 days 10am-5pm.

1427 8/P22 ✓ **Spill the Beans** Dunkeld · 01350 728111 A great wee tearoom on the road to the Cathedral just where you need it in this town so good to wander. Fiona MacPhail gets it right with her mega-cakes (her signature apple and cinnamon meringue!), soups, sandwiches and stovies. Some outside tables. You will need to walk this lot off! Nice, easy 8km loop from corner of the kirkyard (signed). Closed Wed.

1428 8/N22 ✓ **Habitat Café** Aberfeldy · www.habitatcafe.co.uk · 01887 822944 Right on the square in downtown Aberfeldy, the non-compromising Mike Haggerton's paean to coffee and the best cup in the shire (there have been awards). Hot food and snacks and an A for Ambience. Daytime only.

1429 8/R23 ✓ **Taste** St Andrews · 01334 477959 It's a Facebook world here – the best coffee and the best coffee hangout in a student town with a lot of competition. Few seats, many laptops and pads. Always a queue. Go taste why!

1430 8/R24 **The Cocoa Tree Shop & Café** Pittenweem · www.pittenweemchocolate.
DF   co.uk · 01333 312682 Near end of the high street, a chocolate emporium and through the back a busy tea/coffee/choc room with hot snacks, soups, crêpes, cakes and, naturally, hot choco. The wood stove infuses the room with the warm aroma of cinnamon AYR. An excellent brownie! 7 days, daytime only.

1431 8/R24 **Crail Harbour Tearoom** Crail · www.crailharbourgallery.co.uk ·
01333 451896 In cute little Crail, a tearoom where you need it on the road going down to the harbour. Gallery with pics from 'an unnamed local artist'. Lovely, sheltered terrace overlooking the shore. Dressed crab from harbour, herring and dill, flaky salmon and cakes. Perfect! 7 days, daytime only. Closed Jan.

1432 8/Q24   **Campbell's** Falkland · www.campbellscoffeehouse.com · 01337 858738 At The Cross, i.e. the main square, in this, the most pleasant village in Fife, with its Palace (1814/CASTLES) and walks (2003/HILL WALKS). Busy caff with home baking, soup 'n' a sausage, a cuppa and a cake. 7 days 10am-5pm.

1433 8/R25   **Tyninghame Smithy** Tyninghame, nr East Linton · 01620 860581 Set back from the A198 through tiny East Lothian village near **Tyninghame Beach** (2km) and walk (441/BEACHES) also known as St Baldred's Cradle – it's where to go for tea and cake, soup or muffins after your walk. Mary Berry once liked their sponge, apparently. Cosy rooms and outside tables. Some gifts.

1434 8/P24   **The Powmill Milkbar** nr Kinross · 01577 840376 On A977 Kinross (on the M90, junction 6) to Kincardine Bridge road, a real milk bar and real slice of Scottish craic and cake. Apple pie, moist fly cemeteries, big meringues: an essential stop on any Sunday run hereabouts (but open every day). Hot meals, great old-style salads. Local girls! Good place to take kids. Unreconstructed nostalgia. Then: 2042/WALKS.

NORTH

1435 6/R20   ✓✓ **Finzean Tearoom** Finzean · www.finzean.com · 01330 850710 The tearoom and farm shop of the Finzean (pronounced 'Fing-in') Estate on back road between Aboyne and Banchory, a very worthwhile detour. Great food, great views. Report: 1514/FARM SHOPS. Mon-Sat 9am-5pm & Sun from 11am.

1436 5/M17   ✓ **Couper's Creek** Cromarty · www.sutorcreek.co.uk · 01381 600729 Not far (in this small, perfectly presented town) from Graham and Phoebe Fox's original home: the pizza and seafood restaurant **Sutor Creek** (1092/HIGHLANDS). This daytime coffee shop, which also sells great wee Highland gifts (brilliant cards!), does soups (the Cullen skink), salad and sandwiches really well. Enormous cakes you wouldn't want to slice into. Fab ice-cream concoctions. Cromarty great to visit for many reasons (1608/VILLAGES), this is one of them. Website for times.

1437 5/M20   ✓ **Laggan Coffee Shop** nr Laggan · www.potterybunkhouse.co.uk · 01528 544231 On A889 from Dalwhinnie on A9 that leads to A86, the road W to Spean Bridge and Kyle. Lovely Linda's road sign points you to this former pottery, craft shop and bunkhouse (1191/HOSTELS). Great home baking, scones, soup, sarnies and *the* most yummy cakes. Near great spot for forest walks and river swimming (1721/SWIMMING). Open AYR.

1438 6/S19   ✓ **Old Post Office Tearoom** Chapel of Garioch, nr Inverurie · 01467 681660 At the crossroads, so you can't miss it; focal point of the village, Christine Maude's simple fare: cakes, scones (all from local folk) soups and sandwiches. Tiny but tables in the garden. Bennachie is always over there! 10am-4pm. Closed Mon/Tue. AYR.

1439 6/S18   ✓ **Formantine's** Ellon · www.formartines.com · 01651 851123 I found this place (on recommendations) on the B9170 Oldmeldrum–Methlick road on the way to **Haddo** (1872/HOUSES). Clearly, it's a destination in itself, a custom-built café/restaurant and shop/deli with brunch/lunch all day. Lots of local, selective ingredients. Good service. Great for kids; there are walks round the lake. 7 days 9.30am-5.30pm.

1440 6/R20   ✓ **The Black-Faced Sheep** Aboyne · www.blackfacedsheep.co.uk · 01339 887311 Near main Royal Deeside road through Aboyne (A93) and Mark and Sylvi Ronson's excellent coffee shop/gift shop is well loved by locals (and regulars from all over) but is thankfully missed by the bus parties hurtling towards Balmoral. Home-baked breads and cakes. Light specials and good coffee. Their love affair with Italy means specially sourced and imported wines (excellent exclusive house red) and organic olive oil. 10am-5pm, Sun from 11am.

1441 6/N17 ✓ **Logie Steading** nr Forres · www.logie.co.uk · 01309 611733 S of town towards Grantown-on-Spey (A940) – 10km. Or from Carrbridge via B9007. See 2060/WALKS. In a lovely spot near the River Findhorn, a courtyard of fine things (2191/SCOTTISH SHOPS) and the de Oliveiras' **Olive Tree Tearoom** – home bakes, burgers, fishcakes, tartlets; sound local sourcing. Hot food till 3pm. Tables in the courtyard. All in, a vital place to visit. 7 days. Winter hours vary.

1442 4/M15 **Pier Café** Lairg · www.pier-cafe.co.uk · 01549 402971 On the lochside (Loch Shin) on the left of the main road N to Tongue – a grass bank and tiny pier. All gorgeous on a summer's day. Personally run by Catriona and Gregor; home-made (ice cream, chips, all the bakes) and well-sourced from Sutherland's larder. Welcome on the long haul north. Daytime and bistro dinner Fri/Sat. Closed Jan.

1443 5/J17 **Whistle Stop Café** Kinlochewe · 01445 760423 The bright green and yellow old
NC500 village hall at the end of the road through Glen Torridon, just before it meets the A832 to Inverness, where this caff has revived and delighted so many walkers and fellow travellers. Home-made, right-on, welcoming in summer and wood-burning stove in winter. New owners 2019.

1444 5/H16 **Bridge Cottage Café** Poolewe · 01445 781335 In village and near **Inverewe**
NC500 **Gardens** (1553/GARDENS), a cottage, right enough, with crafts/pictures upstairs and parlour teashop run by Spanish people, so not your usual Victoria sponge. Tortilla, rather than baked potatoes and good patisserie. Daytime only. Closed Sat.

1445 4/P14 **Forse of Nature** Latheron · www.forseofnature.com · 01593 741754 On
NC500 the A99 north from Helmsdale to Wick, now part of the NC500. Look for a sign on the road to the left at Latheron, 1km up a long straight drive to a big house (a guesthouse with 6 rooms), a craft gallery and a cool tearoom with home-made food, all a bit of a find. Lots from their garden; hens, pigs. 7 days in season, 10am-6pm.

1446 4/K14 **Secret Tea Garden and Candle Shop** Drumbeg · www.assyntaromas.co.uk In
NC500 Drumbeg but 50m off the amazing B869 road (1679/SCENIC ROUTES), a shack selling home-made soaps and candles and a beautiful wee tea garden out back, where 'mum & son' dispense tea, coffee and exotic cakes (rhubarb and rosehip when I was there). Books to read, fellow travellers to meet. Apr-Sep. Check website for times.

1447 7/J20 **Glenfinnan Dining Car** Glenfinnan · www.glenfinnanstationmuseum. co.uk · 01397 722295 Just off the A830, the Road to the Isles, at the station near the viaduct made famous by the Harry Potter films, an actual carriage with a tiny kitchen from which the Pritchards bring soups, snacks and home baking to your table. This train doesn't go anywhere but is a refreshment break on the 60/80-min viaduct and viewing point walk. Park near the monument (1957/CHARLIE) and do visit the church (1918/CHURCHES). May-Oct. 7 days.

1448 6/S20 **Raemoir Garden Centre** Banchory · www.raemoirgardencentre.co.uk · 01330 825059 On A980, the Deeside road through town, about 3km to a garden centre that has grown into a home-and-garden and lifestyle store. Self-service caff with salad bar, quiches, etc, and cream-laden cakes (though not mine) and beyond the packed emporium a restaurant with extensive menu and more cakes. Always packed; it's a phenomenon. 7 days.

1449 6/R20 **Spider on a Bicycle** Aboyne · www.spideronabicycle.com In Station Sq, off the main A93 through Aboyne, sisters Emma and Hollie Petrie's cool café in a station waiting room with mix 'n' match everything, including the menu. 'Handmade' food focusing on the local but global dishes. 7 days, daytime only.

1450 6/R20 **Platform 22** Torphins · 01339 882807 Torphins is a wee place on the A980 8km N of Banchory. This sweet tearoom 150m up from the crossroads on the B993 to Inverurie is on the site of a former railway station. Emma (cakes 'n all) and David Pattullo work damned hard in the pottery studio/gallery and in the community. Home-made specials, lunch keeps going till 5pm.

SOUTH

1451 7/K27 ✓✓ **GRO Coffee** Irvine Best use satnav/online maps to navigate the Irvine road (GRO too cool for a website or phone number at TGP) for Gordon Rennie's café/restaurant/hangout with an urban vibe, great coffee, baking, hot dishes, and, in evenings, pizza. Has got to be one of the best things about (this) Irvine. Great for kids and lovely garden (though nothing GROs). 7 days.

1452 8/R27 ✓ **Woodside (aka Birdhouse Tearoom)** nr Ancrum · www.
L   woodsidegarden.co.uk · 01835 830315 On B6400 off A68 at Ancrum turn-off. The caff in the shack at the back of the Woodside Garden Centre in the walled garden of **Monteviot House** (1568/GARDENS). Simple, delicious, mostly organic and locally sourced home baking: soup, sandwiches, quiche and splendid cakes. Outside tables on a sheltered lawn. Check for evening meals in the Kailyaird (sic) Restaurant fortnightly Fridays; a local foodie treat. Daytime only.

1453 8/S27 ✓ **The Terrace Café** Floors Castle, Kelso · www.floorscastle.com ·
L   01573 225714 Top garden tearoom inside and out an old outbuilding that forms one side of the estate walled garden (1566/GARDENS) some distance from the Castle (1879/HOUSES). Good, home-made, unpretentious hot dishes and baking: home-cured ham, salads and irresistible cakes and puds and pies. Shop with deli stuff. And the terrace: bliss. Hot food till 2.30pm.

1454 8/R26 ✓ **Flat Cat Gallery Coffee Shop** Lauder · www.flatcatgallery.co.uk · 01578 722808 Opposite Eagle Hotel on Market St. Speeding through Lauder (don't: speed cameras) you might miss Annette and Jacquie's cool coffee spot and proper gallery. Always interesting work, including furniture from Harestanes down the road, and ethnic things. Soup and sandwiches, home baking. 7 days till 5pm.

1455 8/Q27 ✓ **No1 Peebles Road Coffee House** Innerleithen · www.no1peeblesroad. coffee · 01896 830873 Address and statement, perhaps. Well, they are the number one coffee house in these parts with Steampunk (the estimable) coffee, baking and freshly made snacks. Craig Anderson and Emma Jane Perry have quickly established a fuel stop on the bikeathon between Glentress and Traquair. Quite possibly the most empathetic of cycle caffs in these or in any other woods and hills. 8am-4pm (till 6pm Sat/Sun). Closed Tue.

1456 9/M30 ✓ **The Schoolhouse** Ringford · 01557 820250 On A75 10km W of Castle Douglas. A busy road and a perennially busy foodstop where passers-by (maybe surprised at how good it is) and a legion of regulars love fresh, home-made cooking done with integrity and commitment. It's all made here, including daily organic breads, by the amazing Caroline Lawrie. Can take away. 10am-6pm. Closed Wed.

1457 9/L30 ✓ **Caffs in Wigtown** Scotland's booktown and home of the **Wigtown Book**
DF **Festival** 65/EVENTS. **Reading Lasses** 01988 403266 This tiny caff at the
back of one of the main bookshops is a rest and respite from all that browsing.
2-lovely-wifey operation with named, locally sourced ingredients, soup and pies,
salad leaves from garden and home-made cakes. Can be as packed as a bookshelf.
Closed Wed.

1458 9/L30 **Beltie Books** www.beltiebooks.co.uk · 01988 402730 'Beltie' after the Belted
Galloway cow. Andrew Wilson's home cooking and caking; garden. Wed-Mon
daytime only.

1459 9/L30 **Café Rendezvous** 01988 402074 Top of main street. More restauranty than
those above; hot meals. And no books. Good though. 7 days, daytime only.

1460 9/M29 **The Smithy** New Galloway · www.thesmithy-newgalloway.co.uk ·
MAR–OCT 01644 420269 The Smithy has a brilliant location by the burn, with outside
terrace, in a sleepy, one-street town in forest and loch lands. Andrew and Margaret
took over this long-standing caff in 2018: home-baking, soups, toasties. Lunch till
4pm. Closed Tue.

The Best Afternoon Teas

1461 8/M26 ✓ **The Hidden Lane Tearoom** Glasgow · www.thehiddenlanetearoom.com · 0141 237 4391 Beyond Kelvingrove under an arch at the west end of Argyle St where there are many other coffee shops and grazing places, to the end of a backstreet lane which is pure Glasgow, a truly hidden but once found, oft-revisited tearoom. Old style and very new style at the same time. Kirsty Webb and a friendly wee team bake and bring you great cake miraculously from a tiny kitchen. On the tier: 4 sweet, 4 savoury and the scone with clotted cream. Too yum. Noon-5pm, otherwise 10am-5pm (Sat 6pm). Not so hidden anymore!

1462 8/R25 ✓ **Greywalls** Gullane · www.greywalls.co.uk · 01620 842144 The Lutyens manor house and Gertrude Jekyll gardens at this country-house hotel 40 mins E of Edinburgh is the perfect setting for genteel afternoon tea. It's a Roux restaurant (849/LOTHIANS) so expect well-thought-out, smartly delivered niceties, with comfy lounges, outside the gorgeous gardens and croquet! 2.30-5pm.

1463 8/Q25 ATMOS ✓ **Prestonfield** Edinburgh · www.prestonfield.com · 0131 225 7800 This superlative country-house hotel and restaurant on the edge of the city (80/UNIQUE HOTELS), the epitome of gracious living, is an ideal prospect for a proper tea. An art piece of knitted cakes in the hallway may also put you in the mood. A number of sumptuous lounges and locations, tea options and, of course, champagne. 2-7pm. In town, another of James Thomson's esteemed establishments, **The Tower** (0131 225 3003) above and adjacent to the museum, serves tea 2-6pm; wonderful views of the Old Town from the terrace.

1464 8/Q25 ✓ **Palm Court at The Balmoral Hotel** Edinburgh · www.roccofortehotels.com · 0131 556 2414 The grande dame of afternoon tea in the Palm Court beyond the foyer of Edinburgh's landmark hotel. Urbane and soothing (a harpist on the balcony). A cake stand with all you would expect, though not cheap at £40 (with champagne from £55) at TGP. Noon-5pm (you get 2 hours). Book! See 78/UNIQUE HOTELS.

1465 7/K20 L **The Smiddy House** Spean Bridge · www.smiddyhouse.com · 01397 712335 On A82, 14km N of Fort William. Guest house and hugely popular restaurant with big local reputation that (pre-booked) does a specially made afternoon tea in a cosy afternoon-tea-type parlour. Bakewell tart, whisky cake, fruit tarts and an eclectic range of teas. And the right china! Climb something, then treat yourself (possibly with champagne)! Also see 1094/HIGHLANDS.

1466 8/M26 **The Tearooms** Glasgow · www.thebutterflyandthepig.com · 0141 243 2459 The less pub-like, more tearoom-like tearoom of **The Butterfly and The Pig** (504/FOOD PUBS) somewhat sips the zeitgeist but on ever-changing style-driven Bath St, this is a more reflective space. From breakfast to supper but it's in afternoon and high-tea sessions that it comes into its own. 8.30am-5pm.

1467 8/L23 **Mhor 84** nr Balquhidder They've thought of everything at this 'motel' on the A84. Drop by for afternoon tea all afternoon. Goodies from their bakery in Callander (see below) and those meringues! Report: 796/CENTRAL.

The New Artisan Bakers

1468 8/Q25 ✓✓ **Twelve Triangles** 90 Brunswick St, Edinburgh · 0131 629 4664 & 300 Portobello High St · 0131 629 3830 & **Kitchen Table** 148 Duke St · www.twelvetriangles.com All 3 locations (Brunswick St the original) have takeaway and sit-in, and sell their signature sourdough and other delicious breads, the mainstay of their eating-in menu, and pastries and doughnuts. Pioneers of the Real Bread movement. Approach to baking and instore ambience spot on. All daytime only. 7 days. See also 304/TEAROOMS.

1469 5/H20 ✓✓ **The Bakehouse** Mallaig · 01687 462808 Old Quay on the harbour near the yacht pontoons. Matthew and Kate McCarthy's brilliant bakery is quite the best thing that's happened to food in Mallaig since the fish came in. Scottish faves, such as sausage rolls (including black pudding ones), the best sourdough, but also genuine patisserie, the top croissants in the Highlands, their excellent takeaway pizza dome is adjacent. Bakehouse 9am-3pm, Fri/Sat also open 5-9pm. Closed Sun.

1470 8/P22 ✓✓ **Aran Bakery** Dunkeld · www.aran-bakery.com · 01350 727029 Flora Shedden, who reached the final four of the Great British Bake Off, brought her flair and baking skills to Dunkeld and opened up in the main street – you lucky Dunkelders! Breads vary each day, always proper baguettes and croissants, reimagined sausage rolls and unique-to-here cakes. Takeaway sandwiches, etc. Some windowsill seats. 7 days.

1471 8/M25 ✓✓ **Cottonrake Bakery** 497 Great Western Rd, Glasgow · www. cottonrake.com · 07910 282040 One of the first of the bakery new wave taken immediately to heart – the delicious cholesterol-making cakes – now a mainstay of foodie Kelvinside. The baguettes are *sans pareil*. 7 days.

1472 8/L25 ✓✓ **The Bakery by Zique** 79 Lauderdale Gardens, Glasgow · www. byzique.com · 0141 339 6824 Off Clarence Dr, in a heart-of-Hyndland byway, the bakery that supplies **Cafezique** and **Gather by Zique** (487/486/ CASUAL), the 2 destination eateries nearby, with breads, cakes and some other goodies you should perhaps resist but can't. 7 days 9am-6pm.

1473 9/M30 ✓ **Earth Crust Bakery** Castle Douglas · www.earthscrustbakery.co.uk · 01556 502506 Main street, 30m down street on the left at the clocktower. Since Tom and Pavlina Van Rooyen started baking their excellent bread and other goodies in this small bakehouse/takeaway/café, Castle Douglas has begun to fulfil its promise as a 'Food Town' (and see **Mr Pook's Kitchen** 784/SW RESTAURANTS). Ethical, conscientious. Won the Scottish Industry Independent Retailer Award 2017.

1474 8/Q25 ✓ **La Barantine** Edinburgh · www.labarantine.com · 0131 229 0267 Branches in Stockbridge & West Bow. The bakery (with a few seats) that supplies some of the best French-inspired baking in the city to their own and other cafés/coffee shops. Daily fresh à la française. Proper, good patisserie. All 7 days.

1475 8/M26 ✓ **Rawnchy** Glasgow · www.rawnchy.co.uk · 07478 993883 For the love of cake, Poppy Murricane established her bakery/shop in Maryhill Rd in 2016. These are fab cakes that aren't so bad for you: dairy-/gluten-/soy- and refined sugar-free. Supplying many health-conscious cafés and counters, the bright pink shop also sells direct to her adoring regulars, sitting in for coffee – and cake. 7 days.

1476 8/R25 ✓ **Falko** Haddington · www.falko.co.uk · 01620 824824 In the middle of the one-way town centre, facing the High St, Falko's (because it is he, the meister) Konditorei settled here, the bakehouse adjacent consolidated from Edinburgh and Gullane. Traditional German breads and cakes – the spelt and rye, the unique-in-the-UK Bermaline malted bread, the cream-laden (but light) Black Forest Gateau and other seductive slices. German folk come here for bread from all over Scotland. Hot dishes too in the café, like pork schnitzel. Closed Mon/Tue.

1477 8/R25 ✓ **Bostock Bakery** North Berwick & East Linton · 01620 895515 North Berwick at 42 High St, here 5 years, helping to turn it into a town where foodies can get all they want. Signature sourdough breads and renowned patisserie (including the 'Bostock', an almond infused brioche). More recently, the baking Baxters have set up in the main street of East Linton. Both have café seating. NB 7 days; EL closed Mon/Tue.

1478 8/N24 **Hamilton's Cheesecakes** Stirling · 07789 000996 Yes, cheesecakes – only cheesecakes. Not Scottish except for the enterprising Ian Hamilton and that we love these gorgeous sweet things. Individual pots, every conceivable cool flavour displayed irresistibly in a showcase cabinet. And coffee. Go gorge. 7 days.

The Best Scotch Bakers

1479 8/Q23 & 8/R23 ✓✓ **Fisher & Donaldson** Dundee, St Andrews & Cupar · www.fisheranddonaldson.com Main or original branch in main square, Cupar, and a kind of factory outlet up by Tesco, 3 in Dundee (12 Whitehall St, 300 Perth Rd and 83 High St) and Church St, St Andrews. Superior contemporary bakers along traditional lines (born 1919). Surprising (and a pity) that they haven't gone further but they do supply selected outlets with pastries and most excellent Dr Floyd's bread which is as good as anything in the 'artisan' world. Sample also their yum yums, coffee trees, other breads and signature mini apple and rhubarb pies. Dundee Whitehall and Cupar have good tearooms (955/DUNDEE) and the factory one is fab.

1480 8/M24 ✓✓ **Mhor Bread** Callander · www.mhor.net · 01877 339518 W end of main street in busy touristy town. Here forever but taken on by Dick of the food-loving Lewis family of **Monachyle Mhor** (795/CENTRAL) so those pies, cakes, the biggest, possibly the best, tattie scones and sublime doughnuts have all been thrust into the 21st century; your picnic on the Braes is sorted and our favourite Trossachs pit stop! Adjacent café does the bake stuff, plus hot dishes, sandwiches, omelettes and always the scone. The usual MM random furniture. 7 days 7am-5pm; café till 4.30pm.

1481 4/J14 NC500 ✓ **Riverside Bistro, The Lochinver Larder** Lochinver · www.piesbypost.co.uk · 01571 844356 On way into town from Ullapool. A bistro/restaurant mostly and rightly famous for their brilliant pies from the takeaway counter. Huge variety of savoury and fruit from traditional to unique to here. Rapid turnover; always freshly baked. And irresistible puds. Ready sustenance or merely indulgence; you can also get 'em by post. 7 days. Makes those Cornish pasties you find at stations seem even more horrible.

1482 5/M17 **Cromarty Bakery** Cromarty · 013810 600388 For some, a reason to visit this picturesque seaside town. A wee shop but an abundance of speciality cakes, organic bread, rolls and pies, baked daily on premises. Top oatcakes! Also tea, coffee, hot savouries and takeaway. Stick to the traditional and the stodge, though they use old-style ersatz cream. They have also expanded to Fortrose and produce is available elsewhere, e.g. the Storehouse at Evanton. Closed Sun.

1483 8/Q23 **Goodfellow & Steven Dundee, Perth & Fife** · www.goodfellowscakes.co.uk The other bakers in the Fife/Dundee belt (not a patch on Fisher & Donaldson, but hey). G&S have several branches. Good commercial Scotch baking, with the kind of cakes that used to be a treat.

1484 7/G22 **Tobermory Bakery Tobermory** · 01688 302225 In the middle of the postcard houses and shops around Tobermory Bay, this is very much the island bakery. Bread, pies, quiches and an array of old-style fancies and cakes, including the bright yellow pineapple jobs. Some deli stuff. 7 days, daytime only.

1485 6/P17 **The Bakehouse Findhorn** · 01309 691826 The bakery behind the excellent Bakehouse café (1086/HIGHLANDS), where David Boyle turns out a huge range of breads, scones and such like to supply the caff, deli and Findhorn community (1502/DELIS) and other places further and wide. Ryes, spelt, gluten-free and from French country to focaccia. Until the caff opens at 10am you can buy from the bakery door.

1486 8/Q22 **McLaren's Forfar** · www.mclarenbakers.co.uk Also in Kirriemuir. Best in town (and anywhere) for the famous Forfar bridie, a large, meaty shortcrust pasty hugely underestimated as a national (in)delicacy. It's so much better than the gross and grossly overhyped Cornish pasty but it has never progressed beyond its (beefy) Angus heartland; one of the best copies is the home-made bridie that can be found in the café at **Glamis** (1818/CASTLES). 8am-4.15pm. Closed Sun & Thu afternoon. In Forfar, the other bakery **Saddler's** is better for cakes.

1487 8/M26 **Waterside Bakery Strathaven** · 01357 521260 Alexander Taylor's oldest in Scotland (1820) bakery in Strathaven. Some people say Taylor's is one of the reasons for living here. OK, they do good breads, croissants, bics and cakes and the Flour Store Gallery is upstairs – you wouldn't find that at Greggs. Closed Sun (though caff adjacent open).

1488 8/P23 **Murray's Perth** · 01738 624633 At 112 South St in Perth and far and wide (and since 1901!), they know that Murray's Scotch pies are the business. Baked continuously from early till afternoon; there's often a queue. Their sausage rolls, and plain and onion bridies are also top, followed possibly with a perfect pineapple cake. Closed Sun.

1489 8/N23 **Campbell's Bakery Crieff** · 01764 652114 **& Comrie** · 01764 679944 · **www. campbellsbakery.com** On the main streets and across from the main square in Crieff. Traditional bakers, family run; great window displays by Ailsa herself. Soup, coffees and all they make. Great pies, strawberry cakes and the fudge doughnuts. Crieff: 6am-5pm; Comrie: 7am-4.30pm. Closed Sun.

1490 8/M24 **David Bennett & Son Dunblane** · 01786 823212 Actually a butcher's shop – since 1901 – but they come from far for the pies, pies, pies. They're in the window, come at night just to look at them, all sorts they have. Closed Sun.

The Best Ice Cream

1491 8/Q25 ✓✓ **Luca's** Musselburgh · www.s-luca.co.uk · **0131 665 2237** Queues out the door in the middle of a Sunday afternoon in February are testament to the enduring popularity of this much-loved ice-cream parlour. The classic flavours (vanilla, choc and strawberry) and many flashier arrivistes and a plethora of sorbets. In basic and always busy café through the back, The Olympia; you may have to wait there too. Mon-Sat 9am-10pm & Sun 10.30am-10pm. For many, Luca's is simply the best, and folk come from Edinburgh (14km), though there is a branch in town at 16 Morningside Rd (329/CAFÉS). Café upstairs more pizza/pasta and sandwiches. 7 days 9am-10pm. Luca's (wholesale) spreading everywhere. See also 285/KIDS.

1492 9/M31 ✓✓ **Cream o' Galloway** Rainton, nr Gatehouse of Fleet · www.creamogalloway.co.uk · **01557 814040** A75 take Sandgreen exit 2km then left at sign for Carrick. Long a dairy farm producing cheese (now cheese-making again; 4 varieties on sale – the Rainton Tomme is a winner), but it's for the ice cream – available all over Scotland – that C o' G is famous. Nature trail, fab kids' adventure-play area (1758/KIDS; they could spend a day here) and decent organic-type café and Burger Barn with Galloway beef. And there's a dogs-run-free field and a beach at **Sandgreen** (1641/BEACHES). Closed Nov-Jan.

1493 8/R23 ✓ **Jannetta's** St Andrews · www.jannettas.co.uk · **01334 473285** Family firm since 1908. Top of South St and still in the forefront. Look for the queue. Once only vanilla, then Americans at the Open asked for other flavours. Now there are over 50, sorbets and frozen yoghurt and Jannetta's has embraced the development of creative ice-cream cakes. Café and outside tables. 7 days.

1494 8/Q27 ✓ **Caldwell's** Innerleithen · **01896 830382** & Peebles · **01721 729005** The original (and best) in Innerleithen, a ribbon of a town between Peebles and Gala. 2011 was their centenary – yes, they've been making ice cream since 1911. Purists may bemoan the fact that they've exploded into flavours in the 21st century, but their vanilla is king. Jars of sweeties and the (news)papers, hence the early hours: 7 days 6.30am-6pm. Peebles: 7 days 10am-5pm.

1495 8/Q25 ✓ **Mary's Milk Bar** Edinburgh · www.marysmilkbar.com At west end of the Grassmarket, Mary's (for it is she) artisan gelateria – ice cream for the Instagram generation (you gotta get snapped cone in hand with the castle behind you). 12 or so flavours of a contemporary flava: salted caramel, milk, vanilla, chocolate and others (including 2/3 sorbets) that change daily or even hourly. It's made through the back; there's often a big queue. Closed Mon (except Bank Holidays).

1496 8/R25 ✓ **Gelateria Alandas** North Berwick · www.alandas.co.uk · **01620 894444** 1 Quality St, at the end of the town (next to the **North Berwick Fry** 1398/FISH & CHIPS). Bright, brash, shiny ice-cream parlour. Young staff who love the ice cream as much as we do. Took the gold for their chocolate at the Royal Highland Show. Flavours vary, quality not. 7 days 10am-10pm.

1497 8/S20 ✓ **Aunty Betty's** Stonehaven · **01569 763656** On the promenade right next door to the **The Bay** (1379/FISH & CHIPS), always similarly busy. You get your chips, then you get your ice cream and you may have come a long way for them. Betty's is very big on toppings. Signature vanilla and the Scotch tablet. All in all, an irresistible proposition. Noon-10pm (both places).

1498 9/P30 ✓ **Drummuir Farm** Collin, nr Dumfries · www.drummuirfarm.co.uk · 01387 750599 5km off A75 (Carlisle/Annan) road E of Dumfries on B724 (near Clarencefield). A real farm producing real ice cream – still does supersmooth original and honeycomb, seasonal specials; on a fine day, sit out and chill. Indoor and outdoor play areas. Easter-Sep: daily till 5.30pm; Oct-Dec: Sat/Sun till 5pm.

1499 8/Q23 **Visocchi's** Broughty Ferry · www.visocchis.co.uk · 01382 779297 Originally from St Andrews; ice-cream makers for 75 years with legendary caff in Kirriemuir (now no longer connected). So here in Dundee's seaside suburb, a trusty tratt with home-made pasta, as well as the peach melba and a perfectly creamy vanilla. On a sunny day you queue! Closed Mon (unless it's hot). Also 957/DUNDEE.

1500 8/N24 **Allan Water Café** Bridge of Allan · www.allanwatercafe.co.uk · 01786 833060 In early editions of this book, this was an old-fashioned café in an old-fashioned town in the main street (since 1902). Fabulously good fish 'n' chips and ice cream. Now it's taken over the whole block and the ice cream, like everything else, comes in a cabinet of choices. Plus ça change but this ice cream will run and run. 7 days 8am-8.30pm (LO). From 9am Sun.

1501 8/P27 **Taylor's of Biggar** Biggar · www.conesandcandies.co.uk · 01899 220139 Main street (High St). Here for 50 years, a family biz that helps make Biggar a destination and not just a route to the M6 (on the A702). They keep it simple and delicious. 7 days, daytime only.

The Really Good Delis

For Edinburgh listings, see p. 67; for Glasgow, see p. 112.

1502 6/P17 ✓ **Phoenix Findhorn Community** Findhorn · www.phoenixshop.co.uk
Serving the eco-village (1283/RETREATS) and wider community and pursuing a conscientious approach long before it was de rigueur, this is an exemplary and high-quality deli worth the detour from A96 Inverness–Elgin road (and to walk around this village of extraordinary houses). Packed and carefully selected shelves; as much for pleasurable eating as for healthy. Best organic fruit and veg in the NE (note: delivered on Tuesdays). The excellent **Bakehouse** café in Findhorn itself owned by folk who used be here; superb ethical eats (1086/HIGHLANDS). Their breads on sale here. Till 6pm (weekends 5pm).

1503 5/L18 ✓ **Corner on the Square** Beauly · www.corneronthesquare.co.uk ·
NC500 01463 783000 On said corner of the square. Busy with locals and passers-
☕ through, perhaps mainly because of its sit-in coffee-shop fare, including great baking, quiches, scones, soups, etc. But also Gary Williamson's curation and selection of deli produce, cheese, Cromarty bakes (1482/BAKERS) and a great, eclectic wine selection. 7 days. Breakfast-5.30pm (5pm Sat/Sun).

1504 8/N23 ✓ **2 Damned Fine Delis in Crieff: J.L. Gill** 26 W High St · www.
scottishproduce.co.uk · 01764 652396 First and foremost, this extraordinary shop here for '125 years'. West end, near turn to Crianlarich. It's the real epicurean McCoy. Judicious choice of provisions: honey, 10 kinds of oatcakes, lotsa whisky, wine, cheese and cigars – the good things in life. Closed Sun. **McNee's** 23 High St · www.mcneesofcrieff.co.uk · 01764 654582 Near the town clock. Deli/bakers/chocolatiers. An old-fashioned grocer, they make things: great home baking and ready-made meals, home-roasted meats; some sweeties and Italian stuff creeping in ... Open 7 days.

1505 6/Q18 ✓ **Spey Larder** Aberlour · www.speylarder.com · 01340 871243 In deepest
Speyside. A beautiful old shop (1864), conserved, wood and all, by David and Sheana Catto. It's spacious and full of great, often local produce (honeys, bread, game in winter, Speyside chanterelles and, of course, whisky). Nice cheese counter. Local salad boxes; they're always finding new suppliers. Friendly provisioners reside and provide here. Closed Sun.

1506 8/Q23 ✓ **J. Allan Braithwaite** Dundee · 01382 322693 Not by any stretch a deli, but
has to go in these pages for longevity (150 years!), integrity and purity of purpose. A provisioner of teas and coffees long before the caffeine pandemic. Old style, of course. Fab list of both. Here you really do smell the coffee. 9am-5pm. Closed Sun.

1507 8/M23 **Hansen's Kitchen** Comrie · www.hansenskitchen.com · 01764 670253 At
last a deli/café that calm and couthy Comrie deserves. Shelves with selected essentials and a cold counter with delicious, often home-made and locally sourced tasty things: snacks, cheeses (including the Wee Comrie), cakes. Coffee roasted out the back. Couple of tables (hot meals), friendly folk in front and behind the counter. Mon-Sat 8am-5pm (Sun 10am-4pm).

1508 8/Q23 **Heart Space Whole Foods** Dundee · 01382 221721 & St Andrews ·
& 8/R23 01334 208401 · www.wholefoods.heartspacedundee.co.uk Organic and sourced locally provisioner. Good breads. A juice deck out back (Dundee). Good approach and, well, a good vibe. 7 days.

1509 5/M18 **Oil & Vinegar** Inverness · www.oilvinegar.co.uk · 01463 240073 8 Union St, near the train station. Does exactly what it says on the tin and bottle – olives and the stuff that goes with olives, and an exceptional range of vinegars to try from huge flasks – who would think there were so many, so exotic (and the Orkney ones). O&V is a Dutch company; this is their only branch in the UK. A culinary treat in a town with good restaurants but not a lot on the foodie front. Closed Sun.

1510 8/R22 **E&O Fish** East Grimsby, Arbroath On road to harbour. Wholesalers of fish, the door in the wall with the queue outside is their retail 'shop', where they purvey that great Scottish delicacy – the smokie (smoked haddock) and other smoked fish and kippers. This is *the* fish place. 7am-7pm (Sat/Sun from 8am).

1511 8/P23 **Provender Brown** Perth · www.provenderbrown.co.uk · 01738 587300 As we might expect, a decent deli in the city with a vibrant foodie culture. Lots here that's made and sourced locally, including bread and cakes. Good for olives, vacuum-packed products and cheese. Closed Sun.

✓✓ **Pillars of Hercules** nr Falkland Organic grocers with tearoom (1424/TEAROOMS) and outstanding farm shop and deli.

✓✓ **I.J. Mellis** St Andrews, Edinburgh and Glasgow. The cheese guy and other epicurean delights. See www.mellischeese.net.

The Really Good Farm Shops

1512 9/N30 ✓✓ **Loch Arthur Creamery & Farm Shop** Beeswing, nr Dumfries · www.locharthur.org.uk · 01387 259669 Run by Camphill Trust, this is the genuine article and a Thoroughly Good Thing, with many folk who work the fields and the farm, a strong organic agenda, and now a destination for SW foodies and anyone who cares about what they eat. Since the new building, it's a real honeypot! Great bakery (the best bread, cakes and pies), famous organic veg, highly regarded cheeses and the UK's tastiest granola. Meats and eggs. From Beeswing take New Abbey road 1km. Closed Sun.

1513 8/P23 ✓✓ **Gloagburn Farm & Coffee Shop** Tibbermore, nr Perth · www.gloagburnfarmshop.co.uk · 01738 840864 Off A85 Perth–Methven and Crieff road from A9 and ring road at Huntingtower, signed Tibbermore (Tibbermore also signed off A9 from Stirling just before Perth). Through village, second farm on right: a family (the Nivens') farm shop (it all started with a free-range egg) with ducks on the pond and rare-breed pigs out back – excellent fresh produce and, inside, a deli and bustling café, where food (hot dishes, cakes, etc) is exemplary. Lovely eggy things and a signature soufflé. Hot and other food till 5pm. Vacuum-packed meats, frozen meals, fruit 'n' veg, home-made bread, their own oats and many gifty things. A destination only 15 mins from Perth. 7 days.

1514 6/R20 ✓✓ **Finzean Farm Shop & Tearoom** Deeside · www.finzean.com · 01330 850710 On the S side of the river on B976 between Banchory and Aboyne on the Farquharson family's Finzean Estate. Kate and Catriona's very personally run foodie haven, a showcase for local suppliers, in glorious open countryside with views to the hills from the terrace. Local and carefully sourced produce beautifully presented fresh and frozen. Meat and game from the Estate. Cool cookbooks and other good gifties. Hot dishes till 3pm. Cakes that don't rely on cream. Walks, river-swimming and an old kirk nearby (1736/SWIMMING; 1919/CHURCHES). 7 days. See also 1435/TEAROOMS.

1515 8/R24 ✓✓ **Ardross Farm** nr Elie · www.ardrossfarm.co.uk · 01333 331400
Between St Monans and Elie on the A917 Fife coastal route. East Neuk
farm shop, an all-round highly selective provisioner of home-farm produce,
including grass-fed, 21-day hung beef, their own lamb, top venison and a vast array
of seasonal dug vegetables (over 50 varieties, with 7 types of hand-sown potatoes!),
Fiona's pies, ready-made meals. The Pollock family have been here over a century
and they're big supporters of UK farm produce as well as their own. 7 days.

1516 8/P26 ✓✓ **Whitmuir, the Organic Place** Lamancha, nr Peebles · www.
whitmuirtheorganicplace.co.uk · 01968 661147 All-round foodie
destination and fully realised good-life emporium, with shop, art gallery and café/
restaurant. Farm supplies own beef, lamb, pork, eggs and up to 32 different veg
and fruit. Own butchery. A light, well-run place with good attitude and genuinely
organic. Only 40 mins from Edinburgh. 7 days.

1517 8/P24 ✓✓ **Pillars of Hercules** nr Falkland · www.pillars.co.uk · 01337 857749
On A912, 2km from town towards Strathmiglo and motorway since 1983.
A pillar of the organic community and a more ethical way of life. Grocers with
tearoom (1424/TEAROOMS) on farm/nursery where you can PYO herbs. Always
fruit/veg and great selection of dry goods that's a long way from Sainsbury's (there
are supermarket-type trolleys outside) and here long before the organic boom
spread all over this country road; they have a bothy and camping. 7 days.

1518 8/R23 ✓✓ **Balgove Larder** Strathtyrum, nr St Andrews · www.balgove.com ·
01334 898145 On main road S from St Andrews (3km), a perfectly placed,
provisioned and well-run farm shop/home store/café/flower shop and **Steak
Barn** (897/ST ANDREWS) developed with passion from Strathtyrum Farm, which
provides the beef, lamb, pork not only for here but also for many top restaurants in
the area. A celebration of all things East Neuk: Luvians ice cream, Darnley's Gin
(1548/GIN), the oatcakes. Café goes like a fair – 40,000 scones are baked each year!
The non-food section avowedly doesn't sell just 'presents'. 'Night markets' on
mid-month Tuesdays in summer (till 9pm). 7 days 9am-5pm.

1519 8/R22 ✓ **Milton Haugh Farm Shop** Carmyllie · 01241 860579 Off A92 Dundee-
Arbroath road at Carnoustie, follow Forfar road then signs. Enormously popular
faraway farm on B961. Great range of fruit and veg, meats and selected deli fare with
own-label meals, jams, etc. Many different oatcakes. Excellent Corn Kist Coffee Shop
with home-made cakes, soups and specials; from far and wide you come. 7 days.

1520 8/P25 ✓ **Craigie's Farm** nr South Queensferry · www.craigies.co.uk ·
DF 0131 319 1048 Take the South Queensferry exit from dual carriageway N from
Edinburgh, A90 to Forth Road Bridge. Farm signed 2km. Like many on these pages,
these guys saw the potential in farm shopping and grew rapidly from a PYO farm
on the edge of town to a visitor magnet. You can still PYO strawbs and rasps and
other soft fruit (Jun-Aug) but there's a self-service caff (and an outside dog café)
and an emporium of food. Best is their own butchery section but the real attraction
is to sit on a terrace taking tea and cake overlooking rows and fields of fruit like
vineyards in France while the city shimmers in the distance. 7 days.

1521 9/N30 ✓ **Kilnford Barns Farm Shop** Dumfries · www.kilnford.co.uk ·
01387 253087 Edge of town on a roundabout of the A75 heading to
Stranraer. Built around a farm (actually supplied by 3), known for its Beltie (the
Belted Galloway) beef, but also pigs, this is a major farm shop emporium (especially
meats) and café (great burger). Around a courtyard, probably the best local/
seasonal food provisioner in/around Dumfries. 7 days.

1522 8/R25 ✓ **Fenton Barns Farm Shop** nr Drem · www.fentonbarnsfarmshop.com ·
⌨ **01620 850294** Off A1 on A198, then signed by Dirleton, Mhairi and Roy's
country stores/caff is on craft parklet, an old airfield complex. They also look after
St Giles' Cathedral coffee shop in Edinburgh – they never flag, especially since they
opened **Carlyle House** in Haddington (861/LOTHIANS). Organic meats, free-range
eggs, home-made pies, soups, terrines, selected fruit and veg. Home-made
just-about-everything coffee shop in the back (862/LOTHIANS). 7 days.
The Gosford Bothy Farm Shop nearby (Edinburgh side of Aberlady) is especially
good for meats, pies, etc. At entrance to the lovely walk in the **Gosford Estate**
(433/WALKS). Also 7 days.

1523 8/M24 ✓ **The Woodhouse** nr Kippen · **01786 870156** New-build contemporary farm
⌨ shop/deli and airy café, with outside terrace on the Lamb family farm, easily
found on the long, straight A811 Stirling to Loch Lomond road at the first
(Stirling-side) crossroads to Kippen and Thornhill. Big on sustainables. Cheese
counter and Kippen butchers (many sausages), local bread. The caff with salads,
tortes and a roast of the day. A busy little food and fuel stop! 7 days.

1524 8/Q23 ✓ **Cairnie Fruit Farm (and Maze)** nr Cupar · www.cairniefruitfarm.co.uk ·
⌨ **01334 655610** A truly a(maze)ing conversion of a fruit farm into major family
attraction (1750/KIDS) demonstrating if nothing else the inexorable rise of the
strawberry. This and other berries can be picked, purchased and eaten in all
manner of brilliant cakes, with other farm produce and snack food. Main thing
though is the kids' area outside. 7 days, Mar-Oct. Maze: Jul-Oct. Farm is 4km N of
Cupar on minor road past the hospital or 3km from main A92, signed near Kilmany.

1525 8/R23 **Allanhill** nr St Andrews · www.allanhill.co.uk · **01334 477998** 6km out of
⌨ town off Anstruther/Crail road A917. Simple farm shop mainly and café with tables
in the field. Kids' stuff includes animals, hay bales. Great views to St Andrews Bay.
Known for excellent soft fruits, including the elusive blueberry and '1,000 tonnes of
strawberries'. Tearoom has excellent strawberry cakes and a top scone. Kids love it
here. May-Sep.

1526 8/Q24 **Muddy Boots** Balmalcolm · www.muddybootsfife.com · **01337 831222** On
⌨ A914 from A92 S of Cupar, a farm shop with kitchen and crafts and integrity; a full-
on activities play barn for kids. Their home-grown fruit and veg is high quality (the
best raspberries) and they're keen to educate and inspire kids into good country
practice (1751/KIDS). Caff with big central wood stove. 7 days.

▬▬▬ Where To Find Scottish Cheeses...

*The delis on p. 67 and 112 will have good selections (especially Valvona &
Crolla in Edinburgh).*

1527 8/Q25 ✓✓ **I.J. Mellis** Edinburgh, Glasgow & St Andrews · www.mellischeese.
& 8/M25 & net A real cheesemonger. Smell and taste before you buy. Cheeses from
8/R23 all over the UK in prime condition. Daily and seasonal specials. Reports: 357/
EDINBURGH DELIS; 631/GLASGOW DELIS.

1528 8/M25 ✓✓ **George Mewes** Edinburgh & Glasgow · www.
georgemewescheese.co.uk The Byres Rd magnet for anyone with an
epicurean taste: cheese as it should be seen, smelled and eaten. Scottish selection
is just that – a judicious selection (i.e. when they're ripe and ready). Top English
cheeses too. See Glasgow 632/DELIS and Edinburgh 358/DELIS.

1529 8/P25 ✓ **Herbie of Edinburgh** Edinburgh · www.herbieofedinburgh.co.uk · 0131 332 9888 Excellent selection – everything here is the right stuff. Great bread, bagels, etc, from independent baker, home-made hummus and Scottish cheeses. You never get a Brie or a blue here in less than perfect condition.

1530 7/G22 ✓ **Sgriob-Ruadh Farm** Mull · www.isleofmullcheese.co.uk · 01688 302627
L Head out on road to Dervaig, take turning for Glengorm (great coffee shop 1409/TEAROOMS) and watch for sign and track to farm. Past big glass barn, where they live in some kind of blissful bohemia, and follow path to distant doorway into the cheese factory and farm shop (though all there is usually are lovely shit-covered fresh eggs and the cheddar, their new blue and a bit of sausage). **The Glass Barn** tearoom is a must (1410/TEAROOMS). Honesty box when nobody is around.

1531 5/M17 ✓ **The Cheese House** Cromarty · www.cromartycheese.com · 01381 600724 In the old police station, a superb, surprising boutique cheese shop in lovely Cromarty (1608/VILLAGES), specialising in Dutch varieties (they all look glorious), along with local (Highland Fine Cheeses, and the organic vegetarian ones from Connage Cheeses at Ardersier), Humphrey Errington, and the Mulls (above). The biscuits and chutneys to go with. Closed Tue/Wed; 7 days Jul-Sep.

1532 8/Q23 ✓ **The Cheesery** Dundee · www.thecheesery.co.uk · 01382 202160 In Exchange St where there are good caff/restaurants (see Dundee p. 165–7), Stephen and Hilary Barney's cheese place is a foodie oasis in downtown Dundee. Continental, artisan and a dozen selected Scottish. 9.30am-5pm. Closed Sun/Mon.

1533 7/J27 **Arran Cheese Shop** nr Brodick · www.arrancheeseshop.co.uk · 01770 302788 5km Brodick, road to castle and Corrie. Excellent selection of their own (the well-known cheddars) but also Crowdie, Camembert, Brie, Arran and award-winning blue. Selected others. See them being made. Adjacent to Arran Aromatics, an emporium of lotions and potions. 7 days.

1534 5/H18 **West Highland Dairy** Achmore, nr Plockton · www.westhighlanddairy. co.uk · 01599 577203 Charming and shuffly Mr and Mrs Biss still running their great farm dairy shop, selling their own cheeses (goat/cow milk), yoghurt, ice cream, cranachan cheesecake. Signed from village. Highland sylvan setting but no cows in sight. You can learn to make cheese here – they do courses. Kathy's the author of *Practical Cheesemaking*. Usually 10am-4.30pm but phone first.

1535 8/R25 **The Cheese Lady** Haddington · www.thecheeselady.co.uk · 01620 823729 A slice of a shop where Svetlana, for she is the Cheese Lady, carves up artisan and farmhouse cheeses for the burghers of this market town. You'll always find the cheddars – Isle of Mull, Dunlop, and Lanark Blue. Others by season and all the Euro staples. Closed Sun/Mon.

✓✓ **Loch Arthur Creamery** Beeswing, nr Dumfries Their own superlative cheeses and one of the best farm shops/delis in and off the land. Report: 1512/FARM SHOPS.

✓✓ **House of Bruar** nr Blair Atholl Roadside superstore with huge range of everything. Report: 2212/SHOPS.

✓✓ **Cream o' Galloway** Rainton, nr Gatehouse of Fleet Off A75 (2km). Cheese again, as well as the ubiquitous ice cream. 4 new varieties – Carrick, Laganory, Fleet Valley Blue and (my favourite) Rainton Tomme. Order online.

Whisky: The Best Distillery Tours

There are many distilleries (and a plethora of tours of them); some more atmospheric and interesting than others. These are the best:

1536 7/F26

✓✓ **The Islay Malts** Plenty to choose from on this island where whisky rules the waves. Best suggestion: see below, a couple of the big three in the south. They are linked by the **Whisky Path** (walk or cycle from Port Ellen 5km to Ardbeg). Pick **Kilchoman**, small and homely, **Bowmore** because of convenience (and it is good) and **Bruichladdich** because it is a gin distillery too (**The Botanist**). **Kilchoman** First new distillery on Islay in 124 years. Find it in the wild, bleakly beautiful Rhinns; daily tours, with great café 2341/ISLAY (01496 850011). Pronounced 'Kil-homan'.

In the south near Port Ellen, 3 of the world's great malts all in a row on a mystic coast. The distilleries here look like distilleries should:

LLL **Lagavulin** (01496 302749) and **Laphroaig** (01496 302418) offer fascinating tours. Your guide will lay on the anecdotes and explain the process and you get a feel for the life and history, as well as the product of these world-famous places. At Laphroaig there are enhanced (cost and effect) tours, especially their 'Water to Whisky Experience' (book ahead). **Ardbeg** (01496 302244) is perhaps the most visitor-oriented and has a notable café (2340/ISLAY) and makes the most of its (dark olive) brand. All these distilleries are in settings that entirely justify the romantic hyperbole of their advertising. Worth seeing from the outside as well as the factory floor. **Bowmore** (in Bowmore; 01496 810441) has a slick operation that's far from peat-bog standard and their pricey 'Reinventing The Flavour Wheel' and 'Vaults Secrets' tasting tours.

Bruichladdich (01496 850190). On the loch between Bridgend and near Port Charlotte. Both whisky and gin tours (The Botanist, with its 'notes' was here before the tide of Artisan Gin). Ambitious expansion plans at TGP.

THE BEST OF THE SPEYSIDE WHISKY TRAIL

1537 6/Q17
ATMOS

✓ **Strathisla** Keith · www.chivas.com · 01542 783044 Oldest working distillery in the Highlands, literally on the strath of the Isla River; methinks the most evocative atmos of all the Speyside distilleries. Tastefully reconstructed, this is a very classy halt for the malt. Used as the heart of Chivas Regal, the Strathisla though not commonly available is still a fine dram. Various tours, prices and tastings.

1538 6/P18
LL
APR-OCT

✓ **The Glenlivet** nr Tomintoul · www.theglenlivet.com · 01340 821720 Starting as an illicit dram celebrated as far S as Edinburgh, George Smith licensed the brand in 1824 and founded this distillery in 1858, registering the already mighty name so anyone else had to use a prefix. After successions and mergers, independence was lost in 1978 when Seagrams took over. Now owned by Pernod Ricard. The famous Josie's Well, from which the water springs, is underground. Small parties and a walk-through, which is not on a gantry, make the tour satisfying and as popular, especially with Americans, as the product. Excellent reception centre (very frequent tours) with bar/restaurant (food average) and shop; the tour on the website's so good, you probably don't need to go at all, though you won't then get the dram in those hallowed surroundings. 7 days.

1539 6/Q18
LL
☕

✓ **Glenfiddich** Dufftown · www.glenfiddich.com · 01340 820373 Outside town on A941 to Craigellachie by Balvenie Castle ruins. Well-lubricated tourist operation and the only distillery where you can see the whole process from barley to bar (well, not the bottlery). 3 tasting drams. Still very much family run (the only one, their story on the walls); those Grants have done very well. There's an artists-in-residence scheme, with changing exhibitions in summer; gallery by car park (01340 821565). And a good restaurant. AYR.

On the same road you can see a whisky-related craft that hasn't changed. **Speyside Cooperage** is 1km from Craigellachie. See those poor guys from the gantry (no chance to slack). Open AYR. Mon-Fri 9.30am-4.30pm. Good coffee shop.

1540 6/Q17 **Glen Grant** Rothes · www.glengrant.com · 01340 832118 In Rothes on the A941 Elgin to Perth road. Not the most picturesque but a distillery tour with an added attraction, viz. the Victorian gardens and apple orchard reconstructed around the shallow bowl of the glen of the burn that runs through the distillery: there's a lime-tree-lined walk (15 mins) and delightful Dram Pavilion. Owned by Campari, you will be immersed in the history, as well as the process, and tastings before you leave. Mon-Sun 9.30am-5pm (Nov-Mar noon-5pm on Sun).

1541 6/P18 **Cardhu (or Cardow)** Cardow · www.malts.com · 01340 872555 Off B9102 from Craigellachie to Grantown-on-Spey through deepest Speyside, a small if charming distillery with its own community, a millpond, picnic tables, etc. Owned by Diageo, Cardhu is the 'heart of Johnnie Walker' (which, amazingly, has another 30 malts in it). **Knockando** (2167/HERITAGE), a must-visit, is nearby. Open AYR, Mon-Fri (7 days Jul-Sep). Hours vary.

1542 6/P17 **Benromach** Forres · www.benromach.com · 01309 675968 Signed from A96 at Forres. About the smallest working distillery so no bus tours or big tourist operation. Human beings with time for a chat. Rescued by Gordon & MacPhail and reopened 1999. A great introduction to whisky. Check website for opening times.

· ·

1543 8/N21
L
✓ **Edradour** nr Pitlochry · www.edradour.com · 01796 472095 4km from Pitlochry. Picturesque and as romantic as you can imagine the smallest distillery in Scotland to be, producing single malts for blends since 1825 and limited quantities of the Edradour (only 12 casks a week then laid for 10 years, so not easy to find; see website for stockists) as well as the House of Lords' own brand. Guided tour of charming cottage complex every 20 mins. AYR. Closed Sun (& Sat in winter).

1544 5/F18
L
Talisker Carbost, Skye · www.malts.com · 01478 614308 From Sligachan-Dunvegan road (A863) take B8009 for Carbost and Glen Brittle along the S side of Loch Harport for 5km. Skye's only distillery; since 1830 they've been making this classic after-dinner malt from barley and the burn that runs off the Hawkhill behind. The 'Classic Tour' is inexpensive, informative and has a dram in it. Good visitor centre. Apr-Oct 9.30am-5pm (check winter times). **The Oyster Shed** up the hill behind, for excellent seafood to eat in/take away (2300/SKYE). Pub for grub and music nearby: the Old Inn at Carbost.

1545 8/Q26 **Glenkinchie** Pencaitland, nr Edinburgh · www.malts.com · 01875 342012 Only 25km from city centre; one of the most accessible distilleries. Founded in 1837 in a pastoral place watered from the Lammermuirs, 3km from village, with its own bowling green – a trip to the country and a range of whisky tours! 'Whisky in the Wild' tour includes both. State-of-the-art visitor centre. 7 days AYR.

1546 **1/Q10** **Highland Park** **Kirkwall, Orkney** · **www.highlandparkwhisky.com** · **01856 874619** 2km from town on main A961 road S to South Ronaldsay. The whisky is great and the award-winning tour one of the best. The most northerly whisky in a class and a bottle of its own. You walk through the floor maltings and you can touch the warm barley and fair smell the peat. Good combination of the industrial and the traditional (and the Viking hype). Best check website for times.

1547 **8/Q25** **Scotch Whisky Heritage Centre** **Royal Mile, Edinburgh** · **www.scotchwhiskyexperience.co.uk** · **0131 220 0441** On Castlehill, on last stretch to castle (you cannot miss it). Not a distillery of course, but a visitor attraction to celebrate all things a tourist can take in about Scotland's main export. Tours and tours. Shop has huge range. Amber restaurant and café. 7 days 10am-6.30pm (extended hours in summer).

Whisky: The Best Malts Selections

EDINBURGH

Scotch Malt Whisky Society **www.smws.com** · **0131 220 2044** Your search will end here. More a club (with membership), and top restaurant and bar open to the public.
Bennets Bar Report: 365/UNIQUE PUBS.
Kay's Bar Report: 370/UNIQUE PUBS.
The Bow Bar Report: 383/ALES.
Cadenhead's **www.whiskytastingroom.com** · **0131 556 5864** The shrine.
Canny Man's Report: 179/FOOD PUBS.
The Malt Shovel **www.taylor-walker.co.uk** · **0131 225 6843** Unpretentious pub.
Blue Blazer Report: 387/ALES.
Whiski Rooms Report: 250/SCOTTISH.

GLASGOW

 The Pot Still **www.thepotstill.co.uk** · **0141 333 0980** Famously vast collection. Great atmos and the mecca in Glasgow for whisky.

Bon Accord Report: 667/ALES.
The Lismore Report: 665/UNIQUE PUBS.
Ubiquitous Chip Restaurant, bistro and great bar on the corner. Report: 474/HIGH-END RESTAURANTS.
Ben Nevis Report: 666/UNIQUE PUBS.

REST OF SCOTLAND

NORTH

 The Grill **Aberdeen** A bar in Union St, with the definitive tome of Scottish whiskies. Report: 1021/ABERDEEN.

The Torridon **nr Kinlochewe** Classic Highland hotel bar with 360 malts shelf by shelf. And the mountains! Report: 1221/GET-AWAY HOTELS.

Clachaig Inn **Glencoe** Over 100 malts to go with the range of ales and the range of thirsty hillwalkers. Report: 1313/GOOD PUBS.

✓ **The Oystercatcher** **Portmahomack** Gordon Robertson's exceptional malt (and wine) collection in far-flung village. Report: 1106/HIGHLANDS.

✓ **Forss House Hotel** **nr Thurso** Hotel on N coast. Often a wee wind outside; warm up with one of 300 well-presented malts. Report: 1050/HIGHLANDS.

✓ **The Piano Bar at the Glenmoriston Townhouse** **Inverness** Easy-to-decipher malt list in superior, stylish surroundings. Report: 1041/HIGHLANDS.

✓ **The Malt Room** **Inverness** A bar (with bites) down a lane off Church St in town centre. Great list (and gins, cocktails) and a cool hang-out.

✓ **The Anderson** **Fortrose** Amazing collection of over 250 malts (and beers) in atmospheric, small-town hotel bar. And great food! Report: 1071/HIGHLANDS.

✓ **Dornoch Castle Hotel** **Dornoch** Attracts visitors (it is quite castellated) and locals in the bar and garden. Report: 1075/HIGHLANDS.

SPEYSIDE

✓ **Dowans Hotel** **Aberlour** Hotel with lavishly presented showcase in the heart of Speyside. 500+ to choose from. Report: 1028/SPEYSIDE.

✓ **The Craigellachie Hotel** **Craigellachie** Whiskies arranged in stylish bar of this essential Speyside hotel, the river below. Report: 1026/SPEYSIDE.

✓ **Gordon & MacPhail** **Elgin** · **www.gordonandmacphail.com** · **01343 545110** The whisky provisioner and bottlers of the *Connoisseurs Choice* brand you see all over. From humble beginnings over 100 years ago they now supply their exclusive and rarity range to the world. Closed Sun.

✓ **The Whisky Shop Dufftown** **www.whiskyshopdufftown.co.uk** · **01340 821097** The whisky shop in the main street (by the clock tower) at the heart of whisky country. Within a few miles of numerous distilleries, this place stocks all the products (including many halves). Open 7 days.

WEST

✓ **Lochside Hotel** **Bowmore, Islay** · **www.lochsidehotel.co.uk** · **01496 810244** More Islay malts than you ever imagined in a friendly local.

✓ **The Drover's Inn** **Inverarnan** Classic hostelry with around 75 drams and the right atmos to drink them in. Kilty barmen. Report: 1312/GOOD PUBS.

✓ **Sligachan Hotel** **Skye** · **www.sligachan.co.uk** · **01478 650204** On A87 (A850) 11km S of Portree. Nearly 400 malts in Seamus' huge cabin bar. Good ales, including their own (the Cuillin Brewery is here). Report: 2284/SKYE.

Loch Fyne Whiskies **Inveraray** · **www.lochfynewhiskies.com** · **01499 302219** On Main Street (A83), a shop with 400 malts, quaichs, etc.

SOUTH

✓ **Knockinaam Lodge** **Portpatrick** Comfortable country-house hotel; good Lowland selection includes the local Bladnoch. Report: 774/SW HOTELS.

Robbie's Drams **3 Sandgate, Ayr** · **www.robbieswhiskymerchants.com** · **01292 262135** Robin Russell's impressive emporium. Expert and independent. Bottle or case. Collect or order online.

The Best Gin Distillery Tours

Artisan and small-batch gin distilling has expanded exponentially in recent years (and since the last edition of StB). Some of the more ambitious brands have introduced tours of the premises and the process, and have created contemporary visitor attractions. Here are some of the best:

1548 8/R24 **Kingsbarns Distillery** nr Crail · www.kingsbarnsdistillery.com · 01333 451300 A purpose-built, modern distillery and visitor centre on the A917, 5km from Crail beside **Cambo Estate** (881/FIFE; 1305/HOUSE PARTIES); and the **Kingsbarns Golf Course** (2104/GOLF). So, there are many reasons to explore around here and this is one of the most developed of the gin-as-a-way-of-life brands: **Darnley's**. Tours through the day, much branded merchandise and a café. The product available in various bottlings around Fife and beyond.

1549 8/Q25 **Pickering's Gin** Edinburgh · www.pickeringsgin.com · 0131 290 2901 At Summerhall, the unique arts studio, performance and gallery complex (417/GALLERIES) that was Edinburgh's former vet school. Marcus Pickering was manager and protagonist here, making order out of the original chaos, and with partner Matt Gammell turned a couple of unused rooms round the back with passion and an eye for opportunity into a bespoke gin distillery like no other. It's intimate, quirky and tells a good story. You'll find Pickering's all over now, but it starts and continues here. Summerhall, during the Fringe (and actually all year round), is immersive and never stops and has a great bar (362/UNIQUE PUBS), which is where the tour starts.

1550 8/N23 **Strathearn Distillery** Methven, Perthshire · www.strathearndistillery.com · 01738 840100 A tiny farm-/barn-based distillery for whisky and gin – they show you round 'warts and all'. It's amazing what you can do on a farm! Here you muck in and help to make the gin. It's kinda true, anyone can do it. Small and personal and fun. Mon-Fri.

1551 8/Q25 **Edinburgh Gin** 1a Rutland Place, Edinburgh · www.edinburghgin.com · 0131 656 2810 Ideally placed in the west end of the city in Scotland's tourist portal: Edinburgh. The EG distillery tours and the swanky, designery visitor centre have become the first proper gin-based tourist attraction in Scotland. They've opened a new production facility in Leith, but at TGP the 'Discovery Connoisseur' and 'Gin Making' tours are here. There may be a waiting list. The well-turned-out product is increasingly available (worldwide). 7 days.

1552 7/G25 **Lussa Gin** Ardlussa, Isle of Jura · www.lussagin.com · 01496 820196 Based at the far N end of the faraway, starkly beautiful Isle of Jura (2231/ISLANDS) out of the Ardlussa estate, this bespoke 'fresh and zesty' product is 25km and a world away from the internationally renowned Jura Whisky. It's a 'labour of Lussa' for the 3 women who make Lussa Gin happen – numbered bottles, single batches. In a short while, the new spirit of Jura has travelled a long way. Tours available by appointment (you wouldn't want to go that far without having one), though you could just repair to and stay at the **Jura Hotel** (2273/ISLAND HOTELS) and drink in the product and the silence outside.

the
Best
of Outdoor Places

The Best Gardens

☕ signifies notable café.

1553 5/H16
L
NC500
ADMISSION
NTS
☕

✓✓ **Inverewe** Poolewe · www.nts.org.uk · 01445 712952 80km S of Ullapool on A832. World-famous gardens on a Loch Ewe promontory. Beginning in 1862, Osgood Mackenzie made it his life's work and since then people have come from all over the world to admire his efforts. Helped by the ameliorating effect of the Gulf Stream, the wild garden became the model for many others. The walled garden is beyond immaculate: if you were a flower or vegetable, you'd want to be here sheltered, nurtured and inclined to the southern sun (terrace best viewed from the top path by James Reid bench). Guided tours to get the most out of this vast garden or go in the evening when it's quiet! And not to be missed (though visitor volume can blunt the experience) is **Inverewe House** in the midst of your wanderings – the home of Osgood's daughter, the pioneering Mairi Sawyer, who travelled the world plant collecting and who also loved to shop! A £2m brilliant recreation of her life and times and elegant home. **The Bothy** adjacent for refreshments. Shop, visitor centre. Café (Mar-Oct: 10am-4.30pm; hot meals till 3pm), great space, food less so. Gardens AYR till dusk. 45-min 'Pinewood Trail' begins across the road from the café, culminating in a great view.

1554 7/K25
L
MAR-OCT
ADMISSION
☕

✓✓ **Benmore Botanic Garden** nr Dunoon · www.rbge.org.uk · 01369 706261 12km on A815 to Strachur. An outstation of the Royal Botanic Garden in Edinburgh, gifted to the nation by Harry Younger in 1928, but the first plantations date from 1820. Marked walks through formal gardens, woody grounds and pinetum where the air is often so sweet and spicy it seems like the elixir of life (I said this in my first edition – it's still true). Redwood avenue, terraced hillsides, views; a garden of different moods and fine proportions. Good walk, **Puck's Glen**, nearby (2064/WALKS). Café and shop open AYR.

1555 6/S20
L
ADMISSION
NTS
☕

✓✓ **Crathes Castle Gardens** nr Banchory · www.nts.org.uk · 01330 844525 25km W of Aberdeen, just off A93. One of the most interesting tower houses (1883/HOUSES) surrounded by terrific topiary and walled gardens of inspired design and tranquillity (though you're unlikely to have any part of it to yourself). Keen gardeners will be in their scented heaven. The Golden Garden (after Gertrude Jekyll) works particularly well and there's a wild garden beyond the old wall that many people miss. A very *House & Garden* experience, though in summer it's stuffed with people as well as plants. Grounds and Courtyard Café open AYR.

1556 9/N29
ADMISSION

✓✓ **The Garden of Cosmic Speculation** Holywood, Dumfriesshire · www.charlesjencks.com I hesitate to include this extraordinary garden by the landscape artist Charles Jencks because it's only fully open to the public for one day a year in early May (through the Scotland's Gardens Scheme). But it is too remarkable not to include. Laid out in 1988, this extraterrestrial garden of landforms, sculptures, bridges, terraces and architectural works around Portrack, the artist's Georgian farmhouse, remains both a memorial to Jencks's wife Maggie Keswick (who gave her name to the Maggie Cancer Caring Centres) and a place of national importance. Also by Jencks, in the same district and much more accessible is the **Crawick Multiverse** (2179/ART SPACES).

1557 8/P26
LL
ATMOS
ADMISSION

✓✓ **Little Sparta** nr Dunsyre · www.littlesparta.org.uk · 07826 495677 Near Biggar off A702 (5km), go through village then signed. House, in bare hill country, the home of conceptual artist and national treasure, Ian Hamilton Finlay, who died 2006. Gardens lovingly created over years, full of thought-provoking art/sculpture/perspectives (over 250 separate artworks). Unlike anywhere else. A privilege to visit but it is fragile; no dogs or little kids. 700m walk from car park. A bus leaves Edinburgh from the Scottish Poetry Library, first Sat of the month (every Sat in August) at 11.30am. Jun-Sep: check the website, also for how to get the beautiful guide book, *Little Sparta*.

1558 8/L28
ADMISSION
✓✓ **Dumfries House** nr Ochiltree · www.dumfries-house.org.uk · 01290 425959 On the A70 25km E of Ayr. The house, grounds and gardens have been transformed following the intervention of Prince Charles and the Prince's Foundation. There's the house itself (1876/HOUSES), a great café, restaurant and many ways to walk. Several garden areas, including the flagship walled garden (own café and admission) and the 10-acre Arboretum, The Chinese Bridge and marvellous Maze are among many features. As the extensive plantings mature they will be a wonder and a wandering for generations. Check website for times.

1559 8/N23
ADMISSION
✓✓ **Drummond Castle Gardens** Muthill · www.drummondcastlegardens.co.uk · 01764 681433 5km S of Crieff. Signed from A822, 2km from Muthill, then up an avenue of fabulous trees to the most exquisite formal gardens, viewed first from the terrace by the house. A boxwood parterre of a vast St Andrew's Cross in yellow and red (especially antirrhinums and roses), the Drummond colours, with extraordinary sundial centrepiece; 5 gardeners keep every leaf in place. Easter & May-Oct: 7 days 1-5pm (last admission). House not open to public.

1560 9/J31
L
ADMISSION
✓✓ **Logan Botanic Garden** nr Sandhead · www.rbge.org.uk · 01776 860231 16km S of Stranraer by A77/A716 and 2km on from Sandhead. Remarkable outstation of the Edinburgh Botanics, among sheltering woodland in the mild SW. Compact and full of pleasant southern surprises. Less crowded than other exotic gardens. Walled woodland gardens and the Tasmanian Creek. The Gunnera Bog is quite extraterrestrial. Coffee shop decent. Mar-Nov: 7 days 10am-5pm. Sundays in Feb: 10am-4pm for the snowdrops.

1561 7/J24
ADMISSION
NTS
✓✓ **Crarae Garden** Inveraray · www.nts.org.uk · 01546 886614 16km SE on A83 to Lochgilphead. Most gorgeous of the famed gardens of Argyll; peaceful in any season. The wooded banks of Loch Fyne with the gushing Crarae burn are as lush as the Himalayan gorges, where many of the plants originate. Follow the footsteps of plant-hunters and pandas! Open AYR 9.30am-dusk. Visitor centre Apr-Oct. Walks 0.5-2km. Loch Fyne days await you here!

1562 4/N15
LL
NC500
ADMISSION
✓✓ **Dunrobin Castle Gardens** Golspie · www.dunrobincastle.co.uk · 01408 633177 On A9 1km N of town. The Versailles-inspired gardens that sit below the opulent Highland chateau of the Dukes of Sutherland (1829/CASTLES). Terraced, parterred and immaculate, they stretch to the sea. 30 gardeners once tended them, now there are 4 but little has changed since they impressed a more exclusive clientele. Castle open Apr-Oct: 10.30am-last admission 4pm (Jun-Aug 5pm). Garden gate open later.

1563 8/P27
ADMISSION
✓✓ **Dawyck Gardens** nr Stobo · www.rbge.org.uk · 01721 760254 On B712 Moffat road off A72 Biggar-Peebles road, 2km from Stobo. An outstation of the Edinburgh Botanics, though tree planting here goes back 300 years. Sloping grounds around the gurgling Scrape burn which trickles into the Tweed. Landscaped woody pathways for meditative walks. Famous for shrubs, blue Himalayan poppies and Douglas firs. Rare Plant Trail and great walk on 'The John Buchan Way' nearby, 2km off Stobo Rd before Dawyck entrance. Visitor centre with café (home-made food) and shop. Feb-Nov: 10am-6pm (closes earlier in winter).

1564 9/K30
ADMISSION
✓ **Glenwhan Gardens** nr Dunragit, nr Stranraer · **www. glenwhangardens.co.uk** · **01581 400222** Signed from A75 and close to more famous **Castle Kennedy** (also very much worth a visit), this the more edifying labour of love. Up through beechy (and in May) bluebell woods, and through backyards to horticultural haven, teased from bracken and gorse moorland from 1979. Open moorland still beckons at the top of the network of trails through a carefully planted but wild botanical wonder. Many seats for contemplations; some sculpture. Gardens and tearoom Easter-Sep: 10am-5pm. Honesty box Oct.

1565 9/M30
ADMISSION
NTS
✓ **Threave Garden** nr Castle Douglas · **www.nts.org.uk** · **01556 502575** 64 acres of magnificent Victorian landscaping in incomparable setting overlooking Galloway coastline. Gardeners should not miss the walled kitchen garden; horticulturally inspiring and daunting. Garden is part of a vast estate, which includes the castle and a wildfowl reserve. Various walks: a circular Estate Walk 4km with spur (2km return) to the castle. Threave is a bat reserve. You can hire a bat detector with deposit and return next day. Centre open 10am-dusk (other access points for estate AYR).

1566 8/S27
ADMISSION
✓ **Floors Castle Gardens** Kelso · **www.floorscastle.com** · **01573 223333** 3km outside town off B6397 St Boswells. Spacious, immaculate walled gardens some distance from house, it has showpiece herbaceous borders, a 'Tapestry Garden', exquisite glasshouses and a top coffee shop, **The Terrace** (1453/TEAROOMS), and patio. 'Very good roses'. Lovely lawn for kids playing, you lounging. Can get general or separate ticket. Castle: May-Sep 11am-5pm & weekends in Oct; Grounds, gardens & tearoom: AYR. See also 1879/HOUSES.

1567 8/N22
HONESTY BOX
✓ **Cluny House Gardens** nr Aberfeldy · **www.clunyhousegardens.com** · **07818 065966** 3km from Aberfeldy on the back road to Grandtully, described as 'a magical garden for all seasons', as I discovered only in 2018, though it's been here above the Tay for decades. Wendy and John Mattingley tend these verdant 8 acres originally planted by Wendy's parents. Extolled for their enormous Wellingtonias, the wild woodland, atmospheric in any weather, was planted from seed. To underline this, pouches of Cluny seeds are for sale in the hall of the house. The frolicsome colony of red squirrels in the branches above seem unable to believe their luck in being here. Me too. 10am-6pm, AYR. Honesty box.

1568 8/R27
ADMISSION
✓ **Monteviot House Gardens** nr Ancrum · **www.monteviot.com** · **01835 830380** & **Woodside Garden Centre** nr Ancrum · **www. woodsidegarden.co.uk** · **01835 830315** Off A68 at Ancrum, the B6400 to Nisbet (3km), first there's Woodside on left (Victorian walled garden for the house; separate but don't miss) then the mainly formal gardens of the house (home of the Marquess of Lothian); terraced to the river (Teviot). All extraordinarily pleasant. **Woodside** has an organic demonstrations section, other events and a great tearoom (1452/TEAROOMS; 2225/GARDEN CENTRES). House open Jul (not Mon) 1-4.15pm (last entry). Gardens Apr-Oct: noon-4pm (last entry).

1569 7/J23
HONESTY BOX
✓ **Angus's Garden** Taynuilt · **www.barguillean.co.uk** 5km from village (22km from Oban on the A85) along the Glen Lonan road. Take first right after Barguillean Farm. A garden laid out by the family who own the farm in memory of their son Angus, a reporter killed reporting on the war in Cyprus. On the slopes around Angus's Loch, brimful of lilies and ducks and (rescued) swans. Informal mix of tended and uncultivated (though wild prevails), a more poignant remembrance is hard to imagine as you while an hour away in this peaceful place. 9am till dusk. AYR.

1570 8/Q25
L
☑ **Dr Neil's (Secret) Garden** Edinburgh · www.drneilsgarden.co.uk · 07849 187995 Not quite the secret it was (sorry!) but this garden can still feel like your private demesne on the shores of Duddingston Loch. End of the road through Holyrood Park just past Duddingston church; enter through manse gates. Turn right. At end of the manse lawn, a corner gate leads to an extraordinary terraced garden bordering the loch. With wild Arthur's Seat above, you can feel you're in Argyll. The labour of love of Claudia Poitier and volunteers, this is an enchanting corner of the city. 7 days 10am till dusk. The skating minister of the Raeburn painting took off from the restored tower here. Nice café on the way in/out.

1571 7/H24
ADMISSION
NTS
✓ **Arduaine Garden** nr Kilmelford · www.nts.org.uk · 01852 200366 28km S of Oban on A816, one of Argyll's undiscovered arcadias gifted to the NTS who in the current climate struggle to keep it open (in winter get tickets at the hotel). The creation of this (micro)climate in which the rich, diverse vegetation flourished, was influenced by Osgood Mackenzie of Inverewe (above) and its restoration is a testimony to the 20 years' hard labour of the famous Wright brothers. Enter/park by **Loch Melfort Hotel** (728/ARGYLL), gate 100m. Until dusk.

1572 9/M30
ADMISSION
✓ **Cally Gardens** Gatehouse of Fleet · www.callygardens.co.uk · 01557 815029 Off A75 at Gatehouse and through the gateway to **Cally Palace Hotel** (1179/KIDS), this walled garden is signed off to the left before you reach the hotel. Built in the 1770s as the kitchen garden of the big house, it was rescued in 1987 by Michael Wickenden, who transformed it into a haven for gardeners and meticulously gathered, introduced, nurtured and recorded herbaceous plants (over 3,000), many you won't find anywhere else. After Michael's tragic accident on a plant-gathering expedition in Malaysia, this remarkable garden was reopened by Kevin Hughes in summer 2018. Serious stuff, though not suburban neat and tidy. Check website for opening.

1573 7/G26
ADMISSION
✓ **Achamore Gardens** Gigha · www.gigha.org.uk/gardens · 01583 505275 1km from ferry. Walk or cycle (bike hire by ferry); an easy trip. The garden around the island's big hoose, once of the Horlick family, for sale at TGP. Lush tropical plants mingle with early-flourishing rhoddies (Feb-Mar): all due to the mild climate and the devotion of a long roll call of gardeners. 2 marked walks (40 mins/2 hours) start from the walled garden (green route takes in the sea view of Islay and Jura). Density and variety of shrubs, pond plants and trees revealed as you meander in this enchanting spot. Leaflet guides at entrance. Open AYR, 8am-6pm. Honesty box. See 2238/ISLANDS.

1574 6/S20
ADMISSION
NTS
✓ **Drum Castle Rose Garden** nr Banchory · www.nts.org.uk · 01330 700334 1km from A93. In the grounds of Drum Castle (the Irvine ancestral home, though nothing to do with my own Irvines 1827/CASTLES), a superb walled garden that pays homage to the rose and encapsulates 4 centuries of its horticulture. 4 areas (17th–20th centuries). Fabulous, Jul/Aug especially. Apr-Oct: 11am-4pm.

1575 9/M31
ADMISSION
NTS
Hornel Gallery Garden Kirkcudbright · www.nts.org.uk · 01557 330437 The house and atelier of the prolific and notable artist Edward Hornel (1864–1933), who was the most successful of the artists' colony in Kirkcudbright in the early 20th century. He lived here – Broughton House – from 1901 and created a lush, secret garden informed by his travels in Japan. Not extensive but full of interest, it stretches to the mystic tidal river (there's now a small marina over the garden wall), which with the Solway light inspired the artist's work. The colony's story is told at the **Kirkcudbright Galleries** (2187/GALLERIES). House Apr-Oct; garden also open in Feb (for snowdrops, etc – enter by the side gate in the alley).

1576 7/J26   **Ascog Hall Fernery** Rothesay · www.ascogfernery.com · 01700 503461
ADMISSION   Outside town on road to **Mount Stuart** (1871/HOUSES), worth stopping at Ascog
Hall, its small garden and sunken Victorian Fern House, rescued and restored
in 1997. Green and lush and dripping! Easter-Oct: 10am-5pm. And don't miss
Rothesay's Victorian men's loos (women can visit); they are not small.

1577 8/R27   **Priorwood Garden** Melrose · www.nts.org.uk · 01896 822493   Next to
ADMISSION   Melrose Abbey, this tranquil secret garden behind high walls specialises in
NTS   growing flowers and plants for drying. Picking, drying and arranging continuously
in progress. Samples for sale. Run by enthusiasts on behalf of the NTS, they're
always willing to talk stamens with you. Includes a historical apple orchard with
trees through the ages. Laden with apples on a recent visit. Mon-Sat 10am-5pm,
Sun 1-5pm. Closed 4pm winter. A superior shop with flowers and veg from nearby
Harmony Garden, where they hold the book festival (40/EVENTS).

1578 8/Q27   **Kailzie Gardens** Peebles · www.kailziegardens.com · 01721 720007   On
L   B7062 Traquair road. Spacious, well-kept walled garden with informal glasshouses
ADMISSION   and perfect hedges. Informal woodland gardens all eminently strollable. Old-
fashioned roses, wilder bits. Courtyard teashop (though closed at TGP). Kids' corner
and ospreys (Apr-Aug). Fishing ponds. Apr-Oct: 10am-5pm (only grounds in winter).

1579 6/S18   **Pitmedden Garden** nr Ellon · www.nts.org.uk · 01651 842352   35km N of
ADMISSION   Aberdeen, 10km W of A92. Formal French gardens recreated in 1950s on site of
NTS   Sir Alex Seton's 17th-century ones. The 4 great parterres, 3 based on designs for
🍵   Holyrood Palace gardens, are best viewed from the terrace. Charming farmhouse
museum seems transplanted. For lovers of symmetry and an orderly universe (but
there is a woodland walk, wildlife and picnic garden area). May-Sep: 10am-5pm
(last entry).

1580 6/R19   **Pittodrie House** nr Inverurie · www.macdonaldhotels.co.uk · 01467 681444
An exceptional walled garden in the grounds of **Pittodrie House Hotel** at Chapel
of Garioch (985/NE HOTELS). Different gardens compartmentalised by hedges.
500m from house and curiously unvisited by many of the guests, this secret
and sheltered haven is both a kitchen garden and a place for meditations and
reflections (and those wedding photos); chances are you'll have this haven to
yourself, as I have, catching the sun.

1581 7/K24   **Ardkinglas Woodland** Cairndow · www.ardkinglas.com · 01499 600261   Off
ADMISSION   the A83 Loch Lomond–Inveraray road. Through village to signed car park and these
mature woodlands in the grounds of Ardkinglas House on the southern bank near
the head of Loch Fyne. Fine pines include 'the tallest tree in Britain'. Magical at
dawn or dusk. 2km **Loch Fyne Oysters** (1371/SEAFOOD), where there is also the
Tree Shop garden centre, especially good for trees and shrubs.

1582 5/J18   **Attadale Gardens** Strathcarron · www.attadalegardens.com ·
NC500   01520 722603   On A890 from Kyle of Lochalsh and A87 just S of Strathcarron.
ADMISSION   Lovely West Highland home (to the Macphersons, Joanna holds the shears here)
and these delightful gardens near Loch Carron. Exotic specials, water gardens,
collected sculpture, great rhoddies May/Jun. Nursery and kitchen garden. Fern and
Japanese gardens all kept in place by 3 gardeners. A DIY tearoom (honesty box) and
a good café/restaurant. Apr-Oct: 10am-5.30pm. The **Carron Restaurant** nearby
1098/HIGHLANDS is very good.

1583 7/J21   **Ard Daraich Hill Garden** Ardgour · www.arddaraich.co.uk · **01855 841384**
3km S Ardgour at Corran Ferry on A861 to Strontian. A private (50 years), labour-of-love hill and wild garden where you are at liberty to wander. Shores of Loch Linnhe with views of Ben Nevis and Glen Coe – you could be in the Himalayas. Once the home of Constance Spry. Tending to the ericaceous (i.e. specialising in rhoddies), shrubs, trees; birdsong! Open AYR, 7 days. 3 lovely rooms to stay over.

1584 8/M26   **The Hidden Gardens** Glasgow · www.thehiddengardens.org.uk ·
0141 433 2722 This garden oasis in the asphalt jungle of Glasgow's southside was created in the disused wasteland behind The Tramway performance and studio space. A project of environmental theatre group NVA, working with landscape architects City Design Co-operative, this is a very modern approach to an age-old challenge – how to make and keep a sanctuary in the city! It's ageing gracefully. Nice caff. Opening hours vary. Closed Mon.

Royal Botanic Garden Edinburgh Report: 408/ATTRACTIONS.

Mount Stuart Gardens Bute Report: 1871/HOUSES.

Botanic Gardens & Kibble Palace Glasgow Report: 682/ATTRACTIONS.

Kildrummy Castle Hotel nr Alford Report: 1238/SCOTTISH HOTELS.

Castle of Mey Gardens nr Thurso Report: 1815/CASTLES.

Cawdor Castle Gardens nr Nairn Report: 1816/CASTLES.

Brodick Castle Gardens Arran Report: 1819/CASTLES.

Dunvegan Castle Gardens Skye Report: 1821/CASTLES.

Manderston House Gardens Duns Report: 1873/HOUSES.

Learn more about all these gardens and many others in **Scotland for Gardeners** *by Kenneth Cox, published by Birlinn.*

The Best Country Parks

signifies notable café.

1585 9/N28   ✓✓ **Drumlanrig Castle** Thornhill · www.drumlanrigcastle.co.uk ·
ADMISSION   **01848 331555** On A76, 7km N of Thornhill in the west Borders, in whose romance and history it's steeped, much more than merely a country park; spend a good day, both inside the castle (summer only; check website) and in the grounds. Apart from *that* art collection (Rembrandt, Holbein and you may remember the Leonardo got stolen then found, now in the National Portrait Gallery) and the courtyard/stableyard of shops, the delights include a wee tearoom, an adventure playground and regular events programme. Main outdoor focus is on extensive trails for walking (4) and cycling (8). Rik's Bike Shed in the stableyard **01848 330080** is the hub for hiring, fixing and cleaning bikes. Up to 15km round the estate lochs and silvery Nith. Apr-Sep: 10am-5pm.

1586 7/L26 ✓ **Muirshiel Country Park** nr Lochwinnoch · www.clydemuirshiel.co.uk ·
L 01505 614791 Via Largs (A760) or Glasgow (M8, junction 29 A737 then A760
5km S of Johnstone). N from village on Kilmacolm road for 3km then signed.
Muirshiel is name given to wider area but park proper begins 6km on road along the
Calder valley. Despite proximity to the conurbation, this is a wild and enchanting
place for walks, picnics, etc. Trails marked to waterfall and summit views (Windy Hill
an easy 2km). Extensive events programme. Go look for hen harriers. See also 698/
WALKS. Escape!

1587 8/R25 **John Muir Country Park** nr Dunbar · www.eastlothian.gov.uk ·
01620 827459 Named after the 19th-century conservationist who founded
America's national parks (and the Sierra Club), and who was born in Dunbar (his
birthplace is now an interactive museum at 126 High St and the start of The John
Muir Way, which runs across Central Scotland to Helensburgh). This swathe of
coastline to the W of the town (partly known locally as **Tyninghame** 441/BEACHES)
is an important estuarine nature reserve but is good for family walks. Various entry
points: main one is from Dunbar roundabout on A1 back towards North Berwick,
then A1087, 1km; by clifftop trail from Dunbar; or from car park on road into
Dunbar from W at West Barns.

1588 7/L25 **Finlaystone Estate** Langbank · www.finlaystone.co.uk · 01475 540505 A8
ADMISSION to Greenock, Houston direction at Langbank, then signed. Grand mansion home
to chief of Clan MacMillan set in formal gardens in wooded estate. Lots of facilities,
craft shop, leafy walks, walled garden and rather good Garden Café. Apr-Sep: till
5pm; Oct-Mar: till 4pm. An all-round get oot o' the house experience.

1589 8/S27 **Hirsel Country Park** Coldstream · www.dandaestates.co.uk · 01555 851536
On A697, N edge town (direction Kelso). 3,000 acres the grounds of Hirsel House
(not open to public). 2-4km walks through farmland and Dunglass Woods, including
lovely languid lake. Museum, tearoom (7 days) and craft units at the Homestead.

1590 8/N25 **Muiravonside Country Park** nr Linlithgow · www.falkirkcommunitytrust.
org · 01324 590900 4km SW of Linlithgow on B825, or signed from junction 4
of M9 Edinburgh/Stirling. Former farm estate and a park just where you need it,
with 170 acres of woodland walks, parkland, picnic sites and a visitor centre for
school parties or anyone else with an interest in birds, bees and badgers. Ranger
service; guided walks (01324 506119). Great place to walk off that lunch at the
not-too-distant **Champany Inn** (281/BURGERS & STEAKS). Apr-Sep: 8am-8pm
(Oct-Mar till 5pm).

✓✓ **Culzean Castle Park** Ayrshire Superb. Report: 1813/CASTLES.

✓✓ **Haddo House** nr Ellon Beautiful grounds. Report: 1872/HOUSES.

✓ **Mugdock Country Park** nr Glasgow Vast. Report: 694/WALKS.

✓ **Tentsmuir** nr Tayport Estuarine; John Muir, on Tay. Report: 1807/RESERVES.

✓ **Kelburn Country Centre** Largs Report: 1747/KIDS.

The Best Town Parks

1591 8/Q25 ✓✓ **Princes Street Gardens** Edinburgh On S side of Princes St. This former loch, drained when the New Town was built, divided by the Mound, and wrested from 'the landlords' to become a pleasure ground for 'the people' in perpetuity. The eastern half has pitch and putt, the **Scott Monument** (447/VIEWS) and, well, Christmas. The western has its recently restored fountain, open-air café, space for locals and tourists to sprawl on the grass when sunny, the Ross Bandstand – heart of **Edinburgh's Hogmanay** (77/EVENTS) – and the International Festival's fireworks concert (54/EVENTS) and about to be turned into a proper amphitheatre. Workers on lunch, senior citizens on benches, dazed tourists: all our lives are here. Till dusk. Not to forget **The Meadows** – an exceptional asset to the city.

1592 6/S19 ✓✓ **Hazlehead Park** Aberdeen · www.aberdeencity.gov.uk Via Queens Rd, 3km centre. Extraordinary park where the Aberdonians' mysterious gardening skills are magnificently in evidence. Many facilities including a maze, pets' corner, tearoom and there are lawns, memorials and botanical splendours aplenty, especially the azalea garden in spring and roses in summer. Sculpture and serenity!

1593 6/T19 ✓ **Duthie Park** Aberdeen · www.aberdeencity.gov.uk Riverside Dr along River Dee from the bridge carrying main A92 Stonehaven road. The other large well-kept park with duck pond, bandstand, hugely impressive summer rose gardens, carved sculptures and the famous David Welch Winter Garden of subtropical palms/ferns and home to one of the UK's biggest cacti collections.

1594 8/P25 ✓ **Pittencrieff Park** Dunfermline · www.fifedirect.org.uk Extensive park alongside the abbey and palace ruins, gifted to the town in 1903 by Carnegie. Open areas, glasshouses pavilion (more a function room) and café, peacocks, but most notably a deep verdant glen crisscrossed with pathways. Great kids' play area. Lush, full of birds, good after rain, the Park and exploration of Dunfermline's Heritage Quarter, the Abbey and the Carnegie Library, with Richard Murphy's award-winning extension, can make for an elevating afternoon.

1595 8/N23 ✓ **MacRosty Park** Crieff · www.pkc.gov.uk On your left as you leave Crieff for Comrie and Crianlarich; for parking ask locally. A perfect green place on sloping ground to the River Earn (good level walk – Lady Mary's Walk) with tearooms, innovative kids' area, mature trees and superb bandstand. A fine old park. Brilliant for kids.

1596 8/Q24 **Beveridge Park** Kirkcaldy · www.fifedirect.org.uk Another big municipal park with a duck and boat pond, wide-open spaces and many amusements (e.g. bowling, tennis, putting, plootering). **Ravenscraig**, a coastal park on the main road E to Dysart, is an excellent place to walk. Great prospect of the firth and its coves and cruise.

1597 8/R28 **Wilton Lodge Park** Hawick · www.scotborders.gov.uk Hawick not overfull of visitor attractions but it does have a nice park with facilities and diversions enough for everyone, e.g. the civic gallery, rugby pitches (they like rugby a lot in Hawick), a large kids' playground, a seasonal café and lots of riverside walks by the Teviot (you can smell the river banks). Lots of my school friends lost their virginity in the shed here. All-round open-air recreation centre. South end of town by A7. PS: the shed was still there last time I checked.

1598 9/P28   **Station Park**   Moffat · www.visitmoffat.co.uk   On your right as you enter the town from the M74. Well-proportioned people's park; boating pond (with giant swans), 18-hole putting. Annan water alongside offers nice walking. Notable also for the monument to Air Chief Marshall Hugh Dowding, Commander in Chief during the Battle of Britain. 'Never ... was so much owed by so many to so few'.

1599 8/L27   **Dean Castle Park**   Kilmarnock · www.deancastle.com   A77 S, first turn-off for Kilmarnock then signed; from Ayr A77 N, 3rd turn-off. Surprising green and woody oasis in suburban Kilmarnock; lawns and woods around restored castle and courtyard. Urban farm, adventure playground, caff. Hosts **Illuminight** in Oct/Nov (72/EVENTS).

1600 9/M30   **Garries Park**   Gatehouse of Fleet   Notable for its tiny perfect garden which you enter under an arch from the village main street. A wee gem, especially for its flower plantings. Leads to bigger public space (and woody walk 2.5km round S side of village), but pause in the garden and smell those roses. **Galloway Lodge Preserves** (785/SW RESTAURANTS) for lunch, etc.

1601 8/L26   **Rouken Glen & Linn Park**   Glasgow   Both on S side of river. Rouken Glen via
& 8/M26   Pollokshaws/Kilmarnock Rd to Eastwood Toll then right. Visitor area with info centre, garden centre, a café, kids' play area and woodland walks. Linn Park via Aikenhead and Carmunnock road. It's a journey but worth it; this is one of the undiscovered Elysiums of a city that boasts over 60 parks. Activities, wildlife walks, kids' nature trails, horse-riding and Alexander 'Greek' Thomson's **Holmwood House**; open Mar-Oct (NTS).

1602 8/Q23   **Camperdown Park**   Dundee · www.camperdownpark.com   Calling itself a country park, Camperdown is a splendid recreational breathing space for the city and hosts a plethora of distractions – a golf course, a wildlife complex with a great kids' play area (1757/KIDS), and the neoclassical Victorian mansion house, **Camperdown House**, an ongoing project, and events, especially the **Dundee Flower and Food Festival** (62/EVENTS). Situated beyond Kingsway, the ring-route; go via Coupar Angus turn-off. Best walks across the A923 in **Templeton Woods** (2081/WALKS).

1603 6/P17   **Grant Park**   Forres · www.moray.gov.uk   Frequent winner of the Bonny Bloom competitions (a board proclaims their awards) and, with its balance of ornamental gardens, open parkland and woody hillside, this is obviously a carefully tended rose. Good municipal facilities, such as pitch and putt and playground. Cricket in summer and topping topiary. Through woods on Cluny Hill to the Nelson Tower for exercise and view.

1604 8/N25   **Callendar Park**   Falkirk · www.falkirkcommunitytrust.org   Park on edge of town centre, signed from all over. Overlooked by high-rise blocks and near a busy road system, this is nevertheless a beautiful green space with a big hoose (heritage museum with exhibitions), woods and lawns. You can't help feeling they could do with it here. See also **The Kelpies and the Helix** 2/ATTRACTIONS.

The Most Interesting Coastal Villages

1605 5/H18 ✓ **Plockton nr Kyle of Lochalsh** · www.plockton.com A Highland gem
L   12km over the hill from Kyle, clustered around inlets of a wooded bay on Loch
Carron. Cottage gardens down to the bay and their much admired palm trees!
Great walks over headlands. Plockton Inn and on the front the Plockton Hotel have
rooms and pub grub (1073/HIGHLANDS); there's also the estimable **Plockton
Shores** (1091/HIGHLANDS). www.calums-sealtrips.com are a treat (seals and
dolphins almost guaranteed). It's not hard to feel at one with this village (as
generations do).

1606 6/R17 ✓ **Moray Coast Fishing Villages** From Spey Bay (where the Spey slips into the
& 6/S17   sea) to Fraserburgh: some of Scotland's best coastal scenery with interesting
LL   villages in cliff/cove and beach settings. See 1620/BEACHES for the best. Especially
notable are **Portsoy**, with 17th-century harbour (and see 45/EVENTS); **Sandend**,
with its own beach and a fab one nearby at **Sunnyside**; **Pennan**, famous from the
film *Local Hero*; **Gardenstown**, with a walk along the water's edge to **Crovie**
(pronounced 'Crivee'), the epitome of a coast-clinging community (near **Troup
Head** 1791/BIRDS); and **Cullen**, on the A98 with a top café (992/NE RESTAURANTS)
and beach.

1607 1/Q10 ✓ **Stromness Orkney Mainland** 24km from Kirkwall and a different kettle of
fish. Hugging the shore and with narrow streets and wynds, it has a unique
atmos: both maritime and oddly European. Some of the most singular shops you'll
see anywhere and the Orkney folk going about their business. Park near harbour
and walk down the cobbled main street if you don't want to scrape your paintwork.
Great art gallery (2186/GALLERIES).

1608 5/M17 ✓ **Cromarty nr Inverness** At end of road across Black Isle from Inverness
(45km NE); does take longer than you think (well, 30 mins). Village with
times-gone-by atmos without being twee. Lots of kids running about and a pink
strand of beach. Delights to discover include: the East Kirk, plain and aesthetic with
countryside through the windows behind the altar; Hugh (the geologist) Miller's
cottage/Courthouse museum (2173/HISTORY); **Couper's Creek** (1436/TEAROOMS);
Cromarty Bakery (1482/BAKERS); a perfect wee restaurant **Sutor Creek** (1092/
HIGHLANDS); the shore and cliff walk (2092/WALKS); the Pirates' Cemetery, the
obliging dolphins (1792/DOLPHINS), and the not-so-cool oil platforms!

1609 8/N25 **Culross nr Dunfermline** · www.nts.org.uk By A994 from Dunfermline or
NTS   junction 1 of M90 just over Queensferry Crossing (15km). Old centre conserved and
restored by NTS. Mainly residential and not awash with craft and coffee shops.
More historical than quaint; a community of careful custodians lives in the white
and yellow red-pantiled houses. Footsteps echo in the cobbled wynds and those
of the *Outlander* film crews (series 1 & 2). Palace and Town House open Easter-Oct
noon-5pm, weekends Sep/Oct. Interesting back gardens; lovely church at top of hill
(1907/CHURCHES). **Bessie's** café, by the Palace is way better than many by the NTS.
Excellent home baking! 7 days, daytime only.

1610 7/G22 **Tobermory Mull** Postcard/calendar village with painted houses round the bay,
L   and the main town of Mull. Ferry port for Ardnamurchan, but main Oban ferry
is 35km away at Craignure. Usually a bustling harbour front with quieter streets
behind; a quintessential island atmos. Some good inexpensive hotels (and quayside
hostel) well situated to explore the whole island and a great fish restaurant. See
Mull, pages 396-8; 1201/HOSTELS; 1358/SEAFOOD.

1611 7/F26 **Port Charlotte Islay** A township on the Rhinns of Islay, the western peninsula. By A846 from the ports, Askaig and Ellen, via Bridgend, then A847. Rows of whitewashed, well-kept cottages along and back from shoreline. Great wee museum (www.islaymuseum.org), a restaurant, Yan's Kitchen (both Mar-Oct) and the estimable **Port Charlotte Hotel**, with bar and dining room. Town beach and the one between Port Charlotte and Bruichladdich (the war memorial nearby). Quiet and charming, not merely quaint. The road onwards (10km) to **Portnahaven**, (even cuter) far west. See Islay, pages 394–5; 2264/ISLAND HOTELS.

1612 9/N30 **Rockcliffe nr Dumfries** 25km S on Solway Coast road, A710. On the Scottish Riviera, the rocky part of the coast around to **Kippford** (2086/WALKS). A good rock-scrambling foreshore though not so clean, the village with few houses, and repair to the **Anchor** in Kippford for grub and ale (1348/FOOD PUBS).

1613 8/R24 **East Neuk Villages www.eastneukwide.co.uk** The quintessential quaint wee
 & 8/R23 fishing villages along the bit of Fife that forms the mouth of the Firth of Forth. **Crail, Anstruther, Pittenweem, St Monans** and **Elie** have different characters and attractions, especially Crail (1431/TEAROOMS) and Pittenweem harbours; Anstruther is main centre and home of **Fisheries Museum** 2176/HISTORY (see also 1396/FISH & CHIPS; 1776/BIRDS); St Monans for seafood (1357/SEAFOOD); and perfect Elie (1330/FOOD PUBS; 2105/GOLF). Also St Andrews up the road, p. 155–7. Cycling good, traffic in summer not.

1614 8/P25 **Aberdour** Between Dunfermline and Kirkcaldy, 10km E from junction 1 of M90 or go by train from Edinburgh (frequent service: Dundee or Kirkcaldy); delightful station. Walks round harbour and to headland, **Silver Sands** beach 1km.

1615 9/L31 **Isle of Whithorn www.isleofwhithorn.com** Strange faraway village at end of the road, 35km S of Newton Stewart, 6km Whithorn (1863/PREHISTORIC). Mystical harbour where low tide does mean low, saintly shoreline, a sea angler's pub, the **Steampacket** – very good pub grub (1318/GOOD PUBS). Ninian's chapel round the headland underwhelming but you pass the poignant memorial to the *Solway Harvester*. Everybody visiting IoW seems to walk this way.

1616 7/J27 **Corrie Arran · www.visitarran.com** Last but not least, the bonniest bit of
 LL Arran (apart from Kildonan and the glens and the rest), happily reached by bike from Brodick (10km). Many walks from here, including **Goat Fell** (1985/HILLS), but nice just to sit or potter on the foreshore. Hotel has never quite been up to expectations. Animal sculptures and even the boats in the slips of harbours are aesthetic. New seafood café **Mara** at TGP (closed Mon).

Scotland's Superb Beaches & Bays

Well, not all of them! All listed below are in L, LL *and* LLL *settings, obviously.*

1617 4/N12
& 4/M12
& 4/M13
& 4/L12
NC500

✓✓ **North Coast** W of Thurso are some of Britain's most unspoiled and unsung beaches. But no beach bums and no Beach Boys. There are many great little coves, you choose; but those to mention are: **Strathy** and **Armadale** (35km W Thurso), **Farr** and **Torrisdale** (48km), the latter is hugely impressive (the **Bettyhill Hotel** overlooks 1083/HIGHLAND) but Farr is easier to reach, **Coldbackie** (65km) and **Balnakeil** by Durness, 1km W after the craft village (2196/SCOTTISH SHOPS). My favourite (in the far west) is separately acclaimed and claimed ...

1618 4/L12
NC500

✓✓ **Pete's Beach nr Durness** The One of the many great beaches on the North Coast that I've called my own. The hill above it is called Ceannabeinne; you find it 7km E of Durness. Coming from Tongue it's just after where Loch Eriboll comes out to the sea and the road hits the coast again (there's a lay-by opposite and a recent sign calling it after the hill, i.e. not me!). It's a small, perfect cove flanked by walls of coral-pink rock and shallow turquoise sea. Splendid from above (land rises to a bluff with a huge boulder) and from below. Revisiting many times in several aspects (of weather and light), it's never short of magnificent, well, until the bloody zip wire business arrived. There's a great coastal walk to the **Ceannabeinne Township** (2094/WALKS) nearby.

1619 3/E16

✓✓ **Scarista Beach & the Beaches of South Harris** On W coast road S of Tarbert (20km) to Rodel. Scarista is so beautiful that people get married here. Hotel over the road is worth staying just to walk here, but is also a treat retreat (2261/ISLAND HOTELS); there are many cool, self-catering cottages (1244/ LUXURIOUS ISOLATION). Golf on the links (2108/GOLF). This ethereal coast has many extraordinary beaches: immense **Luskentyre** (beach access 4km off main A859) and **Northton**, with the great **Temple Café**. Ask about the machair walk to Toe Head. And camp (1249/WILD CAMPING). It's magnificent on this coast in early evening. The sun also rises.

1620 6/R17
& 6/P17
& 6/S17
& 6/T17

✓✓ **Moray Coast** Many great beaches along coast from Spey Bay to Fraserburgh, notably **Cullen** and **Lossiemouth** (town beaches), and **New Aberdour** (2km from New Aberdour village on B9031, 15km W of Fraserburgh) and **Rosehearty** (8km W of Fraserburgh), both quieter places for walks and picnics. 2 of the great secret beaches on this coast are:
Sunnyside nr Sandend where you walk past the incredible ruins of Findlater Castle on the clifftop (how did they build it? A place, on its grassed-over roof, for a picnic) and down to a cove which on my sunny days has always been perfect. Signed (Findlater) from A98. Take a left from Sandend 16km W of Banff, follow road for 2km, park behind the farm buildings. Walk from here past dovecote, 1km to cliff, then left from the ruin viewpoint. See also 1837/RUINS; 2090/WALKS.
Cullykhan Bay E of Gardenstown signed from the coast road (200m to small car park). A small beach but great littoral for beach scrambling and full of surprises (1980/ENCHANTING PLACES).
Rockpool in Cullen, a great café (992/NE RESTAURANTS).
Shore Inn in Portsoy for harbour pub (1319/GOOD PUBS).

1621 7/G28

✓✓ **Machrihanish nr Campbeltown** Foot of the Kintyre peninsula 10km from Campbeltown. Walk N from Machrihanish village or golf course, or from the car park on A83 to Tayinloan and Tarbert at point where it hits/leaves the coast. A joyously long strand (8km) of unspoiled orange-pink sand backed by dunes and facing the 'steepe Atlantic Stream' all the way to Newfoundland (2107/GOLF). Great accom/eats at **Machrihanish Dunes** and **Royal Hotel** (733/ARGYLL).

1622 7/F24 ✓✓ **Kiloran Beach Colonsay** 9km from quay and hotel, past Colonsay House (8km circular walk); parking and access on hillside. Often described as the finest beach in the Hebrides, it doesn't disappoint, though it can change character. Craggy cliffs on one side, negotiable, rocks on the other, tiers of grassy dunes between. The island was once bought as a picnic spot. This beach was why.

1623 4/K12 ✓✓ **Sandwood Bay Kinlochbervie** This mile-long sandy strand with its old Stack is legendary but there's the problem: too many people, especially since the NC500, come here and you may have to share its glorious isolation. Inaccessibility is its saving grace: it's a 7km walk from the sign off the road at Balchrick (near the cattle grid), which is 6km from Kinlochbervie; allow 3-4 hours return plus time there. More venturesome is the walk from the north and **Cape Wrath** (2084/WALKS). Go easy and go in summer!

1624 3/D18 ✓✓ **South Uist** Deserted but for birds, an almost unbroken strand of beach running for miles down the W coast; the machair is best in early summer (follow the Machair Way). Take any road off the spinal A865; usually less than 2km. Good spot to try is turn-off at **Tobha Mòr** 25km N of Lochboisdale; real blackhouses and a chapel on the way to the sea. Listen to the birds – this is as far away as you can get from the High Streets of life.

1625 7/F26 ✓✓ **Saligo, Machir Bay & The Big Strand Islay** The first two are bays on NW of island via A847 road to Port Charlotte, and B8018 past Loch Gorm; signposting is not good. Wide beaches; remains of war fortifications in deep dunes, Machir perhaps best for beach bums, follow signs for **Kilchoman Distillery**, but Saligo has character (both can be wild). The Big Strand is on Laggan Bay: along Bowmore–Port Ellen road take Oa turn-off, follow Kintra signs. There's camping and great walks in either direction, 8km of glorious sand and dunes (stay/eat **Machrie** golf course and hotel 2259/ISLAND HOTELS). All these are airy ambles under a wide sky. See 2100/GOLF; 2082/WALKS.

1626 3/E14
& 3/G12
& 3/G13 ✓ **The Beaches of Lewis** Perhaps less celebrated than Harris (above), there are numerous enchanting beaches on the Lewis coast; apart from the odd surfie, you're likely to have the strand to yourself. Around **Uig** in the W via A8011, especially **Timsgarry/Ardroil** and go further to legendary **Mangurstadh** into the sunset. Lovely **Loch Croistean Coffee Shop** on the way (2379/HEBRIDES). For the beach at the N end (of the Hebrides), **Port Nis**: keep driving (some interesting stops on the way 1182/HOSTELS; 2161/HISTORY) until you get to this tiny bay and harbour down the hill at the end of the road. **Anthony Barber's Harbour View Gallery** full of his own work (inexpensive and accessible) is worth a visit (Mon-Sat 10am-5pm). 3 more secret beach spots via the B895 15km NW of Stornoway (past Broad Bay) are at the long strand at **Tolsta** and further, at the end of the road, **Traigh Mhor**, and the bridge to nowhere, exquisite **Ghearadha** (pronounced 'Gary').

1627 4/K13 ✓ **Oldshoremore nr Kinlochbervie** The beach you pass on the road to Balchrick, only 3km from Kinlochbervie. It's easy to reach and a beautiful spot: the water is clear and perfect for swimming, and there are rocky walks and quiet places. **Polin** 500m north, is a cove you might have to yourself (1259/WILD CAMPING).

1628 7/J26 ✓ **Ostel Beach/Kilbride Bay** **Millhouse, nr Tighnabruaich** 3km from
Millhouse on B8000 signed Ardlamont (not Portavadie, the ferry), a track to
right before white house (now a café), often with a chain across to restrict access.
Park and walk 1.5km, turning right after lochan. You arrive on a perfect white sandy
crescent known locally as Ostel and, in certain conditions, a mystical place to swim
and picnic. **Arran's north coast** is like a Greek island in the bay.

1629 8/R22 ✓ **Lunan Bay** **nr Montrose** 7km from main A92 road to Aberdeen and 5km of
deep red crescent beach under a wide northern sky. The **But 'n' Ben** in
Auchmithie is an excellent place to start or finish (917/PERTHSHIRE) and good
approach (from south), although **Gordon's** restaurant at Inverkeilor is closer
(915/PERTHSHIRE). You can climb up to the Red Castle. Lunan is often deserted.
The funky **Lunan Bay Diner** is at the car park. 100m to the beach. **St Cyrus** N of
Montrose (a nature reserve) also a lovely littoral to wander. Walk 2km S of village.

1630 4/J14 ✓ **The Secret Beach** **nr Achmelvich** From Achmelvich car park going N, it's
NC500 the next proper bay round, or easier: Lochinver–Stoer/Drumbeg road (1679/
SCENIC ROUTES); lay-by on right 3km after Achmelvich turn-off, 250m beyond sign
for Cathair Estate. Park on the right, cross the road and walk towards the sea (20
mins) following stream (a sign points to Mill). The path is well defined – you step
over the old mill stones. Called **Altanabradhan**, it's the site of an old mill (grinding
wheels still there), perfect for camping and the best sea for swimming in the area.

1631 5/H16 ✓ **Gairloch** A beach I missed until one sunny July afternoon when lots of
NC500 people, but not (and I imagine never) too many, were lying on this perfect
curve of sand, a sheltered bay of Loch Gairloch and swimming in its shallow,
shimmering, non-wavy water. There's a tranquil old graveyard behind (1942/
GRAVEYARDS) and the green golf course beside. Parking and toilets. The longer Big
Sand is 4km W by the campsite (1270/CAMPING WITH KIDS). I must go back.

1632 5/H20 **Camusdarach and the Sands of Morar** **nr Mallaig** 70km W of Fort William
and 6km from Mallaig by a good road, these easily accessible beaches may seem
overpopulated on summer days and the S stretch nearest to Arisaig may have one too
many caravan parks, but they go on for miles and there's enough space for everybody.
The sand is among the best in Scotland with lots of rocky bits for exploration. One
of the best stretches (the bay before the estuary) is **Camusdarach**, signed from the
main road (where *Local Hero* was filmed); further from the road, it is quieter and a
very good swathe of sand. On one early summer evening 2018, it was sublime – we
swam. **Traigh**, the golf course, makes good use of the dunes (2121/GOLF).

1633 4/J16 **Beaches around Gruinard Bay** **by Laide, north of Gairloch** While Gruinard
& 4/J15 Beach itself on the A832 is easily found and accessed (and huge), these 2 I found
NC500 on either side with local intel, both very special. The nearest is at **Mungasdale**,
<500m N, go between fence-post pillars or over a stile by a makeshift pull over
spot – 15-min walk through straggly birch woods to pristine dunes and sand with a
burn. The beach at **Mellon Udrigle** is more widely known and has a car park and a
camping ground (no facilities). A crescent of golden sand and a Stac Polly over the
sea. 6km N from the A832 at Laide.

1634 7/G25 **Lowlandman's Bay** **Jura** Not in itself a beach but a rocky foreshore with ethereal
atmos; great light and space (lovely **Corran Sands** are adjacent; ask directions
locally – recently improved path from Little to Big Corran). Only seals break the
spell. Go right before 3-arch bridge to first group of houses (Knockdrome), through
yard on left and right around cottages to track to Ardmenish. After deer fences, bay
is visible on your right, 1km walk away.

1635 3/C20 **Vatersay south of Barra** The tiny island joined by a causeway to Barra. Twin crescent beaches on either side of the isthmus, one shallow and sheltered visible from Castlebay, the other an ocean beach with more rollers. Dunes/machair; safe swimming. Poignant memorial to a 19th-century shipwreck in the Ocean Bay and another (on the way here) to a plane crash during the war; the wreckage is still there. There's a helluva hill between Barra and Vatersay if you're cycling.

1636 3/C19 **Seal Bay Barra** 5km Castlebay on W coast, 2km after Isle of Barra Hotel through gate across machair where road right is signed Allathasdal a Deas (after a sandy then a rockier cove). A flat, rocky Hebridean shore and skerries, where seals flop into the water and eye you with intense curiosity. The more beachy beach is next to the hotel that you pass on the way.

1637 8/R23 **Fife: West Sands St Andrews** As a town beach, this is hard to beat; it dominates the view to west. Wide swathe not too unclean and sea just about swimmable. Golf courses behind. Consistently gets the Blue Flag, but beach buffs may prefer **Kinshaldy** or **Kingsbarns** (10km S on Crail road), where there is a great beach walk taking in the **Cambo Estate** (881/FIFE) and skirting the great Kingsbarns Golf Course. At the Kingsbarns car park, the caravan dispenses seriously good toasties. And, of course, there's always **Elie**.

1638 7/F23 **The Bay at the Back of the Ocean Iona** Easy 2km walk from the ferry from Fionnphort, S of Mull (2232/ISLANDS) or bike hire from store on your left as you walk into the village (01681 700321). Mostly track: road straight up from the pier, left at the village hall, uphill to Maol Farm and then across the machair. John Smith, who is buried by the abbey, once told me this was his favourite place.
2 great inexpensive hotels on Iona, the **Argyll** and **St Columba** (1171/KIDS).

1639 7/J28 **Silver Sands Kildonan, Arran** In S of island on narrow coast road, S of Whiting Bay signed Kildonan. 500m off A841 at a corner, a grassy terrace on right to park, a staircase to an idyllic Arran hideaway beach. Hotel/bar further along (2315/ARRAN) and nudist beach at Kilmory (go find). **Sannox Bay** N of Corrie where burn comes into the sea also splendid.

1640 4/N16 **Dornoch (& Embo Beaches)** The wide and extensive sandy beach of this
& 4/N15 pleasant town at the mouth of the Dornoch Firth famous for its golf links. Decent accom and bar/food at Dornoch's **Royal Golf Hotel** (1047/HIGHLANDS) and coffee at **Cocoa Mountain**. 4km N, Embo Sands starts with ghastly caravan city, but walk N towards Golspie. Embo is twinned with Kaunakakai, Hawaii. We can dream!

1641 9/J30 **4 Beaches in the far South West** Off A77 before Portpatrick signed Dunskey
& 9/J31 Gardens in summer, follow road signed Killantringan Lighthouse (dirt track) to
& 9/M31 **Killantringan Bay**. Park 1km before lighthouse or walk from Portpatrick following
& 9/L31 the Southern Upland Way. Beautiful bay for exploration. **Sandhead Beach**: A716, S of Stranraer. Shallow, safe waters of Luce Bay (8km of sands). Perfect for families. And **Sandgreen**: off the A75 by Gatehouse of Fleet, signed and go past **Cream o' Galloway** (1758/KIDS) 3km. Lovely wee beach, then the rough road to a southern secret (1681/SCENIC ROUTES), with its small beaches and coves. **Rigg Beach nr Wigtown** 10km S through the Garlieston crossroads, park by Galloway House, walk 500m. Walk to the cliffs. Go from the Wigtown Book Festival (65/EVENTS), or any time.

The Great Glens

All those listed below are in L, LL *and* LLL *settings, obviously.*

1642 5/K18 ✓✓✓ **Glen Affric nr Drumnadrochit · www.glenaffric.org** Beyond Cannich at end of Glen Urquhart A831, 20km from Drumnadrochit on Loch Ness. The 'Glen of a Thousand Whispers', a dramatic gorge that strikes westwards into the wild heart of Scotland. Superb for rambles (2037/GLEN WALKS), expeditions, Munro-bagging (beyond Loch Affric) and even just tootling through in the car. Shaped by the Hydro Board, Loch Beinn a' Mheadhoin adds to the drama. One of the best places in Scotland to appreciate the beauty of Scots pine. Cycling good (bike hire in Cannich and at the campsite) as is the detour to Tomich and **Plodda Falls** (1652/WATERFALLS). Stop at **Dog Falls** (1727/SWIMMING) but do go to the end of the glen.

1643 8/M22 ✓✓✓ **Glen Lyon nr Aberfeldy** One of Scotland's crucial places historically and geographically, much favoured by fishers/walkers/Munro-baggers. Wordsworth, Tennyson, Gladstone and Baden-Powell all sang its praises. The Lyon is a classic Highland river tumbling through corries, gorges and riverine meadows. Several Munros are within its watershed and rise gloriously on either side. Road all the way to the lochside (30km). Eagles soar over the more remote tops at the head of the glen. The **Post Office Tearoom** (01887 866221) halfway round at Bridge of Balgie, does a roaring trade (weekends only in winter) and **Fortingall Hotel** on the way in is indeed a very good inn, if expensive (909/PERTHSHIRE).

1644 7/K21 ✓✓ **Glen Nevis Fort William** Often in film shoots, and easy to see why. Ben Nevis is only part of the magnificent scenery. Many walks and natural wonders (1661/WATERFALLS; 2033/WALKS). West Highland Way emerges here. Visitor centre; cross river to climb Ben Nevis and the walkers' **Ben Nevis Inn** (1140/FORT WILLIAM). A couple of caffs so-so but they're there. This dramatic glen is a national treasure.

1645 7/K22 ✓✓ **Glen Etive nr Ballachulish & Glen Coe** Off from more exalted Glen Coe and the A82 at **Kingshouse** (1060/HIGHLANDS), as anyone you meet there will tell you, this truly is a glen of glens. Treat with great respect while you make it your own. See also 1253/WILD CAMPING; 1717/SWIMMING.

1646 4/M16 **Strathcarron nr Bonar Bridge** You drive up the N bank of this Highland river from the bridge outside Ardgay (pronounced 'Ordguy') which is 3km over the bridge from Bonar Bridge. Road goes 15km to Croick and its remarkable church (1914/CHURCHES). The river gurgles and gushes along its rocky course to the Dornoch Firth and further up there are innumerable places to picnic, swim and stroll. Heavenly here on the warm days of summer 2018.

1647 8/Q21 & 8/P21 **The Angus Glens: Glen Clova**, **Glen Prosen** and **Glen Isla** Isla for drama, Clova for walkers, Prosen for the soul. All via Kirriemuir. Isla to the W is a woody, approachable glen with a deep gorge, on B954 near Alyth (1662/WATERFALLS) and the cosy **Glenisla Hotel**. Others via B955, to Dykehead then road bifurcates. Both glens stab into the heart of the Grampians. Minister's Walk goes between them from behind the kirk at Prosen village over the hill to B955 before Clova village (7km). Glen Clova is a walkers' paradise, especially from Glendoll 24km from Dykehead; limit of road with the Ranger Centre. Viewpoint. Jock's Road to Braemar and the Capel Mounth to Ballater (both 24km). **Glen Clova Hotel** (910/PERTHSHIRE) with famous Loops of Brandy walk (2 hours, 2-B-2); stark and beautiful. **Prosen Hostel** at end of the road is a serene stopover (1190/HOSTELS). The Museum of the Glens in Kirriemuir is sweet and has a surprising homage to AC/DC (no, really!).

1648 9/L29 **Glen Trool nr Newton Stewart** 26km N by A714 via Bargrennan, which is on the **Southern Upland Way** (2026/WALKS). A gentle wooded glen within the vast Galloway Forest Park (one of the most charming, accessible parts). Visitor centre (and café) 5km from Bargrennan. Pick up a walk brochure and walk. Many options (1958/BOB). Start of the **Merrick** climb (1993/HILLS).

1649 8/N23 **The Sma' Glen nr Crieff** Off the A85 to Perth, the A822 to Amulree and Aberfeldy. Sma' meaning small, this is the valley of the River Almond, where the Mealls (lumpish, shapeless hills) fall steeply down to the road. Where the road turns away from the river, the long-distance path to Loch Tay begins (28km). Sma' Glen, 8km, has good picnic spots, but they get busy and midgy in summer.

1650 5/L18 **Glen Strathfarrar Struy** Rare unspoiled glen accessed from A831 leaving Drumnadrochit on Loch Ness via Cannich (30km), or S from Beauly (15km). Signed at Struy, it's a hike (25km) in to tackle the celebrated Munros. For vehicular access check www.thebmc.co.uk before you set off (only 20 cars allowed in each day). 2km to the gate, then 22km to the head of glen past Loch Monar. Good climbing, walking, fishing. No overnight stays. The real peace and quiet!

The Most Spectacular Waterfalls

One aspect of Scotland that really is improved by rain. All the walks to these falls are graded 1-A-1 unless otherwise stated. See p. 12 for walk codes.

1651 5/J19 ✓✓ **Falls of Glomach www.nts.org.uk** 29km E of Kyle of Lochalsh off A87
2-C-3   near Shiel Bridge via Strath Croe to bridge. Walk starts other side; there are
NTS   other ways (e.g. from the SYHA Hostel in Glen Affric) but this is most straightforward. Allow 5/7 hours for the pilgrimage to one of Britain's highest falls (370ft). Path is steep, can be wet with mist and low cloud. Glomach means gloomy and you might feel so, peering into the ravine; from precipice to pool, it's 200m. Vertigo factor and sense of achievement both fairly high. But don't get lost! Consult www.walkhighlands.co.uk or locally. Ranger: 01599 511231.

1652 5/K19 ✓✓ **Plodda Falls nr Tomich · www.glenaffric.org** A831 from Loch Ness to Cannich (20km), then 7km to Tomich, a further 5km up mainly woodland, quite potholed track to car park. 400m walk down through woods of Scots pine and ancient Douglas fir to one of the most enchanting woodland sites in Britain and the Forestry Commission's vertiginous viewpoint over the 150m fall into the churning river below. Pools excellent for swimming. The 'Tweedmouth Trail' is an easy 2.3km loop. Freezes into winter wonderland. Lovely Joyce's **Post Office Café** and hotel in village (1078/HIGHLANDS).

1653 8/N21 ✓ **Falls of Bruar nr Blair Atholl** Close to the main A9 Perth–Inverness road, 12km N of Blair Atholl near **House of Bruar** shopping experience (2212/SHOPS). Consequently, the short walk to lower falls is very consumer-led but less crowded than you might expect. The lichen-covered walls of the gorge below the upper falls (1km) are less ogled and more dramatic. 2.3km circular path well marked; steep/rocky in places. Tempting to swim on hot days (1726/SWIMMING).

1654 7/J27 ✓ **Glenashdale Falls Arran** 3.5km walk from bridge on main road at Whiting
1-B-1   Bay. Signed up the burn side, but uphill and further than you think, so allow 2 hours (return). Series of falls in a rocky gorge in the woods with paths so you get right down to the brim and the pools. Swim here, swim in heaven! There's another waterfall walk, **Eas Mòr**, further S off the A841 at the second Kildonan turn-off. It's under the care of a local ecology group. Steep start but a bracing 1-hour gorge and woodland hike.

1655 5/K16 ✓ **Corrieshalloch Gorge/Falls of Measach** Junction of A832 and A835, 20km
NC500 S of Ullapool. The more dramatic approach is from the car park on the A832
Gairloch road. Staircase to swing bridge from whence to consider how such a wee
burn could make such a deep gash. Very impressive. There's another viewpoint
100m over the bridge and a longer walk from the car park. A must-stop on the way
to/from Ullapool. And see **Inverbroom Estate** (2063/WALKS).

1656 8/P28 ✓ **The Grey Mare's Tail between Moffat & Selkirk** On the wildly scenic A708.
About halfway, a car park and signs for waterfall. 8km from **Tibbie Shiels Inn**
(refreshments, but not recommended for food). There's also a café and wild campsite
here. The lower track takes 10/15 mins to a viewing place still 500m from falls; the
higher, on the other side of the Tail burn, threads between the austere hills and up to
Loch Skene from which the falls overflow (45/60 mins). Then do the circular trail
above you for an all-round satisfying day in the Borders. Mountain goats scamper.

1657 8/N27 ✓ **The Falls of Clyde** New Lanark · www.scottishwildlifetrust.org.uk
Dramatic falls in a long gorge of the Clyde. New Lanark, the conservation village
of Robert Owen, the social reformer, is signed from Lanark. A curious village, a mighty
river. The path to the power station is about 1km, the route more interesting after it, a
1km climb to the first fall (Cora Linn) and another 1km to the next (Bonnington Linn).
One of the mills is a decent family hotel, with some rooms (and 'waterhouses')
overlooking the river. The strange uniformity of New Lanark is oddly poignant when
the other tourists have gone home. When the river is full, the Falls are a wonder.

1658 7/G22 **Eas Fors Mull** On the Dervaig to Fionnphort road 3km from Ulva Ferry; a series
of cataracts tumbling down on either side of the road. Easily accessible from small
car park on left going S (otherwise unmarked). There's a path down the side to the
brink where the river plunges into the sea. On a warm day swimming in the sea
below the fall is a rare exhilaration.

1659 5/G17 **Lealt Falls Skye** Impressive torrent of wild mountain water about 20km N of
2-C-2 Portree on the A855. Look for sign: River Lealt. There's a car park on a bend on right
(going north). Walk to grassy ledges and look over or go down to the beach.
Kilt Rock, a viewpoint much favoured by bus parties, is a few km further (you
look over and along the cliffs). This road has some drop-in caffs, especially the
Ellishadder Art Café (signed to right going N) when open. Also …
Eas Mòr Glen Brittle near end of road. 24km from Sligachan. A mountain waterfall
with the wild Cuillin behind and views to the sea. Approach as part of a serious
scramble or merely a 30-min Cuillin sampler. Start at the Memorial Hut, cross the
road, bear right, cross burn and then follow path uphill.

1660 4/K14 **Eas A' Chual Aluinn Kylesku** Britain's highest waterfall (638ft), near the head
2-C-3 of Glencoul, is not easy to reach. Kylesku is between Scourie and Lochinver off the
main A894, 20km S of Scourie. There are 90-min cruises May-Sep (01971 502231)
from outside the **Kylesku Hotel** (1058/HIGHLANDS). Falls are a rather distant
prospect but the cruise will do you good; baby seals an added attraction Jun-Aug.
There's also a track to the top of the falls from 5km N of the Skiag Bridge on the
main road (4-6 hours return); get directions locally. The water freefalls for 200m,
which is 4 times further than Niagara (take pinch of salt here). You'll need a head for
heights, good footwear (track is often wet) and a map (folk do get lost).

1661 7/K21 **Steall Falls Glen Nevis, Fort William** Take Glen Nevis road at the roundabout
3-A-3 outside town centre and drive to the end (16km) through glen. Start from the second
and final car park, following marked path uphill through the woody gorge with River
Nevis thrashing below. Glen eventually and dramatically opens out and there are great

views of the long veils of the falls. Precarious 3-wire bridge, for which you will also need nerves of steel. (You can see the falls from a distance.) 3km walk, 1.5-2 hours.

1662 8/Q22 **Reekie Linn Alyth** 8km N of town on back roads to Kirriemuir on B951 between Bridge of Craigisla and Bridge of Lintrathen. A picnic site and car park on bend of road leads by 200m to the wooded gorge of Glen Isla with precipitous viewpoints of the defile where Isla is squeezed and falls in tiers for 100ft. Walk further along the glen and look back.

1663 8/M22 **Falls of Acharn nr Kenmore** 5km along S side of Loch Tay on an unclassified road. Walk from just after the bridge going W in township of Acharn; falls are signed. Steepish start then 1km up side of gorge; waterfalls on other side. Can be circular route. Splendid trees!

1664 5/L17 **Rogie Falls nr Strathpeffer** Car park on A835 Inverness–Ullapool road, 5km
NC500 Contin/10km Strathpeffer. Accessibility makes short walk (250m) quite popular to these hurtling falls on the Blackwater River. Bridge (built by the Territorial Army) and salmon ladder (they leap in summer). Woodland trails 1-3km, marked, include a circular route to Contin (2078/WALKS).

1665 4/M15 **Falls of Shin nr Lairg · www.fallsofshin.co.uk** 6km E of town on signed road, car park and falls nearby are easily accessible. Not quite up to the splendours of others here, but one of the best places in Scotland to see Atlantic salmon battling upstream (May-Nov; best late summer). Adventure playground across the road.

■ The Lochs We Love

All those listed below are in L, LL and LLL settings, obviously.

1666 5/J16 ✓✓ **Loch Maree** A832 between Kinlochewe and Gairloch. Dotted with
NC500 islands covered in Scots pine, one hiding some of the best examples of Viking graves and, apparently, a money tree in their midst. Easily viewed from the road which follows its length for 15km. Beinn Eighe rises behind you and the omniscient presence of Slioch is opposite. Aultroy Visitor Centre (5km Kinlochewe), fine walks from lochside car parks, among the largest original Scots pine woodlands in the West Highlands. See 1802/RESERVES.

1667 5/N19 ✓✓ **Loch an Eilean** 4km Inverdruie off the Coylumbridge road from Aviemore. Car park and info board. An enchanted loch in the heart of the Rothiemurchus Forest (2065/WALKS for directions). You can walk right round the loch (5km, allow 1.5 hours). This is classic Highland scenery, a calendar landscape of magnificent Scots pine. Very special.

1668 5/J20 ✓ **Loch Arkaig** 25km Fort William. An enigmatic loch long renowned for its fishing. From the A82 beyond Spean Bridge (at the **Commando Monument** 1893/MONUMENTS) cross the Caledonian Canal, then on by single-track road through the Clunes Forest and the Dark Mile past the Witches' Pool (a cauldron of dark water below cataracts) to the loch. Bonnie Prince Charlie came this way before and after Culloden; one of his refuge caves is marked on a trail.

1669 8/L24 ✓ **Lochs of the Trossachs: Loch Achray** is the small loch at the centre of the
& 7/L24 Trossachs between **Loch Katrine**, on which SS *Sir Walter Scott* and smaller
& 8/M24 *Lady of the Lake* sail 3/4 times a day (01877 376316), and **Loch Venachar**.

The A821 from Callander skirts both Venachar and Achray. Many picnic spots and a fishing centre, and **Venachar Lochside** is excellent (803/CENTRAL). Ben Venue and Ben A'an rise above: great walks (1987/HILLS) and views. A one-way forest road goes round the other side of Loch Achray through Achray Forest (enter and leave from the Duke's Pass road between Aberfoyle and Brig o' Turk). Trail details from forest visitor centre 3km N Aberfoyle. Bike hire at Loch Katrine (01877 376366), Callander or Aberfoyle – best way to see the lochs.

1670 8/L24 **Glen Finglas Reservoir Brig o' Turk** And while we're on the subject of lochs in the Trossachs (see above) here's a fine one to walk to. Although it's man-made, it's a real beauty, surrounded by soft green hills and the odd burn bubbling in. Approach from car park of the rotunda visitor centre on the A821 before Brig o' Turk (3 & 5km circular walks), or from Brig o' Turk itself (1km), then join trails. It's about 5km to the head of the loch and 24km on the Mell Trail round the hill or 12km to Balquhidder: a walk across the heart of Scotland (2040/WALKS). Ranger board gives details. **The Byre** (1345/FOOD PUBS) is nearby across the road.

1671 8/Q20 **Loch Muick nr Ballater** At head of road off B976, the South Dee road at Ballater. 14km up Glen Muick (pronounced 'Mick') to the car park and visitor centre and 1km to the lochside. **Lochnagar** rises above (2019/MUNROS) and walk also begins here for Capel Mounth and **Glen Clova** (1647/GLENS). 3-hour walk around loch; any number of ambles. The lodge where Vic met John is at the furthest point (well, it would be). Open aspect; deer graze. Ranger: 01339 755059.

1672 4/L13 **Loch Eriboll North Coast** 90km W of Thurso. The long sea loch that indents into NC500 the North Coast for 15km and which you drive right round on main A838 (40 mins). Deepest natural anchorage in the UK, exhibiting every aspect of lochside scenery including, alas, fish cages. Ben Hope stands near the head of the loch and there is a perfect beach (my own private Idaho) on the coast (1618/BEACHES). The people who have **Mackay's** in nearby Durness now have 2 luxury, high-spec eco-lodges overlooking the loch at Laid (1246/LUXURIOUS ISOLATION) and halfway up the W bank is the extraordinary art garden of **Lotte Glob** (2183/GALLERIES). Walks from Hope.

1673 9/M30 **Loch Ken between Castle Douglas & New Galloway** · www.lochken.co.uk Loch Ken is long and thin. On spring days it shimmers and lots of people boat and surf and hang out; this is a loch of life. Marina, holiday park and **Galloway Activity Centre** (2149/WATERSPORTS; coffee shop) all thrive on its banks. Then there's New Galloway. Many trails (and deer) around. And the glorious kites!

1674 5/H20 **Loch Morar nr Mallaig** 70km W of Fort William by A850 (a wildly scenic but a smooth route). Morar village is 6km from Mallaig. A single-track road leads from the coast to the loch (500m) then 5km to Bracara. It's the prettiest part with wooded islets, small beaches, lochside meadows and bobbing boats. The road stops at a turning place but a track continues from Bracorina to Tarbet (12km) and it's possible to connect with a boat and sail back to Mallaig on Loch Nevis (check locally). Boat hire on the loch: 01687 462520. Loch Morar, joined to the coast by the shortest river in Britain, also has the deepest water. There is a spookiness about it and just possibly a monster called Morag. Nearby, epic beaches (1632/BEACHES).

Loch Lomond The biggest, not the bonniest, with major visitor centre and retail experience, **Lomond Shores**, at S end near Balloch. Report: 1/ATTRACTIONS.

Loch Ness The longest; and the monster. Report: 3/ATTRACTIONS.

The Scenic Routes

All those listed below are in L, LL *and* LLL *settings, obviously.*

1675 7/K22
ATMOS
NTS

✓✓✓ **Glen Coe** The A82 from Crianlarich to Ballachulish is a fine drive, but from the extraterrestrial Loch Ba onwards, there can be few roads anywhere that bring you into direct contact with such imposing scenery. After Kingshouse and Buachaille Etive Mòr on the left, the mountains and ridges rising on either side of Glen Coe proper invoke the correct usage of the word 'awesome'. The visitor centre sets the topographical and historical scene. See 1313/GOOD PUBS; 2031/WALKS; 1946/BATTLEGROUNDS; 2511/ENCHANTING PLACES; 1203/HOSTELS and great hotels at 1034/1060/HIGHLANDS.

1676 5/H19

✓✓ **Shiel Bridge-Glenelg** The switchback road that climbs from the A87 (Fort William 96km) at Shiel Bridge over the hill and down to the coast opposite the Sleat Peninsula in Skye (short ferry to Kylerhea 7/JOURNEYS). As you climb you're almost as high as the surrounding summits and there's the classic view across Loch Duich to the Five Sisters of Kintail. Coming back you think you're going straight into the loch! It's really worth driving to Glenelg (1865/PREHISTORIC; 1258/WILD CAMPING; 1208/INNS), to Arnisdale and Loch Hourn (16km).

1677 5/H18
NC500

✓✓ **Applecross** www.applecross.uk.com 120km from Inverness. From Tornapress near Lochcarron for 18km. Leaving the A896 seems like leaving civilisation; the winding ribbon heads into monstrous mountains and the high plateau at the top is another planet. It's not for the faint-hearted and Applecross is a relief to arrive in with its campsite and the faraway, famed **Applecross Inn** (1229/GET-AWAY HOTELS). Also see 1263/CAMPING WITH KIDS. This awesome road rises 2,000 feet in 6 miles. See how they built it at the **Applecross Heritage Centre** (2168/HISTORY).

1678 5/J17
NC500

✓✓ **Torridon** Easiest from the A896 between Kinlochewe and Torridon with staggering views along the route of the 3 mighty Torridon mountains: Beinn Eighe, Liathach and Beinn Alligin. There are various starts along this road – this and all other information at the NTS Countryside Centre at the Diabaig turn-off. The single-track road from Torridon village to Diabaig is probably the scenic pinnacle: stop at that bench halfway round and at **Gille Brighde**, the café on the front at Diabaig when you get there (1099/HIGHLANDS). Excellent two-tier accom at **The Torridon** (1221/GET-AWAY HOTELS) and a SYHA tents-only campsite adjacent the Centre. There is much to climb and clamber over here; or merely be amazed. See also 1695/VIEWS.

1679 4/K14
NC500

✓✓ **Lochinver-Drumbeg-Kylesku** The coast road N from Lochinver (35km) is marvellous, essential Assynt. Actually best travelled north-south so that you leave the splendid vista of Eddrachilles Bay (1069/HIGHLANDS) and pass through lochan, moor and even woodland, touching the coast again by sandy beaches (at Stoer, a road leads 7km to the lighthouse and the walk to the **Old Man of Stoer** 2085/WALKS) past the wonderful **Secret Beach** (1630/BEACHES) and approach Lochinver (possible detour to Achmelvich) with a classic long view of Suilven. Take tea 'n' cake at the tea garden **Little Soap 'n' Candles** in Drumbeg (Apr-Oct). Or stock up at the remarkable **Drumbeg Stores** (2218/SHOPS). Get your pies in Lochinver (1481/BAKERS). The Drumbeg viewpoint S of the village is worth a stop 'n' gaze.

1680 4/J15 ✓ **Lochinver-Achiltibuie** S of Lochinver, Achiltibuie is 40km from Ullapool; so this is the route from the north; 28km of winding road/unwinding Highland scenery; through glens, mountains and silver sea. Known locally as the 'wee mad road' (it is maddening if you're in a hurry). Passes Achin's Bookshop (alas for sale at TGP), the path to Kirkaig Falls and the mighty Suilven. Near Achiltibuie there's one of Scotland's most uplifting views (1698/VIEWS).

1681 9/M31 ✓ **The Islands of Fleet** Galloway An enchanting coastal track (it's not really a road) through the hut village – Carrick – which is not even on the map. Off A75 by Gatehouse of Fleet, signed for **Cream o' Galloway** (1758/KIDS), then to Sandgreen (6km from main road). 200m before Sandgreen and its beach 1641/ BEACHES, take the track towards the sea at a corner. Follow this round the hidden coves, headlands, dunes and the shacks always looking out to the islets in Fleet Bay. The derelict building being renovated at TGP. Magic swimming and picnicking and great views before eventually coming back to life in Borgue. Go find!

1682 7/J25 ✓ **Rothesay-Tighnabruaich** A886/A8003. The most celebrated part of this route is the latter, the A8003 down the side of Loch Riddon to Tighnabruaich along the hillsides with the breathtaking views of Bute and the Kyles (can be a lot of vegetation in summer – there's one good high-level lay-by/viewpoint) but the whole way, with its diverse aspects of lochside, riverine and rocky scenery, is supernatural. Includes short crossing between Rhubodach and Colintraive. Good organic restaurant, **Botanica**, in Tighnabruaich (741/ARGYLL).

1683 3/E16 ✓ **The Golden Road** South Harris The main road in Harris follows the W
ATMOS coast, notable for bays and beaches (1619/BEACHES). This is the other, winding round a series of coves and inlets with offshore skerries and a treeless, rocky hinterland: classic Hebridean landscape, especially Finsbay. Tweed is woven; visit and buy (2221/SHOPS). And **Skoon** café 2381/HEBRIDES.

1684 5/G19 **Sleat Peninsula** Skye The unclassified road off the A851 (main Sleat road) especially coming from south, i.e. take road at Ostaig near Gaelic College (good place to stay nearby 2294/SKYE); it meets the coast after 9km. Affords rare views of the Cuillins from a craggy coast. Returning to 'main' road S of Isleornsay, pop into the great hotel pub there, **Eilean Iarmain** (2279/SKYE), or their spruced-up sister pub and hotel **Ardvasar Hotel** in the village near the Armadale ferry.

1685 8/R27 **Leaderfoot-Clintmains** nr St Boswells The B6356 between the A68 and the B6404 Kelso-St Boswells road. This small road, busy in summer, links Scott's View, **Dryburgh Abbey** (1924/ABBEYS; find by following abbey signs) and Smailholm Tower, and passes through classic Border/Tweedside scenery. 500m walk to the Wallace Statue is signed. Don't miss **Irvine's View** if you want to see the best of the Borders (1696/VIEWS).

1686 8/P20 **Braemar-Linn Of Dee** The A93 drive from Ballater to Braemar is beautiful (and now there's **The Fife Arms** 978/NE HOTELS to head for), and then there's 12km of renowned Highland river scenery along the upper valley of the (Royal) Dee. The Linn (rapids) is at the end of the road and the mighty Dee is squeezed until it is no more than 1m wide, but there are river walks (2049/WALKS) and the start of the great Glen Tilt walk to Blair Atholl (2036/WALKS). Deer abound. The whole Deeside road here is fit for a queen and all.

1687 5/L19 **Fort Augustus-Dores** nr Inverness The B862 often single-track road that follows and latterly skirts Loch Ness. Quieter and more interesting than the main W bank A82. Starts in rugged country and follows the straight road built by Wade to tame the Highlands. Reaches the lochside at Foyers and goes all the way to Dores (15km from Inverness) and popular pub for grub, the **Dores Inn** (01463 751203). Fabulous untrodden woodlands near Errogie (marked) and the spooky graveyard adjacent Boleskine House, where Aleister Crowley did his dark magic and Jimmy Page of Led Zeppelin may have done his. 35km total; worth taking slowly.

1688 8/L24 The Duke's Pass, Aberfoyle–Brig o' Turk Of the many roads through the Trossachs, this one is spectacular though gets busy; numerous possibilities for stopping, exploration and great views. Good viewpoint 4km from Loch Achray Hotel, above road and lay-by. One-way forest road goes round Loch Achray and 2 other lochs (Drunkie and Venachar). Good hill-walking starts (1987/1988/1989/HILLS) and Loch Katrine regular daily sailings (2km) Apr-Oct (01877 376316). Bike hire at Loch Katrine (01877 376366), Aberfoyle and Callander. The **Byre** at Brig o' Turk for refreshments (1345/FOOD PUBS).

1689 7/H20 Glenfinnan–Mallaig www.road-to-the-isles.org.uk The A830, aka the **Road to the Isles**. Through some of the most impressive and romantic landscapes in the Highlands, splendid in any weather (it does rain a bit), to the coast at the **Sands of Morar** (1632/BEACHES). This is deepest Bonnie Prince Charlie country (1957/CHARLIE) and demonstrates what a misty eye he had for magnificent settings. A full-throttle biker's dream. The road is shadowed by the West Highland Railway (6/JOURNEYS). Don't miss 1918/CHURCHES and **The Bakehouse** at Mallaig (1469/ARTISAN BAKERS).

1690 7/H21 Lochailort–Acharacle Off from the A830 above at Lochailort and turning S on the A861, the coastal section of this great scenery is superb, especially in the setting sun, or in May when the rhoddies are out. **Glenuig Inn** is a 'green' pub to stop over and eat. This is the road to the **Castle Tioram** shoreline, which should not be missed (1833/RUINS); and glorious Ardnamurchan awaits.

1691 7/H26 Knapdale: Lochgilphead–Tarbert B8024 off the main A83 follows the coast for much of its route. Views to Jura are immense (and on a clear day, Ireland). Not much happens here but in the middle in exactly the right place is the superb **Kilberry Inn** (1206/INNS; 1327/FOOD PUBS). Take it easy on this very Scottish 55km of single track. Short 500m walk to the Coves 3km from Kilberry (looking out to Gigha over the dolphin sea) and to Loch Stornoway – all details at the Inn. There are more folk on bikes on this road than cars – a glorious ride!

1692 8/N22 Amulree–Kenmore Unclassified single-track and very narrow road from the hill-country hamlet of Amulree to cosy Kenmore signed Glen Quaich. Past Loch Freuchie, a steep climb takes you to a plateau ringed by magnificent (far) mountains to Loch Tay. Steep descent to Loch Tay and Kenmore. You may have to open and close the gates. Great walk from car park on left 1km before Kenmore.

1693 8/N23 Muthill–Comrie Pure Perthshire. A route which takes you through some of the best scenery in central Scotland and ends up (best this way round) in Comrie with bar/restaurants and other pleasures (904/918/PERTHSHIRE; 1728/SWIMMING). Leave Muthill (pronounced 'Mew-thil') and the **Barley Bree** (1205/INNS) by Crieff road turning left (2km) into **Drummond Castle** grounds up a glorious avenue of beech trees (gate open 1-5pm, May-Oct). Visit garden (1559/GARDENS); continue through estate. At gate, go right, following signs for Strowan. At first junction, go left following signs (4km). At T-junction, go left to Comrie (7km). Best have a map or GPS, but if not, who cares? It's all bonnie!

The Classic Views

For views of and around Edinburgh and Glasgow see p. 82 and p. 124–5. No views from hill or mountain tops are included here.

1694 5/G17 ✓✓✓ **The Quirang** Skye Best approach is from Uig direction taking the right-hand unclassified road off the hairpin of the A855 above and 2km from town signed Staffin via Quirang (more usual approach from Staffin side is less of a revelation). View (and walk) from car park, the massive rock formations of a towering, contorted ridge. Solidified lava heaved and eroded into fantastic pinnacles. Fine views also across Staffin Bay to Wester Ross. See also 2255/ISLAND WALKS. Flodigarry Hotel has a big view from the terrace 2295/SKYE.

1695 5/J16 ✓✓✓ The views of **An Teallach** and **Liathach**. An Teallach, that great favourite of Scottish hill walkers (40km S of Ullapool by the A835/A832), is best viewed from the side of Little Loch Broom or the A832. The classic view of the other great Torridon mountains (**Beinn Eighe**, pronounced 'Ben-A', and **Liathach** together, 100km S by road from Ullapool) in Glen Torridon and on the road to **Diabaig** (1678/SCENIC ROUTES) 4km from Kinlochewe. This viewpoint is not marked but it's on the track around Loch Clair which is reached from the entrance to the Coulin estate off the A896 (small lay-by), Glen Torridon road (be aware of stalking). Park outside gate; no cars allowed, 1km walk to lochside. These mountains have to be seen to be believed.

1696 8/R27 ✓✓ **Irvine's View** St Boswells The full panorama from the Cheviots to the Lammermuirs. This the finest view in southern Scotland. It's only a furlong further than the famed **Scott's View** (see below): cross the road from Scott's View lay-by through the kissing gate, veering left uphill or through the metal gate 80m along the road following car tracks and veer left to the top of the rise. You'll see the fallen standing stone where I would like my bench. The telecoms monstrosity isn't pleasant but turn your back on it and gaze across the beautiful Borders to another country … you know, England. Excellent café/bookshop/deli in St Boswells (834/BORDERS).

1697 5/G18 ✓✓ **From Raasay** www.raasay.com There are several fabulous views looking over to Skye from Raasay, the small island reached by ferry from Sconser (2230/ISLANDS). The panorama from Dun Caan, the hill in the centre of the island (444m) is of Munro proportions, producing an elation incommensurate with the small effort required to get there. Start from the road to the North End or ask at the rebuilt **Raasay House**, with its café, comfy rooms and great view from the lawn (2291/SKYE).

1698 4/J15 ✓✓ **The Summer Isles** Achiltibuie · www.summer-isles.com The Summer Isles are a scattering of islands seen from the coast of Achiltibuie, the lounge of the **Summer Isles Hotel** (1045/HIGHLANDS), and the terrace of the **Am Fuaran Bar** (1334/FOOD PUBS), and visited by boat from Ullapool. But the best place to see them and the stunning perspective of this western shore is on that road to Altandhu (has other spellings). Best approach is: from Achiltibuie, veer left through Polbain, on and through Altandhu, past turning for Reiff and Blairbuie, then 500m ascending inland. There's a bench (which should have my name on it) and a path (sign for Viewpoint) 50m to little plateau with many cairns and this one of the ethereal views of Scotland. On this same road 500m round the corner, the distant mountains of Assynt all in a row: 2 jaw-dropping perspectives of the Highlands in 5 minutes.

1699 7/K24 ✓✓ **The Rest and Be Thankful** On A83 Loch Lomond–Inveraray road where it's met by the B828 from Lochgoilhead. In summer the rest may be from driving stress and you may not be thankful for the camera-toting masses, but this was always one of the most accessible, rewarding viewpoints in the land. Surprisingly, none of the encompassing hills are Munros but they are nonetheless dramatic.

1700 6/P17 ✓ **Califer nr Forres** 7km from Forres on A96 to Elgin, turn right signed for Pluscarden, follow this road for 5km back towards Forres. You are unaware how high above the coastal plain you are and the lay-by is discreetly located. When you walk across a small park with young memorial trees you are rewarded with a truly remarkable sight – down across Findhorn Bay and the wide vista of the Moray Firth to the Black Isle and Ben Wyvis. There is often fantastic light on this coast.

1701 5/G19 ✓ **Elgol Skye** End of the road, the B8083, 22km from Broadford. The classic view of the Cuillin from across Loch Scavaig and of Soay and Rum. Cruises (Apr-Oct) in the *Bella Jane* (0800 731 3089) or *The Misty Isle* (Apr-Oct, not Sun 01471 866288) to the famous corrie of Loch Coruisk, painted by Turner, romanticised by Sir Walter Scott. A journey you'll remember. 2km from Elgol, **Coruisk House** is one of the great boutique hotels on Skye with excellent dining open to non-res: 01471 866330. There are great Cuillin views also from the **Blue Shed** café en route.

1702 8/Q23 ✓ **The Law Dundee** Few cities have such a single good viewpoint. To N of the centre, it reveals the panoramic perspective of the city on the estuary of the silvery Tay, with its emerging exciting waterfront. Route to Law Rd not easy to follow but walk from town or satnav/Google.

1703 8/R27 ✓ **Scott's View St Boswells** Off B6404 St Boswells to Kelso road (follow Dryburgh Abbey signs). The View, old Walter's favourite (the horses still stopped there long after he'd gone), is 4km along the road (**Dryburgh Abbey** 3km further 1924/ABBEYS). Magnificent sweep of his beloved Border country, but only in one direction. If you cross the road and go through either of the gates and head uphill you'll find **Irvine's View** (see above ... and beyond). Great café/bookshop 834/BORDERS.

1704 8/R27 **Peniel Heugh nr Ancrum** On the subject of great views in the Borders, look no further than this – sentinel of the Borders. Report: 1887/MONUMENTS.

1705 6/N18 **Dulsie Bridge nr Nairn** 16km S of Nairn by the A939 to Grantown-on-Spey, this locally revered but otherwise secret beauty spot is imbued with history. Follow B9007 from Ferness then the signed unclassified road. Park on S side and walk 200m for the best view of the remarkable arched bridge over the charming Findhorn river. Built in 1755, it survived the 'Muckle Spate' of 1829, when the river rose by 40ft. Other walks nearby 2060/WALKS.

1706 7/G21 **Camas Nan Geall Ardnamurchan** 12km Salen on B8007. Coming especially from the Kilchoan direction, a magnificent bay appears below you, where the road first meets the sea. Almost symmetrical with high cliffs and a perfect field (still cultivated) in the bowl fringed by a shingle beach. Car park viewpoint; there is a path down. Ardnamurchan is actually ... awesome.

1707 5/K20 **Glengarry** 3km after Tomdoun turn-off on A87, Invergarry–Kyle of Lochalsh road. Lay-by/viewfinder. An uncluttered vista up and down loch and glen with not a house in sight (pity about the salmon cages). Distant peaks of Knoydart are identified, but not Loch Quoich nestling spookily and full of fish in the wilderness at the head of the glen. Gaelic-named mountains on the board. Bonnie Prince Charlie passed this way. Great hotel at Invergarry (1064/HIGHLANDS).

1708 8/N21 **Queen's View** **Loch Tummel, nr Pitlochry** 8km on B8019 to Kinloch Rannoch. Car park and 100m walk to rocky knoll, where pioneers of tourism, Queen Victoria and Prince Albert, were 'transported into ecstasies' by view of **Loch Tummel** and **Schiehallion** (2011/MUNROS), though the view was named after Isabella, the first wife of Robert the Bruce. Their view was flooded by a hydro scheme after WWII; more recently it spawned a whole view-driven visitor experience. Well, it … makes you wonder!

1709 8/L23 **The Rallying Place of the Maclarens** **Balquhidder** Short climb from behind the church (1938/GRAVEYARDS) along the track 150m then signed Creag an Tuirc, steep at first. Superb view down Loch Voil, the Balquhidder Braes and the real Rob Roy Country and a top bar/restaurant on the A84 on your descent, **Mhor 84** (796/CENTRAL) by the **Monachyle Mhor** people (where you could treat yourself and stay 1220/GET-AWAY HOTELS).

1710 7/L25 **Duncryne Hill** **Gartocharn** Gartocharn is between Balloch and Drymen on the A811 and this view was once recommended by writer and outdoorsman Tom Weir as 'the finest viewpoint of any small hill in Scotland'. Turn up Duncryne road at the E end of village and park 1km on left by a small wood (a sign reads Woods Reserved for Teddy Bears). The hill is only 470ft high and easy, but the view of Loch Lomond and the Kilpatrick Hills is superb.

1711 4/M13 **Tongue** From the causeway across the kyle, or better, follow the minor road to
NC500 Melness, Talmine and the **Craggan Hotel**, a local's choice for grub, on the W side. Look S to Ben Loyal or N to the small islands. There's a lovely, lonely graveyard on the S side of the causeway.

1712 8/N25 **Cairnpapple Hill** **nr Linlithgow** See volcanic geology, a Neolithic henge, east of Scotland agriculture, the Forth plain, the bridges, Grangemouth industrial complex and telecoms masts: not all pretty, but the whole of Scotland at a glance. For directions see 1858/PREHISTORIC.

1713 7/J22 **Castle Stalker View** **Portnacroish** Near Port Appin on main A828 Oban-Fort
L William road. On right going south, the view has been commandeered by the CSV Café, which ain't bad (closed in evenings), but viewpoint can be accessed at all times 50m away from car park. Always impressive, in certain lights the vista of Port Appin, the castle in the fore and Loch Linnhe, is ethereal.

1714 8/R28 **Carter Bar** **English Border, nr Jedburgh** On the A68 Edinburgh-Newcastle road, the last and first view in Scotland just happens to be superb. The Border hill country spread out before you for many long miles. The tear in my eye is not because of the wind, but because this was the landscape of my youth and where I spent my lightsome days. In 2014, I was privileged to give 'The Address' to the Redeswire Stone, which marks the last skirmish between the Scots and English in 1575. It's 200m E of the car park.

1715 4/P12 **Dunnet Head** **between Thurso & John o' Groats** More sense of place than
NC500 Jo'G and it is the most northerly part of the British mainland. Part of extensive RSPB reserve, there are happily more birds than sightseers. View to island of Stoma, Hoy and Orkney Mainland; and those cliffs. A walk (2093/WALKS), and nearby **Mary-Ann's Cottage** (2171/HISTORY) and the venerable **Castle of Mey** (1815/CASTLES) are all on or just off the A836 which takes you here.

The Great Wild Swimming Holes

Take care when swimming in rivers; don't ever take them for granted. Watch the kids. Most of these places are traditional local swimming and picnic spots where people have swum for years but rivers continuously change their course and their nature. Wearing sandals or old sports shoes is the right idea.

1716 5/F18 ✓✓ **The Fairy Pools Glen Brittle, Skye** If you can get anywhere near them on that rare hot day, this is one of the best places on Skye to go; swimming in several clear, deep pools with the massif of the Cuillins around you. One pool has a stone bridge you swim under. Head off A863 Dunvegan road from Sligachan Hotel then B8009 and Glenbrittle road. 7km down just as road begins to parallel the glen itself, you'll see a river coming off the hills. Park where you can. 1-2km walk. Swim with the fairies! Curse the march of tourism and, I guess, early editions of this book.

1717 7/K22 ✓✓ **The Pools in Glen Etive** Glen Etive is a wild, enchanted place where people have been camping for years to walk and climb in Glen Coe area. There are many grassy landings at the riverside, as well as these perfect pools for bathing. The first is about 5km from the main road, the A82 at Kingshouse, but just follow the river and find your own. Take midge cream for evening wear. Lots.

1718 8/S26 ✓✓ **By Elba Bridge nr Abbey St Bathans** Came here years ago then forgot how to find it. There's possibly a better way because this is a 3km walk but it's so worth it – this has one of the longest stretches of pristine water in rocky, wooded surroundings in southern Scotland. Head to Abbey St Bathans from the A1 (12km), go through it and 2km further and park near Toot Corner (signed). At the actual turn, head down through the woods and follow the path to Edin's Hall Broch, from there steep downhill to the river (the Whiteadder) following it until you reach a house and the Elba footbridge. Other side of it, go right to the rocks where you can get in and swim with the fishes!

1719 5/N19 ✓✓ **Feshiebridge nr Aviemore** At the bridge itself on the B970 between Kingussie and Inverdruie. 4km from Kincraig. Great walks here into Glen Feshie and in nearby woodland; under bridge a perfect spot for Highland swimming. Go down to left from south. Rocky ledges, clear water. One of the best – but cold, even in high summer. Further pools nearby and a sculpture trail.

1720 8/N22 ✓✓ **Rumbling Bridge & The Braan Walk nr Dunkeld** Excellent stretch of cascading river with pools, rocky banks and ledges. Just off A9 heading N opposite first turning for Dunkeld, the A822 for Aberfeldy, Amulree (signed Crieff/Crianlarich). Car park on right after 4km. Connects with forest paths (the Braan Walk) to the **Hermitage** (2070/WALKS) – 2km. Fab picnic and swimming spot though take great care. This is the nearest Highland-type river to Edinburgh (about 1 hour). Caketastic tearoom in Dunkeld (1427/TEAROOMS).

1721 5/M20 ATMOS ✓✓ **Strathmashie nr Newtonmore** On A86 Newtonmore–Dalwhinnie (on A9) to Fort William road 7km from Laggan, watch for Forest sign. Car parks on either side of the road; the Druim an Aird car park has finder boards. Great swimming spot, but often campers. Viewpoints, waterfall, pines. If people are here and you want privacy, follow the river; there are many other great pools. Rather good cakes at **Laggan Coffee Shop**, 5km towards A9 (1437/TEAROOMS).

1722 7/K23 ✓✓ **Rob Roy's Bathtub The Falloch Falls, nr Inverarnan** A82 N of Ardlui
ATMOS   and 3km past the **Drover's Inn** (1312/GOOD PUBS). Sign on the right
(Picnic Area) going N. Park, then follow the path. Some pools on the rocky river
course but 500m from car park you reach the main falls and below a perfect round
natural pool 30m across. There's an overhanging rock face on one side and smooth
slabs at the edge of the falls. Natural suntrap in summer (if there is a summer).

1723 5/K19 ✓✓ **Below Plodda Falls nr Tomich** About 30km from Drumnadrochit on
               Loch Ness via the lovely village of Tomich (1078/HIGHLANDS). Short walk to
the well-signposted falls (1652/WATERFALLS) and these serene pools in a
spectacular woodland setting.

1724 8/P27 ✓ **Neidpath Peebles** 2km from town on A72, Biggar road; sign for castle. Park
             by Hay Lodge Park and walk upriver till you're almost underneath the castle.
Idyllic setting of a broad meander of the Tweed, with medieval Neidpath Castle, a
sentinel above. Pools (3m deep in average summer) may be linked by shallow
rapids. Usually a rope-swing on the oak tree at the upper pool. Also see 2053/
WALKS. Swimming here much better recently.

1725 6/N17 ✓ **Randolph's Leap nr Forres** Spectacular gorge on the mythical Findhorn,
             which carves out some craggy scenery on its way to a gentle coast. This
no-longer-secret glade and fabulous swimming hole are behind a wall on a bend of
the B9007 (see 2060/WALKS for directions), S of Forres and Nairn and near **Logie
Steading**, a courtyard of good things (a board there gives directions) and
refreshment (1441/TEAROOMS). One Randolph – or Alistair as the new tale
tells – may have leapt here; we just bathe and picnic under the trees.

1726 8/N21 ✓ **Falls of Bruar nr Blair Atholl** Just off A9, 12km N of Blair Atholl. 250m walk
             from **House of Bruar** car park and shopping experience (2212/SHOPS) to
lower fall (1653/WATERFALLS), where there is a large, accessible and deep pool by
the bridge. Cold, fresh mountain water in a woody gorge. The proximity of the retail
experience can make it all the more … naturally exhilarating.

1727 5/K18 **Dog Falls Glen Affric** Halfway along Glen Affric road from Cannich before loch,
a picnic spot and great place to swim in the peaty waters surrounded by the
Caledonian Forest (with trails). Birds well sussed to picnic crumbs – your car covered
in tits and cheeky chaffinches. Hitchcock or what? (2025/WALKS). Falls (rapids really)
to the left. The more spectacular **Plodda Falls** (1652/WATERFALLS) are nearby.

1728 8/M23 **Near Comrie** 2 great pools near the neat little town in deepest Perthshire. **The
Linn**, the town pool: go over humpback bridge from main A85 W to Lochearnhead,
signed The Ross. Take left fork; after 2km there's a parking place on left. River's
relatively wide, very pleasant spot. For more adventurous, **Glenartney**, known
locally as The Cliffs: go over bridge, the Braco road after 3km signed Glenartney,
past Cultybraggan camp (café and workshops) and then MoD range on left just
before the end-of-the-road sign (200m after boarded-up cottage on right, 5km from
Comrie). Park and walk down to river in glen. With the twin perils of the Army and
the Comrie Angling Club, you might feel you have no right to be here, but you do,
and this stretch of river is marvellous. Respect the farmland. Follow the road further
for picnic spots. Comrie has a great pub/hotel bistro 904/PERTHSHIRE, **Deil's
Cauldron** 918/PERTHSHIRE, **Hansen's Kitchen** 1507/DELIS, and 1489/BAKERS.

1729 7/K26 **Greeto Falls nr Largs** Well known locally; ask for Flatt Rd or head up from the
seafront at Nardini's. Car park at top and you follow the beautiful Gogo Glen path,
past Cockmalane Cottage. Superb views of the Clyde. 3 pools to choose from in the
Gogo Burn near the bridge. Walk can extend to the mast (4km return).

1730 7/H23 **Swimmers' Quarry Easdale** Cross to Easdale on the wee boat (5-min continuous service); see 2163/HISTORY for details. Do visit the museum and the Puffer pub but go beyond scattered houses, following paths to slate quarries full of seawater since 1881, with clear water like an enormous hotel swimming pool. The L-shaped one with its little bench is easiest; the water can be blue like the Aegean.

1731 8/M24 **The Scout Pool & The Bracklinn Falls Callander** The latter are a Callander must-see. Easy to find – signposted from S end of Main St, go uphill to golf course then next car park up on right and from there it's a 2km walk. The Scout Pool is a traditional swimming hole on same river, the Keltie Water, it's a summer thing only. Follow road further 2km from Bracklinn car park till road goes on through iron gate. Park on right. Go downhill 150m, cross wooden bridge then follow river path to right 250m. Access to huge pool dammed by giant boulders. A beautiful secret spot in the woods. Riverscape does change here – reports, please.

1732 9/M30 **The Otter's Pool New Galloway Forest** A clearing in the forest reached by a track, the Raiders' Road, running from 8km N of Laurieston on the A762, and 16km to Clatteringshaws Loch on the A712 (enter from either direction on these roads, both leading to New Galloway). The track is only open March to October and gets busy. It follows the Water of Dee and halfway along – the Otter's Pool. A bronze otter used to mark the spot (it got nicked) and it's a place mainly for kids and paddling; but when the dam runs off it can be deep enough to swim. Sublime on summer days 2018. Road closes dusk. See also 2076/WALKS.

1733 8/R27 **Ancrum** A secret place on the Ale Water (3km out of village towards Lilliesleaf, 250m from farm sign to Hopton – a recessed gate on the right before a bend and a rough track that locals know). A buttercup meadow, a Border burn, a surprisingly deep, secret pool to swim. Go to left of rough vegetation in defile, going downhill follow fence on your right. Cross further gate at bottom (only 100m from road). Arcadia awaits beyond the meadow. In Ancrum, the **Cross Keys** (1339/FOOD PUBS), for ale and excellent food. Nearby, with an approach via A698 to Hawick, is **Born in the Borders**, an all-round retail and refreshment farmyard with brewery (2208/SCOTTISH SHOPS).

1734 8/N24 **Paradise Sheriffmuir, nr Dunblane** A pool at the foot of an unexpected leafy gorge on the moor between the Ochils and Strathallan. Here the Wharry Burn is known locally as 'Paradise' or, contradictorily, the **Devil's Bucket**. Take road from 'behind' Dunblane or Bridge of Allan to the Sheriffmuir Inn (closed); go downhill (back) towards BoA. Park 1km after humpback bridge. Head for the pylon nearest the river and you'll find the pool. Only midges (or rain) will infiltrate your paradise.

1735 6/R20 **Potarch Bridge & Cambus o' May on the Dee** 2 places: the first by the
& 6/Q20 reconstructed Victorian bridge (and near the hotel) 3km E of Kincardine O'Neil. Cambus is another stretch of river E of Ballater (6km). Locals swim, picnic on rocks, etc, and there are forest walks on the other side of road. The brave jump off the bridge at Cambus (in wetsuits). Great tearooms nearby: the **Black-Faced Sheep** and **Spider on a Bicycle** in Aboyne (1440/1449/TEAROOMS) and see below.

1736 6/R20 **The Feugh** The Water of Feugh is the largest tributary of the Dee, with famous falls on the B974 2km S of Banchory. Further along the road towards Aboyne, there are tracks in the beautiful Forest of Birse and some brilliant secret pools and a beautiful tiny kirk (1919/CHURCHES). The folk at the tearoom/farm shop on the nearby **Finzean Estate** (1514/FARM SHOPS), which you should certainly visit, sent me here: down the hill turn right marked 'Forest of Birse', to the sawmill (3km) for the river walk, 2km further for the kirk.

Good Places To Take Kids

⌐ *signifies notable café.*

CENTRAL

1737 8/P25 ✓✓✓ **Edinburgh Zoo** Corstorphine Rd · www.edinburghzoo.org.uk · 0131 334 9171 4km W of Princes St. A large and long-venerated zoo, which is always evolving and where the natural world from the poles to the plains of Africa is ranged around Corstorphine Hill. Enough huge/exotic/ghastly creatures and friendly, amusing ones to fill an overstimulated day. The Budongo Trail chimp enclosure is first class. The penguins do their famous parade at 2.15pm. The beavers are brill, the koalas are cool as ... then there are the Pandas (time-ticketed, you should book in advance). Tian Tian had an issue with her pregnancy, then ... no issue. We and the Chinese await developments. Shop stocked with PC toys and souvenirs. Café. Open AYR. Apr-Sep: 7 days 9am-6pm, reduced hours in winter.

1738 8/L26 & 8/Q25 ✓✓✓ **Riverside Museum** By Clydeside Expressway, Glasgow & **National Museum of Scotland** Chambers Street, Edinburgh World-class and fun and awe. Reports: 674/399/ATTRACTIONS.

1739 8/Q25 ✓✓ **Our Dynamic Earth** Holyrood Road, Edinburgh · www.dynamicearth.co.uk · 0131 550 7800 Edinburgh's major kids' attraction. Report: 405/ATTRACTIONS.

1740 8/Q25 ✓✓ **Museum of Childhood** 42 High Street, Edinburgh · www.edinburghmuseums.org.uk · 0131 529 414242 An Aladdin's cave of toys for all ages. Report: 413/ATTRACTIONS.

1741 8/Q25 ✓✓ **Weehailes Playpark** Newhailes House, Musselburgh · www.nts.org.uk · 0131 653 5599 Splendiferous new (2018) play/adventure park and huge addition to splendid **Newhailes House** (1875/HOUSES). No expense spared here in building an endlessly engaging clamber-all-over activity experience, based a bit on the history of the estate. So well done. Café. Open AYR, daytime.

1742 8/R25 ✓✓ **East Links Family Park** Dunbar · www.eastlinks.co.uk · 01368 863607 Off the A1 and A199 (East Linton to Dunbar road) by the entrance to the John Muir Country Park (well-signed). An easy-going, non-high-tech animal farm and activity centre with inside and outside play areas, go-karts, a train, climbing walls and lots of obliging animals. 7 days 10am-5pm. Combine with **Foxlake** (below) nearby for older kids.

1743 8/R25 ✓ **Foxlake Adventures** nr Dunbar · www.foxlake.co.uk · 01620 860657 & **Reboot Disc Golf** www.rebootdiscgolf.com · 07572 127020 Two related outdoorsy fun things on a lake in a wood on the A199 4km E of Dunbar. At Foxlake you get on a wetsuit, hook on a cable and go wakeboarding. Off the same car park, you take to the woods and throw Frisbees. This is what we do with our leisure time. Kids and (on Foxlake) more daring dads love it. Mar-Dec 9am-dusk. Good caff. **Foxlake also in Dundee** in the harbour by the Apex Hotel.

1744 8/Q25 ✓ **Edinburgh Butterfly Farm & Insect World** nr Dalkeith · www. edinburgh-butterfly-world.co.uk · 0131 663 4932 On A7 signed Eskbank/ Galashiels from ring road (1km). Part of a garden-centre complex. Beauty and the beasties in a creepy-crawly world: delightful butterflies but kids are more impressed by the glowing scorpions, locusts, iguanas and other assorted uglies. Red-kneed tarantula not for the faint-hearted. 7 days 9.30am-5.30pm (10am-5pm in winter).

1745 8/P25 ✓ **Gorgie City Farm** Edinburgh · www.gorgiecityfarm.org.uk · 0131 337 4202 A working farm on busy road in the heart of the city. Friendly domestic animals and people, garden, great playground and café. 7 days, daytime only. Free. Green and fluffy in the concrete jungle.

1746 8/M26 ✓ **Glasgow Science Centre** Pacific Quay · www.glasgowsciencecentre. org · 0141 420 5000 One of Glasgow's most flash attractions. State-of-the-art interactive landmark tower and IMAX. Report: 679/ATTRACTIONS.

1747 7/K26 ✓ **Kelburn Country Centre** Largs · www.kelburnestate.com · L 01475 568685 2km S of Largs on A78. Riding school, gardens, woodland walks up the Kelburn Glen and a visitor section with shops/exhibits/cafés. Notable for its many events and music/arts festival – **Kelburn Garden Party** (44/EVENTS). Wooden stockade for clambering kids; indoor playbarn with quite scary slides. Falconry displays (those long-suffering owls). The Plaisance indeed a pleasant place and the Secret Forest beckons. The graffiti art is ... well, something else! Apr-Oct: 7 days 10am-6pm; winter 10am-4pm. Stock up on ice cream at **Nardini's** famous caff (766/AYRSHIRE).

1748 8/R25 **Yellowcraigs** nr Dirleton Beautiful beach 35km E of Edinburgh via A1, the A198 LL though Dirleton village, then right, for 2km. Big car park. Lovely, scenic strand and dunes (440/BEACHES). Treasure Island play park in the woods is great for kids. Activity and sea air! **Luca's** on the way for ice cream (1491/ICE CREAM).

1749 8/Q25 **The Edinburgh Dungeon** 31 Market St · www.thedungeons.com · 0131 240 1000 Slick but très contrived experience takes you through a ghoulish history of Scottish nasties. Hammy of course, but kids will love the monorail. Opening times vary.

✓✓ **Falkirk Wheel** Falkirk Report: 5/ATTRACTIONS.

FIFE & TAYSIDE

1750 8/Q23 ✓✓ **Cairnie Fruit Farm & Maze** nr Cupar · www.cairniefruitfarm.co.uk · 01334 655610 Leave town by minor road from main street heading past the hospital, signed (4km), or from main A92, signed near Kilmany (3km). A family-run fruit and farm shop/café (1524/FARM SHOPS); hugely popular due to extensive play area using farm materials to amuse kids and get them countrified. This is the Tayside equivalent of Cream o' Galloway (below), this time built around the strawberry rather than the ice cream. They also grow apples and unbelievable quantities of pumpkins. The annually seeded maze in the maize field is major. There are strawberries for tea and other very good grub. Apr-Oct 10am-5pm (9.30am-5.30pm Jul/Aug).

1751 8/Q24 ✓ **Muddy Boots** Balmalcolm · www.muddybootsfife.com · 01337 831222 On A914 S of Cupar. Like Cairnie (above) this is where kids can go wild in the country, but it is no manufactured experience. The goats love being goats, though now for annoying health and safety reasons you can't get near them.

Ditto: the Highland cows! Playbarn, expanded with water slide, and playfields: biking, sledging, jumping (possibly for joy). Great café with centrepiece wood stove. Mon-Sat 9am-5pm (Sun from 10am).

1752 8/P25 ✓ **Deep Sea World** North Queensferry · www.deepseaworld.com · 01383 411880 The aquarium in a quarry which may be reaching its swim-by date. Habitats are viewed from a conveyor belt, from which you can stare at the fish, as diverse divers teem around and above you. Maximum hard sell to this all-weather attraction – the shark capital – but kids like it even when they've been queueing for aeons. Cute seals and sharp sharks! Café is fairly awful, but nice views. Open AYR. 7 days 10am-5pm; weekends till 6pm (last entry 1 hour before).

1753 8/Q23 ✓ **Dundee Science Centre** Greenmarket · www.dundeesciencecentre. org.uk · 01382 228800 Across roundabout from Discovery Point and adjacent **DCA** (2178/GALLERIES). Purpose-built indoor infotainment, this is an innovative and interactive games complex with a message. 7 days 10am-5pm. Average visit time 2-3 hours.

1754 8/Q23 ✓ **Verdant Works** Dundee · www.rrsdiscovery.com · 01382 309060 Near ☕ Westport. Heritage museum that recreates workings of a jute mill. Sounds industrial, but is brilliant for kids and grown-ups. Report: 2158/HISTORY.

1755 8/R23 **Craigtoun Park** St Andrews · www.friendsofcraigtoun.org.uk · 01334 473666 3km SW of St Andrews on the Pitscottie road (enter via Dukes Golf Course). An oasis of fun: bouncy castles, trampolines, putting, crazy golf, boating lake, a train through the grounds, adventure playgrounds and glasshouses. A perfect day's amusement especially for nippers. Opening hours vary. Bar/ restaurant. The **Duke's Clubhouse** adjacent has stunning views. Bus from town.

1756 8/M23 **Auchingarrich Wildlife Park** nr Comrie · www.auchingarrich.co.uk · L 01764 679469 4km from main street over bridge and signed or via Braco off the M9. Conscientious corralling in the Perthshire hills of fluffy, hairy and feathered things, all friendly. Some exotic creatures but mostly familiar. Adventure playground; small flying fox. So-so café; many picnic spots. All on a very informal and approachable scale. 7 days 10am-5pm.

1757 8/Q23 **Camperdown Park** Dundee · www.camperdownwildlifecentre.com · 01382 431811 Large park just off ring road (Kingsway and A923 to Coupar Angus) with wildlife centre and nearby play complex. Animal handling at weekends. Many birds; marmosets, lemurs, the odd bear. Open AYR. Centre 10am-4.30pm, earlier in winter (1602/PARKS).

THE SOUTH & SOUTH WEST

1758 9/M31 ✓✓ **Cream o' Galloway** Rainton, nr Gatehouse of Fleet · www. creamogalloway.co.uk · 01557 814040 There is something inherently good about a visitor attraction based on the incontrovertible fact that human beings love ice cream, especially with a 'pure and simple' message. They now brand themselves 'the Ethical Dairy' and there is an integrity to all they do. Organic café, playbarn, herb garden, karting and fab adventure playground in the woods, part of 5km of child-friendly nature trails. Let's hear it for cows! Feb-Oct 10am-5pm. Allow a few hours. Report: 1492/ICE CREAM. **Sandgreen** 1641/BEACHES.

1759 7/L27 **Kidz Play** Prestwick · www.kidz-play.co.uk · 01292 475215 Off main street at Station Road, past station to beach and to right. Soft-play area in big shed. Everything the little blighters will like in the throwing-themselves-around department. Shriek city. Babies-12. 7 days 9.30am-6pm.

1760 8/Q27
L **Kailzie Gardens** Peebles · www.kailziegardens.com · 01721 720007 All-round family destination 4km from Peebles on B7062. Fishing lochan, osprey-watching (Apr-Aug) though birds are 2km away (as the osprey flies) and marvellous, serene, well-tended gardens (walled and wild); perfectly hedged. Apr-Oct 11am-5.30pm; gardens only in winter.

1761 8/Q27
MAR-SEP **Bowhill** nr Selkirk · www.bowhillhouse.co.uk · 01750 22204 4km from Selkirk on the A708 Moffat–Selkirk road. Bowhill House and Estate, though not offering itself as a kids' 'attraction', is a lovely, woody place for family walking, messing about, mushrooming and getting to feel the trees. Adventure playground. Guided tours only of House (check website), with its world-class art collection. Further down the road St Mary's Loch and the **Grey Mare's Tail** (1656/WATERFALLS) for more outdoors.

1762 8/M25 **Palacerigg Country Park** Cumbernauld · www.northlanarkshire.gov.uk · 01236 720047 6km SE of Cumbernauld off A801, 40 mins from Glasgow. 740 acres of parkland; ranger service, nature trails, picnic area and kids' farm with rare breeds; the longhouses. Golf course and putting green. Changing exhibits about forestry, conservation, etc. Open AYR. 7 days, daylight hours. Café.

✓✓ **Drumlanrig Castle** Thornhill Report: 1585/PARKS.

THE NORTH EAST

1763 6/S17 ✓ **Macduff Marine Aquarium** www.macduff-aquarium.org.uk · 01261 455775 On the seafront E of the harbour, a family attraction for this Moray Firth port. Small but underrated, perhaps because nearby Banff gets more tourist attention, though **Duff House** (2185/GALLERIES) gets fewer visitors than this child-friendly sealife centre. All fish seem curiously happy with their lot, content to educate and entertain. Open AYR 10am-5pm (last admission 4.15pm). Check winter hours.

1764 6/S20 ✓ **The Den & The Glen** Maryculter, nr Aberdeen · www.denandtheglen.co.uk · 01224 732941 Softplay and fibreglass fantasy land in verdant glen 16km S of Aberdeen via B9077, the South Deeside road, a nice drive. Characters from fairy tales dotted around 28-acre park and lots of things to throw yourself around in/on. Older kids may find it tame: no guns, no big technology but nice for little 'uns. Wonderful gardens. 7 days 9.30am-5.30pm (4.30pm last admission), weather permitting.

1765 6/T18 **Aden** Mintlaw · www.adencountrypark.org.uk Pronounced 'Ah-den'. Country park just beyond Mintlaw on A950 16km from Peterhead. Former grounds of mansion with walks and organised activities and events. Farm buildings converted into Farming Heritage Centre, café, etc. Adventure playground. Open AYR.

THE HIGHLANDS & ISLANDS

1766 6/N19 ✓ **Cairngorm Reindeer Herd** Glenmore, nr Aviemore · www.cairngormreindeer.co.uk · 01479 861228 At Glenmore Forest Park, 12km from Aviemore along Coylumbridge Rd, near Glenmore Visitor Centre. Stop at centre (shop, exhibition) to buy tickets and follow the guide in your vehicle up the mountain. From here, a 20-min walk. Real reindeer aplenty in authentic free-ranging habitat (when they come down off the cloudy hillside in winter with snow all around it's very real); they're so … small. 90-min trip 11am AYR and other trips in summer. Wear suitable footwear; phone if weather looks threatening.

1767 5/N19 ✓ **Leault Farm** nr Kincraig · www.leaultworkingsheepdogs.co.uk · **01540 651402** On A9 but easier to find from a sign 1km S of Kincraig on B9152. Working farm with daily sheepdog trials showing an extraordinary facility with dogs and sheep (and ducks). A great spectacle, totally authentic in this setting. Usually 4pm May-Oct (possibly other times). Closed Sat. Sometimes pups to love.

1768 6/N19 ✓ **Landmark Park** Carrbridge · www.landmarkpark.co.uk · **01479 841613** A purpose-built family outdoor activity centre with much to throw yourself into, AV displays and shopping. Great for kids messing about in the woods on slides, in a maze, etc, in a large adventure playground. Plus, the Wildwater Coaster. Fire Tower may be too much for granny but there are fine forest views. Indoors, there's the 'Bamboozeleum'! 7 days 10am-6pm (5pm in winter, 7pm mid-Jul to mid-Aug). Disappointing caff. Great in autumn!

1769 5/N19 ✓ **The Highland Wildlife Park** Kincraig · www.highlandwildlifepark.org. uk · **01540 651270** On B9152 Aviemore-Kingussie. Large drive-through reserve run by Royal Zoological Society with wandering herds of deer, bison, etc, and pens of other animals. Some in habitats, but also cages. Cute, vicious little wildcats! The UK's first polar bear cub arrived to great excitement in 2018, totally upstaging her mum, Victoria, and the snow leopards. Does feel much more natural than a zoo in this swathe of Highland Scotland. Must be time to bring back bears, let the wolves go free and liven up the caravan parks. Open 10am-5pm (Jul/Aug 6pm, winter 4pm).

1770 5/M20 **Highland Folk Museum** Newtonmore · www.highlandfolk.com · MAR-OCT **01540 673551** Just outside town on the A86 to Kingussie and 10 mins from the A9. Historical Highlandish (1700s-1950s) and folksy, but a lovely, interesting place to take kids. Thatched cottages, places to run around, adventure park. Collection of 12,000 artefacts! Apr-Oct.

1771 7/G21 **Nàdurra Visitor Centre** Ardnamurchan · www.nadurracentre.co.uk · **01972 500209** A861 Strontian, B8007 Glenmore 14km. Photographer Michael McGregor's award-winning interactive exhibition (under different owners). Kids enjoy, adults impressed. A walk-through of wildlife, including live pine martens (if you're lucky), herons and CCTV of more cautious creatures. Tearoom. Apr-Oct. Check website for hours.

1772 5/N19 **Loch Insh** Kincraig · www.lochinsh.com · **01540 651272** Watersports centre (2147/WATERSPORTS) but much more on B970 2km from Kincraig (near Kingussie and the A9). Beautiful loch and mountain setting, 2 small beaches and gentle water. Lots of instruction available, wildlife boat trips, biking possibilities and small adventure playground. Good café and terrace overlooking loch: the Boathouse. All-round active day out; there are chalets and a 25-bedroom B&B to stay longer.

The Best Places To See Birds

See p. 302-3 for Wildlife Reserves, many of which are good for birdwatching. All those listed below are in L, LL *and* LLL *settings.*

1773 4/K13 ✔✔ **Handa Island** nr Scourie, Sutherland · www.scottishwildlifetrust. org.uk Take the boat from Tarbet Pier, 6km off A894 5km N of Scourie or from Scourie itself (both 07780 967800) and land on a beautiful island run as a nature reserve by the Scottish Wildlife Trust. Boats (Apr-early Sep though fewer birds after Aug) are continuous depending on demand. Crossing 30 mins. Small reception hut and 2.5km walk over island to cliffs which rise 350m and are layered in colonies, 200,000 strong: fulmars, shags and the UK's largest colony of guillemots. Allow 3-4 hours. Though you must take care not to disturb the birds, you'll be eye to eye with seals and bill to bill with razorbills. Eat at the **Shorehouse** on the cove when you return (1377/SEAFOOD). Mon-Sat. Last return 5pm.

1774 9/P30 ✔✔ **Caerlaverock** nr Dumfries · www.wwt.org.uk · 01387 770200 17km S on B725 near Bankend, signed from road. The WWT Caerlaverock Wetlands Centre is an excellent place to see whooper swans, barnacle geese in their 30-thousand and more (countless hides, observatories, farmhouse viewing tower). Has Fairtrade home-cookin' café as well as farmhouse-style accom with a variety of basic rooms (and a badger feeding station). More than just birds too: natterjack toads, badgers, so not just for twitchers. The Sir Peter Scott hide is pure entertainment. Centre open AYR. 7 days 10am-5pm.

1775 7/F22 ✔✔ **Lunga & The Treshnish Islands** off Mull · www.hebrideantrust.org Sail from Tobermory, Iona/Fionnphort or Ulva ferry on Mull to these uninhabited islands on a 5/6-hour excursion which probably takes in Staffa and Fingal's Cave. Best time is May-July when birds are breeding. Talk of pufflings not making it because parents can't find sand eels seems premature here. Some trips allow 3 hours on Lunga. Razorbills, guillemots and a carpet of puffins oblivious to your presence. This is a memorable day. Boat trips (Ulva Ferry 08000 858786; or 01681 700358 from Fionnphort) from Iona. Trips dependent on sea conditions.

1776 8/R24 ✔✔ **Isle of May** Firth of Forth Island at mouth of Forth off Crail/Anstruther reached by daily boat trips from Anstruther harbour: *The May Princess* (07957 585200; www.anstrutherpleasurecruises.co.uk). Apr-Sep times dependent on tides. Trip 45 mins; allows 3 hours ashore. Or quicker, smaller *Osprey Rib* (07473 631671; www.isleofmayboattrips.co.uk). Can reserve the day before. Island (including isthmus to Rona) 1.5km x 0.5km. Info centre and resident wardens. See guillemots, razorbills and kittiwakes on cliffs; and shags, terns and thousands of puffins. Most populations increasing. This place is strange as well as beautiful. The puffins in early summer are, as always, engaging.

1777 8/R25 ✔✔ **The Bass Rock** off North Berwick · 01620 892838 Temple of gannets. A guano-encrusted massif sticking out of the Forth: their largest island colony in the world. Davie Balfour was imprisoned here in RLS's *Catriona* (aka *Kidnapped II*). A variety of weather-dependent boat trips available Easter-Sep, including landings and safaris (which sell out first). Extraordinary birds, extraordinary experience. For daily trips on *The Sula*: www.sulaboattrips.co.uk, 01620 880770 or enquire at the Seabird Centre (below). **Lobster Shack** on the harbour is brill (1365/SEAFOOD) and many good food options in North Berwick.

1778 8/P22 ✓✓ **Loch of the Lowes** nr Dunkeld · www.scottishwildlifetrust.org.uk ·
01350 727337 4km NE Dunkeld on A923 to Blairgowrie or walk from
Dunkeld main street (2.5km). Superbly managed (Scottish Wildlife Trust) site with
double-floored hide (always open) and other hide (same hours as visitor centre)
and permanent binoculars. Main attractions are the captivating ospreys (from early
Apr-Aug). Nest 100m over loch and clearly visible. Their revival (over 270 pairs now
in UK, 70 in Perthshire alone) is well documented: diary of movements, breeding
history, etc. And a live feed to the feed. Also, the near-at-hand, endless fascination
of watching wild birds, including woodpeckers, and the red squirrels outside the
picture window. Great walks nearby (2043/WALKS), including to Loch Ordie.

1779 6/N19 ✓✓ **Loch Garten** nr Boat of Garten · www.nnr-scotland.org.uk ·
01479 831476 3km village off B970 into Abernethy Forest. Famous for
the ospreys and signed from all round. Best Apr-Jun. 2 car parks: the first has
nature trails through Scots pine woods and around loch; other has visitor centre
with the main hide 250m away: TV screens, binoculars, other wild-bird viewing
and informed chat. Here since 1954, that first pair have done wonders for local
tourism – in fact, they and the RSPB and the army of determined volunteers
practically invented ecotourism! Och, but they are magnificent.

1780 8/Q25 ✓ **The Scottish Ornithologists' Club House** nr Aberlady · www.the-soc.
org.uk · 01875 871330 A198 on the left going into Aberlady from Edinburgh,
opposite Gosford Estate. Not a bird-watching site per se (though between the
Lagoon and the Seabird Centre, below, and near Aberlady Reserve 2km), but an
archive, library and resource centre for lovers of Scottish birds. Light modern
building looks across bay to reserve. Art exhibitions; much to browse. Bird-
watching for beginners courses. Friendly staff. The Society published the definitive
The Birds of Scotland. Open 10am-4pm (noon-6pm weekends in summer). Go in
October, late afternoon, when the geese come in over Aberlady Bay (best viewed
from Kilspindie Golf Club road).

1781 8/Q25 ✓ **The Lagoons** Musselburgh On E edge of town behind the racecourse
(follow road round, take turn-off signed Race Course Parking) at the estuarine
mouth of the River Esk. Waders, sea birds, ducks aplenty and often interesting
migrants on the mudflats and wide littoral. The Lagoons are man-made ponds and
attract big populations (both birds and binocs – there are hides). This is the nearest
diverse-species area to Edinburgh (15km) and is one of the most significant migrant
stopovers in the UK.

1782 8/S20 ✓ **Fowlsheugh** nr Stonehaven · www.rspb.org.uk · 01346 532017 8km S of
Stonehaven and signed from A92 with path from Crawton. Sea-bird city on
2km of red sandstone cliffs up to 200 feet high; take great care. 80,000 pairs of 6
species, especially guillemots, kittiwakes, razorbills but also fulmars, shags and
puffins. Possible to view the birds without disturbing them and discern the layers
they occupy on the cliff face. Best seen May-July and best to go by bike!

1783 7/F25 ✓ **Loch Gruinart, Loch Indaal** Islay RSPB reserve. Take A847 at Bridgend
then B8017 turning N and right for Gruinart. The mudflats and fields at the
head of the loch provide winter grazing for huge flocks of Barnacle and Greenland
geese. They arrive, as do flocks of fellow bird-watchers, in late Oct. Hides and good
vantage points near road. Don't miss beautiful **Saligo Bay** (1625/BEACHES). The
Rhinns and the Oa in the south also sustain a huge variety of birdlife.

1784 1/P10 ✓ **Marwick Head Orkney Mainland** · **www.rspb.org.uk** 40km NW of
Kirkwall, via Finstown and Dounby; take left at Birsay after Loch of Isbister,
cross the B9056 and park at Cumlaquoy. A 4km circular walk. Spectacular sea-bird
breeding colony on 100m cliffs and nearby at the Loons Reserve, wet meadowland,
8 species of duck and many waders. Orkney sites include the Noup cliffs on
Westray, North Hill on Papa Westray and Copinsay, 3km E of the mainland.

1785 7/G23 **Isle of Mull www.rspb.org.uk** Sea eagles. Very successful reintroduction of
these magnificent eagles; a hide with CCTV viewing. By appointment only. Site
changes every year. Mull claims the highest breeding density of golden eagles in
Europe.

1786 8/R25 **Scottish Seabird Centre North Berwick** · **www.seabird.org** · **01620 890202**
Award-winning, interactive visitor attraction near the harbour overlooking Bass
Rock (above) and Fidra. If you don't want to go out there, video and other state-of-
the-art technology makes you feel as if you're with the birds. Viewing deck for the
dramatic diving of the gannets (140km per hour!). Café and shopping where puffins
prevail. Enquire about the (1-hour) boat trips. **Rocketeer Restaurant** adjacent,
The Lobster Shack (1365/SEAFOOD) in summer on the harbour. 7 days.

1787 8/S22 **Montrose Basin Wildlife Centre www.montrosebasin.org.uk** ·
01674 676336 1.5km S of Montrose on A92 to Arbroath. Accessible Scottish
Wildlife Trust centre overlooks estuarine basin hosting residents and migrants.
Good for twitchers, kids. Autumn geese. Visitor centre Mar-Oct daily 10.30am-5pm.
Call for winter hours.

1788 4/N13 **Forsinard Flows Nature Reserve www.rspb.org.uk** · **01641 571225** 44km
from Helmsdale on the A897, or train stops en route to Wick/Thurso. RSPB
(proposed World Heritage site) reserve, acquired after public appeal. 19,000
hectares of the Flow Country and its birds: divers, plovers, merlins and hen harriers
(nest watch in visitor centre). Guided walks and trails. Reserve open AYR; visitor
centre Apr-Oct 9am-5.30pm.

1789 8/Q22 **Loch of Kinnordy Kirriemuir** · **www.rspb.org.uk** · **01577 862355** 4km W of
town on B951, an easily accessible site with 3 hides overlooking loch and wetland
area managed by RSPB. Geese in late autumn, gulls aplenty; always tickworthy.
You may see the vanishing ringlet butterfly. Good deli/café in Kirriemuir (920/
PERTHSHIRE).

1790 6/T17 **Strathbeg nr Fraserburgh** · **www.rspb.org.uk** · **01346 532017** 12km S off
the A952 Fraserburgh–Peterhead road, signed Nature Reserve at Crimond. Wide,
shallow loch close to coastline, a 'magnet for migrating wildfowl'. Marsh/fen,
dune and meadow habitats. In winter 30,000 geese/wigeon/mallard/swans and
occasional rarities like cranes and egrets. 20% of the world's pink-footed geese
drop by. Binocs in visitor centre (8am-6pm, dusk in winter), 3 hides. St Fergus Oil &
Gas terminal does not distract. **Tufted Duck** (989/NE HOTELS) nearby.

1791 6/S17 **Troup Head between Macduff & Fraserburgh, Moray Firth** · **www.rspb.org.**
uk · **01346 532017** Near the cliff-clinging villages of Crovie and *Local Hero* Pennan
on the coastal B9031. Fantastic airy walk from the former (2091/WALKS) or (closer)
directly from the road signed for Northfield following RSPB signs for 2km, then a
1.5km stroll from car park. Puffins, kittiwakes, the whole shebang; and dolphins.

Where To See Dolphins, Whales, Porpoises & Seals

The coast around the north of Scotland has some of the best places in Europe to view whales, dolphins and seals. Boat trips/sealife cruises get you closer but these are the coastal locations for the best sightings. Dolphins are most active on a rising tide, especially May-September.

MORAY & CROMARTY FIRTHS (NEAR INVERNESS)
The population of bottlenose dolphins in this area is about 200. They can be seen all year (mostly Jun-Sep).

1792 5/M17 **Cromarty** Any vantage around town is good, especially South Sutor (2092/COASTAL WALKS), an old lighthouse cottage has been converted into a research station run by Aberdeen University. **Chanonry Point, Fortrose**, through the golf course, E end of point beyond lighthouse is the *best* place to see dolphins from land in Britain. Occasional sightings can also be seen at **Balintore**, opposite Seaboard Memorial Hall; **Tarbat Ness** beyond **Portmahomack**, end of path through reserve further out along the Moray Firth possible at **Burghead**, **Lossiemouth** and **Buckie**, **Spey Bay** and **Portknockie**. Many, many sealife cruises: **Ecoventures www.ecoventures.co.uk · 01381 600323** from Cromarty are hereby recommended. Also check the Dolphin Space Programme, an accreditation scheme for boat operators: **www.dolphinspace.org**.

THE NORTH WEST
On the west coast, especially near Gairloch the following places may offer sightings of orcas, dolphins and minke whales, mainly in summer.

1793 4/H16 **Rubha Reidh** 20km N of Melvaig (unclassified road). Near Gairloch Sands Youth Hostel W of Lonemore. Where road turns inland is a good spot.

1794 5/H17 **Red Point of Gairloch** By B8056 via Badachro round Loch Gairloch. High ground looking over North Minch and S to Loch Torridon. Harbour porpoises often seen from all along this coast.

1795 4/H15 **Greenstone Point** **north of Laide** Off A832 (unclassified road) through Mellon Udrigle round Gruinard Bay. Harbour porpoises Apr-Dec, minke whales May-Oct.

1796 5/F16 **Rubha Hunish** **Skye** The far NW finger of Skye. Walk from Duntulm Castle or Flodigarry. Dolphins and minke whales in autumn.

OTHER PLACES
1797 2/V5 **Mousa Sound** **Shetland** 20km S of Lerwick (1854/PREHISTORIC).

1798 7/F21 **Ardnamurchan** **The Point** The most westerly point (and lighthouse) on this wildly beautiful peninsula. Go to end of road or park near Sanna Beach and walk round. Sanna Beach worth going to just to walk the strand. Visitor centre; tearoom.

1799 8/Q23 **Broughty Ferry** **Fife** Rare but magic! The Esplanade, Castle and by **The Ship Inn** (952/DUNDEE), where you might be having lunch, binoculars provided.

Great Wildlife Reserves

These wildlife reserves are not merely bird-watching places. Most of them are easy to get to from major centres; none requires a permit.

1800 8/S25
NTS

✓✓ **St Abb's Head** nr Berwick · www.nts.org.uk · 01890 771443 9km N of Eyemouth and 10km E of main A1. Spectacular cliff scenery (2087/WALKS), a huge sea-bird colony, rich marine life and varied flora. Good view from top of stacks, geos and cliff face full of serried ranks of guillemot, kittiwake, razorbill, etc. Hanging gardens of grasses and campion. Behind cliffs, grassland rolls down to the Mire Loch and its varied habitat of bird, insect, butterfly life and vegetation. Surprisingly good art gallery (2202/SCOTTISH SHOPS) and NTS interpretation centre in a row of cottages by car park. 1/2/3km walks marked. Disabled access to the Lighthouse on tarmac road behind the cottages. Coffee shop at the car park. The New Inn in Coldingham (3km) for decent pub grub (01890 771315) and 2 good caffs in St Abbs village (a cute harbour) 2km down the road.

1801 6/T18

✓✓ **Sands of Forvie & Ythan Estuary** Newburgh · www.nnr-scotland.org.uk · 01358 751330 25km N Aberdeen. Cross bridge outside Newburgh on A975 to Cruden Bay and park. Path follows Ythan Estuary, bears N and enters the largest undisturbed dune system in the UK (though see below). Dunes in every aspect of formation. Collieston, a 17/18th-century fishing village, and Forvie Centre 4km away. These habitats support the largest population of eiders in Britain (especially June) and huge numbers of terns. It's easy to get lost here, so get lost! Some wish the same would happen to Donald Trump who turned the adjacent dune system into a habitat only for golfers.

1802 5/J17
NC500

✓ **Beinn Eighe** Wester Ross · www.nature.scot Pronounced 'Ben-A'. Bounded by the A832 S from Gairloch and A896 W of Kinlochewe, this first National Nature Reserve in Britain includes remaining fragments of old Caledonian pinewood on the S shore of Loch Maree (largest in West Highlands) and rises to the rugged tops with their spectacular views and varied geology. Excellent wood and mountain trails starting on both roads – from A832 on Loch Maree side there are woodland strolls. Starts to the Beinn (easier) and to the mighty Liathach are from the A896 Glen Torridon road (1695/VIEWS; 1678/SCENIC ROUTES). Hotel (1221/GET-AWAY HOTELS). Great café, **Whistle Stop Café** (1443/TEAROOMS).

1803 7/H24

Scottish Beaver Trial Knapdale · www.scottishbeavers.org.uk In the Knapdale Forest W of Lochgilphead, off the Tayvallich road (B8025) to the Barnluasgan car park and information centre. Introduced in 2009, the trial has been 'an outstanding success', and on a 5km circular walk, there is much evidence of their activity. Early morning and evening there's a good chance of sightings. Their story to be continued. Updates on the website.

1804 8/R25

John Muir Country Park nr Dunbar · www.eastlothian.gov.uk · 01620 827459 Vast park between Dunbar and North Berwick named after the Dunbar-born father of the conservation movement. Includes estuary of the Tyne; part of the park is also known as Tyninghame, and see 441/BEACHES. Diverse habitats: cliffs, sand spits and woodland. Many bird species. Crabs, lichens, sea and marsh plants. Enter at E extremity of Dunbar at Belhaven, off the B6370 from A1; or off A198 to North Berwick. Or better, walk from Dunbar by clifftop trail (2km+) from **The Rocks** (857/LOTHIANS). You could walk to Helensburgh (215km) on the John Muir Way!

1805 7/L26 **Lochwinnoch** www.rspb.org.uk · **01505 842663** 30km SW of Glasgow via M8 junction 28A, then A737 past Johnstone on to A760. Also from Largs 20km via A760. Reserve just outside village on lochside and comprises wetland and woodland habitats. A serious nature centre, incorporating an observation tower. Hides and marked trails; and a birds-spotted board. Shop and coffee shop. Events programme. Good for kids. Visitor centre open 10am-5pm.

1806 5/N20 **Insh Marshes** nr Kingussie · www.rspb.org.uk · **01540 661518** 4km from town along B970 (past Ruthven Barracks), 2,500 acres of Spey floodplain run by RSPB. Trail (3km) marked out through meadow and wetland and a note of species to look out for (including 6 types of orchid, 7 'Red List' birds and half the UK population of goldeneye). Also 2 hides (250m and 450m) high above marshes, vantage points to see waterfowl, birds of prey, otters and deer. Thought to be one of the most important wetland areas in Europe.

1807 8/Q23 **Tentsmuir** between Tayport & Leuchars · www.tentsmuir.org · **01382 553962** N tip of Fife at the mouth of the Tay, reached from Tayport or Leuchars via the B945. Follow signs, taking road that winds for 4km over flat then forested land. Park (car park closes 8.30pm in summer, dusk in winter) and cross dunes to broad strand. Walks in both direction: W back to Tayport, E to Leuchars. Also 4km circular walk of beach and forest. Hide 2km away at Ice House Pond. Seals often watch from waves and bask in summer. Lots of butterflies. Waders aplenty and, to the east, one of UK's most significant populations of eider. Most wildfowl offshore. Check Forestry Commission and Scottish Natural Heritage.

1808 3/C17 **Balranald** North Uist · www.rspb.org.uk · **01463 715000** W coast of North Uist reached by the road from Lochmaddy, then the Bayhead turn-off at Clachan Stores (10km north). This most western, most faraway reach is one of the last redoubts of the disappearing corncrake. Catch its calling while you can.

1809 8/M24 **Flanders Moss** nr Thornhill · www.nnr-scotland.org.uk · **01786 450362** This curious swathe of the Forth valley on the road between Thornhill and Kippen (1km rough track from B822 to car park) is a much revered and well-interpreted ... bog, a kind of micro ecosystem. It's a 'raised bog' and there's a raised walkway around it (1km) and an impressive tower to overlook it. Wet-loving wildlife includes adders, dragonflies and a host of other insects and the birds who feed on them. Then there's the history. This place is a bit of an oddity, central but not overrun. Good grub in Kippen (**The Cross Keys**) and Thornhill (**Lion & Unicorn**) 1329/1332/FOOD PUBS. A very satisfactory afternoon can be had around here.

the Best

of Historical Places

The Best Castles

NTS *National Trust for Scotland. Hours vary. Admission.* HES *Historic Environment Scotland. Standard hours are: Apr-end Sep, 7 days 9.30am– 6pm. Winter hours vary. Admission.*
☕ *signifies notable café.*

1810 8/M24
LLL
ADMISSION
HES

✓✓✓ **Stirling Castle** www.stirlingcastle.scot · 01786 450000
Dominating town and plain, this, like Edinburgh Castle, is worth the hype and history. More aesthetically pleasing, it is, like Edinburgh, a timeless attraction that withstands the waves of tourism as it did the centuries of warfare for which it was built. It does seem a very civilised billet, with gorgeous frescoes, peaceful gardens and cannon-studded rampart walks from which the views are excellent, including the aerial view of the ghost outline of the King's Knot Garden (the Cup and Saucer, as they're known locally). Includes the Renaissance Palace of James V and the Great Hall of James IV restored to full magnificence. Some rock legends have played here and there are many dinners. Unicorn Café is average.

1811 8/Q25
LLL
ADMISSION
HES

✓✓✓ **Edinburgh Castle** www.edinburghcastle.scot · 0131 225 9846
City centre. Impressive from any angle and all the more so from inside. Despite the tides of tourists and time, it still enthrals. Superb perspectives of the city and of Scottish history. Stone of Destiny and the Crown Jewels are the Big Attractions. Café and restaurant (superb views) with efficient but uninspiring catering operation; open only castle hours and to castle visitors. Report: 398/ATTRACTIONS.

1812 6/N17
ADMISSION
NTS

✓✓ **Brodie Castle** nr Forres · www.nts.org.uk · 01309 641371 6-7km W of Forres off main A96. More a (Z-plan) tower house than a castle, dating from 1567. One of the calmest of castle experiences under the conscientious but forward-thinking influences of the NTS. With a minimum of historical hokum, this 16/17th-century, but mainly Victorian, country house is furnished from rugs to moulded ceilings in excellent taste. Every picture (very few gloomies) bears examination. The nursery and nanny's room, the guest rooms, indeed all the rooms, are eminently habitable. Wonderful library. Tearoom inside and out and informal walks in grounds. New 'Playful Garden' for kids. An avenue leads to a lake; in spring the daffodils are famous. Castle open AYR 10am-5pm (check website for winter hours). Grounds open AYR till sunset.

1813 7/K28
LL
ADMISSION
NTS

✓✓ **Culzean Castle** nr Maybole · www.nts.org.uk · 01655 884455
Pronounced 'Cullane'. 24km S of Ayr on A719. Difficult to convey here the scale and the scope of the house and the country park. Allow some hours especially for the grounds. Castle is more like a country house and you observe from the other side of a rope. From the 12th century but rebuilt by Robert Adam in 1775, a time of soaring ambition, its grandeur is almost out of place in this exposed clifftop position. It was designed for entertaining, and the oval staircase is magnificent. Wartime associations (especially with President Eisenhower and you can stay in his suites 761/AYRSHIRE). 560 acres of grounds, including clifftop walk, formal gardens, walled garden (separate admission), Swan Pond (a must) and Happy Valley. Harmonious home farm is visitor centre with exhibits and shop, caffs, etc. The courtyard café especially has great views. And there's a beach. Even the entrance way on the road has been made more welcoming. This really is an appropriate flagship house and gardens experience from NTS. And I remember the Gala Concerts on the Fountain Court (Lou Reed, Patti Smith, Michael Marra)! Open Mar-Oct 10.30am-4pm. Park open AYR. Many special events.

1814 8/Q24
ADMISSION
NTS

✓✓ **Falkland Palace** www.nts.org.uk · **01337 857397** Middle of farming Fife, 15km from M90 junction 8. Not a castle at all, but the hunting palace of the Stewart dynasty. Despite its recreational rather than political role, it's one of the landmark buildings in Scottish history and in the 16th century was the finest Renaissance building in Britain. They all came here for archery, falconry and hunting boar and deer on the Lomonds; and for Royal Tennis which is displayed and explained. Still occupied by the Crichton-Stewarts, the house is dark and rich and redolent of those days of 'dancing and deray at Falkland in the Grene'. Mar-Oct 11am-5pm. Sun noon-5pm. Plant shop and events programme. Superb walks from village (2003/HILL WALKS; 2050/WALKS). See also 1424/TEAROOMS.

1815 4/Q12
L
ATMOS
NC500
ADMISSION
☕

✓✓ **Castle of Mey** nr Thurso · www.castleofmey.org.uk · **01847 851473** Actually near John o' Groats (off A836), castles don't get further-flung than this. Stunted trees, frequent wind and a wild coast but the Queen Mother famously fell in love with this dilapidated house in 1952, filled it with things she found and was given and turned it into one of the most human and endearing of the Royal (if not all aristocratic) residences. Guides tell the story and if you didn't love her already, you will when you leave. Lovely walled garden and animal centre in converted granary with farm animals, including North Country sheep – great for kids. A top tearoom. Mey cattle and produce (cottage pie and crumble). Charles and Camilla still visit. May-Sep (closed 2 weeks end July/early August). Castle 10am-4pm. Simple, elegant hotel on the road (and estate) 1068/HIGHLANDS.

1816 5/N17
ADMISSION
☕

✓ **Cawdor Castle** Cawdor, nr Nairn · www.cawdorcastle.com · **01667 404401** The mighty Cawdor of Macbeth fame. Most of the family clear off for the summer and leave their romantic yet habitable and, yes, ... stylish castle, sylvan grounds and gurgling Cawdor Burn to you. Pictures from Claude to Craigie Aitchison, a modern kitchen as fascinating as the enormous one of yore. Even the tartan passage is nicely done. The burn is the colour of tea. An easy drive (25km) to Brodie (above) means you can see 2 of Scotland's most appealing castles in one day. Shops, courtyard café. 9-hole golf course; trails. These gardens are gorgeous. May-early Oct: 7 days 10am-5pm (last admission).

1817 8/N21
ADMISSION

✓ **Blair Castle** Blair Atholl · www.blair-castle.co.uk · **01796 481207** Impressive from the A9, the castle and the landscape of the Dukes of Atholl (present Duke not present); 10km N of Pitlochry. Hugely popular; almost a holiday-camp atmos. Numbered rooms chock-full of 'collections': costumes, toys, plates, weapons, stag skulls, walking sticks – so many things! Upstairs, the more usual stuffed apartments including the Jacobite bits. Walk in the policies (includes Hercules Garden with tranquil ponds); catch The Whim. Apr-Oct 9.30am-4.30pm (last admission) daily.

1818 8/Q22
LL
ADMISSION

✓ **Glamis Castle** Forfar · www.glamis-castle.co.uk · **01307 840393** 8km from Forfar via A94 or off main A929, Dundee-Aberdeen road (turn-off 10km N of Dundee, a picturesque approach). Fairy-tale castle (pronounced 'Glawms') in majestic setting. Seat of the Strathmore family (Queen Mum spent her childhood here) for 600 years; every room an example of the interior of a certain period. Guided tours (continuous/50 mins long). Restaurant/gallery shop haven for tourists (and for an excellent bridie 1486/BAKERS). Apr-Oct 10am-5.30pm; last entry 60 mins before. Italian Gardens and nature trail well worth 500m walk. 'Prom' concert is held mid-July.

1819 7/J27
ADMISSION
NTS

✓ **Brodick Castle** Arran · www.nts.org.uk · **01770 302202** 4km from town (bike hire 01770 302077 or 01770 302377). Impressive, well-maintained landmark castle, exotic formal gardens and extensive grounds. **Goat Fell** (1985/HILLS) in the background and the sea through the trees. Dating from 13th century and until the 1950s the home of the Dukes of Hamilton. An over-antlered hall leads to liveable rooms with portraits and heirlooms, an atmos of long-ago afternoons. Tangible sense of relief in the kitchens now the entertaining is over. Robert the Bruce's cell less convincing, or it was when visited last. The castle reopens Easter 2019 after a lengthy refurb. Marvellous grounds open AYR (and Goat Fell).

1820 7/H23
LL
ADMISSION
✓ **Duart Castle** Mull · www.duartcastle.com · 01680 812309 A dramatic setting for the 13th-century ancestral seat of the Clan Maclean and home to Sir Lachlan and Lady Maclean. Quite a few modifications over the centuries as methods of defence grew in sophistication but with walls as thick as a truck and the sheer isolation of the place it must have doomed any prospect of attack from the outset. Now a happier, homelier place, the only attacking that gets done these days is on scones and cake in the superior tearoom. Apr: Sun-Thu 11am-4pm. May-Oct: 7 days 10.30am-5.30pm. Diverse event programme in summer months.

1821 5/F17
ADMISSION
Dunvegan Castle Skye · www.dunvegancastle.com · 01470 521206 3km Dunvegan village. Romantic history and setting, though more baronial than castellated, the result of mid-19th-century restoration that incorporated the disparate parts. Much more recent restorations of the castle and the 30,000-acre estate presided over by the 30th MacLeod of MacLeod. Necessary crowd management leads you through a series of rooms where the Fairy Flag, displayed above a table of exquisite marquetry, has pride of place. Gardens, perhaps lovelier than the house, down to the loch; boats leave the jetty to see the seals. Busy café, The Macleod Tables (though food disappointing; there's always **Jann's** in the village 2305/SKYE). Open Apr-Oct: 7 days 10am-5.30pm. Loch cruises from the jetty. Don't miss the **St Kilda Shop** on the drive in (2220/SHOPS).

1822 5/J18
LLL
ADMISSION
Eilean Donan Dornie · www.eileandonancastle.com · 01599 555202 On A87, 13km before Kyle of Lochalsh. A calendar favourite, often depicted illuminated. Inside is a generous portion of history (American size). The Banqueting Hall with its Pipers' Gallery must make for splendid dinner parties for the Macraes. Much military regalia among the bric-a-brac, but also the impressive Raasay Punchbowl partaken of by Johnson and Boswell. Mystical views from ramparts, as well as the more ersatz human story below the stairs. Closed Jan. Check website for times.

1823 8/N22
ADMISSION
Castle Menzies nr Aberfeldy · www.menzies.org · 01887 820982 In Tay valley with spectacular ridge behind (**Walks In The Weem Forest**, part of the Tummel Valley Forest Park; separate car park). On B846, 5km W of Aberfeldy, through Weem. The 16th-century stronghold of the Menzies (pronounced 'Mingiss'), one of Scotland's oldest clans. Sparsely furnished with odd clan memorabilia, the house nevertheless conveys more of a sense of Jacobite times than many more brimful of bric-a-brac. Bonnie Prince Charlie stopped here on the way to Culloden. Open farmland situation, so manured rather than manicured grounds. Good refreshment options in Aberfeldy (1419/1428/TEAROOMS; 923/PERTHSHIRE). Apr-Oct 10.30am-5pm (Sun 2-5pm).

1824 8/P23
ADMISSION
Scone Palace nr Perth · www.scone-palace.co.uk · 01738 552300 Pronounced 'Skoon'. On A93 road to Blairgowrie and Braemar. A 'great house', the home to the Earl of Mansfield and gorgeous grounds. Famous for the Stone of Scone (aka The Stone of Destiny) on which the kings of Scots were crowned, and the Queen Vic bedroom. Maze and pinetum. Many contented animals greet you and a plethora of peacocks. Annual Game Fair and The Rewind Oldie Music Fest is in late July. The kids were here 2018 for the BBC's Big Weekend. Disappointing café but courtyard pleasant. Apr-Oct: 7 days 9.30am-5pm. Winter hours vary.

1825 8/R24 **Kellie Castle nr Pittenweem · www.nts.org.uk · 01333 720271** Major castle
ADMISSION in Fife. Dating from 14th century and restored by Sir Robert Lorimer, his influence
NTS evidenced by magnificent plaster ceilings and furniture. Notable mural by Phoebe
Anna Traquair. The gardens, nursery and kitchen recall all the old Victorian virtues.
The old-fashioned roses still bloom for us. Check website for opening hours.

1826 6/R19 **Craigievar Castle nr Banchory · www.nts.org.uk · 0844 493 2174** 15km N
ADMISSION of main A93 Aberdeen–Braemar road between Banchory and Aboyne. A classic
NTS (and pink) tower house, perfect like a porcelain miniature. Random windows,
turrets, balustrades. Set among sloping lawns and tall trees. Limited access to halt
deterioration; you are spared the shuffling hordes. Tours only. Apr-Sep. No caff.

1827 6/S20 **Drum Castle (the Irvine Ancestral Home) nr Banchory · www.nts.org.uk ·**
ATMOS **01330 700334** Please forgive this, the longest entry in this section. 1km off main
ADMISSION A93 Aberdeen–Braemar road between Banchory and Peterculter and 20km from
NTS Aberdeen centre. For 24 generations this has been the seat of the Irvines. My ain
folk! 4 times I've signed the visitor book and each time have wandered through the
accumulated history hopeful of identifying with something. Gifted to one William
De Irwin by Robert the Bruce, it combines the original keep (the oldest intact
tower house in Scotland), a Jacobean mansion and Victorian expansionism. Hugh
Irvine, the family 'artist', whose extravagant self-portrait as the Angel Gabriel raised
eyebrows in 1810, does seem like my kind of chap; at least more interesting than
most of my soldiering forebears. Give me a window seat in that library! Grounds
have an exceptional walled rose garden (Apr-Oct: 11am-4pm 1574/GARDENS). Tower
can be climbed for great views. Some pleasant walks from the car park. Check
website for castle hours.

1828 6/Q20 **Balmoral Castle nr Ballater · www.balmoralcastle.com · 01339 742534**
LL On main A93 between Ballater and Braemar. Limited house access (i.e. only the
ADMISSION ballroom: public functions are held here when They're in residence and some
corporates). Grounds with Albert's wonderful trees are more rewarding. For royalty
rooters only, and if you like Landseers … Crathie Church along the main road has
a good rose window, an altar of Iona marble. John Brown is somewhere in the old
graveyard down track from visitor centre, the memorial on the hill is worth a climb
for a poignant moment and view of the policies (1895/MEMORIALS). Crathie services
have never been quite the same Sunday attraction since Di and Fergie on a prince's
arm (bring it on, Harry and Meghan). 7 days, from end March to end July.

1829 4/N15 **Dunrobin Castle Golspie · www.dunrobincastle.co.uk · 01408 633177** The
LL largest house in the Highlands, the home of the Dukes of Sutherland who once
NC500 owned more land than anyone else in the British Empire. It's the first Duke who
ADMISSION occupies an accursed place in Scots history for his perceived inhumane replacement,
in these vast tracts, of people with sheep. His statue stands on Ben Bhraggie above
the town (1892/MONUMENTS). Living the life of imperial grandees, the Sutherlands
transformed the castle into a *château* and filled it with their … wealth. Once there
were 100 servants for a house party of 20 and it had 30 gardeners. Now it's a leisure
industry and the gardens are beyond fabulous (1562/GARDENS). The castle and
separate museum are open Apr-Oct 10.30am-4.30pm (5pm Jun-Sep).

Crathes nr Banchory Reports: 1555/GARDENS; 1883/HOUSES.

Fyvie Aberdeenshire Report: 1882/HOUSES.

The Most Interesting Ruins

HES Historic Environment Scotland. Standard hours are: Apr-end Sep 7 days 9.30am-5.30pm; Oct-Mar 9.30am-4.30pm. Local and winter variations. Call 0131 668 8831 to check. Most HES properties carry admission. Membership: 0131 668 8600, any manned sites or www.historicenvironment.scot ☕ signifies notable café.

1830 8/N25
HES
✓✓✓ **Linlithgow Palace** Linlithgow · www.historicenvironment.scot · 01506 842896 Impressive from the M9 and from the southern approach to this most agreeable of West Lothian towns, but don't confuse the magnificent Renaissance edifice with St Michael's Church next door, topped with its controversial crown and spear spire. From the Great Hall, built for James I, King of Scots, with its huge adjacent kitchens, and the North Range with loch views, you get a real impression of the lavish lifestyle of the court. Not as busy as some HES attractions on this page but it is fabulous. King's Fountain restoration added to the palace appeal. A music fest, 'Party at the Palace', is held in early Aug.

1831 9/P30
LL
HES
☕
✓✓ **Caerlaverock Castle** nr Dumfries · www.historicenvironment.scot · 01387 770200 17km S by B725. Follow signs for Wetlands Reserve (1774/ BIRDS) but go past road end (can walk between). Fairy-tale fortress within double moat and manicured lawns, the daunting frontage being the apex of an unusual triangular shape. Since 1270, the bastion of the Maxwells, the Wardens of the West Marches. Destroyed by Bruce, besieged in 1640. The whole castle experience is here and the – Power of The Lawn. Café in the Boathouse at Glencaple 7km away. On the Nith, very Solway!

1832 8/S20
LL
✓ **Dunnottar Castle** nr Stonehaven · www.dunnottarcastle.co.uk · 01569 762173 3km S of Stonehaven on the coast road just off the A92. Like Slains further north, the ruins are impressively and precariously perched on a clifftop. Historical links with Mary, Queen of Scots (the odd night), Wallace and even Oliver Cromwell, whose Roundheads besieged it in 1650. The Crown Jewels of Scotland were once held here. 400m walk from car park. Clifftop walk from Stonehaven (2km) or take 'The Land Train' from Market Sq (seasonal). Castle AYR.

1833 7/H21
L
ATMOS
✓ **Castle Tioram** nr Acharacle · www.tioram.org Pronounced 'Cheerum'. A romantic ruin on a tidal island where you don't need the saga to sense the place. 5km from A861 just N of Acharacle signed Dorlin. 5km then park by Dorlin Cottage. Serenely beautiful shoreline then walk across a short causeway. You can go to Tioram but not enter. A great hike, 'the Silver Walk', starts here (8km).

1834 6/P17
HES
✓ **Elgin Cathedral** Elgin · www.historicenvironment.scot · 01343 547171 Follow signs in town centre. Set in a meadow by the river, a tranquil corner of this busy market town, the scattered ruins and surrounding graveyard of what was once Scotland's finest cathedral. The nasty Wolf of Badenoch burned it down in 1390, but there are some 13th century and medieval renewals. The octagonal chapterhouse is especially revered, but this is an impressive and evocative slice of history. HES have made great job of restorations. Tower can be climbed. Around the corner, there's the Biblical Garden planted with species mentioned in the Bible. Gardens open May-Sep.

1835 6/Q19
L
ATMOS
HES
✓ **Kildrummy Castle** nr Alford · www.historicenvironment.scot · 01975 571331 15km SW of Alford on A97 near the hotel (1238/SCOTTISH HOTELS) and across the gorge from its famous gardens. Most complete 13th-century castle in Scotland, an HQ for the Jacobite uprising of 1715 and an evocative

site. Here the invitation in the old HS advertising to 'bring your imagination' is truly valid. Apr-Sep 9.30am-5.30pm. Now head for the gardens (400m).

1836 3/C20 ✓ **Kisimul Castle** Barra · www.historicenvironment.scot · 01871 810313
LLL The medieval fortress, home of the MacNeils that sits on a rocky outcrop in
HES the bay 200m offshore. Originally built in the 11th century, it was burnt in the 18th and restored by the 45th chief, an American architect, but was unfinished when he died in 1970. An essential pilgrimage for all MacNeils, it is fascinating and atmospheric for the rest of us, a grim exterior belying an unusual internal layout – a courtyard that seems unchanged and rooms betwixt renovation and decay. Easter-Oct: 7 days. Gift shop. Last boat 4.30pm.

1837 6/R17 ✓ **Findlater Castle** nr Cullen Ruin of a marvellous castle on a mystical coast.
LLL On the way to **Sunnyside** (1620/BEACHES). Signed off A98 Banff-Inverness (3km): park behind the farmyard, pass the impressive doocot; you don't see the castle until walking through the cornfields. The 13th–15th-century ruin is built into the promontory, fortified by nature. A board at the clifftop viewpoint depicts it in its glory – but how did they build it? This is a ruin of ruins though intriguingly you can't really reach it.

1838 7/H23 ✓ **Dunollie Castle** Oban · www.dunollie.org · 01631 570550 Just outside
APR-OCT town via Corran Esplanade towards Ganavan. An iconic ruin recently consolidated into part of a new historic attraction – The Laird's (or 1745) House Museum – but mainly worth a visit for views of the bay and Lismore, and its 'enchanting' woodlands.

1839 8/R21 **Edzell Castle** Edzell · www.historicenvironment.scot · 01356 648631 3km
HES village off main street, signed. Pleasing red sandstone ruin in bucolic setting – birds twitter, rabbits run. The notable walled parterre Renaissance garden, created by Sir David Lindsay way back in 1604, is the oldest preserved in Scotland. The wall niches are nice. Lotsa lobelias! (Jun-Sep). Mary, Queen of Scots was here (she so got around). Gate on the road is closed at night.

1840 5/M17 **Fort George** nr Inverness · www.historicenvironment.scot · 01667 460232
HES On promontory of Moray Firth, 18km NE of Inverness, via A96 by Ardersier. A vast site – one of the most outstanding artillery fortifications in Europe. Planned after Culloden as a base for George II's army and completed 1769, it remains unaltered and allows a very complete picture. May provoke palpitations in the nationalist heart, but it's heaven for militarists and altogether impressive (don't miss the museum). It's hardly a ruin, of course, and still occupied by the Army. 7 days 9.30am-4/5.30pm.

1841 7/H25 **Tarbert Castle** Tarbert, Argyll · www.tarbertcastle.info Strategically and dramatically overlooking the sheltered harbour of this epitome of a West Highland port. It's for the timeless view rather than an evocation of tangible history (Robert the Bruce connected) that it's worth finding the way up. Access from Harbour Rd. 10 mins up, then 20- and 40-min walks from there.

1842 7/K23 **Kilchurn Castle** Loch Awe · www.historicenvironment.scot Romantic ruin
L at the head of awesome Loch Awe, reached by a 1km walk from the car park off the
HES main A85, 5km E of Lochawe village. You go under the railway line. A very pleasant spot for loch reflections; and your own. Apr-Sep.

1843 8/R23
HES

St Andrews Cathedral St Andrews · www.historicenvironment.scot · 01334 472563 The ruins of the largest church in Scotland before the Reformation, a place of great influence and pilgrimage. St Rule's Tower and the jagged fragment of the huge West Front, in their striking position at the convergence of the main streets and overlooking the sea, are remnants of its great glory. Find a great photographic book: *St Andrews A Portrait of a City* by Adamson & Macintyre. 7 days AYR.

1844 8/Q26
HES

Crichton Castle nr Pathhead · www.historicenvironment.scot · 01875 320017 3km W of A68 at Pathhead (28km S of Edinburgh) or via A7 turning E, 3km S of Gorebridge. Massive Border keep dominating the Tyne valley in pristine countryside. Apr-Sep: Mon-Wed & Sat, 9.30am-5pm (last entry). Nearby is the 15th-century collegiate church. 500m walk from Crichton village. Good picnic spots below by the river though may be overgrown in summer.

1845 8/R25
LL
HES

Tantallon Castle North Berwick · www.historicenvironment.scot · 01620 892727 5km E of town by coast road; 500m to dramatic clifftop setting with views to **Bass Rock** (1777/BIRDS). Dates from 1350; massive curtain wall to see it through stormy weather and stormy history. The Red Douglases and their friends kept the world at bay. Wonderful beach nearby (442/BEACHES). Open AYR.

1846 5/L18
LLL
HES

Urquhart Castle Drumnadrochit · www.historicenvironment.scot · 01456 450551 28km S of Inverness on A82. The classic Highland fortress on a promontory overlooking Loch Ness visited every year by bus loads and boat loads of tourists. Photo opportunities galore among the well-kept lawns and extensive ruins of the once formidable stronghold of the Picts and their scions, finally abandoned in the 18th century. Visitor facilities almost cope with demand. Open AYR.

1847 8/M24
HES

Doune Castle Doune · www.historicenvironment.scot · 01786 841742 Follow signs from centre of village which is just off A84 Callander–Dunblane road. Overlooking the River Teith, the well-preserved ruin of a late 14th-century courtyard castle with a great hall and another draughty room where Mary, Queen of Scots once slept. Is a location for many films (famously *Monty Python and the Holy Grail*) and TV series (*Game of Thrones* and *Outlander*). Nice walk to the meadow begins on track to left of castle; you can swim from the riverbank. Good view from the top but a narrow, steep climb. **Buttercup Café** in the village is good (1423/ TEAROOMS).

1848 6/T18
LL
ATMOS

Slains Castle nr Cruden Bay 32km N of Aberdeen and 2km W of Cruden Bay, from unmarked car park (Meikle Partans) on bend of the A795 (a white track leads to the ruins, very potholed at the start, but OK), or walk from village. You see its craggy outline then walk 1km. Obviously because of its location, but also because there's no reception centre/postcard shop or proper signposts, this is an evocative ruin. Your imagination, like Bram Stoker's (who was inspired after staying here to write *Dracula*), can be cast to the winds. The seat of the Earls of Erroll, it has been gradually disintegrating since the roof was removed in 1925. Once, it had the finest dining room in Scotland. The waves crash below, as always. Be careful!

1849 8/S27
L

Hume Castle Hume, nr Kelso This imposing, well-preserved ruin sits above the road and the countryside between Greenlaw and Kelso. Its impressive walls here since the 18th century from a 13th-century fortification. Marvellous views across the Merse as far as the English border.

The Best Prehistoric Sites

HES *Historic Environment Scotland. Standard hours are: Apr-end Sep 7 days 9.30am-5.30pm; Oct-Mar 9.30am-4.30pm. Local and winter variations.* ☕ *signifies notable café.*

1850 1/P10
L
ADMISSION
HES

✓✓✓ **Skara Brae** Orkney Mainland · www.historicenvironment.scot · 01856 841815 32km Kirkwall by A965/B9655 via Finstown and Dounby. Excellent visitor and orientation centre. Can be a windy (500m) walk to this remarkable shoreline site, the subterranean remains of a compact village 5,000 years old. It was engulfed by a sandstorm 600 years later and lay perfectly preserved until uncovered by the laird's dog after another storm in 1850. Now it permits one of the most evocative glimpses of truly ancient times in the UK.

1851 1/Q10
FREE
HES

✓✓ **The Standing Stones of Stenness** Orkney Mainland · www.historicenvironment.scot Together with the **Ring of Brodgar** and the great chambered tomb of **Maes Howe**, all within 18km of Kirkwall, these are as impressive ceremonial sites as you'll find anywhere. From same period as Skara Brae. The individual stones and the scale of the Ring are very imposing and deeply mysterious. The burial cairn is the finest megalithic tomb in the UK. 500m walk from the visitor centre. Guided tour only. Note: tunnel entry is only 1m high! Seen together, they stimulate even the most jaded sense of wonder.

1852 3/F14
FREE
HES
☕

✓✓ **The Callanish Stones** Lewis · www.historicenvironment.scot · 01851 621422 24km from Stornoway. Take Tarbert road and go right at Leurbost. The best-preserved and most unusual combination of standing stones in a ring around a tomb, with radiating arms in cross shape. Predating Stonehenge, they were unearthed from the peat in the mid-19th century and are the Hebrides' major historical attraction. Other configurations nearby. At dawn and dusk, hardly anyone else is there. Visitor centre has a couthy caff, art & craft not so good. See also 2384/HEBRIDES.

1853 5/M18
ATMOS
FREE
HES

✓ **Clava Cairns** nr Culloden · www.historicenvironment.scot · 01667 460232 Here long before the most infamous battle in Scottish and other histories; another specially atmospheric place. Not so well signed but continue along the B9006 towards **Cawdor Castle**, that other great historical landmark (1816/CASTLES), taking a right at the Culloden Moor Inn; follow signs for Clava Lodge holiday homes, picking up Historic Scotland sign to right. Chambered cairns in a grove of trees. They're really just piles of stones but the death rattle echo from 5,000 years ago is perceptible to all, especially when no one else is there. Remoteness probably inhibits New Age attentions and allows more private meditations in this extraterrestrial spot.

1854 2/V5
LL
FREE
HES

✓ **Mousa Broch** Shetland · www.historicenvironment.scot · 01856 841815 On island of Mousa off Shetland mainland 20km S of Lerwick. To see it properly take the Mousa Boat (www.mousa.co.uk 07901 872339) from Sandsayre Pier. Takes 15 mins. Isolated in its island fastness, this is the best-preserved broch in Scotland. Walls are 13m high (originally 15m) and galleries run up the middle, in one case to the top. Solid as a rock, this example of a uniquely Scottish phenomenon would have been a very des res. Also **Jarlshof** in the S next to Sumburgh airport has remnants and ruins from Neolithic to Viking times, with especially impressive wheelhouses.

1855 8/M22 ✓ **Crannog Centre** Kenmore, nr Aberfeldy · www.crannog.co.uk ·
ADMISSION 01887 830583 On S Loch Tay road 1km Kenmore. Superb reconstruction of
Iron Age dwelling (there are several under the loch). Credible and worthwhile
archaeological project, great for kids: conveys history well. Displays in progress and
human story told by pleasant, costumed humans. Apr-Oct 10am-5.30pm. Great
waterfall walk at Acharn, 2km (1663/WATERFALLS). Eat Aberfeldy (923/PERTHSHIRE;
1419/TEAROOMS) and a great café, **Habitat Café** (1428/COFFEE).

1856 7/H24 ✓ **Kilmartin Glen** nr Lochgilphead · www.historicenvironment.scot An
FREE important, easily accessible area. Possibly start 2km S of Kilmartin and 1km
HES (signed) from A816, and across road from car park – 2 distinct stone circles from a
long period of history between 3000–1200 BC. Story and speculations described on
boards. Pastoral countryside and wide skies. Look for the 'cup and saucer'! There
are apparently 150 other sites in the vicinity (c. 800 'ancient monuments'), and an
excellent museum and café (closed for refurbishment till 2021; see www.kilmartin.
org). See also **Dunadd** (1991/HILLS) for perspective of the whole area.

1857 1/Q12 ✓ **Tomb of the Eagles** Orkney Mainland · www.tomboftheeagles.co.uk ·
ATMOS 01856 831339 33km S of Kirkwall at the foot of South Ronaldsay; signed from
ADMISSION Burwick. A relatively recent discovery, the excavation of this cliff cave is on private
land. You call in at the visitor centre first and they'll tell you the story. There's a
2km walk then you go in on a skateboard – no, really! Allow time; ethereal stuff.
Mar-Oct 9.30am-5.30pm (by appointment Nov-Feb).

1858 8/N25 **Cairnpapple Hill** nr Linlithgow · www.historicenvironment.scot ·
ADMISSION 01506 634622 Approach from the Beecraigs road off W end of Linlithgow main
HES street. Go past the Beecraigs turn-off and continue for 3km. Cairnpapple is
signed. Astonishing Neolithic henge and later burial site on windy hill with views
from Highlands to Pentlands. Atmosphere made even more strange by the very
21st-century communications mast next door. Cute visitor centre! Summer only
9.30am-5.30pm but site can be accessed any time. See also 1712/VIEWS.

1859 9/L30 **Cairnholy** between Newton Stewart & Gatehouse of Fleet · www.
FREE historicenvironment.scot 2km off main A75. Signed from road. A mini-Callanish
HES of standing stones around a burial cairn on very human scale and in a serene
setting with another site (with chambered tomb) 150m up the farm track. Excellent
view – sit and contemplate what went on 4,000–6,000 years ago and a great place
to watch the sunrise over the Solway.

1860 8/R21 **The Brown and White Caterthuns** Kirkton of Menmuir, nr Brechin & Edzell
L · www.historicenvironment.scot 5km uphill from war memorial at Menmuir,
FREE then signed 1km: a steep pull. Lay-by with obvious path to both on either side
HES of the road. White easier (500m uphill). These Iron Age hilltop settlements give
tremendous sense of scale and space and afford an impressive panorama of the
Highland line. Colours refer to the heather-covered turf and stone of one and the
massive collapsed ramparts of the White. Sit here for a while and picture the Pict.

1861 4/Q13 **The Grey Cairns of Camster** nr Wick · www.historicenvironment.scot ·
FREE 01667 460232 20km S of Wick, a very straight road (signed for Cairns) heads
HES W from the A9 for 8km. The cairns are instantly identifiable near the road and
impressively complete. The 'horned cairn' is the best in the UK. In 2,500 BC these
stone-piled structures were used for the disposal of the dead. You can crawl inside
them if you're agile (or at night, brave). There are many other sights signed off the
A9/99 but also interesting and nearby is:

1862 4/Q14   **Hill o' Many Stanes** nr Wick · www.historicenvironment.scot ·
NC500   **01667 460232** Aptly named place with extraordinary number of small standing
FREE   stones; about 200 in more than 22 rows. If fan shape were complete, there would
HES   be 600. Their very purposeful layout is enigmatic and strange.

1863 9/L31   **The Whithorn Story** Whithorn · www.whithorn.com · 01988 500508
ADMISSION   Excavation site (though not active), medieval priory, shrine of St Ninian, visitor
centre and café. More than enough to keep the whole family occupied. Enthusiastic
staff. Christianity? Look where it got us: this is where it started in Scotland. Also
1615/VILLAGES. Easter-Oct: 7 days 10.30am-5pm.

1864 8/M25   **Bar Hill** Twechar, nr Kirkintilloch A fine example of the low ruins of a Roman
FREE   fort on the Antonine Wall, which ran across Scotland for 200 years early AD. Great
place for an out-of-town walk (705/VIEWS).

1865 5/H19   **Glenelg Brochs** Glenelg · www.historicenvironment.scot · 01667 460232
FREE   110km from Fort William. Glenelg is 14km from the A87 at Shiel Bridge (1676/
HES   SCENIC ROUTES). The brochs are 5km from Glenelg village in beautiful Glen Beag.
The 2 brochs, Dun Troddan and Dun Telve, are the best-preserved examples on the
mainland of these mysterious 1st-century homesteads. Easy here to distinguish
the twin stone walls that kept out the cold and the more disagreeable neighbours.
Brilliant pub (food and rooms) in village (1208/INNS).

1866 3/D17   **Barpa Langass** North Uist 8km S of Lochmaddy, visible from main A867 road,
FREE   like a stone hat on the hill (200m walk). A squashed beehive burial cairn dating
from 1,000 BC, the tomb of a chieftain. It's largely intact and the small and nimble
can explore inside, crawling through the short entrance tunnel and down through
the years. Nice hotel nearby (1231/GET-AWAY HOTELS), where a circular walk starts,
taking in this site and the loch (direction board 2.5km).

1867 6/S19   **Aberdeenshire Prehistoric Trail: East Aquhorthies Stone Circle** nr Inverurie ·
FREE   www.historicenvironment.scot · 01667 460232 4km from Inverurie. Signed
HES   from B993 from Inverurie to Monymusk. A circle of pinkish stones with 2 grey
sentinels flanking a huge recumbent stone set in the rolling countryside of the Don
Valley. **Bennachie** over there, then as now (2000/HILLS)!

1868 6/S18   **Loanhead of Daviot Stone Circle** nr Inverurie · www.historicenvironment.
ATMOS   scot Head for the village of Daviot on B9001 from Inverurie; or Loanhead,
FREE   signed off A920 between Oldmeldrum and Insch. The site is 500m from top
HES   of village. Impressive and spooky circle of 11 stones and one recumbent from
4,000/5,000 BC. Unusual second circle adjacent encloses a cremation cemetery
from 1,500 BC. Remains of 32 people were found here. Obviously, an important
place. God knows what they were up to.

1869 6/R19   **Tomnaverie Stone Circle** nr Tarland & Aboyne · www.historicenvironment.
FREE   scot · 01667 460232 Less visited or even known than the above so here you really
HES   are likely to take in its mystery and the panoramic view of bucolic Aberdeenshire
and distant Lochnagar without distraction. An easily imaginable circle from 2,500
BC: a long time then! Leave A93 near Aboyne Academy for Tarland, 6km just before
the town, 300m uphill walk from car park.

Great Country Houses

NTS *National Trust for Scotland. Hours vary. Admission.*
HES *Historic Environment Scotland. Standard hours are: Apr-end Sep 7 days*
9.30am-5.30pm; Oct-Mar 9.30am-4.30pm. Local and winter variations. All
charge admission.
⌨ *signifies notable café.*

1870 8/R27 ✓✓ **Abbotsford House** nr Melrose · www.scottsabbotsford.com ·
01896 752043 The beautiful home built by Sir Walter Scott and lived in until his death. Scott was once the world's most successful novelist and the man who practically invented the romantic image of Scotland and, in so doing, tourism. A recent major makeover returned the house to its original splendour – it's exactly as he left it, and the gardens are pristine and peaceful. Lovely aspect overlooking the Tweed, all strollable and it's on the Borders Abbeys Way (www. bordersabbeysway.com). Other excellent Borders walks from car park across the road, e.g. Cauldshiels Loch; great views. Interpretation and exhibition building as you arrive and **Ochiltree's** café/restaurant above – a terrace offers a first aerial view of the policies. Mar-Nov 10am-4/5pm.

1871 7/K26 ✓✓ **Mount Stuart** Bute · www.mountstuart.com · 01700 503877
L Unique Victorian Gothic house; echoes 3rd Marquess of Bute's passion for
ATMOS mythology, astronomy, astrology and religion. Such splendour in intimate and
⌨ romantic atmos: Italian antiques, notable paintings, fascinating detail with humorous touches. The chapel, the Marble Hall and the Rock Garden all superb. Equally grand gardens with fabulous walks and some sea views. Stylish visitor centre. Main café in courtyard behind the house; hot food. Annual art commissions in house and gardens. Mar-Oct 11.30am-4pm. Best check whether it's a day for hourly guided tours or free-flow admission. Grounds 10am-6pm. Allow time here.

1872 6/S18 ✓✓ **Haddo House** nr Ellon · www.nts.org.uk · 01651 851440 Designed by
L William Adam for the Earl of Aberdeen, the Palladian-style mansion itself
NTS by guided tour only (must book) but the extensive, superb grounds open always.
⌨ Not so much a house, more a leisure land in the best possible taste; grounds with bluebells, wild garlic then autumn trees, a pleasant café, estate shop and gentle education. Grand house, full of things; the basements are where to ponder. Glorious window by Burne-Jones in the chapel. Occasional afternoon teas followed by evening service: heaven (May-Oct)! Limited programme of other events. Most folk come for the walks, including to the lake and down the Scots Mile. Au naturel kids' Adventure Playgrounds. Gardens AYR till sunset.
EAT Café in the courtyard but outside by the car park is **Mrs Smith's**: more home-made and has outside tables. 7 days AYR.

1873 8/S26 ✓✓ **Manderston** Duns · www.manderston.co.uk · 01361 883450 Off
LL A6105, 2km down Duns–Berwick road. Swan song of the Great Classical
ATMOS House, one of the UK's finest examples of Edwardian opulence. *The* Edwardian country house of (once) TV fame. The family still lives here. Below stairs as fascinating as up (the famous silver staircase!); sublime gardens (do see the woodland garden across the lake and the marble dairy). May-Sep: Thu/Sun 1.30pm-4.15pm (last entry). Gardens 11.30am-dusk AYR.

1874 8/Q27 ✓✓ **Traquair House** Innerleithen · www.traquair.co.uk · 01896 830323
L 3km from A72 Peebles–Gala road. Archetypal romantic Border retreat steeped in Jacobite history (the famous Bear gates). Human proportions, liveability and lots of atmos. An enchanting house, a maze (20th century) and tranquil duck pond in the garden. Traquair ale still brewed. **Garden Café** much improved of late (1420/TEAROOMS). Pottery and other craft shop. Apr-Oct: House 11am-5pm (Oct 11am-4pm, Nov weekends only). Notable events programme, including main Traquair Fayre (May) and Festival of Literature & Thought (Aug).

1875 8/Q25 ✓✓ **Newhailes House** Musselburgh · www.nts.org.uk · 0131 653 5599
NTS Well signed from Portobello end of Musselburgh (3km), Newhailes is an
☐ NTS flagship project stabilising this microcosm of 17th-/18th-century history uniquely intact here. Great rococo interiors, very liveable, especially library. A rural sanctuary near the city: parklands, shell grotto, summer house. Brilliant new adventure park (1741/KIDS). Tours last 1 hr 15 mins, noon-3.30pm, book online.

1876 8/L28 ✓✓ **Dumfries House** nr Ochiltree · www.dumfries-house.org.uk ·
☐ 01290 425959 One of the finest Palladian mansions in the country saved for the nation by a consortium led by Prince Charles (and £5 million from the Scottish Government). The 750 acres and 18th-century apartments with their priceless Chippendale furniture and pristine artefacts are to open to the public, as are the emerging landscaped gardens (1558/GARDENS). Great walks in the grounds; café, guest house (760/AYRSHIRE) and restaurant. Check website for hours.

1877 8/T26 ✓ **Paxton House** nr Berwick · www.paxtonhouse.co.uk · 01289 386291
Off B6461 to Swinton and Kelso, 5km from A1. Country park and Adam mansion with Chippendales and Trotters; the picture gallery is a National Gallery outstation. 80 acres of woodlands to walk. Good adventure playground. Restored Victorian boathouse and salmon-fishing museum on the Tweed. Red squirrel hide. Event programme including indoor and outdoor performance. Sweet terraced riverside garden and superb walk along the Tweed to the historic Union Bridge (1km) is a must. Tours (1 hr) 4 times a day, Mar-Nov 10am-5pm. Sundays only in winter. Garden 10am-sunset.

1878 8/Q25 ✓ **Gosford House** nr Aberlady · www.gosfordhouse.co.uk · 01875 870808
On A198 between Longniddry and Aberlady, Gosford Estate is behind a high wall and strangely stunted vegetation. Imposing house with centre block by Robert Adam and the wing that you can visit by William Young who did Glasgow City Chambers. The Marble Hall houses the remarkable collections of the unbroken line of Earls of Wemyss and priceless art, informally displayed. Phone for opening times and tours. Walk in the superb grounds, snack at the **Bothy** farm shop/café (signed). Edinburgh side of Aberlady (car park closes 5pm). See 433/WALKS.

1879 8/S27 **Floors Castle** Kelso · www.floorscastle.com · 01573 223333 More a vast
LL mansion than old castle, the ancestral home of the Duke of Roxburghe overlooks,
☐ with imposing grandeur, the town and the Tweed. 18th-century with later additions. You're led round lofty public rooms, past family collections of fine furniture, tapestries and porcelain. Priceless; spectacularly impractical. Marvellous walled garden (1566/GARDENS) and tearoom **The Terrace Café** (1453/TEAROOMS), with separate entrance and another café by the house. May-Oct 11am-5pm. Gardens and Terrace Café AYR.

1880 8/R27 **Mellerstain House** nr Gordon/Kelso · www.mellerstain.com · 01573 410225
Home of the Earl of Haddington, signed from A6089 (Kelso–Gordon) or A6105
(Earlston–Greenlaw). One of Scotland's great Georgian houses, begun by William
Adam in 1725, completed by Robert. Outstanding decorative interiors (the ceilings
are *sans pareil*) especially the library, and spectacular exterior 1761; it is truly a
stately home. Easter weekend and Fri-Mon, May-Oct. Courtyard teahouse by the
guys from **Hoebridge Inn** (836/BORDERS), 11am-4.30pm. Fab gardens (11am-5pm)
and grounds with sculpture, walks to the River Eden and round the lake.

1881 8/R26 **Thirlestane Castle** Lauder · www.thirlestanecastle.co.uk · 01578 722430
2km off A68. Castellated/baronial seat of the Earls and Duke of Lauderdale and
family home of the Maitlands. Extraordinary staterooms, especially plasterwork;
the ceilings must be seen to be believed. The nurseries (with toy collection),
kitchens and laundry are more approachable. Adventure playground. Quiet
meadow. May-Sep: Sun-Thu 10am-4pm.

1882 6/S18 **Fyvie Castle** nr Fyvie · www.nts.org.uk · 01651 891266 40km NW of
NTS Aberdeen, an important stop on the Castle Trail, which links the great houses of
☞ Aberdeenshire. Before opulence fatigue sets in, see this pleasant baronial pile first.
Inhabited till 1980s, it feels less remote than most. 13th-century origins; Edwardian
interiors. Fantastic roofscape and ceilings. Restored racquets court and, yes,
bowling alley. Good tearoom. Tree-lined acres; lochside walks. Apr/May & Sep/Oct:
Sat-Wed 11am-5pm; Jun-Aug: 7 days 11am-5pm. Grounds AYR.

1883 6/S20 **Crathes Castle** nr Banchory · www.nts.org.uk · 01330 844525 25km W of
L Aberdeen on A93. In superb gardens (1555/GARDENS), a fairy-tale castle: a 16th-
NTS century tower house that is fascinating to visit. Up and down spiral staircases and
☞ into small but liveable rooms. The notable painted ceilings and the Long Gallery at
the top are all worth lingering over. 350 years of the Burnett family are ingrained in
this oak. Apr-Oct 10.30am-4.45pm; till 3.45pm winter. Last entry 45 mins before.
Big event programme. Rangers on hand. Grounds AYR 9.30am-dusk. Go Ape
playground. Courtyard tearoom and nearby 994/NE RESTAURANTS.

✓✓ **Drumlanrig Castle** Thornhill The art! The courtyard, the park. Report:
1585/PARKS.

▆▆ Great Monuments, Memorials & Follies

These sites are open at all times and free unless otherwise stated.

1884 7/F27 ✓✓ **The American Monument** Islay · www.islayinfo.com On the SW
1-A-2   peninsula of the island, known as the Oa (pronounced 'Oh'), 10km from
LL Port Ellen. A monument to commemorate the shipwrecks nearby of 2 American
ATMOS ships, the *Tuscania* and the *Otranto*. The obelisk overlooks this sea – which is often
beset by storms – from a spectacular headland, a sometimes disquieting place, a
reminder of 2 tragedies in one year, 1918: one a U-boat attack, the other an
accident. Take road from Port Ellen past Maltings, marked Mull of Oa, then 8km.
Signed off the road. Park, then a spectacular 1.5km clifftop walk to monument. Can
do 6km round trip. Birdlife good in Oa area (RSPB reserve).

1885 8/N24 ✓ **Wallace Monument** Stirling · www.nationalwallacemonument.com ·
LL   01786 472140 Visible for miles and with great views, though not as dramatic
as Stirling Castle. Approach from A91 or Bridge of Allan road. 150m walk from car
park (or minibus) and 246 steps up. Victorian gothic spire marking the place where

Scotland's great patriot swooped down upon the English at the Battle of Stirling Bridge. Mel Gibson's *Braveheart* increased visitors mid-90s. Thankfully, Mel Gibson's film has also been consigned to history! In the 'Hall of Heroes' the heroines section requires a feminist leap of the imagination. The famous sword is very big. Clifftop walk through Abbey Craig woods is worth detour. Monument open daily AYR. Caff not great. Nice woodland walks.

1886 5/F16 **The Grave of Flora MacDonald** Skye Kilmuir on A855, Uig–Staffin road, 40km N of Portree. A 10ft-high Celtic cross supported against the wind, high on the ridge overlooking the Uists from whence she came. Long after the legendary journey, her funeral in 1790 attracted the biggest crowd since Culloden. The present memorial replaced the original, which was chipped away by souvenir hunters. Dubious though the whole business may have been, she still helped to shape the folklore of the Highlands.

1887 8/R27 **Peniel Heugh** nr Ancrum Pronounced 'Pinal-Hue'. An obelisk visible for miles
LL and on a rise offering some of the most exhilarating views of the Borders. Also known as the Waterloo Monument, it was built on the Marquess of Lothian's estate to commemorate the battle. It's said that woodland on the slopes around represents the positions of Wellington's troops. From A68 opposite Ancrum turn-off on B6400, go 1km past Monteviot Gardens up steep, unmarked road to left (cycle sign; monument not marked) for 150m; sign says Vehicles Prohibited, etc. Park, walk up through woods. Great organic caff nearby (1452/TEAROOMS) – you can start the hike from here.

1888 8/R25 **The Hopetoun Monument** Athelstaneford, nr Haddington · **www.**
L **eastlothian.gov.uk** The 30m needle atop a rare rise in East Lothian (Byres Hill) and a great vantage point from which to view the county from the Forth to the Lammermuirs and Edinburgh over there. Off A6737 Haddington to Aberlady road on B1343 to Athelstaneford. Car park and short climb. Tower usually open and viewfinder boards at top but take a torch – it's a dark climb (132 steps). Good gentle ridge walk east from here.

1889 8/P25 **The Tower at the House of the Binns** nr Linlithgow · **www.nts.org.uk** Off
NTS A904 W from the access road at the Forth Road Bridge. This is the perfect chess-piece castle or tower that sits so proudly on the horizon with its saltire blowing behind the NTS-managed House of the Binns. The austere house, home of the Dalyell family since 1612 (including Our Tam who asked the famous West Lothian Question), ain't intrinsically interesting (Jun-Sep: Sat-Wed 2-5pm) but the view of the Forth from the tower, which was built for a bet and cost £29 10 shillings, is splendid. Park by the house and walk 250m. Grounds open AYR till 7pm/dusk.

1890 8/N25 **The Pineapple** Airth · **www.landmarktrust.org.uk** · **01628 825925** From Airth N of Grangemouth, take A905 to Stirling and after 1km the B9124 for Cowie. It sits on the edge of a walled garden at the end of the drive. 45ft high, it was built in 1761 as a garden retreat by an unknown architect and remained 'undiscovered' until 1963. How exotic the fruit must have seemed in the 18th century, never mind this extraordinary folly. Grounds open AYR. Oddly enough, you can stay here (2 bedrooms, Landmark Trust). The gardens are kept by NTS (National Trust for Scotland) and there's a figure-of-eight walk that takes in Dunmore village and the River Forth.

1891 4/L12 **John Lennon Memorial** Durness In a garden created in 2002 (a BBC *Beechgrove*
NC500 *Garden* project) amazing in itself surviving these harsh, very northern conditions, an inscribed slate memorial to JL, who for many years as a child came here with

his aunt for the hols. 'There are places I'll remember all my life' from *Rubber Soul*. Who'd have thought that song (*In My Life*) was about here? There's also a piece by national treasure, ceramic artist **Lotte Glob** (2183/GALLERIES). Garden upkept by volunteers.

1892 4/N15 **The Monument on Ben Bhraggie** Golspie Atop the hill (pronounced 'Brachee')
L that surmounts the town, the domineering statue and plinth (over 35m) of the
NC500 dreaded first Duke of Sutherland; many have campaigned to have it demolished,
yet it survives. Climb from town fountain on marked path. The hill racers go up in
minutes but allow 2 hours return. His private view along the NE coast is superb
(1829/CASTLES; 1562/GARDENS) and for background 2165/HISTORY.

1893 7/K20 **The Commando Monument** nr Spean Bridge On prominent rise by the A82
L Inverness to Fort William road, where the B8004 cuts off to Gairlochy 3km N of
Spean Bridge. Commemorates the Commandos who gave their lives in WWII and
who trained in this area. Spectacular vista and poignant memorial garden to troops
lost in more recent conflicts, including the Iraq and Afghan wars.

1894 7/H23 **McCaig's Tower or Folly** Oban Oban's great landmark on Battery Hill, built
L in 1897 by McCaig, a local banker, to give 'work to the unemployed' and as a
memorial to his family. Built from Bonawe granite, it's like a temple or coliseum
and time has mellowed whatever incongruous effect it may have had originally.
The views of the town and the bay are magnificent and it's easy to get up from
several well-signed points in town centre.

1895 6/Q20 **The Victoria Memorial to Albert** Balmoral Atop the fir-covered hill behind
L the house, she raised a monument, the **Albert Cairn**, whose distinctive pyramid
shape can be seen peeping over the crest from all over the estate. Desolated after
his death, the broken-hearted widow had this memorial built in 1862 and spent so
much time here, she became a recluse; the British Empire trembled. Path begins
at shop on way to Lochnagar distillery, 45 mins up, 460 feet above sea level. OK
Balmoral, (1828/CASTLES): but all the longing and love for Scotland can be felt here,
the estate laid out below. Renewed interest following Victoria films and TV, so expect
company. The fabulous new **Fife Arms** 978/NE HOTELS is nearby, at Braemar.

1896 9/L30 **Murray's Monument** nr New Galloway Above A712 road to Newton Stewart,
about halfway between. A fairly austere needle of granite to commemorate a
'shepherd boy', one Alexander Murray, who rose to become a professor of Oriental
Languages at Edinburgh University in the early 19th century. A 10-min walk up
for fine views of Galloway Hills; pleasant waterfall – The Grey Mare's Tail, 500m
circular walk. Just as he, barefoot ...

1897 8/R27 **Smailholm Tower** nr Kelso & St Boswells · www.historicenvironment.scot ·
L **01573 460365** The classic Border tower that inspired Sir Walter Scott; plenty of
ATMOS history and romance in a bucolic setting. Picnic or whatever. Good views from its
ADMISSION crags. Smailholm was a subject of the pioneer of photography, W. H. Fox Talbot,
HES in what became the first photographic coffee-table book. Oh Instagram, how far
we've come. Near main road B6404 or off smaller B6937 – well signposted. Apr-
Sep 9.30am-5.30pm. But fine to visit at any time (1685/SCENIC ROUTES).

Scott Monument Princes Street, Edinburgh Report: 447/VIEWS.

The Most Interesting Churches

Generally open unless otherwise stated; those marked * have public services.

1898 8/Q26
L
ATMOS
ADMISSION

✓✓✓ ***Rosslyn Chapel** Roslin · www.rosslynchapel.com · 0131 440 2159 12km S of Edinburgh city centre. Take A702, then A703 from ring-route road, marked Penicuik. Roslin village 2km from main road and chapel 500m from village crossroads above Roslin Glen. Medieval but firmly on the world map because of *The Da Vinci Code*. Grail seekers have been coming forever but now a whole experience – chapel, tour, visitor centre, coffee and gift shop – is available. Teems with tours in summer yet no doubting the atmos in this temple to the Templars, all holy, meaningful stuff, if somewhat over the heads of most. But it is a special place after the major restoration, and is a working Episcopalian church. Mon-Sat 9.30am-4.30pm (last admission), Sun noon-4.15pm (last admission). Walks in the glen can begin here (after the orange house), see 429/WALKS. Café is so-so.

1899 7/K23
LL
ATMOS

✓✓ ***St Conan's Kirk** Loch Awe · www.stconanskirk.org.uk · 01838 200298 A85 33km E of Oban. Perched among trees on the side of Loch Awe, this small but spacious church seems to incorporate every ecclesiastical architectural style. Its building was a labour of love for one Walter Campbell, who was perhaps striving for beauty rather than consistency. Though modern (begun by him in 1881 and finished by his sister and a board of trustees in 1930), the result is a place of ethereal light and atmos, enhanced by and befitting the inherent spirituality of the setting. There's a spooky carved effigy of Robert the Bruce, a cosy cloister and the most amazing flying buttresses. Big atmos.

1900 1/R11
LL
ATMOS
ADMISSION

✓✓ **The Italian Chapel** Lamb Holm, Orkney · www.visitorkney.com · 01856 872856 8km S of Kirkwall at Lamb Holm, the first causeway on the way to St Margaret's Hope. In 1943, Italian PoWs transformed a Nissen hut, using the most meagre materials, into this remarkable ornate chapel completed at the end of the war in 1945. The meticulous *trompe l'œil* and wrought-iron work are a touching affirmation of faith. Open AYR, daylight hours. At the other end of the architectural scale, **St Magnus Cathedral** in Kirkwall is a great edifice, but also imbues spirituality.

1901 8/M25
ADMISSION

✓✓ **Queen's Cross Church** 870 Garscube Road, Glasgow · www. mackintoshchurch.com · 0141 946 6600 Set where Garscube Rd becomes Maryhill Rd at Springbank St. C.R. Mackintosh's only church. Fascinating and unpredictable in every part of its design. Some elements reminiscent of Glasgow School of Art (built in the same year 1897) and others, like the tower, evoke medieval architecture. Bold and innovative, now restored and functioning as the HQ of The Mackintosh Society and an event space. Apr-Oct: Mon-Fri 10am-5pm; Nov-Mar: Mon, Wed, Fri 10am-4pm. No services. See 717/MACKINTOSH.

1902 9/N28
L
ATMOS

✓ ***Durisdeer Parish Church** nr Abington & Thornhill · www. scotlandschurchestrust.org.uk Off A702 Abington–Thornhill road and 3km off the Edinburgh road, near **Drumlanrig** (1585/PARKS). If I lived near this delightful village in the hills, I'd go to church more often. It's exquisite and the history of Scotland is in the stones. The Queensberry marbles (1709) are displayed in the north transept (enter behind church) and there's a cradle roll and a list of ministers from the 14th century. The plaque to the two brothers who died at Gallipoli is especially touching. Covenanter tales are writ on the gravestones.

1903 7/K26 ✓ ***Cathedral of the Isles** Cumbrae · www.cathedraloftheisles.org · 01475 530006 Frequent ferry service from Largs is met by bus for 6km journey to Millport. Lane from main street by Newton pub, 250m, then through gate. The smallest cathedral in Europe, one of Butterfield's great works (other is Keble College in Oxford). Here, small is outstandingly beautiful and absolutely quiet except Sundays in summer when there are concerts. Can stay (1289/RETREATS); see also 1406/CAFÉS.

1904 6/Q19 ✓ **The Chapel at Migvie** nr Tarland & Aboyne An extraordinary tiny chapel on a farm in the midst of Aberdeenshire, hardly known, rarely visited. And yet when you open the door (and wait) the lights go on to reveal a Tardis-like space somewhere between a crypt and an art gallery. Local artists working with glass, stone, paint and poetry have created this homely homage by Philip Astor, in memory of his mum and dad. Wonderfully affecting. To find this very secret place head N from Dinnet on the A93 halfway between Ballater and Aboyne, past the signed **Burn o' Vat** (1978/ENCHANTING PLACES) on the A97 for 12km, Migvie, a farming hamlet, 2km E. You'll see it, then you'll get it! It's always open.

1905 3/E16 **St Clement's** Rodel, South Harris · www.historicenvironment.scot Tarbert
FREE 40km. Classic island kirk in Hebridean landscape. Go by the **Golden Road** (1683/
HES SCENIC ROUTES). Simple cruciform structure with tower, which the adventurous can climb. Probably influenced by Iona. Now an empty but atmospheric shell, with blackened effigies and important monumental sculpture. Goats in the churchyard graze among the headstones of all the young Harris lads lost at sea in the Great War. There are other fallen angels on the outside of the tower.

1906 3/D19 ***St Michael's Chapel** Eriskay, nr South Uist/Barra · 01878 700305 That rare example of an ordinary modern church (centenary 2002) without history or grand architecture, which has charm and serenity, and imbues the sense of well-being that a religious centre should as the focal point of a relatively devout Catholic community who care for it. Overlooking the Sound of Barra. Edifying whatever your religion.

1907 8/N25 ***Culross Abbey Church** www.historicenvironment.scot Top of Forth-side
FREE village of interesting buildings and winding streets (1609/VILLAGES). Worth hike up
HES winding hill (signed; ruins adjacent) for views and for this well-loved and cared-for church. Great stained glass window, often full of flowers (though not on my last visit. Come on, ladies of the parish!).

1908 8/M24 ***Dunblane Cathedral** www.dunblanecathedral.org.uk · 01786 825388
HES Huge nave of a church, charmingly asymmetrical, built around a Norman tower (from David I) on the Allan Water and restored 1892. The wondrously bright stained glass is mostly 20th century. The poisoned sisters buried under the altar helped change the course of Scottish history. A contemplative place! Once when I was there our Andy (Murray) got married. See also 1346/FOOD PUBS; 1490/BAKERS.

1909 6/T19 ***St Machar's Cathedral** Aberdeen · www.stmachar.com · 01224 485988
The Chanonry in Old Aberdeen off St Machar's Drive about 2km from centre. Best seen as part of a walk round the old village within the city occupied mainly by the university. The cathedral's fine granite nave and twin-spired West Front date from 15th century, on site of 6th-century Celtic church. Noted for heraldic ceiling and 19/20th-century stained glass. Seaton Park adjacent has pleasant Don-side walks and there's the old Brig o' Balgownie. Church 9.30am-4.30pm, 10am-4pm winter.

1910 8/R27 ***Bowden Kirk nr Newtown St Boswells** Signed from A68 (the A699), 500m off the main street. Beneath the **Eildons** (2004/HILL WALKS) in classic rolling Border country, an atmospheric 17th-century kirk of 12th century origin. Beautiful setting in one of southern Scotland's prettiest villages. Sun service 9.30am. Eat in Melrose or St Boswells p. 146–7.

1911 8/S26 **Fogo Parish Church Fogo, nr Greenlaw** Go find this sweet historic church by the Blackadder, the quintessential Berwickshire river. 17th century from 12th century origins: lairds' lofts, box pews. Rural and spiritual; be alone.

1912 8/Q25 ***The East Lothian Churches Aberlady, Whitekirk, Athelstaneford &**
& 8/R25 **Garvald** 4 charming churches in bucolic settings; quiet corners to explore and reflect, though sadly these churches are not usually open. Easy to find. All have interesting local histories and in the case of Athelstaneford, a national resonance: a vision in the sky near here inspired the flag of Scotland, the saltire. The spooky Doocot Heritage Centre behind the church explains. Aberlady is my favourite; Garvald a days-gone-by village with pub.

1913 8/P25 **Abercorn Church nr South Queensferry** Off A904. 4km W of roundabout at Forth Bridge, just after village of Newton, Abercorn is signed. 11th-century kirk nestling among ancient yews in a sleepy hamlet, untouched since Covenanter days. St Ninian is said to have preached to the Picts here and though hard to believe, Abercorn was once on a par with York and Lindisfarne in religious importance. Church usually open. Walk in woods from corner stile or the Hopetoun Estate.

1914 4/L16 **Croick Church Bonar Bridge · www.croickchurch.com** 16km W of
L Ardgay, just over the river from Bonar Bridge and through the splendid glen of
ATMOS **Strathcarron** (1646/GLENS). This humble and charming church is remembered for its place in the story of the Highland Clearances. In May 1845, 90 folk took shelter in the graveyard around the church after they had been cleared from their homes in nearby Glencalvie. Not allowed even in the kirk, their plight did not go unnoticed and was reported in *The Times*. The harrowing account is there to read, and the messages they scratched on the windows. Sheep graze all around then and now. The **Carron Restaurant** is a surprisingly good foodstop nearby.

1915 8/L26 ***Thomas Coats Memorial Church Paisley · www.paisley.org.uk** Built by Coats (of thread fame), an imposing edifice, sometimes called the Baptist cathedral of Europe. A monument to God, prosperity and the Industrial Revolution. Viewing by arrangement 0141 587 8992. Sun service 11am.

1916 8/R25 ***The Lamp Of The Lothians St Mary's Collegiate Haddington · www.**
stmaryskirk.co.uk Signed from east main street. A beautiful town church on the River Tyne, with good stained glass and interesting crypts and corners. Obviously at the centre of the community, a lamp as it were, in the Lothians. Tours, brass rubbings (Sat). Music some summer Sundays. Coffee shop and gift shop. Don't miss the ancient orchard and St Mary's Pleasance medicinal garden: contemplate your condition. Daily and Sunday service.

1917 8/P22 ***Dunkeld Cathedral www.dunkeldcathedral.org.uk** In town centre by lane to the banks of the Tay at its most silvery. Medieval splendour among lofty trees. Notable for 13th-century choir and 15th-century nave and tower. Parish church open for edifying services and other spiritual purposes. Lovely summer recitals. Good marked circular walk from corner of kirkyard (5km) and welcome tearoom, **Spill the Beans**, in the lane (1427/TEAROOMS), and the **Aran Bakery** (1470/ ARTISAN BAKERS) in the main street.

1918 7/J20   **St Mary & St Finnan Church**   Glenfinnan · www.glenfinnanchurch.org · 01687 450223   On A830 Fort William–Mallaig Road to the Isles (1689/SCENIC ROUTES), a beautiful Catholic church in a spectacular setting that's just so harmonious: the soft sandstone, the pale oak floors, the marble, the glass. Queen Vic said she never saw a lovelier or more romantic spot (though she said that a lot). Late 19th century. Open daily, Sunday mass 1pm.

1919 8/R20   **Forest of Birse Kirk**   nr Aboyne   A tiny church in the middle of nowhere, the hills all around, a footpath to Aboyne (6km). Actually on the Finzean Estate (they told me about this in the **Finzean Tearoom** 1514/FARM SHOPS) and I set off to find it. Bottom of the hill from the shop, turn right signed Forest of Birse, past the sawmill about 5km following the very walkable River Feugh. A simple house of God on a grassy landing by the river, built 1890, always open. Edification. Make this pilgrimage. If you let me know what day in 2018 I left my name in the visitors' book, I will buy you dinner at the Boat Inn in Aboyne. This is a test!

St Giles' Cathedral   Edinburgh   Report: 414/ATTRACTIONS.

▪ The Great Abbeys

NTS *National Trust for Scotland. Hours vary. Admission.*
HES *Historic Environment Scotland. Standard hours are: Apr-end Sep 7 days 9.30am-5.30pm; Oct-Mar 9.30am-4.30pm. Local and winter variations.*

1920 7/F23   ✓✓ **Iona Abbey**   www.historicenvironment.scot · 01681 700512   This
ATMOS   hugely significant place of pilgrimage for new age and old age pilgrims and
HES   tourists alike is reached from Fionnphort, SW Mull, by frequent CalMac Ferry (a 5-min crossing). Walk 1km. Here in 563 AD St Columba began his mission for a Celtic church that changed the face of Europe. Cloisters, graveyard of Scottish kings and, marked by a modest stone, the inscription already faded by the weather, the grave of John Smith, the patron saint of New Labour. Ethereal, clear light through the unstained windows may illuminate your contemplations. Great sense of being part of a universal church and community. Regular services. Good shop (2206/SCOTTISH SHOPS) and nearby galleries. Residential courses and accom (MacLeod Centre adjacent, 01681 700404). For many, this is best thing on or off Mull.

1921 6/P17   ✓✓ **Pluscarden Abbey**   between Forres & Elgin · www.
ATMOS   pluscardenabbey.org · 01343 890257   The oldest abbey monastic community still working in the UK, in one of the most spiritual of places. Founded by Alexander II in 1230 and being restored since 1948. Benedictine services (starting with Vigil and Lauds at 4.30am through Prime-Terce-Sext-None-Vespers and Compline at 7.50pm) open to the public. The ancient honey-coloured walls, brilliant stained glass, monks' Gregorian chant: the whole effect is a truly uplifting experience. The bell rings down the valley. Services aside, open to visitors 4.30am-8.30pm. See also 1284/RETREATS.

1922 8/L26   ✓✓ **Paisley Abbey**   www.paisleyabbey.org.uk · 0141 889 7654   In the town centre. An abbey founded in 1163, razed (by the English) in 1307 and with successive deteriorations and renovations ever since. Major restoration in the 1920s brought it to present-day cathedral-like magnificence. Exceptional stained glass (the recent window complementing the formidable Strachan East Window), an impressive choir and an edifying sense of space. Sunday services are superb, especially full-dress communion and there are open days and concerts. Mon-Sat 10am-3.30pm. Café/shop.

1923 8/R28 ✓✓ **Jedburgh Abbey** www.historicenvironment.scot · 01835 863925
HES   The classic abbey ruin; conveys the most complete impression of the Border abbeys built under the patronage of David I in the 12th century. Its tower and remarkable Catherine window are still intact. Excavations have unearthed a 12th-century comb. It's now displayed in the excellent visitor centre, which brilliantly illustrates the full story of the Abbey's amazing history. Best view from across the Jed in the Glebe. My home town; my abbey!

1924 8/R27 ✓✓ **Dryburgh Abbey** nr St Boswells · www.historicenvironment.scot ·
ATMOS   01835 822381 One of the most evocative of ruins, an aesthetic attraction
HES since the late 18th century. Sustained innumerable attacks from the English since its inauguration by Premonstratensian Canons in 1150. Celebrated by Sir Walter Scott, buried here in 1832 (with his biographer Lockhart at his feet), its setting, among huge cedar trees on the banks of the Tweed is one of pure historical romance. 4km A68. See also 1703/VIEWS. Hotel adjacent not what it was. Eat nearby at **Main Street**, **Buccleuch Arms** or **Hunters Stables** (834/829/846/BORDERS).

1925 9/N30 **Sweetheart Abbey** New Abbey · www.historicenvironment.scot ·
HES 01387 850397 12km S by A710. The endearing and enduring warm red sandstone abbey in the shadow of Criffel, so named because Devorguilla de Balliol, devoted to her husband (he of the Oxford college), founded the abbey for Cistercian monks and kept his heart in a casket which is buried with her here. No roof, but the tower is intact. Cutesy Abbey Cottage tearoom has good, comforting food and even its own cookbook (so-so gift shop). Gaze at the ruins while eating your soup and cake.

1926 8/R27 **Melrose Abbey** www.historicenvironment.scot · 01896 822562 Another
HES romantic setting, the abbey seems to lend class as well as history to the whole town. Once again built by David I (what a guy!) for Cistercian monks from Rievaulx from 1136. It once sustained a huge community, as evinced by the widespread excavations. There's a museum of abbey, church and Roman relics; and possibly Robert the Bruce's heart, excavated in the gardens. Tempting Tweed walks start here. You can't miss the **Greenhouse Café** on the corner and there are numerous good food options in Melrose, p. 146-7.

1927 8/R22 **Arbroath Abbey** www.historicenvironment.scot · 01241 878756 25km N
HES of Dundee. Founded in 1178 and endowed on an unparalleled scale, this is an important place in Scots history. It's where the Declaration was signed in 1320 to appeal to the Pope to release the Scots from the yoke of the English (you can buy facsimiles of the yellow parchment; the original is in the Scottish Records Office in Edinburgh – oh, and tea towels). It was to Arbroath that the Stone of Destiny (on which Scottish kings were traditionally crowned) was returned after being 'stolen' from Westminster Abbey in the 1950s and is now at Edinburgh Castle. Great interpretation centre before you tour the ruins.

The Most Interesting Graveyards

1928 8/M26
LL
ATMOS

✓✓ **Glasgow Necropolis** The vast burial ground at the crest of the ridge running down to the river that was the focus of the original settlement of Glasgow. Everything began at the foot of this hill and, ultimately, ended at the top, where many of the city's most famous (and infamous) sons and daughters are interred within the reach of the long shadow of John Knox's obelisk. Generally open dawn till dusk, most atmos if you can get this very Glasgow experience to yourself (possibly best not alone, though there is CCTV).

1929 8/Q25
ATMOS

✓ **Edinburgh Canongate Kirkyard** On left of Royal Mile going down to Palace. Adam Smith and the tragic poet Robert Fergusson revered by Rabbie Burns (who raised the memorial stone in 1787 over his pauper's grave) are buried here in the heart of Auld Reekie on the Heritage Trail. Tourists can easily miss this one, though not **Greyfriars**, a place of ancient mystery, famous for the much Instagrammed wee dog who guarded his master's grave for 14 years; for the plundering of graves in the early 18th century for the Anatomy School; and for the graves of Allan Ramsay (prominent poet and burgher), James Hutton (the father of geology), William McGonagall (the 'world's worst poet') and sundry serious Highlanders. Annals of a great city are written on these stones. **Dean Cemetery** is an Edinburgh secret; my New Town lips are sealed.

1930 7/G25

✓ **Isle of Jura: Killchianaig graveyard in the north** Follow road as far as it goes to Inverlussa, graveyard is on right, just before hamlet. Mairi Ribeach, buried here, apparently lived until she was 128. **In the south at Keils** (2km from road N out of Craighouse, bearing left past houses in Keils and through the deer fence), her father is buried and he was 180! Both sites are beautiful, isolated and redolent of island history, with much to reflect on, not least the mysterious longevity of the inhabitants and that soon many of us may live this long.

1931 5/L18

✓ **Chisholm Graveyard nr Beauly** Last resting place of the Chisholms and 3 of the largest Celtic crosses you'll see anywhere, in a secret, atmospheric woodland setting. 15km W of Beauly on A831 to Struy after Aigas dam and 5km after golf course on right-hand side; 1km before Cnoc Hotel opposite Erchless Estate and through a white iron gate on right. Walk 150m on mossy path. Go find!

1932 5/J19
LL

✓ **Clachan Duich nr Inverinate** A beautiful stonewalled graveyard at the head of Loch Duich just S of Inverinate, 20km S of Kyle of Lochalsh. A monument on a rise above, a ruined chapel and many, many Macraes, this a delightful place to wander with glorious views to the loch and the mountains.

1933 7/J21

Eilean Munde nr Ballachulish The island and graveyard in Loch Leven around the chapel of St Fintan Munnu who travelled here from Iona in the 7th century; the church was rebuilt in the 18th. Notable apart from mystery and history because of the Stewarts buried here, also the MacDonalds and Camerons who maintained it despite their conflicts. You'll need a wee boat or boat trip (SeaXplorer – 01855 413203) by the **Isles of Glencoe Hotel** (1178/KIDS).

1934 7/H28

Campbeltown Cemetery One of the nicest things about this end-of-the-line town is the cemetery. At the end of a row of posh houses, the original merchant and mariner owners of which are interred in the leafy plots next door. Still in use after centuries of commerce and seafaring, it has crept up the terraces of a steep and lush overhanging bank. The white cross and row of WWII headstones are affecting. **Royal Hotel** for sustenance (733/ARGYLL).

1935 7/K28   **Kirkoswald Kirkyard nr Maybole & Girvan** On main road through village between Ayr and Girvan. The graveyard around the ruined kirk and famous as the burial place of the characters in Burns' most famous poem, *Tam o' Shanter*. A must for Burns fans and famous-grave seekers, with Souter Johnnie and Kirkton Jean buried here. **Souter Johnnie** himself gives his name to the restaurant and pub across the road: a great grub stop.

1936 8/Q26   **Humbie Churchyard nr Humbie** 25km SE of Edinburgh via A68 (turn-off at Fala). Deep in the woods with the burn besides, this is as reassuring a place to be buried as you could wish for; if you're set on cremation, come here and think of earth. I wrote this 25 years ago; these decisions ever closer.

1937 8/R27   **Ancrum Churchyard nr Jedburgh** The quintessential country churchyard; away from the village (2km along B6400), by a lazy river (the Ale Water, crossed to a farm by a humpback bridge) with a chapel in ruins. Elegiac and deeply peaceful. Great river swimming spot nearby (1733/SWIMMING). The **Cross Keys** for food and ale to live by 1339/FOOD PUBS.

1938 8/L23   **Balquhidder Churchyard** Chiefly notable as the last resting place of one Rob Roy MacGregor who was buried in 1734 after causing a heap of trouble hereabouts and raised to immortality by Sir Walter Scott and then Michael Caton-Jones (the movie). Despite well-trodden path, setting is poignant. Sunday evening concerts have been held in the kirk Jul/Aug (check locally). Nice walk from back corner to the waterfall and then to **Rallying Place** (1709/VIEWS). Great long walk (13km) to **Brig o' Turk** (2040/WALKS). Refresh at **Mhor 84** (796/CENTRAL).

1939 8/N24   **Logie Old Kirk nr Stirling** A crumbling chapel and an ancient, lovingly restored graveyard at the foot of the Ochils. The wall is round to keep out the demons, a burn gurgles beside and there are some fine and very old stones going back to the 16th century. Take road for Wallace Monument off A91, then first right. The old kirk is 500m beyond the new. The interpretation board is sponsored by the enigmatic-sounding Sons of the Rock. Continuing on this steep narrow road (then right at the T-junction) takes you on to the **Ochils** (2005/HILL WALKS).

1940 4/P14   **Tutnaguail Dunbeath** There are various spellings of this enchanting cemetery
    NC500   5km from Dunbeath, Neil Gunn's birthplace. Found by walking up the strath he describes in his book *Highland River* (1965/LITERARY PLACES). With a white wall around it, this graveyard, which before the Clearances once served a valley community of 400 souls, can be seen for miles. Ask at heritage centre for route or see **www.dunbeath-heritage.org.uk**.

1941 8/Q23   **Birkhill Cemetery Dundee** Opened in 1989. Part of the city's Templeton Woods across the road (to Coupar Angus from the dual carriageway) from **Camperdown Park** (1602/PARKS; 2081/WALKS), this well-laid-out cemetery is a revelation. No other graveyard on these pages seems so well kept and well used. Garlands of flowers on the graves. Aesthetic and reflective. Many Islamic graves, a woodlands burial section beyond and the 'Baby Green' is particularly affecting.

1942 5/H16   **Gairloch Old Graveyard** On the left as you arrive in Gairloch from the S by
    NC500   the golf course (where you park). Looking over the lovely bay and beach (1631/BEACHES), a green and tranquil spot to explore. Osgood Mackenzie of **Inverewe Gardens** (1553/GARDENS) is buried in the bottom-right corner (facing the sea) under a simple Celtic cross, wild ferns behind, among many other Mackenzies.

The Great Battlegrounds

NTS *National Trust for Scotland. Hours vary. Admission.*

1943 5/M18
ATMOS
NTS
✓✓ **Culloden** nr Inverness · www.nts.org.uk · 0844 493 2159 Signed from A9 and A96 into Inverness and about 8km from town. This state-of-the-art visitor centre with 'voices of history' puts you in the picture. There's a 10-min rooftop perspective or a 40-min through-the-battlefield walk. Positions of the clans and the troops marked out across the moor; flags enable you to get a real sense of scale. If you go in spring, you see how wet and miserable the moor can be (the battle took place on 16 April 1746). No matter how many other folk are there wandering down the lines, a visit to this most infamous of battlefields can still leave a pain in the heart. Centre opening times vary but generally 9am-5.30pm. Ground open at all times for more personal Cullodens.

1944 8/N24
NTS
✓✓ **Bannockburn** nr Stirling · https://battleofbannockburn.com · 01786 812664 4km town centre via Glasgow road or junction 9 of M9 (3km), behind a hotel (not recommended), a state-of-the-art visitor centre, where you can actually play the game of Battle. Ticket allows film view, exhibition then the game to play or just watch. Some visitors might be perplexed as to why 24 June 1314 was such a big deal for the Scots and, apart from the 250m walk to the flag and the huge statue, there's not a lot doing in the field. But the battle against the English did finally secure the place of Robert I (the Bruce) as King of Scots, paving the way for the final settlement with England 15 years later. The best place to see the famous wee burn is from below the magnificent Telford Bridge (nearby, ask!). Controversies still rage among scholars on many aspects but nobody would question its significance. In 2014, a festival 'Bannockburn Live', for which I was the Director, celebrated the battle's 700th anniversary.

1945 5/G18
Battle of the Braes Skye 10km Portree. Take main A87 road S for 3km then left, marked Braes, for 7km. Monument is on a rise on right. The last battle fought on British soil and a significant place in Scots history. When the Clearances, uninterrupted by any organised opposition, were virtually complete and vast tracts of Scotland had been depopulated for sheep, the Skye crofters finally stood up in 1882 to the Government troops and said enough is enough. A cairn has been erected near the spot where they fought on behalf of 'all the crofters of Gaeldom', a battle which led eventually to the Crofters Act which has guaranteed their rights ever since. At the end of this road at Peinchorran, there are fine views of Raasay (which was devastated by clearances) and Glamaig, the conical Cuillin, across Loch Sligachan.

1946 7/J21
LLL
ATMOS
Glen Coe Not much of a battle, of course, but one of the most infamous massacres in British history. Much has been written (John Prebble's *Glencoe* and others) and a discreetly located visitor centre provides audiovisual scenario. MacDonald Monument near Glencoe village and the walk to the more evocative Signal Rock where the bonfire was lit, now a happy woodland trail in this doom-laden landscape. Many other great walks. See 1971/ENCHANTING PLACES; 1313/GOOD PUBS.

1947 1/Q11
Scapa Flow Orkney Mainland & Hoy · www.scapaflow.co.uk · 01856 791300 Scapa Flow, surrounded by various of the southern Orkney islands, is one of the most sheltered anchorages in Europe. Hence the huge presence in Orkney of ships and personnel during both wars. The Germans scuttled 52 of their warships here in 1919 and many still lie in the bay. The *Royal Oak* was torpedoed in 1939 with the loss of 833 men. Much still remains of the war years: the rusting hulks, the shore

fortifications, the Churchill Barriers and the ghosts of a long-gone army at Scapa and Lyness on Hoy. Evocative visitor centre, museum (temporarily at the Hoy Hotel, Lyness, reopens 2020) and naval cemetery at Lyness. Open Mar-Oct.

1948 8/R27 **Lilliard's Edge nr St Boswells** On main A68, look for Lilliard's Edge Caravan Park 5km S of St Boswells; park and walk back towards St Boswells to the brim of the hill (about 500m), then cross rough ground on right along ridge, following tree-line hedge. Marvellous view attests to strategic location. 200m along, a cairn marks the grave of Lilliard who, in 1545, joined the Battle of Ancrum Moor against the English 'loons' under the Earl of Angus. 'And when her legs were cuttit off, she fought upon her stumps'. An ancient poem etched on the stone records her legendary … feet. Hardly anyone goes/finds this place. Thanks to readers Dougie Cameron and Donna Allen who did (I know, I still owe you dinner).

1949 8/N21 **Killiecrankie nr Pitlochry** The first battle of the Jacobite Risings where, in July
NTS 1689, the Highlanders lost their leader Viscount (aka Bonnie) Dundee, but won the battle, using the narrow Pass of Killiecrankie. One escaping soldier made a famous leap. Well-depicted scenario in visitor centre; short walk to 'The Leap'. Battle viewpoint and cairn is further along road to Blair Atholl, turning right and doubling back (3km from visitor centre). You get the lie of the land from here. Many good walks and the lovely **Killiecrankie Hotel** (905/PERTHSHIRE) for rest, refreshments and excellent food.

Mary, Charlie & Bob

HES *Historic Environment Scotland. Standard hours are: Apr-end Sep 7 days 9.30am–5.30pm; Oct-Mar 9.30am–4.30pm. Local and winter variations.*

MARY, QUEEN OF SCOTS (1542–87)
Linlithgow Palace Where she was born. Report: 1830/RUINS.

Holyrood Palace Edinburgh And lived. Report: 402/ATTRACTIONS.

1950 8/M24
LL
HES
Inchmahome Priory Port of Menteith · www.historicenvironment.scot Priory ruins on the Isle of Rest in Scotland's only lake. Here the infant queen spent her early years cared for by Augustinian monks. A short boat journey. Signal the ferryman by turning the board to the island, much as she did. Apr-Oct: 7 days. Last trip 4.15pm (Oct till 3.15pm). **Lake Hotel** adjacent for great food (799/CENTRAL).

1951 8/R28
Mary, Queen of Scots' House Jedburgh In gardens via Smiths Wynd off main street. Historians quibble but this long-standing museum claims to be *the* house where she fell ill in 1566 but still made it over to visit the injured Bothwell at Hermitage Castle 50km away. Tower house in good condition; displays and well-told saga. Me and my brother used to play tennis in the garden. Mar-Nov.

1952 8/P24
L
HES
Loch Leven Castle nr Kinross · www.historicenvironment.scot · 01577 862670 Well signed! The ultimate in romantic penitentiaries on the island in the middle of the loch, visible from the M90. Not much left of the ruin to fill the fantasy, but this is where Mary spent 10 months in 1568 before her famous escape and final attempt to get back the throne. Sailings Apr-Oct 10am–4.15pm last sailing (Oct 3.15pm), from the pier in Pier Rd, Kinross (a café serves as you wait). Small launch, a 10-min trip, return as you like.

1953 9/M31
HES
Dundrennan Abbey nr Auchencairn · www.historicenvironment.scot Mary got around and there are innumerable places where she spent the night. This was where she spent her last one on Scottish soil, leaving next day from Port Mary (nothing to see there but a beach, 2km along the road skirting the sinister MoD range, the pier long gone). The Cistercian abbey (established 1142) which harboured her on her last night is now a tranquil ruin.
'In my end is my beginning,' she said, facing her execution 19 years later.

1954 8/R25
Her 'death mask' is displayed at Lennoxlove House nr Haddington · www.lennoxlove.com It does seem small for someone who was supposedly 6 feet tall! Lennoxlove on road to Gifford. Apr-Oct Wed/Thu/Sun. Tours 12/1/2/3.30pm.

BONNIE PRINCE CHARLIE (1720–88)

1955 3/D19
L
Prince Charlie's Bay or Strand Eriskay The uncelebrated, unmarked and quietly beautiful beach where Charlie first landed in Scotland to begin the Jacobite Rebellion. Nothing much has changed (except the pier for Barra ferry is adjacent) and this crescent of sand with soft machair and a turquoise sea is still a special place. 1km from township heading south; best approach from township, not the ferry road – it's a small beach along from the harbour. See also 2240/ISLANDS.

1956 5/H20
L · ATMOS
Loch Nan Uamh, The Prince's Cairn nr Arisaig Pronounced 'Loch Na Nuan'. 7km from Lochailort on A830 (1690/SCENIC ROUTES), 48km Fort William. Signed

from the road (100m lay-by), a path leads down to the left. This is the traditional spot where Charlie embarked for France in September 1746, having lost the battle and the cause. The rocky headland also overlooks the bay and skerries where he'd landed in July the year before to begin the campaign. This place was the beginning and the end and it has all the romance necessary to be utterly convincing. Is that a French ship out there in the mist? The movie still awaits.

1957 7/J20
LL
NTS

Glenfinnan www.visitglenfinnan.co.uk Here he raised his standard to rally the clans to the Jacobite cause. For a while on that day in August 1745 it looked as if few were coming. Then pipes were heard and 600 Camerons came marching from the valley (where the viaduct now spans). That must have been one helluva moment. It's thought that he actually stood on the higher ground but there is a powerful sense of place and history here. The visitor centre has an excellent map of Charlie's path through Scotland – somehow he touched all the most alluring places! Climb the tower or take the long view from Loch Shiel (1676/SCENIC ROUTES). Nice church 1km (1918/CHURCHES); notable hotel and bar (1239/SCOTTISH HOTELS). Walk to the Harry Potter viaduct via the **Dining Car** (1447/TEAROOMS).

Culloden nr Inverness Report: 1943/BATTLEGROUNDS.

ROBERT I, THE BRUCE (1274-1329)

1958 9/L29

Bruce's Stone Glen Trool, nr Newton Stewart 26km N by A714 via Bargrennan (8km to head of glen) on the **Southern Upland Way** (2026/WALKS). The fair **Glen Trool** is a celebrated spot in Galloway Forest Park (1648/GLENS). The stone is signed (200m walk) and marks the area where Bruce's guerrilla band rained boulders onto the pursuing English in 1307 after routing the main army at Solway Moss. Good walks, including to **Merrick** which starts here (1993/HILLS).

1959 8/N24

Bannockburn nr Stirling The climactic battle in 1314, when Bruce decisively whipped the English and secured the kingdom (though Scotland was not legally recognised as independent until 1329). The scale and even the excitement of the skirmish can be visualised in the fancy (new 2014) visitor centre. See 1944/BATTLEGROUNDS.

1960 8/R22
HES

Arbroath Abbey Not much of the Bruce trail here, but this is where the famous Declaration was signed that was the attempt of the Scots nobility united behind him to gain international recognition of the independence they had won on the battlefield. What it says is stirring stuff; the original is in Edinburgh. Great interpretation centre. 9.30am-5.30pm. See 1927/ABBEYS.

1961 8/P25
HES

Dunfermline Abbey Church www.dunfermlineabbey.co.uk Here, some tangible evidence: his tomb. Buried in 1329, his remains were discovered wrapped in gold cloth when the site was being cleared for the new church in 1818. Many of the other great kings, the Alexanders I and III, were not so readily identifiable (Bruce's ribcage had been cut to remove his heart). With great national emotion he was reinterred under the pulpit. The church (as opposed to the ruins and Norman nave adjacent) is open Easter-Oct, winter for services. See as part of a walk round 'The Heritage Quarter'. Include the **Carnegie Library** and **Pittencrieff Park** (1594/PARKS).

1962 8/R27
HES

Melrose Abbey On his deathbed Bruce asked that his heart be buried here after it was taken to the Crusades to aid the army in their battles. A likely lead casket thought to contain it was excavated from the chapter house and it did date from the period. It was reburied here and is marked with a stone. Let's believe in this! See 1926/ABBEYS.

The Important Literary Places

1963 7/K28 **Robert Burns (1759-96) Alloway, Ayr & Dumfries · www.robertburns. org** A well-marked heritage trail through his life and haunts in Ayrshire and Dumfriesshire. **Alloway:** A good start with the (NTS) restoration of **Burns Cottage www.burnsmuseum.org.uk** and, 1km away, the state-of-the-art **Museum**. Here, the bard has a legacy and interpretive centre worthy of his international stature and appeal (2153/HISTORY). Both open 7 days. Also in Alloway, the Auld Brig o' Doon and the Auld Kirk where Tam o' Shanter saw the witches dance are evocative, the Monument and surrounding gardens are poetically perfect (if you're in a musing mood). Elsewhere:
Ayr: The Auld Kirk off main street by river; graveyard with diagram of where his friends are buried; open at all times. **Dumfries:** The house where he spent his last years and mausoleum 250m away at back of a kirkyard stuffed with extravagant masonry. His howff in Dumfries, the **Globe Inn**, is very atmospheric – established in 1610 and still going strong. 10km N of Dumfries on A76 at **Ellisland Farm** (home 1788-91) possibly the most interesting site. The farmhouse with genuine memorabilia, e.g. his mirror, fishing rod, a poem scratched on glass, original manuscripts. There's his favourite walk by the river where he composed *Tam o' Shanter* and a strong atmos about the place. Open 7 days summer, closed Sun/Mon in winter. **Poosie Nansie's**, the pub he frequented in Mauchline, is perhaps disappointing. **Brow Well** near Ruthwell on the B725 20km S of Dumfries and near **Caerlaverock** (1774/BIRDS), is a quieter place, a well with curative properties where he went in the latter stages of his illness.

1964 8/S21 **Lewis Grassic Gibbon (1901-35) Arbuthnott, nr Stonehaven · www. grassicgibbon.com** Although James Leslie Mitchell left the area in 1917, this is where he spent his formative years. Visitor centre (01561 361668; Mar-Oct: 7 days 10am-4.30pm) at the end of the village (via B967, 16km S of Stonehaven off main A92) has details of his life and can point you in the direction of the places he writes about in his trilogy, *A Scots Quair*. The first part, *Sunset Song*, as depicted in the Terence Davies 2015 film, is generally considered to be one of the great Scots novels and this area, the **Howe of the Mearns**, is the place he so effectively evokes. Arbuthnott is reminiscent of 'Kinraddie' and the churchyard 1km away on the other side of road (the Kirk of St Ternan) still has the atmosphere of that time of innocence before the war which pervades the book. His ashes are here in a grave in a corner; the inscription: 'the kindness of friends/the warmth of toil/the peace of rest'. From 1928 to when he died 7 years later, at the age of only 34, he wrote an incredible 17 books. From the Kirk go downhill to right, the wooden bridge over the Bervie: the Mearns as was. And thanks, Stewart Gibb.

1965 4/P14
NC500 **Neil Gunn (1891-1973) Dunbeath, nr Wick · www.neilgunn.org.uk** Scotland's foremost writer on Highland life, perhaps not receiving the recognition he deserves, was brought up in this North East fishing village and based 3 of his greatest yarns here, particularly *Highland River*, which must stand in any literature as a brilliant evocation of place. The **Strath** in which it is set is below the house (nondescript, next to the shop) and makes for a great walk (2052/WALKS). Commemorative statue by the harbour, not quite the harbour you imagine from the books. The excellent heritage centre (**www.dunbeath-heritage.org.uk**) depicts the Strath on its floor and has all info. Gunn also lived for many years near **Dingwall** and there is a memorial on the back road to Strathpeffer and a wonderful view in a place he often walked (on A834, 4km from Dingwall).

1966 8/Q27 **James Hogg (1770–1835) St Mary's Loch, Ettrick** The Ettrick Shepherd who wrote one of the great works of Scottish literature, *The Private Memoirs and Confessions of a Justified Sinner*, was born, lived and died in the valleys of the **Yarrow** and the **Ettrick**, some of the most starkly beautiful landscapes in Scotland. **St Mary's Loch** on the A708 28km W of Selkirk: there's a commemorative statue looking over the loch and the adjacent and supernatural seeming Loch of the Lowes. On the strip of land between is **Tibbie Shiels** pub (and hotel), once a gathering place for the writer and his friends (e.g. Sir Walter Scott) though now closed. Across the valley divide (11km on foot, part of the **Southern Upland Way** 2026/WALKS), or 25km by road past the Gordon Arms, Yarrow, is the remote village of **Ettrick**, another monument and his grave (and Tibbie Shiels') in the churchyard.

1967 8/R27 **Sir Walter Scott (1771–1832) Abbotsford, Melrose** No other place in Scotland (and few anywhere) contains so much of a writer's life and work. This was the house he rebuilt from the farmhouse he moved to in 1812 in the countryside he did so much to popularise. The house, even recently lived in by his descendants, is now a major Borders tourist attraction (1870/HOUSES), sympathetically restored and with an excellent visitor centre and café (open AYR). Pleasant grounds and topiary, and walks by the Tweed which the house overlooks. House and gardens open Mar-Nov. His grave is at **Dryburgh Abbey** (1924/ABBEYS). There are monuments to Walt famously in Edinburgh (447/VIEWS) and in George Square, Glasgow.

1968 8/Q25 **Robert Louis Stevenson (1850–94) Edinburgh** Though Stevenson travelled widely – lived in France, emigrated to America and died and was buried in Samoa – he spent his first 30 years in Edinburgh. He was born and brought up in the New Town, living at **17 Heriot Row** from 1857-80 which is still lived in (not open to the public). Most of his youth was spent in this newly built and expanding part of the city in an area bounded then by parkland and farms. Both the Botanics (408/ATTRACTIONS) and **Warriston Cemetery** are part of the landscape of his childhood. However, his fondest recollections were of the **Pentland Hills** and, virtually unchanged as they are, it's here that one is following most poignantly in his footsteps. The cottage at **Swanston** (a delightful village with some remarkable thatched cottages reached via the city bypass/Colinton turn-off or from Oxgangs Rd and a bridge over the bypass; the village nestles in a grove of trees below the hills and is a good place to walk from), also the ruins of **Glencorse Church**. A pleasant walk in Colinton Dell (**Water of Leith** 423/WALKS) can include **Colinton Parish Church**, where Stevenson often visited his grandfather, who was the minister. In 2013 a statue of RLS as a child was installed here. **The Writers' Museum** at Makars' Court has exhibits (and of many other writers). The **Hawes Inn** in South Queensferry where he wrote *Kidnapped* has had its history obliterated in brewery makeovers but is currently an OK stay (858/LOTHIANS).

1969 8/Q25 **J. K. Rowling (b.1965) Edinburgh · www.jkrowling.com** Scotland's most successful and revered writer ever as the creator of Harry Potter was famously an impecunious single mother scribbling away in Edinburgh coffee shops. The most mentioned is opposite the Festival Theatre and is now **Spoon** (126/BRASSERIES); the **Elephant House** on George IV Bridge makes the most of a tenuous connection. Harry Potter country as interpreted by Hollywood can be found at **Glenfinnan** (1957/CHARLIE) and **Glen Coe**, especially around the **Clachaig Inn** (1219/INNS).

1970 8/Q25 **Irvine Welsh (b.1958), Alexander McCall Smith (b.1948), Ian Rankin (b.1960) and Val McDermid (b.1955)** have an international readership, homes in Edinburgh and all have their haunts.

The Most Enchanting Places

1971 7/K22   **The Lost Valley (Coire Gabhail)** Glen Coe The secret glen where the ill-fated
    2-B-2   MacDonalds hid the cattle they'd stolen from the Lowlands and which became
     LLL   (with politics and power struggles) their undoing. A narrow, wooded cleft takes
  ATMOS   you between the imposing and gnarled 3 Sisters hills and over the threshold (God
    knows how the cattle got there) and into the huge bowl of Coire Gabhail. The place
    envelops you in its tragic history, more redolent perhaps than any of the massacre
    sites. Park on the A82 6.5km from the visitor centre (300m W of the white
    bungalow) by the road (2 car parks always busy). Follow clear path down to and
    across the River Coe. Ascend keeping burn to left; 1.5km further up, it's best to ford
    it. Allow 3 hours. See also 1946/BATTLEGROUNDS.

1972 4/Q13   **The Whaligoe Steps** Ulbster 10km S of Wick. 100m to car park by an unsigned
     LL   road off the A99 at the (modern) telephone box near sign for the Cairn of Get. Short
  NC500   walk from the car park at the end of cottage row to this remarkable structure hewn
    into sheer cliffs, 337 steps down to a grassy platform – the Bink – and an old fishing
    station. From 1792, creels of cod, haddock and ling were hauled (by women) up
    these steps to the merchants of Wick and Lybster. 1,000 barrels of herring were
    landed here in 1792. Consider these labours as you follow their footsteps in this
    wild and enchanting place. No rails and can be slippy. Davy Nicolson (who lives in
    the row) may be your unofficial (but impassioned) guide. There is a café at the top
    of the steps, which some locals like, others not.

1973 8/Q25   **Under Edinburgh Old Town** Visit Mary King's Close, a medieval street under the
    Royal Mile closed in 1753 (**The Real Mary King's Close** www.realmarykingsclose.
    com; 0131 225 0672); and the Vaults under South Bridge – built in the 18th century
    and sealed up around the time of the Napoleonic Wars (**Mercat Tours** www.
    mercattours.com; 0131 225 5445). History underfoot for unsuspecting tourists and
    locals alike. Glimpses of a rather smelly subterranean life way back then. It's dark
    during the day, and you wouldn't want to get locked in.

1974 1/P10   **Yesnaby Sea Stacks** Orkney Mainland · www.visitorkney.com A clifftop
     LL   viewpoint that's so wild, so dramatic and, if you walk near the edge, so precarious
    that its supernaturalism verges on the uneasy. Shells of lookout posts from the
    war echo the melancholy spirit of the place. ('The bloody town's a bloody cuss/No
    bloody trains, no bloody bus/And no one cares for bloody us/In bloody Orkney' –
    first lines of a poem written then, a soldier's lament). Near Skara Brae, it's about
    30km from Kirkwall and way out west. Follow directions from **Marwick Head**
    (1784/BIRDS).

1975 5/F17   **The Fairy Glen** Skye A place so strange, it's hard to believe that it's merely a
     LLL   geological phenomenon. Entering Uig on the A855 (becomes A87) from Portree,
  ATMOS   take road on right by the Uig Hotel marked Balnaknock for 2km and you enter an
    area of extraordinary conical hills which, in certain conditions of light and weather,
    seems to entirely justify its legendary provenance. Your mood may determine
    whether you believe they were good or bad fairies, but there's supposed to be an
    incredible 365 of these grassy hillocks, some 35m high – well, how else could they
    be here? As at Skye's Fairy Pools, prepare for campervan chaos.

1976 5/M18   **Clava Cairns** nr Inverness Near **Culloden** (1943/BATTLEGROUNDS) these curious
  ATMOS   chambered cairns in a grove of trees near a river in the middle of 21st-century
    nowhere. A place to make you feel a glow or a creeping chill (1853/PREHISTORIC).

1977 5/M17
ATMOS

The Clootie Well **between Tore & Avoch** Spooky place on the road towards Avoch and Cromarty 4km from the A9 roundabout at Tore, N of Inverness. Easily missed, though there is a marked car park on the right side of the road going east. What you see is hundreds of rags or clouts: pieces of clothing hanging on the branches of trees around the spout of an ancient well, where the wearer might be healed. They go way back up the hill behind and though some may have been here a long time, this place seems to have been commodified like everywhere else, so there's plenty of new socks and branded T-shirts. Weird that people still 'hang out' here!

1978 6/Q20
L

Burn o' Vat **nr Ballater · www.visitdeeside.org.uk** This impressive and rather spooky glacial curiosity on Royal Deeside is a popular spot and well worth the short walk. 8km from Ballater towards Aberdeen on main A93, take B9119 for Huntly for 2km to the car park at the Muir of Dinnet Nature Reserve – driving through forests of strange spindly birch. Some scrambling to reach the huge 'pot' from which the burn flows to Loch Kinord. SNH visitor centre. Forest walks, 1.3km circular walk to Vat, 6km to loch. Busy on fine weekends, it's uncanny when deserted.

1979 9/N29
ATMOS

Crichope Linn **nr Thornhill** A supernatural sliver of glen inhabited by water spirits of various temperaments (and midges). Some parts of the path narrow. Take road for Cample on A76 Dumfries to Kilmarnock road just S of Thornhill; at village (2km) there's a wooden sign so take left for 2km. Discreet sign and gate in bank on right is easy to miss, but park in quarry 100m further on. Take care – can be wet and very slippy. Gorge is a 10-min schlep from the gate. We saw red squirrels! **Durisdeer Church** nearby is also enchanting (1902/CHURCHES).

1980 6/S17
LL

Hell's Lum Cave **nr Gardenstown, Moray Firth Coast** Locally popular but still secret beach picnic and combing spot E of Gardenstown off the B9031 signed for **Cullykhan Bay** 1620/BEACHES. From car park (200m from main road), you walk down to bay and can see on left a scar on the hill which marks the lum, approached along the shoreline via a defile known as the Devil's Dining Room. Local mythology surrounds this wild curiosity. In the cave you may hear what sounds like children crying.

1981 8/R24

Dunino Den **Strathvithie, nr Crail** Alerted to this ancient, sacred and mysterious place off the B9131 in deepest Fife by a reader and others who went to find it, but I only recently found it myself. There's a church (signed) which probably occupies a stone-circle site (some stones dated AD 800). A pathway by the graveyard leads to a promontory above the Kinaldy Burn. The pools here are reputedly where the druid priests made human sacrifices to appease the gods. Steps lead to a narrow gorge – The Den – where a Celtic cross has been carved into the rock face. I was there on a windy, monochrome day in winter. It is certainly a powerful, even spooky place. Walk through the woods can be circular back to the road (3km).

The Necropolis **Glasgow** Report: 1928/GRAVEYARDS.

Loanhead of Daviot Stone Circle **nr Inverurie** Report: 1868/PREHISTORIC.

the
Best
of Strolls, Walks
& Hikes

Favourite Hills

Popular and notable hills in the various regions of Scotland but not including Munros or difficult climbs. Always best to remember that the weather can change very quickly. Take an OS map on higher tops. See p. 12 for walk codes.

1982 4/K14
2-C-3

✓✓ **Suilven** Lochinver From close or far away, this is one of Scotland's most awe-inspiring mountains. The 'sugar loaf' can seem almost insurmountable, but in good weather it's not so difficult. Route from Inverkirkaig, 5km S of Lochinver on road to Achiltibuie, turns up track by fabled Achin's Bookshop, hopefully still there when you read this, on the path for the Kirkaig Falls; once at the loch, you head for the Bealach, the central waistline through an unexpected dyke and follow track to the top. The slightly quicker route from the N (Glencanisp) following a stalkers' track that eventually leads to Elphin, also heads for the central breach in the mountain's defences. Either way it's a long walk in; 8km before the climb. Allow 8 hours return. At the top, the most enjoyable 100m in the land and below – amazing Assynt. 731m. Take OS map.

1983 4/J15
2-B-3

✓✓ **Stac Pollaidh/Polly** nr Ullapool This hill described variously as 'perfect', 'preposterous' and 'great fun'; it certainly has character and, rising out of the Sutherland moors on the road to Achiltibuie off the A835 N, demands to be climbed. Route everyone takes is from the car park by Loch Lurgainn 8km from main road. The last lap to the pinnacles is exposed and can be off-putting. Best half-day hill climb in the North. 613m. Allow 3-4 hours return. NB: Be alert to erosion of the path (that our footsteps make).

1984 4/K14
2-B-3

✓✓ **Quinag** nr Lochinver Pronounced 'Koonyag'. Like Stac Polly (above), this Corbett has amazing presence and seems more formidable than it actually is. Park off the A894 – great views from several viewpoints N of Kylesku – where great seafood awaits (1096/HIGHLANDS). An up-and-down route can take in 6 or 7 tops in your 5-hour expedition (or curtail). Once again, awesome Assynt!

1985 7/J27
2-B-2

✓ **Goat Fell** Arran Starting from the car park by the Arran Brewery/The Wineport Café, 3km from town, or from Corrieburn Bridge S of Corrie further up the coast (12km). A worn path, a steady climb, rarely much of a scramble; a rewarding afternoon's exertion. Some scree and some view! 874m. Usually not circular. Allow 5 hours. Brodick best for refreshments.

1986 7/K24
2-B-3

✓ **The Cobbler (aka Ben Arthur)** Arrochar Perennial favourite of Glasgow hillwalkers and, for sheer exhilaration, the most popular of the Arrochar Alps. A good path ascends from the A83 on the other side of Loch Long from Arrochar (park in lay-bys near Succoth road end; there are always loads of cars) and takes 2.5-3 hours to traverse the up 'n' down route to the top. Just short of a Munro at 881m, it has 3 tops, of which the N peak is the simplest scramble (central and S peaks for climbers). Where the way is unclear, consult map/fellow travellers.

● ●

5 MAGNIFICENT HILLS IN THE TROSSACHS

1987 8/L24
2-B-3

✓ **Ben Venue & Ben A'an** 2 celebrated tops in the Highland microcosm of the Trossachs around Loch Achray; strenuous but not difficult and with superb views. Ben Venue (729m) is more serious; allow 4-5 hours return. Start from Kinlochard side at Ledard or more usually from Loch Katrine corner, the car park before Loch Achray Hotel. Ben A'an (pronounced 'An'), 454m, starts with a steep climb from the main A821 near the same corner before the Tigh Mor timeshare apartments. Some slithering (recent timber ops). An awesome stone staircase leads to an easy scramble at top. Allow 2-3 hours. Many others do walk this way. Refresh at **The Byre** (1345/FOOD PUBS).

1988 8/L23
2-B-3
Ben Shian Strathyre Another Trossachs favourite and not taxing. From village main road (the A74 to Lochearnhead), cross bridge opposite Munro Inn, turn left after 200m, then path on right after 50m. A steep start through woods. Overlooking village, views to Crianlarich and Ben Vorlich (see below). 600m. 3 hours return.

1989 8/L24
1-B-1
Doon Hill The Fairy Knowe, Aberfoyle Legendary hillock, only 2.5 hours return from Aberfoyle, so a gentle elevation into faery land. The tree at the top is the home of the People of Quietness; one local minister had the temerity to tell their secrets (in 1692) and paid the price thereafter. Go round it 7 times and your wish will be granted, go round backwards at your peril (you wouldn't, would you?). From main street take Manse Rd. 1km past cemetery, then signed.

1990 8/L24
2-B-3
Ben Ledi nr Callander A Corbett (879m, seems higher than it is), the Trossachs spread before you as you climb. W from town on A84 through Pass of Leny. First left over bridge to car park. Well-trodden path, ridge at top. Return via Stank Glen then follow river. Allow 4 hours. **The Lade Inn** for a (choice of 200) beers (1324/REAL-ALE PUBS), and **Mhor Bread** for the picnic (1480/BAKERS).

● ●

1991 7/H24
1-A-1
✓ **Dunadd Kilmartin** Halfway from Kilmartin on A816. Less of a hill, more of a lump, but it's where they crowned the kings of Dalriada for half a millennium. Rocky staircases and soft, grassy top. Stand there when the Atlantic rain is sheeting in and ... you get wet, presumably like the kings did. Or when the light is good you can see the glen and distant coast. **Kilmartin House Museum** nearby for info and great food (2172/HISTORY; 1414/TEAROOMS) – closed Sep 2019-2021.

1992 9/N30
2-A-2
Criffel New Abbey, nr Dumfries 12km S by A710 to New Abbey, which Criffel dominates. It's only 569m, but seems higher. Exceptional views from top as far as English lakes. Granite lump with brilliant outcrops of quartzite. The annual race gets up and back to the Abbey Arms in under an hour; you can take it easier. Start from village, or 3km S of village, the turn-off from the A710, 100m from one of the curious painted bus shelters signed for Ardwell Mains Farm. Over there the Solway shimmers.

1993 9/L29
2-B-3
Merrick nr Newton Stewart Go from bonnie Glen Trool via Bargrennan 14km N on the A714. **Bruce's Stone** is there at the start (1958/BOB). The highest peak in southern Scotland (843m), it's a strenuous though straightforward climb, a grassy ridge to the summit and glorious scenery. 6 hours.

1994 8/R25
BOTH 1-A-1
North Berwick Law The conical volcanic hill, a beacon in the East Lothian landscape. **Traprain Law** nearby (signed from A1), is higher, easy and celebrated by rock climbers, but has major prehistoric significance as a hill fort citadel of the Goddodin and a definite aura. NBL is also simple and rewarding – leave town by Law Rd, path marked beyond houses. Car park and picnic site. Views 'to the Cairngorms'(!) and along the Forth. Whalebone at the top. Many food options in North Berwick.

1995 8/R28 **Ruberslaw** **Denholm, nr Hawick** This smooth hummock above the Teviot valley
2-A-2 affords views of 7 counties, including Northumberland. Millennium plaque on top.
At 424m, it's a gentle climb, taking about 1 hour from the usual start at Denholm
Hill Farm (be aware of livestock). Leave Denholm at corner of green by post office
and go past war memorial. Take left after 2km to farm. **Ruberslaw Wild Woods
Campsite**, one of Scotland's best (1261/CAMPING WITH KIDS).

1996 8/N27 **Tinto Hill** **nr Biggar & Lanark** A Clyde Valley landmark and favourite climb in
2-A-2 South/Central Scotland, with easy access to start from Fallburn on the A73 near
Symington, 10km S of Lanark. Park 100m behind Tinto Hills farm shop. Good,
simple track there and back though it has its ups and downs before you get there.
Braw views. 707m (it's a Graham). Allow 2.5 hours.

1997 7/L24 **Conic Hill** **Balmaha, Loch Lomond** An easier climb than the Ben up the road
2-A-2 and a good place to view it from. Conic, on the Highland fault line, is one of the first
Highland hills you reach from Glasgow. Stunning views also of Loch Lomond from
its 361m peak. Ascend through woodland from the corner of Balmaha (the visitor
centre) car park. Watch for buzzards and your footing on the final crumbly bits.
Easy walks also on the nearby island, **Inchcailloch** (2068/WALKS). 1.5 hours up.

1998 8/N21 **Ben Vrackie** **Pitlochry** Small mountain, magnificent views. **Moulin Inn** to
2-A-2 return to for pub grub (1322/REAL-ALE PUBS). Woods, moorland, a loch and a bit of
a steep finish (at 841m, it's a Corbett). For the start, take A924 from Moulin (1.5km
uphill from Pitlochry), going straight ahead when the road turns left to the car park
300m further on. Track well signed and obvious. 4 hours.

1999 8/P23 **Kinnoull Hill** **Perth** Various starts from town and A85, e.g. Manse Rd and the
1-A-1 Quarry car park. The wooded ridge above the Tay with its tower and incredible
views to S from the precipitous cliffs. Surprisingly extensive area of hillside
(Kinnoull Hill Woodland Park) can include Deuchny Hill, and it's not difficult to
get lost. Look for the 'Arboretum'. The leaflet/map from Perth tourist information
centre helps. Quarry car park a good start (though not signed as such) – it's a local
lurve spot after dark.

2000 6/R19 **Bennachie** **nr Aberdeen** The must-do-one-day hill, an easy 528m, often busy
2-B-2 at weekends but never lets you down. Various trails take you to 'the Taps' from 3
main car parks. (1) From the Bennachie Centre (01467 681470): 10km N of Inverurie
on the A96, take left to Chapel of Garioch (pronounced 'Geery'), then left (it's
signed). (2) 16km N of Inverurie on the A96, take the B9002 through Oyne, then
signed on left – picnic here among the pines. (3) The Rowantree car park 5km N
of Monymusk towards Blairdaff – the longer though easier walk in. All car parks
have trail-finders. From the fortified top you see Aberdeenshire. Allow 3 hours.
Bennachie's soulmate, **Tap o' Noth**, is 20km W. Easy approach via Rhynie on A97
(then 3km). Refresh: **Old Post Office**, Chapel of Garioch 1438/TEAROOMS.

2001 3/C20 **Heaval** **Barra** The mini-Matterhorn that rises above Castlebay is an easy and
2-B-2 rewarding climb. At 383m, it's steep in places but never over-taxing. You see 'the
road to Mingulay'. Start up hill through Castlebay, park behind the new-build house
and find path via Our Lady, Star of the Sea. 1.5 hours return.

Hill Walks

The following ranges of hills offer walks in various directions and more than one summit. They are all accessible and fairly easy. See p. 12 for walk codes.

2002 5/G18 **Walks on Skye** Obviously many serious walks in and around the **Cuillin** (2020/ MUNROS; 2030/WALKS), but almost infinite variety of others. Can do no better than read a great book, *50 Best Routes on Skye and Raasay* by Ralph Storer (available locally), which describes and grades many of the must-dos.

2003 8/P24 **Lomond Hills nr Falkland** The conservation village lies below a prominent ridge
3-10KM easily reached from the main street, especially via Back Wynd (off which there's a
CIRC car park). More usual approach to both East and West Lomond, the main tops, is
XBIKES from Craigmead car park 3km from village towards Leslie trail-finder board. The
2-A-2 celebrated Lomonds (aka the Paps of Fife), aren't that high (West is 522m), but they can see and be seen for miles. Also: easy start from radio masts 3km up road from A912 E of Falkland. 1432/TEAROOMS and 4 pubs in the village.
An easy rewarding single climb is **Bishop Hill**. Start 100m from the church in Scotlandwell. A steep path (150m down main road) veers left and then there are several ways up. Allow 2.5 hours. Great view of Loch Leven and a good swathe of Central Scotland. Sheep tracks down to Kinnesswood (park a second car to save walk back). Gliders overhead from the airstrip below.

2004 8/R27 **The Eildons Melrose** The 3 much-loved hills or paps visible from most of the
3KM central Borders and easily climbed from the town of Melrose which nestles at their
CIRC foot. Leave main square by road to station (the Dingleton road); after 100m a path
XBIKES begins between 2 pebble-dash houses on the left. You climb the smallest first, then
1-A-2 the highest central one (422m). You can make a circular route of it by returning to the golf course. Allow 2 hours. Good pub and food options in Melrose; p. 146-7.

2005 8/N24 **The Ochils** Usual approach from the 'hillfoot towns' at the foot of the glens that
2-40KM cut into their south-facing slopes, along the A91 Stirling-St Andrews road. Alva,
SOME CIRC Tillicoultry and Dollar all have impressive glen walks easily found from the main
XBIKES streets where tracks are marked (2041/GLEN WALKS). Good start near Stirling from
1/2-B-2 the Sheriffmuir road uphill from Bridge of Allan about 3km, look for pylons and a lay-by on the right (a reservoir just visible on the left). Usually other cars here. A stile leads to the hills which stretch away to the east for 40km and afford great views for little effort, e.g. from Dumyat (3 hour return) though the highest point is Ben Cleugh at 721m. Swimming place nearby is 'Paradise' (1734/SWIMMING).

2006 8/R26 **The Lammermuirs** The hills SE of Edinburgh that divide East Lothian's rich
5-155KM farmlands from the Borders' Tweed valley. Mostly high moorland but there's
SOME CIRC wooded gentle hill country in the watersheds of the southern rivers and
MT BIKES spectacular coastal scenery between Cockburnspath and **St Abb's Head** (1800/
1/2-B-2 RESERVES; 2087/WALKS). Eastern part of the **Southern Upland Way**, follows the Lammermuirs to the coast (2026/WALKS). Many fine walks begin at Whiteadder Reservoir car park (A1 to Haddington, the B6355 through Gifford), then 10km to a mysterious loch in the bowl of the hills. Also, the 10km 428m Priestlaw Hill circuit to the south and the Sparleton Hill loop, 10km, 465m, and around **Abbey St Bathans** (head off A1 at Cockburnspath): through village to Toot Corner

(signed 1km) and off to left, follow path above valley of Whiteadder to Edin's Hall Broch (2km) and then find a sublime swimming spot at **Elba (Swing) Bridge** (1718/SWIMMING). Circular walks possible; ask in village. **The Yester Estate** near Gifford is nearer Edinburgh and a good foothill option (435/WALKS).

2007 5/L17 **Knockfarrel Dingwall to Strathpeffer** A walk (around 8km) between the two
3KM   towns N of Inverness along the ridge between the A834 and A835 that includes
CIRC   Knockfarrel, an Iron Age fort site on a raised plateau with views of the valleys, Loch
XBIKES   Ussie and the Cromarty Firth. Non-taxing, hugely rewarding and damned pleasant.
1-A-2   Find starts in either town or drive to Knockfarrel from the A835 Dingwall–Contin
NC500   road off the A9, turning at the sign for the red kites. Go past kite turn-off to the
T-junction, turn left and 500m further, finish on a rough track to the car park.

2008 8/S27 **The Cheviots** Not strictly in Scotland but they straddle the border and Border
history. Many fine walks start from Kirk Yetholm (such as the Pennine Way
stretching 400km S to the Peak district and **St Cuthbert's Way** 2029/WALKS),
including an 8km circular route of typical Cheviot foothill terrain. Many walking
guides available at Border tourist centres. Most forays start at Wooler, 20km from
Coldstream. Cheviot itself (815m) is a boggy plateau; Hedgehope via the Harthope
Burn more fun. In 2014 I was privileged to give 'The Redeswire Address' at the
Redeswire Stone by **Carter Bar** (1714/VIEWS).

2009 8/N23 **The Knock Crieff** The short, steep-to-start, wooded hill above Crieff. Easy to
5KM · CIRC   access (follow signs for **Crieff Hydro** 1166/KIDS 2km further and park) with great
XBIKES   views across Strath Earn. Only recently climbed by me, a good after-lunch or
2-A-2   before-dinner constitutional.

Campsie Fells nr Glasgow Report: 695/WALKS OUTSIDE GLASGOW.

The Pentlands nr Edinburgh Report: 427/WALKS OUTSIDE EDINBURGH.

Some Great Easy Munros

There are almost 300 hills in Scotland over 3,000ft as tabled by Sir Hugh Munro in 1891. Those selected here have been chosen for their relative ease of access both to the bottom and thence to the top. Tackle only what is within your range of experience and ability. All these offer rewarding climbs. None should be attempted without proper clothing (especially boots) and sustenance. You may also need an OS map or GPS thing. Never underestimate how fast weather conditions can change in the Scottish mountains.

2010 7/L24 **Ben Lomond Rowardennan, Loch Lomond** Many folks' first Munro, given
proximity to Glasgow (soul and city). It's not too taxing a climb and has rewarding
views (in good weather). 2 main ascents: the tourist route is easier, from toilet
block at Rowardennan car park (end of road from Drymen), well-trodden all the
way; or 500m up past Youth Hostel, a path follows burn – the Ptarmigan Route.
Steeper but quieter, more interesting. Circular walk possible. 974m. 3 hours up.

2011 8/M22 **Schiehallion nr Kinloch Rannoch** Fairy Hill of the Caledonians and a bit of a
must (though very busy). New path c/o John Muir Trust over E flank. Start Braes of
Foss car park 10k from KR. 10km walk, ascent 750m. 5 hours. 1,083m.

2012 8/P21 **Càrn Aosda Glenshee** Very accessible, starting from Glenshee ski car park; follow ski tow up. Ascent only 270m of 917m, so bag a Munro in an hour. Easier still, take chairlift to Cairnwell, take in peak behind and then Càrn Aosda – and you're doing three Munros in a morning (cheating, but hey). The Grampian Highlands unfold. Another easy (500m to climb) Munro nearby is **Carn an Tuirc** from the A93.

2013 5/M20 **Meall Chuaich Dalwhinnie** Starting from verge of the A9 S of Cuaich at Cuaich cottages. Ascent only 623m, though the total walk is 14km. Follow aqueduct to power station then Loch Cuaich. An easily bagged 951m.

2014 5/J16 **An Teallach Torridon** Sea-level start from Dundonnell on the A832 S of Ullapool. One of the most awesome Scots peaks, not the ordeal it looks. Path well trodden; great scrambling opportunities for the nimble. Peering over the pinnacle of Lord Berkeley's Seat into the void is a jaw-drop. Take a day. 1,062m.

2015 5/H17 **Beinn Alligin Torridon** The other great Torridon trek. Consult regarding start at NTS Countryside Centre on corner of Glen Torridon–Diabaig road. Car park by bridge on road to Inveralligin and then Diabaig (1678/SCENIC ROUTES), where there's a brill wee bistro, the **Gille Brighde** (1099/HIGHLANDS). Walk through woods over moor by river. Steepish pull up on to the Horns of Alligin. You can cover 2 Munros in a circular route that takes you across the top of the world. 985m. Then you could tackle **Liathach** (trickier); **Beinn Eighe**, also from a start on Glen Torridon road (probably easiest).

2016 7/G23 **Ben More Mull** The cool, high ben sits in isolated splendour, the only Munro bar the Cuillin not on the mainland. Sea-level start from the bridge over the Scarisdale river on the coast road B8035, 5km SW of Gruline, that skirts the southern coast of Loch Na Keal, then a fairly clear path through river gorge and rocky landscape. Tricky near the top but breathtaking views over the islands. 966m. 6/7 hours.

2017 4/L13 **Ben Hope nr Tongue** The most northerly Munro and many a bagger's last; also a good one to start with. Steep and craggy with splendid views, the approach from the south is relatively easy and takes about 5 hours there and back. Go S from Hope (on the A38) on the unclassified road to Strathmore. 927m.

2018 5/L17 **Ben Wyvis nr Garve** Standing apart from its northern neighbours, you can feel the presence of this mountain from a long way off. North of main A835 road Inverness–Ullapool and very accessible from it, park 6km N of Garve (48km from Inverness) and follow marked path by stream and through the shattered remnants of what was once a forest (replanting in progress). Leave the dereliction behind; the summit approach is by a soft, mossy ridge. Magnificent 1,046m.

2019 8/Q20 **Lochnagar nr Ballater** Described as a fine, complex mountain, its nobility and mystique apparent from afar, not least Balmoral Castle. Approach via Glen Muick (pronounced 'Mick') road from Ballater to car park at Spittal of Glen Muick at the loch (1671/LOCHS). Path to mountain well signed and well trodden. 18km return, allow 6-8 hours. Steep at top; the loch supernatural. Apparently on a clear day you can see the Forth Bridge. 1,155m.

2020 5/G19 **Blà Bheinn Skye** Pronounced 'Blahven'. The magnificent massif, isolated from the other Cuillin, has a sea-level start and seems higher than it is. The *Munro Guide* describes it optimistically as 'exceptionally accessible'. It has an eerie jagged beauty and – though some scrambling is involved and it helps to have a head for exposed situations – there are no serious dangers. Take B8083 from Broadford to Elgol through Torrin, park 1km S of the head of Loch Slapin, walking W at Allt na Dunaiche along N bank of stream. Blà Bheinn is an enormously rewarding climb. Rapid descent for scree runners, but allow 8 hours. 928m. The Blue Shed on the road overlooking loch should not be missed (1402/CAFÉS).

2021 8/M22   **Ben Lawers**   **nr Killin**   The massif of 7 summits, including 6 Munros that dominate the N side of Loch Tay, linked by a 12km twisting ridge that only once falls below 800m. If you're fit, you can do the lot in a day starting from the N or Glen Lyon side. Have an easier day of it knocking off Beinn Ghlas then Ben Lawers from the Lawers car park, 5km off the A827. 4/5 hours. Refresh at Aberfeldy: 923/PERTHSHIRE; 1419/1428/TEAROOMS.

2022 8/M22   **Meall Nan Tarmachan**   **nr Killin**   The part of the ridge W of Lawers (above), which takes in a Munro and several tops, is one of the easiest Munro climbs and is immensely impressive. Start 1km further on from Lawers car park down 100m track and through gate. Slog to start. 12km walk, climb 800m, allow 6 hours.

2023 5/H19   **Ladhar Bheinn**   **Knoydart**   Pronounced 'Larven'. 1 of 3 Munros on the Knoydart Peninsula – many a bagger's last call but not least (though all 3 can be done together). 1,020m.

▰▰ Long Walks

These walks require preparation, maps, good boots, etc. Don't carry too much. Sections are always possible. See p. 12 for walk codes.

2024 7/K23   **2-B-3**   ✓ **The West Highland Way** www.west-highland-way.co.uk The 150km walk which starts at Milngavie 12km outside Glasgow and goes via some of Scotland's most celebrated scenery to emerge in Glen Nevis before the Ben. The route goes like this: Mugdock Moor–Drymen–Loch Lomond–Rowardennan–Inversnaid–Inverarnan–Crianlarich–Tyndrum–Bridge of Orchy–Rannoch Moor–Kingshouse Hotel–Glen Coe–The Devil's Staircase–Kinlochleven. The latter part from Bridge of Orchy is the most dramatic. **Bridge of Orchy Hotel** (01838 400208; 1211/INNS. Best; not cheap!) and the newly smart **Kingshouse** (1060/HIGHLANDS) are both historic staging posts, as is the **Drover's Inn**, Inverarnan (1312/GOOD PUBS). When booking accom, allow time for fatigue; don't carry a lot.
START Officially at Milngavie (pronounced 'Mill-guy') Railway Station (regular services from Glasgow Central and Queen Street, also buses from Buchanan St Bus Station), but actually from Milngavie shopping precinct 500m away. However, the countryside is close. From other end on Glen Nevis road from roundabout on A82 N from Fort William. The Way is well marked; there's a good *Official Pocket Companion* or download from website.

2025 5/J19   **& 5/K19**   **2-C-3**   ✓ **Glen Affric** In enchanting Glen Affric and Loch Affric beyond (2025/WALKS; 1642/GLENS; 1727/SWIMMING), some serious walking begins on the 32km Kintail trail. Done either west-east starting at Morvich, 2km from A87 near Shiel Bridge, or east-west starting at the Affric Lodge 15km W of Cannich. Route can include one of the approaches to the **Falls of Glomach** (1651/WATERFALLS).

2026 9/P28   **2-B-3**   **The Southern Upland Way** www.southernuplandway.gov.uk 350km walk from Portpatrick across the Rhinns of Galloway, much moorland, the Galloway Forest Park, the wild heartland of Southern Scotland, then through **James Hogg**

country (1966/LITERARY PLACES) to the gentler east Borders and the sea at Pease Bay (official end, Cockburnspath). Route is Portpatrick-Stranraer-New Luce-Dalry-Sanquhar-Wanlockhead-Beattock-St Mary's Loch-Melrose-Lauder-Abbey St Bathans. The first and latter sections are the most obviously picturesque but highlights include Loch Trool, the Lowther Hills, St Mary's Loch, Traquair, Melrose and the River Tweed. Usually walked west-east, the Southern Upland Way is a formidable undertaking. Info from **Ranger Service** (West section: 07834 567893; East section: 01835 826750).
START Portpatrick by the harbour and up along the cliffs past the lighthouse. Or Cockburnspath. Map is on side of shop at the Cross.

2027 6/Q18
1-A-3

The Speyside Way www.speysideway.org A long-distance route that generally follows the valley of the River Spey from Buckie on the Moray Firth coast to Aviemore in the foothills of the Cairngorms, with a side spur to Tomintoul over the hill between the River Avon (pronounced 'A'rn') and the River Livet (24km). The main stem of the route largely follows the valley bottom, criss-crossing the Spey several times – a distance of around 100km, and is less strenuous than Southern Upland or West Highland Ways. The Tomintoul spur has more hill-walking character and rises to a great viewpoint at 600m. Throughout the walk you are in whisky country with opportunities to visit **Cardhu**, **Glenlivet** and other distilleries nearby (1541/1538/WHISKY). Info from **Ranger Service** (01340 881266).
START Usual start is from Spey Bay 8km N of Fochabers (from Buckie adds another 8km); the first marker is by the banks of shingle at the river mouth.

2028 8/Q22
2-B-3

The Cateran Trail Named after the Caterans who were marauding cattle thieves, this 100km hike crosses their old stamping ground, the splendid hills and glens of Angus and Perthshire. Splendid circular from a start at Blairgowrie and 4/5 days to complete; there are also 5 sections: Blairgowrie-Bridge of Cally-Glenshee-Glen Isla-Alyth. Inn options on the way, especially **The Strathardle Inn** www.strathardleinn.co.uk · **01250 881224**, a classic walkers' pub/bistro/hotel.

2029 8/S27
2-A-3

St Cuthbert's Way From Melrose in the Borders (where St Cuthbert started his ministry) to Lindisfarne on Holy Island off Northumberland (where he died) via St Boswells-Kirk Yetholm-Wooler. 100km but many sections easy. Bowden-Maxton and a stroll by the Tweed especially fine. Causeway to Holy Island a treat at the end. Good refreshment options Melrose and St Boswells.

Serious Walks

None of these should be attempted without OS maps, equipment and preparation. Hill- or ridge-walking experience may be essential. See p.12 for walk codes.

2030 5/G19
3-C-3

The Cuillin Mountains Skye Much scrambling and, if you want it, serious climbing over these famously unforgiving peaks. The Red ones are easier and many walks start at the **Sligachan Hotel** on the main Portree-Broadford road (2284/SKYE). In July there's a hill race up Glamaig, the conical one overlooking the hotel. Most of the Black Cuillin, including the highest, Sgurr Alasdair (993m), and Sgurr Dearg, 'the Inaccessible Pinnacle' (978m), can be attacked from the campsite or the youth hostel in Glen Brittle. Good guides are *Introductory Scrambles from Glen Brittle* by Charles Rhodes, or *50 Best Routes in Skye and Raasay* by Ralph Storer, both available locally, but you will need a map. See also 2/ATTRACTIONS; 1189/HOSTELS; 1659/WATERFALLS; 2020/MUNROS; 1716/SWIMMING.

2031 7/K22 **Aonach Eagach Glen Coe** One of several possible major expeditions in the Glen
3-C-3 Coe area and one of the world's classic ridge walks. Not for the faint-hearted or
the ill-prepared. It's the ridge on your right for almost the whole length of the glen
from Altnafeadh to the road to the **Clachaig Inn** (rewarding refreshment). Start
from main road, at (very small) car park opposite the one for the **Lost Valley** (1971/
ENCHANTING PLACES). Stiff pull up then the switchback path across. There is no
turning back. Scary pinnacles two-thirds over, then one more Munro and the knee-
trembling, scree-running descent. On your way, you'll have come close to heaven,
seen Lochaber in its immense glory and reconnoitred some fairly exposed edges
and pinnacles. Go with somebody good as I once did. See also 1675/SCENIC ROUTES;
1313/GOOD PUBS; 1203/HOSTELS; 1946/BATTLEGROUNDS.

2032 7/K22 **Buachaille Etive Mòr Glen Coe** In same area as above, another of the UK's
3-C-3 best high-level hauls. Not as difficult or precarious as the Eagach and long loved by
climbers and walkers, with stunning views from its several false summits to the actual
top with its severe drops. Start on main Glen Coe road. 5km past reborn **Kingshouse
Hotel** (1060/HIGHLANDS). Well-worn path. Allow 6/7 hours return. 1,022m.

2033 7/K21 **Ben Nevis** Start on Glen Nevis road, 5km Fort William town centre (by bridge from
2-B-3 visitor centre). Ascent starts from Achintee Farm and the **Ben Nevis Inn** (handy
afterwards 1140/FORT WILLIAM). This, 'The Mountain Path', is the most popular and
safest route. Allow the best part of a day (and we do mean the best – the weather
can turn quickly here). For the more interesting and tougher arete route, allow
8/9 hours. There are accidents on this mountain even with experienced climbers
so take great care. It is the biggest, though not perhaps the best; you can see 100
Munros on a clear day (i.e. about once a year). You climb it because ... you have to.
1,344m.

2034 5/J19 **The Five Sisters of Kintail & The Cluanie Ridge** Both generally started from
3-C-3 A87 along from **Cluanie Inn** (1317/GOOD PUBS) and they will keep you right; usually
walked east to west. Sisters is an uncomplicated but inspiring ridge walk, taking in
3 Munros and 2 tops. It's a hard pull up and you descend to a point 8km further up
the road (so arrange transport). Many side spurs to vantage points and wild views.
The Cluanie or south ridge is a classic which covers 7 Munros. Starts at inn; 2 ways
off back on to A876. Both can be walked in a single day (Cluanie allow 9 hours).
From Morvich off A87 near Shiel Bridge another long-distance walk starts to **Glen
Affric** (2025/WALKS).

2035 6/N19 **Glenmore Forest Park** From Coylumbridge and Loch Morlich; 32km through the
3-C-3 **Rothiemurchus Forest** (2065/WALKS) and the famous **Lairig Ghru**, the ancient
right of way through the Cairngorms which passes between Ben Macdui and
Braeriach. Ascent is over 700m and going can be rough. This is one of the great
Scottish trails. At end of June, the Lairig Ghru Race completes this course
east-west in 3.5 hours, but generally this is a full-day trip. The famous shelter,
Corrour Bothy between Devil's Point and Càrn a' Mhàim, can be a halfway house.
Near Linn of Dee, routes converge and pass through the ancient Caledonian Forest
of Mar. Going east-west is less gruelling and there's Aviemore to look forward to!

Glen & River Walks

See also Great Glens, p. 279-80. See p.12 for walk codes.

2036 8/N21
UP TO 17KM
CIRC
XBIKES
1-B-2

✓ **Glen Tilt Blair Atholl** A walk of variable length in this classic Highland glen, easily accessible from the old Blair Rd off main Blair Atholl road near Bridge of Tilt Hotel, car park by the (very) old bridge. Trail leaflet from park office and local tourist information centres. Fine walking and unspoiled scenery begin only a short distance into the deeply wooded gorge of the River Tilt, but to cover the circular route you have to walk to Gilbert's Bridge (9km return) or the longer trail to Gow's Bridge (17km return). Begin here also the great route into the Cairngorms leading to the Linn of Dee and Braemar, joining the track from Speyside which starts at **Feshiebridge** (1719/SWIMMING) or **Glenmore Forest** (2071/WALKS).

2037 5/J19
5/8KM
CIRC
BIKES
1-B-2

✓ **Glen Affric Cannich, nr Drumnadrochit** Easy short walks are marked and hugely rewarding in this magnificent glen well known as the first stretch in the great east-west route to Kintail (2025/WALKS) and the **Falls of Glomach** (1651/WATERFALLS). Starting point of this track into the wilds is at the end of the road at Loch Affric; there are many short and circular trails indicated and in Forestry Commission's free guide, locally available. Track closed in stalking season. Easier walks in famous Affric forest from car park at **Dog Falls**, 7km from Cannich (1727/SWIMMING). Waterfalls and spooky tame birds. Good idea to hire bikes at Drumnadrochit or Cannich (01456 415364). See also 1642/GLENS.

2038 4/J14
6KM
CIRC
XBIKES
1-B-2
NC500

✓ **Glen Canisp and the Inver River Lochinver** An enchanting river and woodland walk, with a middle section up an easy hill. A 6km 'loop' in a broad sweep round the back of Lochinver. Best from N to S starting on the bridge at the junction of the road to Baddidarach, on fisherman paths along the river, among beautiful mixed trees with some Scots pine. Well maintained and signed, you ascend 75m to fine views with Suilven presiding, and back into the village via **Glencanisp Lodge** (1067/HIGHLANDS). Don't forget the pies at the **Riverside Bistro** (1481/BAKERS).

2039 8/M24
4KM
XCIRC
1-B-1

✓ **The Darn Walk** A perfect amble in any season following the Allan Water between Bridge of Allan and Dunblane. Sometimes on the banks, at others high above; the river in different aspects totally endears itself. The path crosses two tumbling tributaries, the Wharry Burn and Cock's Burn (can be tricky). Not circular, so two cars needed, or the bus, or best, the train. Starts by BoA station at the bridge, Henderson St to Blairforkie Dr – 500m, then a gap in the wall and a sign for 'Dunblane 2.5 miles'. Enter Dunblane across the golf course. Allow 2 hours one way. **Jam Jar** or **Allan Water Café** in BoA for refuel (802/CENTRAL; 1405/CAFÉS).

2040 8/L24
18KM
XCIRC
XBIKES
2-B-2

✓ **Glenfinglas and Balquhidder to Brig o' Turk** Easy amble through the heart of Scotland via Glen Finglas (1670/LOCHS) from the car park on the A821 with a handy pub (1345/FOOD PUBS). The complete walk not circular (so best to arrange transport). Usual start at Balquhidder graveyard (1938/GRAVEYARDS), then Ballimore and past Ben Vane to the reservoir and Brig o' Turk (5 hours). Starts for shorter walks at B o' T and on the A821. And many options both short and long from the Visitor Centre.

2041 8/N24
3KM + TOPS
CIRC
XBIKES
1-A-2

✓ **Dollar Glen Dollar** The classic fairy glen in central Scotland, positively hoaching with water spirits, reeking of ozone and euphoric after rain. 20km by A91 from Stirling or 18km from M90 at Kinross junction 6. You walk by the Burn of Care and the Burn of Sorrow. Start at side of the volunteer-run museum or golf club, or further up road (signed Castle Campbell) where there are 2 car parks, the top one 5 mins from castle. The castle at head of glen is open 7 days, last entry 5.30pm (Oct-Mar 4pm) and has boggling views. There's a circular walk back (3km) or take off for the Ochil Tops, the hills surrounding the glen. There are also first-class walks up the glens of the other hillfoot towns, Alva and Tillicoultry, which also lead to the hills (2005/HILL WALKS).

2042 8/N24
3KM
CIRC
XBIKES
1-A-1

✓ **Rumbling Bridge nr Dollar** Formed by another burn off the Ochils, an easier short figure-of-eight walk in a glen with something of the chasmic experience, and added delight of the unique double bridge (built 1713). At the end of one of the walkways under the bridge you are looking into a Scottish jungle landscape as the Romantics imagined. Near Powmill on A977 from Kinross (junction 6, M90) then 2km. Up the road is The **Powmill Milk Bar** serving very traditional home-made food for over 40 years. It's 5km W on the A977. 7 days, daytime only.

2043 8/P22
16KM
CIRC
BIKES
1-A-2

✓ **Loch Ordie nr Dunkeld** Not a walk through a specific glen or riverside but one which follows many burns past lochs and ponds, skirts some impressive hills and is all in all a splendid and simple hike through glorious country almost Highland in nature but close to the Central Belt. Loch Ordie is halfway on a loop that starts at a bend on the A923 Blairgowrie road on left about 7km from Dunkeld, after the turn-off for Loch of the Lowes (near the sign and gateway to Cardney House) or signed from Butterstone 7km (and can combine with walk to Loch of the Lowes 3km). Deuchary Hill, the highest here at 509m, can be climbed on a non-circular path from the main circuit. This is one of the best, most scenic walks in Perthshire. Mostly level.

2044 8/Q21

✓ **Glen Clova Walks** Most walked of the Angus glens. Many start from end at Acharn, especially W to Glen Doll (ranger centre for orientation, etc). Also enquire at **Glen Clova Hotel** (1227/GET-AWAY HOTELS) – 2-hour Loops of (Loch) Brandy walk starts here – and repair there afterwards (great walkers' pub). Easy!

2045 8/R23
BIKES
1-A-1

✓ **The Lade Braes St Andrews** Unlike most walks on these pages, this cuts through the town itself following the Kinness Burn. But you are removed from all that! Start at Westport at the traffic lights just after the garage on Bridge St or (marked) opposite 139 South St. Trailboard and signs. Through Cockshaugh Park (side spur to Botanics on opposite bank) and the leafy glen and green sward at the edge of this famously fine town. Ends in a duck pond. You pass the back gardens of some very comfortable lives. 2 routes are described in *St Andrews Local Walks* available at the TIC.

2046 5/M17
BIKES
1-A-1

✓ **The Fairy Glen Rosemarkie** On the Black Isle. On the main A832, the road to Cromarty, 150 metres after the Plough Inn on the right, a car park and information board. Beautiful, easy 3km walk with gorge, 2 waterfalls and some great birdlife. Can finish on Rosemarkie beach to picnic and look for dolphins. Some superb trees. Eat in **Cromarty** (1608/VILLAGES).

2047 8/L24
2-7KM
CIRC
1-A-1

✓ **Loch Ard Walks nr Aberfoyle** Pleasant Trossachs ambles through mixed forestry by Loch Ard and other lochans. Start around Milton on the B829 3km W of Aberfoyle. Trailboards. 4 walks marked, from 3-14km, one a 'Sculpture Trail'. Wildlife abounds. A good family outing.

2048 8/N23
8KM · XCIRC
XBIKES
1-B-1

✓ **River Earn Perthshire** An easy riverside amble in Perthshire between Crieff and Muthill. Not circular so two cars best or bus. I'd recommend starting at Crieff, from the corner of the Stuart Crystal Visitor Centre, on the road between the towns. Follow the yellow arrow waymarkers and take care not to miss the one in

Sallyardoch Wood near the end. No effort, and an unsung, surprising and beautiful river to follow. Great food at **The Barley Bree** in Muthill (1205/INNS). Improved track and bridge at TGP.

2049 8/P20
2-8KM
XCIRC
XBIKES
1-B-2

The River Quoich nr Braemar A memorable Highland walk in upper Deeside beyond Braemar (3km). Start at the Linn of Quoich at end of the road past Mar Lodge. Woods to wander and a good path as far as the Cleric's Stone, a huge erratic. The river at its most beguiling and spectacular views of Beinn a' Bhùird. Walk as far as you wish (up to 14km). This gem recommended by Brian Louden.

2050 8/Q24
3KM
CIRC
XBIKES
1-A-2

The Maspie Den, Falkland Fife If you're in Falkland for the Palace (1814/CASTLES) or the tearoom (1432/TEAROOMS), this amble up an enchanting glen is a must. Go through village then signed Cricket Club for Falkland Estate and School – car park just inside gate (with map) – and further on to the Info Hub, staffed by enthusiastic volunteers. Glen and refurbished path up the macadam road are obvious. Gushing burn, the '**Temple of Decision**', waterfalls – you can even walk behind one! Then take to the hills (2003/HILLS).

2051 4/N15
6KM
CIRC
XBIKES
1-B-1
NC500

The Big Burn Walk Golspie A non-taxing, perfect glen walk through lush diverse woodland. 3 different entrances, including car park marked from A9 near Dunrobin Castle gates, but most complete starts beyond Golspie Inn and Sutherland Stonework at the end of the village. Go past derelict mill and under aqueduct following river. A supernature trail unfolds with ancient tangled trees, meadows, waterfalls, cliffs and much wildlife. 3km to falls, return via route to castle woods for best all-round intoxication.

2052 4/P14
5KM
XCIRC
XBIKES
1-B-1
NC500

The Strath at Dunbeath The glen or strath so eloquently evoked in Neil Gunn's *Highland River* (1965/LITERARY PLACES), a book that is as much about the geography as the history of his childhood. Starting below the row of cottages on your left after the flyover going N near the much older Telford Bridge. A path follows the river for many miles. A leaflet from the Dunbeath Heritage Centre points out places on the way as well as having a map on its entire floor. It's a spate river and in summer becomes a trickle; hard to imagine Gunn's salmon odyssey. It's only 500m to the broch, but go into the more mystical hinterland (1940/GRAVEYARDS).

2053 8/Q27
5/12KM
CIRC
XBIKES
1-A-1

Tweedside Peebles etc The riverside trail that follows the Tweed from town (Hay Lodge Park), past Neidpath Castle (1724/SWIMMING), and on through classic Border wooded countryside, crossing river either 2.5km out (5km round trip), or at Manor Bridge 6km out (Lyne Footbridge, 12km). *Walking in the Scottish Borders* and many Tweedside trail guides. Other good Tweedside walks between **Dryburgh Abbey** and Bemersyde House grounds (1685/SCENIC ROUTES) and at **Newton St Boswells** by the golf course. Great pub-grub/tearoom options in **Melrose**, p. 146-7, and in St Boswells, especially **Main Street Trading** (834/BORDERS).

2054 8/L27
3/5KM
CIRC · XBIKES
1-A-1

Failford Gorge nr Mauchline Woody gorge of the River Ayr. Start from bridge at Ayr end of village on B743 Ayr–Mauchline road (4km Mauchline). Easy, marked trail. Pub in village. Particularly notable for food is the **Sorn Inn** near Mauchline (1328/FOOD PUBS). Bucolic Ayrshire at its best.

2055 8/M23
3/5KM
CIRC
XBIKES
1-A-1

Glen Lednock nr Comrie Walk to the gorge from Comrie or take the car further into the glen to reservoir (9km) for more open walks. From town take right off main A85 (to Lochearnhead) at the excellent **Deil's Cauldron** bar/restaurant (918/PERTHSHIRE). Walk and Deil's Cauldron (waterfall and gorge) are signed after 250m. Walk takes less than 1 hour and emerges on road near the **Melville Monument** (cross road and find paths up through trees for great views back towards Crieff, 1 hour return). There's also the start of a hike up Ben Chonzie, 6km up glen at Coishavachan. This is one of the easiest Munros (931m) with a good path and great views, especially to NW.

2056 6/R17
1-A-1
Bridge of Alvah Banff Details at 2077/WALKS, mentioned here because the best bit is by the river and the bridge itself. The single-span crossing was built in 1772 and stands high above the river in a sheer-sided gorge. The river below is deep and can look wild. In the right light it's almost Amazonian. Walk takes 1.5 hours from **Duff House** (2185/GALLERIES). There's a picture of Alvah upstairs in the collection.

2057 8/R21
2KM
XCIRC
XBIKES
1-A-1
The Gannochy Bridge & The Rocks of Solitude nr Edzell 2km N of village on B966 to Fettercairn. There's a lay-by after bridge and a blue wooden door on left (you're in the Edzell Woods and grounds of Burn House). Through it is another 'beech tree' world with a path above the rocky gorge of the River North Esk (3km). Huge stone ledges over dark pools. You don't have to be alone (or maybe you do).

2058 9/L29
1-B-2
Glen Trool nr Newton Stewart A simple non-clambering, well-marked route round Loch Trool. A circular 8km but with many options. And a caff at the visitor centre. See also 1648/GLENS.

Woodland Walks

See p.12 for walk codes.

2059 7/G21
✓✓ **Ardnamurchan** For anyone who loves trees (or hills, great coastal scenery and raw nature), this far-flung peninsula is a revelation. Approach from S via Corran ferry on A82 S of Fort William or N from Lochailort on A830 Mallaig–Fort William road (1689/SCENIC ROUTES) or from Mull. Many marked and unmarked trails (see Ariundle below) but consult online or locally. To visit Ardnamurchan is to fall in love with Scotland again and again. Woods especially around Loch Sunart. Good family campsite at **Resipole** (1269/CAMPING WITH KIDS) and lovely food at Lochaline (1085/HIGHLANDS).

2060 6/N17
1-4KM
CIRC
XBIKES
1-A-2
✓✓ **Randolph's Leap nr Forres** On the B9007. Spectacular gorge of the gorgeous Findhorn river lined with beautiful beech woods and a great place to swim or picnic (1725/SWIMMING). Go **either**: 10km S of Forres on the A940 for Grantown, then the B9007 for Ferness and Carrbridge. 1km from the sign for **Logie Steading** (2191/SCOTTISH SHOPS) and 300m from the narrow stone bridge, there's a pull-over place on the bend. The woods are on the other side of the road. **Or**: take the A939 S from Nairn or N from Grantown-on-Spey and at Ferness take the B9007 for Forres. Approaching from this direction, it's about 6km along the road; the pull-over is on your right. This is one of the sylvan secrets of the North. Trailboard at site and at Logie Steading, from which it's a 3.5km walk return, so I'd say simply head from here; there's a great café (and browsing opportunities).

2061 7/J23
2-8KM
CIRC
XBIKES
2-A-2
✓✓ **Lochaweside** Unclassified road on N side of loch between Kilchrenan and Ford, centred on Dalavich. Illustrated brochure available from local hotels around Kilchrenan and Dalavich post office, describes 6 walks in the mixed, mature forest all starting from car parking places on the road. 3 starting from the Barnaline car park are trail-marked and could easily be followed without a guide. Avich Falls route crosses River Avich after 2km with falls on return route. Inverinan Glen is always good. The timber trail from the Big Tree/Cruachan car park 2km S of Dalavich takes in the loch, a waterfall and it's easy on the eye and foot (4km). The track from the car park N of Kilchrenan on the B845 back to Taynuilt is less travelled but also fine. Pub at Kilchrenan.

2062 7/J24
3KM
CIRC
XBIKES
1-A-1

✓ **Inveraray Castle Estate** I don't actually list Inveraray in Best Castles in *StB*, but the gardens and especially the woodland walks on the estate are superb in any season. Two main routes to follow, one around the policies and another up to the folly (not more than an hour) for great views. Castle (or its tearoom with pictures from *Downton's* Scottish episode, which was filmed here). Apr-Oct, grounds AYR. There's also a good tearoom in the village, **Brambles** 732/ARGYLL, and the estimable **George Hotel** 725/ARGYLL.

2063 5/K16
1/7KM
CIRC
XBIKES
1-A-2
NC500

✓ **Inverbroom Estate Walks Lael, nr Ullapool** 15km S of Ullapool on the A835, 2 car parks marked Lael Forest Garden are the start/finish for 2 circular walks, one short (45 mins, 1.2km) in the forest alone and around a magical waterfall, and the other via the village of Auchindrean across the road and along the River Broom almost as far as the **Corrieshalloch Gorge** (1655/WATERFALLS). Equally rewarding for effort. Good leaflet guide from Ullapool tourist information centre.

2064 7/K25
3KM
CIRC
XBIKES
1-B-1

✓ **Puck's Glen nr Dunoon** Close to the gates of the **Younger Botanic Garden at Benmore** (1554/GARDENS), on the other side of the A815 to Strachur, 12km N of Dunoon. A short, exhilarating woodland walk from a convenient car park. Ascend through trees then down into a fairy glen, follow the burn back to the road. Some pools to be swum.

2065 5/N19
1-B-2

✓ **Rothiemurchus Forest nr Aviemore** The place to experience the magic and the majesty of the great Caledonian Forest and the beauty of Scots pine. Approach from B970, the road that parallels the A9 from Coylumbridge to Kincraig/Kingussie. 2km from Inverdruie near Coylumbridge follow sign for Loch an Eilean; one of the most perfect lochans in these or any woods. Loch circuit 5km (1667/LOCHS). Info and sustenance from the fine farm shop at the Rothiemurchus visitor centre at Inverdruie (**Druie**, their café; daytime only).

2066 5/M20
3KM
CIRC
XBIKES
1-A-1

✓ **Uath Lochans Rothiemurchus** A less frequented place and a very fine walk in the same neck of the woods as one of several around Glen Feshie. Off the B970 between Kincraig and Coylumbridge/Aviemore signed Glen Feshie, 2km to car park on the right. 3 walks marked around the lochans, all a dawdle. The best takes you around Farleitter Crag with views over the treetops (red route is not as long as it says, maybe 1.5 hours).

2067 7/H21
5KM
CIRC
MT BIKES
1-B-2

✓ **Ariundle Oakwoods Strontian** 35km Fort William via Corran Ferry. There are many walks around Loch Sunart and Ariundle. Rare oak and other native species. You see how very different Scotland's landscape was before industrialisation. Start over town bridge, turning right for Polloch. Go on past Ariundle Centre, with good home baking in the café, and park. Walks are well marked.

2068 7/L24
3KM
CIRC
1-A-2

✓ **Inchcailloch Island Loch Lomond** Surprisingly large island near Balmaha, criss-crossed with easy, interesting woodland walks (<1km) with the loch always there through the trees. A pleasant afternoon option is to row there from Balmaha Boatyard (£10 a boat at TGP). They also run a regular ferry; 01360 870214.

2069 8/N22
3.5KM
CIRC
XBIKES
1-A-2

✓ **The Birks o' Aberfeldy** Circular walk through oak, beech and the birch (or birk) woods of the title, easily reached and signed from town main street (1km). Steep-sided wooded glen of the Moness Burn with attractive falls, especially the higher one spanned by bridge where the 2 marked walks converge. This is where Burns 'spread the lightsome days' in his eponymous poem. Allow 2 hours. Excellent tearoom and all-round life enhancer, **The Watermill**, back in town (1419/TEAROOMS) and the **Three Lemons** (923/PERTHSHIRE). Great coffee at **Habitat Café** (1428/TEAROOMS).

2070 8/N22
1–3KM
CIRC
XBIKES
1–A–1

The Hermitage Dunkeld On A9 2km N of Dunkeld. Popular, easy, accessible walks along glen and gorge of River Braan with pavilion overlooking the falls and, further on, Ossian's Cave. Also, uphill Craigvinean walks start here to good viewpoint (2km). Several woody walks around Dunkeld/Birnam – there's a good leaflet from the tourist information centre. 2km along river is **Rumbling Bridge**, a deep gorge, and beyond it great spots for swimming (1720/SWIMMING). Good tearoom in Dunkeld (1427/TEAROOMS) and bakery/caff (1470/ARTISAN BAKERS), and river terrace bar at the **The Atholl Arms**. The **Enchanted Forest** event in October brings the forest to life and light.

2071 6/N19

Glenmore Forest Park nr Aviemore Along from Coylumbridge (and adjacent Rothiemurchus) on road to ski resort, the forest trail area centred on Loch Morlich (sandy beaches, good swimming, watersports). Visitor centre has maps of walk and bike trails and an activity programme. Glenmore Lodge (01479 861256) is Scotland's Outdoor Training Centre and well worth a visit. They know a thing or two about walking!

2072 5/H20

Knoydart Community Woodlands by Inverie On Knoydart Peninsula. Ferry from Mallaig or walk in from Glenfinnan (25km). Historic and restored woodlands around Inverie Village, part of the Knoydart walking experience (there are coastal walks, Corbetts and Munros) 2023/MUNROS. www.knoydart.org. See 1252/CAMPING.

2073 7/J22
<1–5KM
CIRC
1–B–1

Sutherland's Grove Barcaldine 10km N of Oban on the A828. Accessible and easy walking where paths are well signed (maps usually available in the car park). Notable for splendid Douglas firs (from 1870), gorge and waterfalls. 5 walks from <500m to 5km.

2074 8/M24
2 OR 4KM
CIRC
XBIKES
1–A–1

Above the Pass of Leny Callander A walk through mixed forest (beech, oak, birch, pine) with great Trossachs views. Start from main car park on A84, 4km N of Callander (Falls of Leny are on opposite side of road, 100m away). Various options marked and boarded where marshy. Another short but glorious walk is to the **Bracklinn Falls** – signed off E end of Callander Main St; start by the golf course (1km; see also 1731/SWIMMING). Also loop to the Crags (adding another 2km).

2075 8/M21
2–15KM
CIRC
BIKES
1–B–2

Loch Tummel Walks nr Pitlochry Mixed woodland N of Loch Tummel, reached by the B8019 from Pitlochry to the visitor centre at **Queen's View** (1708/VIEWS), 01796 473123; and walks in the Allean Forest, which take in some historical sites (a restored farmstead, standing stones), start nearby (2–4km). There are many other walks in area: the Forestry Commission brochure is available locally.

2076 9/L29

The New Galloway Forest Huge area of forest and hill country with every type of trail, including part of **Southern Upland Way** from Bargrennan to Dalry (2026/WALKS). Visitor centres at Kirroughtree (5km Newton Stewart) and Clatteringshaws Loch on the Queen's Way (9km New Galloway). Glen and Loch Trool are very fine (1648/GLENS); and walks (up to 5km) around Laurieston. **The Smithy** by the bridge in New Galloway for sustenance (1460/TEAROOMS). There's a river pool on the Raiders' Road (1732/SWIMMING). One could ramble on ...

2077 6/R17
7KM · CIRC
XBIKES
1–A–2

Duff House Banff Duff House is the major attraction around here (see also 2185/GALLERIES), but if you've time it would be a pity to miss the wooded policies and the meadows and riverscape of the Deveron. To the Bridge of Alvah where you should be bound is about 7km return; 1.5 hours return. See also 2056/WALKS.

2078 5/L17
1–4KM
CIRC · XBIKES
1–A–2
NC500

Torrachilty Forest & Rogie Falls nr Contin & Strathpeffer Enter by old bridge just outside Contin on main A835 W to Ullapool or further along (4km) at Rogie Falls car park. Shame to miss the falls (1664/WATERFALLS), but the woods and gorge are pleasant enough if it's merely a stroll you need. **Ben Wyvis** further up the road is the big challenge (2018/MUNROS).

2079 6/N19 **Abernethy Forest nr Boat of Garten** 3km from village off B970, but hard to miss because the famous ospreys are signposted from all over (1779/BIRDS). Nevertheless, this woodland reserve is a tranquil place among native pinewoods around Loch Mallachie with dells and trails. Many other birdies twittering around your picnic. They don't dispose of the midges.

2080 6/Q17 **Fochabers** On main A96 about 3km E of town are some excellent woody and winding walks around the glen and Whiteash Hill (2-5km). Further W on the Moray Coast is **Culbin Forest**: head for Cloddymoss or Kintessack off A96 at **Brodie Castle** 12km E of Nairn (1812/CASTLES). Acres of Sitka (spruce) in a sandy coastal forest. Worth going to **The Bakehouse** in Findhorn for sustenance (1086/HIGHLANDS).

2081 8/Q23 **Templeton Woods Dundee** Extensive and atmospheric woodlands on the edge of Dundee, just beyond the Kingsway dual carriageway. Turning is 3km on Coupar Angus road after Camperdown Park. Many trails to walk or bike; visitor centre, a tower and a wee lochan. Red squirrels and roe deer may scamper. **Birkhill Cemetery** on the way in is a joy (1941/GRAVEYARDS).

Dumfries House nr Ochiltree Wooded policies, farmland and extensive new gardens in development. Report: 1558/GARDENS.

Coastal Walks

See p.12 for walk codes.

2082 7/F26
XCIRC
XBIKES
2-B-2
✓✓ **Kintra Islay** From Port Ellen on the Bowmore road take Oa turn-off: 2km to Kintra turn-off, then 4km. Park in old farmyard by campsite (1256/WILD CAMPING). A fabulous beach (1625/BEACHES) runs in opposite direction and the notable golf course behind it (2100/GOLF). You are invited to 'Walk on the Wild Side' along N coast of the Mull of Oa, an area of diverse beauty with a wonderful shoreline. The **American Monument** walk is spectacular (1884/MONUMENTS).

2083 6/T18 ✓✓ **The Bullers of Buchan nr Peterhead** 8km S of Peterhead on A975 Cruden Bay road. Park and walk 100m to cottages. To the N is the walk to Boddam and Longhaven Nature Reserve along dramatic cliffs and S past **Slains Castle** (1848/RUINS). The Bullers is at start of walk, a sheer-sided hole 75m deep with outlet to the sea through a natural arch. Walk round the edge, looking down on layers of birds (who may try to dive-bomb you away); it's a wonder of nature on an awesome coast. Take great care (and a head for heights).

2084 4/K12 ✓✓ **Cape Wrath & The Cliffs of Clo Mor** Britain's most northwesterly point reached by ferry from 1km off A838, 4km S of Durness; a 10-min crossing then 60-min minibus ride to Cape. Ferry holds 12 and runs May-Sep (call for times: 01971 511246) or ferryman direct (07719 678729): John Morrison on his boat for over 30 years. At 281m Clo Mor are high though not the UK's highest. For cliffs, ask to be put off the bus (which goes to the Stevenson lighthouse) and reduce the walk to 3km. The caff here **Ozone**, is always open '24/7' (really?). Around 8 trips a day, weather and MoD range permitting. Bikes are OK. Easter-Sep. In other direction, the 28km to Kinlochbervie is one of Britain's most wild and wonderful coastal walks. Beaches include **Sandwood** (1623/BEACHES).

2085 4/J14
1-B-2
NC500

✓ **Old Man of Stoer nr Lochinver** Easy, exhilarating and spectacular walk to the dramatic 70m sandstone sea stack. Start at lighthouse off unclassified road 14km N of Lochinver on the Drumbeg road (1679/SCENIC ROUTES). Park and follow sheep tracks; cliffs are high and steep. 7km round trip; 2/3 hours. Then find the **Secret Beach** (1630/BEACHES).

2086 9/N30
1-A-2

✓ **Rockcliffe to Kippford** An easy and can be circular stroll along the 'Scottish Riviera' through woodland near the shore (2km) past the Mote of Mark, a Dark Age hill fort with views to Rough Island. The better clifftop walk is in the other direction to Castlehillpoint. **The Anchor** in Kippford (1348/FOOD PUBS) for pub and grub.

2087 8/R25
5-10KM
CIRC
XBIKES
1-B-2

✓ **St Abb's Head nr Berwick** Among the most dramatic coastal scenery in southern Scotland, scary in a wind, rhapsodic on a summer's day. Extensive wildlife reserve and trails through coastal hills and vales to cliffs. Best to park at visitor centre on St Abbs village road 3km from A1107 to Eyemouth and follow route (1800/RESERVES). 30 mins to cliffs, walks marked 1/2/3km. Nice caff, interpretation centre, gallery (2202/SCOTTISH SHOPS). Decent pub grub at **New Inn**, Coldingham, and 2 good caffs in St Abbs village (2km) and at **The Craw Inn** (1349/FOOD PUBS).

2088 5/H18
NC500

Applecross This far peninsula is marvellous for many reasons (1677/SCENIC ROUTES) and there are fine walks in and around Applecross Bay foreshore, including river and woodland strolls. See *Walks on the Applecross Peninsula*, available locally.

2089 7/H21
10KM RETURN
XCIRC
BIKES
1-B-1

Singing Sands Ardnamurchan 2km N of Acharacle, signed for Arivegaig. 3km to Arivegaig and park before wooden bridge (gate may be locked). Cross wooden bridge, following track round side of Kentra Bay. Follow signs for Gorteneorn, and walk through forest track and woodland to beach. As you pound the sands they should sing to you whilst you bathe in the beautiful views of Rum, Eigg, Muck and Skye (and just possibly the sea). 'Beware unexploded mines', a notice says.

2090 6/R17
8KM · XCIRC
XBIKES
1-A-1

East From Cullen Moray Coast This is the same walk mentioned with reference to **Sunnyside** (1620/BEACHES), a golden beach with a fabulous ruined castle (**Findlater**) that might be your destination (1837/RUINS). There's a track E along from harbour. 2 hours return. A superb coastline. Eat at **Rockpool** (992/NE RESTAURANTS).

2091 6/S17

Crovie–Troup Head Moray Coast Another Moray Coast classic that takes in the extraordinary cliff-clinging village of Crovie and the bird-stacked cliffs of the headland. Start at car park and viewpoint above Crovie, 15km E of Banff off B9031. Park and walk over the headland, then follow path to Troup Head. 5km return. The 'official' shorter walk (1.5km) from RSPB car park 2km off B9031 E of Crovie/ Gardenstown, signed for Northfield. Big sky and sea and birdlife.

2092 5/M17
5KM
CIRC
XBIKES
1-A-1

The South Sutor Cromarty The walk, known locally as 'The 100 Steps', though there are a few more than that, from Cromarty village (1608/VILLAGES; 1436/ TEAROOMS; 1092/HIGHLANDS) round the tip of the S promontory at the narrow entrance to the Cromarty Firth. E of village past bowling green then up through woods to headland. Good bench! Go further to top car park and viewpoint panel. Perhaps return by road. Dolphins are often in that sea!

2093 4/Q12
2KM
CIRC
XBIKES
1-B-2
NC500

St John's Point & Scotland's Haven East Mey, nr John o' Groats A short, secret walk between Thurso and John o' Groats on this northernmost headland. Prince Charles walks here (really!). Brilliant views to Dunnet Head and S Orkney. Follow signs then pass the **Castle of Mey** (1815/CASTLES). After 2km turn left. Park at cottages and go through long gate at the bend of the road, finding a path to right of the gorse heading for the sea. You don't see the stacks, the Men of Mey, where the 5 tides meet, till you're almost there. Following track to right mostly carved out of heather you arrive at a narrow, steeply banked cove called Scotland's Haven. A perfect shelter! Then back. 1 hour.

2094 4/L12
1KM · CIRC
XBIKES
1-B-2
NC500

Ceannabeinne Township Trail nr Durness This is the walk near my favourite beach (1618/BEACHES), 7km E of Durness. There's a lay-by; marker boards direct you on the path, relating the story of the township abandoned in 1842. A short, life-enhancing stroll through history (the 'Durness Riots'!) and splendid coastal scenery in spite of that fecking unsightly zip line!

2095 8/Q24
2-B-2

The Fife Coastal Path and The Chain Walk Elie Adventurous headland scramble at the W end of Elie (and Earlsferry). Go to end of the road then by path skirting golf course towards headland. Hand- and footholds carved into rock with chains to haul yourself up. Emerge by Shell Bay Caravan Park or down steps (1 hour circular). Watch the tide. **The 19th Hole** is the must-eat (1331/FOOD PUBS).

2096 8/Q23
1-A-1

The North Fife Coastal Path Wormit Less celebrated, less known than above but much less footfall and lots of interest. Start from furthest W houses in Wormit near the Tay Bridge (to Dundee). Head through woods and gorge on a simple path to lovely **Balmerino**. You can start at Newport and finish at Newburgh (28km), but this 8km (return) section is a very rewarding stroll by the Tay. Refresh at **The View** in Wormit 888/FIFE.

2097 7/J26
2-B-2

Cock of Arran Lochranza This round trip usually starts at Lochranza castle. A breathtaking coastal trail round the N end of the island (see 2250/ISLAND WALKS). Great for twitchers, ramblers, fossil hunters and geologists. Strong boots advisable. Approximately 4 hours, around 12km.

2098

Island Coasts See Fantastic Walks in the Islands, p. 380-2, but also these:

5/E18

Duirinish coast on **Skye**, a long (8-12 hours) route with some of the best coastal architecture in the UK: sea arches, waterfalls, stacks. For starts, consult locally.

5/F19

Minginish coast, also on **Skye**, with views to the small isles, Hebrides and the Cuillin. Fantastic geology and sea eagles above. 6-8 hours.

1/P11

The Old Man of Hoy from Rackwick on Hoy. 10km of epic coast. Ferry from Stromness then minibus.

2099 8/Q23
3KM
XCIRC
1-A-1

Broughty Ferry Esplanade Broughty Ferry This is a very different walk/stroll from others on these pages, no wild coast here but nonetheless an engaging and pleasant pursuit only 20 mins from Dundee centre. Head to the front (The Tay Estuary Waterfront) in 'The Ferry' (many good food and drink options, see p. 165-7) towards the castle. Beyond is 'The Esplanade' and a 3km easy, breezy beach walk to Monifieth. Highlights are the Barnhill Rock Garden, the 'swimming zone' – they are proud of this beach – and the customary beverage stop at the **Glass Pavilion** (959/DUNDEE). There may be dolphins!

the Best

of Outdoor Activities

Good Golf Courses In Great Places

Scotland has many world-renowned, historic and championship courses – Gleneagles, St Andrews, Carnoustie; in Ayrshire and in East Lothian. They need no further endorsement from StB. However, here are others less well known. Great because of splendid surroundings, ambience, for offering a unique quality of experience – and good golf.

2100 7/F26 ✓ **Machrie** Islay · 01496 302310 7km Port Ellen. Worth going to Islay just for
LL the golf, **The Machrie Hotel**, having undergone major refurbishment, reopened 2018 (2259/ISLAND HOTELS). Old-fashioned course to be played by feel and instinct. Splendid, often windy isolation. The notorious 17th, Iffrin (it means Hell), vortex-shaped from the dune system of marram and close-cropped grass, is one of many great holes. 18 holes.

2101 8/S27 ✓ **Roxburghe Hotel Golf Course** nr Kelso · www.roxburghe.net ·
01573 450333 Only championship course in the Borders. Designed by Dave Thomas along banks of River Teviot. Part of the Floors Castle estate. Open to non-res. Bar/lounge/clubhouse. **The Roxburghe Hotel** reopens 2019 after a major refurbishment. See also 824/BORDERS.

2102 4/N16 ✓ **Royal Dornoch** www.royaldornoch.com · 01862 810219 Sutherland
LL championship course laid out by Tom Morris in 1877. Has been declared 5th
NC500 best course in the world outside the US, but not busy or incessantly pounded. No poor holes. Stimulating sequences. Probably the most northerly great golf course in the world – and not impossible to get on. Sister course the **Struie** also a treat.

2103 5/N17 ✓ **Nairn** www.nairngolfclub.co.uk · 01667 453208 Traditional seaside links,
L one of the easiest championship courses to get on. Good clubhouse, friendly folk. (Nairn Dunbar across town also has good links.) Handicap certificate required for both.

2104 8/R24 ✓ **Kingsbarns** www.kingsbarns.com · 01334 460860 Between Crail and St
L Andrews, one of Fife's newest and Scotland's best courses. In all top rankings. Challenging and a beautiful location on a secret coast. Not cheap.

2105 8/R24 ✓ **Elie** www.golfhouseclub.co.uk · 01333 330301 Splendid open links kept
in top condition; can be windswept. The starter has his famous periscope and may be watching you. Adjacent 9-hole course, often busy with kids, is fun (01333 330955).

2106 8/Q25 ✓ **Musselburgh Links** www.musselburgholdlinks.co.uk · 0131 653 5122
The original home of golf (recorded here in 1672), but this 9-hole links run by the local authority is not exactly top turf and is enclosed by Musselburgh Racecourse. Nostalgia still appeals though. **Royal Musselburgh** (01875 810276; www.royalmusselburgh.co.uk) nearby for the serious game. Dates to 1774, fifth-oldest in Scotland. On both you play through history.

2107 7/G28 ✓ **Machrihanish** www.machgolf.com · 01586 810213 & **Machrihanish**
LL **Dunes** nr Campbeltown · www.machrihanishdunes.com ·
01586 810000 Among the dunes and links of the glorious 8km stretch of the **Machrihanish Beach** (1621/BEACHES). The Atlantic provides thunderous applause. See 733/ARGYLL.

2108 3/E16 ✓ **Harris Golf Club** Scarista, Isle of Harris · www.harrisgolf.com ·
LLL 01859 550226 Phone number is for the secretary but no need to ring: just
turn up on the road between Tarbert and Rodel and leave £20 in the box. First tee
commands one of the great views in golf and throughout this basic but testing
course, you are looking out to sea over **Scarista Beach** (1619/BEACHES) and bay.
The sunset may put you off your swing. 9 holes. Closed Sun.

2109 3/C19 ✓ **Askernish** South Uist · www.askernishgolfclub.com · 01878 700628
Another superb Hebridean dunes and machair course first laid out by Tom
Morris in 1891, rescued and reopened in 2008. 'One of the most natural golf
courses in the world'. 5km N of Lochboisdale, 1km from A865 to the sea. 18 holes.
Café in the clubhouse.

2110 9/N30 ✓ **Southerness** Solway Firth · www.southernessgolfclub.com ·
L 01387 880677 25km S of Dumfries by A710. A championship course on links
on the silt flats of the firth. Despite its prestige, visitors do get on. Start times
available 10am-noon and 2-4pm. There are few courses as good as this at these
prices. Under the wide Solway sky, it's pure … southerness.

2111 8/P22 ✓ **Rosemount** Blairgowrie · www.theblairgowriegolfclub.co.uk ·
01250 872622 Off A93, S of Blairgowrie. An excellent, pampered and
well-managed course in the middle of green Perthshire, an alternative perhaps to
Gleneagles, usually easier to get on and rather cheaper.

2112 6/N19 ✓ **Boat of Garten** www.boatgolf.com · 01479 831282 Challenging,
picturesque course in town where ospreys have been known to wheel
overhead. Has been called the Gleneagles of the North; certainly the best around,
though not for novices. 18 holes.

2113 5/M16 ✓ **Tain** www.tain-golfclub.co.uk · 01862 892314 & **Brora** www.broragolf.
& 4/N15 co.uk · 01408 621417 2 northern courses that are a delight to play on. Tain
L designed by Tom Morris in 1890. Brora stunning, with good clubhouse, hotel
NC500 (1046/HIGHLANDS) and coos on the course. With the Royal Dornoch (above), they're
a roving-golfer must.

2114 5/H16 **Gairloch** www.gairlochgolfclub.co.uk · 01445 712407 S of town on A832,
L it overlooks the bay and a perfect, pink, sandy beach (1631/BEACHES). Small
NC500 clubhouse with honesty box out of hours. Not the most agonising course; and on
a clear day with views to Skye, you can forget agonising over anything. 9 holes.

2115 9/M29 **New Galloway** www.newgallowaygolfclub.com · 01644 420737 Local course
on S edge of this fine wee toon. Almost all on a slope but affording great views
of Loch Ken and the Galloway Forest behind. No bunkers and only 9 short holes,
some steep, but exhilarating play. Easy to get on, except Sun. Just turn up.

2116 8/R28 **Minto** Denholm · www.mintogolf.co.uk · 01450 870220 9km E of Hawick.
Spacious parkland in Teviot valley. Best holes 3rd, 12th and 16th. **Vertish Hill**
www.hawickgolfclub.com · 01450 372293 · Hawick A more challenging hill
course. Both among the best in Borders. 18 holes. Best holes 2nd and 18th.

2117 8/R25 **Gifford** www.giffordgolfclub.com · 01620 810591 Dinky 9-hole inland course
on the edge of a charming village, bypassed by the queue for the big East Lothian
courses and a guarded secret among regulars. Generally OK, but phone starter
(above) for availability. I was touched when they wrote to thank me for this entry a
few editions back. *Golf World* once called it 'the best 9 holes in Scotland'.

2118 **5/L17** **Strathpeffer** **www.strathpeffergolf.co.uk** · **01997 421219** Very hilly (we do
    NC500 mean hilly) course full of character and with exhilarating Highland views. Small-
town friendliness. You play up there with the gods and other old codgers. 18 holes.

2119 **6/P17** **Elgin** **www.elgingolfclub.com** · **01343 542338** 1km from town on A941 Perth
road. Many memorable holes on moorland/parkland course in an area where links
may lure you to the coast at **Nairn** (above) or **Lossiemouth**. 18 holes.

2120 **4/L12** **Durness** **www.durnessgolfclub.org** · **01971 511364** The most northerly golf
    LL course on mainland UK, on the wild headland by Balnakeil Bay, looking over to
    NC500 Faraid Head. The last hole is over the sea. Only open since 1988, it's already got cult
status. 2km W of Durness. 9 holes.

2121 **5/H20** **Traigh** Arisaig · **www.traighgolf.co.uk** · **01687 450337** A830 Fort William–
    LL Mallaig road, 2km N Arisaig. Pronounced 'Try' and you should. The islands are set
out like stones in the sea around you and there are 9 hilly holes of fun. Has been
called 'the most beautiful 9 holes in the world'.

The Best Cycling

EASY CYCLING

2122 8/Q27 ✓ **The Borders** The Borders with its gentle hills, river tracks and low urbanisation has been paving the cycleway both for mountain biking (see below) and for more leisurely and family pursuits. Good linkage and signage and many routes, e.g. the 4 Abbeys, the Tweed Cycleway, the Borderloop and individual trails. **Glentress**, by Innerleithen, now a top cycling hub. **'Tweedlove'** is an international love-of-cycling festival in late May (31/EVENTS). Cycling guides and downloads widely available. There's ample choice for all abilities and ages. See also 7 Stanes (below).

2123 6/P18
20KM
CAN BE CIRC
✓ **Speyside Way: Craigellachie-Ballindalloch** The cycling part of the Way (2027/WALKS), with great views; it's flat and there are no cars. Goes past distilleries. Circular by return on minor roads.
START Craigellachie, by ranger's office.

2124 8/L24
11KM
CAN BE CIRC
✓ **The Trossachs nr Aberfoyle & Callander · www.trossachs.co.uk** Many low-level lochside trails and long-distance routes, including the West Loch Lomond Cycle Path and Sustrans Route 7. Good runs are Aberfoyle–Callander (20km, all off-road) and the Loch Ard Circle from Aberfoyle going W (signed Inversnaid Scenic Route) or Loch Katrine to Callander. Bike hire Loch Katrine, Callander, Aberfoyle.

2125 7/K26 ✓ **Cumbrae** For an island day out, take ferry from Largs (every 15 mins, 30 mins in winter) to beautiful Cumbrae (visit the classic **Ritz** 1406/CAFÉS). 4 or 5 routes around the island. One a stiff pull to a great viewpoint. Others stick to sea level. Consult locally. Circular with extension to Barbay Hill, 15km. All these roads are quiet.

2126 9/N28 ✓ **Drumlanrig nr Thornhill** Also in the SW. In the Drumlanrig Estate (1585/PARKS) around the River Nith, lochs and forest. 8 routes from 3-15km. Bike hub in the stableyard by the castle for bike hire, maintenance, even showers. **Rik's Bike Shed**: 01848 330080.

2127 8
55KM
CIRC
Forth & Clyde Canal, Glasgow–Falkirk Wheel East out of the city, urban at first then nice in the Kelvin Valley; Kilsyth Hills to the north. Falkirk Wheel 5/ATTRACTIONS.
START The Maryhill Locks, Maryhill Rd. And check the brilliant hire project www.nextbike.co.uk/en/ in Glasgow.

2128 9/L30
15KM
CAN BE CIRC
Glentrool nr Newton Stewart Two routes from visitor centre (1648/GLENS; 1958/BOB). Deep in the forest and well signed. Briefly joins public road. The 7 Stanes sections can be difficult (see below). Also **Clatteringshaws**: various routes around the loch including the Raiders' Road (1732/SWIMMING).
START Glentrool visitor centre off A714. Bike hire at **Kirroughtree** and network of trails listed from here (see below).

2129 8
12KM/VARIOUS
CIRC
Edinburgh Trails There is a vast network of cycle and towpaths especially N of the New Town. Another good run is to Balerno from Union Canal towpath in Lower Gilmore Place. End at Balerno High School.

2130 5/N19
20KM
CIRC
Loch an Eilean nr Aviemore Lots of bike tracks here in the Rothiemurchus Forest. This one goes past one of Scotland's most beautiful lochs (1667/LOCHS) and you can go further to Loch Insh via Feshiebridge and around Glen Feshie.
START Signed from B970 at Coylumbridge. Lotsa bike hire in Aviemore.

MOUNTAIN BIKING

2131 8 & 9 ✓✓ **7 Stanes Borders & South West** · www.7stanes.com Ambitious and hugely popular network of bike trails in S of Scotland, different lengths and abilities in each of 8 places, which include **Glentress/The Tweed Valley** (see below), **Newcastleton**, **Forest of Ae**, **Dalbeattie**, **Mabie**, **Glentrool** (see above), and **Kirroughtree** (see above). Routes at all levels. Built by bikers. Many challenges. Good signage throughout.

2132 8/Q27 ✓✓ **Glentress Forest nr Peebles** · www.glentressforest.com Meticulously constructed mountain-bike trails. Well signed and well used from 2 car park starts in this hugely popular national cycling centre, with café, shop (Alpine Bikes) and many facilities, including showers. 'Roompods' to stay in. Many food and drink options in Peebles and Innerleithen, p. 146–7, especially **No1 Peebles Road Coffee House**, a true caff for cyclists (1455/COFFEE). Trails for all levels, plenty of flowing descents and drops. The serious downhill stuff is nearby at **Traquair**, where the **7Stanes** cross-country route also starts (see above).

2133 8/M26 ✓ **Cathkin Braes Country Park Glasgow** Host of the 2014 Commonwealth Games mountain bike competition. Car park at the top of the park is a good starting point to the trails, which offer technical biking and great views.

2134 7/K21 ✓ **Nevis Range nr Fort William** · www.nevisrange.co.uk Hosts the Mountain Bike World Cup on the Witch's Trails. For downhill adrenaline junkies take the gondola up. It's not all hardcore; there are terrains and routes to suit all. Pinemarten café at car park and Snowgoose Restaurant & Bar 650m up the mountain. Bike hire Nevis Range, Inverlochy. For more downhill action head to **Glencoe Mountain Resort**.

2135 6/R20
25KM
CIRC
Glen Tanar Royal Deeside · www.glentanar.co.uk Good way to encounter this beautiful glen in the shadow of Mount Keen. Quite difficult in places.
START Tombae on the B976 opposite junction of A97 and A93.

2136 7/K21
XCIRC
Great Glen, Fort William–Loch Lochy Easy at first on the Caledonian Canal towpath. Later it gets hilly with long climbs. Great views.
START Neptune's Staircase at Banavie near Fort William.

2137 8/P21
25KM
CIRC
Perthshire & Angus, Glenfernate–Blair Atholl Beautiful Highland trail that takes in forests, lochs and **Glen Tilt** (2036/WALKS). Mainly rough track. Follow directions from tourist information centre leaflets.
START On the A924 14km E of Pitlochry, 500m E of school.

The Open-Air Swimming Pools

2138 8/S20 ✓ **Stonehaven Outdoor Pool** Stonehaven · www.stonehavenopenairpool. co.uk · **01569 762134** The Friends of Stonehaven Outdoor Pool won the day (eat your hearts out North Berwick) and saved a great pool that goes from length to strength. Fabulous 1930s Olympic-sized heated saltwater pool (85ft). Midnight swims from 10pm Jul/Aug on Wednesdays (is that cool, or what?). Jun-Sep only: 10am-7.30pm (10am-6pm weekends). Heated salt-water heaven (28°). **The Bay** top fish 'n' chips and **Aunty Betty's** ice cream on the prom nearby (1379/FISH & CHIPS; 1497/ICE CREAM).

2139 7/K25 ✓ **Gourock Bathing Pool** Gourock · **01475 213122** The only other open-air (proper) pool in Scotland that's still open – historic and recently refurbished. On coast road S of town 45km from Glasgow. 1950s-style leisure. Heated (to 29°C), so it doesn't need to be a scorcher (brilliant, but can get chock-a-block). May-Oct weekdays until 7.30/8pm, weekends 4.30pm.

2140 4/Q13 ✓ **The Trinkie** Wick On S side of town, follow cliff walk up from harbour or by NC500 car through housing estate. 2km. Not an organised set-up but a pool sluiced and filled by the sea within a natural formation of rocks. A bracing stroll, never mind immersion. Needs TLC. Wickers also go to the North Baths near the harbour (Wick side) and opposite the wee lighthouse. 2 rare open-air swim spots in the far north: midnight midsummer swimming. Anyone?

2141 7/G22 **The Bathing Pool** Glengorm Estate, Mull A pool sluiced and filled by the sea by an Iron Age fort on the headland of this beautiful estate 7km N of Tobermory off the Dervaig road. Some seaweed fringing but once it was filled with white sand (they say one day it may be restored). In the meantime, for swimming baggers and the like. 45 mins from the best coffee shop on Mull (1409/TEAROOMS), the walk described (2249/ISLAND WALKS), and you can stay and lord it up in the castle (2347/MULL). Watch for cows.

2142 8/R23 **The Step Rock Pool** St Andrews Shallow bathing pool between West Sands and East Sands beaches below the Aquarium and the **Seafood Ristorante** (1366/SEAFOOD). Since 1903, when the gentlemen used to swim here naked, a shallow alternative to the colder sea (and the East Sands Leisure Centre). Costumes advised. Has given its name to the local swimming club.

Especially Good Watersports Centres

2143 8/R24 ✓ **Elie Watersports** Elie · www.eliewatersports.co.uk · **01333 330962** Great beach location in totally charming wee town where there's enough going on to occupy non-watersporters. Easy lagoon for first timers and open season for inexperienced users. Wind-surfers, kayaks, water-skiing. Also mountain bikes and inflatable 'biscuits'. See also 1330/FOOD PUBS; 2105/GOLF.

2144 7/K26 ✓ **Scottish National Watersports Centre** Cumbrae · www. nationalcentrecumbrae.org.uk · **01475 530757** Frequent ferry from Largs (centre near ferry terminal so 5km Millport) then learn how to pilot things that float. Scotland's premier instructor facility, though not a drop-in facility. Great range of courses. Bunk-room accom.

2145 8/P25 ✓ **Port Edgar Watersports** South Queensferry · www. portedgarwatersports.com · 0131 331 3330 End of village between the Road Bridge and the new bridge. Major marina, watersports centre. Berth your boat, hire dinghies (big range). Big tuition programme for kids and adults, including canoes. Home to Port Edgar Yacht Club. Down The Hatch café and **Scott's**, the big new bar/restaurant (870/LOTHIANS).

2146 8/M26 ✓ **Strathclyde Country Park** www.visitlanarkshire.com · 01698 402060 Major watersports centre 15km SE of Glasgow and easily reached from Central Scotland via M8 or M74 (junction 5 or 6). 200-acre loch and centre with instruction on sailing, canoeing, windsurfing, water-skiing. Hire canoes, Lasers and Wayfarers, windsurfers and trimarans. Olympic-standard rowing (as seen on TV).

2147 5/N19 ✓ **Loch Insh** Kincraig · www.lochinsh.com · 01540 651272 On B970, 2km from Kincraig towards Kingussie and the A9. Marvellous loch site launching from gently sloping dinky beach into the shallow forgiving waters of Loch Insh. Hire of canoes, dinghies, windsurfers and rowing boats. Minibus to Kingussie, row back on the Spey. Archery and mountain biking. An idyllic place to learn anything. Sunset from the balcony restaurant, the Boathouse. Chalets and B&B. Sports Apr-Oct.

2148 6/N19 ✓ **Loch Morlich Watersports Centre** nr Aviemore · www.lochmorlich.com · 01479 861221 By Glenmore Forest Park, part of the plethora of outdoor activities hereabouts (skiing, walking, etc). This is the loch you see from Cairngorm and just as picturesque from the woody shore. Surprising coral-pink beach! Canoes, kayaks, rowing boats and dinghies with instruction in everything. Evening hire possible. Coffee shop up top. Good campsite adjacent (1262/CAMPING WITH KIDS).

2149 9/M30 ✓ **Galloway Activity Centre** Loch Ken, nr Castle Douglas · www.lochken. co.uk · 01556 502011 15km N on A713 to Ayr. Dinghies, wind-surfers, canoes, kayaks, tuition, biking. Also the Climbing Tower (so you zip-wire and take that leap of faith). Mountain biking, laser tag and archery. Accom in yurts, cabins and a bunkhouse. All this by a serene and forgiving loch by the Galloway Forest (1673/LOCHS). Phone for times and courses. Café open Mar/Apr-Oct; book in winter.

The Best Surfing Beaches

It is true: Scotland has some of Europe's best surfing beaches.

2150 4/P12 ✓✓ **North Coast: Thurso** Surf City. Some say the best surfing in Europe.
NC500 Waves in town at river mouth. Steep barrelling. **E of Thurso:** Torrisdale and Farr Bay. **Isle of Lewis** Go N of Stornoway, off Barvas, N of just about anywhere. Leave the A857 and your day job behind.

2151 7/E22 ✓ **West Coast: Isle of Tiree** Exposed to all the Atlantic swells, gorgeous little
& 7/G27 Tiree ain't just great for windsurfing. Stay at Millhouse, a self-catering hostel. **Machrihanish** Near Campbeltown at the foot of the Mull of Kintyre. Long strand to choose from (1621/BEACHES). Clan Skates in Glasgow (0141 339 6523) has up-to-date info.

2152 8/S25 ✓ **East Coast: Pease Bay** S of Dunbar near Cockburnspath on the A1. The nearest surfie heaven to the capital. The not-very-nice caravan site has parking and toilets. Very consistent surf; popular. Info and surf school from **Momentum** www. momentumsurfshop.com. Many other beaches here on E Lothian/Berwickshire coast, including **Coldingham** and **Belhaven**. **Nigg Bay** S of Aberdeen, and the **Granite Reef** and **Lunan Bay** (1629/BEACHES), N of Aberdeen, around Fraserburgh (the broch).

the
Best
of Consuming
Passions

Best History & Heritage

For Edinburgh museums, see p. 73–6; Glasgow museums, see p. 118–21.
☕ *signifies notable café.*

2153 7/K28
☕
✓✓ **Robert Burns Birthplace Museum** Alloway, Ayr · www.
burnsmuseum.org.uk · **01292 443700** Here in douce wee Alloway, the
restored cottage where Burns was born and the brilliant contemporary museum/
gallery/coffee shop, an appropriate paean to his memory, an evocation of his times
and works and both interesting and fun places to visit. Cottage is a row of rooms
with set pieces and slightly unnerving voiceovers. The museum has state-of-the-
art and technology exhibits exploring not just the well-kent and comic aspects
(*Tam o' Shanter, Auld Lang Syne*, the Kilmarnock Edition) but the wider implications
of his national significance and a modern translation of his influence. Serene
gardens, red roses. A caff you wouldn't write a poem about; maybe the wild birds. A
world-class encomium! Open AYR.

2154 8/R25
☕
✓✓ **National Museum of Flight** nr Haddington · www.nms.ac.uk ·
0300 123 6789 3km from A1. In the old complex of hangars and Nissen
huts by East Fortune, an airfield dating to WWI with a large collection of planes
from gliders to jets and especially wartime memorabilia respectfully restored and
preserved. Inspired and inspiring displays; not just boys' stuff. Marvel at the bravery
and sense the unremitting passage of time. Airship R34 made its historic Atlantic
crossings from East Fortune. Concorde is indeed an 'experience': hugely impressive
outside, claustrophobic in (especially queueing to leave). But did David Frost and
Joan Collins ever join the Mile High Club? Annual air show mid-July. Recent 'hangar
developments'. 7 days 10am-5pm (4pm in winter).

2155 8/Q23
✓✓ **RRS Discovery** www.rrsdiscovery.com · **01382 309060** & **HMS
Unicorn** www.frigateunicorn.org · **01382 200900** · **both Dundee**
The two historic ships that define both the old seafaring and the new tourist-
attracting port of Dundee city, landmarks in the waterfront now surmounted by the
V&A (4/ATTRACTIONS). No doubting the *RRS Discovery* – built in Dundee and the
boat that took Scott and Shackleton on the British National Antarctic Expedition in
1901 – and *HMS Unicorn*, launched in 1824, the world's last intact warship – are
beautiful to look at and fascinating to visit. 7 days 10am-6pm.

2156 7/H23
☕
✓✓ **Atlantic Islands Centre** Isle of Luing · www.atlanticislandscentre.
com · **01852 314096** Great contemporary building telling the story of
Luing and the Slate Islands. A superb day out only 40 mins from Oban: take scenic
B844 12km S of Oban, then the B8003 at the fork for the ferry at Cuan (also 12km);
ferry every half hour (fewer in winter), 3 mins on board. Fine walking but best by
bike (hire nearby 01852 314274) or car. Orientation/interpretation then explore the
island. Café has great community baking. See also Easdale below.

2157 8/R24
ATMOS
✓✓ **The Secret Bunker** nr Crail · www.secretbunker.co.uk ·
01333 310301 The nuclear bunker and regional seat of government in the
event of nuclear war: a twilight labyrinth beneath a hill in rural Fife so vast, well
documented and complete, it's both fascinating and chilling. Few museums are as
authentic or as resonant, even down to the claustrophobic canteen with bad food.
Makes you wonder what 300 people would have made of it, incarcerated there,
what the Cold War was all about and what secrets the MoD is brewing these days
for the wars yet to come. Mar-Oct 10am-5pm (last entry).

2158 8/Q23
✓✓ **Verdant Works Dundee** · www.verdantworks.com · **01382 309060**
West Henderson's Wynd near Westport. Award-winning, superior heritage museum that for once justifies the accolades. The story of jute and the city it made. Immensely effective high-tech and designer presentation of industrial and social history. Excellent for kids (the Red Box!). Guided tours by volunteers, many of whom worked in the mills. Lofty High Mills event space. Café. Mon-Sat 10am-6pm; winter: Wed-Sat till 5pm and closed Mon/Tue. Sun from 11am.

2159 4/Q13
NC500
✓✓ **Wick Heritage Centre Bank Row, Wick** · www.wickheritage.org · **01955 605393** Amazing volunteer-run civic museum, jam-packed with items about the sea, town and that hard land. Upstairs and downstairs, stretching halfway along the street. Few places have so much meticulously gathered that lovingly portrays and evokes the spirit of a place. The much-used words 'secret gem' are entirely appropriate here. Easter-Oct 10am-last entry 3.45pm. Closed Sun.

2160 4/H16
NC500
✓ **The Russian Arctic Convoy Project Aultbea** · www.theracmproject.org · **01445 731137** On the A832 by Aultbea, S of Laide, a small, fascinating, possibly vital exhibition 'centre' just off the road that follows Loch Ewe, which in World War II was the UK headquarters for operations in the North Atlantic and Arctic waters convoying armaments and supplies beyond the reach of German aircraft to the Allies and very good friends – the Russians – who were fighting the good fight with us. Important now to remember that! There were 1,000 ships in the bay, 3,000 men lost their lives, it was 'the worst journey in the world' (Churchill). Strangely affecting collection of memorabilia. Apr-Oct 10am-4pm. Closed Sun.

2161 3/F13
ATMOS
HES
✓ **The Blackhouse at Arnol Lewis** · www.historicenvironment.scot · **01851 710395** A857 Barvas road from Stornoway, left at junction for 7km, then right through township for 2km. A blackhouse with earth floor, bedboxes and central peat fire (no chimney hole), occupied by the family and their animals. Remarkably, this house was lived in until the 1960s. Smokists may reflect on that peaty fug. Open AYR. 9.30am-5.30pm (4.30pm in winter, Oct-Feb). Closed Sun. See also the extraordinary **Gearrannan Blackhouse Village**, 10km S (halfway to the **Callanish Stones** 1852/PREHISTORIC), where some of the thatched cottages are available for self-catering and there is a hostel and a café, 9.30am-5.30pm. See 1182/HOSTELS.

2162 4/P15
NC500
✓ **Timespan Helmsdale** · www.timespan.org.uk Far-northern town, where a historic strath comes down to the sea, was a special place (presumably) then and now. This museum and arts centre records and cleverly presents this, well, span of time. Makes you think! Great wee café by the bridge in its geology garden. Fish 'n' chips at **La Mirage** (1107/HIGHLANDS). Mar-Oct 10am-5pm (reduced winter hours).

2163 7/H23
LL
ATMOS
✓ **Easdale Island Folk Museum** www.easdalemuseum.org On Easdale, an island/township reached by a 5-min (continuous) boat service from Seil 'island' at the end of the B844 (off the A816, 18km S of Oban – you just press the button and it comes!). Something special about this grassy hamlet of whitewashed houses on a rocky outcrop, which has a tearoom/bar, **The Puffer** (01852 300022; www.pufferbar.com), a gallery and a craft shop, and this museum across the green. The history of the place (a thriving slate industry erased one stormy night in 1881, when the sea drowned the quarry 1730/SWIMMING) is brought to life in displays from local contributions. Easter-Sep 11am-5pm.

2164 **2/V5** ✓ **Shetland Museum & Archives** Lerwick · www.shetland-museum.org.
  L   uk · **01595 695057** Impressive, landmark, purpose-built contemporary space
ATMOS developed from what remained of the Lerwick waterfront. 60,000 images bringing
the story of these fascinating islands to life. Also the **Up-Helly-Aa** story (15/
EVENTS)! **Hays Dock Café/Restaurant** worth a visit in its own right. And **The
Mareel** 2419/SHETLAND. 7 days 10am-5pm (Sun from noon).

2165 **4/M12** ✓ **Strathnaver Museum** Bettyhill · www.strathnavermuseum.org.uk ·
  L   **01641 521418** On N coast and NC500, 60km W of Thurso, in a converted
NC500 church that is very much part of the whole appalling saga, a graphic account of the
Highland Clearances told through the history of this fishing village and the strath
that lies behind it, whence its dispossessed population came; 2,500 folk were
driven from their homes – it's worth going up the valley (from 2km W along the
main A836) to see (especially at Achenlochy) the beautiful land they had to leave in
1812 to make way for sheep. Detailed leaflet of Strath to follow by car and foot.
Open Apr-Oct: Mon-Sat 10am-5pm. Find the poignant and beautiful **Rosal
Clearance Township** about 6km from A836 via B871, 45-min walk from the car
park. Café on roadside by museum for sustenance.

2166 **4/P12** ✓ **Caithness Horizons** Thurso · www.caithnesshorizonsmuseum.com ·
NC500 **01847 896508** Town centre via pedestrianised main street. Another
surprising, incredibly well-conceived and laid-out collection of all things of the far
north, from the Picts and Vikings to Dounreay, including the recreation of the
control panel for the old reactor, cup of tea and a Bourbon biscuit on the desk.
These stories are compelling and well told. Tue-Sat 10am-5pm.

2167 **6/P18** ✓ **Knockando** nr Aberlour, Speyside · www.kwc.co.uk · **01340 810345** On
the B9102 off the A95 below Grantown-on-Spey and Keith, well signposted.
Lovingly restored cottage woolmill complex in woody, watery Speyside setting. With
reactivated Victorian machinery, this mill has been continuously running for over
200 years and all its history is here. You can still buy their products or just sit in
wonder by the stream. Mar-Oct: Tue-Sun 10am-4pm. Check winter times.

2168 **5/H18** ✓ **Applecross Heritage Centre** www.applecrossheritage.org.uk Along the
  L   strand from the **Walled Garden** (1088/HIGHLANDS) and **Applecross Inn**
NC500 (1229/GET-AWAY HOTELS) adjacent the lovely church built on an ancient monastery,
a well-designed building and lay-out of the story of this remarkable, end-of-the-
world community. Reading room with comfy chairs! 10am-4pm. Not weekends in
winter.

2169 **6/T17** ✓ **The Museum of Scottish Lighthouses** Fraserburgh · www.
  L   lighthousemuseum.org.uk · **01346 511022** At Kinnaird Head near the
harbour. A top attraction, so signed from all over. Purpose-built and very well done.
Something which may appear of marginal interest made vital. In praise of the prism
and the engineering innovation and skill that allowed Britain once to rule the seas
(and the world). A great ambition (to light the coastline) spectacularly realised. *At
Scotland's Edge* by Allardyce and Hood is well worth taking home, as is Bella
Bathhurst's *The Lighthouse Stevensons*. Timed tours include the lighthouse (72 steps
and a ladder). 10am-5pm (last tour 4pm).

2170 5/H18
LL

✓ **Bright Water Visitor Centre & Gavin Maxwell House** Eilean Ban, Skye ·
www.eileanban.org · 01599 530040 You don't have to be a Maxwell fan,
Ring of Bright Water reader or otter-watcher to appreciate the remarkable
restoration of this fascinating man's last house on the island under the Skye
Bridge. Skye is a natural haven and the Stevenson Lighthouse superb. The centre
supports a number of natural heritage and wildlife projects. Contact centre for
guided tours of the cottage, the lighthouse and the hide (otters not guaranteed but
quite likely, book and meet at Otter Gate on the bridge). Apr-Oct: Mon-Fri
10am-4pm.

2171 4/P12
NC500

Mary-Ann's Cottage Dunnet · www.caithness.org On N coast off A836 from
Thurso to John o' Groats, signed at Dunnet; take the road for Dunnet Head. Lived in
till 1990 by Mary-Ann Calder, 3 generations of crofters are in these stones. But not
nostalgic or heritage heavy, just an old lady's house, the near present and past and
still the geraniums! Compare to that other old lady's house 10 mins up the road
(**Castle of Mey** 1815/CASTLES). Jun-Sep 2-4.30pm.

2172 7/H24

Kilmartin House Museum nr Lochgilphead · www.kilmartin.org ·
01546 510278 N of Lochgilphead on A816. Centre for landscape and archaeology
interpretation – so much to know of the early peoples and Kilmartin Glen is
littered with historic sites. Intelligent, interesting, run by a small independent
trust. Excellent organic-ish café (1414/TEAROOMS) and bookshop without the usual
tat. Some nice Celtic carvings. Guided tours of the glen in summer. Museum and
tearoom closing autumn 2019 until 2021 for extensive refurbishment.

2173 5/M17

Cromarty Courthouse Museum Church St · www.cromarty-courthouse.org.
uk · 01381 600418 Housed in an 18th-century courthouse, this award-winning
museum uses moving, talking models to bring to life a courtroom scene and
famous Cromarty figures to paint the varied history of this special town (1608/
VILLAGES). Noon-4pm. Closed Fri/Sat. **Hugh Miller's Birthplace** is next door. Born
in 1802 and best known as the father of geology, he was remarkable in many ways
and this tells his singular story. Apr-mid Oct noon-4pm.

2174 5/F16

Skye Museum of Island Life Kilmuir · www.skyemuseum.co.uk ·
01470 552206 On A855 Uig-Staffin road 32km N of Portree. The most authentic
of several converted cottages on Skye where the crofter's life is recreated for the
enrichment of ours. The small thatched township includes agricultural implements
and domestic artefacts, many illustrating an improbable fascination with the royal
family. **Flora MacDonald's Grave** nearby (1886/MONUMENTS). Apr-Oct 9.30am-
5pm. Closed Sun.

2175 7/J24

Auchindrain nr Inveraray · www.auchindrain.org.uk · 01499 500235 8km
W of town on A83. A whole township reconstructed to give a very fair impression
of both the historical and spatial relationship between the cottages and their
various occupants. Longhouses and byre dwellings; their furniture and their ghosts.
Tearoom. Apr-Oct: 7 days 10am-5pm.

2176 8/R24

Scottish Fisheries Museum Anstruther · www.scotfishmuseum.org ·
01333 310628 In and around a cobbled courtyard overlooking the old fishing
harbour in this busy East Neuk town. Excellent evocation of traditional industry still
alive (if not kicking). Impressive collection of models and actual vessels including
those moored at adjacent quay. Crail and Pittenweem harbours nearby for the full
picture (and fresh crab/lobster). Open AYR. 10am-5.30pm, Sun 11am-5pm (closed
4.30pm in winter). 1396/FISH & CHIPS a must!

The Special Galleries & Art Spaces

For Edinburgh, see p. 77; Glasgow, p. 126. ☕ signifies notable café.

2177 8/P25 ☕ ✓✓ **Jupiter Artland** Wilkieston · www.jupiterartland.org · 01506 889900 W of Edinburgh. Not a public gallery as such but a world-class open-air artland assembled by Robert and Nicky Wilson in the groves and gardens of their home, Bonnington House. In an unfolding story, some of the UK's leading artists have been commissioned to produce site-specific work for you to discover: Andy Goldsworthy, Anthony Gormley, Anish Kapoor and an enormous landform by Charles Jencks which you pass through when you arrive; many others. Phyllida Barlow to mark Jupiter's 10th anniversary. This is art exposure and extraordinary patronage on a grand scale. There are temporary exhibitions in the courtyard gallery. Workshops and courses. Best get directions from the website. Allow 3 hours on site. Book online. May-Sep: Thu-Sun 10am-5pm. Lovely courtyard café an artwork in itself by Nicolas Party.

2178 8/Q23 ☕ ✓✓ **Dundee Contemporary Arts** Dundee · www.dca.org.uk · 01382 432000 State-of-contemporary-art gallery (by award-winning architect Richard Murphy) with great café (946/DUNDEE), well-selected designer shop and cinema. It once transformed the cultural face of Dundee and it is often worth travelling to/from the Central Belt if you're interested in cutting-edge contemporary art. Well used, well loved!

2179 8/M28 ✓✓ **Crawick Multiverse** nr Sanquhar · www.crawickmultiverse.co.uk The latest major project by renowned landscape artist Charles Jencks (1556/GARDENS), privately funded on land of the Duke of Buccleuch estates. This beautiful massive intervention of stone and earth and grass has all the hallmarks of his work, transforming an opencast coalmine into an enduring and edifying public space. Just N of the village after the school then right on the B740, 1.5km from Sanquhar station. The **Blackaddie Hotel** for food (783/SW RESTAURANTS).

2180 8/P23 ✓ **The Fergusson Gallery** Perth · www.museumsgalleriesscotland.org.uk In distinctive round tower (a former waterworks). The assembled works on two floors of J.D. Fergusson (1874-1961) and his partner Margaret Morris. Though he spent much of his life in France (illustrated here), he had an influence on Scottish art and was pre-eminent among The Colourists. It's a long way from Perth to Antibes 1913 but these pictures are a draught of the warm south. Some temporary exhibitions. Tue-Sat 10am-5pm. Open Sun in summer.

2181 8/Q24 ✓ **Kirkcaldy Galleries** Kirkcaldy · www.onfife.com · 01592 583206 Near railway station, but ask for directions (it's easy to get lost). One of the best galleries in central Scotland; recently refurbished. Splendid introduction to the history of 19th-/20th-century Scottish art. Lots of Colourists/McTaggart/Glasgow Boys. And Sickert to Redpath. And famously the only public collection in Scotland showing Scotland's 'best-selling artist': one Jack Vettriano, who was a Fife lad.

2182 9/M31 NTS ✓ **Hornel Gallery** Kirkcudbright · www.nts.org.uk · 01557 330437 Hornel's (Broughton) house is a fabulous evocation with a collection of his work and atelier as was. 'Even the Queen was amazed'. Beautiful, atmospheric garden stretches to the river. Apr-Oct noon-5pm. Garden AYR. The **Jessie M. King House**, is 100m down the same road towards the Tolbooth (not open to the public).

2183 4/L13
NC500

✓ **Lotte Glob's Gallery and Garden** Loch Eriboll · www.lotteglob.co.uk ·
01971 511727 In Laid, on western shore of Loch Eriboll and the main road N
to Durness, you enter through the Glob-like gateposts into Lotte's extraordinary
world, her distinctive ceramic works of art perfectly at home in this wild landscape.
Studio and gallery (but more a trail of rough tracks). Just wander, it is uniquely
special!

2184 6/P17

✓ **Moray Art Centre** Findhorn · www.morayartcentre.org · **01309 692426**
Part of the Findhorn Community/Foundation/park and eco-village. Another
very good reason for visiting this life-affirming place. Fascinating building by Randy
Klinger (2007) in keeping with the creative and ingenious architecture all around
you with an interesting programme of exhibitions and workshops. Tue-Sat.

2185 6/R17
☕

✓ **Duff House** Banff · www.nationalgalleries.org · **01261 818181** Nice walk
and easy to find from town (it's a major attraction). Important outstation of
the National Galleries of Scotland in meticulously restored Adam house with
interesting history and spacious grounds. Ramsays, Raeburns, Gainsboroughs,
portraiture of mixed appeal and an El Greco. Go further up the Deveron for a
pleasant stroll (2077/WALKS). Nice tearoom. AYR (weekends in winter).

2186 1/Q10

✓ **The Pier Arts Centre** Stromness, Orkney · www.pierartscentre.com ·
01856 850209 On main street (1607/VILLAGES), a gallery on a pier which
could have come lock, stock and canvases from Cornwall. Permanent St Ives-style
collection assembled by one Margaret Gardiner: Barbara Hepworth, Ben Nicholson,
Paolozzi and others shown in a sympatico environment with the sea outside.
Important early-20th-century pictures complemented by work of recent
contemporaries. Partners with the Tate. A rare treat! Tue-Sat 10.30am-5pm.

2187 9/M31

✓ **Kirkcudbright Galleries** Kirkcudbright · www.kirkcudbrightgalleries.
org.uk · **01557 331276** Opening 2018, the Galleries, over 4 floors opened in
the Old Town Hall on St. Mary St to tell the story and focus attention on the colony
of artists who settled and worked in SW Scotland's most beguiling town. Though
Hornel (see above) and Jessie M. King were leading lights, there were many others
and the group had a national impact. The Kirkcudbright story is told on the ground
floor, with temporary exhibitions above. This is well worth a visit. 7 days.

2188 7/F22
☕

✓ **Calgary Art In Nature** Calgary, Mull · www.calgaryartinnature.co.uk
Contemporary artwork and sculpture to be found on a trail through the woods
adjacent to the wonderful beach at **Calgary Bay** on the far W coast of Mull and an
exhibition gallery space. The project of Matthew Reade, who ran the Calgary
Farmhouse Hotel (the great **Café at Calgary Arts** remains, Easter-Nov), the 1km
trail is fun rather than thought provoking, but it's a great idea, and nice for kids.

2189 6/T19

✓ **Aberdeen Art Gallery** Schoolhill, Aberdeen · www.aagm.co.uk ·
01224 523700 Major gallery with temporary exhibits and eclectic and
significant permanent collection from Impressionists to 19th- and 20th-century
British and Scottish and contemporary artists. Reopened after a major refurb.

2190 8/R22

✓ **Hospitalfield** Arbroath · www.hospitalfield.org.uk · **01241 656124** An
arts centre in a historic (Arts & Crafts) house, 400m from the A92, S of the
centre (at McDonald's), with artists in residence. The collection and interiors are
fascinating and the legacy of artist and collector Patrick Allan-Fraser (1812–1890).
Only open Wed 2-5pm. The café in the walled garden is open Wed & Sat 11am-
4pm. Hospitalfield curated Scotland's 'pavilion' at the Venice Biennale 2015.

Best Shopping for Scotland

✐ signifies notable café.

2191 6/N17
✔✔ **Logie Steading** nr Forres · www.logie.co.uk · 01309 611378 In beautiful countryside 10km S of Forres, signed from A940 Forres–Grantown-on-Spey road. Near pleasant woodlands and brilliant picnic spots (2060/WALKS), with lovely walled garden around the big house nearby (Apr-Dec). Much better than your usual crafty courtyard to visit and browse. Includes Giles Pearson's Country Furniture, a second-hand bookshop and the **Olive Tree Café**, a home-baking tearoom with integrity. Seems fitting as the estate was built with the fortune of the guy who invented the digestive biscuit! 1441/TEAROOMS. 7 days.

2192 6/P17
✔✔ **Johnston's Cashmere Centre** Elgin (the HQ), also Hawick, St Andrews & London · www.johnstonscashmere.com Johnston's is, as they say, one of the last of the Mohicans actually making textiles in Scotland. They are 'the only British mill to transform fibre to garment' (yarns spun at their factory in Elgin and made into garments in the Borders). They stock their own ranges, including couture cashmere, many of which are sold internationally, as well as other quality brands. This extensive mill shop, the high-quality and classy 'home' section, heritage centre and café is a serious visitor attraction hereabouts. The jumpers, bunnets and cardies are more classic than cool but they won't fall apart and they ain't made in China. Lovely garden adjacent the pulsating mill with free tours Mon-Fri (30 mins) from the wool store through dyeing, pearling, spinning and weaving into their cloth and scarves. You will want to buy something! Mon-Sat 9am-5.30pm, Sun 11am-5pm. Near the Cathedral (1834/RUINS).

2193 5/N16
✔ **Anta Factory Shop** Fearn · www.anta.co.uk · 01862 832477 Off B9175 from Tain to Nigg ferry, 8km through Hill of Fearn, at disused airfield. Shop with adjacent pottery. Also in Edinburgh, Glasgow and London. Anta is a classy brand: distinctively but not too tartan. Fabrics; rugs and throws, and ceramics/stoneware. You can commission furniture to be covered in their material. Pottery tour by arrangement. Open summer daily 9.30am-5.30pm (Sun 11am-5pm). Ring for winter hours. Pottery: Mon-Fri only. Nice café shuts 4pm.

2194 8/R24
✔ **Crail Pottery** Crail · www.crailpottery.com · 01333 451212 At the foot of Rose Wynd, signposted from main street (best to walk). In a tree-shaded Mediterranean courtyard and upstairs attic, a cornucopia of brilliant and useful things by the prolifically talented Grieve family since 1965. Huge variety of useful and beautiful ceramics still being made downstairs. This is *the* East Neuk memento. Open 9am-5pm (weekends from 10am). Don't miss the harbour nearby, one of the most romantic neuks in the Neuk. Good tearoom on way (1431/TEAROOMS).

2195 5/N16
NC500
✔ **Tain Pottery** Tain · www.tainpottery.co.uk · 01862 894112 Off the A9 just S of Tain (opposite side of A9 to road signed for Anta at Fearn; see above). Big, welcoming working pottery, big stuff and often bold design, hand-painted and very popular (they do the National Trust for Scotland and are stocked all over the UK). Daily in summer, 9am-6pm (Sat/Sun 10am-5pm). Closed Sun in winter.

2196 4/L12
NC500
✔ **Balnakeil** Durness From Durness and the A836, take Balnakeil and Faraid Head road for 2km W. Founded in the 1960s in what one imagines was a haze of hash, this craft village is still home to downshifters and creatives, i.e. talented people. Paintings, pottery, print-making, glass, wood and jewellery in prefab huts where community members work and hang out (the site was an early-warning

station). **Cocoa Mountain** (01971 511233) make here their heavenly thin chocolate you get all over the north, including Dornoch, and have a chocolate bar open AYR (9am-6pm; 11am-4pm in winter). Discreetly round the back is **The Café**, the best place to eat in this NW corner (1403/CAFÉS).

2197 8/R27 ✓ **Harestanes Countryside Centre** nr Jedburgh Off A68 at Ancrum, the B6400 to Nisbet. Farm steading complex on Monteviot Estate (1568/GARDENS) with café/exhibition/superior crafts, including the excellent **Buy Design** offering beautiful furniture (there are woodworking courses here), ceramics and glass. Also **Mary's Dairy** (she even makes the cones for the very sweet ice cream). Easter-Oct 10am-5pm; check website for times in winter. Event programme and walks (get Harestanes Path leaflet at the visitor centre) – go through the door in the wall to the Teviot walks and St Cuthbert's Way. Better tearoom 1km down the road at **Woodside** (1452/TEAROOMS). Harestanes is a genuinely good facility for craftmakers and visitors.

2198 8/Q24 ✓ **Maspie House Gallery** Falkland · www.maspiehousegallery.com · 01337 857735 Small up and downstairs gallery near The Cross in downtown Falkland, Fife's most pleasant village to visit (1814/CASTLES; 2050/WALKS; 1432/CAFÉS). John McLaren shows work from his own talented family and other local artists, and he has 'the eye', so some interesting pictures in various mediums, and ceramics. Tue-Sat 11am-4pm. 2-bedroom B&B adjacent.

2199 5/F18 ✓ **Skye Makers Gallery** Dunvegan · www.skyemakers.com · 01470 521666 Karen Redfern's 2-floor gallery on Dunvegan main street, the road to the castle (1821/CASTLES), a curated one-stop central location for many of Skye's best artists. A part of 'Art Skye', a creative trail illustrated in a readily available booklet. I particularly liked the photography of Ronald MacDonald and Russell Sherwood, and the wood sculpture of John Parsons. Also the engravings of the Raven Press Gallery, which is in Glendale near **The Three Chimneys** 1204/INNS. Karen also produces a beautiful art magazine *Skye Makers*.

2200 4/J14 & 4/K15 NC500 ✓ **Highland Stoneware** Lochinver · 01571 844376 & Ullapool · 01854 612980 · www.highlandstoneware.com On road to Baddidarach as you enter Lochinver on A837; and on way N beyond Ullapool centre. A large-scale pottery business including a shop/warehouse and open studios that you can walk round (Lochinver is more engaging). Similar to the ceramica places you find in the Med, but less terracotta: more painted and heavy-glazed stoneware in set styles. Many broken plates adorn your arrivals. Great selection; pricey, but you may have luck in the Lochinver discount section. Mail-order service. 9am-6pm weekdays. Check website for weekend/winter hours.

2201 8/Q25 ✓ **Kinloch Anderson** Edinburgh · www.kinlochanderson.com · 0131 555 1390 A trek from uptown but firmly on the tourist trail and so much better than the High St, i.e. the tartan-tainted Royal Mile. Independent, family-run company since 1868, they are experts in Highland dress and all things tartan; they've supplied *everybody*. They design and manufacture their own tartans, have a good range of men's tweed jackets; even rugs. Mon-Sat 9am-5.30pm.

2202 8/S25 **Number Four** St Abbs · www.numberfourgallery.co.uk · 01890 771111 It's the number 4 cottage in the row by the car park and interpretation centre at the start of the walks to glorious **St Abb's Head** (1800/RESERVES; 2087/WALKS). This very personal 'art and craft gallery' is perhaps much better than it has to be. Thrives because of the good taste and judgement of Jenny and all-round artist Chris. Hard not to find something here to adorn or enhance your life. From £10 to £1,000. Open AYR. Closed Wed.

2203 5/F17   **Edinbane Pottery** Skye · www.edinbane-pottery.co.uk · 01470 582234
500m off A850 Portree (22km) to Dunvegan road. Since 1971, Stuart Whatley's
great working pottery has been making wood-fired and salt-glazed pots of all
shapes and for every purpose. A family business where the various processes can
often be seen in progress. AYR: Mon-Fri 9am-6pm; Easter-Oct: 7 days. 2 great
places in the village to stay and eat (2285/2308/SKYE).

2204 5/F17   **Skye Silver** Colbost · www.skyesilver.com · 01470 511263   10km Dunvegan
on B884 to Glendale. Since 1974, reputable jewellery made and sold in an old Skye
schoolhouse in a distant corner; **The Three Chimneys** restaurant and **Red Roof**
nearby. Well-made Celtic designs; good gifts. Check website for opening times. Big
online.

2205 6/P17   **Findhorn Pottery** Findhorn, nr Forres · www.findhornpottery.com ·
01309 691601   Deep in both the Findhorn Community (since 1971) and the
spreading park, it's more than interesting to wander through the eco-village to this
long-standing pottery and shop. 3 potters work away here and their ware is for sale.
It's the real deal! Apr-Oct 10.30am-5.30pm (from noon Sun). From 1pm Nov-Mar
(closed Mon/Tue). They never stop turning.

2206 7/F23   **Iona Abbey Shop** Iona   Via CalMac ferry from Fionnphort on Mull. Crafts
     HES   and souvenirs across the way in separate building. Proceeds support a worthy,
committed organisation. Christian literature, tapes, etc, but mostly artefacts from
nearby and around Scotland. Celtic crosses much in evidence, but then this is
where they came from! Also on the way to and from the abbey, **Aosdana** gallery
(jewellers) and **Oran Creative Crafts** in restored steadings are good to browse.

2207 9/M30   **Galloway Lodge Preserves** Gatehouse of Fleet · www.gallowaylodge.co.uk ·
     ☕   01557 814001   On High St, same building as the PO. Packed with local jams,
marmalades, chutneys and pickles. Scottish pottery by Scotia Ceramics, Highland
Stoneware and Dunoon. Good presents and jam for you. 10am-5pm. Self-service
coffee shop, home-made and old-style – good for mum, gran and bairns! See 785/
SW RESTAURANTS.

2208 8/R27   **Born in the Borders** nr Jedburgh · www.bornintheborders.com ·
01835 830495   On the A698 Hawick–Jedburgh off the A68 Edinburgh road.
Transformed farmyard on the Teviot with a deli, shop, café and microbrewery.
Takes 'Borders' literally, so provisions from Northumberland in the deli. A well-
promoted Borders stop and shop (and eat). Microbrewery open for look-see, Dark
Horse, Foxy Blonde (and they nabbed 'Flower of Scotland') on the shelves. 7 days.

2209 7/J21   **Crafts & Things** nr Glencoe village · www.craftsandthings.co.uk ·
     ☕   01855 811325   On A82 between Glencoe village and Ballachulish, across from Loch
Leven. Long here, an eclectic mix, a myriad of things. Mind, body and mountain
books, a trove of Scottish-crafted jewellery, easy on the eye art (upstairs) and
reasonably priced knit/outerwear. Good coffee shop doing salads, sandwiches, ice
cream and home baking. 7 days until 5pm.

The Very Special Independent Shops

🍵 *signifies notable café.*

2210 6/S19
🍵 ✓✓ **Hammerton Store** Aberdeen · www.hammertonstore.co.uk · 01224 324449 On road W to Deeside somewhere in a suburb. Susan Watson's love affair with Aberdeen and life. Not only a deli, more a superior provisioner where essentials include kindling, Katy's eggs, art, travelling rugs, cool pottery, cookery books. Susan properly selects and sources everything. Provenance is not an idle gesture – she goes to Lewis to see the gin being made (there are many others in the cabinet, there long before the boom). Bakes are from the estimable Alice of Bakery Lane. Tables inside and on the corner, where you can snack and reflect how nice it would be to have a place like this in your neighbourhood. Mon-Fri 8am-6pm; Sat/Sun 8.30am-5pm. Long may independence and good taste prevail.

2211 8/R27
🍵 ✓✓ **Main Street Trading Company** St Boswells · www. mainstreetbooks.co.uk · 01835 824087 On Main St just off A68. All-round very good thing for the Borders: a well-thought-out and browsable bookshop and café on the street, with excellent home-made food (834/BORDERS) and, across a courtyard, a deli and 'home shop', with Scottish and elsewhere gifts and handcrafted homeware. 10 years ago, Bill and Roz Delaney and a great team created a distinctive Borders destination (next best thing to the railway!). Closed Mon.

2212 8/N21
LL
🍵 ✓✓ **House of Bruar** nr Blair Atholl · www.houseofbruar.com · 01796 483236 Extraordinarily successful countryside mall. The shopaholic honeypot on A9 N of Blair Atholl. In the various floors and chambers they sell an enormous range of clothes, textiles and anything you might need for the home, garden or body. It really can claim to be the Harrods of the North. The vast food section sells the best of Scottish everything, with some top-end brands, more Scotch eggs, smoked salmon (and Lindt chocolate) than you ever thought existed, and there's always a queue at the huge self-service café with tables in and out. (There often seems more folk here than in Pitlochry.) Strategically placed where you want to stop on the A9, Bruar is the best of the roadside retail explosion. Falls nearby for non-retail therapy (1653/WATERFALLS). 7 days 9am-5pm.

2213 8/L23
✓ **Mhor In Store** nr Balquhidder · www.mhor.net · 01877 384691 On the A84, on the right heading west beside **Mhor 84**, the roadside inn (796/CENTRAL), a new star in the Mhor constellation of cool, stylish places to eat/sleep/drink and now shop. An idiosyncratic and random collection, from outdoorsy to urban chic; a bazaar of beautiful thingies – some might even be useful, e.g. walking sticks. Thu-Sun 10am-5pm.

2214 8/N22
& 8/Q25
✓ **Homer** Aberfeldy · 01887 820802 & Edinburgh · 0131 225 3168 · www. athomer.co.uk Born out of **The Watermill** (1419/TEAROOMS) and also in (a separate shop) the main street and 8 Howe St, in Edinburgh's New Town, floors of furniture, ceramics, textiles and kitchenware that complement the core bookshop and upstairs gallery that Kevin and Jayne Ramage started in 2005. Irresistible adjuncts to the good life selected with impeccable taste. Love from Scotland.

2215 8/N22 ✔ **The Highland Chocolatier** Grandtully · www.highlandchocolatier.com ·
☕ 01887 840775 Part of **Legends** coffee shop (1426/TEAROOMS), Iain Burnett's chocolateria is a Perthshire destination in itself. A splurge of artisan chocolate-makers in recent years but Iain's meticulously crafted and beautifully presented individual and boxed chocs are in a class of their own. Indulge. 7 days 10am-5pm.

2216 9/N29 ✔ **Thomas Tosh** Thornhill · www.thomastosh.com · 01848 331553 Near
☕ the crossroads in East Morton St. Mr T. Tosh was a local guy lang syne, not the proprietor of this lofty emporium in an old parish hall, in the often sped-through but delightful toon of Thornhill. Great taste here in all manner of essential and gifty things, ceramics, furniture, prints and especially books selected by Messrs O'Keefe & Cripps. The café does great home baking, soups, coffee. Licensed. Occasional events; they bring culture to this part of the county.

2217 1/Q10 ✔ **Judith Glue** Kirkwall, Orkney · 01856 874225 & Bridge St, Inverness ·
01463 248529 · www.judithglue.com Opposite the cathedral in Kirkwall. Distinctive handmade jumpers, the runic designs are signature. Also the individual Highland and Orkney ceramics and jewellery, condiments and preserves. Landscape prints of Orkney are by twin sister, Jane. See also 2387/2396/ORKNEY. Mon-Sat 9am-6pm (longer hours in summer), Sun from 11am.

2218 4/K14 ✔ **Drumbeg Village Stores** Drumbeg · www.drumbegstores.co.uk ·
L 01571 833235 On the single-track road that runs from Kylesku to Lochinver,
NC500 halfway along, amid some of the most spectacular scenery in Scotland (1679/ SCENIC ROUTES), a wonderful wee store in tiny Drumbeg township. Shopkeeper Wendy Glover stocks essentials and Scottish produce from craft beers to her own baking, fruit & veg and coffee. Couple of tables outside overlooking the road. Bringing a whole new dimension to the 'shop local' mantra, at least she'll never have to compete with Tesco.

2219 5/H16 ✔ **Hillbillies and the Mountain Coffee Co.** Gairloch · 01445 712316 In the
NC500 middle of the straggly town amid great coastal (and mountain) scenery, a
☕ bookshop/coffee shop totally at one with its location and the people who appreciate it. Inspired selection of outdoor, thought-provoking and just good books. Maps, great stuff for presents and the caff with bagels, soup and great tea and Mountain Coffee list. Go buy a book! 9am-6pm. Closed Dec-Feb.

2220 5/F17 **St Kilda Shop** Dunvegan, Skye · 01470 521206 Unique little shop by the Estate offices and the pier on the way in/out of the castle itself (1821/CASTLES). The Macleods (whose domain you're in) and the MacDonalds fought over St Kilda, Scotland's island of the soul (2236/ISLANDS). Short of going there, everything you might like to know about it is presented here; many books. Also Harris Tweed and other handmade things to wear or give. Same hours as castle.

2221 3/E15 **Harris Tweed & Knitwear** Tarbert & Plocrapool · www. harristweedandknitwear.co.uk · 01859 502040 Catherine Campbell's warehouse and shop in Tarbert and croft/shop. Exhibition in the Old School on the Golden Road 5km S of Tarbert, a homage to Marion Campbell, the doyenne of croft-based weaving. Bales of tweed in Tarbert with knitwear and clothing at the adjacent shop and in the schoolhouse. Closed Sun.

Not Just Garden Centres, More A Way Of Life

☕ signifies notable café. Others may have cafés that have not been recommended.

2222 8/P25 ✔✔ **Dougal Philip's New Hopetoun Gardens** nr South Queensferry ·
☕ www.newhopetoungardens.co.uk · 01506 834433 On the A904. 40 years on, the ever-expanding and meticulously nurtured prize bloom of Scottish garden centres sprawling aesthetically among trees with many different zones and demonstration gardens (including Oriental and Scottish). Everything you could ever grow or put in a Scottish garden. Acres of accessories; from bird feeders to statuary of every age. Orangery tearoom has verdant views and tasty home-made stuff. Open AYR 10am-5.30pm. Tearoom closes 4.30pm. 'Art in the Garden' event Jul/Aug.

2223 8/P23 ✔✔ **Glendoick** Glencarse, nr Perth · www.glendoick.com ·
☕ 01738 860205 Take slip road off the A85, 10km from Perth, in the fertile Carse of the Tay. A large family-owned garden centre long a destination; adjacent, their famous rhododendron and azalea gardens – the (Cox) family garden, 2km up the road, open for snowdrops (Feb) and rhoddies and azaleas (Apr to mid-Jun) is remarkable. Garden centre is well laid out, with friendly, informed staff. Lovely pagoda garden. Nice (recently expanded) coffee shop with some home baking, hot meals; big on soups. Good bookshop, their 'Food Library', including Kenneth's own splendid books – the lavishly illustrated *Woodland Gardening* published 2018 (see Best Gardens, p. 264-9). You could spend hours here! 7 days till 5.30pm/5pm winter.

2224 7/J22 ✔ **Kinlochlaich Garden** Appin · www.kinlochlaichgardencentre.co.uk ·
01631 730342 On main A828 Oban–Fort William road just N of Port Appin turn-off, the West Highlands' largest nursery/garden centre. Set in a large walled garden filled with plants and veg soaking up the climes of the warm Gulf Stream. The Hutchisons nurture these acres enabling you to reap what they sow. With an array of plants on offer it's like visiting a friend's garden and being able to take home your fave bits. Charming cottages and apartments. For the treehouse, book well ahead. 7 days 9.30am-5pm (dusk in winter).

2225 8/R27 ✔ **Woodside** nr Ancrum · www.woodsidegarden.co.uk · 01835 830315 On
☕ B6400 off A68 opposite Ancrum turn-off just past **Harestanes** (2197/ SCOTTISH SHOPS) and before **Monteviot** (1568/GARDENS), this is Emma and Stephen Emmerson's conscientiously run nursery in a walled garden of the big hoose that overlooks the Teviot. Beautiful, quiet place with displays, events and organic agenda. They really care about their plants, the wildlife and yours. Best tearoom around in a wooden cabin in corner (1452/TEAROOMS). 7 days 10am-5pm. A walk starts here to **Peniel Heugh** and the view (1887/MONUMENTS).

2226 6/S20 **Raemoir Garden Centre** Banchory · www.raemoirgardencentre.co.uk ·
☕ 01330 825059 On A980 off main street 3km N of town. A garden centre that grew into a massive roadside emporium à la House of Bruar on a side road in Deeside (and on a taste bypass). Still, it's packed with people and the stuff they browse and buy. Café and restaurant are a destination in themselves (1448/TEAROOMS). Somewhere there are plants! 7 days 9am-6pm. Café till 5.30pm, restaurant till 4pm.

2227 9/M30 **Cally Gardens** Gatehouse of Fleet · www.callygardens.co.uk · **01557** 815029 An extraordinary assemblage of herbaceous perennials in a gorgeous walled garden. Comprehensive sales online but great to visit when open; check hours on website and also see 1572/GARDENS.

2228 8/Q23 **Turriff's** Broughty Ferry · **01382 778488** A wee nursery/farm shop/garden centre that's been here for decades, deep in the Dundee suburbs (though only a few minutes from the main road into 'The Ferry' off Victoria Rd). The garden is set around a lovely old mansion, which houses on its ground floor **Jessie's**, a superb tearoom (948/DUNDEE). A horticultural haven in a precisely cultivated and somewhat encroaching suburban landscape. An experience for all the family (many recent kids' activities added) and still in the same family. 7 days.

2229 8/R25 **Smeaton Nursery Gardens** East Linton · www.smeatonnurserygardens. co.uk · **01620 860501** 2km from village on North Berwick road (signed Smeaton). Up a drive in an old estate is this walled garden going back to the early 19th century. Wide range; good for fruit (and other) trees, herbaceous, etc. Nice to wander round, an additional pleasure is the Lake Walk halfway down the drive through a small gate in the woods. 1km stroll round a secret finger lake in magnificent mature woodland (10am-dusk 436/WALKS). Mon-Sat 9.30am-4.30pm, Sun 10.30am-4.30pm. Laid-back tearoom.

the
Best
of Skye & The Islands

The Best of Islands

2230 5/G18 ✓✓ **Raasay** A small car ferry (car useful, but bikes best) from Sconser (between Portree and Broadford) on Skye takes you to this, the best of places. The distinctive flat top of Dun Caan presides over an island whose history and natural history is Highland Scotland in microcosm. The village Inverarish, with rows of mining-type cottages, is 1km from the new jetty, which is by the 'big house', home to the excellent outdoor centre. Risen from the ashes of a fire which gutted most of it in 2009, **Raasay House** is also a hotel, café/bar, restaurant and library, and hosts a full activity programme for groups or individuals (2291/SKYE). The views from the lawn, or the viewpoint above the House, or better still from Dun Caan with the Cuillin on one side and Torridon on the other, are exceptional (2245/ISLAND WALKS). There's a ruined castle, a secret rhododendron-lined loch, seals, otters and eagles. Many walks on hill, shore or woods; free guides at the House or ferry to show you where! Find **'Calum's Road'** and read the book. Much to explore, spend a day or days, but go quietly here.
Regular CalMac ferry from Sconser on Skye (0800 066 5000).

2231 7/G25 ✓✓ **Jura** Small regular car ferry from Port Askaig on Islay or from Tayvallich in Argyll takes you to a different world. Jura is remote, scarcely populated and has an ineffable grandeur indifferent to the demands of tourism. Ideal for wild camping, and there's a great hotel and pub (2273/ISLAND HOTELS) in the only village (Craighouse) 12km from ferry at Feolin on the 'Long' road, and at the N end **Ardlussa House** (2335/JURA), on the estate where they make the highly regarded **Lussa Gin** (1552/GIN). Walking guides available at the hotel and essential, especially for the Paps, the hills that maintain such a powerful hold over the island. Easiest climb is from Three Arch Bridge; allow 6 hours. Evans' Walk, starting 1km N of the bridge is easier, still boggy. The distillery where The Jura comes from is not as beautiful as the drink it produces – tours www.jurawhisky.com. **Corryvreckan** whirlpool is another lure – boat tours (07976 280195); impressiveness depends upon tides. Barnhill, Orwell's house where he wrote *1984*, isn't open but there are many fascinating side tracks: the wild W coast; around Loch Tarbert; and the long littoral between Craighouse and Lagg. Also 1634/BEACHES; 1930/GRAVEYARDS. With the one 'Long' road and over 5,000 deer, the sound of silence is everything. And ask locally about 'T on the Beach' (Lussa Beach in the north) – a real treat. Bike hire (07436 886621).
CalMac (0800 066 5000) 7 days, 5-min service from Port Askaig. Passenger-only ferry from Tayvallich to Craighouse twice daily Easter-Sep (07768 450000). For bike hire in Craighouse, ask at the hotel.

2232 7/F23 ✓✓ **Iona** 150,000 visitors a year, but Iona still enchants (as it did the Colourists and centuries of pilgrims), especially if you can get away to the **Bay at the Back of the Ocean** (1638/BEACHES) or sit in one of the many gardens. Or stay: **Argyll Hotel** best 01681 700334 (1225/GET-AWAY HOTELS); **St Columba Hotel** near the abbey has more rooms and its garden 01681 700304 (2353/MULL); or B&B. There's a great hostel and now **Iona Pods** (1184/HOSTELS). Abbey shop and nearby galleries (2206/SCOTTISH SHOPS). Pilgrimage walks on Tuesday (10am from St John's Cross). Bike hire from Finlay Ross shop (01681 700357). Everything about Iona is benign; even the sun shines here when it's raining on Mull and corncrakes thrive while elsewhere they disappear.
Regular 15-min CalMac service from Fionnphort till 6pm, earlier in winter (0800 066 5000).

2233 7/F24 ✓✓ **Colonsay** www.colonsay.org.uk Accessible to day-trippers but time ashore is short so you need to arrange accom. The (7 x 16km) island is a haven of wildlife, flowers and beaches (1622/BEACHES) and a serene and popular stopover. Single-track roads great for cycling. 250m from the ferry, the eponymous hotel is congenial, convenient and way better than you might expect (2269/ISLAND HOTELS). Great bar; self-catering units nearby. Some holiday cottages and many B&Bs (check Colonsay website); camping not encouraged. Bar meals and supper at the hotel and **Pantry** at the pier. A wild 18-hole golf course and bookshop – yes, a bookshop adjacent (summer 3-5.30pm, closed Sun). Semi-botanical gardens at Colonsay House, with Garden Café adjacent, and fine walks, especially to Oronsay (2252/ISLAND WALKS). Don't miss the house at Shell Beach, which sells oysters and honey.
CalMac from Oban (or Islay). Crossing takes just over 2 hours. Times vary.
0800 066 5000.

2234 5/G20 ✓✓ **Eigg** www.isleofeigg.net Run by a community (heritage) trust, this small, perfectly formed island seems in robust health, with the first wind/water and solar-powered electricity grid in the world, and a growing, proactive population that many other islands would (and possibly will) die for. A wildlife haven for birds and sealife; otters, eagles and seal colonies. There's a friendly tearoom at the pier (boat hours only in winter); home baking, licensed; evening meals in summer. The irrepressible Sue Kirk runs the shop and Lageorna, which has a restaurant (01687 460081). There's also a B&B at Kildonan (01687 482446), a GH, and lovely cabins at Tigh an Sithean (01687 460049), near the Singing Sands (with other good walks). Check website for other B&Bs. **Glebe Barn** is a brill wee hostel 01687 315099 (1197/HOSTELS). Great walk to Sgurr An Eigg, an awesome perch on a summer's day (2258/ISLAND WALKS). Great events programme, including summer music fests **Fèis Eige** and **The Howlin' Fling**.
CalMac (from Mallaig) 0800 066 5000 or from Arisaig. Arisaig Marine
(01687 450224) 7 days in summer. Phone for other timings. No car ferry. Day trips to
Rum and Muck. Bike hire 07855 363252.

2235 5/F20 ✓✓ **Rum** www.isleofrum.com The large island in the group S of Skye, off the coast at Mallaig. The CalMac ferry plies between Canna, Eigg, Muck and Rum but not too conveniently and it's not easy to island-hop and make a decent visit. Rum, the most wild and dramatic, has an extraordinary time-warp mansion in Kinloch Castle, which is mainly a museum (guided tours tie in with boat trips). An ambitious campaign afoot at TGP to transfer the castle from SNH to community ownership, restoring accom, café and bar. Of all heritage sites in the islands, this is a must to visit. There are fine trails, climbs, bird-watching spots (largest shearwater population in the world!). 2 simple walks are marked for the 3-hour visitors, but the island reveals its mysteries more slowly. The Doric temple mausoleum to George Bullough, the industrialist whose Highland fantasy the castle was, is a 9km (3-hour) walk across the island to Harris Bay. Sighting the sea eagles (the first to be reintroduced into the UK) will stay with you all summer. Lovely **Ivy Cottage GH** does evening meals and picnics (www.ivycottageisleofrum.co.uk; 01687 462744; Apr-Sep).
CalMac ferry from Mallaig direct (twice a week) or via Eigg (2 hours 15 mins). Better
from Arisaig (Murdo Grant 01687 450224), summer only (can get 3 hours ashore).

2236 3/C16 ✓✓ **St Kilda** www.kilda.org.uk There's nothing quite like St Kilda … anywhere. By far the most remote and removed of the islands here, it is an expedition to reach and one of a physical, cultural and spiritual nature. A spectacular World Heritage site, run by NTS, it occupies a special place in the

Scottish heart and soul. Now much more accessible, with several day-trip options, you will be among many photographers, birdwatchers, archaeologists and divers (very clear waters); then you leave! No catering. Tiny pre-book campsite.
To visit: Kilda Cruises (www.kildacruises.co.uk) 01859 502060 from Leverburgh, Harris, and from Uig on Skye 07836 611699.

2237 7/E22 ✓✓ **Isle of Tiree** www.isleoftiree.com It is an isle, not just an island – flat, with lovely sand and grass and the weather's usually better than the mainland. High sun levels and a bit of wind does keep away the midges. Lots of outdoor activities: famously, windsurfing, but kayaking, bird-watching and other gentle pursuits. The **Scarinish Hotel** (www.tireescarinishhotel.com) and the **Tiree Lodge Hotel** (www.tireelodge.co.uk) are there but not much loved. There are 3 guest houses, a wee hostel (01879 220435), a campsite and a more than a couple of places to eat: amazing, really, in 30 square miles. And there are 2 festivals, music in July and windsurfing in October (48/67/EVENTS). Tiree has a unique character different to the islands on this page. But you may long for trees.
Daily flights from Glasgow (www.flybe.com; Tiree airport 01879 220456). CalMac (0800 066 5000) ferries from Oban (daily in summer, about 4 hours).

2238 7/G26 ✓✓ **Gigha** www.gigha.org.uk Romantic small island off Kintyre coast with classic views of its island neighbours. Easy mainland access (20-min ferry) contributes to an island atmos without a feeling of isolation (and yippee, no caravans!). Like Eigg, Gigha was bought by the islanders, so its fragile economy is dependent on your visit. The island is run by a heritage trust. **Achamore Gardens** (1573/GARDENS) are a big attraction (the house may yet become a hotel) and the **Gigha Hotel** (2276/ISLAND HOTELS) provides comfortable surroundings. All very relaxed and friendly. The **Boathouse Café** (www.boathousegigha.co.uk) by the ferry for lunch and dinner is superb under Gordon McNeill (Mar-Sep: 01583 505123). 3 B&Bs. Many trails and tracks; ask locally for leaflet. Bike, kayak hire, etc, by the ferry 01583 506520. Double Beach is where the Queen once swam off the royal yacht – two crescents of sand either side of the N end of Eilean Garbh isthmus.
CalMac ferry from Tayinloan on A83 (0800 066 5000), 27km S of Tarbert (Glasgow 165km). One an hour in summer, fewer in winter.

2239 7/F22 ✓✓ **Ulva** www.isleofulva.com Off W coast of Mull; boat leaves from the hamlet of Ulva Ferry on B8073 26km S of Dervaig. Idyllic wee island with 5 well-marked walks, including to the curious basalt columns similar to Staffa, or by causeway to the smaller island of Gometra; plan routes at the **Boathouse** interpretive centre and tearoom (with Ulva oysters, home-cooked food 9am-4.30pm Easter-Sep, not weekends, except Sun Jun-Aug). Sheila's (thatched) Cottage faithfully restored tells the Ulva story. No accom though camping can be arranged (01688 500264). A charming Telford church has services 4 times a year. Ulva is a perfect day away from the rat race of downtown Tobermory (and everywhere else)! In 2018, Ulva passed from private hands to the (Mull) community and campaigners. Check locally as to how this affects ongoing facilities for visitors.
All-day 5-min service (not Sat; Sun summer only) till 5pm.

2240 3/D19 ✓✓ **Eriskay** www.visitouterhebrides.co.uk Made famous by the sinking nearby of the SS *Politician* in 1941 and the salvaging of its whisky cargo, later immortalised by Compton Mackenzie in *Whisky Galore*, this Hebridean gem has all the idyllic island ingredients: perfect beaches (1955/CHARLIE), a lovely church, **St Michael's** (1906/CHURCHES), a hill to climb, a pub (called **The Politician** and telling the story round its walls; it sells decent pub food all day in summer), and the causeway to South Uist (the road cuts a swathe across the

island). Limited B&B and no hotel, but camping is OK if you're discreet. Eriskay and Barra together – the pure island experience.
CalMac ferry from Barra (Aird Mhor) 40 mins (0800 066 5000): 5 a day in summer, winter hours vary.

2241 3/F15 **The Shiants** www.shiantisles.net 3 magical, uninhabited (save for 250,000 birds) tiny islands off E coast of Harris. Read about them in one of the most detailed accounts (a love letter) to any small island ever written: *Sea Room* by Adam Nicolson, the guy who owns them. There's a bothy and it's possible to visit by visiting first his website or www.hebridean-whale-cruises.co.uk out of Gairloch.

2242 7/H22 **Lismore** www.isleoflismore.com Sail from Oban (car ferry) or better from Port Appin 5km off the main A828 Oban–Fort William road, 32km N of Oban; there's a seafood bar/restaurant/hotel (1372/SEAFOOD) to sit and wait. A road runs down the centre of the island (heritage centre and a rather good café halfway). Both till 4pm in season though check (www.lismoregaelicheritagecentre.org; 01631 760020). There are many hill and coastal walks; even the near end round Port Ramsay feels away from it all. History, natural history and air. Island bike hire from Port Appin (01631 730391). **Kerrera** is also a great excursion from Oban (ferry from Gallanach, 10 mins along the coast, takes only a few minutes) and another more peaceful world. Great **Tea Garden** (753/OBAN) and basic bunkhouse, via a well-marked (with teapots!) 1-hour walk.
CalMac (0800 066 5000) service from Oban, 4 or 5 times a day (2 on Sun). From Port Appin (32km N of Oban) several per day, 5 mins. Last back 8.15pm; 9.45pm Fri & Sat; 6.35pm winter, but check (01631 562125).

2243 7/F22 **Staffa** For many, a must, especially if you're on Mull. The geological phenomenon of Fingal's Cave and Mendelssohn's homage are well known. But it's still impressive. Several boat-trip options, many including the Treshnish Islands.
Trips from Mull (08000 858786). From Iona/Fionnphort (01681 700338 or 01681 700358). From Oban (01631 730686).

2244 7/H24 **Isle of Luing** A small (6km-long) fascinating island reached by regular ferry (takes cars) 24km S of Oban (0800 066 5000). See 2156/HISTORY.

Fantastic Walks In The Islands

For walk codes, see p. 12.

2245 5/G18
1 0KM
XCIRC
XBIKES
2-B-2

Dun Caan **Raasay** Still one of my favourite island walks – to the flat top of a magic hill, the one you see from most of the E coast of Skye. Take ferry (2230/ISLANDS). Walk guides at ferry or **Raasay House** (hotel, café, activity centre 2291/SKYE). Routes via old iron mine, near Inverarish village or shorter from road to N end. Amazing views – the island enchants.

2246 3/E15
1 2KM RETURN
XCIRC
XBIKES
2-B-2

Glen Uladail **North Harris** Take B887 W from N of Tarbert (on A859) almost to the end (where at Hushinish there's a good beach), but go right (towards the power station) before the big house (1303/HOUSE PARTIES). Park here or further in and walk to dam (3km from road). Take right track round reservoir and left around the upper loch. Over the brim you arrive in a wide, wild glen; an overhang 2km ahead is said to have the steepest angle in Europe and is favoured by extreme climbers. Go quietly; if you don't see deer and eagles here, you're making too much noise on the grass. On the way, 7km from the main road turn-off at **Meavaig**, there's a car park – a track leads up Glen Meavaig 2km to the North Harris Eagle Observatory. The longest single path in the Western Isles – **Meavaig to Bogha Glas** (16km) can be started at carpark either end.

2247 3/G13
& 3/G12
3-11KM · CIRC
XBIKES ·
2-B-2
Walks on Lewis 2 coastal walks in the N of Lewis. **Tolsta Head** via B895 NE of Stornoway and its continuation to the car park of **Traigh Mhor** (1626/BEACHES). Head for the cliffs of the Head; walk combines magnificent sands, big cliffs and impressive sea stacks. **The Butt of Lewis** from Port Nis going N as far as you can get in the Hebrides. Start at the cemetery by Eoropaidh Beach. A fine, airy walk on mainly grassy paths, heading first for the Stevenson lighthouse. Can shorten to 3km or do fuller circuit.

2248 7/G23
15/20KM
XCIRC
XBIKES
2-B-2
Carsaig Mull In S of island, 7km from A849 Fionnphort–Craignure road near Pennyghael. 2 walks start at pier: going left towards Lochbuie for a spectacular coastal/woodland walk past Adnunan Stack (8km); or right towards the imposing headland where, under the cliffs, the Nuns' Cave was a shelter for nuns evicted from Iona during the Reformation. Nearby is a quarry, the stone from which was used to build Iona Abbey. Much further on (12km Carsaig), at Malcolm's Point are the extraordinary Carsaig Arches, carved by wind and sea (take great care!).

2249 7/G22
3KM
CIRC
XBIKES
2-B-2
Glengorm Estate nr Tobermory, Mull Old, accessible estate 7km N of Tobermory off Dervaig road with 3 easy-to-find-and-follow routes. Good map in **The Coffee Shop** (1409/TEAROOMS), one of the best on Mull for sustenance before and after (it can get windy on the headlands). Walks vary from less than 30 mins (the Flat Rock), through 1 hour (the Fort and bathing pool 2141/OPEN-AIR POOLS) to 1.5 hours (Mingary Point). Some magical geomorphology you can climb. If you stay in **Glengorm Castle** (2347/MULL), you can do the lot at your ease.

2250 7/J26
11KM
CIRC
XBIKES
2-B-2
Cock of Arran Lochranza Start and finish at Lochranza church on A841 and follow the signs to the magnificent shoreline via Newton. Divers and ducks share the littoral with seals. Look for Giant Centipede fossil trail, and *Hutton's Unconformity*, a big deal in the geology world. Further on at opening of wall, pace 350 steps and turn left up to Ossian's Cave. Path crosses Fairy Dell Burn and eventually comes out at Lochranza Bay. Allow 4/5 hours and stout boots.

2251 7/J27
6KM
CIRC
XBIKES
2-B-2
Holy Isle by Arran The small island that sits so greenly and serenely in Lamlash Bay is 1km away by hourly ferry (less frequently in winter; 01770 700463). Holy Isle is known as the spiritual sanctuary and World Peace Centre project of **Samye Ling Monastery** (1282/RETREATS) but you can freely walk around the littoral and easily to the top of the presiding single hill (Mullach Mòr). It's natural, beautiful and spiritual; a walk to cherish.

2252 7/F24
12 + 6KM
XCIRC
BIKES
1-A-2
Colonsay www.colonsay.org.uk See 2233/ISLANDS. From hotel or the quay, walk to Colonsay House and its lush, overgrown intermingling of native plants and exotics (8km round trip); Garden Café. Or to the priory on Oronsay, the smaller island. 6km to the Strand (you might get a lift with the postman) then cross at low tide, with enough time (at least 2 hours) to walk to the ruins. Allow longer if you want to climb the easy peak of Ben Oronsay. Tide tables at hotel. Nice walk also from **Kiloran Beach** (1622/BEACHES) to Balnahard Beach – farm track 12km return.

2253 5/G17
30KM
XCIRC
XBIKES
The Trotternish Ridge Skye The 30km high-level ridge walk, as opposed to The Quirang and The Old Man of Storr (see below for both), also offers many shorter walks without climbing or scrambling, but to take in the whole in a circular walk, start at the **Lealt Falls** (1659/WATERFALLS) car park on the A855 Staffin road.

2254 5/G17 **The Old Man of Storr** Skye The enigmatic basalt finger visible from the Portree-
9KM Staffin road (A855). Start from car park on left, 12km N from Portree. There's a
CIRC well-defined path through afforestation towards the cliffs and a steep climb up the
XBIKES grassy slope to the pinnacle which towers 165ft tall. Great views over Raasay to
2-B-2 the mainland. Lots of space and rabbits and birds, who make the most of it, but an
increasingly popular pilgrimage, so much human company, too. 3km, climb 250m.

2255 5/G17 **The Quirang** Skye See 1694/VIEWS for directions to start point. The strange
6KM formations have names (e.g. The Table, The Needle, The Prison) and it's possible
CIRC to walk round all of them. Start of the path from the car park on the Uig–Staffin
XBIKES road is easy. At the first saddle, take the second scree slope to The Table, rather
2-B-2 than the first. When you get to The Needle, the path to the right between two giant
pinnacles is the easiest of the 3 options. From the top you can see the Hebrides.
This place is supernatural; anything could happen. So be careful.

2256 5/G18 **Scorrybreac** Skye A much simpler prospect than the above and more quietly
3KM spectacular but mentioned here because anyone can do it; it's only 3km (or longer
CIRC 6.5km to the Storr Lochs) and it's more or less in Portree. Head for **Cuillin Hills**
XBIKES **Hotel** off Staffin Rd out of town (2290/SKYE). Shoreline path signed below hotel.
1-A-1 Passes Black Rock, where once Bonnie Prince Charlie left for Raasay; continues
round hill. Nice views back to the bright lights and pink and pastel houses of Portree.

2257 1/Q11 **Hoy** Orkney There are innumerable walks on the scattered Orkney Islands; on
20/25KM a good day, head to the N of Hoy for some of the most dramatic coastal scenery
CIRC anywhere. Ferries from Houton. Stromness via Graemsay, met by a minibus or a
MT BIKES car ferry from Houton E of Stromness with 20km drive to start of walk. Make tracks
2-B-2 N or S from junction near Moaness pier and don't miss the landmarks, the bird
sanctuaries and of course the Old Man himself if you've got the time (4 hours). See
2098/WALKS.

2258 5/G20 **An Sgurr** Eigg Unmissable treat on Eigg. Take to the big ridge. Not a hard pull;
extraordinary views and island perspective from the top. See 2234/ISLANDS. Start
from the ferry pier, 3 hours.

▬▬▬ The Best Island Hotels

This section excludes Skye which has its own hotel listings, p. 386–9.

2259 7/F26 ✓✓ **The Machrie** Islay · www.themachrie.com · 01496 302310 The
47 ROOMS long-established hotel (and golf course) in the middle of Islay on the long
£LOTS road near the airport, practically rebuilt by Campbell Gray Hotels in one of the most
anticipated transformations (the hotel, the golf course, the island) of 2018. It was a
long time coming, but the results are impressive. Upstairs restaurant (called '18')
and the Stag Lounge make the most of the view (the Links, the ocean, the sunset)
and their Islay whisky collection. Haven't visited at TGP. Reports, please.

2260 3/F14 ✓✓ **Lews Castle** Stornoway, Lewis · www.naturalretreats.co.uk ·
23 ROOMS 01625 416430 Overlooking the town, a reconstructed landmark. It was
L the home of Lord Leverhulme, given to the town in perpetuity, abandoned then
££ renovated to an impressive standard (certainly upstairs) into a hotel with suites and
self-catering apartments for individual (average stay is 3–4 nights) or exclusive use.
Bedrooms are spacious; kitchen/lounges have (mostly) views across the extensive
grounds to the port and the sea, and are light and contemporary with tasteful

furnishings and art. Downstairs, a bar, a café/restaurant **The Storehouse**, a shop, a ballroom and a 'state room' for afternoon tea. No country-house/posh castle aura. Similarly, the grounds (at TGP, soon to be restored gardens) are open at all times, with great cycling and walking trails. Sympathetically managed by Natural Retreats, who are also in John o' Groats (1084/HIGHLANDS), this is approachable luxury with every convenience and great for families.

2261 3/E16
6 ROOMS · DF
LL · NO TV
MAR-DEC
£££

✓✓ **Scarista House** South Harris · www.scaristahouse.com · 01859 550238 21km Tarbert, 78km Stornoway. On the W coast famous for its beaches and overlooking one of the best – 200m across the road by the postbox on the Hebridean Way (1619/BEACHES). Tim and Patricia Martin's civilised retreat and home from home. Fixed menu in dining rooms, the sea over there. No phones or other intrusions (though Wi-Fi and TV in the kitchen); many books. The golf course up the road is exquisite. Good family hotel but delightfully laid-back. Great suites.

£££ **EAT** A fixed menu but the place to eat in these Hebrides. 4 courses; good value for this quality. Notify fads and diets. Open to non-res. 2 lovely dining rooms.

2262 1/Q10
8 ROOMS
££

✓✓ **The Storehouse** Kirkwall, Orkney · www. thestorehouserestaurantwithrooms.co.uk · 01856 252250 As the website says, this is a ground-floor restaurant with (comfortable, contemporary) rooms above, a long labour-of-love conversion of a historic storehouse in downtown Kirkwall and an island hotel in the far north of everything that could be in any modern city hotel quarter.

EAT The Leonards café and restaurant – look no further for eats (except maybe Judith Glue, same owner, same town 2395/ORKNEY).

2263 7/F26
11 ROOMS
DF
££

✓✓ **Bridgend Inn** Bridgend, Islay · www.bridgend-hotel.com · 01496 810212 Near Bowmore on the Port Askaig road. I love this comfortable roadside hostelry, long a fixture on the island by the A846/A847 crossroads and a gathering place for locals and visitors. Owned by Islay Estates, it has an easy-going bar (with food), a lounge for tea and timeless afternoons, and a dining room opening on to lovely gardens. Bedrooms in simple, good taste are inexpensive. Manager Lorna McKechnie heads a very naturally friendly team. Good art on the walls everywhere. A peaceful retreat from mainland life!

2264 7/F26
10 ROOMS
L
££

✓✓ **Port Charlotte Hotel** Port Charlotte, Islay · www. portcharlottehotel.co.uk · 01496 850360 The epitome of the comfy island inn. Modern, discreet approach to guests. Sea swishing below; very much at the heart of this fine whitewashed village (1611/VILLAGES). Good whisky choice, traditional music (Wed & Sun) and good grub in the bar; restaurant dining room, with conservatory and sea-gazing terrace. Tourists in summer, twitchers in winter. The Allisons support local and Scottish artists (on the walls) and music, and Grahame sings in the Gaelic choir. The beating heart of Islay!

2265 7/J27
28 ROOMS
(HOUSE) +
36 (SPA)
DF · ££

✓✓ **Auchrannie** Brodick · www.auchrannie.co.uk · 01770 302234 More a resort than merely an island hotel but one that brings the outside in. And offers a huge range of outdoor activities. Tops for families (kids) but caters well for grown-ups without. Choice of restaurants, pools and types of accom. See 2312/ARRAN.

2266 7/G22
6 ROOMS
NO PETS
APR-OCT
££

Highland Cottage Tobermory, Mull · www.highlandcottage.co.uk ·
01688 302030 Breadalbane St opposite Tobermory fire station. Street above harbour (from roundabout on road from Craignure). Small, comfy rooms named after islands. This is a well-run cottage-boutique; both cosy and chic. Small, maybe, but perfectly formed: relax into Jo Currie's simply delicious, easy-going fine dining. Dave your amiable host. They know good food and they know Mull. It's the place to eat. Dining without fuss in a perfect parlour. Also 2345/MULL.

2267 7/J27
22 ROOMS
££

Douglas Hotel Brodick, Arran · www.thedouglashotel.co.uk ·
01770 302968 The new esplanade: where the Ardrossan ferry comes in. The Douglas has redefined Brodick for visitors, with attention to detail (well-chosen art, good lighting) and to service, overseen by local owner Sean and sister Elaine Henry. You're plugged in very comfortably to Arran. Mandy Todd has a firm, light touch in The Bistro. See also 2313/ARRAN.

2268 7/J27
13 ROOMS
££

Glenisle Hotel Lamlash, Arran · www.glenislehotel.com · 01770 600559
There's a choice of decent hotels on Arran and to urban standards. The smart, comfortable Glenisle also has the advantage of being in Lamlash (5km Brodick), so relaxing and buzzy at the same time. Overlooks bay and **Holy Isle** (2251/ISLAND WALKS). Nice bar and restaurant and garden terrace on the bay, and other good eating options nearby. Has a Michelin recommendation. New owners 2018 continuing a high standard. See also 2314/ARRAN.

2269 7/F24
10 ROOMS
L
MAY-SEP
££

Colonsay Hotel www.colonsayestate.co.uk · 01951 200316 Long-established, well run, and generally a superb island hotel, 400m from the ferry on this island perfectly proportioned for short stays (2233/ISLANDS). The laird (and wife) and their partners have turned this into a contemporary destination hotel. Calm public rooms and buzzy bar (especially quiz nights). Mobiles only work in the garden. House and garden to visit and stunning beach 5km. On your bike.

2270 7/F22
10 ROOMS
££

Coll Hotel www.collhotel.com · 01879 230334 Julie and Kevin Oliphant and daughter Laura continue to win accolades for their exemplary island hotel and restaurant on Coll, which to my shame and frustration I have never visited (yes, J & K, I'm still relying on other reports). But I know it's got a great island garden, a deck overlooking the sea and that big reconstruction brings a new larger restaurant that has 'amazing views', a public and lounge bar in a new extension. It's an ambitious and laudable leap of faith. All the bedrooms are in the old house. Coll is now designated a Dark Sky destination because of its very low light pollution – so look up! I imagine it's kind of perfect! Coll is 2.5/3 hours from Oban. Ferries sail AYR.

2271 7/F26
13 ROOMS
DF
££

The Islay Hotel Port Ellen, Islay · www.theislayhotel.com · 01496 300109
On corner where the ferry comes in. Completely refurbished by well-versed locals with a kind of Islay crowdfunding community buy-in. This hotel and bar are close to all island matters and yet the public rooms and bedrooms are light and contemporary – you feel you could be on any mainland. Very close to the big 3 distilleries: Laphroaig, Lagavulin and Ardbeg. Restaurant does get mixed reviews.

2272 7/F26
17 ROOMS
££

The Harbour Inn Bowmore, Islay · www.bowmore.com · 01496 810330
Owned by the parent company (Beam Suntory) of Bowmore Distillery, this top island restaurant with rooms is 2 doors up from the harbour in the centre of the main town on lovely, quite lively Islay. Rooms, 7 in the main building, 5 in the 'Old Bakery' across the road and 5 nearby 'cottages', are all contemporary and comfy. Lounge with views and a notable restaurant, especially seafood. Bar with malts and bar meals (LO 9.30pm).

2273 7/G25 ✓ **Jura Hotel** Craighouse · www.jurahotel.co.uk · **01496 820243** 12km
17 ROOMS from Islay ferry at Feolin. The island hub run with Jura style by Andy and Cath
L McCallum and a young, obliging team. Bedrooms are simple and serviceable,
NO TV though not large and no TV. Bar for all local craic; they make their eclectic clientele
£ welcome. Food in both bar and dining room best it's been for years under Stuart
Russell. All home-made, including pasta and top granola for breakfast. Everything
you'll need, including Wi-Fi. Camping on their grassy field to the sea is free. See
2231/ISLANDS.

2274 3/C20 **Castlebay Hotel** Castlebay, Barra · www.castlebay-hotel.co.uk ·
15 ROOMS **01871 810223** Prominent position overlooking bay and ferry dock. You see where
LL you're staying long before you arrive. Old-style holiday hotel at the centre of Barra
FEB-DEC life. Perhaps upgrading would spoil its charm though the bedrooms have improved
££ a tad. OK restaurant and bar meals. Adjacent bar, famed for craic and car culture,
has more than a dash of the Irish (1316/GOOD PUBS) and a busy pool table. Sea view
superior rooms worth the extra.

2275 3/C20 **Isle of Barra Beach Hotel** Tangasdale · www.isleofbarrahotel.co.uk ·
15 ROOMS **01871 810383** A 3km hop from Castlebay on Tangasdale Beach, a quiet, very
L island location with wide views from the spacious lounge. Accom on brilliant Barra
DF is often hard to come by (demand always seems to exceed supply). Though the
MAY-SEP hotel could benefit from a titivation, location's the thing: you might be lucky to get
££ in here. Good reports for food. They have electric bikes.

2276 7/G26 **Gigha Hotel** Gigha · www.gighahotel.com · **01583 505254** A short walk
12 ROOMS from the ferry on an island perfectly proportioned for a short visit; easy walking
££ and cycling. Residents' lounge peaceful, with dreamy views to Kintyre. Menu with
local produce, e.g. Gigha prawns, scallops and the halibut. Island life without the
remoteness. See also 2238/ISLANDS.

 ✓ **Argyll Hotel & St Columba Hotel** Iona Reports: 1210/INNS; 2353/MULL.

✓ **Amhuinnsuidhe Castle** Harris · **01859 560200** 6km N of Tarbert, then
12km to the W. Wild, real, luxurious, great food and fishing. Report: 1303/
HOUSE PARTIES.

The Best of Skye

The Bridge Unromantic but easy and free; from Kyle.
CalMac Ferry www.calmac.co.uk · 0800 066 5000 Mallaig–Armadale, 30 mins. Tarbert (Harris)–Uig, 1 hour 35 mins, as Mallaig.
The Best Way to Skye Glenelg–Kylerhea www.skyeferry.co.uk 5-min sailing. Continuous Easter–Oct. Winter sailings – check tourist information centre. Community run. See 7/JOURNEYS.

WHERE TO STAY ON SKYE

2277 5/F17
6 ROOMS
£LOTS

✓✓ **The House Over-By at The Three Chimneys** Colbost · www.threechimneys.co.uk · 01470 511258 7km W of Dunvegan by the B884 to Glendale. When Eddie and Shirley Spear transformed their house over-by into the House Over-By, it was the first boutique-style accom in the Highlands. Refurbished recently and now many years later it's still a model of understated luxury in a wild and woolly place. From inside your double-level suite you can contemplate the hill, the happy sheep and the loch below. Rooms are adjacent/over-by from the accolade-laden restaurant (in world's top lists). Separate dining room for a healthy breakfast transforms into a light conservatory lounge in the evening.
EAT After the long hike across the courtyard or a drive from the rest of the world you deserve a treat! With chef Scott Davies and a top team. See below.

2278 5/H19
19 ROOMS
DF
£LOTS

✓✓ **Kinloch Lodge** Sleat · www.kinloch-lodge.co.uk · 01471 833333 Just S of Broadford, 55km Portree. The ancestral but not-at-all imposing home of Lord and Lady Macdonald, with newer-build house adjacent – adding 10 superbly appointed rooms – with its own spacious, country drawing room. It's a family affair with Isabella most hospitably in charge. Lady Mac is Claire Macdonald of cookery fame; which may set the tone of your expectations but the accolade-laden menu is down to the executive chef, Marcello Tully, and you can bet that dinner in the perfect Highland lodge dining room is an epicurean experience to relish. Comfy bar and lounge for pre and après, Skye and the sky outside.
EAT At Lady Claire and Marcello's elegant table. See below.

2279 5/H19
12 ROOMS
4 SUITES
L
ATMOS
££

✓✓ **Eilean Iarmain** Sleat · www.eileaniarmain.co.uk · 01471 833332 15 mins S of Broadford. Tucked into the bay, Lady Lucilla Noble's Gaelic inn, with its great pub and good dining, provides sympatico, comfortable base in S of the island. Their famously Gaelic approach to hospitality (no TVs except in the suites but there is Wi-Fi), gives this place the indefinable 'it'. The ethics and principles of Lucilla's late husband, the eminent proponent of the dynamic Gaelic culture and environment, Sir Iain Noble, still prevail from 1976. It hasn't compromised much and doesn't have to. Bar is local craic central. 6 rooms in main hotel, garden rooms in the house overby. Also 4 suites in steading with grassy terrace to the shore (and they do have TV). Shop and gallery adjacent. They have their own 'Gaelic whisky' Poit Dhubh (an old illicit still is on view) and in 2018 their own gin – the complete Highland experience. You wander down to the quay for mobile phone reception; you don't want to go anywhere else.
££ **EAT The Praban Bar** for atmos and excellent bar food; dining room for fine dinner, both under chef Virgil Tiskus.

2280 5/G19
5 ROOMS
L
££

✓✓ **Coruisk House** Elgol · www.coruiskhouse.com · 01471 866330 20km from Broadford on the beautiful and relatively good road to Elgol, views of the mighty Blà Bheinn (Blaven) – you are heading for Turner country 1701/ VIEWS. 2km from Elgol harbour, an elegantly proportioned house, white outside and in (lime-washed pine in a conservatory the length of the house), and white and light in rooms and bathrooms. The whole effect is tasteful simplicity with hand-picked furnishings, decor, photographs. Clare and Iain have furnished a **Soho Farmhouse** far from everywhere, where you can really relax, walk, take *the* boat trip (8/JOURNEYS) and come back for Clare's 4/2/4 course dinner which hits all the right notes. 3 rooms, 2 suites (which do have small white TVs). You will love it here, as they do.

• •

THE SONAS COLLECTION HOTELS

3 highly individual boutique hotels by Anne Gracie and the late Ken Gunn:

2281 5/H19
18 ROOMS
NO PETS
££

✓ **Duisdale House** Sleat · www.duisdale.com · 01471 833202 Only 4km up the road from Toravaig (below) nearer to Broadford, Anne Gracie's bigger hotel in the south, refurbished boutique-style to a high standard (big wallpapers, luxe bathrooms). Hot tub on the garden deck; the gardens themselves quite gorgeous. Also the larger restaurant of the two; a little more casual. Eat especially in summer in the light conservatory or the intimate firelit lounge.

£££ **EAT** Either Toravaig (a little more formal) with chef Miles Craven, or Duisdale with Brian Ross – both excellent eats in the south.

2282 5/H19
9 ROOMS
NO PETS
££

✓ **Toravaig House Hotel** Sleat · www.skyehotel.co.uk · 01471 833231 Main road S from Broadford to Armadale. Anne's personally run hotel along with Duisdale above; two brilliantly positioned places to eat and stay on Skye. Small and charming with bold, contemporary refurbished rooms and pleasing restaurant with fine understated dining.

2283 5/F17
18 ROOMS
NO PETS
£££

✓ **Skeabost Country House Hotel** nr Portree · www.skeabosthotel.com · 01470 532202 11km W of Portree on the A850, the Dunvegan road. After the above, Sonas acquired this venerable Skye chateau, with a historic and stately interior. The conservatory, panelled dining room, original billiard room (and table), loads of public space and some sumptuous bedrooms have been upgraded and remodelled in the contemporary house style. There are 5 'Pier' rooms overlooking the loch, 4 in the 'Garden' and many to be added 2019 in the 'stable' block. Exquisite grounds, including the babbling River Snizort (hotel has fishing rights for 8 miles and own ghillie) and a sweet little 9-hole (though can do 18) golf course.

• •

2284 5/G18
21 ROOMS
DF
L
££

✓ **Sligachan Hotel** Sligachan · www.sligachan.co.uk · 01478 650204 The landmark and historic Sligachan Hotel at the crossroads of Skye, recently refurbished and hauled into the 21st century by the Coghill family, who've been here for generations. They've made a great job and it's now a civilised hub for all things outdoors and the good life generally. Rooms contemporary, a great bar, **Seamus'** (2309/SKYE FOOD), a microbrewery and a famous campsite across the road (1266/CAMPING). It's Skye totale.

2285 5/F17
6 ROOMS
££

✓ **Edinbane Lodge** Edinbane · www.edinbanelodge.com · 01470 582217 In the village just off the A850 Portree to Dunvegan road. This restaurant with rooms is the first (ambitious) solo venture of highly regarded Skye chef Colin Montgomery. I saw it as a building site in 2018, by the time you read this I have no doubt it will be another destination on the big island where now things change fast. Mark my words, but reports, please.

2286 5/G18 ✓ **Viewfield House** Portree · www.viewfieldhouse.com · 01478 612217
11 ROOMS   One of the first hotels you come to in Portree on the road from S (driveway
NO TV   opposite gas station). Traditionalists and comfortablists need look no further.
APR-OCT   Individual, grand but somehow modern, full of antiques and memorabilia, though
££   not at all stuffy (except the animals and raptors in the hall). There's purposefully no
TV. This historic and rambling house is also one of the best value-for-money hotels
on the island. Log fires; supper available if you want but many Portree options.
Croquet and a grass tennis court (just waiting to be revived). Track through the
woods to town (15 mins). Iona Macdonald Buxton is your genial host.

2287 5/F17 ✓ **Greshornish Country House** Greshornish · www.greshornishhouse.
10 ROOMS   com · 01470 582266 Pronounced 'Gresh-nish'. Off A850 Portree–Dunvegan
LL   road about halfway, then 6km along Loch Greshornish to delightful isolation.
££   Comfy, spacious, airy rooms presented with some taste (nice pics) by local
entrepreneur Campbell Dickson – who also has **The Portree Hotel** (below) and
whose parents used to own the house. Log fires, billiard room, candlelit dinners.
A good retreat (available for exclusive use).

2288 5/G18 **Bosville Hotel** Portree · www.bosvillehotel.co.uk · 01478 612846
20 ROOMS   Refurbished rooms and a place to eat at the top of the brae heading N from centre
£££   on the road to Staffin. **Dulse & Brose** restaurant (2301/SKYE RESTAURANTS); urban
standard of comfort and at the very heart of Portree.

2289 5/G18 **Marmalade Hotel** Portree · www.marmaladehotel.co.uk · 01478 611711
8 ROOMS   Leave from corner of main square, go uphill away from sea and keep going 1.5km.
£££   Unlikely, almost suburban location until you see the view (from gardens and 4 of
the 8 rooms). Rooms are above the busy bar/restaurant, which is popular with
locals, especially for pizza. Friendly staff (and friendly midges if you're out on the
lawn in summer).

2290 5/G18 **Cuillin Hills Hotel** Portree · www.cuillinhills-hotel-skye.co.uk ·
29 ROOMS   01478 612003 On the edge of Portree (off road N to Staffin) near water's edge.
££   Secluded mansion-house hotel with nice conservatory. Great views from most
rooms and the 2 dining areas. Superb terrace/lawn. Nice walk round the bay can
start from the garden (2256/ISLAND WALKS).

2291 5/G18 **Raasay House** Raasay, off Skye · www.raasay-house.co.uk · 01478 660300
22 ROOMS   The 'big house' in a classic setting on Raasay, the best of islands (2230/ISLANDS), a
DF   short ferry from Sconser, halfway between Broadfoot and Portree. An ill wind and a
££   fire razed most of the building in 2009, but it was extensively and sympathetically
restored into an all-round Skye asset: hotel, café, restaurant, bar, library and quite
brilliant activity centre. Many walks. 3 levels of room, including posh. Raasay will
enfold you from here.

2292 5/G18 **The Portree Hotel** Somerled Sq, Portree · www.theportreehotel.com ·
26 ROOMS   01478 612511 On the corner of the square in very downtown Portree with a busy
NO PETS   bar and café/restaurant. Recently extensively refurbished in contemporary style, a
££   mid-price stopover. Other eating options nearby.

2293 5/G18 **Rosedale Hotel** Beaumont Cres, Portree · www.rosedalehotelskye.co.uk ·
20 ROOMS   01478 613131 A traditional, long-established (almost historic) Portree hotel on the
NO PETS   corner of the bay and harbour, refurbished and reimagined by energetic new owner
L · APR-NOV   Neil Beaton. Inexpensive by Portree/Skye standards. Rooms vary. Small upstairs
££   restaurant. Car park by arrangement in summer.

2294 5/G19
85 ROOMS
£

Sabhal Mòr Ostaig Sleat · www.smo.uhi.ac.uk · **01471 888000** Pronounced 'Sawal More Ostag', the Gaelic College off A851 N of Armadale. Otherwise student accom but excellent inexpensive rooms (£40 single/£80 twin) on an expensive island in modern builds overlooking Sound of Sleat. The penthouse is spectacular. Breakfast and dinner in bright refectory; there's also a café and a shop. You could learn Gaelic!

2295 5/G17
11 + 7 ROOMS
MAR-OCT
£LOTS

Flodigarry Hotel www.hotelintheskye.co.uk · **01470 522203** In a glorious elevated setting looking over to Staffin Island in the far N of Skye (35km from Portree on A855, mostly single-track road). Recommended in early editions of *StB*, this much-loved mansion hotel went through a patchy patch, but new owners have refurbished and boldly blinged up to a high spec. Front rooms have truly spectacular views (and are priced accordingly). Flora MacDonald's (actual) cottage adjacent has 7 additional rooms. Bar's nice.

THE BEST RESTAURANTS ON SKYE

2296 5/F17
£LOTS

✓✓ **The Three Chimneys** Colbost · www.threechimneys.co.uk · **01470 511258** 7km W of Dunvegan on B884 to Glendale. There has been a lot of water under that Bridge but after more than 25 years of this book and their restaurant, Shirley and Eddie Spear's Three Chimneys, in a converted cottage on the edge of the best kind of nowhere, is still where you kinda must go on Skye. This was the first restaurant in Scotland to prove that it didn't matter where you were – if the food and atmos were right, people would find you. Now look how many have followed in their footsteps. With chef, Scott Davies, the Chimneys goes from delicious strength to strength. They shop local for everything (Skye supplies hugely improved following their example), from Glendale leaves to local langoustines. Fastidious, smart service, a voluble and persuasive sommelier, and a strong kitchen team. It's a long road to Colbost but by the start of your starter you know why you came. They can recommend some B&Bs when their own rooms are (as usual) full. Lunch Mar-Nov, dinner AYR.

2297 5/H19
£LOTS

✓✓ **Kinloch Lodge** Sleat · www.kinloch-lodge.co.uk · **01471 833333** In S on Sleat Peninsula, 55km S of Portree signed off the main Sleat road along a characterful track. The Macdonald family home and hotel offers a taste of the high life without hauteur; their pics and portraits surround you as you start with drinks in the drawing rooms and move to the elegant dining room. Lady Claire herself no longer in the kitchen – it's maestro and mentor to many of the new hot Skye chefs, Marcello Tully's food that you come to adore. 5 courses (fixed menu, with 2-choice main, so flag up fads/diets) or 7-course 'tasting' and 'special'. Great écossais/français cheeseboard with flight option. It's an 'experience Skye through food' thing, as the sun goes down outside the windows between the portraits, and the curtains are drawn. There's also afternoon tea.

2298 5/G18
£££

✓✓ **Scorrybreac** Portree · www.scorrybreac.com · **01478 612069** Scorrybreac House is indeed a house in Bosville Terrace on the road to Staffin. Small (8 tables) and widely thought to be just about perfect, this started as a pop-up by Calum Munro (son of Donnie, notable Scottish musician and man about Skye) but became the must-go eatery. Simple approach with a light, confident and imaginative touch: just very fine cooking. Calum's new exciting and ambitious hotel project in Portree's Square opening at TGP.

2299 5/F17 ✓✓ **Lochbay Restaurant** Stein · www.lochbay-restaurant.co.uk · LL ✓✓ 01470 592235 12km N of Dunvegan off A850. Small, celebrated, ATMOS accoladed seafood bistro with chef/patron Michael Smith sending out great £££ seafood from a tiny kitchen. Report: 1359/SEAFOOD.

2300 5/F18 ✓ **The Oyster Shed** Carbost · 01478 640383 Paul McGlynn, the oyster £ ✓ farmer's farm shop and seafood takeaway, behind the Talisker Distillery, via an atrocious road – and that was before the campervan overload of 2018. Oysters, naturally, and lobster, crab, langoustines. BYOB. A foodie corner of Skye worth weaving through the potholes to find. Daytime only. Check times in winter. See 1362/SEAFOOD.

2301 5/G18 **Dulse & Brose** Portree · www.dulsebrose.com · 01478 612846 Long the ££ place to eat at the top of the town, the restaurant of the Bosville Hotel got a new name, a new look and new everything some years back. Sassy, casual dining; this is well-turned-out food in a bistro setting. Open AYR.

2302 5/G18 **Café Arriba** Portree · www.cafearriba.co.uk · 01478 611830 Upstairs café £ at the top of the road down to the harbour. A funky, bright, long-established and kinda boho caff on Skye with a view of the bay. Eclectic home-made food changes daily, always vegetarian, some vegan. Big breakfasts till 4pm. Cosmo cuisine and atmos. It pulls off the trad yet contemporary trick. 7 days 8am-6pm.

2303 5/F18 **The Old School Restaurant** Dunvegan · www.oldschoolrestaurant.co.uk ££ · 01470 521421 On main road away from castle, for over 30 years a perennially popular family-run bistro, much loved for local food and approach. Not so old school, just solid: all the favourites are here. Lunch, summer only Wed-Sun, dinner 7 nights AYR.

2304 5/E17 **Red Roof Skye** Glendale · www.redroofskye.co.uk · 01470 511766 Way out ££ NW at Glendale (beyond the Three Chimneys, above). In 2018, Gareth, Petri and Hanna reopened the white bothy with the red roof as a croft-to-table restaurant. Set 3-course menu. Jun-Oct. Tue-Thu only. Always loved locally. Check website for current info.

2305 5/F18 **Jann's Cakes** Dunvegan · 01470 521730 Main road out of village, A863 to £ Broadford. A wee shack really but where Jann (and Lewis) Dove turn out an amazing array of heavyish but heavenly home-made cakes, bread, chocolates, soup and, yes, curries, tagines and other scrumptious and unlikely world food. If you love chocolate, you'll love Jann's cakes. Though locals mutter about the price of a slice, this is a great wee find! 11am-5pm, AYR.

2306 5/G18 **Caledonian Café** Portree · www.caledoniancafe.co.uk · 01478 612553 On £ the main street. Simple, serviceable and busy caff open long hours in summer for hungry tourists who don't want to cough up loadsa dosh to eat. Hot specials and usual caff fare. Home baking and home-made ice cream. 7 days 9am-9pm.

2 GOOD SEAFOOD RESTAURANTS IN PORTREE

2307 5/G18   **Sea Breezes** Quay St · www.seabreezes-skye.co.uk · 01478 612016 &
££   **Lower Deck** 1 Douglas Row · www.lowerdeckseafoodrestaurant.co.uk ·
01478 613611 Similar offerings, take them as you find them (they're near each
other). Unreconstructed seafood cafés, local, reliable. Mar-Oct. Lunch & LO
9/10pm.

GOOD PUB FOOD ON SKYE

2308 5/F17 ✓ **Edinbane Inn** www.edinbaneinn.co.uk · 01470 582414 The new owners
££   (2017) have transformed the village inn into where to go for casual food and a
craic-culture destination. Always buzzing. 6 nice rooms upstairs.

2309 5/G18 ✓ **Seamus' @ The Sligachan Hotel** www.sligachan.co.uk · 01478 650204
£   A quite brilliant pub/gathering place in the centre of the island (2284/SKYE
HOTELS) for walkers, climbers, campers – everybody. A big food operation all day
from lunch. Microbrewery, ales and loadsa whisky. Legendary ceilidhs.

2310 5/H19 ✓ **The Praban Bar @ Hotel Eilean Iarmain** Sleat · www.eileaniarmain.
££   co.uk · 01471 833332 On its own quay, in its own key and in its own world.
15 mins S of Broadford, this bar practically defines Gaelic culture and hospitality.
Chef Virgil Tiskus has upped the game foodwise, but it's just great to be here.
Regular proper ceilidhs.

2311 5/F17   **The Stein Inn** nr Waternish · www.stein-inn.co.uk · 01470 592362 Off B886,
££   about 10km Dunvegan. In row of cottages on the shore of Loch Bay. Over 200 years
old, the 'oldest inn on Skye', with great pub (open fire, OK grub lunch and dinner).
Waternish is a very special spot. Top seafood restaurant adjacent (1359/SEAFOOD).

WHAT TO SEE ON SKYE

The Cuillin Mountains (2/ATTRACTIONS); **Raasay** (2230/ISLANDS), (2245/
ISLAND WALKS); **The Quirang** (1694/VIEWS), (2255/ISLAND WALKS); **Old Man
Of Storr** (2254/ISLAND WALKS); **Dunvegan** (1821/CASTLES); **Eas Mòr** (1659/
WATERFALLS); **Elgol** (1701/VIEWS); **Skye Museum Of Island Life** (2174/HISTORY);
Flora MacDonald's Grave (1886/MONUMENTS); **Skye Silver**, **Edinbane Pottery**
(2204/2203/SCOTTISH SHOPS); **Fairy Pools** (1716/SWIMMING); **Duirinish** and
Minginish (2098/WALKS).

The Best of Arran

CalMac Ferry www.calmac.co.uk · **0800 066 5000** Ardrossan–Brodick, 55 mins. 6 per day Mon-Sat, 4 on Sun. 0800 066 5000. Ardrossan–Glasgow, train or road via A77/A71 1.5 hours. Claonaig-Lochranza, 30 mins. 9 per day (summer only). The best way to see Arran is on a bike (hire: 01770 302077 or 01770 302377).

WHERE TO STAY ON ARRAN

2312 7/J27
28 ROOMS
(HOUSE) +
36 (SPA)
DF
££

✓✓ **Auchrannie** Brodick · www.auchrannie.co.uk · **01770 302234** Once an old mansion, now expanded into a holiday complex that caters for all sorts but brilliant for families (1167/KIDS). House has best rooms, eats (Eighteen69 restaurant and bistro Brambles) and small pool. The Spa Resort, like a Holiday Inn in the country, has good modern rooms, the bigger pool and leisure facilities. Juice Bar here means Scottish 'juice'. Upstairs restaurant Cruize a bit Glasgow Airport but fits all sizes! Plenty indoors for Arran weather but also out: Arran Adventure Centre on hand.

2313 7/J27
22 ROOMS
££

✓ **Douglas Hotel** Brodick · www.thedouglashotel.co.uk · **01770 302968** On the front where the ferry comes in, you can't miss it even at night, lit large. High-quality and complete renovation of the old Douglas by returned local lad Sean Henry raising the game on Arran immeasurably. Contemporary design and fixtures, well selected art. A local Local on the front and revamped bistro restaurant. See also 2267/ISLAND HOTELS.

2314 7/J27
13 ROOMS
££

✓ **Glenisle Hotel** Lamlash · www.glenislehotel.com · **01770 600559** This carefully refurbished and rethought hotel in Lamlash looking out to Holy Isle, with new owners Anne and Neil Kennedy maintaining pre-eminence here. Local stone, colour and texture in evidence in well-appointed bedrooms, bar and restaurant. Calm, efficient and friendly: a perfect stay in lovely Lamlash. Good bistro and outside terrace/garden overlooking the bay. See also 2268/ISLAND HOTELS.

2315 7/J28
15 ROOMS
DF
L
££

Kildonan Hotel Kildonan · www.kildonanhotel.com · **01770 820207** In the S of the island (Brodick 16km) on a beautiful strand overlooking Pladda Island and lighthouse; Ailsa Craig spectral beyond. Great outside terrace (with big arty stones) for gazing out to sea. Happy, popular bar with grub and conservatory dining room. Nearby beach (1639/BEACHES) and waterfall (1654/WATERFALLS) also. Somehow it's a bit special.

Lochranza Youth Hostel Report: 1202/HOSTELS.

Glen Rosa Campsite 4km Brodick. Bucolic. Report: 1254/WILD CAMPING.

WHERE TO EAT ON ARRAN

2316 7/J27 ✓ **The Glenisle Bistro** Lamlash Civilised contemporary dining. See 2314/
£ ARRAN HOTELS.

2317 7/J26 ✓ **Stags Pavilion** Lochranza · www.stagspavilion.com · 01770 830600
££ Adjacent to the golf course in Lochranza in the N of the island, locals make the
journey here from all over (you probably have to book). Rino Pisano brings an
Italian influence to a seasonal menu. Nice building (the former clubhouse), atmos
and garden. Closed Wed.

2318 7/J27 ✓ **The Drift Inn** Lamlash · www.driftinnarran.com · 01770 600608 Just off
££ the main road, by the sea. Hugely popular pub for atmos and grub, probably
the most rockin' place to eat on the island (occasional live music). Some
imaginative combos and faves. Seaside garden. Wed-Sun: noon till late.

2319 7/J27 ✓ **Douglas Hotel Bistro** Brodick · www.thedouglashotel.co.uk ·
££ 01770 302968 Contemporary dining in bar and bistro. See above.

2320 7/J27 **Brodick Bar & Brasserie** Brodick · 01770 302169 Possibly best bistro/pub food
££ in Brodick, with recent new owners. Goes like a fair and can feel like a canteen on
summer evenings. Long blackboard menu. Pizzas. Lunch & LO 9pm. Bar till late.
Closed Sun.

2321 7/J27 **Felicity's** Whiting Bay · www.felicitysarran.co.uk · 01770 700357 Restaurant
£ of the former Eden Lodge Hotel on the long front of Whiting Bay, 15km S of Brodick.
Felicity Young just makes everything: sandwiches to cakes to chargrilled dishes and
pizza. Tables overlook the bay. All-day lunch and then 5-9pm.

2322 7/J27 **Old Pier Tearoom** Lamlash · 01770 600249 On Shore Rd, the main road
£ through Lamlash, a wee traditional café with very good home baking especially the
sausage rolls and the scones. Soups and hot dishes but must leave room for those
cakes. 7 days, daytime only. Check winter opening hours.

WHAT TO SEE ON ARRAN

2323 7/J27 ✓ **Brodick Castle** 5km walk or cycle from Brodick. Impressive museum and
NTS gardens. Flagship NTS property. Reopening 2019. Report: 1819/CASTLES.

2324 7/J27 **Goat Fell** 6km/5-hour great hill walk starting from the car park at Cladach near
2-A-2 castle and Brodick, or sea start at Corrie. Report: 1985/HILLS.

2325 7/J27 **Glenashdale Falls** 4km, but 2-hour forest walk from Glenashdale Bridge at
1-B-1 Whiting Bay. Steady, easy climb, sylvan setting. And **Eas Mòr**. Report: 1654/
WATERFALLS.

2326 7/J26 **Arran Distillery** In Lochranza. Visitor centre, tour and tasting of the Arran Single
Malt. 7 days. Winter hours vary (01770 830264).

2327 7/J27 **Machrie Moor Standing Stones** Off main coast road 7km N of Blackwaterfoot.
Various assemblies of Stones, all part of an ancient landscape. We lay down there.

2328 7/J27 **Glen Rosa & Glen Sannox** Fine glens: Rosa near Brodick, see 1254/WILD
& 7/J26 CAMPING; and fabulous **beaches** (1639/BEACHES).

The Best of Islay & Jura

CalMac Ferry www.calmac.co.uk · **0800 066 5000** Kennacraig–Port Askaig, 2 hours; Kennacraig–Port Ellen, 2 hours 10 mins (0800 066 5000). Port Askaig–Feolin, Jura: (01496 840681) 5 mins, frequent daily. Passenger ferry from Tayvallich near Crinan, Easter-Sep: 07768 450000. **By Air: Flybe** www.flybe.com · **0871 700 2000** Glasgow to Port Ellen Airport in S of Islay.

WHERE TO STAY ON ISLAY & JURA

2329 7/F26
£LOTS

✓✓ **The Machrie** nr Port Ellen, Islay Top island golfing and whisky hotel, transformed and reopened 2018. Report: 2259/ISLAND HOTELS.

2330 7/F26
11 ROOMS · DF
££

✓✓ **Bridgend Inn** Islay · www.bridgend-hotel.com · **01496 810212** Middle of island on road from Port Askaig, 4km Bowmore. Superb roadside inn with good pub meals, dining and cosy rooms. Report: 2263/ISLAND HOTELS.

2331 7/F26
10 ROOMS
L
££

✓✓ **Port Charlotte Hotel** Islay · www.portcharlottehotel.co.uk · **01496 850360** Restored Victorian inn and gardens overlooking sea in conservation village. Restful place and views. Good bistro-style menu. Eat in bar/ conservatory or dining room. Top terrace on the sea. Report: 2264/ISLAND HOTELS.

2332 7/F26
17 ROOMS
££

✓✓ **The Harbour Inn** Bowmore, Islay · www.bowmore.com · **01496 810330** Harbourside inn with conservatory lounge, Schooner bar for seafood lunch and less formal supper, and dining room with Mod-Brit menu. Bedrooms have all mod cons; owned by the Distillery. Conservatory on the loch. Report: 2272/ISLAND HOTELS.

2333 7/F26
13 ROOMS
DF · ££

✓ **The Islay Hotel** Port Ellen · www.theislayhotel.com · **01496 300109** In the S of the island, and very close to the ferry terminal. A friendly contemporary hotel, restaurant and bar. Report: 2271/ISLAND HOTELS.

2334 7/G25
17 ROOMS
L · NO TV
£

✓ **Jura Hotel** Craighouse · www.jurahotel.co.uk · **01496 820243** The island hotel and all-round social centre does all you want it to (including free camping and use of their facilities). Good bar, fortunately very good food (there's nowhere else). One of the friendliest and quietly contemporary hotels in the islands. Situated in front of the distillery by the bay. Report: 2273/ISLAND HOTELS.

2335 7/G25
5 ROOMS
DF
L
NO TV
£

✓ **Ardlussa House** Jura · www.ardlussaestate.com · **01496 820323** Hard to be more far-flung than this: the Ardlussa Estate occupies the N of Jura and this lived-in family house is a welcome destination after a single-track journey (28km from Craignure) on the 'Long Road'. 5 rooms (2 with superb views), 8 bathrooms. Convivial dinner with all their own venison, pork, lobsters and garden veg. The Fletchers share their splendid wild backyard with you. No TVs in rooms, phone reception dodgy; this is real island life. George Orwell's house is on their land. Home of **Lussa Gin** 1552/GIN. Ask about 'T on the Beach' (they know everything about Jura). Kids run free.

2336 7/F26
5 ROOMS
NO PETS
££

Kilmeny Country House nr Ballygrant, Islay · www.kilmeny.co.uk · **01496 840668** Margaret and Blair Rozga's top-class guest house 500m off the road, 6km S of Port Askaig (the ferry). Though small, big attention to detail. No evening meals but a house-party atmos and an Aga in the parlour.

2337 7/F26

12 ROOMS

NO PETS

££

Glenegedale House nr Port Ellen, Islay · www.glenegedaleguesthouse. co.uk · **01496 300400** On the main A846 long straight road opposite the airport – planes could practically land on the garden. You'll never find a homelier airport hotel than Graeme and Emma Clark's luxury guest house. Comfy and with eye to design (Timorous Beastie wallpaper). Home cooking and now licensed. New courtyard rooms to come at TGP.

2338 7/F26

Camping/Caravan Site Kintra Farm, Islay · www.kintrafarm.co.uk · **01496 302051** Off main road to Port Ellen; take Oa road, follow Kintra signs 7km. Jul-Aug. Grassy strand, coastal walks. See 1256/WILD CAMPING.

2339 7/F26

Islay Youth Hostel Port Charlotte · www.syha.org.uk · **01496 850385** Sleeps 30. In a converted whisky warehouse.

WHERE TO EAT ON ISLAY & JURA

✓ **The Harbour Inn, Port Charlotte Hotel & Bridgend Inn** See above. Best bets for dinner.

2340 7/F26

£

✓ **Ardbeg Distillery Café** nr Port Ellen, Islay · www.ardbeg.com · **01496 302244** 5km E of Port Ellen on the whisky road. Great local reputation for food. Beautiful vaulted ceiling (the Kiln Room). Food home-made, as are those Ardbegs. Most vintages and cool clothing to boot. Mon-Fri (7 days Jun-Aug) 10am-LO 4pm. Gets busy (there's an overspill room). You may wait. Closed weekends in winter.

2341 7/F26

£

Kilchoman Distillery Café Rockside Farm, Islay · www.kilchomandistillery. com · **01496 850011** The small distillery in the NW off the A847 from Bridgend (12km). This caff has much to like, especially the secret-recipe Cullen skink. Mon-Sat 10am-5pm (not Sat in winter).

2342 7/F26

£

Peatzeria Bowmore, Islay · www.peatzeria.com · **01496 810810** In downtown Bowmore overlooking lochside. A proper stone-baked and innovative (black pudding, crab, scallops, Islay lobster) pizzeria with other Islay-Italia dishes in small, bright, up-and-down room and covered outdoor terrace. Local and global!

WHAT TO SEE ON ISLAY & JURA

Islay: The Distilleries especially Ardbeg (good café), Lagavulin and Laphroig (classic settings), all by Port Ellen; **Bowmore** perhaps more convenient (1536/WHISKY); **Wildlife Info & Field Centre** at Port Charlotte; **American Monument** (1884/MONUMENTS); **Oa & Loch Gruinart** (1783/BIRDS); **Port Charlotte** (1611/VILLAGES); **Kintra** (2082/WALKS); **Finlaggan**, the romantic, sparse ruin on island in Loch Finlaggan: last home of the Lords of the Isles. Off A846 5km S of Port Askaig; **Islay House Square** A courtyard of local craft and food producers (batik, marmalade, Islay Ales, art gallery/framers) behind Islay House – enter off Port Askaig–Bowmore road by Bridgend.

Jura: See 2231/ISLANDS; **The Paps of Jura and Evans' Walk**; **Killchianaig, Keils** (1930/GRAVEYARDS); **Lowlandman's Bay, Corran Sands** (1634/BEACHES).

CalMac Ferry www.calmac.co.uk · 0800 066 5000 Oban–Craignure, 45 mins. Main route: 6 a day. Lochaline–Fishnish, 15 mins. 9-15 a day. Kilchoan–Tobermory, 35 mins. 7 a day (Sun in summer only). Winter sailings: call CalMac/see website.

WHERE TO STAY ON MULL

2343 7/G23
7 ROOMS/5 COTTS
£LOTS

✓✓ **Tiroran House** Tiroran · www.tiroran.com · 01681 705232 A treat and a retreat way down in the SW of Mull near Iona. Light, comfy house in glorious gardens with excellent food and flowers. Sea eagles fly over. Report: 1222/ GET-AWAY HOTELS.

2344 7/G22
4 ROOMS
NO PETS/KIDS
££

✓✓ **Strongarbh House** Tobermory · www.strongarbh.com · 01688 302319 Behind and above the landmark Western Isles (see below), a smart and exceptional B&B – cosy library, a 'gallery space', afternoon tea on arrival. Jane Wilde and Adrian Lear have built a taste oasis.

2345 7/G22
6 ROOMS
NO PETS
APR-OCT · ££

✓ **Highland Cottage** Tobermory · www.highlandcottage.co.uk · 01688 302030 Opposite fire station on street above the harbour. Like a country house, well, … a country cottage in town. A top dining room. Report: 2266/ ISLAND HOTELS.

2346 7/F23
17 ROOMS
APR-OCT · ££

✓ **Argyll Hotel** Iona · www.argyllhoteliona.co.uk · 01681 700334 Near ferry and on seashore overlooking Mull on road to abbey. Laid-back, cosy accom, home cooking, good vegetarian. Report: 1210/INNS.

2347 7/G22
5 ROOMS
££

✓ **Glengorm Castle** nr Tobermory · www.glengormcastle.co.uk · 01688 302321 Minor road on right going N outside Tobermory (6km) takes you to this fine castle on a promontory set in an extensive estate which is yours to wander (excellent walks 2249/ISLAND WALKS). Fab views over to Ardnamurchan, little peaks to climb and a natural bathing pool (2141/OPEN-AIR POOLS). Spacious bedrooms (old-style comfy) in family home (the Nelsons) – use the library, complimentary bar and grand public spaces. Loads of art, lawn and gardens. Excellent self-catering cottages on estate. B&B only. And 1409/TEAROOMS.

2348 7/G22
12 ROOMS
££

✓ **The Mishnish** Tobermory · www.themishnish.co.uk · 01688 302500 Rooms above the once legendary Mishnish Pub. It may have lost some of its music and mystique but this is now a well-refurbished hotel, with a restaurant and bar that still retain some of the old vibe. One bedroom has a Jacuzzi! The Mish now and forever at the heart of the matter on Mull.

2349 7/G22
7 ROOMS
DF
£

The Bellachroy Hotel Dervaig · www.thebellachroy.co.uk · 01688 400314 Dating from 1608 no less, this is a well-known watering hole and hotel in the delightful village of Dervaig between Tobermory and the beautiful beach (and sculpture trail) at Calgary. Christine Weaver and Anthony Ratcliff have turned it into a bit of a gastropub and it's a good base for exploring Mull away from the hubbub of Tobermory.

2350 7/G22
26 ROOMS
£

Western Isles Hotel Tobermory · www.westernisleshotel.com · 01688 302012 At the end of the bay high above the harbour, this Tobermory landmark has one of the most commanding positions of any hotel in Scotland, with spectacular views from (some) rooms, conservatory brasserie, dining room and especially the terrace. Its chequered history of ownership seems to continue. Needs TLC and a lotta cash. Transforming it would also transform Tobermory.

2351 7/H22
82 ROOMS
£
Isle of Mull Hotel Craignure · www.crerarhotels.com · 01680 812544
Strung-out, low-rise hotel round Craignure Bay near the ferry from Oban (hotel can pick you up); hotel with the largest number of rooms on Mull. Decent rooms, spa and pool. Bit of a drive to an alternative restaurant (which you will want to find).

2352 7/G22
15 ROOMS
DF
££
Tobermory Hotel Tobermory · www.thetobermoryhotel.com · 01688 302091
On the waterfront. Creature comforts, open fires, great outlook in the middle of the bay. 10 rooms to front, upper with coombed ceilings; all recently refurbished and contemporary. Related to Galleon Grill (see below) nearby. Very much downtown Tobermory, this is an excellent place to locate for all Mull meanderings.

2353 7/F23
27 ROOMS
MID MAR-OCT
£
St Columba Hotel Iona · www.stcolumba-hotel.co.uk · 01681 700304
Shares some ownership and ideals of the Argyll (above) and nearby, on the road to the Abbey. Larger and more purpose-built than the Argyll, so some uniformity in rooms. Nice views; extensive lawn and organic market garden. Relaxing and just a little religious. Menu with good vegetarian options varies. Several single rooms.

Camping Tobermory on the Dervaig Rd, Craignure (1267/CAMPING WITH KIDS). Calgary Beach and at Loch Na Keal shore (1251/WILD CAMPING).

Tobermory Youth Hostel In main street on bay. Report: 1201/HOSTELS.

WHERE TO EAT ON MULL

2354 7/G22
L
££
✓✓ **Café Fish** Tobermory · www.thecafefish.com · 01688 301253 Jane McDonald and chef Liz McGougan's deliciously informal 'café' restaurant upstairs in the white building at the pier on corner of the bay. Bright, bustling upstairs room and terrace on the dock – Johnny's boat at the quayside supplies the shellfish, arriving around 4pm every day; they're wheeched upstairs. All else is properly sourced (they close in winter, partly because supplies cannot be guaranteed) and 'the only thing frozen are our fisherman'. God and St Peter alone know how they produce that long, diverse, imaginative menu from the tiny, tiny kitchen. Sensible wine list, nice puds. Lunch & 5.30-10pm (LO). Mar-Oct.

2355 7/F23
£££
✓✓ **Ninth Wave** nr Fionnphort · www.ninthwaverestaurant.co.uk · 01681 700757 In the S of Mull near the ferry for Iona (1.5 hours to Tobermory). This highly regarded off-the-road-and-map restaurant is the epitome of destination dining. Canadian Carla Lamont in the kitchen and the garden, John out front (in a kilt) and on the boat. The terroir supplies your table in this surprisingly contemporary croft conversion in the quiet deep south. Simple choice, fixed-price menu fine-dining style. Easter-Oct. Closed Mon/Tue. Dinner only. Book!

2356 7/G22
£
✓✓ **Glengorm Farm Coffee Shop** nr Tobermory Excellent daytime eats outside Tobermory. The best casual daytime dining. Report: 1409/TEAROOMS. And see Tobermory Bakery, below.

2357 7/G22
££
✓ **Highland Cottage** Tobermory · www.highlandcottage.co.uk · 01688 302030 Informal but fine-ish dining on Mull. Only limited availability for non-res so get in touch to enquire and hopefully enjoy Jo Currie's creative and dab hand in the kitchen. See 2266/ISLAND HOTELS.

2358 7/G22 **The Bellachroy Hotel** Dervaig · www.thebellachroy.co.uk · 01688 400314
££ Some might say The Bellachroy *is* Dervaig. Now a destination for lunch and dinner. Craft beers and good wine list, especially Bordeaux. See also above.

2359 7/F22 **The Café @ Calgary Arts** Calgary · www.calgary.co.uk · 01688 400256 A
£ great wee café just where you need it by the sculpture trail (2188/ART SPACES). Easter-Nov.

2360 7/G22 **The Glass Barn @ Sgriob-Ruadh Farm** nr Tobermory ·
£ www.isleofmullcheese.co.uk · 01688 302627 On the road to Dervaig (2km). A uniquely vibey tearoom out on its own in the farmyard and dairy where they make the Mull cheddars. See also 1410/TEAROOMS.

2361 7/G22 **The Galleon Grill** Tobermory · www.galleongrill.com · 01688 301117 Just
£ off the main street behind the post office. Same folk have the Tobermory Hotel (above). Mainly steaks but also seafood. Could be in a city somewhere. Liked by locals and TripAdvisors. 7 days.

2362 7/G22 **Hebridean Lodge** Tobermory · www.hebrideanlodge.co.uk · 01688 301207
££ On the way into the town from Craignure and the south. Upstairs restaurant above picture-framers and gallery. Home cooking and bakery with good local reputation. Check website for times.

2363 7/G22 **Tobermory Bakery** Tobermory · www.glengormcastle.co.uk · 01688 302225
£ Tom and Marjorie Nelson's Main St bakery-deli with quiches, salads and old-fashioned fancies. Related to gorgeous Glengorm. See 1484/BAKERS.

2364 7/G22 **The Fish & Chip Van aka The Fishermen's Pier** Tobermory · 01688 302390
£ Tobermory's famous meals-on-wheels under the clock tower on the bay. Fresh, al fresco: usually a queue. However, they don't actually make those chips! Open 7 days in summer 12.30pm-9pm. Closed Sun in winter. Report: 1391/FISH & CHIPS.

WHAT TO SEE ON MULL

Duart Castle 5km Craignure. Seat of Clan Maclean. Impressive from a distance, homely inside. Good view of clan history and from battlements. Tearoom (1820/CASTLES). **Eas Fors** Waterfall on Dervaig to Fionnphort road. Very accessible series of cataracts tumbling into the sea (1658/WATERFALLS). **Ulva & Iona** (many references). **The Treshnish Isles** (from Ulva Ferry or Fionnphort). Marvellous trips in summer (1775/BIRDS); walks from **Carsaig Pier** and on **Glengorm Estate** (2249/ISLAND WALKS); or up **Ben More** (2016/MUNROS); **Croig** and **Quinish** in north, by **Dervaig** and **Lochbuie** off the A849 at Strathcoil, 9km S of Craignure: these are all serene shorelines to explore. **Aros Park** forest walk, from Tobermory, about 7km round trip.

The Best of The Outer Hebrides

CalMac Ferry www.calmac.co.uk · 0800 066 5000 Ullapool–Stornoway, 2 hours 40 mins (not Sun). Oban/Mallaig–Lochboisdale, South Uist and Castlebay, Barra, up to 6.5 hours. Uig on Skye–Tarbert, Harris (not Sun) or Lochmaddy, North Uist, 1 hour 40 mins. Also Leverburgh, Harris–Berneray (not Sun) 1 hour.
By Air: Flybe www.flybe.com · 0871 700 2000 from Inverness/Glasgow/Edinburgh. Otter to Barra/Benbecula from Glasgow (1/2 a day).

WHERE TO STAY IN THE OUTER HEBRIDES

2365 3/E16
6 ROOMS
DF · LL · NO TV
MAR–DEC
£££
£££

✓✓ **Scarista House** South Harris · www.scaristahouse.com · 01859 550238 20km S of Tarbert. Cosy haven near famous but often deserted beach; this celebrated retreat offers the real R&R and a lovely dinner. Also self-catering accom. Dog-friendly and kid-friendly – it's an all n' all. Report: 2261/ISLAND HOTELS; 1169/KIDS.
EAT Intimate dining, probably best on Harris.

2366 3/E14
7 ROOMS
DF · LLL · NO TV
MAY–SEP
££

✓ **Baile-Na-Cille** Timsgarry, West Lewis · www.bailenacille.co.uk · 01851 672242 Near Uig 60km W of Stornoway. This is about as far away as it gets but guests return again and again to the Gollins' house overlooking that incredible beach. Hospitable hosts allow you the run of their place – the books, the games room, the tennis court, walled flower garden and perhaps others of the many beaches nearby (1626/BEACHES). All home-made grub (bread, ice cream, etc) in communal dining room with amusing Rocket (sic) overtones. Highly individual home away from home that's decent value. A set menu and especially good for families (1170/KIDS).
££ **EAT** Beautiful beach view and a unique dining experience open to non-res.

2367 3/G13
4 ROOMS
L
£

✓ **Broad Bay House** Back, Lewis · www.broadbayhouse.co.uk · 01851 820990 11km N of Stornoway on E of island on the sea via B895 to Back. High approval ratings for this purpose-built bungalow with big, light dining and lounge area and outside deck. Spacious, contemporary rooms with big TV, iPod docks, etc. Ian and Marion solicitous but discreet. Ian knows everywhere you might want to go and you'll want to stay a while in this chilled-out back of beyond, e.g. **Tolsta** and beaches north (1626/BEACHES). Cheese/seafood platter evenings with home-made bread.

2368 3/E15
21 ROOMS
££

✓ **Hotel Hebrides** Tarbert, Harris · www.hotel-hebrides.com · 01859 502364 Contemporary boutique-style new-build hotel right by the pier where the boat comes in, so convenient and probably just what you want (the Harris Hotel below is perhaps cosier). Rooms, restaurant and bar are light, uncluttered modern. Possibly the best contemporary hotel in the Hebrides!

2369 3/E15
23 ROOMS
NO PETS
££

✓ **Harris Hotel** Tarbert, Harris · www.harrishotel.com · 01859 502154 In the township near the ferry terminal, in the same family since 1904, and like the Hebrides above, a good base for travels in North/South Harris. These quite different hotels are among the best in Lewis. Variety of public rooms here and diverse range of bedrooms (view/non-view, refurbished/non-refurbished, standard/superior), some of which are large and very nice. Friendly and well run. Food not a strong point, but adequate in the hotel-like dining room. Both bar and conservatory have atmos and there's a great garden.

2370 3/D17 ✓ **Hamersay House** Lochmaddy, North Uist · www.hamersayhouse.co.uk ·
8 ROOMS   **01876 500700** A contemporary new-build hotel: bathrooms refurbished 2018
DF   by the people who have **Langass Lodge** (see below; Apr-Oct) so best standard of
££   style and efficiency in these far-flung islands, where the beaches and the sky are
immense. Leisure Club includes sauna/steam. Good brasserie. Open AYR.

2371 3/E14   **Uig Lodge** Uig, Lewis · www.uiglodge.co.uk · **01851 672396** West Lewis but
10 ROOMS   decent road most of the way. 1km from Uig community stores and close to an
L   amazing beach and others nearby (1626/BEACHES). Well known and regarded for
££   their salmon smokery, but lovely rooms in a laid-back lodge. Same folk building a
new restaurant on the road, open 2019.

2372 3/F14   **Royal Hotel** Stornoway, Lewis · www.royalstornoway.co.uk · **01851 702109**
24 ROOMS   The most central and urbane of the 3 main hotels in town, all owned by the same
££   family. HS-1 bistro and Boatshed Restaurant for dining. The **Cabarfeidh Hotel**
www.cabarfeidh-hotel.co.uk · **01851 702604** may have the best bedrooms.
The **Caladh Inn** www.caladhinn.co.uk · **01851 702740** This inn, pronounced
'Cala', and its caff Eleven, with popular self-service buffet, are possibly best value.
These hotels are about the only places open in Lewis on Sunday. Best all-round for
buzz and rendezvous is the Royal.

2373 3/F13   **Borve Hotel** Borve, North Lewis · www.borvehousehotel.co.uk ·
9 ROOMS +   **01851 850223** 32km N of Stornoway on a mainly long, straight road to Port
4 CHALETS   of Ness. Surprisingly contemporary though perhaps a little soulless hotel, with
££   boutique-style rooms. Bar and restaurant are busy with locals at weekends. The
smartest stay north of Stornoway; they should revisit the art.

2374 3/D19   **Polochar Inn** South Uist · www.polocharinn.com · **01878 700215** S of
11 ROOMS   Lochboisdale near Eriskay causeway (and ferry for Barra). An 18th-century inn at
NO PETS   the rocky end of the Uists. Excellent value, good craic and the view/sunset across
LL   the sea to Barra. Rooms refurbished to good standard. The pub-grub menu uses
££   local produce. LO 8.45pm.

 Lews Castle Stornoway, Lewis Quite exceptional. Report: 2260/ISLAND
HOTELS.

✓ **Amhuinnsuidhe Castle** Amhuinnsuidhe, Harris Real castle and fishing
lodge, chic at a price. Report: 1303/HOUSE PARTIES.

Langass Lodge North Uist Best bet in the Uists (and see Hamersay House
above, same ownership). Report: 1231/GET-AWAY HOTELS.

Castlebay Hotel Castlebay, Barra Overlooks ferry terminal in the village, superb
views. Decent dining (better than was). Atmospheric bar. Reports: 2274/ISLAND
HOTELS; 1316/GOOD PUBS.

Isle of Barra Beach Hotel Tangasdale, Barra Great setting, though mixed
reviews. Report: 2275/ISLAND HOTELS.

Hostels Simple hostels within hiking distance. 2 in Lewis, 3 in Harris, 1 each in
North and South Uist. Am Bothan at Leverburgh is independent and funky.
The Blackhouse Village in North Lewis is exceptional (1182/HOSTELS).

2375 3/F14 ✓ **Digby Chick** Stornoway, Lewis · www.digbychick.co.uk · **01851 700026**
£££ Undoubtedly and for over 30 years, the place to eat in Stornoway and the contemporary dining standard that no one else has matched. Chef/proprietor James Mackenzie creative and au courant in the kitchen. Seafood a speciality; a solid reputation. Can't go wrong here. Mon-Sat lunch & LO 8.30pm.

2376 3/F14 ✓ **Blue Lobster** Stornoway, Lewis · **07909 728548** Perceval Square, on the £ harbour where big windows and an enclosed terrace look out on fishing boats and across to Lews Castle. Café and gift shop with good things and home-made food. Best casual drop-in in town.

2377 3/E16 ✓ **Croft 36** Northton, Harris · www.croft36.com · **01859 520779** On the £ road into village 1.5km A859 north of Leverburgh. The best kind of pop-up, a community and visitor service. A shack where you'll find (all home-made) bread, pies, cakes, ready-made meals to heat up, from wild rabbit pastries to frangipanes. You leave the money in an honesty box. And it works. Mon-Sat, daytime only.

2378 3/F13 ✓ **40 North** Bragar, Lewis · www.40northfoods.co.uk · **01851 710424** In a £ modern house conservatory (**The Verandah**) and an outhouse (**The Croft Kitchen**) at Bragar, a township along the A858 near the **Blackhouse at Amol** (2161/HERITAGE) about 20 mins NW of Stornoway, a restaurant and a takeaway respectively that folk come to from miles around. The takeaway queue waits in the kitchen; everybody speaks Gaelic. Eclectic menu in both, great desserts. Lunch & LO 7.30pm. Closed Sun/Mon.

2379 3/E14 ✓ **Loch Croistean Coffee Shop** nr Uig, Lewis · **01851 672772** About 30 mins L from Stornoway on the road into the sunset, Marianne Campbell's schoolhouse £ converted into a tasteful, laid-back tearoom and restaurant. Simple good food; soup, sandwich and cake, all home-made, and lovely buffet suppers (Fri/Sat in season). Music and film nights. Mon-Sat noon-8pm (winter Wed-Sat). Closed Jan/Feb.

2380 3/F15 ✓ **North Harbour Bistro & Tearoom** Isle of Scalpay · **01859 540218** 20 L mins (10km) S of Tarbert but E to Scalpay (by the bridge) in the village ££ overlooking the harbour. George Lavery's good-food destination restaurant has garnered great reviews and feedback since it opened 2014. Cheffy, contemporary food, but small, so book for dinner. All-day menu till 9pm. Closed Sun. BYOB, though licence in progress at TGP.

2381 3/E16 ✓ **Skoon Art Café** South Harris · www.skoon.com · **01859 530268** Near £ the **Golden Road** (1683/SCENIC ROUTES) 12km S of Tarbert or follow the sign off A859, then 4km to Geocrab (pronounced Jocrab). Andrew and Emma Craig's café in a gallery (his work on the walls). All done well – interesting soups, great home baking. Apr-Sep: Tue-Sat daytime only; weekends in winter (or check).

2382 3/C20 **Café Kisimul** Barra · www.cafekisimul.co.uk · **01871 810645** On the 'main ££ street' of Castlebay down to the quay and overlooking the 'castle' in the bay, a surprising Indian (with some Italian dishes!) restaurant that's rather good. Not a lot of choice on Barra so all the more welcome. Mar-Sep: 7 days lunch & dinner. Weekends only in winter.

2383 3/F14 **The Thai Café** Stornoway, Lewis · **01851 701811** Opposite police station. ££ Though there are palms outside in the sometimes rainswept street, you couldn't be further from Phuket. Mrs Panida Macdonald's restaurant an institution here;

you may have to book. Good atmos and real Thai cuisine. Still a surprising find (the furthest Thai in the west?).

2384 3/F14
£
Coffee Shops: An Lanntair Gallery Stornoway, Lewis · **www.lanntair.com & Callanish Visitor Centre** Callanish, Lewis · **www.callanishvisitorcentre. co.uk** An Lanntair, an all-embracing arts and cultural centre, is a great rendezvous spot and has a good view of the ferry terminal. Lunch & evening menu. The Callanish caff is far better than most visitor centres. Open till 8pm in summer. See also 1852/PREHISTORIC. Both closed Sun.

2385 3/E16
£
The Anchorage Leverburgh, South Harris · 01859 520225 Sally Lessi's all-round family restaurant/café/bar at the pierhead where the boat leaves for Berneray and the Uists. Much better than your average terminal caff with most stuff home-made and cooked to order. Friendly! Mar-Sep (weekends in winter) noon-9pm. Closed Sun.

2386 3/D17
£
Stepping Stone Restaurant Balivanich, Benbecula · 01870 603377 8km from main A855. Nondescript building in ex- (though sometimes operational) military air base. Served the Forces, now the tourists – it aims to please. 7 days lunch & dinner (winter hours may vary). Menu changes through day.

✓✓ **Scarista House** South Harris A 20-min Tarbert/45-min Stornoway drive for best dinner on Harris. Fixed menu. Book. Reports: 2261/ISLAND HOTELS; 2365/HEBRIDES HOTELS.

The Boatshed at The Royal Hotel & The Cabarfeidh Hotel both Stornoway Best hotel options and your **only decent Sunday options on Lewis**.

WHAT TO SEE IN THE OUTER HEBRIDES

Eriskay & Mingulay (2240/ISLANDS); **Golden Road** (1683/SCENIC ROUTES); **Beaches** At Lewis, South Harris and South Uist (1626/1619/1624/BEACHES); **Balranald Reserve** (1808/RESERVES). **Scarista Golf** (2108/GOLF); **Surfing** (2150/ SURFING BEACHES). **St Clement's Church & St Michael's Church** (1905/1906/ CHURCHES); **Blackhouse at Arnol** (2161/HISTORY); **Barpa Langass & Callanish Stones** (1866/1852/PREHISTORIC); **Harris Tweed** (2221/SHOPS).

The Best of Orkney

Northlink Ferries www.northlinkferries.co.uk · **0845 600 0449** Kirkwall: from Aberdeen – Tue, Thu, Sat, Sun, 6 hours; Stromness from Scrabster – 2/3 per day, 2 hours. John o' Groats to Burwick (01955 611353), 40 mins, up to 4 a day (May-Sep only). **Pentland Ferries** www.pentlandferries.co.uk · **01856 831226** from Gills Bay (near John o' Groats) to St Margaret's Hope – 3 a day, 1 hour. **By Air: Flybe** www.flybe.com · **0871 700 2000** To Kirkwall from Aberdeen, Edinburgh, Glasgow and Inverness.

WHERE TO STAY IN ORKNEY

2387 1/Q10
8 ROOMS
££

✓ **The Storehouse** Kirkwall · www.thestorehouserestaurantwithrooms. co.uk · **01856 252250** Judith Glue (see below) and David Spence opened this smartest place in town in 2018 transforming a B-listed store in the heart of Kirkwall into a ground-floor restaurant and shop with excellent contemporary rooms above. All in good taste, pulling Kirkwall onwards and upwards. What took them so long? (Answer: the massive job, the meticulous attention to detail.) See also 2262/ISLAND HOTELS.

2388 1/Q10
8 ROOMS
NO PETS
££

✓ **Foveran Hotel** St Ola · www.thefoveran.com · **01856 872389** A964 Orphir road; 5km from Kirkwall. Recent renovation has raised this in-the-country hotel to the most contemporary rural stay on the Mainland. This Scandinavian-style, low-rise hotel is a friendly, informal place, with the top restaurant and a top view hereabouts. They use local ingredients (food and the folk). Great value. Small but comfy and light rooms; garden overlooks Scapa Flow.

2389 1/Q10
10 ROOMS
££

The Lynnfield Kirkwall · www.lynnfield.co.uk · **01856 872505** Holm Rd adjacent to **Highland Park** (1546/WHISKY) and overlooking the town. Kirkwall's most comfy old-style, sporting 4 stars and with good local reputation for food, wine and whisky. And congeniality.

2390 1/Q10
16 ROOMS
££

Merkister Hotel Harray · www.merkister.com · **01856 771366** Overlooking loch, N but midway (15 mins) between Kirkwall and Stromness. A fave with fishers and twitchers; handy for archaeological sites and possibly the Orkney outdoorsy hotel of choice. Rooms small and B&B-ish; good bar meals.

2391 1/Q10
42 ROOMS
£

Stromness Hotel Stromness · www.stromnesshotel.com · **01856 850298** Orkney's biggest hotel at the heart of the Orkney matter and overlooking the harbour. Rooms so-so but very good value. Even has lifts. Central and picturesque. Flattie Bar a wee gem. Victorian Garden behind.

2392 1/Q9
L

✓ **Bis Geos Hostel & Cottages** Westray · www.bisgeos.co.uk · **01857 677420** Hostel with 2 self-catering cottages. Traditional features and some luxuries.

2393 1/Q9

✓ **The Barn** Westray · www.thebarnwestray.co.uk · **01857 677214** Near Pierowall. 4-star self-catering hostel in renovated stone barn. Great views.

2394 1/Q10

Kirkwall Peedie Hostel Ayre Rd, Kirkwall · **01856 875477** On the front. Private bedroom (3), sleep 2 or 4, own keys.

WHERE TO EAT IN ORKNEY

2395 1/Q10 ✓✓ **The Leonards @ The Storehouse** Kirkwall, Orkney · www.
££ thestorehouserestaurantwithrooms.co.uk · 01856 252250 The ground-floor restaurant in a painstakingly converted historic building with a private dining area and open kitchen. In one stroke Kirkwall eating out is bang up to date. Orkney produce. Accessible good food for well, everybody. 7 days breakfast/lunch/dinner. Closely related to:

2396 1/Q10 ✓ **Judith Glue Café and Restaurant** Kirkwall · www.judithglue.com ·
££ 01856 874225 Can't miss it opposite St Magnus Cathedral. An eating-out place that serves and champions Orkney produce: the ale, the seafood, the cheese, Orkney ales, the Highland Park. JG long known for the knits and quality souvenirs (and puffin stuff). Home-made, blackboard menu. 7 days AYR; times vary.

2397 1/Q10 ✓ **Foveran Hotel** St Ola · www.thefoveran.com · 01856 872389 5km
££ Kirkwall, so a short hop by car or taxi from downtown. Good, locally sourced food in a contemporary, smart room with The View. See above.

2398 1/Q10 **The Lynnfield** Kirkwall · www.lynnfield.co.uk · 01856 872505 Some
££ traditionalistas say the best hotel meal in Kirkwall. See above.

2399 1/Q10 **The Hamnavoe Restaurant** Stromness · 01856 850606 Off main street. The
££ Taylors here since 2003. Seafood is their speciality, especially lobster and crab. Apr-Oct: lunch weekends only, dinner Tue-Sun 6.30pm-9pm. Nov-Mar: open weekends only.

2400 1/Q10 **Julia's Café & Bistro** Stromness · www.juliascafe.co.uk · 01856 850904
£ Home baking, blackboard and vegetarian specials opposite harbour. A favourite with the locals. Gets busy – fill yourself up before the ferry journey! Open AYR. Rare early opening. 7 days 9am-5pm (from 10am Sun). Phone for winter opening hours.

2401 1/Q10 **Birsay Bay Tearoom** Birsay · www.birsaybaytearoom.co.uk · 01856 721399
£ N of mainland, 30 mins Kirkwall, a wee tearoom between Marwick and Brough Head (with the lovely walk between them). It's near 'the Palace' ruin, so head for that. There is also a walk at low tide to the island. Home bakes, and greenhouses where the tomatoes and leaves come from. 7 days, daytime only.

2402 1/Q10 **Lucano** Kirkwall · 01856 870319 In a pleasant back street of the town away
£ from the harbour, a very serviceable and welcome Italian restaurant with all the stuff you'd expect and want. 7 days lunch & dinner.

WHAT TO SEE IN ORKNEY

2403 1/P10 ✓✓✓ **Skara Brae** 25km W of Kirkwall. Amazingly well-preserved
HES 5,000-year-old village. Report: 1850/PREHISTORIC.

2404 1/Q10 ✓✓ **Standing Stones of Stenness, The Ring of Brodgar, Maes Howe**
W of Kirkwall on A965. Vibrations! Report: 1851/PREHISTORIC.

2405 1/R11 ✓✓ **The Italian Chapel** 8km S of Kirkwall at first causeway. A special act of
faith. Inspirational and moving. Report: 1900/CHURCHES.

2406 1/P11 **The Old Man of Hoy** On Hoy; 30-min ferry 2 or 3 times a day from Stromness.
3-hour walk along spectacular coast. Report: 2098/ISLAND WALKS.

2407 1/P10   **Yesnaby Sea Stacks** 24km W of Kirkwall. A precarious clifftop at the end of the world. Report: 1974/ENCHANTING PLACES.

2408 1/P10   **Skaill House** by Skara Brae · www.skaillhouse.co.uk · **01856 841501** 17th-century mansion built on Pictish cemetery. Set up as it was in the 1950s; with Captain Cook's crockery in the dining room looking remarkably unused. Apr-Sep: 7 days 9.30am-6pm (or by appointment). Tearoom and visitor centre and HES link with Skara are adjacent.

Also: **St Magnus Cathedral** (1900/CHURCHES); **Stromness** (1607/VILLAGES); **The Pier Arts Centre** (2186/GALLERIES); **Tomb of the Eagles** (1857/PREHISTORIC); **Marwick Head** and many of the smaller islands (1784/BIRDS); **Scapa Flow** (1947/BATTLEGROUNDS); **Highland Park Distillery** (1546/WHISKY).

The Best of Shetland

Northlink Ferries www.northlinkferries.co.uk · **0845 600 0449** Aberdeen-Lerwick: Mon, Wed, Fri – departs 7pm, 12 hours. Tue, Thu, Sat, Sun – departs 5pm (via Orkney).
By Air: Flybe www.flybe.com · **0871 700 0535** To Sumburgh from Aberdeen, Inverness, Glasgow and Edinburgh.

WHERE TO STAY IN SHETLAND

2409 2/U4   ✓ **Burrastow House** Walls · www.burrastowhouse.co.uk · **01595 809307**
6 ROOMS   40 mins from Lerwick. Most guides and locals agree this is the place to stay on
LL   Shetland. Peaceful Georgian house on a quiet bay with views to island of Vaila.
APR-OCT   Wonderful home-made/produced food. Full of character with food (set menu;
££   order day before) service. Rooms probably the best on the island.

2410 2/V5   ✓ **Scalloway Hotel** Scalloway · www.scallowayhotel.com · **01595 880444**
23 ROOMS   10km W of Lerwick on a picturesque waterfront, the McKenzies have built a
DF · ££   strong reputation for food and comfy, contemporary rooms.
£££   **EAT** Closest to a fine-dining dinner on Shetland. Excellent value.

2411 2/U3   **Busta House Hotel** Brae · www.bustahouse.com · **01806 522506**
22 ROOMS   Pronounced 'Boosta'. Historic country house at Brae just over 30 mins from
££   Lerwick (1 hour airport). Elegant and tranquil. High standards. Comfy rooms named
after islands. Excellent food; famously great malt selection.

2412 2/V5   **The Lerwick Hotel** Lerwick · www.shetlandhotels.com · **01595 692166**
35 ROOMS   Short walk to downtown Lerwick. Along with Kveldsro Hotel (same ownership),
££   probably the best in town. Brasserie restaurant.

2413 2/U6   **The Spiggie Hotel** Dunrossness · www.thespiggiehotel.co.uk ·
6 ROOMS   **01950 460409** 8km Sumburgh Airport, 32km Lerwick. Overlooks RSPB reserve of
££   Spiggie Loch. Small, personally run country hotel. Especially good for bar meals.

2414 2/U3 **St Magnus Bay Hotel** Hillswick · www.stmagnusbayhotel.co.uk ·
33 ROOMS 01806 503372 Far away in the NW of the mainland, 50km (50 mins) from Lerwick
££ on the Hillswick coast, a distinctive, wooden-built (in 1900) hotel (renovation
ongoing). Have to admit I still haven't been here but all reports are good; everyone
calls it 'charming'.

2415 2/V4 **Westings, The Inn On The Hill** Whiteness · 01595 840242 12km from Lerwick.
6 ROOMS Breathtaking views down Whiteness Voe. Excellent base for exploring. Old-style
££ bedrooms. Large selection of real ales. Campsite alongside.

2416 2/V5 **Islesburgh House Hostel** Lerwick · www.shetland.gov.uk · 01595 745100
Beautifully refurbished and central. A 5-star hostel. Open AYR.

2417 2 **Camping Bods** (fisherman's barns). Cheap sleep in wonderful seashore settings:
The Sail Loft at Voe; **Grieve House** at Whalsay; **Windhouse Lodge** at Mid Yell;
Voe House at Walls; **Betty Mouat's Cottage** at Dunrossness; **Johnnie Notions**
at Eshaness. Take sleeping mats. Check tourist office for details: 01595 693434.

WHERE TO EAT IN SHETLAND

✓ **Scalloway Hotel** Scalloway See above.

2418 2/V5 ✓ **Hay's Dock Café Restaurant** Lerwick · www.haysdock.co.uk ·
££ 01595 741569 Part of the Shetland Museum & Archive. Contemporary,
beautiful space with great views of Lerwick Harbour. Excellent, all-day café, dinner.

2419 2/V5 ✓ **Mareel** Lerwick · www.mareel.org · 01595 745500 Landmark purpose-
£ built entertainment and community centre on Lerwick waterfront, embedded
in the natural and cultural landscape of Shetland. Great cinema, great café and bar.
Daytime (from 10am, salads, sandwiches, the oatcakes) or evening menu till 9pm.
Bar later. Lovely light through those windows here, in this, the Shetland hub. My
last visit to Lerwick for the Film Festival meant Mareel and Hay's Dock adjacent
were the alternating great food options.

2420 2/U3 ✓ **Frankie's** Brae · www.frankiesfishandchips.com · 01806 522700 Busta
£ Voe and the marina great asset to Shetland eating out (or in). Takeaway and
caff. Local seafood, home baking, sustainable fish policy. Many awards including
No 1 in the National Fish & Chip Awards 2015. 9.30am-8pm. Sun from noon
(not in winter).

2421 2/V5 **The String** Lerwick · 01595 694921 A quartet of local lads crowdfunded and
£ then opened this well-thought-out café-restaurant and music venue in 2018.
Casual dining with a seafood slant, for lunch and dinner and their chef Akshay
Borges, live music and cultural events. Haven't visited at TGP. 11am-10pm (5pm
Tue). Late bar at weekends. Closed Mon.

2422 2/V5 **The Dowry** Lerwick · 01595 692373 Café/restaurant (and beer shop) also new
£ 2018, taking its name from the 'dowry payment' by which Shetland (and Orkney)
were pawned to Scotland by the King of Denmark, Norway and Sweden in the
16th century. It has a Scandic vibe and look, but no smørrebrød or pricey foraged
menus here. Contemporary both small and sharing plates, and craft beers aplenty.
Breakfast through to 9pm (later at weekends). Closed Sun.

2423 2/V5 **Fjara Café Bar** Lerwick · **www.fjaracoffee.com** · **01595 697388** Near Tesco,
£ but on the wee peninsula jutting out into Brewick Bay – seal spotting territory.
Simple home baking and local produce. Supper at night, including burgers. 8am-
10pm (bar until midnight Fri/Sat).

2424 2/V5 **The Olive Tree** Lerwick · **01595 697222** Nice deli/café/takeaway in the Toll
£ Clock Shopping Centre. Home-made stuff. Daytime only.

2425 2/V5 **The Peerie Shop Café** The Esplanade, Lerwick · **www.peerieshop.co.uk** ·
£ **01595 692816** Great shop and caff in downtown Lerwick, with home baking. A
local delicacy! The place to hang out in Lerwick. 9am-6pm. Closed Sun.

2426 2/U3 **The Mid Brae Inn** Brae · **01806 522634** 32km N of Lerwick. 7 days lunch &
££ supper till 8.45pm (9.30pm weekends). Big portions of filling pub grub.

WHAT TO SEE IN SHETLAND

✓ **Mousa Broch & Jarlshof** Report: 1854/PREHISTORIC. Also **Clickimin** broch.

✓ **Shetland Museum & Archives** Lerwick Report: 2164/HISTORY.

2427 2/U5 **St Ninian's Isle** Bigton 8km N of Sumburgh on West Coast. An island linked
by exquisite shell-sand. Hoard of Pictish silver found in 1958 (now in Edinburgh).
Beautiful, serene spot.

2428 2/V5 **Scalloway** 10km W of Lerwick, a township once the ancient capital of Shetland,
dominated by the atmospheric ruins of Scalloway Castle.

2429 2/V5 **Noup of Noss** Isle of Noss, off Bressay 8km W of Lerwick by frequent ferry
to Bressay and then wee boat (also by boat trip direct from Lerwick; check tourist
information centre); limited in winter. Spectacular array of wildlife.

2430 2/V5 **Up-Helly-Aa** **www.uphellyaa.org** Festival in Lerwick on the last Tuesday in
January. Ritual with hundreds of torchbearers and much fire and firewater. Norse,
northern and pagan. A wild time can be had. See 15/EVENTS.

2431 2/V5 **Sea Races** The Boat Race every midsummer from Bergen in Norway. Part of the
largest North Sea international annual yacht race.

2432 2/V4 **Bonhoga Gallery & Weisdale Mill** Weisdale · **www.shetlandarts.org** ·
01595 830400 Former grain mill housing Shetland's first purpose-built gallery.
Good café.

Maps

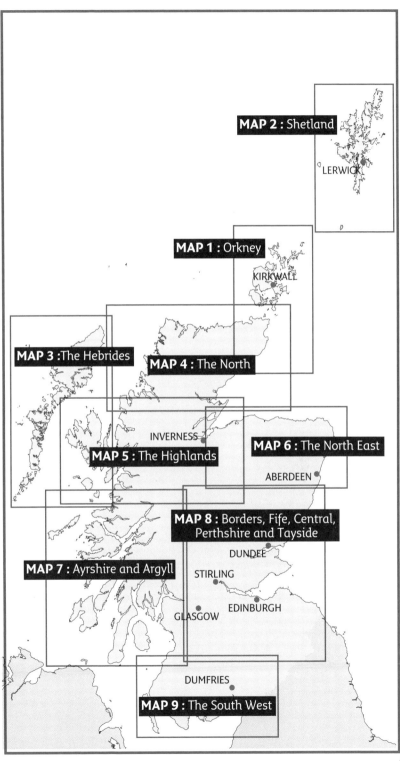

MAP 2 : Shetland

LERWICK

MAP 1 : Orkney

KIRKWALL

MAP 3 :The Hebrides

MAP 4 : The North

MAP 5 : The Highlands

INVERNESS

MAP 6 : The North East

ABERDEEN

MAP 8 : Borders, Fife, Central,
Perthshire and Tayside

DUNDEE

STIRLING

MAP 7 : Ayrshire and Argyll

GLASGOW

EDINBURGH

DUMFRIES

MAP 9 : The South West

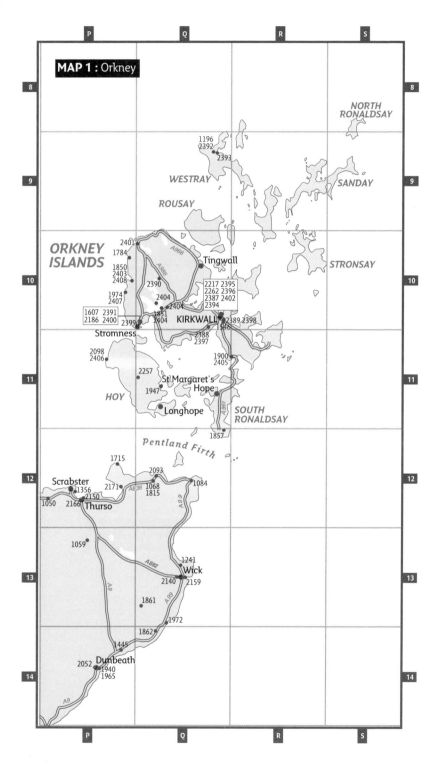

MAP 1 : Orkney

NORTH RONALDSAY

ORKNEY ISLANDS

WESTRAY

ROUSAY

SANDAY

STRONSAY

2401
1784

1850
2403
2408

1974
2407

1607 2391
2186 2400

2390

2404

2257

2098
2406

2399

1947

A966

A986

Tingwall

2217 2395
2262 2396
2387 2402
2394

2404
2404
1851
2404

KIRKWALL

2388
2397

2389 2398
1546

1900
2405

St Margaret's
Hope

HOY

Longhope

SOUTH
RONALDSAY

A961

1857

Stromness

Pentland Firth

1715

Scrabster

1356

2150

1050   2166 Thurso

2171

2093

A836 1068
1815

1084

A99

1059

A882

1241

Wick

2140   2159

1861

A99

1972

1862

1445

2052   Dunbeath
        1940
        1965

A9

A9

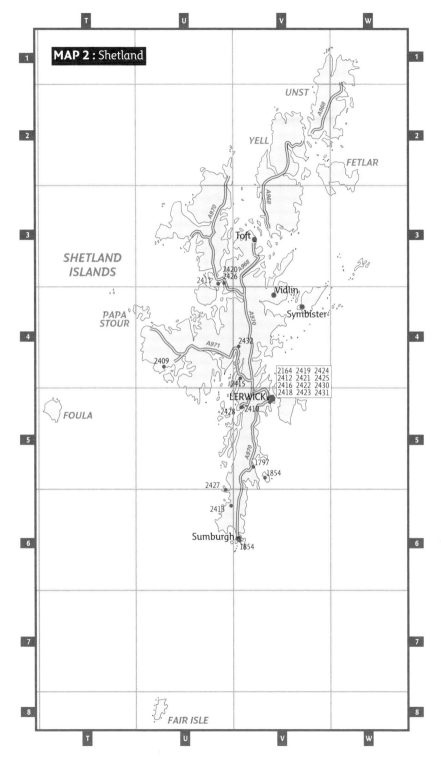

MAP 2 : Shetland

UNST

YELL

FETLAR

A968

A970

A968

Toft

SHETLAND
ISLANDS

2420
2426
2411

Vidlin

Symbister

PAPA
STOUR

A971

2432

2409

2164 2419 2424
2412 2421 2425
2416 2422 2430
2418 2423 2431

2415

LERWICK

2428   2410

FOULA

A970

1797

1854

2427

2413

Sumburgh

1854

FAIR ISLE

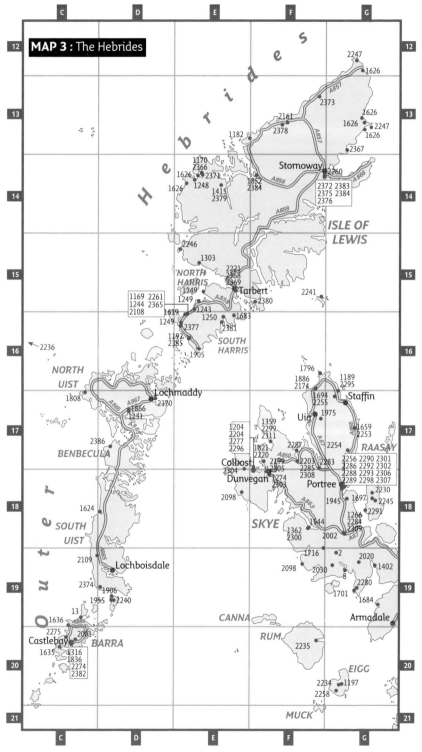

MAP 3 : The Hebrides

H e b r i d e s

ISLE OF
LEWIS

Stornoway

NORTH
HARRIS

Tarbert

SOUTH
HARRIS

NORTH
UIST

Lochmaddy

BENBECULA

SKYE

SOUTH
UIST

Lochboisdale

Colbost
Dunvegan

Uig

Staffin

RAASAY

Portree

Armadale

CANNA

Castlebay

BARRA

RUM

EIGG

MUCK

O u t e r

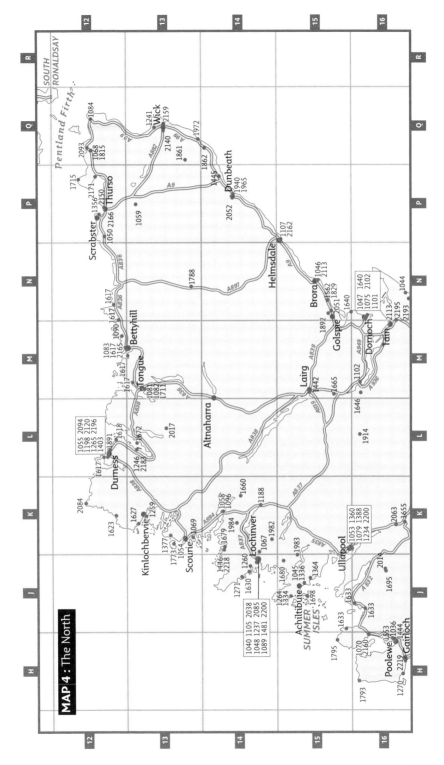

MAP 4 : The North

SOUTH RONALDSAY

Pentland Firth

Scrabster
Thurso
Wick
Dunbeath
Helmsdale
Brora
Golspie
Dornoch
Tain
Bettyhill
Tongue
Lairg
Altnaharra
Durness
Kinlochbervie
Scourie
Lochinver
Achiltibuie
SUMMER ISLES
Ullapool
Poolewe
Gairloch

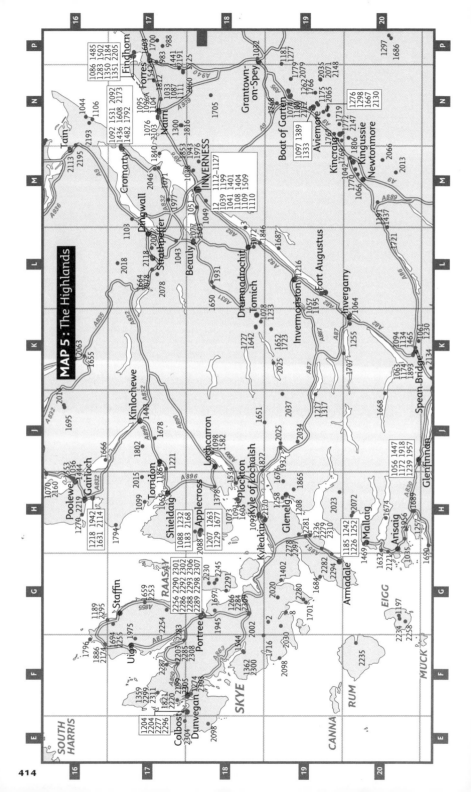

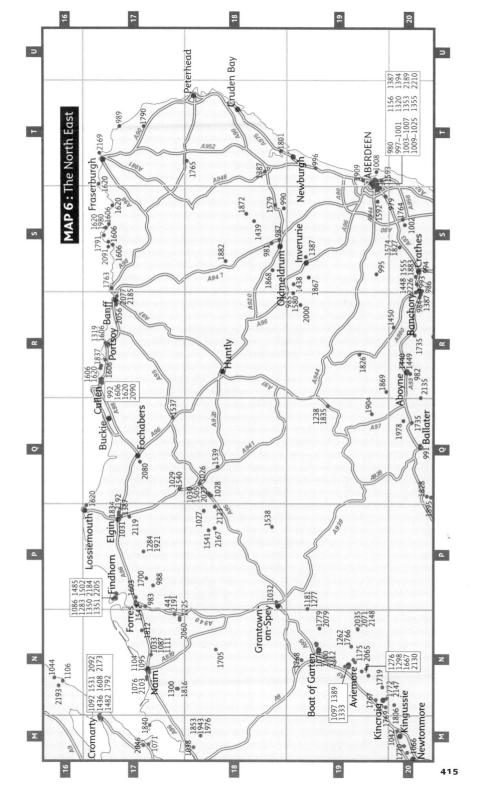

MAP 6: The North East

415

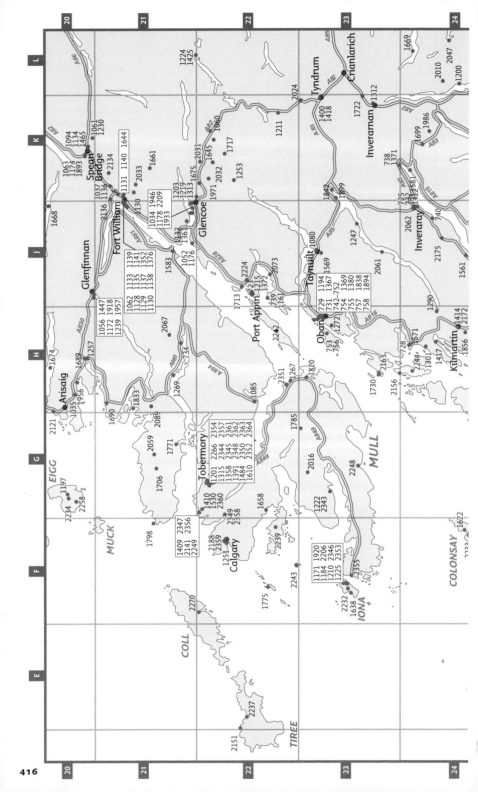

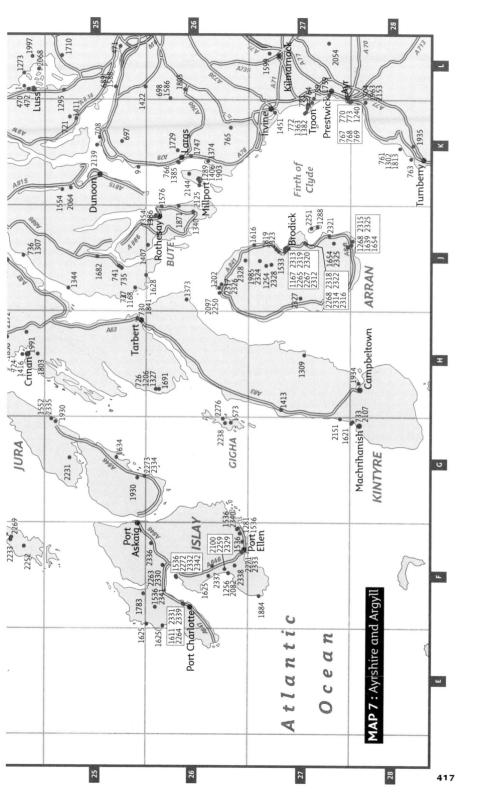

MAP 7 : Ayrshire and Argyll

417

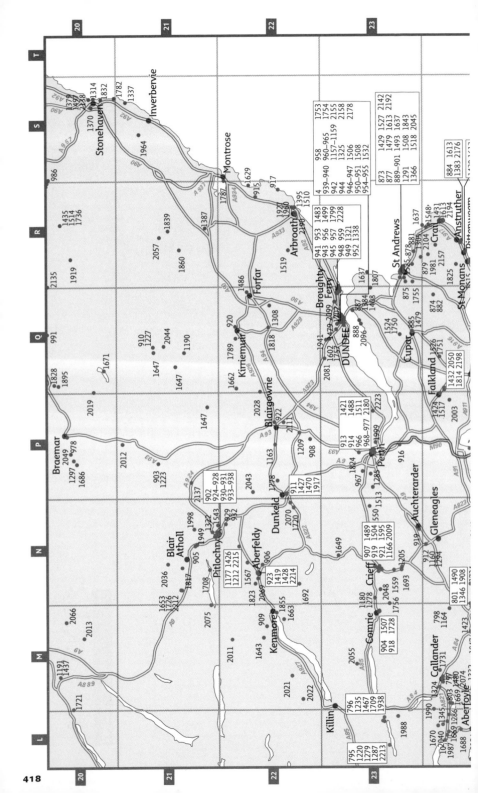

418

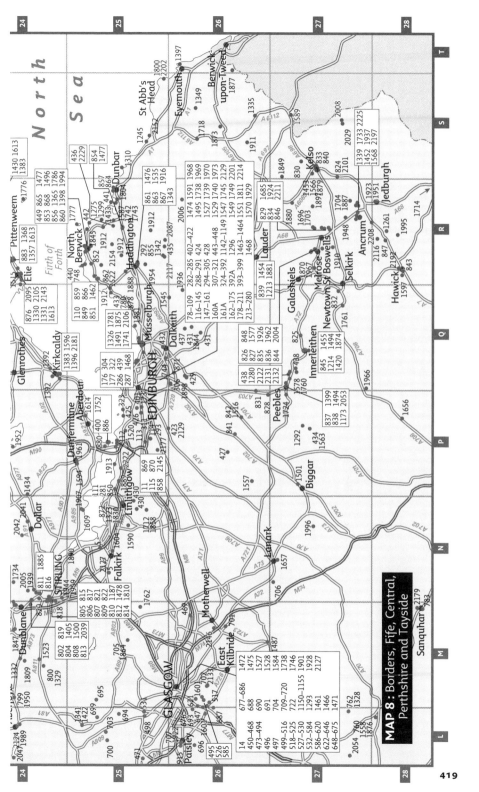

MAP 8 : Borders, Fife, Central, Perthshire and Tayside

419

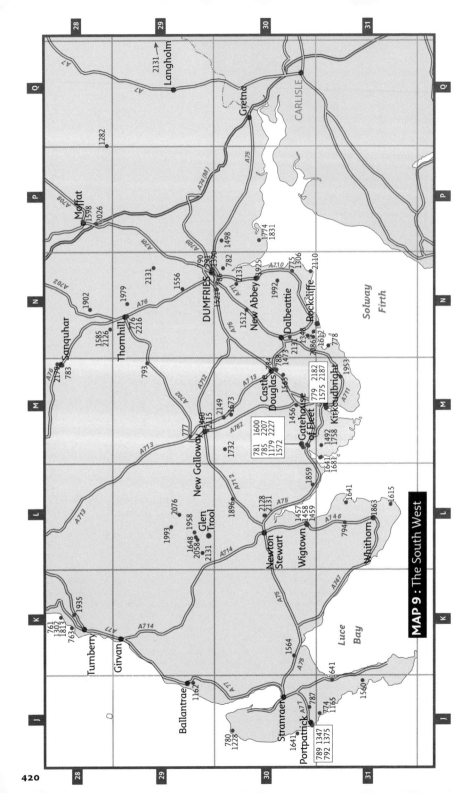

MAP 9 : The South West

420

Index